DOCTOR  WHO

THE ENCYCLOPEDIA

THE DEFINITIVE GUIDE TO THE HIT BBC SERIES

GARY RUSSELL

BBC
BOOKS

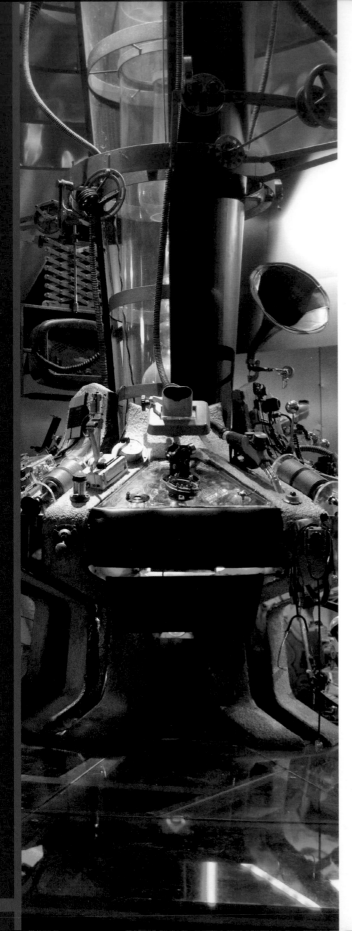

1 3 5 7 9 10 8 6 4 2

Published in 2011 by BBC Books, an imprint of Ebury Publishing.
A Random House Group Company

Doctor Who is a BBC Wales production for BBC One.
Executive producers: Steven Moffat, Caroline Skinner and Piers Wenger

As this book went to press, episodes 6.8 to 6.13 were being finalised for
transmission. There may subsequently have been some minor changes that
were made too late to be included here.

The Random House Group Limited Reg. No. 954009

Addresses for companies within the Random House Group can be found
at www.randomhouse.co.uk

A CIP catalogue record for this book is available from the British Library.

ISBN 978 1 849 909 426

Commissioning editor: Albert DePetrillo
Editorial manager: Nicholas Payne
Project editor: Steve Tribe
Designer: Richard Atkinson
Production: Phil Spencer

Printed and bound in China by C & C Offset Printing Co., Ltd.

To buy books by your favourite authors and register for offers,
visit www.randomhouse.co.uk

INTRODUCTION

Welcome back — has it been nearly four years since the last edition of this book?

If you don't have that version (and why not?), let me explain — this is an alphabetical catalogue of everything in televised Doctor Who between 2005 and now. More than 3,500 entries and nearly 200,000 words later and we have it, from 'Rose' right up to 'The Wedding of River Song'.

Once again, I've had amazing help from my very own team of Silents on this — checking my facts, my grammar, my tenses and querying, more than once, my choices. So, in no particular order, thanks to everyone who helped on that first edition, and for this second one: Andrew Pixley, Paul McFadden, Edward Russell, Amy Oakes, Dave Turbitt, Phil Ford, Brian Minchin, Lindsey Alford, Caroline Henry, Nicholas Pegg, Anwen Aspden, Marie Brown, Matthew Cox, Stephen Nicholas, Steff Morris, Ceres Doyle, Nerys Davies, Scott Handcock and, most importantly of all, James DeHaviland and Jenni Fava, whose attention to detail made my life so much easier. Thanks, both of you — unsung heroes no longer!

Thanks also to the team behind the book, Albert DePetrillo at BBC Books, Steve Tribe, sage and sensible editor, and Richard Atkinson, the design genius. Thanks as always to Steven Moffat, Russell T Davies, Julie Gardner, Phil Collinson, Marcus Wilson, Piers Wenger, Beth Willis, Sanne Wohlenberg, Tracie Simpson, Peter Bennett, Susie Liggat, Caroline Skinner and Denise Paul, without whom the last few years simply wouldn't have been any fun . . .

This book is dedicated with so much love and fondness to three friends and colleagues whose presence is missed daily and whose contribution to the history of this brilliant programme is impossible to put into words — Barry Letts, Elisabeth Sladen and Nicholas Courtney.

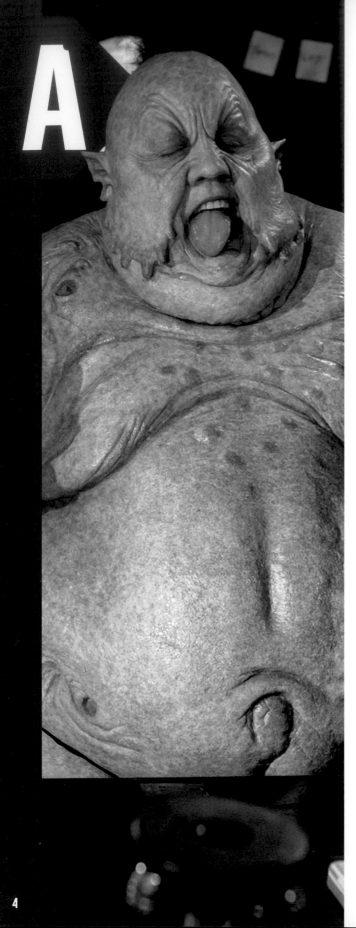

Abaddon: Legendary demon name, one of many attributed to the Beast throughout the galaxies. (2.8, 2.9)

ABBA: Swedish pop group that Rose Tyler saw play live at Wembley in November 1979 while the Doctor hunted the Graske. (AotG)

Abberline, Inspector Frederick: Chief Inspector of London's Metropolitan Police in 1888, charged with solving the Jack the Ripper murders. Madame Vastra found and ate the killer, later telling her aide Jenny to contact Abberline and tell him Jack's reign of terror was over. (6.7)

Aberdeen: Queen Victoria was travelling there by coach rather than train as a tree had reportedly been placed on the line, possibly a precursor to an assassination attempt. (2.2) At the time of her original journeys alongside the Doctor, Sarah Jane Smith's home was in South Croydon and that's where the Doctor told her he had brought her to when it was time for them to part ways. After the TARDIS left her, Sarah Jane realised she wasn't in Hillview Road, Croydon at all, but in Aberdeen. (2.3)

'Abide with Me': 19th-century Christian anthem, sung by the drivers from the New New York Motorway as they reclaimed the Overcity after the Doctor freed them. (3.3)

Abomination, the: The Dalek Emperor referred to Rose Tyler as this when she returned to the Game Station, the power of the time vortex coursing through her being. She used this power to obliterate him, his Daleks and their fleet from existence. (1.13) The Supreme Dalek used the phrase to describe the insane Dalek Caan. (4.12)

Abzorbaloff, the: The name taken by a creature from the planet Clom, twin world to Raxacoricofallapatorius. Disguised as the human Victor Kennedy, he absorbed humans into his flesh for food, whilst searching for the Doctor so he could steal his TARDIS. He carried a silver-topped claw-shaped cane, which was actually a limitation-field creator that kept him compressed after he had absorbed the humans. When Elton Pope broke the cane, the final four victims – Ursula Blake, Colin Skinner, Bridget and Bliss – fought back. The Abzorbaloff died as he exploded and his remains were in turn absorbed by the earth under the concrete paving stones of London. (2.10) Davros taunted the Doctor about how many people had died trying to help him over the years, and this made the Doctor recall the victims of the Abzorbaloff. (4.13) (Played by PETER KAY)

Academy, the: Ancient seat of learning for Time Lords on Gallifrey. Time Lords entered it as Novices at 8 years of age, after viewing the Untempered Schism. It was destroyed along with the rest of Gallifrey at the end of the Last Great Time War. (3.12)

Academy of the Question, the: See *The Silence*

A

Acetic acid: A useful defence against the calcium-based Raxacoricofallapatorians who made up the Family Slitheen. Jackie Tyler used vinegar to defeat the Slitheen that threatened her and Mickey Smith. (1.5)

Acorah, Derek: Presenter of the series *Most Haunted*, he bemoaned the fact that, as ghosts were now everywhere, he was out of a job. (2.12)

Action Procedures: A series of standard orders actionable by the commander of World State bases. Procedure One required a sealed lockdown. Procedure Five required the destruction of a base via its nuclear core being overloaded. (4.16)

Adams, Douglas: Author of the *Hitchhiker's Guide to the Galaxy* series of novels. After defeating the Sycorax Leader, the Doctor likened himself to the books' lead character, Arthur Dent, since he was wearing pyjamas and a dressing gown, as Dent did throughout his travels. (2.X)

Adams, John: Second President of the United States of America and one of the Founding Fathers. A street in Florida was named after him, and the Doctor realised that the little girl trapped inside a NASA spacesuit was located nearby. (6.1)

Addams: Vinvocci salvager, whose ship the *Hesperus* was in orbit while she and her fellow Vinvocci, Rossiter, pretended to be humans, using a Shimmer. They seemed to be working for Joshua Naismith, attempting to repair the Immortality Gate, but in fact they knew exactly what it really was, since it was Vinvocci-built. They were trying to transport it off Earth. Instead, Addams teleported the Doctor and Wilfred Mott to the *Hesperus*. When the *Hesperus* flew down to Earth, Addams manned the rear laser guns to shoot down the warheads the Master fired at them. After the Doctor and Wilfred left the ship, Rossiter and Addams flew it home. (4.17, 4.18) (Played by SINEAD KEENAN)

Adelaide: South Australian city where Ed Gold was born. (4.16)

Adherents of the Repeated Meme: Robotic servants of the Lady Cassandra aboard Platform One, bringing with them the deadly Spider robots. When they arrived in the Manchester Suite, the Steward introduced them as representing Financial Family Seven, but the Doctor quickly realised this was a ruse and exposed them as frauds, at which point they were all deactivated. (1.2) (Voiced by SILAS CARSON)

Adipose: Living fat creatures. When humans ingested Adipose Capsules, the creatures grew within the fatty deposits of their bodies, then detached themselves. Their departure gave the impression that the capsules provided an instant weight-loss drug. The Adipose young were collected by  Matron Cofelia, who planned to deliver them to the Adiposian First Family, despite the fact that using Earth as a breeding planet was in contravention of the Shadow Proclamation. (4.1) In the alternative world where Donna Noble never met the Doctor, the USA saw 60 million people dissolved into Adipose, with Adiposian spaceships collecting the creatures from every major city. (4.11) As she saw her mother and fiancé change into the Master in front of her and her memories started to return, Donna Noble remembered the Adipose. (4.17) An Adipose young was in the bar on Zog where the Doctor introduced Captain Jack Harkness to Midshipman Alonso Frame. (4.18)

Adipose Capsule: Diet pills made and distributed by Adipose Industries to slimmers in London. In fact, the pills contained the dormant DNA of Adipose young, which attracted the fat and eventually left the human host while they slept, a process called parthenogenesis. They then returned independently to Adipose Industries, ready to be sent home. (4.1)

Adipose Industries: False firm set up by Matron Cofelia on Earth, in London, to distribute the Adipose Capsules. Donna Noble and the Doctor separately pretended to be Health and Safety inspectors to gain access to their sales records. The firm gave away a free gold pendant with each box of pills, but this actually contained bioflip-digital-stitch circuitry that Matron Cofelia could track the hatching Adipose young with after parthenogenesis. (4.1)

Adipose 3: An Adiposian breeding world, it was one of the planets the Daleks had stolen and placed a second out of sync with the universe, to help power the Reality Bomb. (4.12, 4.13)

Adiposian First Family: Employed Matron Cofelia to create a new generation of Adipose on Earth after their breeding planet, Adipose 3, was lost. They came to Earth to collect the youngsters after the Doctor alerted the Shadow Proclamation to what was going on, and they killed Cofelia to ensure her silence following the exposure of this illegal activity. (4.1)

Africa: Second largest continent on Earth. Tom Milligan was working with children there at the time the Sontarans set up their ATMOS invasion attempt. (4.4) The UN Air Force retreated across the northern part because they were unable to defeat the Daleks. (4.12)

Aga Khan University: Multinational university. Tarak Ital attended the Pakistan section, based in Karachi. (4.16)

Age of Steel: The Cyber Controller on 'Pete's World' declared that, with its army becoming fully operational, Earth was now in the Age of Steel. (2.6)

Agorax: One of the players of *The Weakest Link* aboard the Game Station. When he lost the final round, the Anne Droid appeared to disintegrate him, but in truth he was transmatted over to the Dalek mothership and turned into part of the growing Dalek army created by the Emperor. (1.12) (Played by DOMINIC BURGESS)

Aickman Road: Colchester street where Craig Owens lived, at number 79, a single-storey flat which had been given the appearance of a two-storey building by the perception filter used by a time engine that had landed on the original roof. The time engine originally belonged to the Silence and the Academy of the Question, and was controlled by a human avatar to entice humans in. (5.11) When the Doctor saw another time engine being used by the Silence in America, he recalled the one in Aickman Road. (6.2)

Air corridor: The Doctor used the TARDIS to create one for River Song to escape into after she jumped from the *Byzantium* towards the Doctor's ship. (5.4)

A

Air Force One: Personal aircraft of the President of the United States of America. It brought President Winters to Britain, along with a cadre of UNIT troops, to take over the Toclafane situation from Harry Saxon. (3.12)

Aitchinson-Price: Author of a book that was the definitive account of Mafeking, according to John Smith, the history teacher at Farringham School for Boys. (3.8)

Air Raid Warden: Man responsible for ensuring that the lights of London were extinguished whenever there was an air-raid warning. He was horrified when the whole of London was lit up during such an attack, unaware that this was part of the Daleks' plan. He was very relieved when, after the Doctor stopped the Daleks, the lights went out again, saving London from a bombing. (5.3) (Played by COLIN PROCKTER)

which he repeatedly had cut down until it was the correct size, they hoped that the beam of moonlight created would be enough to destroy the Haemovariform. They were correct, though neither lived to see their work come to fruition. (2.2)

Alan [1]: London man who, like his children, had A+ blood and thus was affected by the Sycorax's blood control. (2.X) (Played by SIMON HUGHES)

Alan [2]: Chiswick resident who disobeyed the Daleks and, with his wife Laura and son Simon, fled back into their house. The Daleks then blew the house to pieces with the family inside as an example to other humans. (4.12) (Played by GARY MILNER)

Alaya: Silurian warrior who hated humanity and wanted nothing more than to provoke a war between the species. She deliberately infected Tony Mack with Silurian venom, knowing this would provoke his already edgy daughter – whose son and husband had previously been taken by the Silurians – into attacking and killing her. The plan succeeded: Alaya died and, when Rory Williams returned the body, her sister Restac immediately declared war on the human race. (5.8, 5.9) (Played by NEVE McINTOSH)

Albert, Prince of Saxe-Coburg and Gotha: Beloved husband to Queen Victoria, he died in 1861. Foreseeing the danger of the Haemovariform rumoured to exist in the lands around the Torchwood Estate, Albert, along with his friend Sir George MacLeish, built a huge telescope. Linking it to the fabled Koh-I-Noor diamond,

Albert Hall: Impressive London venue built to honour Albert, consort to Queen Victoria. It was hosting a Promenade concert when a Graske escaped the TARDIS via a portal, and the Doctor retrieved it after asking the conductor of the orchestra to play his special composition, 'Music of the Spheres'. (MotS)

Albino Servant: Worker at the Shadow Proclamation, who foresaw Donna Noble's fate. (4.12) (Played by AMY BETH HAYS)

Albion Hospital: Situated in the City of London, bordering the East End, Albion Hospital was where the augmented pig was taken to be examined by undercover Torchwood scientist Toshiko Sato. (1.4) In 1941, Dr Constantine was the last of the hospital's inhabitants to succumb to the Chula virus that turned people into gas-mask zombies. Later, he and the hospital's patients and staff were returned to a better state of health than they had been in before. (1.9, 1.10)

Alex: Husband of Claire, and resident of Rowbarton House. After unsuccessfully trying to have children, he suddenly had a son, George. George was in fact an alien, a Tenza who placed himself in their flat and altered himself to become exactly what they had always wanted, using a perception filter to subtly change their and their neighbours' memories of his 'being born'. Alex was drawn, along with the Doctor, into the nightmarish world George had created when he believed he was being rejected. Alex convinced George that he was loved – bringing back to reality everyone

A

primitive portable television to the mast. This would enable the Wire to disseminate itself further afield, creating the Time of Manifestation. The Doctor was able to briefly turn the portable TV that Mr Magpie had built from a receiver into a transmitter and beamed the Wire back onto an early Betamax video recorder. (2.7)

Alexandria: Lobos Caecilius hoped to get a contract supplying marble to the granaries of this Grecian city. (4.2)

Alf: A young boy Nancy agreed to look after on the streets of Blitzed London, brought to her by another lad, Jim. Alf had been evacuated from London to stay with a family on a farm, but was abused by a man there. Like all the kids now in Nancy's care, he had then fled back home to London. (1.9, 1.10) (Played by BRANDON MILLER)

trapped in the giant doll's house that had become their prison. Having realised the truth about him, Claire and Alex allowed George to stay, living as their son, and loving him just as if he were really their biological offspring. (6.9) (Played by DANIEL MAYS)

Alexandra Palace: Originally built in 1873 as North London's answer to the Crystal Palace, in 1936 it ceased being an exhibition centre and became the home for the BBC's first experiments in live television broadcasts – it remained an essential part of the BBC's transmissions until the mid 1960s, although the mast still broadcasts today. The Wire instructed Magpie to go there and hook up a

Alfava Metraxis: Seventh planet of the Dundra System in the Garn Belt, and originally the home world to the two-headed Aplans. Four hundred years after the Aplans died out, six billion humans colonised the planet, unaware they were in imminent danger. This was because the Aplans' Maze of the Dead beneath the surface had become the resting place for a colony of Weeping Angels, who killed everyone until they ran out of energy. When a Weeping Angel in its hold caused the *Byzantium* to crash there, the Angels regenerated, feeding off the ship's radiation. They were eventually all destroyed by the time field that opened on the ship after the Doctor and Amy Pond arrived. (5.4, 5.5)

Alfie: School classmate to Mandy Tanner and Timmy Winters. (5.2)

Algy: British army officer who was with Captain Jack Harkness when the latter spotted Rose Tyler hanging on the mooring rope of a loose barrage balloon while a German air raid was under way in Blitzed London. Later, on duty at the Limehouse Green railway yard where the crashed Chula medical ship was stored, he became infected by the gas-mask illness. He was eventually cured by the Chula nanogenes. (1.9, 1.10) (Played by ROBERT HANDS)

Ali, Mrs: In the artificial world created by CAL for Donna Noble to live in, Mrs Ali was another of the residents at the sanatorium where Donna had been for two years, attended by Doctor Moon. (4.9)

Alien: The Doctor considered the first two *Alien* films to be good examples of 'escaping from difficult predicaments' movies. (DL)

Alien world: A beautiful red-hued planet with massive creatures wheeling in the air, to which the Doctor took Rose Tyler. While there, he asked her how long she would stay with him. For ever was her response. (2.12)

Alignment of Exedor, the: Seventeen galaxies in perfect unison, locked in a time stasis field. The Doctor had only one chance to ride the TARDIS into it. (6.12)

Alison: The Doctor named a galaxy this on his way to the Ood-Sphere when answering Ood Sigma's projected song. (4.17)

Alistair: Chief of Security aboard the starship *Byzantium*, where River Song had been placed on dispensation from the Stormcage Facility. He was trying to recapture her when she escaped into the TARDIS. He was killed when the

Byzantium crashed onto Alfava Metraxis. (5.4) (Played by SIMON DUTTON)

Alliance of Shades, the: Mysterious alien organisation who ensured that humanity was kept ignorant of alien incursions on Earth as often as possible. They utilised androids dressed like Men in Black to clear up after them. The Androids, led by Mister Dread, were eventually deprogrammed in 1972 by the Alliance. (DL)

Allhallows Street: Street in Southwark where the crooked house stood that the Carrionites used as their base of operations. (3.2)

Alpha Ceti Beta 6: A very bright star, according to the Doctor. (AG02)

Alpha Class: Designation of the type of space station Platform One was – i.e. top of the range. (1.2)

Alpha Geminorum: A star distant from Earth. Castor 36, the new world promised to Luke Rattigan by the Sontarans, allegedly existed beyond it. (4.4, 4.5)

Alpha-Mezon Gun: Energy weapon used by River Song to destroy the stone Dalek that patrolled the National Museum (5.13) and the Silence that had kidnapped Amy Pond. (6.2)

Ambassador of Thrace: Lady Cassandra O'Brien attended a drinks party in his honour one night, when a dying man approached her and told her she was beautiful. She remembered this as being the last time anyone told her that. In truth, the dying man was herself, transplanted into the failing body of Chip. (2.1)

Ambassadors from the City State of Binding Light: Guests aboard Platform One for the Earthdeath spectacle. (1.2)

Ambrose Hall: A children's home where the orphaned schoolgirl Nina lived. (2.3)

Ancient Britain: Referred to in questions by the Anne Droid aboard the Game Station, during the *Weakest Link* quiz. (1.12)

Anderson: One of Captain Rory Williams's soldiers within Area 52. He wore an Eye Drive to keep him aware of the Silence at all times. He was killed when they escaped their water chambers. (6.13) (Played by MATT DOLMAN)

Andrew: One of the Lever Room operators responsible for bombarding the Wall with particle energy via the giant Levers during a 'ghost shift'. He was killed by Cyberleader One, who arrived to take over Torchwood Tower. (2.12)

Angela: Chittering alien who worked for Dorium Maldovar at his bar. She gave Dorium a Vortex Manipulator for River Song, but Dorium wasn't pleased to see it still attached to a Time Agent's wrist. (5.12) (Played by ALAN GLET)

Angelica: One of the guests at Donna Noble and Lance Bennett's wedding. She wasn't being particularly helpful during the confusion after Donna vanished on her way to the altar. (3.X)

Angelo, Cleric: One of Father Octavian's troopers. He was killed in the catacombs by a Weeping Angel. (5.4) (Played by TROY GLASGOW)

Angelo, Father: Leader of the Brethren, who worshipped the Haemovariform and brought it to the Torchwood Estate. Having taken over the House and imprisoned its occupants, he forced Sir Robert MacLeish to act as if nothing had changed when Queen Victoria arrived. When he revealed his true motives, Queen Victoria shot him dead. (2.2) (Played by IAN HANMORE)

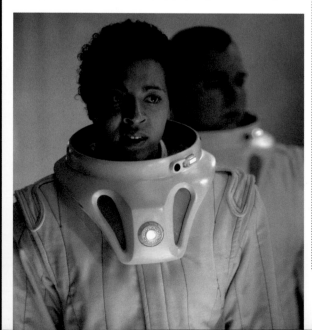

Angelo, Jeff: Grandson of Mrs Angelo. The Doctor used his laptop to communicate with all the leading science stations and scientists of the world. He left Jeff to coordinate with them the broadcasting of the simple message 'Zero' that would draw the Atraxi back to Earth and straight to Leadworth, to recapture Prisoner Zero. (5.1) (PLAYED BY TOM HOPPER)

Angelo, Mrs [1]: In the artificial world created by CAL for Donna Noble to live in, Doctor Moon claimed his stomach was slightly upset by Mrs Angelo's rhubarb surprise. (4.9)

Angelo, Mrs [2]: Resident of Leadworth and friend of Amy Pond – although she assumed Amy was a nurse, or a nun, not a kissogram. She lived with her grandson Jeff, and it was her TV that the Doctor watched when he realised the Atraxi were broadcasting their message on every frequency. (5.1) (Played by ANNETTE CROSBIE)

Anghelides Equation: Mathematical conundrum solved in 14 hours by Jones, the computer guarding the Poseidon Community. (AG04)

Anita [1]: One of the archaeological team that Strackman Lux brought to The Library. She was befriended by the Doctor after becoming infected by the Vashta Nerada because she was so brave about it; however, the Vashta Nerada eventually killed her and used her spacesuit to communicate with him. Her brain patterns were saved onto the data core and when River Song found herself living in the core's fantasy world, Anita was there too. (4.8, 4.9) (Played by JESSIKA WILLIAMS)

Anita [2]: One of the crew aboard the *Teselecta*. She was injured by the Anti-Bodies but teleported away, along with the rest of the crew. (6.8) (Played by AMY CUDDEN)

Annalise: 20-year-old ditzy girl, who had an affair with Clive Jones (she claimed he seduced her) and ultimately set up home with him. She attended Leo Jones's 21st birthday event (although allegedly only bought him a bar of scented soap) and got into an argument with Francine Jones, Clive's wife over Annalise's tanning tones. Annalise then stormed off into the night, pursued by an angry Clive. (3.1) (Played by KIMMI RICHARDS)

Anne Droid: Quizmaster of *The Weakest Link*, a robot with what appeared to be a disintegrator blaster in its mouth, but was in fact a transmat beam, sending losing contestants over to the Dalek mothership, where they were turned into part of the growing Dalek army created by the Emperor. The Anne Droid was later reprogrammed to defend the station against the Daleks but was exterminated on Floor 495. (1.12, 1.13) (Voiced by ANNE ROBINSON, played by ALAN RUSCOE)

A

A

Anne Marie: One of Donna Noble's co-workers at Jival Chowdry's photocopying business in the alternative world where Donna never met the Doctor. Donna reckoned Anne Marie was responsible for nicking the firm's cash kitty. (4.11)

Anne, Princess: Princess Royal in the 21st-century royal family. Rose Tyler wondered if she was a werewolf. (2.2)

Annie: Dying sister of Charlie in the London of 1605. (AG05)

Anomaly Exhibition, the: An exhibition of historical impossibilities at the National Museum, which included the Pandorica and two stone Daleks. (5.13)

'Another Rock 'n' Roll Christmas': 1984 hit for Gary Glitter. It was playing in the house where the Graske replaced the parents with changelings. (AotG)

Anti-Bodies: The Justice Department Vehicle *Teselecta* contained Anti-Bodies, robotic assassins that would erase real criminals from within the ship once they were brought aboard. The crew of the *Teselecta* were safe from the Anti-Bodies provided they wore special wristbands that identified them as non-hostile. In an attempt to gain control of the ship, Amy Pond soniced the wristbands and deactivated them throughout the ship, causing the crew to teleport safely to their mothership in orbit, leaving Amy and Rory Williams controlling it. (6.8) (Voiced by JONATHAN HART)

Anti-Gravity Clamps: Tritovore technology which held the crystal nucleus that powered their ship's engines in place. The Doctor used the clamps to make the number 200 bus fly out of the sand of San Helios and back to Earth through the wormhole created by the Stingrays. (4.15)

Anti-Matter Monsters: Sarah Jane Smith told Rose Tyler that during her time travelling with the Doctor, they had fought these creatures. (2.3)

DOCTOR WHO THE ENCYCLOPEDIA

A

Antiplastic: The Doctor had a vial of this in case he couldn't persuade the Nestene Consciousness to leave Earth voluntarily. Although an Auton took it from the Doctor, Rose Tyler knocked into the Auton, causing it to drop the antiplastic onto the liquid-plastic form of the Consciousness. (1.1)

Anura: Planet almost entirely covered with water, with only tiny islands just far enough above sea level to require its inhabitants to be amphibious. However, on long journeys away from Anura, the Anurans required portable water tanks to keep them breathing. Ulysses Mergrass, who the Doctor met on Myarr, came from Anura. (TIQ)

Apalapucia: Pleasure planet and hub of 10,000 cultures, where Amy Pond was separated into a different time stream from the Doctor and Rory Williams, and ended up living a lifetime there, waiting for them to rescue her. The planet was under quarantine due to an outbreak of the lethal Chen7 plague. It only affected life forms with two hearts, such as the Apalapucians and Time Lords. Although Amy was safe, the automated Handbots would try and 'save' her, which in turn would kill her. (6.10)

Aplans: Two-headed race which lived on Alfava Metraxis centuries before humans colonised it. Deep below the planet, in their Maze of the Dead, a colony of Weeping Angels existed, waiting to regenerate themselves. (5.4, 5.5)

Apollo 11: The first moon-landing mission, with astronauts Neil Armstrong, Michael Williams and Buzz Aldrin. The Doctor intercepted Neil Armstrong's famous 'One giant step for a man' speech to insert subliminal images of a Silent saying humanity should kill it on sight, ensuring that it would be seen every time anyone ever saw that recording. (6.2)

Appian Way: Major Roman road which the Doctor made a pun about to Donna Noble as they escaped the Sibylline Sisterhood in Pompeii. (4.2)

Apple Grass: Kind of sweet-smelling grass found on the slopes overlooking the New Atlantic on New Earth. (2.1) Cheen had heard that the air in Brooklyn smelled of apple grass. (3.3)

Appleton, Alistair: Presenter of the television show *Ghostwatch*, which examined the phenomena of the ghosts appearing all over the world. When the ghosts were revealed to be Cybermen, he was killed live on television. (2.12)

Apprehension, Mister: One of the Alliance of Shades' Men in Black androids. He was put out of action by an arrow fired by one of Night Eagle's Shoshoni tribesmen. (DL)

Arcadia: The site of a major battle in the Last Great Time War. The Doctor was there and watched as the Daleks fled from it. (2.13) He later took Amy Pond there, but presumably to an earlier time zone. (5.10)

Archangel Network:

Communications system in the United Kingdom launched by Harry Saxon. Via its 15 satellites in orbit around Earth, the Master beamed down the four-beat pulsing rhythm with which he hypnotised the population of Britain into voting for him (it was roughly 98 per cent successful). Most of the broadband and mobile phones used in Britain during Saxon's time, including Martha Jones's phone, utilised the Archangel network. The Doctor used the network against the Master, by tuning his mind into it over his year in captivity and linking telepathically with all the humans already enslaved by the pulse-beat. Boosted by the empathic chant of 'Doctor' from people across the

A

world, as inspired by Martha Jones, the Doctor was able to use the Archangel network to psychically reverse the ageing process the Master had put him through. With the boost of power this gave him, the Doctor briefly accessed almost preternatural powers, becoming impervious to the Master's laser screwdriver simply by exercising his belief that it wouldn't harm him. The Master's spell over humanity broken, the Doctor and Captain Jack Harkness were able to rid Earth of the Toclafane. (3.12, 3.13)

Archbishop of Canterbury: According to the Doctor's psychic paper when Craig Owens read it, the Doctor was the Archbishop's 'special favourite'. (5.11)

Archer, Jeffrey: Politician and author whose books could be found in The Library. (4.8)

Architect: The architect of the Blaidd Drwg Project died when he was run over in bad weather by the Lord Mayor of Cardiff, Margaret Blaine. (1.11)

Archive Six: Where records were kept aboard the Game Station referring to contestants being transmatted into the game areas. The Female Programmer headed to Archive Six to discover more about the Doctor, but the Controller forbade it, stating that Archive Six was out of bounds. The old Spike Room from which Cathica Santini Khadeni had destroyed the Jagrafess, Archive Six was where the Controller hid the TARDIS from the Dalek monitoring devices. (1.12)

Arctic Circle: Northernmost area on Earth. A scientific research base there was attacked by Cybermen who had been buried under the ice for centuries. (AG02)

Arctic Desert: Area on Earth that Lady Cassandra O'Brien claimed her mother had been born in. (1.2)

Ardennes: Region of France where the Doctor, armed with just a bow and arrow, once rescued Charlemagne from an insane computer. (4.7)

Are You Being Served?: British 1970s sitcom set in a fictional department store. The Doctor quoted the opening lines to the theme song as he exited the elevator at the top of the Empire State Building. (3.5)

Area 51: See *Dreamland*

Area 52: A similar set-up to Dreamland but, in the alternative Earth reality created when River Song changed time, it was built within a pyramid in Egypt and housed Silence immersed in water. (6.13)

Argonne National Laboratory: Chicago-based science establishment where Steffi Ehrlich studied when she went to America from Germany. (4.16)

Arianna: Greek mate of Jackie Tyler's who once successfully sued the local council for suggesting she looked Greek. She was Greek. She received £2,000. (1.1)

Arizona: American state. The Glen Canyon Dam was situated there. (6.2)

Arkiphets, the: Devotees of one of the religions practised in the 42nd century. (2.9)

Armitage: Schoolboy at Farringham School for Boys in 1913, who knew the drill for defending the school when the Family of Blood attacked. (3.9)

Armstrong, Neil: The first man to step onto the moon. Richard Lazarus estimated that his own work with the Genetic Manipulation Device would prove as important to mankind as that achievement. (3.6) The Doctor intercepted Neil Armstrong's famous 'One giant step for a man' speech to insert subliminal images of a Silent saying humanity should kill it on sight, ensuring that it would be seen every time anyone ever saw that recording. (6.2)

A

Army of Meanwhiles and Never-Weres: Participants in the Time War, controlled by the Couldhavebeen King. (4.18)

Arthur [1]: A white horse that wandered from 1744 Paris to the 51st-century SS *Madame de Pompadour* via a time window. The Doctor later rode Arthur back to France via the time window overlooking the Ballroom in 1758 Versailles. (2.4)

Arthur [2]: Young son of Eleanor, the President, who received a head injury at Zarusthra Bay, and was tended to by the Sontaran nurse Strax. (6.7) (Played by HENRY WOOD)

Arthur Dent: Fictional character from Douglas Adams's *Hitchhiker's Guide to the Galaxy* series of novels. The Doctor likened himself to Dent after defeating the Sycorax Leader, because he was wearing pyjamas and a dressing gown, as Arthur Dent had throughout his travels. (2.X)

As You Like It: A play by William Shakespeare. The Doctor quoted the phrase 'All the world's a stage' to the writer, thus providing him with part of the play's prologue. (3.2)

Ascension: The event the Cybermen on Earth in 1851 were preparing for, when a Dreadnought-class battleship, a CyberKing, was to be launched. (4.14)

Ascension Islands: Henry Van Statten's aide Diana Goddard stated that the Dalek in Van Statten's Vault had come to Earth over 50 years previously, in the early 1960s, and crashed on 'the Ascension Islands'. It is not known if she meant Ascension Island itself or one of its neighbours, St Helena or Tristan da Cunha (which itself is actually five islands). (1.6)

Ascinta: A civilisation lost during the Last Great Time War. (2.3)

Asgard: Professor River Song wondered if the Doctor had joined her for their picnic at Asgard at the time they met at The Library. He hadn't. (4.8)

Ashington: Schoolboy at Farringham School in 1913, who was told to fetch water for the Vickers Gun before the Family of Blood attacked. (3.9)

Ashton, Dev: Oldest crewman aboard the SS *Pentallian*, on his final tour of duty. He was a mechanic and engineer and was caught by Korwin McDonnell. Whereas McDonnell had vaporised his previous victims, with Ashton he transferred a portion of the sun he was consumed by into him, thus creating two agents for the sun amongst the crew. The sun-possessed Ashton then wrecked the ship's systems, meaning that the generators could not be brought back online to jump-start the engines. He then jettisoned an escape pod containing Martha Jones and Riley Vashtee towards the sun, and attacked captain Kath McDonnell in the medcentre. She overpowered him and pushed him into a stasis chamber, activating the cryofreeze unit, destroying the sun parts of him, leaving just his dead body. (3.7) (Played by GARY POWELL)

Asquith, General: Army officer in charge of investigating the Big Ben incident. After seeing the augmented pig at Albion Hospital, he went to 10 Downing Street to discover Joseph Green had been appointed Acting Prime Minister. Convinced the actual Prime Minister had been kidnapped by extraterrestrials, Asquith threatened to remove Green from power – until he was killed and his body used by one of the Slitheen family. The Slitheen version of Asquith then added to the military's confusion rather than aiding it, enabling the Family Slitheen to carry out their audacious plan. Asquith's Slitheen version was later killed when 10 Downing Street was destroyed by a sub-Harpoon missile. (1.4, 1.5) (Played by RUPERT VANSITTART)

Asteroid 7574B: Precise location of the *Infinite*, provided by the datachip possessed by Mergrass. (TIQ)

Astronaut Girl: See *Song, River*

Athelstan, King: English King around AD 924, whose court the Doctor visited. He was given the Cup of Athelstan by King Hywel of the Welsh. (4.15)

Atif: Freelance reporter who tried to sell a story about the Torchwood Institute to the editor of *The Examiner* after being given stolen papers by a disgruntled Torchwood employee. The editor, however, betrayed him to Torchwood, who took him away. (2.12T) (Played by SHANE ZAZA)

Atillo, Lieutenant: One of the security officers on the rocket silo base on Malcassairo, charged with ensuring the human refugees there got safely aboard the rocket. When the rocket was about to launch, Atillo joined his fellow humans and headed for Utopia. Whether he or his descendants were turned into the Toclafane by the Master is unknown. (3.11) (Played by NEIL REIDMAN)

Atkins Diet, the: According to Lance Bennett, Donna Noble talked excitedly about this dietary fad. (3.X)

ATMOS: Atmospheric Omission System. On the face of it, the perfect catalytic converter for cars on Earth – reducing CO_2 emissions to zero via an ionising nano-membrane carbon dioxide convertor. A vast majority of vehicles around the world had one fitted – from the taxi that came to collect Stacy Campbell (4.1) to UNIT vehicles (4.4). It was developed by Luke Rattigan and made him a fortune, but it had in fact been augmented by the Sontarans to emit a gas lethal to humans that would make Earth breathable for them and their newly hatched clones. This gas was hidden in a secret compartment in a temporal pocket, just one second out of sync with real time. The gas was a Caesofine Concentrate, which contained carbon monoxide, hydrocarbons, nitrogen oxides, bosteen and probic 5. After the Sontaran plan was defeated, people started removing the ATMOS from their cars very quickly. Another aspect to the ATMOS was an in-built SatNav that gave the Sontarans limited control over vehicles. (4.4, 4.5) (Voiced by ELIZABETH RYDER) In the alternative world where Donna Noble never met the Doctor, ATMOS succeeded in killing large numbers of people until

A

Torchwood put an end to the scheme, although at great personal cost to themselves. (4.11)

Atmospheric Converter: The Doctor built one of these out of odds and ends of human and Sontaran technology he found at the Rattigan Academy. Firing it into Earth's atmosphere ignited the Caesofine Concentrate and so rid the planet of the poison gas from the ATMOS devices. (4.5)

Atom Clamps: Objects used in Bowie Base One. The Doctor didn't need them — he had Gadget! (4.16)

Atraxi: Aliens represented by a huge eye. Prisoner Zero had escaped from them and into Leadworth. The Atraxi traced it to Earth, preparing to destroy the planet if Prisoner Zero was not surrendered to them. The Doctor delivered Prisoner Zero back to them, warning them to stay away from Earth in future as he was its protector (5.1) (VOICED BY DAVID DE KEYSER) One of the races that formed the Pandorica Alliance, they were taken back to Earth's past by the Daleks. (5.12) The story that the Doctor had driven the Atraxi off Earth with a good telling off survived into the 51st century. (6.7)

powered TARDISes and it would reuse limbs and organs from the dead pilots to keep the Patchwork People alive. Auntie finally died when the Doctor's TARDIS, its personality matrix downloaded into another dead humanoid, Idris, was inhabited by House and taken across the Void towards the Doctor's universe. (6.4) (Played by ELIZABETH BERRINGTON)

Attila the Hun: Fifth-century Mongol warlord. According to the Doctor, the city of Venice was founded by refugees fleeing his campaigns. (5.6)

Attlee, Clement: Leader of the Opposition and Winston Churchill's deputy during the coalition that governed Britain during the Second World War. As Lord Privy Seal, Attlee was responsible for bringing the Cabinet together while Churchill worked from the War Rooms beneath London. Churchill told Lillian Breen to contact Attlee and arrange a meeting to discuss the Dalek threat. (5.3)

Augurs: City elders and intellectuals in the Roman Empire who claimed to have special powers allowing them to see the future. Lucius Petrus Dextrus was Chief Augur of Pompeii. (4.2)

Auntie: One of the Patchwork People, a humanoid woman trapped on the sentient asteroid House. She was kept alive by House over many centuries to act as a lure for Time Lords and other travellers who were drawn into House's pocket universe. House fed off the rift energy that

Australasia: The Emperor Dalek's forces bombed this Earth continent in 200,100. (1.13)

Auto-Gloves: Device worn on Roman Groom's hands, and later by the Doctor, with which he remotely controlled Gadget. (4.16)

Automated Decency Filter: Felman Lux installed these in his Courtesy Nodes to ensure that private messages sent to and from visitors remained polite. (4.8, 4.9)

Autons: Animated plastic shop-window dummies brought to life by the Nestene Consciousness when it landed on Earth, fleeing from the Time War. They carried lethal energy blasters in their right hands and were responsible for a massacre in a shopping arcade in South London witnessed by Clive Finch and his family, Jackie Tyler (1.1) and Elton Pope (2.10). A group of Autons who believed they were truly human were established in AD 102 as part of the trap laid by the Pandorica Alliance. Amongst them was an Auton replica of Rory Williams drawn from a photo of him dressed as a legionnaire and Amy as a policewoman from her kissogram days. River Song said she once dated an Auton duplicate. (5.12, 5.13)

Auvers-sur-Oise: North-western region of Paris, where Vincent Van Gogh was living when the Doctor and Amy Pond visited him. He planned to paint a church there — and the Doctor had spotted, in an exhibition centuries later, that he had painted a Krafayis in the window of the church and wanted to find out why. After defeating the Krafayis, the Doctor and Amy returned to the future and saw that the painting no longer had the creature painted into it. (5.10)

Avatar Hologram: Part of the mechanism aboard the Silence and Academy of the Question time engine that had landed on top of 79 Aickman Road and disguised itself as a second-floor flat. In an attempt to find a pilot capable of launching it again, the time engine created a series of human avatars designed to appeal to passers-by, to ensure they would come into the 'flat'. The time engine would then try and turn them into a pilot, accidentally killing them and reducing their bodies to a liquid that began to stain the ceiling of Craig Owens's flat below. (5.11) (Played by DARRELL HEATH, ANDY JONES & ELLIE CURSIO)

AVC: Registration name of one of the British spitfires shot down engaging German Messerschmitts and Heinkels. (5.3)

Avery, Captain Henry: Legendary English pirate who disappeared in 1699. Taking the ship *Charles II* and renaming it *Fancy*, Avery spent a few years as a notorious pirate, amassing a vast treasure. Shortly after he'd stolen the Mogul of India's treasure, Avery's vessel became becalmed and, one by one, its crew were taken by a Siren after they became injured and gained a black spot on their palms. The Doctor tried to use the TARDIS to get the remaining crew, including Avery's son Toby, off the *Fancy*, but the TARDIS was damaged and the Siren took that too. When Rory and then Toby were taken, Avery accepted the Doctor's plan – to be deliberately injured, so the Siren would take them too. Waking up on a Skerth ship, the Doctor realised the Siren was just a holographic automatic medical interface. All Avery's crew, including Toby, had been 'repaired' but would die if they left the medical fields of the ship. Realising that his son was far more important than treasure, Avery elected to sail the Skerth ship across the stars with his son and crew at his side. (6.3) He and his son were amongst the people the Doctor called in favours from during his attack on Demon's Run. The two Averys stopped Kovarian escaping with Melody Pond. (6.7) (Played by HUGH BONNEVILLE)

Avery, Toby: Henry Avery's young son, who had stowed away aboard the *Fancy* some weeks after his mother had passed away. Dying of typhoid fever, he already had a black spot on his palm when Avery found him, but he had been protected from the Siren because he was hiding inside a wooden barrel. However, during a storm, Toby ventured above deck and, when he grabbed his father's coat, the last piece of stolen treasure aboard fell out. This gave the Siren access to Toby, and she took him. They later found Toby aboard the Skerth ship; if they returned to Earth, Toby would die but by staying on the Skerth ship, he was safe. Avery opted to stay with Toby and they set out to explore the stars. (6.3) Toby and his father were amongst the people the Doctor called in favours from during his attack on Demon's Run. The two Averys stopped Kovarian escaping with Melody Pond. (6.7) (Played by OSCAR LLOYD)

Avix Patrol: A Sontaran squad, part of Field Major Kaarsh's team on Earth in 1605. (AG05)

Axons: Energy-vampires that the Master had once been forced to bring to Earth. He and the Axons were defeated by the Doctor. The Master reminded the Doctor of this when taunting him over his current defeat. (3.13)

Azlok, Lord Knight: Commander of the Viperox Battle Drones on Earth, answering only to his Queen, who was living deep beneath the ground, breeding new warriors. Azlok deceived Colonel Stark of the Dreamland military base into helping him search for an Endymide genetic weapon that had been specifically designed to wipe the Viperox out. Stark believed it was a superweapon he could use as a deterrent against the Soviet Union. When the Doctor exposed Azlok, he turned on Stark and the humans but was driven off Earth by the TARDIS sound systems, which the Doctor put on a frequency so painful to Viperox that they all fled. (DL) (Voiced by DAVID WARNER)

B

Babbington, Lady: Socialite whose pearls had recently been stolen from under her nose by the mysterious Unicorn, according to Lady Clemency Eddison. (4.7)

Back to the Future: The Doctor used this 1985 movie and its time-travelling lead character, Marty McFly, to explain to Martha Jones the complexities of the Infinite Temporal Flux. (3.2)

Bad Wolf: A phrase scattered across time and space by Rose Tyler after she had looked into the heart of the TARDIS and absorbed the power of the time vortex. It followed the Ninth Doctor and Rose throughout their travels, until Rose realised it was a message from herself in the future, linking the Bad Wolf Corporation to the present day, and proving that she had to return to the Doctor and save him on board the Game Station. The phrase first appeared when the Moxx of Balhoon was heard talking about 'the Bad Wolf scenario' on Platform One. (1.2) Gabriel Sneed's maid, Gwyneth, spoke of seeing 'the Big Bad Wolf' when she read Rose's mind. (1.3) A young spray-painter wrote 'BAD WOLF' on the side of the TARDIS. (1.4, 1.5) In 2012, Henry Van Statten used 'Bad Wolf One' as the call sign for his helicopter. (1.6) In the year 200,000, Satellite Five was responsible for broadcasting several thousand TV channels, among them 'Bad WolfTV'. (1.7) In 1987, a street poster was defaced with the words 'Bad Wolf', not far from where Pete Tyler was originally killed. (1.8) In 1941, the German bomb due to land on the Chula ambulance was labelled 'Schlechter Wolf'. (1.10) In contemporary Cardiff, Blon Fel Fotch Pasameer-Day Slitheen adopted 'Blaidd Drwg' as the name for her nuclear power station, and the Doctor realised for the first time that the

phrase had been stalking them through time. (1.11) The Doctor and his companions were then abducted from the TARDIS to the Game Station, formerly Satellite Five, and now home to the Bad Wolf Corporation. (1.12) It was their logo that Rose had scattered throughout space and time. The words also appeared on a poster in a South East London café and as graffiti on the Powell Estate. (1.13, 2.1) The Host would later associate Rose Tyler with 'the Wolf' when speaking with her in Scotland, 1879. (2.2) According to Victor Kennedy's research, a Bad Wolf virus

was also responsible for corrupting Torchwood's documentation on Rose Tyler. (2.10) When Rose became trapped on 'Pete's World', the Doctor sent a projection of himself across the Void and it emerged in Norway, on Dårlig Ulv Stranden, otherwise known as Bad Wolf Bay. (2.13) The Japanese translation, *akurō*, appeared on one of the many cars trapped within the New New York Motorway in the year 5,000,000,053. (3.3) Rose Tyler whispered the words to the dying Donna Noble so that, when she was returned to her real body, she could tell the Doctor – because he'd know it was warning that the barriers between the dimensions of reality were coming down. On Shan Shen, everything written suddenly read as the words 'Bad Wolf' until the TARDIS left the planet. (4.11) The Doctor took Rose and his human double back to Bad Wolf Bay to start a new life together. (4.13)

Bahrain: Gulf state, visited by Donna Noble's friend Veena Brady. (4.1)

Bailey, Dolly: Cheeky and cheerful host of the Elephant Inn, who provided rooms for William Shakespeare, the Doctor and Martha Jones. She discovered Lilith the Carrionite guiding Shakespeare's hand as he wrote the climax of *Love's Labour's Won*. Helped along by Lilith, she died of fright. (3.2) (Played by ANDRÉE BERNARD)

Baines, Jeremy: Unpleasant bullying older boy at Farringham School for Boys, he was a snob and a racist. When he left the school grounds illicitly one night to retrieve beer stashed in a tree in Blackdown Woods near Cooper's Field, he witnessed the arrival of the Family of Blood's spaceship. He found a way in and was murdered by the Family, who opted to use his body as a vessel for Son of Mine to inhabit. (3.8) (Played by HARRY LLOYD)

Baker, Matt: TV presenter on *Blue Peter*, who demonstrated how to make a cake shaped like the spaceship which had crashed into Big Ben. (1.4)

Balamory: Township which the Doctor pretended he was from when posing as Doctor James McCrimmon upon meeting Queen Victoria in 1879. Balamory is actually a fictional Scottish island created in a television programme for children 123 years later. (2.2)

Balmoral Castle: Queen Victoria's Scottish home in Aberdeenshire. She was travelling there when her party stopped en route at Sir Robert MacLeish's Torchwood House for a night's rest. (2.2)

Baltazar, Scourge of the Galaxy: A tyrannical despot from the planet Triton. He was about to obliterate Earth in the 40th century when the Doctor destroyed his ship, which he had grown from the metals on the planet Pheros. After his arrest (he was betrayed by his companion, Caw, for three bars of gold), he was placed in a cell on the prison planet Volag-Noc. There he discovered the story of the *Infinite* and, upon his release many years later, he set about finding the datachips that would create a 3D map to lead him to the legendary vessel. He set in motion a task for the Doctor, sending him on a quest to collect

the chips and planning to relieve him of them later. When they found the location of the *Infinite*, Baltazar left the Doctor on Volag-Noc for three years, while heading to the fabled ship in the TARDIS with Martha Jones. But the *Infinite* was of no real use, and the Doctor had Baltazar imprisoned in Volag-Noc once again for the murders of Kaliko, Mergrass and Gurney, the people who originally had the datachips. (TIQ) (Voiced by ANTHONY HEAD)

Banana daiquiri: The Doctor claimed to have invented this cocktail a couple of centuries early, while drunk at a party with Madame de Pompadour in 18th-century France. (2.4)

Bandogge: Mongrel dogs used to guard Bedlam. As a demonstration for visitors, they would sometimes be set upon the inmates for sport. The jailer at Bedlam offered to put on such a show for the Doctor and his friends. (3.2)

Bannakaffalatta: Diminutive Zocci travelling aboard the *Titanic* who flirted with Astrid Peth, and was one of the guests who visited Earth. Bannakaffalatta was in fact a cyborg due to injuries and used his electromagnetic

power source to destroy some of the Heavenly Host, sacrificing his life in the process. (4.X) (Played by JIMMY VEE, voiced by COLIN McFARLANE)

Bannerman Road: Street in Ealing where Sarah Jane Smith lived, with her son, Luke, and Mr Smith, their computer. For a short while, the Jacksons lived opposite. (4.12, 4.13, 4.18)

Banto's DVD Store:
Selling new and second-hand DVDs, this was the shop on Queen Street that Larry Nightingale worked at when Sally Sparrow came to tell him about Kathy's disappearance. The shop was owned by Banto (played by IAN BOLDSWOTH), and amongst the DVDs on display were *Acid Burn*, *City Justice*, *Candy Kane*, *Angel Smile* and *Shooting the Sun*. While there, Sally also saw more of the recorded message from the Doctor; Larry explained to her that it was on 'Easter eggs' across 17 unrelated DVDs. Later, Sally and Larry bought Banto out and took on the shop for themselves, selling antique books and rare DVDs. (3.10)

Barbarella: The Doctor likened the effect Rose's contemporary clothes would have on the people of Naples in 1860 to Jean-Claude Forest's comic-strip heroine, famed for wearing not very much at all. (1.3)

Barcelona: Capital city of Catalonia, Spain. The Doctor was not thinking of taking Rose Tyler there, but instead to the planet Barcelona, where dogs had no noses, on a Tuesday in October of 5006, at 6pm. (1.13, BA) The Doctor told the Caecilius family that Donna Noble was from there. (4.2)

Barclay: Teenager and almost qualified car mechanic aboard the number 200 bus to Brixton when it went through a wormhole to San Helios. He was on his way to see his girlfriend Tina. He proved resourceful and smart on San Helios, and

the Doctor recommended him to Captain Magambo as a potential recruit for UNIT. (4.15) (Played by DANIEL KALUUYA)

Barman [1]: Passed a note from the Doctor to Captain Jack Harkness in the Zaggit Zagoo bar on Zog concerning Midshipman Frame. (4.18) (Played by JAKE APPLEBEE)

Barman [2]: Pointed out where Gideon Vandaleur was to the Doctor. (6.13) (Played by SEAN BUCKLEY)

Barnaby: Orphan, and friend of Charlie, who had become a cutpurse on the streets of London in 1605. (AG05) (Voiced by CHRIS JOHNSON)

Barnes, Oliver: One of the Silver Cloak, who drove their Sparrow Lane minibus. He took a bit of a shine to the Doctor, although, unlike Minnie Hooper, refrained from pinching his bum. (4.17) (Played by BARRY HOWARD)

Barren Earth Scenario: A study from the 'Pete's World' version of the Torchwood Institute reported that, as male fertility dropped, life spans in the western world were decreasing. (2.5)

Bartle, Mr: Marketing Manager of Ood Operations, who thought his boss Halpen was an idiot. He was murdered by Ood Delta Fifty and when Halpen discovered what Bartle thought of him, he had all Bartle's family's benefits negated. (4.3) (Played by PAUL CLAYTON)

Bartock, Daniel: Representative from the Ethics Committee on Sanctuary Base 6 who, according to the Beast, was a liar. He formed something of a flirtatious relationship with Rose Tyler and it was his idea to create a psychic flare that would disable the Ood and perhaps break the hold over them which the Beast had. When that was successful, he, Rose, Toby Zed and Zachary Cross Flane escaped on a shuttleship from Krop Tor as the planet was sucked towards the nearby black hole. (2.8, 2.9) (Played by RONNY JHUTTI)

Basic 5: The telepathic level upon which the Ood communicated with one another. It rose to Basic 30 when the Beast first made contact with them and then, as they attacked the humans on Sanctuary Base 6, peaked at a massive Basic 100, which should have killed them but didn't. (1.8, 1.9)

Bastic bullets: Weaponry that Captain Jack Harkness told the doomed humans aboard the Game Station would be effective against Dalek armour. He was wrong, however, and the bastic bullets failed. (1.13)

Battersea: Area of South West London, famous for its disused power station. On 'Pete's World', John Lumic's Cybus Industries had converted the power station into a massive Cyber-conversion factory. (2.5, 2.6)

Battery Park: Area of New New York, from where Brannigan and Valerie set out, five miles back from Pharmacytown. They had left it twelve years before the Doctor's arrival. (3.3)

Battle of Canary Wharf: Popular name given to the battle on 21st-century Earth between the Cybermen and the Daleks. (2.12, 2.13) The Cybermen and Daleks were returned to the Void, although the four-strong Cult of Skaro escaped. (3.4, 3.5) Captain Jack Harkness later investigated the lists of the dead or missing and found Rose Tyler's name among them, but was relieved to

learn from the Doctor that she, her mum, Jackie, and Mickey Smith were all alive and well, though trapped on the parallel Earth known as 'Pete's World'. (3.11)

Battle of Trafalgar: The Doctor told Rose he could take her to witness this. (2.2)

Battle of Waterloo: The final battle in the war between the British and Napoleon Bonaparte's French army in June 1815. John Smith, the fictional character created by the chameleon arch to exist in Farringham School for Boys in 1913, was teaching the boys in his class about the battle. (3.8)

Baudouin I: King of the Belgians in 1953 – the Doctor's psychic paper convinced a security guard at Alexandra Palace that that was who the Doctor was. (2.7)

Bavaria: Modern name for Saxe-Coburg, as the Doctor explained to Rose Tyler. (2.2)

Baxter: A schoolboy at Farringham School for Boys in 1913, he was popular with the older boys for stashing beer in Blackdown Woods outside the school grounds. (3.8)

Baxter, Geoffrey: UNIT adviser in their Mission Control base beneath the Tower of London. As his blood group was A+, he was hypnotised by the Sycorax. (2.X) (Played by IAN HILDITCH)

Baxters, the: Guests at the wedding of Stuart Hoskins and Sarah Clark. They hadn't arrived. (1.8)

B

Bazoolium: A ceramic which changes temperature to predict the weather. Rose Tyler obtained a jar constructed from it at a bazaar on an asteroid and gave it to her mum, Jackie, as a gift. (2.12)

Bear River Massacre: A famous battle between the US army and the Native American Shoshoni tribe in 1863, in which the tribe were all but wiped out. Jimmy Stalkingwolf reminded Cassie Rice and the Doctor that his people believed the military had been running roughshod over the dwindling Shoshoni ever since. (DL)

Bear With Me: One of the programmes broadcast from the Game Station. Three people had to live with a bear. The Doctor liked the celebrity edition, in which the bear climbed into a bath. (1.12)

Beast, the: A legendary creature of evil, imprisoned beneath the surface of Krop Tor by the Disciples of Light, when our universe didn't exist. Its gaolers placed it there because the planet was in a permanent geo-stationary orbit around the black hole later referred to as K 37 Gem 5. If the Beast was freed, the planet would crash into the black hole, destroying itself and the Beast. However, the Beast managed to transfer its consciousness into humans, firstly a crewman called Curt, whose mind broke under the strain, then later archaeologist Tobias Zed and a group of Ood, willing to sacrifice its huge demonic body for a chance to spread its evil throughout the universe of the 42nd century. When it was threatened, it placed all of its mind in Toby Zed, but Rose Tyler ejected Toby into space where he and the trapped consciousness of the Beast were destroyed for good in the event horizon of the black hole, followed shortly after by its now empty body, which was drawn, along with the planet Krop Tor itself, into the black hole. (2.8, 2.9) (Voiced by GABRIEL WOOLF)

Beatbox Club: South London nightclub, where Sarah Clark had been the night she met Stuart Hoskins. (1.8)

Beatles, The: British pop group of the 1960s and early 1970s. The crew of the SS *Pentallian* had set a trivia question on one of their door seals, asking who had had the most UK number one hits before the download era – Elvis or The Beatles. (The Beatles lost!) The Doctor quoted one of their songs, 'Here Comes The Sun', as the ship neared the living sun. (3.7) Their first two albums were one of the highlights of 1963, according to the Doctor. (AG01) The Doctor wanted to join them. (6.13)

Beatrice: One of Donna Noble's co-workers at Jival Chowdry's photocopying business in the alternative world where Donna never met the Doctor. Donna suspected Bea of writing her redundancy notice on Chowdry's behalf. Donna stole Bea's stapler, but gave her a toy cactus. (4.11)

Beckham, Victoria: According to Lance Bennett, Donna Noble talked excitedly about this former Spice Girl, known as Posh Spice, and whether she was pregnant. (3.X)

B

Bedlam: Common name for Bethlem Royal Hospital. (3.2)

Bee: One of Sarah Clark's guests, expected at her wedding, but who hadn't shown up. (1.8)

Bees: Donna Noble told the Doctor that a large proportion of the world's bees had recently inexplicably disappeared. (4.1) She mentioned it again on the Ood-Sphere. (4.3) In the alternative world where Donna never met the Doctor, her mum noted the bees had disappeared. (4.11) The Doctor realised the migrant bees were using a wavelength to find their way home, to Melissa Majorica. Having sensed the danger that the Daleks represented, they left Earth and went home. (4.12)

Beethoven, Ludwig van: 18th-century German composer, often cited as one of the greatest who ever lived, who was tragically deaf by the time he was 30, although he carried on composing. The Doctor reckoned he learnt to play the organ by hanging around with Beethoven. (3.6)

Beijing: Capital of China. Martha Jones claimed to have gone there and collected one of the phials of liquid needed to arm the gun she was allegedly preparing to kill the Master with. (3.13) The Master took control of 2.5 million Chinese soldiers there, all of which were in fact him. (4.18)

Belgium: European country on Earth. The Fifth and Tenth Doctors, after a time collision occurred, reasoned that the resultant explosion would create a hole in the space/time vortex the size of Belgium. (TC) Agatha Christie said she decided to make Hercule Poirot a Belgian because they make lovely buns. She may not have been entirely serious. (4.7)

Bell family: Florizel Street residents and recent purchasers of a television set on which they could watch the Queen's Coronation. (2.7)

Bell, Alexander Graham: Scottish thinker, generally recognised as the inventor of the telephone in 1876 in America. The very first phone call, made by Bell to his assistant Thomas Watson, bled through onto both Sonny Hoskins' portable phone and Rose Tyler's anachronistic mobile phone in 1987. This was just as a time breach occurred, as a result of Rose saving her father's life earlier. (1.8)

Bell, Doctor Joseph: The Doctor, posing as Doctor James McCrimmon, told Queen Victoria that he studied under Bell at Edinburgh University. (2.2)

Ben [1]: School classmate to Mandy Tanner and Timmy Winters. (5.2)

Ben [2]: White House worker who was apparently tall and a bit of a *Star Trek* fan, according to Joy. (6.1)

Benjamin: Nephew of Abigail Pettigrew. He, his Aunt Isabella, his son and daughter visited Kazran Sardick to beg to be allowed to 'borrow' Abigail for Christmas Day. Because they still owed 4,500 Gideons, Sardick refused. When the Doctor went back through time, trying to change Sardick's past, he took Abigail to the family on Christmas Eve, when Benjamin was just a young boy. The Doctor tried a variety of card tricks on Benjamin, who remained unimpressed, if amused. (6.X) (Played by STEVE NORTH and BAILEY PEPPER)

Bennett, Geologist Mia: Crewmember on the Bowie Base One Mars mission, secretly involved with the base's nurse, Yuri Kerenski. Born in Houston, Texas, her father, Peter, was a famous astronaut and geologist, and Mia

B

followed in his footsteps. Along with Yuri and Captain Adelaide Brooke, she survived the attack by the Flood and was safely returned to Earth by the Doctor in the TARDIS. Freaked out by all the deaths she had witnessed, on top of the dimensional transcendentalism of the TARDIS, she fled, closely followed by Yuri. She and Yuri later learned that Adelaide had died and gave glowing testimonials to her bravery, which helped inspire Adelaide's granddaughter Susie to follow in her footsteps. (4.16) (Played by GEMMA CHAN)

Bennett, Lance: Personnel officer at HC Clements, who made a deal with the Empress of the Racnoss. In exchange for supplying her with a sacrificial victim, who could be imbued with Huon particles and become a key to unlock the ship at the centre of Earth, the Secret Heart, where the Racnoss young were imprisoned, he would get to explore the stars with her. Meeting Donna at work, he faked a relationship with her as he fed her Huon liquid every day, hidden in cups of coffee. He was even willing to go through with marrying her but the hormones in Donna's body, excited by the wedding, caused the Huon particles to react early and she was drawn into the Doctor's TARDIS. Pretending to go along with the returned Donna and the Doctor, Lance betrayed them to the Empress. However, when the Doctor escaped with Donna, the Empress, now knowing exactly how much Huon energy a human body could take, force-fed Lance more Huon particles, turning him into a spare key. Eventually tiring of her plaything, the Empress threw Lance down to the centre of the planet and, as his body hit the Secret Heart, it opened and the Racnoss children escaped, most likely eating Lance's body along the way. (3.X) (Played by DON GILET)

Bennett, Stan and Iris: Lance Bennett's parents, who were at the church when Donna Noble disappeared during her wedding to their son. They later partied at the reception, and Stan was injured when the Christmas baubles exploded under the direction of the Roboforms. (3.X) (Played by ASH CRONEY, SANDRA SCOTT)

Benson, Sophie: A friend of Craig Owens. The two of them actually loved each other, but neither was brave enough to say so and they ended up almost losing one another after Sophie, encouraged by the Doctor, decided to

move abroad to work with primates. As she was coming to say one last farewell to Craig, she was tricked into entering the apartment above Craig's. In fact this was a spaceship with a time engine that was looking for a new pilot. Sophie's desire to leave was the psychic power it needed, but Craig persuaded her to stay and this conflicting information destroyed the ship. The Doctor left Sophie and Craig to start a new life together, happily in love at last. (5.11) After marrying Craig, they had a baby, Alfie. Sophie left Craig to look after Alfie for a weekend while she went to help her mate Melina and thus missed the Doctor's return to their lives. (6.12) (Played by DAISY HAGGARD)

Bergerac: BBC Television detective series set on Jersey, about Sergeant Jim Bergerac. Jim Purcell was appalled to find a repeated episode on television one night. (6.9)

Bering Strait: A strait running between East Russia and Alaska. The Master and the Toclafane had turned Russia into the massive Shipyard Number One, which ran from the Black Sea to the Bering Strait. (3.13)

Berlin: Capital of Germany. The TARDIS went there in 1938 after Melody Zucker shot the Time Rotor. The Doctor, Melody, Amy Pond and Rory Williams met Adolf Hitler and encountered the *Teselecta* there. (6.8)

Bernard: Jim Purcell's bulldog, which went everywhere with him on the Rowbarton House estate. (6.9) (Played by ELVIS)

Bernard Quatermass, Professor: Fictional scientist who Doctor Malcolm Taylor had named a unit of measurement after. (4.15)

Bessan: Home world of a race who resembled bats. The Krillitanes invaded and dominated Bessan, and absorbed the inhabitants' physical characteristics. (2.3)

Betamax: Domestic videotape system available from 1975. The Doctor stored the defeated Wire on a Betamax tape in 1953 and claimed he was going to record over it. (2.7)

Bethlem Royal Hospital: London institute for the insane, based in Bishopsgate. The Doctor, William Shakespeare and Martha Jones headed there to visit Peter Streete, who had been incarcerated under terrible conditions after talking about witches. (3.2)

Betty, Aunty: Eddie Connolly's sister who, with her husband John and pet terrier, visited Eddie's house to watch the Coronation on his new television set. She suggested that Eddie should beat Tommy Connolly, to stop him growing up a 'mummy's boy'. (2.7) (Played by JEAN CHALLIS)

Betty Boop: Cartoon heroine created by Max Fleischer. One of her cartoons, 'Betty Boop and Grampy', was showing as part of the Entertainment System aboard the *Crusader 50*. (4.10)

Bev: Friend of Jackie Tyler. (1.1) She was in the wedding party at Stuart Hoskins' marriage to Sarah Clark in 1987 when Pete Tyler died. (1.8) Jackie was gossiping on the phone with her when Rose returned home after being attacked by the Roboform mercenaries. She later called Jackie to tell her it was snowing. (2.X) (Played by EIRLYS BELLIN)

Bexley: South London town on the border with Kent. Martha Jones and Thomas Milligan planned to stay overnight in slave quarters there whilst on their

way to a North London UNIT base. Martha found a chance to tell her story about the Doctor there, before she was interrupted by the Master who came to find her. Thomas Milligan tried to protect Martha, but was lasered down on the streets by the Master. (3.13)

Bianca: A Venetian flower-seller who almost became a victim of Francesco Calvierri until Amy Pond and Rory Williams interrupted him. (5.6) (Played by GABRIEJELA PALINIC)

Big Ben: Colloquial name for the clock attached to Westminster Palace, home of the British Parliament – Big Ben is actually the bell, the tower structure is St Stephen's Tower. In 1941, Rose Tyler and Captain Jack Harkness danced on his invisible Chula warship in front of the clock face during the Blitz. (1.9) The clock, bell and tower top were destroyed in 2006 when a spaceship piloted by an augmented pig crashed through it before landing in the River Thames. (1.4) Rebuilding work was still going on by the time the Sycorax ship arrived over London the following Christmas. (2.X) The Doctor found himself suspended over it as his out-of-control TARDIS spun towards Earth. (5.1)

Big Brother: One of the many 'games' being played on the Game Station and broadcast throughout Earth – there were 60 *Big Brother* contests going on simultaneously throughout the Game Station. Like all the games, losing appeared to be instantly fatal, although in fact eviction from the *Big Brother* house involved being transported to the Dalek mothership and turned into part of the growing Dalek army created by the Emperor. (1.12)

Big Brother 504: An earlier *Big Brother* series than the one the Doctor found himself part of aboard the Game Station, in which the contestants had rebelled and walked out. After that, all Game Station studios were locked with a deadlock seal to prevent a repeat of that situation. (1.12)

Biggin Hill: Kent village and home to a major airfield during the Second World War. A number of squadrons were despatched from there to deal with German fighters by Group Captain Childers's team in the Cabinet War Rooms. (5.3)

Biggles: Amy Pond's favourite cat when she was younger. (6.10)

Biggs, Ronald: Great Train Robber from the 1960s, who fled to Brazil and remained there in hiding, because Brazil and Britain had no extradition treaty. The Doctor likened the Plasmavore's hiding on Earth to Biggs in Brazil, as the Judoon could not track it down on Earth. (3.1)

Binary 9: Access to information about John Lumic, including passcodes and logins for Cybus Industries, were found by Pete Tyler and transmitted on wavelength 657 using binary 9, which he then passed to the Preachers in the guise of Gemini. Mickey Smith subsequently used the same path to access the code that disabled the Cybermen's emotional inhibitors on 'Pete's World'. (2.6)

Binary dot tool: A device the Doctor used to construct a portable scanner to help him find the Isolus Podship. (2.11)

Biocattle: The Sisters of Plenitude tried using biocattle to cultivate their cures and vaccines, which failed, so they bred New Humans instead. (2.1)

Biochip: All of the crew of Sanctuary Base 6 had a biochip implanted in them, so their whereabouts could be monitored and they were locatable in an emergency. (2.8, 2.9)

Bio-Convention: On 'Pete's World', the Bio-Convention was a piece of legislature from the Ethical Committee that the Cybus Industries Ultimate Upgrade Project contravened. (2.5)

Biodamper: The Doctor gave one of these to Donna, in the shape of a ring, hoping it would keep her hidden from the Roboform Santas that were pursuing her. However, the Roboforms were still able to find her at her non-wedding

B

reception, because the Huon particles in her blood were so old that a biodamper could not conceal them. (3.X)

BIS: See *Brandon's Information Solutions*

Bishop, Detective Inspector: Baffled policeman in North London, charged with investigating the outbreak of faceless people. He locked the victims in a cage for their own safety and, when he encountered the Doctor, discovered that an alien criminal called the Wire was responsible, shortly before he too fell victim and lost his face. Once the Wire was defeated, his face returned and Bishop was able to resume his duties. (2.7) (Played by SAM COX)

Bishop, the: Local church leader whose son drowned. The body looked a mess but, as a favour, Cardiff undertaker Gabriel Sneed used all his embalming skills to make the body look cherubic. (1.3)

Bistro 10: Cardiff Bay restaurant where the Doctor and Margaret Blaine dined. (1.11)

'Bitey': Nickname the Doctor gave to the Cybermat he reprogrammed to attack the Cybermen in Colchester. The Cybermen stomped upon 'Bitey', destroying it. (6.12)

Black Death, the: Pestilence that regularly afflicted London, most likely a mutation of the bubonic plague. William Shakespeare's son Hamnet was a victim and it was grief over his death that saw Shakespeare at his lowest ebb, almost incarcerated in Bedlam for a while, enabling the Carrionites to use his words of despair to access Elizabethan England. (3.2)

Black, Doctor: Art academic at the Musée D'Orsay in Paris, who believed Vincent Van Gogh to be the finest painter of all time. (5.10) (Played by BILL NIGHY)

Black Gold, the: The pirate ship owned by Captain Kaliko. It patrolled Bouken, a desert planet OilCorp were sucking dry of its natural resources in an oil-starved 40th century, then selling them at inflated prices. (TIQ)

Black hole: Deep-space phenomenon. The one designated K 37 Gem 5 was connected by a gravity funnel to the planet Krop Tor, impossibly in orbit around it. When the funnel finally collapsed, Krop Tor was drawn back towards the black hole. The survivors aboard Sanctuary Base 6 tried to use an escape shuttle to flee the black hole but were pulled back after the Beast, in its human host Toby Zed, was sucked into the event horizon. Using the TARDIS, the Doctor drew the shuttle to safety, but Krop Tor was eventually destroyed within the black hole's event horizon. (2.8, 2.9)

Black hole converters: Technology the Master had placed within his 2,000 war rockets, with which he planned to destroy planets and convert them into black holes. With his plans on the verge of failing, he threatened to set the black hole converters off on Earth, but the Doctor pointed out that this would kill him. The Master relented, passing over his wristwatch, which contained the detonator. (3.13)

Black Rod: Parliamentary official in 1605, charged with keeping the King's ceremonial treasures safe, as well as being a master swordsman. He was briefly taken over by the Sontarans but freed from their control by Rory Williams. (AG05) (Voiced by MILES RICHARDSON)

Black Sea: Inland sea, stretching between Russia and the south-eastern end of Europe. The Master and the Toclafane had turned Russia into the massive Shipyard Number One which ran from the Black Sea to the Bering Strait. (3.13)

Black Void: Area in the Citadel on Gallifrey where Lord President Rassilon's War Council met during the Time War, and where he addressed the

legion of Time Lords awaiting his commands. Aware that Gallifrey was timelocked, Rassilon plotted the Ultimate Sanction, but to do this he needed help from outside Gallifrey. From within the Black Void, Rassilon sent a thought impulse back through time to form a link within the Master's mind, via which Gallifrey and the Time Lords could be brought back into existence. (4.17, 4.18)

Blackbeard: 18th-century English pirate, real name Edward Teach, famed for lighting matches within his huge beard and frightening his foes, who believed he resembled the devil. The Doctor cited him as a great warrior commander to Martha Jones. (TIQ)

Blackdown Woods: Jeremy Baines, a pupil at Farringham School for Boys, was sent there to retrieve beer but became intrigued by a spaceship that landed in Cooper's Field. (3.8)

Blackfriars: Area of London, on the north bank of the Thames, where Mr Crane collected Morris and the other homeless, an act videotaped by Jake Simmonds on 'Pete's World'. (2.5)

Blaidd Drwg: Welsh for 'Bad Wolf'. It was the name selected by Blon Fel Fotch Pasameer-Day Slitheen, posing as Margaret Blaine, for the nuclear power plant she intended to destroy. The resultant energy would have enabled her to open the rift above Cardiff and escape. (1.11)

Blaine, Margaret: An MI5 officer who was murdered by the Family Slitheen and her body used so the Slitheen could infiltrate the British government after everyone's attention was diverted by the Big Ben incident. She was responsible for the Prime Minister. (1.4, 1.5) She was the only Slitheen to escape the bombing of 10 Downing Street by activating a short-range teleport device concealed in her earrings and brooch. She ended up on the Isle of Dogs in East London and later made her way to Cardiff, where she became the Mayor, pushing through the construction of the Blaidd Drwg nuclear facility. A scale model of the facility was built on the back of a tribophysical waveform macro-kinetic extrapolator. Not having the power to use it herself, she was hoping that a nuclear meltdown would supply the energy she needed to open the space and time rift running through Cardiff and power up the extrapolator. As it turned out, the arrival of the TARDIS and Captain Jack's wiring up of the extrapolator to the ship's console supplied the very power she needed. Despite the Doctor's best attempts to get Margaret to recognise the error of her ways, she still tried to kill Rose Tyler to ensure the Doctor took her away from Earth. Instead, the extrapolator's power, mixed with that of the rift and the time machine itself, opened up the heart of the TARDIS. Margaret gazed into the pure energies of the time vortex and reverted to an egg. The Doctor took the egg back to Raxacoricofallapatorius in the hope that, reborn, Margaret might take a different path. (1.11) (Played by ANNETTE BADLAND)

Blair, Tony: Former Prime Minister of Great Britain, and possibly the one murdered by the Family Slitheen. (1.4) Mickey Smith commented that 'Pete's World' was perhaps a parallel world where Blair never got elected. (2.5)

Blake: One of the soldiers under Captain Reynolds protecting Queen Victoria in 1879. (2.2)

Blake, Major Richard: UNIT officer in charge of the Sycorax situation. He briefed Harriet Jones and Daniel Llewellyn on the protocols of dealing with extraterrestrial beings and was with them both when they were teleported aboard the Sycorax ship. After the death of Llewellyn, Blake tried to protect Harriet Jones, but died when the Sycorax Leader struck him with his energy whip. (2.X) (Played by CHU OMAMBALA)

Blake, Ursula: Caught up in the events surrounding the Sycorax invasion on Christmas Day, Ursula had gone to Trafalgar Square in London that night, to celebrate being alive. While there, she took a photo of the Doctor, which led to her meeting Colin Skinner, and then the other members of a group of Doctor-fans who later became known as LINDA. Ursula was especially drawn

to Elton Pope and they started a mild relationship. When Victor Kennedy, in reality the alien Abzorbaloff, infiltrated LINDA, only Ursula and Elton stood up to him, and Ursula was, like Skinner and the other LINDA members before her, absorbed into his skin. When Elton broke the Abzorbaloff's cane, Ursula and the others managed to exert enough pressure internally that the Abzorbaloff exploded. The Doctor was able to restore Ursula's life essence as she had been the last one absorbed, and so she survived as a face embedded in a concrete slab, living in Elton's flat. (2.10) Davros taunted the Doctor about how many people had died trying to help him over the years, and this made the Doctor think of Ursula. (4.13) (Played by SHIRLEY HENDERSON)

Blanche: One of the WAAF personnel working for Winston Churchill in the Map Room in the Cabinet War Rooms beneath London. (5.3) (Played by NINA DE COSIMO)

Blasco, Dee Dee: Young, enthusiastic research assistant to Professor Hobbes, travelling with him on the *Crusader 50*. She didn't really like the Professor much and was far more interested in her thesis about the Lost Moon of Poosh. Her father had been a mechanic so she understood the way the *Crusader 50* worked and could reassure the other passengers that they weren't going to suffocate when it got stranded. When an entity took over the mind of one of the other passengers, Sky Silvestry, Dee Dee veered from a belief in the Doctor to fearing him, eventually joining in the attempt to throw the Doctor out onto the surface. However, after Sky's villainy was revealed and she was destroyed, Dee Dee realised her error. (4.10) (Played by AYESHA ANTOINE)

Blazen Scale: Method of monitoring energy in the 42nd century. The energy readings from beneath Krop Tor were over 90 statts, enough energy to fuel the Empire. (2.8)

Bliss [1]: An artistic member of LINDA, Bliss was the first victim of the Abzorbaloff, ending up as part of his posterior, although he told LINDA that she had left to get married. When the absorbed victims fought back to explode the Abzorbaloff, Bliss died alongside her fellow LINDA teammates, Bridget and Colin Skinner. (2.10) (Played by KATHRYN DRYSDALE)

Bliss [2]: A new Mood Patch developed in New New York in 5,000,000,029. It mutated quickly into an airborne virus and killed everybody in the Overcity in seven minutes. Only the Face of Boe and Novice Hame, protected by his smoke, survived and set about ensuring those living in the Undercity and on the Motorway could survive. (3.3)

Bloodtide, Mother: One of the Carrionites who had escaped into Elizabethan England, seeking to have William Shakespeare write the words that, when spoken at the end of his play *Love's Labour's Won*, would open a portal in time and space and release the rest of the Carrionites from the Deep Darkness into which the Eternals had cast them at the dawn of time. When William Shakespeare turned their spellcasting back on them, Mother Bloodtide and the other

Carrionites were trapped inside their crystal ball for eternity. (3.2) (Played by LINDA CLARK)

Blowfish: Piscine aliens which travelled to Stonehenge as part of the Pandorica Alliance. When the Pandorica opened and history was stopped, the Alliance were reduced to fossils. (5.12) (Played by CHRIS BARBER)

Bloxham Road: Street close to the Powell Estate, where the Sycorax teleport sent the Doctor, Mickey Smith, Rose Tyler, Alex Klein and Harriet Jones. (2.X)

Blue Division: A troop of security guards under the command of Bywater, working for Henry Van Statten in his Vault, deep below Utah. (1.6)

Blue Peter: Children's television magazine programme. Presenter Matt Baker demonstrated how to make a cake shaped like the spaceship that had crashed into Big Ben. (1.4)

Blyton, Enid: Successful British children's author of the 20th century. Donna Noble assumed it would be difficult to find Enid having tea with her fictional creation, Noddy. (4.7)

Boardwalk, the: A bar that Donna Noble's mate Mooky suggested they spent Christmas Eve at in the alternative world where Donna never met the Doctor. (4.11)

Boatswain, the: Second-in-command of Avery's pirate crew aboard the *Fancy*. He taunted Avery's son, Toby, about Avery being a pirate and in anger Toby stabbed at him, injuring him. The Boatswain lasted longer than the rest of his shipmates as the Doctor had ensured there were no reflective surfaces in the magazine, where he was tied up after trying to mutiny. However the chains that held him were reflective and the Siren eventually got him. He was later found alive aboard the Skerth ship, being tended to by the Siren. He joined Avery exploring the universe. (6.3) (Played by LEE ROSS)

Bob: Huw Edwards' fellow commentator at the Olympic Games Opening Ceremony. Bob was in the Stadium when the Isolus extracted everyone, Bob included, and placed them in an ionic holding pen. He was later returned when the Isolus left Earth safely. (2.11)

Bob, Cleric: One of Father Octavian's troopers. He was killed in the catacombs by the Weeping Angel from Razbahn which then used his voice to contact the Doctor. (5.4, 5.5) (Played by DAVID ATKINS)

Bobby: One of the Silver Cloak who Wilfred Mott asked to ring the skiffle band. (4.17)

Boemina: The alleged name to be given to the Face of Boe's offspring, according to the *Boewatch* programme on Bad WolfTV. (1.7)

Boer War: More accurately the Second Boer War, fought between the British and the Transvaal allies over the ever-growing British Empire and ownership of the precious jewels and mineral ores in Africa. Joan Redfern's husband Oliver died at the battle of Spion Kop in January 1900. (3.8)

Boeshane Peninsula: A tiny colony, where Captain Jack Harkness grew up. He was later the colony's first successful applicant to the Time Agency. This achievement got his image on posters, and he was referred to as the Face of Boe. (3.13)

Boewatch: A programme about the Face of Boe on Bad WolfTV, which was reporting his pregnancy when the Doctor and Rose Tyler visited Satellite Five. (1.7)

'Bohemian Rhapsody': Song written by Queen. Rocco Colasanto led everyone in a rousing chorus of it in their house in Leeds in the alternative world where Donna Noble never met the Doctor. (4.11)

Boléro: 1928 ballet work, composed by Maurice Ravel. Toby Zed listened to this while working on the ancient Veltino inscriptions he had found on the surface of Krop Tor. The music switched off when the Beast contacted his mind. (2.8)

Bonaparte, Napoleon: French general and later his country's Emperor, who was a brilliant strategist and campaigner. He dominated much of Western Europe during the early 19th century. The Doctor cited him as a great warrior commander to Martha Jones. (TIQ) According to the Doctor, he loved Venice. (5.6) The bottle of wine the Doctor brought to Lake Silencio had been given to him (or rather, thrown at him) by Napoleon. (6.13)

Bone Meadows: Standing on Alfava Metraxis with the Doctor, River Song wondered if they had done the Bone Meadows yet. (5.4)

Bosley: Barney Collins's dog, which was duplicated by the Prisoner Zero multiform. (5.1)

Bosteen: Part of the chemical compound that the Sontarans used in the ATMOS devices. (4.4, 4.5)

Bosphorus: Turkish restaurant in Cardiff Bay, where Captain Jack Harkness entertained the Doctor, Rose Tyler and Mickey Smith with his tales of life as a Time

Agent. The Doctor's holiday mood was broken when he saw a photograph of Margaret Blaine on the front page of the *Western Mail*. (1.11)

Boston Tea Party: The Doctor told Rose Tyler that he had been present in December 1773 at the start of the American Revolution, actually pushing boxes onto the decks of the British ships ready to have their contents tipped overboard. (1.3)

Boudicca: English queen of Norfolk who led an uprising against the invading Romans in AD 61. She came so close to success that Emperor Nero almost

considered withdrawing his garrisons from the British Isles, but ultimately she was defeated in the West Midlands. The Doctor cited her as a great warrior commander to Martha Jones. (TIQ)

Bougainvillea: South American evergreen plant. The Doctor could smell them on Messaline, where the terraforming device known as the Source had begun its work in an enclosed area. (4.6)

Bouken: Desert world overrun by the oil rigs owned by OilCorp, who were sucking the planet dry of its natural resources in an oil-starved 40th century and selling them on at inflated prices. OilCorp's biggest opponents were a number of pirates who would attack the rigs and steal the oil, selling it at low prices to poorer planets. (TIQ)

Bowie Base One: Named after British singer David Bowie who had a hit single 'Life On Mars?', Bowie Base One was the first experimental scientific research establishment set up by the World State on Mars in 2058. There a group of humans tried to see if the planet could be colonised. Constructed in Liverpool and built in kit form on Mars as a series of connected domes (medical, engineering, bio, etc.), the base was deliberately built over the Gusev Crater because the ice floe beneath could potentially supply water. However, deep within the frozen water lived a microscopic sentient life force, the Flood. In 2059, the Flood began to infiltrate the crew via the water they used. It took the humans over one by one, until Captain Adelaide Brooke blew the base to pieces with its nuclear core. Established history stated that when it was destroyed, all hands died with it. The Doctor changed that when he saved three of the crew and took them home to Earth. (4.16)

Boxer: Mate of Leo Jones, who was visiting Brighton with Leo, Shonara and Keisha when Harry Saxon kidnapped Leo's parents and eldest sister. (3.12)

Boy: Young member of a family whose Christmas was almost ruined when his parents were kidnapped by the Graske and replaced with changelings. But the real parents were swiftly returned, none the wiser. (AotG) (Played by JAMES HARRIS)

Braccatolian space: An area in which the Master planned to open up a rift and launch war rockets containing black hole converters through it, which would herald the dawn of his New Time Lord Empire. (3.13)

Bracewell, Professor Edwin: Winston Churchill's chief scientist who was believed to have invented the 'Ironsides' as weapons with which to win the Second World War. When the Doctor discovered that the Ironsides were Daleks, he realised that Bracewell was in fact an android built by the Daleks, with a positronic brain. He was powered by an Oblivion Continuum in his chest, which could be remotely detonated. The real Bracewell had existed at some point as the android had his memories – especially those of an old flame called Dorabella and of growing up with his parents in a post office in Paisley. These were so deeply implanted that he had no idea he wasn't real. After the Daleks were defeated, largely thanks to Bracewell's scientific knowledge, the Doctor and Amy Pond made sure he escaped the Cabinet War Rooms to try and start his life over again and find Dorabella. (5.3) Churchill subsequently retained his services, and Bracewell later showed him a Van Gogh painting, *The Pandorica Opens*, when he realised it contained a message for the Doctor. (5.12) (Played by BILL PATTERSON)

Brady, Veena: Mate of Donna Noble. She once went to Bahrain. Donna used her as an alibi to explain to Sylvia Noble why she was going away for a while. In fact she was leaving Earth along with the Doctor. (4.1) Sylvia told Donna she asked Veena about this, but Veena had known nothing about it. (4.4) In the alternative world where Donna never met the Doctor, Veena was one of the mates Donna was out drinking with when the Empress of the Racnoss attacked Earth. (4.11) Veena was famous for getting two-for-one lagers from the local off-licence because she fancied the salesman with a goatee beard. After Donna had lost all her memories of the Doctor, Veena was the first person she spoke to about the planets in the sky. (4.13) (Played by SUZANN McLEAN)

Brakovitch: Someone from Captain Jack Harkness's past, according to one of his amusing anecdotes. (1.11)

'Brand New Key': Originally a hit for Melanie in 1971, Bliss and Ursula of LINDA sang this song together at one of their meetings. (2.10)

Brandon, Joe: A resident living close to Deffry Vale High School who first brought the UFOs to the attention of local newspapers. (2.3T)

Brandon's Information Solutions: Call centre where Craig Owens worked and met Sophie Benson. When the stain on the ceiling of his apartment poisoned him, Craig fell ill so the Doctor took his place for the day, representing Craig at a team meeting and getting Craig's ideas for improvements agreed. (5.11)

Brannigan family: Thomas Kincade Brannigan (played by ARDAL O'HANLON) was an eccentric Catkind car driver in the Motorway tunnels of New New York who, along with his human wife Valerie (played by JENNIFER HENNESSEY) and their litter of kittens, offered the Doctor a lift. Brannigan initially thought the Doctor was a little bit dim, then quite rude, but after a while gained a great deal of respect for the Time Lord. Valerie was amused by the Doctor at first, but got anxious about his influence when he began insisting that, with three adults aboard, they should head to the Fast Lane to find Martha Jones. She was adamant she would not take her kittens down there. The Brannigans' car was one of the first to get out of the Motorway system and up to the Overcity once the Doctor had opened up the roof. (3.3)

Branson Inheritance, the: Independent space agency (presumably named after British entrepreneur Richard Branson) in the 2050s. Ed Gold wondered if the Doctor represented them when he arrived inexplicably at Bowie Base One on Mars. (4.16)

Breakfast: BBC television magazine programme, broadcast in the alternative timeline created when River Song opted not to kill the Doctor. On one edition of the show, presenters Bill Turnbull and Sian Williams interviewed author Charles Dickens about his new Christmas television play. (6.13)

Brecon: When the Doctor pointed upwards to indicate where the Gelth had come from, undertaker Gabriel Sneed assumed he meant this picturesque rural area north of Cardiff, famous for the Brecon Beacons. (1.3)

Breen, Lilian: One of the WAAF personnel working for Winston Churchill in the Map Room in the Cabinet War Rooms beneath London. Her boyfriend Reg was killed in action over the English Channel. (5.3) (Played by SUSANNAH FIELDING)

Brethren: The Monks of St Catherine, who worshipped the Haemovariform and brought it to the Torchwood Estate, locked within its current Host. Having taken over Torchwood House and imprisoned Lady Isobel and the staff, the monks' leader, Father Angelo, forced Sir Robert McLeish to act as if nothing had changed when Queen Victoria arrived to stay. (2.2)

Brian: A name the Doctor would often give people whose real name he couldn't remember. (6.9)

Bridge Street: Road in London where the Doctor, Rose Tyler, Pete Tyler and the Preachers planned to meet up after escaping the Cybermen on 'Pete's World'. (2.6)

Bridget: A young single mum, she had come to London to search for her missing daughter, who had got into drugs. Bridget joined the LINDA group to find the Doctor too. She travelled down from the north of England for each meeting but one day stopped coming, shortly after her romance with Colin Skinner had begun to blossom. Victor Kennedy told Skinner that he could help

him find her but, in truth, Bridget had already been absorbed by Kennedy's real persona, the Abzorbaloff. When the absorbed victims fought back to explode the Abzorbaloff, brave Bridget died alongside her beloved Skinner. (2.10) Davros taunted the Doctor about how many people had died trying to help him over the years, and this made the Doctor think of Bridget. (4.13) (Played by MOYA BRADY)

B

Bridget Jones: Fictional character who appeared in books by Helen Fielding, which could be found in The Library. (4.8)

Brighton: East Sussex city, home of Roedean School, which Lucy Saxon had attended, and where Leo Jones had taken his family for a break when Martha Jones tried to warn him about Harry Saxon. (3.12) The Doctor had a bad beach holiday there once. (AGO3)

Bringer of Night: Legendary demon name, one of many attributed to the Beast throughout the galaxies. (2.8, 2.9)

Britain's Got Talent: ITV talent show. A Colchester girl called Nina tried to get onto it, but was rejected. (6.12)

Britain's Next Top Model: Reality show on Sky Living, enjoyed by Essex shop worker Kelly. (6.12)

British Empire: Part of Yvonne Hartman's ideology for Torchwood was to re-establish the British Empire that had existed during the reign of Torchwood's founder, Queen Victoria. (2.12)

British Rocket Group: Research group from the 1960s whose skills and expertise were still influencing projects such as Guinevere One four decades later. (2.X)

Brixton: South West London suburb. After undergoing a metacrisis, Donna Noble's mind started to overload with information absorbed from the Doctor's memories, and 'Brixton' was one of the words she muttered. (4.13) It was the final destination of the bus, number 200, on its journey from Victoria Station on the night it went through a wormhole and ended up on San Helios. (4.15)

Broadback Lane: East London street, along which the children from the Ingleby Workhouse were being led on their way to build the engine for the CyberKing. (4.14)

Broadfell, HMP: London Prison where Lucy Saxon was secretly detained, and where Harry Saxon's followers arranged to bring the Master back to life. Because Lucy Saxon interfered with the procedure, the prison was destroyed in a huge explosion, and only the Master survived. Joshua Naismith gained access to the CCTV footage of the aftermath and saw the newly reborn Master flee. (4.17)

Broadmarsh Street: In the fiction the TARDIS created for the human-Doctor's background, John Smith believed he had grown up on this road in Radford Parade, Nottingham. (3.9)

Broadsword: Call sign used by Group Captain Childers to communicate with the three spitfire pilots – Danny Boy, Jubilee and Flintlock – sent into outer space via Bracewell's gravity bubble. (5.3)

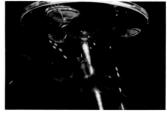

Broff: One of the players of *The Weakest Link* aboard the Game Station. After Fitch's apparent death, Broff tried to escape the studio so the Anne Droid seemed to disintegrate him. In truth, he was transmatted over to the Dalek mothership and turned into part of the growing Dalek army created by the Emperor. (1.12) (Played by SEBASTIAN ARMESTO)

Broken K Ranch: Place where Jimmy Stalkingwolf worked. Cattle there had been killed by what Cassie Rice reckoned was a cougar but Jimmy wasn't convinced. The Doctor discovered it was actually a Viperox Battle Drone practising its hunting skills. (DL)

B

Brook Street: West London street where Donna parked her mother's car. She left the keys in a rubbish bin and asked Rose Tyler to tell Sylvia where they were if she came looking. (4.1)

Brooke, Captain Adelaide: Commander of Bowie Base One on Mars. A pioneer of space exploration (she was the first Briton on the moon), even her achievements would eventually be dwarfed by those of her granddaughter, Susie Fontana-Brooke. Londoner Adelaide was a tough no-nonsense commander who would go to any lengths to protect her crew and their mission. She had an undisclosed history with her deputy, Ed Gold, which brought them into conflict as often as it had them working well together. Adelaide originally went into space because of the Daleks (her parents vanished during a Dalek invasion) — the Dalek that spotted her let her live which the Doctor reasoned was because it recognised her importance to the future. After the Flood infiltrated Bowie Base One, Adelaide realised that she had to take any measures to stop them reaching Earth and ultimately prepared to sacrifice herself and her remaining crew in a nuclear explosion, which is how the Doctor understood history would report it. Her death inspired Susie to become a space pioneer, so when the Doctor saved Adelaide — determined to ignore the Laws of Time — he changed the future. Adelaide realised that the future was more

important than either of them and she shot herself, rather than do anything that would alter Susie's destiny, much to the Doctor's horror. (4.16) (Played by LINDSAY DUNCAN and RACHEL FEWELL)

Brooke, Emily: Daughter of Adelaide Brooke and mother to baby Susie. (4.16) (Played by LILY BEVAN)

Brooke, Mr: Adelaide Brooke's father who hid his daughter in the attic during the Dalek invasion of Earth. He went out to find Adelaide's missing mother but neither of them were ever seen again. Most likely they became part of the Daleks' early Reality Bomb experiments. (4.16) (Played by CHARLIE DE'ATH)

Brooklyn: Part of New New York where it was said that there were jobs aplenty, wooden houses and air that smelled of apple grass. Access to it was via the Brooklyn Flyover, ten miles from Pharmacytown, a six-year trip (approximately) via the Fast Lane. (3.3)

Brooklyn Turnoffs 1 and 2: Parts of the New New York Motorway which were closed to traffic. (3.3)

Buchanan, Joe: Gambler and player, who was transported to the God Complex along with Rita, Howie Spragg and Gibbis. His biggest fear was ventriloquists' dummies, but it was his faith in luck that eventually made him a victim of the Minotaur which guarded the holographic prison, and he died there. (6.11) (Played by DANIEL PIRRIE)

Bucket, Lorna: Young woman from the Gamma Forests who met the Doctor as a child and ran with him through the forests. In the language of Lorna's people, the word 'Doctor' meant 'great warrior' and that was what he was to her. Aware that the Clerics and Headless Monks were combining forces in an effort to find and kill the Doctor, Lorna infiltrated Demon's Run, but slipped away when the Doctor was exposed and joined in the fight alongside Amy Pond, Rory Williams, Strax, Vastra and Jenny against the monks. Previously, she had presented Amy with an embroidered prayer leaf with 'Melody Pond' stitched into it, but written in

the language of the Gamma Forests, which Amy couldn't read and the TARDIS took a long time to translate. After the battle, Lorna was mortally wounded, but before she died she was reunited with the Doctor, who told her he remembered her as a little girl. Shortly after she died, the TARDIS finally translated the prayer leaf. Instead of saying 'Melody Pond', it gave the name in the language of the Gamma Forests: 'River Song'. (6.7) (Played by CHRISTINA CHONG)

Buckingham Palace: The Doctor managed to stop the starliner *Titanic* crashing into the Queen's official residence, much to her gratitude. (4.X) In the parallel world where Donna Noble never met the Doctor, the *Titanic* crashed into it, destroying the south of England in a nuclear explosion. (4.11) The TARDIS was parked there one Easter when the Doctor took an unplanned trip to San Helios on a London bus. (4.15) Liz Ten lived there aboard *Starship UK*. (5.2) The Palace was damaged during the Blitz when the Daleks caused all the lights of London to illuminate. (5.3) In the alternative London created by River Song's refusal to kill the Doctor and therefore disrupt established history, the Palace was renamed the Buckingham Senate and was home to the Holy Roman Emperor, Winston Churchill. (6.13)

Bucknall House: Block of the Powell Estate where the Tyler family lived at number 48.

Budapest: Hungarian capital. Martha Jones claimed to have gone there and collected one of the phials of liquid needed to arm the gun she was supposedly preparing to kill the Master with. (3.13)

Buffalo: Codeword Mickey Smith used to gain access to the UNIT computer system. (1.5)

Bugs Bunny: Warner Brothers cartoon character, famed for his 'What's Up, Doc' catchphrase. The Doctor told Jimmy Stalkingwolf that as Jimmy wasn't Bugs Bunny, he shouldn't call him 'Doc'. (DL)

Bundeswehr: German unified military organisation where Steffi Ehrlich trained before moving to the RWTH to train with the Space Program. (4.16)

Burbage, Richard: Actor, of the Lord Chamberlain's Men. In 1599, he played the King of Navarre in both *Love's Labour's Lost* and *Love's Labour's Won* and was due to speak the closing passage which would bring the Carrionites to Earth. (3.2) (Played JALAAL HARTLEY)

Bursar: The financial administrator at Farringham School for Boys. The latest, Mr Phillips, was murdered by Son of Mine, who inhabited the body of schoolboy Jeremy Baines. (3.8, 3.9)

Busboy: Worked at Gloria's Golden Grill in Utah and served the Doctor with a coke. (6.1) (Played by EMILIO AQUINO)

Businessman: Driver of a car on the New New York Motorway, occupying the final lane before the Fast Lane, a thousand feet below. He gave the exhausted Doctor a glass of water, witnessed the Macra thrashing about in the fumes, and was then surprised by the arrival of Novice Hame. (3.3) (Played by NICHOLAS BOULTON)

Butcher's boy, the: A boy Gwyneth, the maid at Gabriel Sneed's undertakers, had her eye on. (1.3)

Butetown: A district of Cardiff. Madame Mortlock, a medium, was based there when it was the main dockland area for the city during Victorian times. (1.3)

Butler: In service to the Duke of Manhattan, and present when he was cured of Petrifold Regression in the Hospital run by the Sisters of Plenitude. (2.1) Although he survived the attack by the New Humans, it seems almost certain he later died as a victim of the mutated Bliss virus that wiped out the majority of New Earth's population. (3.3) (Played by STUART ASHMAN)

Buzzer: Morpeth-Jetsan contractor, working at the St John's crystal-diluric acid farm, whose dad was a postman. He was in his rig-harness, asleep while his Ganger was working, when the solar tsunami hit St John's, giving his Ganger a sense of individuality and a desire to be a separate living person. Buzzer was taught to build a house of cards — a trait shared by his Ganger. As the Gangers and the human originals found themselves in conflict, Buzzer's Ganger was killed by Foreman Cleaves, causing the rest of the Gangers to regroup and decide to destroy the humans for good. The real Buzzer, believing that Jennifer Lucas was trapped somewhere, went to find her and Rory Williams. However, Jennifer was dead and Buzzer encountered the deranged Jennifer Ganger, which literally ate him alive. (6.5, 6.6) (Played by MARSHALL LANCASTER)

By the Light of the Asteroid: Soap opera on Sto, featuring amongst other things, twins and the many husbands of Joofie Crystalle, watched by the Van Hoffs. Foon Van Hoff had to answer questions on it to win their trip aboard the starliner *Titanic*. The Doctor had also seen it. (4.X)

Byron, Lord George Gordon: 19th-century poet who, according to the Doctor, loved Venice. (5.6)

Bywater: Security Commander in the Vault, Henry Van Statten's underground bunker. Charged with overseeing the Dalek on its escape from the Cage, he sent one of his officers, De Maggio, on escort detail, to ensure Rose Tyler and Adam Mitchell's safety, before engaging in combat — and was the first of the Vault staff to be exterminated by the Dalek's re-energised blaster. (1.6) (Played by JOHN SCHWABB)

Byzantium: Professor River Song wondered if the Doctor had met her at the crash of the *Byzantium* at the time they met at the Library. He hadn't. (4.8) River was aboard the Galaxy-class starliner, a category 4, when she realised it carried a Weeping Angel in its vault. After River escaped the ship, the Angel caused a phase-shift in the warp engines, causing it to crash on Alfava Metraxis, where an entire army of Angels was waiting. They fed upon the radiation from the crashed ship, regenerating themselves and then pursued the Doctor, Amy Pond, River and some Clerics through the Maze of the Dead. (5.4, 5.5) After leaving the *Byzantium* crash site, River travelled to Earth and the past, to meet up with Amy and Rory Williams and told them the Doctor was still alive. (6.13)

C

Caan, Dalek: Former Attack Squad Leader of the Thirtieth Dalek Assault Squad, later one of the Cult of Skaro, who brought the Genesis Ark to Earth in the Void Ship, after the Time War ended. (2.12, 2.13) After fleeing the Battle of Canary Wharf via an emergency temporal shift, along with the rest of the Cult, Caan ended up in Manhattan in 1930, where he was the Cult's go-between with Mr Diagoras, eventually bringing Diagoras to the Transgenic Lab to take part in the Final Experiment. Dalek Caan patrolled the sewers, sometimes alone, sometimes with Thay. Caan led the attack on Hooverville and exterminated its leader, Solomon. After realising that Dalek Sec had betrayed them, the rest of the Cult accepted Caan as their new leader and he wired himself up to their Battle Computer to guide and ultimately exterminate their new Dalek-Human army. When confronted by the Doctor, Caan once again activated an emergency temporal shift and escaped. (3.4, 3.5) Fleeing Earth, he deliberately headed back to the Last Great Time War, where he rescued Davros from the jaws of the Nightmare Child. As a result, Caan was driven insane but was now able to observe and understand the various timelines that crossed the universe and so manipulated them, first to bring the Doctor and Donna Noble together, then to spark the metacrisis that resulted in the creation of a human Doctor and boosted Donna's mind to Time Lord levels. This enabled the Doctor and his friends to stop Davros and the Supreme Dalek from rebirthing a whole new Dalek race because Caan saw that this could only destroy reality for ever. Caan, chained and trapped in the Crucible's Vaults, was destroyed along with the Crucible after successfully manipulating the Doctor into defeating Davros and stopping the Reality Bomb being detonated. (4.12, 4.13) Despite her memory having been wiped, after the arrival of the Master on Earth and his subsequent attempt to turn humanity into himself, Donna Noble recalled Caan as her mind subconsciously fought the Master's influence (4.17, 4.18) (Operated by DAVID HANKINSON (2.12, 2.13), BARNABY EDWARDS, NICHOLAS PEGG (3.4, 3.5), BARNABY EDWARDS (4.12, 4.13), voiced by NICHOLAS BRIGGS)

Cabinet War Rooms, the: Winston Churchill's top secret base of operations during the Second World War, built beneath the streets of London. (5.3)

Caecilius, Evelina: Elder child in the Caecilius family who was hoping to join the Sibylline Sisterhood, due to her consistent inhaling of the Pyrovillian dust being pumped into the family house via the vents beneath the building, which were also causing her to transform into living stone. When the Pyroviles were destroyed and time returned to its correct track, Evelina's gifts disappeared, her stone arm reverted to flesh and bone, and she eventually enjoyed a typical Roman teenager's life in the country's capital city. (4.2) (Played by FRANCESCA FOWLER)

Caecilius, Lobos: Head of the house in the Caecilius home in Pompeii. A marble merchant by trade, he had been employed by Lucius Dextrus Petrus to construct one of the six marble circuit boards needed by the Pyroviles to repower their ship. A Pyrovile rampaged through his home but was destroyed by the Doctor, who was eventually able to take the family to safety on the hills above

Pompeii, from where they witnessed the city die. He eventually set up a successful new marble business in Rome. (4.2) (Played by PETER CAPALDI)

Caecilius, Metella: Wife of Lobos Caecilius and fiercely proud of her children especially Evelina, who she wanted to see join the Sibylline Sisterhood. Along with the rest of her family, she was saved by the Doctor and eventually set up a new life with them in Rome. (4.2) (Played by TRACEY CHILDS)

Caecilius, Quintus: Lazy, indolent but smart youngest child of the Caecilius family. He helped the Doctor break into Lucius Dextrus Petrus's home and, for all his cynicism about his sister's prophetic gifts, he was extremely protective of her. When his family moved to Rome he began training as a doctor. (4.2) (Played by FRANCOIS PANDOLFO)

Caesar: The Doctor told Rose he could take her to witness the Roman Emperor Gaius Julius crossing the Rubicon. (2.2) Thanks to River Song's hallucinogenic lipstick, the Auton Romans near Stonehenge believed the Doctor was Caesar, in this case most likely Marcus Ulpius Nerva Traianus, aka Trajan. (5.12)

Caesofine Concentrate: The gas which the ATMOS device emitted, which would turn Earth into clonefeed, the amniotic fluid necessary if Earth was to become a breeding colony for the Sontarans. However its weakness was that it was volatile and would ignite easily, so the Doctor was able to destroy it by firing energy from an atmospheric converter he built. (4.4, 4.5)

Cain, Officer Margaret: Maggie Cain was working in the Bowie Base One bio-dome when her friend Andy Stone became the first victim of the Flood. It then attacked her, but initially left her body unchanged, accessing her voice and memories in order to infiltrate the main dome. Once inside, and having

learnt of the volume of water Earth offered, subterfuge was no longer necessary. Through Maggie, the Flood led the other taken over human bodies in an attack on the rest of the domes. Maggie's body infiltrated the escape shuttle Ed Gold was preparing, and infected him, although he destroyed the shuttle with his last vestige of humanity. Maggie's body was destroyed along with the Flood in the nuclear explosion that smashed Bowie Base One. (4.16) (Played by SHARON DUNCAN-BEWSTER)

Cairo: Capital of Egypt. Amy Pond took the Doctor on a train there after rescuing him from the Holy Roman Empire in Britain. (6.13)

CAL: See *Lux, Charlotte Abigail*

Calcium: One of the main constituents of Raxacoricofallapatorians, the race to which the Family Slitheen belonged. Realising that the compression field they used to fit inside their human skinsuits had weakened their physical bodies, the Doctor suggested acetic acid as a good weapon against them. (1.4, 1.5)

Caledonia Prime: Water riots were in their third day in the Glasgow region of Caledonia Prime, according to Channel McB. (1.7)

Calhoon, Sergeant: UNIT officer charged with filtering all the reports to Captain Magambo at the Gladwell road tunnel. (4.15)

California: Western state of America, which was settled in the 19th century around the San Andreas Fault, a geological flaw in the landmass. Many of the earthquakes that have plagued the region are attributable to the fault as the two plates that make up the fault move northwards and southwards. The Doctor likened the rift threaded through Cardiff to California on the San Andreas Fault. (3.11) The Doctor, Kazran Sardick and Abigail Pettigrew visited it on Christmas Eve, 1952. (6.X)

Calisto B: The Doctor visited a drinking den in the dockyards on this planet, looking for Father Gideon Vandaleur. (6.13)

C

reflected the heat of the sun's rays at him so Francesco exploded in the heat. (5.6) (Played by ALEX PRICE)

Calvierri, Rosanna: Posing as the matriarch of an established Venetian family, Rosanna was really the last of the Saturnyne Sisters of the Water, who, to escape the time field that had erased Saturnyne, brought the survivors of her race to Earth. She was the only female and disguising her characidic appearance with a perception filter, she and her son Francesco, would entice young women into their 'school' and then turn them via blood transfusion into Saturnyne women so they could breed with the 10,000 male Saturnynes swimming in the canals of Venice. The Doctor stopped her plan and, realising that her race was doomed, Rosanna threw herself into the canals. Her 'sons' fed on her. (5.6) (Played by HELEN McCRORY)

Calvierri Girls, the: A group of Venetian girls brought to Rosanna Calvierri's 'school' by citizens who needed prestige or couldn't afford to keep their daughters. The girls were supposedly taught how to be 'ladies' and were often seen walking along the streets of Venice with their parasols, looking very prim and proper. In truth, Rosanna Calvierri and her son Francesco were Saturnynes – piscine vampiric aliens who were turning the girls into their own race so they could breed with the 10,000 male Saturnynes living in the canals of the city. The girls were killed when Guido, father of one of their number Isabella, blew them, and himself, up with TNT. (5.6) (Played by ELIZABETH CROFT, GABRIELA MONTARAZ, HANNAH STEELE, SONILA VIESHTA and GABRIELLA WILDE)

Calisto Pulse: Used to disarm micro-explosives. River Song paid Dorium Maldovar for her Vortex Manipulator with one of these. She exchanged it for the Manipulator as she had slipped a micro-explosive into Dorium's drink. (5.12, 5.13)

Call My Bluff: One of the programmes broadcast from the Game Station. It used real guns. (1.12)

Callufrax Minor: One of the planets stolen by the Daleks and secreted a second out of sync within the Medusa Cascade. The Doctor eventually returned it to its rightful place in space and time. (4.12, 4.13)

Calvierri, Francesco: Rosanna Calvierri's son. Though fiercely loyal and devoted to his mother, he was a bit of a loose cannon, and would occasionally venture into the streets of Venice to taste human flesh. After discovering the truth about the Saturnynes, Amy Pond and Rory Williams cornered Francesco and, while Rory took him on in single combat, Amy

Calypso, Sally: Holographic news reporter beamed directly into the cars travelling on the New New York Motorway. Most of her reports were of car accidents, car-jackings and current traffic and weather conditions, and they were being generated automatically by the Senate building under the control of the Face of Boe, who wished the inhabitants of the Motorway to believe life above it was perfectly normal. (3.3) (Played by ERIKA MACLEOD)

Cambodia: Donna Noble was aware that to go to Cambodia required inoculations, so she wondered if going to other planets with the Doctor would require similar immunisation. (4.1)

Cambridge University: Harry Saxon allegedly attended this university, and had a particular prowess for rugby and athletics. (3.12) Adelaide Brooke attended it. (4.16)

Campbell, Stacy: Young woman who used the Adipose Capsules to lose weight – successfully shedding eleven pounds in five days – and making her feel confident enough to dump her boyfriend. Visiting her Haringey home, Donna Noble accidentally activated Stacy's free 'pendant', which caused the Adipose to hatch from her en masse, killing her. (4.1) (Played by JESSICA GUNNING)

'Camptown Races': Popular 19th-century song, written by Stephen Foster. When the Doctor had been poisoned by cyanide and was trying to mime what would help him, Donna Noble suggested he was miming this song. (4.7)

Canary Wharf: Colloquial name for the tower at One Canada Square, although Canary Wharf is actually the business district it sits in. The main tower was taken over by the Torchwood Institute as their London base until the defeat of the Cybermen and Daleks in what became known as the Battle of Canary Wharf. (2.12, 2.13)

Candleford Street: London street where Roger Davey lived, at number 16. (4.1)

Candy, Professor: Archaeology professor at the Luna University. River Song studied under him. (6.8) (Played by PAUL BENTLEY)

Cane: Victor Kennedy/the Abzorbaloff carried this disguised limitation-field creator. When Elton Pope broke it, the Abzorbaloff was destroyed. (2.10)

Cane, Biff: Loud but pleasant passenger aboard the *Crusader 50*, on holiday with his family. His jocularity soon turned to aggression after an alien entity breached the transporter and took over Sky Silvestry, especially when his wife became frightened, and eventually he led an attack on the Doctor, planning to throw him out onto the planet's surface, believing he was the real monster. After the Hostess sacrificed herself to destroy Sky and the creature within her, Biff and his family were safe. (4.10) (Played by DANIEL RYAN)

Cane, Jethro: Teenage son of Biff and Val Cane, a bit emo and for most of the time the Doctor's only ally aboard the *Crusader 50*. Even he turned against him in the end, although he refused to physically drag the Doctor towards the exit until his father insisted. (4.10) (Played by COLIN MORGAN)

Cane, Val: Biff's wife and seemingly a fun-loving woman, but when the alien entity that took over Sky Silvestry started using Val's voice, her instinctive bigotry emerged, making her more negative and spiteful than normal. She was

the first to convince everyone the Doctor was the enemy until It was proven to be Sky. She tried to say she knew it was Sky all along until a look from the Doctor silenced her. (4.10) (Played by LINDSEY COULSON)

Cape Kennedy: NASA's Florida space centre from where they launched space missions. There, the Doctor accessed the Saturn 5 rocket, carrying Apollo 11, but was captured by security and held until President Nixon was taken there In the TARDIS by River Song and Rory Williams. (6.1, 6.2)

Cappuccino!: Coffee house where Sally Sparrow read the letter from her old friend Kathy Nightingale, detailing her life in the past. (3.10)

Capricorn, Max: CEO of Max Capricorn Cruiseliners on Sto for 176 years. His body had decayed over that time but he'd placed himself within the cybernetic Max-Box to preserve his head. His own company had voted him off the board. He planned for his own luxury liner, *Titanic*, to be struck by meteoroids, hopefully killing everyone aboard. The crippled ship would then crash into Earth creating a nuclear devastation, although Max himself would remain safe within an Omnistate Impact Chamber. He hoped his board would then be indicted for mass murder – the ultimate revenge. Max had arranged to be collected from Earth and retire to a new life on Penhaxico Two. He was killed when Astrid Peth drove a fork-lift truck into the Max-Box, sending him and her to their deaths in the nuclear engines below. (4.X) (Played by GEORGE COSTIGAN)

Captain, the [1]: Commanding officer aboard the *Thrasymachus*, the galaxy-class starship, with 4,003 people aboard that was about to crash into the planet Ember. She tried to plead with Kazran Sardick to help her save everyone, but he was completely uninterested. (6.X) (Played by POOKY QUESNEL)

Captain, the [2]: Military officer who set out in a helicopter to rescue the humans trapped in the St John's monastery, besieged by their rogue Gangers (6.5, 6.6) (Voiced by DARRYL ADCOCK)

Captain Troy Handsome: The Doctor claimed to be this fictional character from International Rescue, based on the TV series *Thunderbirds*, when confronting the Avatar hologram created by the time engine on Aickman Road. (5.11)

Car 10hot5: Registration details of the car occupied by Ma and Pa before it was destroyed by the Macra living below the Fast Lane, part of the New New York Motorway. (3.3)

Car 465diamond6: The car registered to Milo and Cheen. (3.3)

Cardiff: The capital city of Wales. The Doctor and Rose first visited it on Christmas Eve 1869, when they helped stop a Gelth invasion through the rift in space and time that crossed the city. (1.3) They returned to the city in late 2006 to enable the TARDIS to ingest some rift energy and discovered a member of the Slitheen family planning to destroy the city by using an energy extrapolator combined with the destruction of a new nuclear facility to tear open the rift, enabling her to pilot the extrapolator home. (1.11) Captain Jack Harkness later joined a small Torchwood team to monitor the rift directly under Roald Dahl Plass, where the TARDIS had been parked. He was recovering from injuries alone in the Torchwood Hub when he heard the TARDIS materialise directly above, the energy shaking his base. He raced to the surface, eager to contact the Doctor again. Seeing him on the TARDIS monitor but unwilling to face his old friend, the Doctor tried to leave, but Jack was quicker and he was holding on to the exterior shell of the TARDIS as it dematerialised. (3.11) After the defeat of the Master and the Toclafane, the Doctor returned Jack to Cardiff Bay. (3.13) Torchwood Three helped defend Earth against the Daleks and, using rift energy, bring it back to its rightful place in space and time. (4.12, 4.13)

C

Cardiff Gazette: Local newspaper for which Cathy Salt worked as a journalist. (1.11)

Cardiff Heritage Committee: A team who were electrocuted in a swimming pool, ostensibly due to normal wear and tear of pools. (1.11)

Carlo: Steward in the House of Calvierri, and loyal to Rosanna and Francesco until he realised they were aliens. As Rosanna tried to flood Venice, Carlo fled the house, taking as much of the Calvierri gold and jewellery as he could carry. (5.6) (Played by SIMON GREGOR)

Carmen: London woman who was on the number 200 bus when it was transported to San Helios. Mildly sensitive to psychic energy, she heard the population of San Helios cry out as they died, an echo of which flowed back through the wormhole to Earth – increased by the three alien suns around San Helios. Ever since she was young she had heard voices and could make predictions: over the years, she had consistently won small amounts on the lottery with her husband, Lou. After the Doctor got them safely back to Earth, Carmen told the Doctor that something was returning through the dark and that 'he' would knock four times. (4.15) (Played by ELLEN THOMAS)

Carnivorous Skulls: Guardians in the Labyrinth of Skulls, keeping enemies out of the Seventh Transept of the Headless Monks. The skulls may well have once belonged to those who eventually became Headless Monks. They protected the Doctor and Dorium Maldovar from Gantok by eating him. (6.13)

Carpenter, John: Movie director, responsible for the 1982 version of *The Thing*, which the Doctor referred to when he and Amy Pond approached the deserted Arctic Geological Survey Base in Zebra Bay. (AG02)

Carrionites: Female-dominated species which existed when the universe was young, based in the 14 stars of the Rexel Planetary Configuration. As a species, they were cast into the Deep Darkness by the Eternals, who, legend had it, used the Rexel stars as a prison door. Three Carrionites escaped back to 16th-century England through the words of a despondent William Shakespeare – Carrionite science being based on sensing emotions such as grief and suffering and using them to manipulate matter via words, shapes, numbers and names. They then had Peter Streete design a 14-sided amphitheatre that would channel their energies back into the Deep Darkness when the correct words were spoken aloud at the epicentre of the structure – a moment the Carrionites referred to as the Hour of Woven Words. Their true form was more akin to a giant skeletal raven or crow but, by using words, the three Carrionites could reshape themselves into more humanoid form. This required a lot of energy, so they usually appeared aged

and ugly. The three Carrionites failed in their attempt to create a Millennium of Blood on Earth by allowing the others out of the Deep Darkness. The portal was sealed once more by William Shakespeare and the Doctor, and the three Earth-based Carrionites were trapped within a crystal ball for eternity. (3.2) The Doctor kept their crystal ball in a box in the TARDIS, under 'C' for Carrionites. (4.7)

Carter [1]: One of Cline's soldiers on Messaline – he was responsible for using the Doctor's DNA to create Jenny. He was killed in a Hath attack. (4.6) (Played by AKIN GAZI)

Carter [2]: Captain of the Justice Department Vehicle *Teselecta*. He oversaw the operation on Earth to kill Adolf Hitler, before realising they were too early in Hitler's time stream. After bringing Amy Pond and Rory Williams aboard,

he lost control of the ship temporarily to them, but later got it back. Feeling that he owed the Doctor a favour, he turned the *Teselecta* into a duplicate of the Doctor, handing control over to him. (6.8, 6.13) (Played by RICHARD DILLANE)

Carter, Penny: Science correspondent of *The Observer*, who was suspicious of Miss Foster and Adipose Industries and attempted to sneak into the building late at night to spy on the company. Miss Foster, who was actually Matron Cofelia, found Penny and held her captive and she only escaped once the Adiposian First Family arrived to take away the Adipose young and kill Matron Cofelia. (4.1) (Played by VERONA JOSEPH)

Cartwright, Lucy: Six-year-old girl who was skipping along the lane in her home village of Farringham when she was kidnapped by a Scarecrow, one of the soldiers created by the Family of Blood. Taken back to their invisible ship, she was murdered, and her form taken on by Daughter of Mine, who then returned to Lucy's home and killed her parents. (3.8) (Played by LAUREN WILSON)

Carver, Doctor: Medic at Leadworth Hospital, with whom Rory Williams had shared his concerns about the coma patients he had witnessed walking around the village. Carver later told Rory's boss, Doctor Ramsden about the conversation. (5.1)

Casanova, Giacomo: 18th-century Venetian poet and adventurer whom, the Doctor remembered, he owed a chicken. (5.6)

Cash: One of Cline's soldiers on Messaline. He was killed in a Hath attack. (4.6) (Played by BEN ASHLEY)

Casp, Matron: Leader of the Sisters of Plenitude, she controlled the experiments on the humans in the secret Intensive Care Unit beneath the Hospital on New Earth. Fleeing from the infectious patients, Casp fell to her death in a lift shaft when a patient grabbed her ankle, spreading its numerous viruses to her immunity-free body. (2.1) (Played by DONA CROLL)

Caspian Sea: The largest landlocked expanse of water on Earth, part of the Russian landmass. Dagestan was on its shores, which was where Yuri Kerenski's brother lived. (4.16)

Cassandra: See *O'Brien Dot Delta Seventeen, Lady Cassandra*

Cassavalian Belt: Star system that contained the planet Sto. (4.X)

Cassini couple: Elderly married ladies, who had been driving on the Motorway for 23 years – theirs was one of the first cars to set off. Although this was a year after the Bliss-mutated Mood Patch had wiped out the Overcity, it is unknown if the earlier drivers were aware of the disaster that had befallen their fellow New New Yorkers. Alice (played by BRIDGET TURNER) was the driver; May (played by GEORGINE ANDERSON) was a car spotter and was able to identify the car that had kidnapped Martha Jones for the Doctor. (3.3)

Castor 36: World far beyond Alpha Geminorum, which Luke Rattigan believed the Sontarans would transport him and his students to. General Staal implied it was a complete fabrication. (4.4, 4.5)

Catesby, Robert: Leader of the 13 plotters who planned to blow up the House of Lords in 1605. (AG05) (Voiced by ALEXANDER VLAHOS)

Cathy Gale: Fictional adventuress from the British TV series *The Avengers* who was one of the highlights of 1963, according to the Doctor. (AG01)

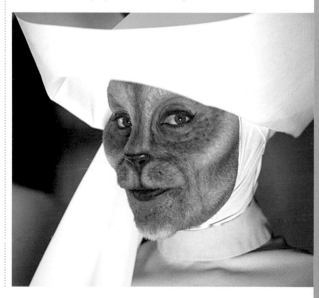

C

Catkind: Feline race found in Galaxy M87, many of whom shared the planet New Earth with the variety of humans living there. Amongst the Catkind on New Earth were the Sisters of Plenitude, Brannigan (who married a human) and Javit. (2.1, 3.3)

Catrigan Nova: A planet possessing whirlpools of gold. The Master offered to take Tanya, his masseuse, there after he'd established his New Time Lord Empire. (3.13)

Catrin: Little girl from London who, like her father and brother, had A+ blood, and thus was affected by the Sycorax's blood control. (2.X)

Catullus, Gaius Valerius: Roman poet whose Latin works were the subject of prep for Hutchinson's class at Farringham School for Boys. Unwilling to do it himself, Hutchinson forced brighter pupil Timothy Latimer to do it for him. (3.8)

Cavill, Mr: Third officer and helmsman aboard the starliner *Titanic*. He was presumably killed when the meteoroids struck the ship. (4.X)

Caw: Baltazar's ally, Caw was a gold-eating bird from the planet Pheros. His biomechanical race, formed from a living metal, was powered by fusion reactors. He was working for Baltazar and rescued him from his destroyed ship, but subsequently betrayed Baltazar to the authorities for gold bars. Years later, he

was reunited with a forgiving Baltazar and they set in motion the trap to retrieve the *Infinite*, with Caw charming the Doctor and Martha Jones into going on a quest. Caw also gave Martha a brooch, which was in fact his son, Squawk, who relayed details of where the TARDIS was going back to Caw and thus Baltazar. When the final datachip leading to the location of the *Infinite* had been recovered, Caw flew Baltazar to Volag-Noc, but Caw was shot in the fusion chamber by Gurney, and died, apologising to Martha, on the icy surface of the planet. (TIQ) (Voiced by TOBY LONGWORTH)

Celestial Belt of the Winter Queen: A descendant of Adelaide Brooke reached this distant solar system. (4.16)

Central Intelligence Agency: American investigative agency. Howie Spragg believed that his internment within the God Complex might be part of a CIA plot. (6.11)

Central Park: Vast open parkland at the heart of Manhattan's midtown area. It was in the southern end that Solomon presided over the Hooverville that had been erected there. (3.4, 3.5)

Central World Authority: Cyberleader One demanded of Yvonne Hartman that he address such an official body on Earth, but she pointed out there wasn't one. Cyberleader One opted to create one there and then, with himself at its head. (2.13)

Ceres System: Secondary location of the *Infinite*, its whereabouts provided by the datachip possessed by Kaliko. (TIQ)

Chaka Demus 'n' Pliers: American male singing duo (Demus's real name was John Taylor; Pliers' was Everton Bonner), cited by Elton Pope as an example of a good use of 'n' in a phrase, along with fish 'n' chips and rock 'n' roll. Hence LINDA — the London Investigation 'N' Detective Agency. (2.10)

Chambers: The areas in the Cyber-conversion factory in the 'Pete's World' Battersea Power Station, where the humans were either upgraded or incinerated. Chambers 5, 6, 8, 9, 10, 11 and 12 were all cited. (2.6)

Chambers, Mark: Deceased man who donated his face to be used on a Courtesy Node in the Library. (4.8) (Played by JOSHUA DALLAS)

Chambers, Mr: Conductor and leader of the band that played at the dance in the Farringham village hall. He was disintegrated by Father of Mine. (3.8) (Played by PETER BOURKE)

Chambers, Suzette: Friend of Sylvia Noble, who worked for Jival Chowdry's photocopying business and was one of the Wednesday Girls. She had lost some weight after using Adipose Capsules and was later affected by unexpected parthenogenesis in the wine bar, along with a number of other customers. However, she was safe after the Doctor stopped Matron Cofelia's scheme. (4.1) After the ATMOS scare, Sylvia wanted to check up on her. (4.5) In the alternative world where Donna Noble never met the Doctor, Suzette introduced Donna to Chowdry and she got a job as his secretary. (4.11) (Played by SUE KELVIN)

Chameleon arch: A device in the Doctor's TARDIS that enabled him to rewrite every single cell of his biology and become a human, John Smith. The process was painful. His essence was then stored within a special Gallifreyan fob watch. The Master also used one of these to become Professor Yana. (3.8, 3.9, 3.11)

Chan, Bau and Ru: Friends of the Tylers and Smiths from the Powell Estate. They berated Rose for her year-long absence and the effect it had had on Mickey Smith. (1.4) On 'Pete's World', Ru told Rita-Anne that Ricky Smith had been seen with the Preachers. (2.5) (Played by BASIL CHUNG and FIESTA MEI LING)

Chancellor, the: Time Lord official and member of Rassilon's Council. He approved the Ultimate Sanction and travelled to Earth with Rassilon. He was driven back into the Time War by the enraged Master. (4.18) (Played by JOE DIXON)

Chancellor Street: Street in London where Martha Jones encountered the Doctor for the first time as he removed his tie to prove to her later self that he could travel in time. (3.1)

Chandrakala, Miss: Housekeeper at Eddison Hall and Lady Clemency's confidante. She'd been in India with her Ladyship and was the only other person aware of her pregnancy and perhaps its alien origins. She was killed when the Vespiform pushed a stone gargoyle down onto her from the roof of the Hall. (4.7) (Played by LEENA DHINGRA and SUKHI KAUR)

Changelings: False humans, used by the Graske to replace people they kidnapped, which the Graske would then exploit to create mayhem. (AotG)

Channel 44,000: Channel broadcasting the version of *Big Brother* that the Doctor found himself part of aboard the Game Station. (1.12)

Chantho: Last surviving member of the Malmooth race, which had originally lived in the Conglomeration on Malcassairo. Chantho worked alongside Professor Yana as both his scientific assistant and his friend. However, when she saw him become the Master after he opened his Gallifreyan fob watch, she realised he had to be stopped. The Master instead electrocuted her but, with her dying breath, Chantho shot him, causing him to regenerate inside the Doctor's TARDIS. (3.11) Davros taunted the Doctor about how many people had died trying to help him over the years, and this made the Doctor think of Chantho. (4.13) (Played by CHIPO CHUNG)

Chapel of Rest: Room within Gabriel Sneed's undertakers where the recently deceased were laid in their coffins. (1.3)

Chaplin, Charlie: British silent movie star and director. When Donna absorbed the Doctor's knowledge after undergoing a metacrisis, she asked to meet him. (4.13)

Charlemagne: The Doctor said he once rescued Charlemagne, 8th-century King of the Franks, from an insane computer in the Ardennes (4.7)

Charles: 17th-century nobleman, who was less than happy to find the Doctor hiding naked under the skirts of Matilda. Amy Pond and Rory Williams read about this incident in the book *Myths and Historical Impossibilities*. (6.1) (Played by PAUL CRITOPH)

Charles II: 17th-century English king. The Doctor offered Martha Jones the chance to meet him, but she declined. (3.13)

Charles, Oliver: Transport Liaison Officer at 10 Downing Street, who was murdered and his body used for a few weeks by a member of the Family Slitheen. During this time, he enjoyed a number of sexual liaisons, with Charles's wife, his mistress and a young farmer. However, Oliver Charles wasn't that important to the Slitheen's plan and so, when the opportunity came to get rid of it and wear the body of General Asquith, he took it, discarding Charles's empty skin and dumping it in the cupboard where Harriet Jones was hiding. (1.4) (Played by ERIC POTTS)

Charlie: Orphaned boy who was trying to save his dying sister, Annie, when he followed a Rutan trail that led him to the cellars beneath Parliament in 1605. He was captured by the Rutan Host. (AG05) (Voiced by JAMIE ORAM)

Charlie Brown: After undergoing a metacrisis, Donna Noble's mind started to overload with information and Charlie Brown was one of the people she said she'd like to meet, before remembering he was fictional, a cartoon character created by Charles Shultz. (4.13)

Chaudhry, Nasreen: Head of the Discovery Drilling Project in South Wales. She had been given the job of finding alternative energy sources beneath the ground, unaware that her drill had in fact disturbed a Silurian hibernation colony in the Silurian city below ground. Along with Tony Mack and his family, she joined the Doctor hiding in the village church when Silurian warriors attacked. Realising that the Doctor planned to follow them back to their city, she accompanied him in the TARDIS and eventually found herself acting as a human ambassador, alongside Amy Pond, trying to come to a deal with Silurian elder, Eldane. However, Tony had been stung by a Silurian tongue and the venom in his body was mutating him and there was no time to find a cure. Tony allowed himself to be put into suspended animation, to wake up in 1,000 years, and Nasreen opted to do the same. (5.8, 5.9) (Played by MEERA SYAL)

Chavic Fice: When the government there collapsed, many of the non-human races that existed within the Fourth Earth Empire ceased visiting Satellite Five. (1.7)

Check-in Girl: Hologramatic worker at Twostreams who helped Amy Pond select a destination on Apalapucia. (6.10) (Played by JOSIE TAYLOR)

Cheem: See *Forest of Cheem*

Cheen: A young woman in New New York, she was heading to Brooklyn with Milo, who was seeking a job in the Foundries there, thus creating a new home for them and their unborn son away from Pharmacytown. She and Milo kidnapped Martha Jones so that they could legitimately register as having three adults aboard their car and gain access to the Fast Lane. Once down there, the car was attacked by the Macra, and Milo switched off everything in the vehicle to avoid

attracting the creatures' attention. Realising that they would quickly run out of air, Milo, Cheen and Martha made the decision to reactivate the car and take their chances of getting away from the Macra. When the Doctor reopened the cover of the Motorway, Milo and Cheen were able to return to the Overcity and start a new life up there. (3.3) (Played by LENORA CRICHLOW)

Chelonians: Testudine reptiles who travelled to Stonehenge, as part of the Pandorica Alliance. (5.12)

Chen, San: In physics, San Chen, not San Hazeldine, discovered the 15-10 Barric Fields. Rodrick didn't know this when asked by the Anne Droid in *The Weakest Link* aboard the Game Station. (1.12)

Chen7: Plague that, once contracted, was lethal within one day to people with two hearts, such as the Apalapucians and Time Lords. (6.10)

Chenna: Young Torchwood Archivist aboard Sanctuary Base 6. She discovered her friend Curt in Captain Walker's quarters, his face bearing strange tattoos, his mind completely destroyed. Exactly what happened to Chenna and Curt after this is unknown but, by the time the Doctor and Rose Tyler arrived on

Sanctuary Base 6, they were no longer present, and no mention was made of Curt's markings when a similar fate befell Toby Zed. (2.9T) (Played by ALYS THOMAS)

Chernobyl: Mr Cleaver indicated in his online comments about the Blaidd Drwg project that it could end up more devastating than this 1986 Ukrainian nuclear power station disaster. (1.11)

Chester, Charlie: British stand-up comedian and presenter. After undergoing a metacrisis, Donna Noble's mind started to overload with information, and Charlie Chester was one of the people she said she'd like to meet. (4.13)

Chez Alison: Shop where Donna Noble got her wedding dress. Unsurprisingly, she didn't ask them to put pockets in the dress. (3.X)

Chicane, Heidi: Singer at the Laurenzi theatre, originally slated to sing the lead number, 'Heaven Or Hell', in the New York Revue, but she broke her ankle and Tallulah had to step up and take her place. Tallulah maintained she had had nothing to do with Heidi's accident. (3.4)

Chicken, Mr: The occupier of 10 Downing Street in 1730, visited by the Doctor, who recalled him as 'a nice man'. Two years later, the building was officially declared the Prime Minister's residence, although it was another three years before Mr Chicken moved out and Robert Walpole became the first Prime Minister to live there. (1.5)

Chief Steward: Officer aboard the starliner *Titanic* when it was struck by meteoroids. He survived and, along with the Doctor, tried to rally the other survivors. When he opened a bulkhead which he didn't realise had been directly hit by a meteoroid, he was sucked out into space and killed. (4.X) (Played by ANDREW HAVILL)

Chieftain: Leader of the cannibalistic Futurekind, who started the hunt for Padra Fet Shafe Cane. After the humans had left Malcassairo, he took his people into the empty Silo base and, although there was a brief hunt for the Doctor's party, once they too had gone the Futurekind were left alone on the planet to starve. (3.11, 3.12) (Played by PAUL MARC DAVIES)

Child: Pompeian boy briefly separated from his mother during the eruption of Vesuvius. Donna Noble tried to save them both, but they ignored her and ran away to their deaths. (4.2)

Child Princess: Young member of the Royal family on Padrivole Regency Nine who, with her blonde curls, pink cheeks and simpering voice, had been a target for a Plasmavore, who drained her blood. The Plasmavore was later executed for the murder. (3.1)

Childers, Group Captain: One of the RAF personnel working for Winston Churchill in the Map Room in the Cabinet War Rooms beneath London. (5.3) (Played by TIM WALLERS)

Children [1]: The two daughters of a female coma patient in Leadworth Hospital were created as extensions of Prisoner Zero when it took their mother's form to communicate with the Doctor. (5.1) (Played by EDEN MONTEATH and MERIN MONTEATH)

Children [2]: A group of youngsters watched the Doctor return to the TARDIS in Colchester. Years later, they would recall the moment, and River Song would research them in an effort to understand the Time Lord's motives. (6.12) (Played by JOHN WILLIAM CARTER, ELLIE ROSE, MORGAN PIRIE and CHANTELE EVANS)

Children of Skaro: Dalek Caan described the Cult of Skaro by this name to the Doctor and Martha Jones in the Transgenic Lab, whilst waiting for the results of Dalek Sec's attempt to combine his body with that of the human, Mr Diagoras. (3.4)

Children of the Motorway: Name given to those kittens and babies born while their parents drove along the New New York Motorway. (3.3)

Children of Time, the: A term used by Dalek Caan and Davros to describe the Doctor's companions who would end up in the Medusa Cascade. These were Sarah Jane Smith, Captain Jack Harkness, Mickey Smith, Donna Noble, Martha Jones and Rose Tyler. (4.12, 4.13)

China: Listing things of importance that happened in 1979, the Doctor told Rose Tyler that China invaded Vietnam. (2.2) Martha Jones walked across the Earth telling her story about the Doctor, preparing people for the right moment to chant his name. Amongst the places she went to were the Fusion Mills of China. She also told Professor Docherty she had been to Beijing, to collect part of the weapon she wanted to kill the Master with. (3.13) One of the early ATMOS victims died there. Their nuclear weapons were primed and ready to strike the Sontaran mothership in Earth's orbit. (4.5) Unlike the Britain of the alternative world where Donna Noble never met the Doctor, where there was a fuel shortage, China was choked by ATMOS gas. (4.11) The Doctor told Lady Christina de Souza that he observed the war between China and Japan (whether this was the First or Second Sino-Japanese War wasn't clear). (4.15) The Master took over the Red Army in Beijing. (4.18) Amy Pond and Rory Williams visited the Liao Dynasty in the 12th century to get a takeaway meal. (AG05)

Chip: A force-grown clone (possibly grown from the cells of Lady Cassandra O'Brien). He served Cassandra loyally and, when she was exposed as being behind the events on Platform One and her skin burst, Chip rescued her brain and frame

and recreated her using salvaged skin from her posterior. With his henna tattoos and limited life span, Chip's devotion annoyed Cassandra until she realised that he was willing to sacrifice his life to keep her alive by donating his body to her mind. After she entered Chip's body, the Doctor took her back in time to meet her original human self. Before dying in Cassandra's arms, Chip/Cassandra became the last person to tell her earlier self that she was beautiful. Cassandra never forgot this, and Chip's markings became her favourite pattern, later leading her to create Chip in the image of Chip. (2.1) (Played by SEAN GALLAGHER)

Chip Type: The Nurse on Satellite Five initially offered a Type One Chip to Adam Mitchell. It would be implanted into the back of his skull and cost 100 credits. He opted for the Type Two, implanted into his forehead and giving full access to the information spikes and thus the entire history of the human race, which was activated at the click of his fingers. It cost 10,000 credits, but the Doctor had arranged unlimited funds for him. The procedure took a picosurgeon just ten minutes. (1.7)

Chisholm: Archaeologist and Chief Engineer at the Zebra Bay Arctic Base which was attacked by Cybermen. He managed to escape but remained utterly traumatised by his experiences. He was later bitten by a Cybermat and his arm turned into a cyberarm, but he used the inbuilt gun to destroy the Cyberleader. He was later reverted to his human form and waited for help from Fort Cecil and UNIT. (AG02) (Voiced by BARNABY EDWARDS)

Chiswick: Area in West London where Donna Noble and Lance Bennett were due to get married. (3.X) Donna was born there and the whole Noble family lived there. (4.3, 4.4, 4.5, 4.11, 4.12, 4.13, 4.17, 4.18) Donna claimed to be from 'the Chiswick Nobles' to appear titled at Lady Eddison's garden party. (4.7)

Chiswick High Road: Donna Noble drove down this road on her way to accept a job with HC Clements. (4.11)

Chloe: School classmate to Mandy Tanner and Timmy Winters. (5.2)

Chowdry, Jival:
Owner of a photocopying business in Merchant Street. He employed Donna Noble as his secretary in the alternative world where Donna never met the Doctor but later had to let her go when money was tight. In the real world, Donna had rejected Chowdry's offer and instead gone to work for HC Clements. (4.11) (Played by BHASKAR PATEL)

Chrissie: One of Jake Simmonds' troopers, brought over from 'Pete's World' to Rose's Earth to fight the Cybermen, and then the Daleks. He ordered her to monitor the Cybermen's communications from the Lever Room. (2.13)

Christian, Cleric: One of Father Octavian's troopers. He was killed in the catacombs by a Weeping Angel. (5.4) (Played by MARK SPRINGER)

Christianity: One of the many religions practised in the 42nd century. (2.9) Lobos Caecilius wasn't keen on his son Quintus socialising with Christians at the Thermopolium. (4.2)

Christie, Agatha Mary Clarissa: 20th-century writer of crime fiction. The Doctor offered Martha Jones the chance to meet her, but she declined. (3.13) However, Donna Noble got to meet her at a garden party hosted in Agatha's honour by Lady Clemency Eddison on the day before she disappeared for eleven days in 1926. At this point, Agatha had just discovered her husband's infidelity and was the author of only six books, most famously featuring her Belgian detective Hercule Poirot. It was these books which Lady Clemency had read voraciously, their plots and twists and turns being transmitted telepathically via the Firestone gem she wore to the Vespiform that was Clemency's illegitimate son. The Vespiform turned to murder, inspired by the books, until the Doctor, Donna Noble and Agatha exposed the Reverend Golightly as the changeling. Feeling guilty over the murders, Agatha stole the Firestone and led the Vespiform away from Eddison Hall. She threw the gem into a lake, and the Vespiform followed and drowned. With the psychic link between her and the Vespiform broken, Agatha's memory was erased and, ten days later, she arrived at a hotel in Harrogate, with no apparent memory of what had occurred at Eddison Hall or even that she had been there. (4.7) (Played by FENELLA WOOLGAR)

Chula: Advanced warrior race, one of whose ships Captain Jack Harkness had commandeered from a Chula woman, reprogramming its onboard computer (played by DIAN PERRY) to consider him as its owner. It had a powerful tractor beam, and could become invisible, as camouflage. Like all Chula ships, its internal air was saturated with nanogenes, intelligent subatomic robots which could repair living tissue. Jack, a conman, had also stolen a Chula medical ship and sent it ahead to crash on Earth, hoping to draw out Time Agents, convince them it was valuable and sell it to them before a German bomb destroyed it, but not before he'd fled with their payment (he had calculated exactly when it was due to strike). Unknown to Jack, the medical ship leaked on impact and the nanogenes escaped into the air there. Those particular nanogenes had not been programmed to recognise human beings, and the first contact they made was with a recently deceased child, Jamie, wearing a gas mask. Assuming all humans were 'empty' of life, they reanimated him, the gas mask now blended into his flesh, and proceeded to make contact with other humans, making flesh-and-bone gas masks and scars identical to Jamie's grow on their bodies. When the nanogenes encountered the DNA of both dead Jamie and his living mother, they recombined to bring Jamie back to full health. The Doctor was then able to programme the nanogenes to bring all the other affected humans back to perfect health, which included making a lot of them fitter than they had been before. Jack's ship was destroyed when he used the tractor beam to capture the detonating German bomb and hold it in a deteriorating stasis. He was rescued by the Doctor's TARDIS. (1.9, 1.10)

Church at Auvers, The: Painting by Vincent Van Gogh on display at the Great Exhibition in Paris. The Doctor and Amy Pod spotted a Krafayis in the painting and went back to meet Vincent and stop it. Afterwards, the Krafayis vanished from the painting. (5.10)

Church of the Tin Vagabond: One of the many religions practised in the 42nd century. (2.9)

Christine: One of the psychologists that Aunt Sharon sent young Amelia Pond to see, although in the post-Pandorica timeline, it was because Amelia claimed that stars existed rather than because of the Raggedy Doctor. Christine took Amelia out and showed her the blank night sky to prove that no such thing as stars existed (which they hadn't because the exploding TARDIS created a total event collapse), but Amelia was sure she knew the stars should have existed. (5.13) (Played by FRANCES ASHMAN)

Christmas Carol in Prose, Being a Ghost Story of Christmas, A: Published in 1843 by Charles Dickens, this was one of his most successful novels, originally written as a means to pay off debts. Dickens travelled to Cardiff in 1869 to give a charity reading of the story. (1.3)

Christopher: Name adopted by a Vespiform that landed in Delhi in 1885 and romanced Lady Clemency Eddison. He died during the monsoon later that year, leaving the unwed Clemency carrying his child. (4.7) (Played by DAMIEN MANTOULAN)

Chronomites: Blue four-dimensional creatures that lived in the space/time vortex. Touching them made skin feel itchy. They lived their lives in a perpetual eternal time loop, reliving their existence over and over again. (AG03)

Chronon Blocker: The Doctor needed to build one of these on Skaro, to stop the time paradox that the Daleks had created from killing Amy Pond, who was fading from existence due to having never been born after the Daleks destroyed Earth in 1963. (AG01)

Churchill, Winston Spencer: Conservative Prime Minister of Great Britain, the Queen's Coronation took place in 1953 during his third term of office. The Doctor was appalled to see the British police operating clandestinely on the streets of Muswell Hill, surprised that such things could happen in Churchill's Britain. (2.7) Vivien Rook likened Harry Saxon to Churchill. (3.12) He telephoned the Doctor in the TARDIS, asking him to pay him a visit as he had a potential problem. (5.2) He and the Doctor were old friends, with Churchill being aware of regeneration and the TARDIS – indeed, he was looking for ways to gain access to the ship's secrets. He called the Doctor and Amy Pond to Earth because he was initially mistrustful of the Ironsides, war machines built by his chief scientist Bracewell. By the time the TARDIS arrived, however, Churchill had decided the Ironsides project was too important to the war effort to worry about them. The Doctor was horrified to discover the Ironsides were actually Daleks and tried to convince Churchill and Bracewell to destroy them, but they didn't believe him. When the Daleks revealed their true colours, Churchill put Bracewell to work to find ways of stopping them. When the Dalek threat was averted, Churchill tried one last time to palm the TARDIS key from the Doctor – and succeeded, although Amy spotted this and exposed his sleight of hand. (5.3) When Edwin Bracewell later came to see him, bringing Van Gogh's painting *The Pandorica Opens*, Churchill phoned the Doctor but got through to River Song instead. (5.12) In the alternative London created by River Song's refusal to kill the Doctor and therefore disrupt established history, Churchill was Holy Roman Emperor, and had the Doctor, or as he now knew him, the Soothsayer, imprisoned. (Played by IAN McNEICE)

'Circle Of Life': Oscar-nominated song from the movie *The Lion King*, written by Tim Rice and Elton John. The Doctor quoted the opening lyrics to the Sycorax Leader. (2.X)

Citadel: Huge capital city of the Time Lords on Gallifrey, protected by a huge glass dome that was irreparably damaged during the Time War. (3.12, 3.13, 4.18)

City of Binding Light, the: Remarkable place that sent Ambassadors to Platform One to witness Earthdeath. (1.2)

'Clair de Lune': Musical composition which should have been heard coming from the ice cream van in Leadworth when, instead, it broadcast the Atraxi voice. (5.1)

Claire: Nurse, wife of Alex, and resident of 58 Rowbarton House. After unsuccessfully trying to have children, she suddenly had a son, George. George was in fact an alien, a Tenza, who placed himself in their flat and altered himself to become exactly what they had always wanted, using a perception filter to subtly change their memories – and their neighbours' memories – of his 'being born'. After realising the truth about George, Claire and Alex allowed him to stay, as their son, loving him just as if he were really their biological offspring. (6.9) (Played by EMMA CUNNIFFE)

Clancy's Garage: Car-repair shop where Mickey Smith worked. (2.X)

Clare: One of Melina's many crises that, along with her Dylan crisis, caused Sophie Benson to have to leave Craig Owens's flat to go and sort out. (5.11)

Clark, Farmer: Slightly pompous man who ran Oakham Farm in the village of Farringham. He spotted a Scarecrow in one of his fields, which seemed to wave to him. Investigating, he was set upon by a horde of Scarecrows, which took him to the Family of Blood's invisible spaceship. There he was murdered, and his body inhabited by Father of Mine. (3.8) (Played by GERARD HORAN)

Clark, Sarah: It was on the way to pregnant Sarah's wedding to Stuart Hoskins that Pete Tyler was killed in a hit-and-run car accident. However, when Rose Tyler saved her father's life, time was disturbed, enabling the antibody-like wraiths, the Reapers, to spill into the world of 1987, wiping people out of time and feeding off the resultant chronal energy. Stuart and Sarah had met when she had lost her purse outside the Beatbox Club and couldn't get a cab home. After Pete Tyler sacrificed his life, thus mending the wound in time, the wedding took place, with no one recollecting any of what had occurred other than the unfortunate death of Pete outside the church. (1.8) (Played by NATALIE JONES)

Clark, Sheila: 37-year-old Colchester resident who was killed by the Cybermen and her body used for spare parts. (6.12)

Classic Earth: The National Trust had rearranged the naturally shifting continents of Earth, so it once again resembled what was known as 'Classic Earth' to observers from space. (1.2)

Claude: The trainee Mechanic aboard the *Crusader 50* on the planet Midnight. He shared the cabin with Driver Joe and died alongside him when the creature living on the planet's surface ripped the cab away from the rest of the craft. (4.10) (Played by DUANE HENRY)

Claudio: Roman soldier who was unaware he was actually an Auton duplicate until his pre-programming kicked in and he helped drag the Doctor into the Pandorica. (5.12) (Played by MARCUS O'DONOVAN)

Clavadoe: In the Pan Traffic Calendar, the month of Hoob is followed by Pandoff, not Clavadoe. Fitch didn't know this when asked by the Anne Droid in *The Weakest Link* aboard the Game Station. (1.12)

Cleaver, Mr: Welsh nuclear adviser, charged by the government with investigating the Blaidd Drwg Power Station project. He realised that the power station was badly designed, fearing that the suppression pool would cause the hydrogen recombiners to fail. Thus the containment isolation system would collapse, resulting in a meltdown – a potential nuclear explosion which would take most of South Wales with it. After posting some of his fears on Clive Finch's internet site, by then run by Mickey Smith, he reported his findings to the Mayor of Cardiff, former MI5 operative Margaret Blaine, only to discover as she decapitated him that she was actually an alien: Blon Fel Fotch Pasameer-Day Slitheen, a member of the Family Slitheen. (1.11) (Played by WILLIAM THOMAS)

Cleaves, Miranda: Foreman of the Morpeth-Jetsan contractors, working at the St John's crystal-diluric acid farm. She was in her rig-harness when the solar tsunami hit St John's and gave her Ganger a sense of individuality and a desire to be a separate living person. As the Gangers and the human originals found themselves in conflict, Miranda made the first error by killing Buzzer's Ganger, enraging the other Gangers. Although she remained the de facto leader of the humans, her Ganger allowed Jennifer Lucas's Ganger to take charge of the Gangers. When the real

Miranda contacted the military to ask for aid, the Ganger Miranda was able to work out the password and intercept the rescue helicopter. However, as the struggle got more desperate, the Doctor was able to make the two Mirandas realise that both sides were at fault and the real enemy was Jennifer. Miranda and her Ganger both suffered from headaches, the result of a fatal parietal clot. Exhausted, the Ganger Miranda teamed up with the Ganger Doctor to blow St John's up, killing Jennifer and themselves. The real Doctor took the real Miranda and the Gangers of Dicken and Jimmy Wicks to safety in the TARDIS. After curing her clot, the Doctor took Miranda and Dicken to Morpeth-Jetsan to begin a campaign to seek equality for Gangers. (6.5, 6.6) (Played by RAQUEL CASSIDY)

Clement Street: Address in Barnet where Colin Stretton lived at number 41. (4.1)

Clements, HC: Owner of a security company that was actually a subsidiary of the Torchwood Institute. One of his employees, Lance Bennett, was secretly working for the alien Empress of the Racnoss and, possibly through Lance's duplicity, HC Clements ended up as food, killed and prepared for her children to eat once they emerged from their entombment at the centre of planet Earth. Rather unkindly, due to his distinctive footwear, his employees often referred to him as the Fat Cat in Spats. (3.X)

Cleopatra, Queen: Mickey Smith and Rose Tyler discussed the fact that the Doctor once mentioned he knew, and clearly got on well with, the legendary Queen of the Nile. He referred to her as 'Cleo'. (2.4) River Song used the hallucinogenic lipstick to convince a legion of Auton Romans in AD 102 that she was Cleopatra, even dressing for the part. (5.12) The Holy Roman Emperor thought she was a dreadful woman but an excellent dancer. He had met up with her in Gaul. River Song managed to get access to the pyramids in Egypt from her thanks to her hallucinogenic lipstick. (6.13)

Clerics: Military force, whose organisation was based upon religious hierarchies, from the 51st century. A group of Clerics, under a Bishop, Father Octavian, were brought to Alfava Metraxis by River Song to help the Doctor stop the Weeping Angels. (5.4, 5.5) Some years later, using the asteroid Demon's Run as a base, the Clerics teamed up with another religious order, the Headless Monks, to try and find the Doctor, who they perceived as a huge threat to them. They kidnapped Amy Pond, replacing her with a Flesh version aboard the TARDIS and watched over her as she gave birth to Melody Pond aboard the asteroid, before taking the baby away as part of their plan. However, the Doctor was able to manipulate the Clerics, led by Colonel Manton, into almost turning against the Monks and, in the confusion, the Clerics were overpowered and escorted from Demon's Run by the Judoon and Silurians. (6.7)

Cliff: One of Donna Noble's co-workers at Jival Chowdry's photocopying business in the alternative world where Donna never met the Doctor. Donna reckoned he should be sacked because he didn't do anything, as far as she could see. (4.11)

Cliffs of Oblivion: A natural structure on Midnight where a glacier of sapphires shattered when it fell from the top of the cliff face. According to Professor Hobbes, this was nonsense as sapphire is an aluminium oxide and the planet's surface was just a compound silica and iron pigmentation. (4.10)

Clifton's Parade: Road in South East London where Mickey Smith was when he heard the TARDIS materialisation sound as it brought Rose Tyler home after Emergency Programme One had been activated. (1.13) Mickey's dad, Jackson, used to work at a key-cutter's there before he went to Spain. (2.5)

Cline: Soldier on Messaline and number two to General Cobb. After the Doctor showed both the humans and the Hath on Messaline the truth of their situation, Cobb tried to shoot him, but hit Jenny instead, so Cline took Cobb into custody. Cline was present later when Jenny's Time Lord DNA, boosted by the Source, enabled her body to regenerate itself, and he watched as she stole a shuttlecraft and fled into space. (4.6) (Played by JOE DEMPSIE)

Clive: A footman in the service of the MacLeish family in Torchwood House. He was killed by the Haemovariform. (2.2)

Clockwork Robots: Repair androids aboard the SS *Madame de Pompadour*, who were following their programming and trying to repair the ship after it was caught in an ion storm. Their programming slightly corrupted, they had already used the bodies of the human crew to try and operate the ship, but to no avail. They reasoned that they required the brain of the original Madame de Pompadour, and used time-window technology aboard the ship and localised teleports to access different times in French history until they found her. The Doctor broke the time-window connections to the 51st century and, after deactivating themselves, the Robots stayed inert in 18th-century Versailles. (2.4)

Cloister Bell: The TARDIS's internal alarm system, which rings when the ship is in imminent danger. (BA, 3.13, TC, 4.11, 4.16, 5.1, AG03, 6.3, 6.4)

Clom: Twin world to Raxacoricofallapatorius and home to the vile Abzorbaloff. (2.10) It was one of the planets stolen by the Daleks and secreted a second out of sync within the Medusa Cascade. The Doctor eventually returned it to its rightful place in space and time. (4.12, 4.13) It had a Disneyland, which boasted the Warpspeed Death Ride. (6.10)

Clonemeat: The Sisters of Plenitude tried using clonemeat to cultivate their cures and vaccines, but it failed, so they bred the New Humans instead. (2.1)

Clonepods: Small one-person shuttle craft operated by Sontaran troopers. (4.4, 4.5)

Clovis, Frau: Fastidious PA to the Duke of Manhattan, present when he was cured of Petrifold Regression in the Hospital run by the Sisters of

C

Plenitude in New New York. (2.1) Although she survived the attack by the New Humans, it seems almost certain she later died as a victim of the mutated Bliss virus that wiped out the majority of New Earth's population. (3.3) (Played by LUCY ROBINSON)

Clown, the: One of the images found in a room in the holographic hotel within the God Complex. As it carried a balloon, it may have represented Tim Nelson's fear. (6.11) (Played by DAMON JEFFREY)

Co-pilot: One of the crew of the *Thrasymachus*, a galaxy-class starship that was about to crash on the planet Ember. (6.X) (Played by MICAH BALFOUR)

Cobb, General: Leader of the human military on Messaline. Ruthless and determined to use any means to wipe out the Hath, his world fell apart when the Doctor exposed the truth — that the humans and Hath were on the same side and the war had been fought for only seven days by clones. Angrily, he tried to silence the Doctor by shooting him, but killed the Doctor's daughter, Jenny, instead. Cobb was placed under arrest by his own men. (4.6) (Played by NIGEL TERRY)

Cobb, John: Notorious housebreaker, hanged on the Tyburn Tree. (AG05)

Code Nine: The emergency codeword used by the government to flag up a sighting of the Doctor. When Jackie Tyler called to let the authorities know the Doctor was in South East London, Indra Ganesh, a junior secretary for the Ministry of Defence, told General Asquith that a Code Nine was confirmed, unaware that Asquith was by then an alien. (1.4) Harriet Jones asked Major Blake of UNIT if a Code Nine had indicated the presence of the Doctor as the Sycorax ship approached Earth. (2.X)

Code Red: UNIT call-sign meaning alien activity had been discovered on Earth. (4.4, 4.5) UNIT Control in Geneva sent a worldwide Ultimate Code Red as Dalek ships approached the planet. (4.12) Captain Magambo issued one when she feared Stingrays would emerge from the wormhole growing inside the Gladwell road tunnel. (4.15)

Code-Wall: The Doctor suggested River Song establish one of these around The Library, via a quarantine beacon. (4.8)

Cofelia, Matron: Extraterrestrial nanny from the Five-Straighten Classabindi Nursery Fleet. She was employed by the Adiposian First Family to create a breeding colony of Adipose young on Earth after Adipose 3 disappeared. She established Adipose Industries in London and, as Miss Foster, began distributing diet pills that converted natural fat into the Adipose young, giving the impression of being an instant weight-loss solution. The Doctor alerted the Shadow Proclamation to Cofelia's incursion, and they in turn chastised the Adiposian First Family. When the Adiposian ship arrived on Earth to collect their young, they killed Cofelia to hide any potential witnesses from the Shadow Proclamation. (4.1) (Played by SARAH LANCASHIRE)

Coffa: One of Jabe's associates aboard Platform One from the Forest of Cheem. He was distressed to hear of Jabe's death from the Doctor. (1.2) (Played by PAUL CASEY)

Colasanto, Rocco: Avuncular Italian family patriarch, who jollied along everyone billeted to live at number 29, in Leeds, in the alternative world where Donna Noble never met the Doctor. He used to run a newsagents in Shepherds Bush. He and Wilfred Mott formed a friendship, which was cut short when the whole extended Colasanto family were taken away, allegedly

to a work camp when non-Britons had their social status lowered – although Wilfred and Donna suspected it was something far more sinister. (4.11) (Played by JOSEPH LONG)

Colchester: Essex town, where Craig Owens and Sophie Benson lived. (5.11, 6.12)

Cold Lamentation: A Time Lord occasion. On the night before this the Master, as a child, looked into the Untempered Schism and was slowly driven insane from that point on, because Lord President Rassilon sent him the sound of drumming, the rhythm of four – a Time Lord heartbeat – through the Schism and into his mind. (4.18)

Cole, Mr: Master of the Hazel Street Workhouse in Victorian London. He was captured by the Cybermen and put under their control via an earpiece control device. He then took all the children in his Workhouse to the Cybermen to be used in the construction of the engine for the CyberKing. Mr Cole's usefulness over, Miss Hartigan killed him, via the earpiece. (4.14) (Played by MICHAEL BERTENSHAW)

Collection Squad: Elite Adipose Industries team whose job it was to collect stray and unscheduled Adipose young that hatched too early. (4.1)

Colleen: One of the strongest players of *The Weakest Link* aboard the Game Station, who banked loads of money. When she lost a round, the Anne Droid

appeared to disintegrate her but, in truth, she was transmatted over to the Dalek mothership and turned into part of the growing Dalek army created by the Emperor. (1.12) (Played by KATE LOUSTAU)

Collins, Barney: One of the coma patients at Leadworth Hospital, with whom Prisoner Zero made a psychic connection, creating a body for itself from Barney's memories of himself and his dog, Bosley. (5.1) (PLAYED BY MARCELLO MAGNI)

Collins, Jackie: Author of the novel *Lucky*. Rodrick didn't know this when asked by the Anne Droid in *The Weakest Link* aboard the Game Station. (1.12)

Collins, Miss: One of Joshua Naismith's staff who was badly burned as a child. She was a test subject for the Immortality Gate, which successfully regenerated her skin. When the Master used the Gate to imprint himself on every human on Earth, Miss Collins became the Master too. When she was restored, she fled the Naismiths' house with the rest of the staff and guards. (4.17, 4.18) (Played by NICCI SICHEY)

Coltrane, Alice: In the alternative world where Donna Noble never met the Doctor, Alice was with Donna, Veena and Mooky in the pub when the Racnoss Webstar attacked Earth. Alice was even more alarmed because she was adamant she could see something on Donna's back, although no one else could. (4.11) (Played by NATALIE WALTER)

Coltrane, Miss: Woman sent to Leeds, when the South of England was declared inhospitable after the *Titanic* crashed in the alternative world where

Donna Noble never met the Doctor. She was to live on the same street as the Nobles, but at number 8. (4.11)

Commandant, the: German officer in charge of Stalag Luft 14. The Doctor attempted to lead allied prisoners of war in an escape attempt, but their escape tunnel ended in the Commandant's office. Amy Pond and Rory Williams read about this incident in the book *Myths and Historical Impossibilities*. (6.1)

Commander [1]: Troop commander in the Weapons Testing Area of Van Statten's Utah base, he tried to stop the Dalek getting any further out of the complex. He died, along with all his men, plus countless lab technicians and office workers when the Dalek electrocuted them after setting off the water sprinkler system. (1.6) (Played by JOE MONTANA)

Commander [2]: One of the leaders of the Roman forces on Salisbury Plain in AD 102. He believed he was a human but was actually an Auton duplicate. He worked out that River Song wasn't really Cleopatra and assigned the Auton duplicate of Rory Williams to accompany her to Stonehenge. (5.12) (Played by CLIVE WOOD)

Communicator: Device the Doctor created and gave to Amy Pond and Rory Williams while they were on their honeymoon, to let them know when he was coming to collect them. Amy later used it to talk directly to the Doctor when he was on Ember and she was trapped aboard the *Thrasymachus*. (6.X)

Compact Laser Deluxe: Weapon used by Captain Jack Harkness to destroy Trine-E and Zu-Zana aboard the Game Station. No one wanted to ask where it was concealed, as he was naked when he produced it. (1.12)

Conceptual Space: The TARDIS had just entered this when the ship made an emergency landing which resulted in the exterior materialising inside for safety but creating a time loop. (S)

Condensate Wilderness: The reduction of reality into which the whole universe was becoming condensed. The humans on Malcassairo hoped that Utopia was far enough beyond this to provide refuge. (3.11)

Condition Red [1]: An alert status that enabled an Earth Empire Security Commander to shoot dead anyone he or she felt compromised a situation. Mr Jefferson threatened to shoot Toby Zed on Sanctuary Base 6 under the terms of such an alert. (2.8)

Condition Red [2]: Codeword within the Saxon administration to imply a plan had gone wrong. The Sinister Woman referred to Clive Jones warning

Martha Jones to stay away from the family home as a Condition Red. (3.12) When the Jones family and Captain Jack Harkness, aboard the *Valiant*, tried to stage an assassination attempt on the Master's life, a Condition Red alert went out. (3.13)

Conductor: Leader of the orchestra in the Albert Hall, who allowed his musicians to play the Doctor's composition 'Music of the Spheres', despite being distracted by a Graske. (MoS) (Played by BEN FOSTER)

Conglomeration: The city on Malcassairo in which the Malmooth had lived before their virtual extinction. (3.11)

Connery, Sean: Scots actor whose portrayal of James Bond was one of the highlights of 1963, according to the Doctor. (AG01)

Connie: Child at the reception for Donna Noble and Lance Bennett's non-wedding. Donna checked up on her after the attack by the Roboform Santas. (3.X)

Connolly, Eddie: Husband to Rita and father to Tommy, who lived with them and his mother-in-law in Horizel Street, Muswell Hill, North London. An ex-serviceman since the Second World War, Eddie's pride and patriotism bordered on extremism. He was scared by the changes occurring in 1950s Britain, realising they didn't fit his view of the world, which manifested itself as bullying towards his wife and son. When the Doctor visited his home and embarrassed him before his family, he got worse and had the faceless Grandma (who actually owned the house) removed by the police. When Rita discovered that Eddie had done this to her mother, and to other friends and neighbours, she threw him out of the house in front of other members of their family. (2.7) (Played by JAMIE FOREMAN)

Connolly, Rita: Downtrodden wife to the bullish Eddie Connolly, who insisted that Rita prepare for a party to celebrate the Coronation, putting up decorations and flags as well as providing food and drink for his family. During the Coronation party, Rita finally decided she had taken enough from Eddie and threw him out of their house when she realised it had been her husband who had shopped their neighbours and friends and her mother to the police after they had lost their faces to the power of the Wire. (2.7) (Played by DEBRA GILLETT)

Connolly, Tommy:
Teenaged son of the bullying Eddie Connolly, closer to his mum, Rita,

and his grandmother than Eddie would have liked. Tommy realised that the Doctor might be able to explain what had happened to his grandmother, who had lost her face, and joined him on his trip to Alexandra Palace to defeat the Wire. After Rita threw Eddie out of their home, Rose Tyler persuaded Tommy that, whatever Eddie's faults, he was still his father, and so the boy helped carry his dad's bags to wherever he ended up. (2.7) (Played by RORY JENNINGS)

Constantine, Doctor: The last person in Albion Hospital to be affected by the gas-mask virus created by the Chula nanogenes, he was able to show the Doctor that the seemingly dead patients were just immobile until triggered by something. Like the 4-year-old boy they were now based upon, the only question in their minds was 'Are you my mummy?' Constantine had done some experimental therapy with the 'empty' child in room 802 and recorded it – his empathy existing perhaps due to the fact he had lost his own children and grandchildren to the war. Eventually Constantine succumbed and became a gas-mask zombie like the others, threatening the Doctor, Rose Tyler and Captain Jack Harkness. When the nanogenes later recognised the correct human DNA, they repaired all those who had been infected, restoring Constantine, who was then able to carry on his good work at the hospital. (1.9, 1.10) (Played by RICHARD WILSON)

Control and Application of Gunpowder, The: A book in Sir Robert MacLeish's library. (2.2)

C

Control Voice: One of the military commanders of the Earth Empire, contacted by Pilot Kelvin on Myarr. (TIQ) (Voiced by BARNEY HARWOOD)

Controller [1]: Young unnamed woman plugged directly into the Game Station who monitored all its broadcasts. She had been sent insane by the demands of her job – having been doing it since the age of 5. However, she had

also been planning the downfall of the Daleks ever since she had learned of the Doctor's existence, and she was responsible for transporting him, Rose Tyler and Captain Jack Harkness to the Game Station. The Male and Female Programmers believed she would not recognise the Doctor's existence as he was not a member of staff, but in fact the Controller had been watching him for years. When solar flares disrupted the Station's transmissions, the Daleks could not monitor events there, and she was able to explain to the Doctor what was going on. Although the disruption then ended, she gave the Doctor partial coordinates for the Dalek fleet, knowing that the Daleks could now hear her – which they did. They transported her to their ship and exterminated her. (1.12) Davros taunted the Doctor about how many people had died trying to help him over the years, and this made the Doctor think of the Controller. (4.13) (Played by MARTHA COPE)

Controller [2]: The role assumed by Dalek Caan after the Cult had deemed Dalek Sec no longer capable of leading them. As such, he wired himself into the machinery in the Transgenic Lab and monitored the results of the Final Experiment. From there he was able to send a massive mental pulse of energy into the brains of every single Dalek-Human hybrid and kill them instantly after they had destroyed Daleks Thay and Jast. (3.5)

Controller [3]: Road-management controller whose responsibilities included overseeing traffic in the Gladwell road tunnel. (4.15) (Played by JUNE CAMPBELL DAVIES)

C

Cook [1]: One of the household of Lady Isobel MacLeish, she survived the Werewolf attack on Torchwood House. (2.2) (Played by SUZANNE DOWNS)

Cook [2]: In charge of feeding the boys and staff at Farringham School for Boys. (3.8)

Cook [3]: Worked for Sarah, preparing burgers for the homeless and was killed by the Master. (4.17) (Played by JIMMY MACK)

Cooper, Gwen: Operative working for Captain Jack Harkness at Torchwood Three in Cardiff. In the alternative world where Donna Noble never met the Doctor, she died aboard the mothership of the Tenth Sontaran Battle Fleet. (4.11) She and Ianto Jones worked with Jack in their base, the Hub, to try and stop the Daleks and later helped the Doctor bring Earth back to its correct place in space, using the power of Cardiff's rift. (4.12, 4.13) (Played by EVE MYLES)

Cooper, Miss: Villager at the dance in Farringham when the Family of Blood attacked, killing Mr Chambers and demanding the Doctor hand himself over to them. She may well have been the daughter of the man who owned Cooper's Field. (3.9)

Cooper's Field: Area of Farringham where the Family of Blood landed their invisible spaceship, just on the border of Blackdown Woods. (3.8, 3.9)

Copacabana Beach: Popular resort in Rio de Janeiro, Brazil, which Martha Jones randomly elected to visit in the TARDIS. (TIQ)

Copper, Mr: The official historian aboard the luxury starliner *Titanic*. Originally from Sto, Mr Copper was something of a fraud – his actual knowledge of Earth, its history, people and customs was entirely misconstrued, and indeed his Earthonomics degree was bought from Mrs Golightly's Happy Travelling University and Dry Cleaner's after he'd given up a career as a travelling salesman. He was one of the few survivors of the *Titanic* but, having been exposed as a fake, he knew his career was over and he was likely to be sent to jail on Sto. The Doctor took him to Earth and left him there to start a new life. Mr Copper actually had a million pounds of Earth currency. (4.X) He used that money to establish the Mr Copper Foundation, which created the technology that enabled Harriet Jones to set up a subwave network between the Doctor's old friends. (4.12) (Played by CLIVE SWIFT)

Cordolaine Signal: A signal transmitted by the Sontarans that excited the copper surface of normal Earth bullets, causing them to expand within the gun's barrel, and thus not fire. Colonel Mace overcame this problem by using bullets not coated in copper. (4.4, 4.5)

Cornwall: South-westernmost part of Britain, where Alan and Maria Jackson were holidaying when the Daleks moved Earth to the Medusa Cascade. (4.12)

Corporation, the: The company that owned various space stations such as Platform One and were responsible for programming the Control Computers which ran them. (1.2)

Corsair, the: A Time Lord adventurer, famous for his Ouroboros tattoo, and admired and respected by the Doctor, regardless of whatever regeneration he (or sometimes she) was in. The Doctor was lured to House's asteroid by a Psychic Container, seemingly despatched by the Corsair. The Corsair, however, was long since dead, along with his TARDIS. The Corsair's right arm was later worn by Auntie, whilst Uncle had his spine and kidneys. (6.4)

Corvin, Sister: One of the Catkind Sisters of Plenitude. She wrote a thesis about the migration of sentience, referring to the process as the Echo of Life. (2.1)

Costard: Character from *Love's Labour's Lost* and *Love's Labour's Won*, played by William Kempe, a member of Shakespeare's company. (3.2)

Cotter Palluni's World: The Doctor wanted to take Donna Noble there to see the Lightning Skies. (4.4)

'Could It Be Magic': Barry Manilow song, covered by Take That and playing in the wine bar where the Wednesday Girls met. (4.1)

Couldhavebeen King, the: Participant in the Time War. (4.18)

Countdown: One of the programmes broadcast from the Game Station. Contestants had 30 seconds to stop a bomb detonating. (1.12) It was an updated version of a British quiz show broadcast by Channel 4; in the erased 2009 timeline that followed the Toclafane domination of Earth, Professor Docherty reminisced that she used to enjoy *Countdown*, presented by either of the Deses (Lynam or O'Connor). (3.13)

Crabtree: Thuggish plain-clothed policeman who assisted Detective Inspector Bishop in taking away the faceless people of Muswell Hill in 1953. (2.7) (Played by IEUAN RHYS)

Crack in the Wall: See *Time Field*

Craddock, Phyllis 'Fanny': British television cook from the 1950s to the 1970s, whom the Doctor referred to as one of the greatest chefs on Earth. (TIQ)

Crane, Matt: Torchwood operative based in the Lever Room in the Torchwood Tower. He spotted the TARDIS at the Powell Estate, much to the delight of Torchwood's CEO, Yvonne Hartman. Matt was later led to the upper floors of the Tower, where he was killed by the Cybermen and reanimated via a Cybus Industries ear pod that was connected directly into his cerebral cortex. When the Doctor discovered this, he jammed the signal to the ear pods and the already dead Matt died once again. (2.12) (Played by OLIVER MELLOR)

Crane, Mr: John Lumic's right-hand man on 'Pete's World'. He had worked alongside Lumic for many years and knew how ruthless his boss could be. He had no conscience when it came to fooling London's homeless that he could give them food, instead having them converted into Cybermen. However, when Lumic activated the ear-pod signal that would blank everyone's mind, Mr Crane realised it was meant to include him. He confronted Lumic and tried to kill him, but a Cyberman electrocuted him. (2.5, 2.6) (Played by COLIN SPAULL)

'Crazy Little Thing Called Love': Top Five 1979 song by Queen, which was played at Amy Pond and Rory Williams's wedding. The Doctor taught some kids his Drunk Giraffe dance to it. (5.13)

Credit Five: Form of currency, resembling thin metal strips, on Satellite Five. (1.7)

Creet: Orphaned refugee child who assisted Lieutenant Atillo in the Silo base on Malcassairo. He helped reunite the Shafe Cane family and later went aboard the rocket to Utopia, telling Martha Jones that his mother believed the skies above Utopia were full of diamonds. When Martha Jones heard this phrase repeated by the inhabitant of one of the Toclafane spheres, she realised who the Toclafane really were. (3.11) (Played by JOHN BELL)

Crespallions: Blue-skinned race charged with running Platform One. Some Crespallions were of average humanoid height, others no taller than human children. (1.2)

Crimean War: 19th-century war fought by Britain and her allies against the Russians. The doorman at the village hall in Farringham was a veteran of the war. (3.8)

Crime Crackers: Television programme that alerted the public to the disappearances of the children from Stratford in 2012. (2.11T)

Crispin, Cleric: One of Father Octavian's troopers. He was killed in the *Byzantium*'s Forest Vault when he approached the time field. (5.4, 5.5) (Played by STEPHEN MARTIN-WALTERS)

Croatia: Eastern European country. One of the residents of Rowbarton House was originally from there, although he now worked in London as a traffic warden. (6.9)

Crofter: Travelling through the moorlands of Scotland in 1840, he was killed by the original werewolf that had crash-landed on Earth 300 years earlier. (2.2T) (Played by ALAN DORRINTON)

Cronkite, Walter Jr: American news anchor for CBS – he was reporting on Neil Armstrong's successful moon landing in 1969 when the

Doctor's pre-programmed subliminal message about the Silence flashed up. (6.2)

Croot, Billy: Local man who asked Jackie Tyler out while Rose was missing for a year. (1.4)

Croot, Mrs: Resident of South East London, who Elton Pope met. She told him where Jackie Tyler lived. Presumably the mother of Billy. (2.10) (Played by BELLA EMBERG)

Crosactic Energy: The Doctor planned to use this to stun the Krafayis in the church at Auvers. (5.10)

Crosbie: Housemate alongside Strood and Lynda in the *Big Brother* house when the Doctor was transported in. Shortly after, she was the eighth housemate to be evicted. A great cook, she apologised for stealing Lynda Moss's soap and, although apparently disintegrated, she was in fact transmatted over to the Dalek mothership to be turned into part of the growing Dalek army created by the Emperor. (1.12) (Played by ABI ENIOLA)

Cross Flane, Zachary: Second-in-command of the Torchwood Archive's Sanctuary Base 6, he took charge after the death of Captain Walker when their ship crashed on Krop Tor after encountering the black hole which the planet

C

was orbiting. Not really wanting the command, he nevertheless successfully dealt with the attack by the Beast imprisoned beneath the planet's surface and took the survivors away in a shuttle ship. Just when they thought they were safe, they found themselves drawn towards the black hole, but were saved by the Doctor using the TARDIS's force fields to protect the ship and drag it away. (2.8, 2.9) (Played by SHAUN PARKES)

Crossgate Cabs: London taxi firm. The Doctor, Martha Jones and Captain Jack Harkness watched a television in its window and discovered that the Master had set them up as public enemies. (3.12)

Crown and Anchor, the: Colchester pub which boasted a Sunday soccer league team, who were due to play Craig Owens's King's Arms team the week after the Doctor played. (5.11)

Croydon: At the time of her original journeys alongside the Doctor, Sarah Jane Smith's home was in South Croydon and that's where the Doctor told her he had brought her to when it was time for them to part ways. After the TARDIS left her, Sarah Jane realised she wasn't in Hillview Road, Croydon at all, but in Aberdeen. (2.3)

Crucible, the: The Dalek space station at the heart of the rift in the Medusa Cascade, powered by a heart of Z-Neutrino energy. It was destroyed by the actions of Donna Noble after she underwent a metacrisis. (4.12, 4.13)

Cruciform: When the Dalek Emperor took possession of this towards the end of the Time War, the Master realised his people, the Time Lords, were defeated and fled, turning himself human via a chameleon arch and becoming Professor Yana. (3.12)

Crusader 50: One of a number of Crusader craft used by the Leisure Palace Company to show visitors the sights of Midnight. *Crusader 50* was the vehicle the Doctor took to see the Cliffs of Oblivion. It was a small, enclosed coach, with entertainment systems, a hostess and piloted by a driver and a mechanic. (4.10)

Cryo-Cave: Place beneath Elliot Sardick's house, built over a fog lake, where he stored the cryogenic chambers. (6.X)

Cryofreeze: Part of the stasis chamber in the medcentre aboard the SS *Pentallian*. Kath McDonnell used it to kill Dev Ashton when he was sun-possessed, and the Doctor made Martha Jones use it to try and freeze the sun out of him when he too became sun-possessed. (3.7)

Cryogenic Chambers: Coffin-like devices into which Elliot Sardick, and later his son Kazran, installed the dying people of Ember who were put up by their families as collateral against the money loaned to them by the Sardicks. Abigail Pettigrew was one of these people. (6.X)

Crystal-Dilurgic Acid: Volatile and incredibly dangerous natural acid found in Earth's lower mantle. Rising to the crust via natural wells, the Morpeth-Jetsan company had alpha-grade industrial stations across the world farming the acid under military contracts. Because the acid was so instantly lethal to humans, even encased in protective suits, the Morpeth-Jetsan company developed a substance called the Flesh, from which they created Gangers, duplicates of their staff with exact memories and skills downloaded into them to farm the stuff. (6.5, 6.6)

Crystal Feast, the: The name given to Christmas by the original colonists on Ember. (6.X)

Crystal Nucleus: Organic structure that powered the engines of the Tritovore ship held in place by magnetic clamps. With the ship irreparably crippled, the Doctor planned to get the crystal's clamps back to the number 200 bus and take the passengers and Tritovores back to Earth with it, although the Tritovores didn't survive a Stingray attack. The clamps raised the bus out of the sand, enabling it to fly home through the wormhole created by the approaching Stingrays. (4.15)

Cult of Skaro, the: Legendary group of four Daleks, appointed by the Emperor during the Time War to think and plan, each having a degree of individuality and emotion denied most rank-and-file Daleks. They gave themselves names, Caan, Jast, Thay, and their leader, a Black Dalek, was Sec. They fled the end of the Time War, a limited time-travel capability built into each of them, unaware that the Emperor had survived, and they hid, along with the Genesis Ark containing millions of Dalek prisoners, in the Void, waiting for the chance to ease themselves into reality. Once this had been achieved, Sec released the Dalek prisoners and began a war against both humans and Cybermen. However, when the Doctor reopened the Void, all the Daleks were in danger of being drawn back in. Ultimately every Dalek, plus the empty Ark, was returned to the Void apart from the four members of the Cult, who used an emergency temporal shift to escape the carnage. (2.12, 2.13) They ended up trapped in 1930, in Manhattan, with no supplies and little energy. Realising that their future might lie in genetic experimentation to create a new race of Daleks, they oversaw the construction of the Empire State Building, intending to use it as a conductor for

gamma radiation caused by a solar flare. The radiation would then carry the Dalek Factor into nearly a thousand specially prepared unconscious humans. This Final Experiment would provide the Cult with a new army. However, they had not foreseen that Dalek Sec's desire to merge his consciousness with a human body, creating the Dalek Sec Hybrid, would in turn give him a conscience and a degree of humanity. Sec turned against his fellow Daleks and they exterminated him. Not long after, their Dalek-Human army, influenced by the addition of Time Lord DNA courtesy of the Doctor, turned on the Cult – both Thay and Jast were destroyed before Caan exterminated all the Dalek-Humans. The Doctor tried to appeal to Caan, now the last Dalek in the universe, but Caan activated an emergency temporal shift and vanished. (3.4, 3.5) Caan voyaged back to the Time War and rescued Davros, the Daleks' creator, from the jaws of the Nightmare Child, and the experience drove him insane. He and Davros were later imprisoned by the Supreme Dalek, who referred to Caan as the Abomination. (4.12, 4.13)
(Operated by BARNABY EDWARDS, NICHOLAS PEGG, DAVID HANKINSON, ANTHONY SPARGO, DAN BARRATT, voiced by NICHOLAS BRIGGS)

C

Cult of Vulcan: A group of six men led by Lucius Petrus Dextrus in Pompeii who followed the fire god Vulcan and what they believed were his Gods of the Underworld, the Pyroviles. They were all killed when Vesuvius erupted. (4.2)

Cup of Athelstan: Golden ornamental drinking vessel presented to King Athelstan by Hywel, King of the Welsh, in the tenth century. Around a thousand years later, it was on display in the International Gallery when Lady Christina de Souza stole it and smuggled it onto the number 200 bus. She was

subsequently taken to San Helios, where the Doctor used the Cup to weld together the bus and Tritovore technology and so activate the magnetic clamps that would enable the bus to fly. This damaged the Cup beyond repair. (4.15)

Curbishley, Colonel Hugh: Lady Clemency Eddison's husband, who caught influenza in 1918 and had been confined to a wheelchair ever since. He was fiercely loyal to his family, turning a blind eye to his son's homosexuality and willing to move heaven and earth for his beloved wife. However, part of his life was a sham – the wheelchair wasn't necessary at all; he stayed in it because he believed that Lady Clemency only remained with him out of pity and that if she knew he was as able-bodied as she, she would leave him. He was wrong. (4.7) (Played by CHRISTOPHER BENJAMIN)

Curbishley, Rt Hon Roger: Only son of Hugh Curbishley and Lady Clemency Eddison. He was due to inherit his mother's estate one day, although, as a gay man, he was unlikely to further the family tree. He was having a relationship with the Hall's footman, Davenport. Roger was murdered – stabbed in the back with a dinner knife – by the Vespiform that was in fact his half-brother. (4.7) (Played by ADAM RAYNER)

Curt: Young Torchwood Archivist aboard Sanctuary Base 6 who was charged with going through Captain Walker's personal belongings after his death. Amongst them, he found the book of hieroglyphs and maps Walker had been given by McMillan on Earth. As soon as he touched it, he heard the Beast speak to him. The book then burst into flames and Curt tried to escape. When he was found moments later by fellow crewmember Chenna, his face was covered in alien tattoos, identical to the ones from the destroyed book, and his mind was completely broken. It is unknown what Curt's final fate was but he was presumably no longer alive by the time the Doctor and Rose Tyler arrived on Sanctuary Base 6, and no mention was made of Curt's markings when a similar fate befell Toby Zed. (2.8T, 2.9T) (Played by KENON MANN)

Custody Sergeant: Police officer who released Melody Zucker into Amy Pond's care. (6.8) (Played by GARRY LLOYD GEORGE)

Cwmtaff: Village in South Wales where Nasreen Chaudhry set up her drilling project, employing a number of the locals. When dead bodies started disappearing from the cemetery, the police were called but before they got there, the TARDIS arrived. The village was later sealed off by an energy barricade erected by the Silurian base below the surface, and it only vanished when the base was shut down. (5.8, 5.9)

Cyber Control: The heart of the Cyber-conversion factory on 'Pete's World', where the Doctor, Rose and Pete Tyler met the Cyber Controller, who had once been John Lumic. It was destroyed in a massive explosion that obliterated the factory and the Controller itself. (2.6)

Cyber Controller: Advanced Cyberform on 'Pete's World', powered via a massive energy throne it sat in, akin to the wheelchair John Lumic, its creator, had used. Lumic's brain was placed inside the Controller, but even that wasn't enough to outwit the Doctor. After the rest of the Cyberforms had their emotional inhibitors switched off, they went insane and rampaged through Cyber Control, destroying everything. The Controller eventually left its throne and pursued the Doctor, Rose Tyler and Pete Tyler up a rope ladder to the Cybus Industries zeppelin. Pete used the Doctor's sonic screwdriver to cut the rope

ladder, and the Controller plummeted to its destruction amidst the exploding Cyber-conversion factory below. (2.6) (Played by PAUL KASEY, voiced by ROGER LLOYD PACK) The Cybermen trapped beneath the Sanderson & Grainger department store sought out a human to become their new Cyber Controller and selected Craig Owens for the task as the Doctor wasn't compatible with Cyber technology. However, Craig overloaded their emotional inhibitors and destroyed them and their ship. (6.12)

CyberKing: A massive dreadnought-class Cybership, shaped like a Cyberman, utilised on the frontline of planetary incursions. It could walk independently, striding across London, approximately 200 feet high. At its heart was a Cyber factory ready to convert millions into Cybermen. Its mouth held the control chamber where the pilot sat. The CyberKing in Victorian London was piloted by Miss Mercy Hartigan, her mental powers increased by the Cybermen, but driven by her emotions as much as by Cyber technology. After the Doctor freed her mind, Miss Hartigan used that power to destroy the control room and herself, and the Doctor transported the crippled ship into the space/time vortex where it disintegrated. (4.14) The Doctor realised that the time field opening up all over the universe and erasing people and events from memory might explain why no one remembered the CyberKing attacking London. (5.5)

Cyberleaders: During the attempted invasion of Earth, Cyberleader One was responsible for taking over Torchwood Tower. He was later destroyed by Jake Simmonds's troopers from 'Pete's World', but all his knowledge was instantly downloaded into another Cyberman, who became Cyberleader Two. That Cybermen was about to convert Jackie Tyler when the upgrading to Cyberleader occurred, and Jackie was able to escape in the momentary confusion. (2.12, 2.13)

C

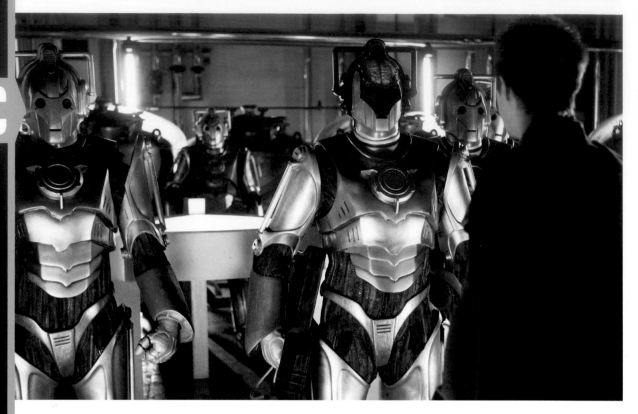

An advanced form of Cyberleader led the small group of Cybermen who built a CyberKing in Victorian London. It was destroyed by an angry Mercy Hartigan after she had been augmented with Cyber technology. (4.14) (Played by PAUL KASEY, voiced by NICHOLAS BRIGGS) One was frozen beneath the Arctic Circle for nearly 10,000 years, until awoken by the nanovirus-infected Elizabeth Meadows, who the Cyberleader then killed. He in turn was killed by Chief Engineer Chisholm using Cyber technology against him. (AG02) (Voiced by

NICHOLAS BRIGGS) Rory Williams demanded the Cyberleader of the Twelfth Cyber Legion tell him where to find Amy Pond. (6.7) (Played by JON DAVEY, voiced by NICHOLAS BRIGGS)

Cybermats: Metallic rodent-like creatures used by the Cybermen to convert humans into Cyberslaves, by injecting them with a nanovirus, in the Arctic Circle. (AG02) They also fed off human brain waves. The Doctor tested his Ganger's memory by asking for a definition of them. (6.6) The Cybermen buried beneath the Sanderson & Grainger department store in Colchester, Essex used Cybermats to siphon off electricity to help revitalise them. The Doctor reprogrammed one to attack them, but the Cybermen stomped on it, crushing it. The Doctor had nicknamed it 'Bitey'. (6.12)

Cybermen: Intended as the next level of mankind, the Cybermen were created on 'Pete's World' by John Lumic, who was investigating means of prolonging his own degenerating life span. The result of the Cybus Industries Ultimate Upgrade project, these Cybermen consisted of a human brain welded directly into a steel exoskeleton, suspended within a cradle of copyrighted chemicals. Beneath the chest plate, metal gears and servos were intertwined with human flesh, threaded throughout the suit with strings of tissue to serve as a central nervous system. Emotions were inhibited, and all humanity removed, turning the Cyberform into a simple drone, although the suits themselves could also function without a human subject. Immensely strong and invulnerable to attack, the Cybermen were able to dispense a lethal electrical charge through their

C

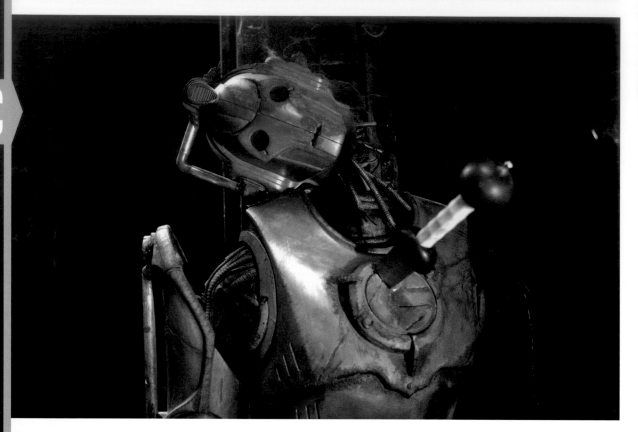

hands, and later developed laser weaponry, which they concealed in their forearms. Although impervious to bullets, a Cyber suit could be rendered inoperative by means of an electromagnetic bomb or Dalek gun, and could be destroyed in its entirety by a direct bazooka blast. In the event of a Cyberman's destruction, their knowledge was retained within a central consciousness and could be downloaded into another drone if necessary. By transmitting a signal via the Cybus Industries ear pods, Lumic was able to lure the entire population of London into Battersea Power Station, where they were then subjected to the Upgrade process. Reject stock was incinerated on site, and pre-converted Cybermen were kept suspended in Deepcold storage tunnels until required. The Doctor and his companions were later able to deactivate the signal transmitting to the emotional inhibitors, and destroyed the factory, freeing the surviving humans and driving the Cybermen mad in the process. However, with Cybus factories still in operation over seven continents, Mickey Smith remained on 'Pete's World' to help Pete Tyler and Jake Simmonds combat the remaining Cyber threat. (2.5, 2.6)

Although Pete Tyler eventually managed to assert a degree of control, Earth's new Golden Age under the auspices of President Harriet Jones meant that many people opted not to destroy the surviving Cybermen, arguing they had rights as living beings. Three years later, the Cybermen had vanished — heading into the Void and crossing over into the 'real' Earth, initially appearing as 'ghosts', and successfully transposing five million Cybermen across the planet, before revealing their true form to the world. Following their arrival en masse, Cyberleader One took control of operations, using a camera located in a Cyberform's forearm to

transmit a message of triumph to the world. Basing themselves in the Torchwood Tower at Canary Wharf, the Cybermen went out onto the streets, taking people away for upgrading. They then encountered the Daleks, offering them an alliance, which the Daleks rejected, thus beginning a war between the two alien races, with humanity caught in the middle. As the Cyberman fatalities mounted, they began the emergency upgrading of Torchwood personnel, and attempted a retreat through the Void, but were stopped by Yvonne Hartman's Cyberform. The Doctor and Rose Tyler managed to reopen the Void, drawing nearly all the Cybermen and Daleks back inside, sealing them inside the Void, unable to enter any other world for all eternity. (2.12, 2.13)

A small group of Cybermen escaped the Void by using the Daleks' Dimension Vault to get to Earth, although back in Victorian times. Bereft of technology, the Cybermen opted to use whatever they could to jury-rig a CyberKing. Needing a mind to pilot it, the Cybermen enslaved Mercy Hartigan, who in turn brought children into a workhouse to actually build the CyberKing's engines. The Doctor was able to use the energy from the Cybermen's Infostamps to override the Cybermen's control over Miss Hartigan and she in turn destroyed all the Cybermen and their slaves, the Cybershades as well as herself. The Doctor then beamed the CyberKing into the space/time vortex. (4.14)

The head of a non-Cybus Industries Cyberman from the 'real' universe was in the exhibit room in Henry Van Statten's base deep under the surface of Utah. (1.6) The Tenth Doctor tried to work out where in the Fifth Doctor's timeline he met him by asking if he'd met the Cybermen yet. (TC) The Doctor kept things relating to the

Cybermen in a box lettered 'C' in the TARDIS. (4.7) The Doctor cited his defeat of the Cybermen to the Atraxi as a reason to fear him. (5.1) Cybermen travelled to Stonehenge, as part of the Pandorica Alliance. When the Pandorica opened and history was stopped, the Alliance was reduced to fossils. (5.12, 5.13) A troop crashed under the Arctic Circle 10,000 years ago. Their sentient Mothership later sent out Cybermats to convert the local humans into Cyberslaves to free the trapped Cybermen. The Doctor reprogrammed the nanoforms inside their body chemistry to attack their hosts, which they did, wiping the Cybermen out. (AG02) Rory Williams infiltrated the Twelfth Cyber Legion to find out where Amy Pond was being held – because he and the Doctor knew the Cybermen were monitoring the entire quadrant. (6.7) A Cybership crashed on Earth hundreds of years ago, and over time the Sanderson & Grainger department store was built over the top of it. When the corroded Cybermen awoke, they began killing locals and using their body parts to replenish themselves. They were destroyed when Craig Owens overloaded their emotional inhibitors as they tried to convert him into a new Cyber Controller. (Voiced by NICHOLAS BRIGGS)

Cyberpunk Girls: A couple of teenaged Japanese drivers on the New New York Motorway. When the Doctor entered their car, he borrowed a blue scarf to keep the exhaust fumes from choking him. (3.3) (Played by NAOMI HAYAMA, KAMAN CHAN)

Cybersentry: A damaged Cyberman watched over the Pandorica at Stonehenge and tried to attack Amy Pond but Rory Williams destroyed it. (5.12) (Played by TIM BAGGALEY)

Cybershades: When Cybermen found themselves stranded in Victorian London, bereft of all but primitive power supplies, they took animals bodies, such as cats and dogs and augmented them with their own technology, creating cybernetic beasts that could run fast, up and down walls and infiltrate small areas. As she destroyed the Cybermen, Miss Hartigan also wiped out all the Cybershades with a mind-blast. (4.14)

Cyberslaves: Half-human, half-Cyberman drones created by the Cybermats. Unable to create full Cybermen from the humans they found, these

halfway versions were used to work on the Cybership buried under the ice in the Arctic Circle. They were slowed down by the frequencies issued by the Doctor's sonic screwdriver. After the Doctor reversed the nanovirus, the Cyberslaves became normal, if very confused, humans once again. (AG02)

Cyborg Caravans: Traveller society on Sto, where cyborgs were still considered second-class citizens. Mr Copper enjoyed their company and they had often given him shelter when he was a travelling salesman. (4.X)

Cybus Industries: Established in 'Pete's World' in 1982. By 2001, it had estimated profits of $78 billion. (2.5T) It had almost complete control of the communications market, and it was via the Cybus ear pods worn by most of society that Cybus was able to bring people to their factories for the Ultimate Upgrade – to become Cybermen. Among the other sub-companies that Cybus Industries owned or ran were Vitex, International Electromatics, IE24, Cybus Finance, Cybus Properties and Cybus Network. The latter was the primary communications provider on 'Pete's World', providing access to communications, the internet and countless other forms of information. (2.5, 2.6)

Cyclo-Steinham Core: Power unit for the Infostamps the Cybermen had used to learn all they could about Victorian London. The energy, when released from the end of the Infostamp, could destroy Cybermen. (4.14)

Cynaps: One of Cybus Industries' technological advances on 'Pete's World'. It was the process by which the human brain, once placed in the Cyberform head, could interact with the steel exoskeleton – referred to as the Ultimate Upgrade. (2.5)

D

Da Costa: UNIT worker in New York who was present when Earth was moved to the Medusa Cascade. She was probably later exterminated by the Daleks. (4.12)

Dad: A London man kidnapped by the Graske at Christmas, and replaced with a changeling. He was eventually returned home with no memory of his experiences. (AotG) (Played by NICHOLAS BEVENEY)

Daemos: Civilisation which had the concept of evil represented by a horned beast in its culture. (2.9)

Dagestan: Russian republic where Mikhail Kerenski and his husband George lived. (4.16)

Dagmar Cluster: Location of the SS *Madame de Pompadour* in the 51st century, two and a half galaxies away from Earth. (2.4)

Daily Contemplation: Every day at the same time, the drivers of the cars on the New New York Motorway took a few moments to sing together, as one voice, a hymn to celebrate their lives. (3.3)

Daily Courier: Newspaper that reported on Agatha Christie's disappearance in 1926. (4.7)

Daily Download: On 'Pete's World', Cybus Industries regularly downloaded information such as news, weather, sport, TV schedules, lottery numbers and a daily joke directly into people's ear pods. (2.5)

Daily Telegraph: British daily broadsheet newspaper, read by the Abzorbaloff before it revealed its true self to Elton Pope and Ursula Blake. (2.10)

Daisy's Wild Ride: Young children's book by Bob Graham, that educates children in basic science. The Doctor was delighted that Craig Owens was reading this to Alfie. (6.12)

Dalek embryo: An early aborted experiment in creating new Daleks by the Cult of Skaro resulted in failed Dalek embryos being flushed into the Manhattan sewer system in 1930. The Doctor found one and, after discovering its DNA type was 467-989, realised that he was facing his old foes. (3.4)

Dalek Paradigm: After activating the Progenitor device, the last of the old Time War Daleks were destroyed by a superior, new Dalek council, known as the new Dalek Paradigm. This consisted of a Drone, a Scientist, a Strategist, the Eternal and the Supreme. (5.3)

Dalek Stratagem: The Dalek Emperor's plan for humanity in 200,100. Having set the Jagrafess up in Satellite Five 191 years previously, the

Daleks had been manipulating humanity, first through news broadcasts, later through the quiz and game shows, gradually building up a new army harvested from the 'losing' contestants, transported there illegally by the Controller. The Daleks had been waiting just on the edge of Earth's solar system – 200 ships, containing almost half a million new Daleks, ready to dominate the galaxy. As the plan neared completion, Rose Tyler absorbed the Time Vortex from the heart of the TARDIS and was able to erase the Daleks, their ships and the Emperor himself from all existence, and the galaxy was saved. (1.12, 1.13)

Dalekanium: The metal which laces a Dalek's polycarbide armoured shell. Slats of this were attached to the mooring mast atop the Empire State Building so that, when struck by a bolt of gamma radiation, they would conduct the pulse precisely into the bodies of the comatose humans in the Transgenic Lab. (3.4, 3.5) The Doctor needed a Dalekanium Coil to build the Chronon Blocker. (AG01)

Daleks: Secured within tank-like life-support machines, the Daleks were genetically engineered on the planet Skaro to be emotionless killers – their primary function to simply conquer and destroy all other life across the universe and to ensure the survival and purity of the Dalek race. Bred as soldiers, the Daleks lived for commands, and elected designated controllers to coordinate units via a military computer.

Protected by a polycarbide outer shell, with a force field capable of melting bullets on impact, the Daleks were almost completely invulnerable. They were armed with a projected energy weapon that scrambled internal organs and killed on impact, fitted to a midsection that could rotate 360 degrees, and their only weaknesses were concentrated gunfire aimed at their eyepieces and an assault using their own weaponry. Most Daleks were also equipped with a multi-functional sucker arm, capable of manipulating computer equipment, reading brainwaves, detecting pulses and performing intelligence scans. It could also be used as a rudimentary weapon, suffocating victims and collapsing their skulls when otherwise low on energy. Although Daleks were equipped with these basic appendages, others could also be fitted, such as more advanced weaponry or assault claws capable of cutting through doors.

Designed for survival, the Dalek casing formed the perfect life-support system, capable of moving across any terrain, in space, or underwater, and affording visual contact between units. Within this shell sat the Dalek itself – fundamental DNA type 467-989 – secured into position by a series of metal clamps and pistons cut into the flesh, surrounded by a series of controls. Daleks could draw back these casings, exposing themselves to the world outside, or pulling other beings inside. As part of their organic nature, the Daleks were also capable of basic telepathy, harnessing their wills to manipulate the feelings of those around them, and could project ideas across space into the minds of potential allies. They were said to have disappeared from space following the Tenth Dalek Occupation, but went to fight against the Time Lords in the Last Great Time War. The Time War ended when the Doctor – known in the legends of Skaro as 'the Oncoming Storm' – destroyed both civilisations.

A single Dalek survived, however, insane and alone in 2012. It fell through time, crashing into the Ascension Islands in the middle of the 20th century, and burning in a crater for three days before it was rescued. For 50 years it was sold at private auction from one collector to another, before coming to the attention of billionaire Henry Van Statten, who imprisoned it in chains as the prize of his collection and named it the 'Metaltron'. It was tortured in an attempt to make it talk, and so shielded itself from the humans, causing men to burst into flames on contact. Transmitting a distress signal, the Dalek slowly discovered itself to be the last survivor of its race, and manipulated Rose Tyler into rejuvenating its physical form, the Daleks having evolved an ability to use temporal radiation as a power supply during the Time War. Contaminated with Rose's human DNA, however, this Dalek then began mutating, eventually opting to exterminate itself through fear of what it might otherwise become. (1.6)

Far into the future, the Dalek Emperor had also survived, hiding in the depths of space. Although crippled, its ship remained alive, and the Emperor shaped the development of Earth through its news and television output, guiding humanity's progress for centuries. It waited patiently, then infiltrated the systems of Earth, harvesting dispossessed humans and nurturing them in Dalek form: a new army of Daleks and a fleet of 200 ships. The Emperor soon proclaimed himself to be God, creating new life in his image, claiming Earth as a Dalek Paradise. It then perished alongside every other Dalek in the universe when Rose Tyler absorbed the power of the Time Vortex and reduced them to atoms. (1.12, 1.13)

D

Although every Dalek in the universe had now been destroyed, a secret order had escaped shortly before the end of the Time War: the Cult of Skaro. Above and beyond the Emperor, who had established the Cult to think and reason outside the Dalek norm, these four Daleks had fled into the Void between different realities. They emerged from their Void Ship in Earth's Torchwood Institute in 2007, just as Cybermen from a parallel world had taken over the planet. The Cult promptly declared war. They primed the Genesis Ark and unlocked it in the skies over London, releasing millions of Daleks from within. These were later all drawn back into the Void, however, when the Doctor briefly reopened the breach between realities. (2.12, 2.13)

The Cult of Skaro performed an emergency temporal shift to escape the Doctor's trap, and relocated themselves to 1930s New York, draining their power cells in the process. The Cult's leader, Dalek Sec, then initiated research into the conception of Dalek-Human hybrids, and sacrificed his own existence in an attempt to ensure the survival of Dalek-kind. Daleks Jast and Thay were later exterminated by their own Dalek-Human hybrids, and Dalek Caan performed an emergency temporal shift in order to escape. Just one Dalek, in the whole of the universe. . . (3.4, 3.5)

Now led once again by their creator Davros, rescued from the Time War to build a new Dalek empire, the Daleks planned to detonate a Reality Bomb that would destroy all life outside the Medusa Cascade. The Daleks' power was turned back on them by Donna Noble after she had undergone a metacrisis with the Doctor (4.12, 4.13) During their invasion of Earth they took a number of Londoners, including Adelaide Brooke's parents, and killed them in their Reality Bomb experiments. A lone Dalek found Adelaide but inexplicably spared her life – the Doctor thought that the Dalek may have recognised Adelaide's importance to the future and spared her. (4.16) The Doctor cited his defeat of the Daleks to the Atraxi as a reason to fear him. (5.1)

The last three Daleks from the Medusa Cascade located a Dalek Progenitor device but, because their DNA was no longer pure Dalek, the Progenitor did not recognise them as the superior race. When the Daleks tricked the Doctor into

confirming who they were, his testimony activated the Progenitor, which created a brand new paradigm of Daleks, purebred and powerful. They swiftly exterminated the last of Davros's Daleks and used a time corridor to escape the Doctor. (5.3)

An alternative Emperor, based in the city of Kalaann, planned to change the time continuum and ensure a new Dalek timeline came into existence where they were never defeated, by controlling the Laws of Time. Using the Eye of Time, the Daleks had changed history and destroyed most of Earth in 1963. Travelling to Skaro, the Doctor and Amy Pond used the Eye to put time back on the right track and thus ensure the Dalek invasion had never happened. (AG01)

The Supreme, the Eternal and a Drone travelled to Stonehenge, leading the Pandorica Alliance. When the Pandorica opened and history was stopped, the Alliance was reduced to fossils. Two of the fossilised stone Daleks were later transported around the world with the Pandorica, watched over by the Lone Centurion. When the Pandorica reopened in 2010, a fragment of its restorative energies touched one of the stone Daleks returning it to life, but it was destroyed by River Song. (5.12, 5.13)

Lady Silver Tear died when the Minotaur in the God Complex used her fear of Daleks against her. (6.11)

(Operated by DAN BARRATT, STUART CROSSMAN, BARNABY EDWARDS, DAVID HANKINSON, NICHOLAS PEGG and ANTHONY SPARGO, voiced by NICHOLAS BRIGGS)

Damascus Road: North London street where Mr Magpie abandoned the faceless Rose Tyler in 1953. (2.7)

Dame Kelly Holmes Close: A residential street in Stratford, East London, named after the British Olympic runner, from which children had been inexplicably disappearing in 2012. (2.11)

Dancer: One of Avery's pirate crew aboard the *Fancy*. When Amy Pond took up a sword to try and protect the Doctor, both Dancer and Rory Williams were cut by Amy and black spots appeared on their palms. When the Siren came for them, Dancer was seemingly disintegrated before everyone's eyes. He was later found alive aboard the Skerth ship, being tended to by the Siren. He joined Avery exploring the universe. (6.3) (Played by CHRIS JARMAN)

Danes, Mr: Joshua Naismith's major domo. He looked after the Master while he was a prisoner in Naismith's home. When the Master used the Gate to imprint himself on every human on Earth, Danes became the Master too. When he was restored, he fled Naismith's house with the rest of the staff and guards. (4.17, 4.18) (Played by SIMON THOMAS)

'Daniel': A 1973 top five hit for Elton John – possibly the record that inspired Elton Pope's parents to name him after their favourite singer. (2.10)

Daniels Family [1]: Southampton-based family that the Doctor befriended, apparently stopping them from boarding the RMS *Titanic* before its fateful voyage in 1912. (1.1)

Daniels Family [2]: One of the dislocated families from the South of England in the alternative world where Donna Noble never met the Doctor. Like the Nobles, they were sent to a street in Leeds, to live at number 15. (4.11)

'Danny Boy': The Nurse on Satellite Five told Adam Mitchell that one recipient of the Type Two information spike chip used to whistle this 20th-century Celtic song, written by Frederick Weatherly, to activate his chip. (1.7)

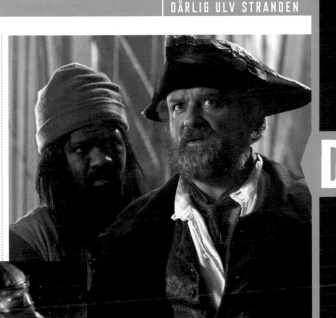

Danny Boy: Code name for the leader of the three spitfires sent into outer space via Bracewell's gravity bubble to destroy the Daleks' transmitter. He was the only survivor of the attack. (5.3) (Played by CHRISTOPHER MILLER, voiced by MARK GATISS) The pilot was re-engaged by the Doctor, this time to take out the communications array on Demon's Run in the 51st century, which his squad successfully did before returning to their own time. (6.7) (Voiced by MARK GATISS)

Darforth, Melanie: Bought Adipose capsules from Adipose Industries. (4.1)

Darillium: The Eleventh Doctor took River Song to Darillium, aware that she was destined to die soon at The Library, although River didn't know. He gave her a sonic screwdriver with a secret neural relay inside which would save and store her brainwaves. He took her to see the Singing Towers and cried, but wouldn't tell her why. (4.9)

Dark Matter Reefs: An area of space, most likely unexplored, towards the edge of the known universe. Utopia wasn't quite as far as the Dark Matter Reefs, nor the Wildlands. (3.11)

Dark Times: Period of Gallifreyan history, about 4.6 billion years ago. According to the Doctor, the Nestenes, the Racnoss and the Great Vampires rampaged through space back then, as did the legendary Great Old Ones. The Fledgling Empires, amongst which were the Gallifreyans, banded together to fight these foes. (3.X, TIQ)

Dårlig Ulv Stranden: The beach in Norway in 'Pete's World' where the Doctor, as a hologram, and Rose Tyler, were reunited for two minutes, able to say a final, heartfelt goodbye. It translates into English as Bad Wolf Bay. (2.13) The Doctor took Rose and his half-human double back there to start a new life together. (4.13)

Dartmore Road: Street in Tower Hamlets where Ciaran Thompson lived at number 9A. (4.1)

Data Core: See *CAL*

Daughter of Mine: One of the Family of Blood, who took on the form of Lucy Cartwright and murdered her parents and, later, the headmaster of the local school, Mr Rocastle. Once the Doctor had regained his Time Lord form, he tricked the Family and blew up their spaceship. The Doctor trapped Daughter of Mine – still in Lucy's form – within the refractive index of a mirror. She was to inhabit the dark recesses of a mirror, all mirrors, for eternity, the Doctor returning to visit her once a year, every year. (3.8, 3.9) (Played by LAUREN WILSON)

Dave [1]: One of Sarah Clark's guests due at her wedding, who hadn't shown up. (1.8)

Dave [2]: Dave was Huw Edwards' fellow commentator at the Olympic Games Opening Ceremony, observing the Torch-bearer's route. (2.11)

Dave [3]: Best man at Rory Williams's wedding to Amy Pond. (5.13) (Played by WILLIAM PRETSELL)

Davenport: Footman at Eddison Hall, engaged in a romantic relationship with Roger Curbishley. Donna Noble felt sorry

for him after Curbishley was murdered because, due to the social mores of the time, Davenport couldn't be seen to grieve publicly or be comforted by anyone. (4.7) (Played by DANIEL KING)

Davey, Roger: Haringey man (not a Catkind) who used Adipose Capsules to diet and lost 14 kilos in two weeks. He had what he believed was a faulty burglar alarm that went off at 1.10am every day. He complained about the burglar alarm to *Watchdog*. In fact, it was the fleeing Adipose leaving his house via the cat flap that caused the alarm to go off. (4.1) (Played by MARTIN BALL)

Davinadroid: Robotic voice that controlled the *Big Brother* house aboard the Game Station. (1.12) (Voiced by DAVINA McCALL)

Davros: Driven, megalomaniac, genius-level scientist from the planet Skaro who, after being injured during a war, created the Daleks. Confined to a mobile life-support machine, Davros was eventually betrayed by the Daleks but returned to lead them against Gallifrey in the Last Great Time War alongside the Emperor Dalek. Davros was apparently lost during the first year of the war, when his command ship flew into the jaws of the Nightmare Child at the Gates of Elysium. However, Dalek Caan, last survivor of the Cult of Skaro, himself a Time War survivor, jumped back in time and rescued Davros from the Nightmare Child, and together they created a new Dalek Empire, using cells from Davros's own body to clone new Dalek mutants. These new Daleks, led by the Supreme Dalek, distrusted Davros and feared the now insane Caan and sealed them into the Vaults

D

within the Dalek Crucible, a vast space station at the heart of the Medusa Cascade. The Supreme Dalek ordered them to create the Reality Bomb, with which the Daleks would destroy everything outside the Cascade — but the Doctor and his Children of Time stopped the Reality Bomb going off and destroyed all the Dalek technology within the Crucible. Davros was trapped in the rubble of the Vaults, and the Doctor was forced to leave him to die... (4.12, 4.13) As she saw her mother and fiancée change into the Master in front of her, Donna Noble remembered Davros as her memories started to come back. (4.17) (Played by JULIAN BLEACH)

Dawkins, Richard: Renowned evolutionary biologist who was the first person on Earth to publicly state that 26 planets hadn't been drawn to Earth but the planet had instead moved to join with them. (4.12) Amelia Pond's Aunt Sharon didn't trust Richard Dawkins or the 'star cults' that believed the skies had once been full of stars. (5.13)

D'Étoiles, Madame: Jeanne-Antoinette ('Reinette') Poisson married Charles-Guillaume d'Étoiles in 1741 but divorced him four years later when she became the King's consort and moved into the Palace at Versailles as Madame de Pompadour. The Doctor referred to her as Madame d'Étoiles when he worked out who she was. (2.4)

De Chateauroux, Madame: Mistress of King Louis XV of France, whose death in 1744 enabled Jeanne-Antoinette Poisson to become his new consort. (2.4)

De Florres: One of Avery's pirate crew aboard the *Fancy*. When the crew hid from the Siren in the bilge-water-infested hold of the ship, a leech bit into his leg and the Siren claimed him. He was later found alive aboard the Skerth craft, being tended to by the Siren. He joined Avery exploring the universe. (6.3) (Played by TONY LUCKEN)

De Maggio: An officer in Bywater's security detail in the Vault of Henry Van Statten's underground base. She was charged with getting Rose Tyler and Adam Mitchell to safety after the Dalek broke free. Having slaughtered her comrades, the Dalek caught up with the fleeing trio in a stairwell.

Relieved, assuming the Dalek couldn't climb after them, they were astonished when it began to elevate. De Maggio sent the youngsters on, trying to negotiate with the Dalek, to no avail. Finally, she opened fire, and it exterminated her. (1.6) (Played by JANA CARPENTER)

De Niro, Robert: Mickey Smith mimicked De Niro as Travis Bickle, quoting his 'You lookin' at me?' moment from *Taxi Driver* while aboard the SS *Madame de Pompadour*. (2.4)

De Rossi's: The wine bar where Sylvia Noble and Suzette Chambers met up with the other Wednesday Girls. (4.1)

De Souza, Lady Christina: Aristocratic thief who stole priceless objets d'art partially because her father had lost a lot of money to the Icelandic banks, but more for the kicks. Along with her partner Dimitri, she stole the Cup of Athelstan from the International Gallery but was almost caught by DI McMillan, who had been on her trail for a long time. She jumped onto a number 200 bus to Brixton, where she met the Doctor. Together with the other passengers, they entered a wormhole and were sent to San Helios. Lady Christina quickly took charge and efficiently organised the passengers into trying to find a way to get the bus out of the sinking sands. Intrigued by the Doctor, she followed him to the Tritovore ship where her thieving abilities came in handy when retrieving a crystal nucleus and its magnetic holding clamps from the bottom of a gravity well. On their successful return to Earth, the Doctor wouldn't let her join him in the TARDIS but did ensure she eluded McMillan and his men, enabling her to escape them in the flying bus. (4.15) (Played by MICHELLE RYAN)

Death in the Clouds: In a box marked 'C' in the TARDIS, filed under 'Agatha Christie', the Doctor had a copy of this Christie novel, with a picture of a wasp on the front, suggesting that deep within her subconscious, maybe she hadn't completely forgotten the Vespiform – although the wasp in the novel is normal sized. (4.7)

Deathless Prince: Legendary demon name, one of many attributed to the Beast throughout the galaxies. (2.8, 2.9)

Debbie: Friend of Jackie Tyler's who lived on the Powell Estate and had a friend on the *Mirror* newspaper. (1.1)

Deep Darkness: Prison dimension into which the Eternals cast the Carrionites within the Rexel Planetary Configuration. (3.2)

Deep Realms: Area of space where the Isolus began their journey thousands of years ago. (2.11)

Deepcold 6: Underground area leading to the Cyber-conversion factory in Battersea Power Station on 'Pete's World'. The Doctor and Mrs Moore entered the factory via this area and found it full of immobile Cybermen. (2.6)

Defabricator: A device operated by the robots Zu-Zana and Trine-E aboard the Game Station as part of their *What Not to Wear* programme. It literally disintegrated fabrics and saved time disrobing. Captain Jack Harkness later adapted it as a weapon and destroyed a Dalek with it. (1.12, 1.13) Jack took it to Earth when he left the Game Station, storing it at Torchwood Three in Cardiff. When he faced the Daleks again, he took it with him, and used it to destroy the Supreme Dalek aboard the Dalek Crucible. (4.12, 4.13)

DEFCON One: NATO state-of-emergency code. It implied that NATO were ready to use a nuclear strike on the Sontaran mothership. (4.4, 4.5)

Defence 05: The Dalek stratagem for teleporting insurgents away from endangering the Crucible. (4.12, 4.13)

Deffry Vale High School: Selected by Brother Lassar of the Krillitanes to be the base for their plan to solve the Skasas Paradigm. Mickey Smith drew the Doctor and Rose Tyler's attention to it after reports in the press of UFO activity in the area three months earlier. The Krillitanes used Krillitane Oil to improve the mental capacity of the students, but the building was blown up by a self-sacrificing K-9, to destroy the alien invaders. (2.3) A web page about the school was seen by the Doctor when he accessed a mobile phone with his sonic screwdriver to search for HC Clements. (3.X)

Delaney, Trisha: Shop assistant who Mickey Smith told Rose Tyler he was dating to make her jealous. Rose, who knew Trisha's brother Rob, believed Mickey was lying, as Trisha was not his type. (1.11)

Delaware III, Canton Everett: Former FBI agent, who was forced out of the Bureau because he wanted to marry a black man. In 1969, President Nixon brought him in to investigate the strange phone calls he was getting from a child, because Nixon needed someone with training but no loyalty to the FBI. When the Doctor, River Song, Amy Pond and Rory Williams turned up in the White House, Canton was won over by them, and realised the Doctor could help the President. He travelled with the Doctor to Florida and found an abandoned warehouse, where the child was supposedly hiding. As well as the child, locked into a NASA spacesuit, they discovered the Silence. Over the next three months, Canton pretended to be working with the FBI again, tracking down River, Amy and Rory while building a prison around the Doctor at Area 51 in Nevada. In truth, Canton was gathering them all together so they could work out a plan of action to stop the Silence. He and Amy travelled to a Florida orphanage, Graystark Hall, where the child had been placed some years earlier. The Silence occupied the orphanage, to protect the child, a girl, and captured Amy. Canton filmed a Silent telling him to kill it, which the Doctor later broadcast in a series of subliminal segments in the television coverage of the first moon landing. Although Canton was unable to have the marriage he wanted, he at least got the respect of Nixon. Forty-two years later, the older Canton brought gasoline to Lake Silencio, as instructed by the Doctor and watched as the astronaut girl murdered him and helped burn the Doctor's body. (6.1, 6.2) (Played by WILLIAM MORGAN SHEPPARD and MARK SHEPPARD)

Delerium Archive: Museum built onto an asteroid. It was the final resting place of the Headless Monks and was where River Song left the Home Box from the Byzantium for the Doctor to find. (5.4)

Delhi: Capital city of India where, in the year of the monsoons, Lady Clemency Eddison met a Vespiform posing as a human called Christopher. He later drowned when the river Jumna flooded. (4.7)

Delta Fifty, Ood: Red-eyed Ood that murdered Ood Operations Marketing manager Bartle and then fled into the wastelands. Away from the factory, his red-eye faded but he was gunned down by the guards and died in front of the Doctor and Donna Noble, trying to reconnect to his fellow Ood by singing. (4.3) (Played by PAUL KASEY, voiced by SILAS CARSON)

Delta wave: Trapped on the Game Station, facing half a million Daleks, the Doctor opted to use the station's resources as a huge transmitter, and created a Delta Wave, using Van Cassadyne energy. The Wave would fry anything in its path. The Emperor foresaw this and reminded the Doctor that using the Delta Wave would indeed wipe out the Daleks, but it would also kill everything between them, including the population of Earth. In the end, faced with the choice of using the Delta Wave or not, the Doctor resigned himself to failing, and the Wave was never activated. (1.13)

Demon's Run: Asteroid owned by the Headless Monks in the 51st century. There, the

Clerics and Headless Monks combined forces to launch their attack on the Doctor, fearing him as their greatest enemy. The pregnant Amy Pond was kidnapped by the Clerics and placed on Demon's Run, where a woman called Madame Kovarian oversaw the delivery of her baby daughter, Melody. Once the Doctor and Rory Williams knew about Demon's Run, they set about gathering a huge army of the Doctor's allies who owed him favours. These included Dorium Maldovar, Madame Vastra, Commander Strax and a platoon of Judoon. Rory tried to get River Song involved, but she refused because she knew that the battle of Demon's Run would be the Doctor's darkest hour, when he would rise high and then fall far — and she explained she could not be there until the very end, because it was the day that he would finally find out who she was. The battle was fought and a number of people died, but Kovarian escaped with Melody Pond, planning to turn her into a living weapon with which to destroy the Doctor for ever. (6.7)

Den Watts: Fictional character from the BBC soap opera *EastEnders*, whose ghost had returned to plague current publican Peggy Mitchell. (2.12)

Dennison, Sergeant: DI McMillan's second-in-command during the chase to capture Lady Christina de Souza, code number Tango 183. He set up a roadblock at the north end of the Gladwell tunnel expecting to see the bus with Christina aboard pull up, but it didn't emerge from the tunnel. (4.15) (Played by GLENN DOCHERTY)

Dent Road: Street HMS Broadfell was on. (4.17)

Derek: A mate of Rose's at Henrik's, she assumed he was responsible for setting up a prank to trap her in the basement of the store. (1.1)

Desk Sergeant: Police officer at the station Sally went to, who wasn't too interested until she mentioned Wester Drumlins. He then asked her to wait while he fetched DI Billy Shipton. (3.10) (Played by RAY SAWYER)

Desktop Theme: The TARDIS internal design can be easily reconfigured and redesigned, which the Doctor calls the desktop theme. Possible themes include wood, coral and leopard pattern. (TC)

Dewey Decimal Classification: A system of organisation, used mostly in libraries, in which books are ordered in increasing numerical order based upon the decimal number they have been assigned. Donna Noble mastered this in two days, when she worked at Hounslow Library. (4.6)

Devon: One of the county tower blocks on *Starship UK*. (5.2)

Dextrus, Lucius Petrus: Chief Augur of the Pompeii City Government and also leader of the Cult of Vulcan. As an augur, he had a psychic link with the Pyroviles. The secondary timeline caused by their arrival on Earth and the space-time rift opened by the eruption of Vesuvius gave Lucius a genuine ability to see the future and interpret it in ways the people of Pompeii would understand. The Pyroviles charged him with obtaining marble circuit boards, which acted as energy converters when assembled together to repower their crashed ship. After taking the circuit boards to Vesuvius and handing them over to the Pyroviles, he was killed when the volcano began to erupt. (4.2) (Played by PHIL DAVIS)

Diagoras, Mr: Former soldier and building foreman. The Cult of Skaro offered Diagoras a chance to improve his position in life, and they gave him the opportunity to prove himself by overseeing the construction of the top floors of the Empire State Building, including the fixing of a section of Dalek Thay's Dalekanium armour to the mooring mast. Dalek Sec, impressed by Diagoras, realised he now had the last component he needed for the Final Experiment and had Diagoras brought to him. Opening his casing, Sec drew Diagoras into himself, physically merging their two bodies, resulting in Sec's Dalek form gaining mobility via Diagoras's body, creating a template for the Cult's Dalek-Human army. However, in absorbing Diagoras, Sec also gained a rudimentary conscience and began to question exactly what Daleks were. If there was anything left of Diagoras himself after this process, apart from his torso, it was lost for ever when Dalek Sec was betrayed by his fellow Daleks and exterminated. (3.4, 3.5) (Played by ERIC LORENS)

Diamond Plains, the: Area on Midnight where the Leisure Palace was situated. (4.10)

Diary Room: Area of the *Big Brother* house aboard the Game Station where the contestants could talk freely without their fellow housemates hearing. (1.12)

Dicken: Morpeth-Jetsan contractor, working at the St John's crystal-diluric acid farm. He was in his rig, asleep while his Ganger was working, when the solar tsunami hit St John's, giving his Ganger a sense of individuality and a desire to be a separate living person. As the Gangers and the human originals found themselves in conflict, Dicken stuck close to Foreman Cleaves and the Doctor and witnessed the death of Jimmy Wicks and his dying acceptance of his Ganger as another version of him. When both sides came under attack from the deranged Ganger of Jennifer Lucas, Dicken and his Ganger worked together to try and trap Jennifer in a corridor, but the door locks were damaged. The real Dicken sacrificed himself to Jennifer, giving his Ganger time to seal the door and save everyone else from Jennifer's onslaught. The Ganger Dicken, his form set permanently as Dicken after travelling in the TARDIS, returned to Morpeth-Jetsan with Foreman Cleaves

to start building a better relationship between mankind and the Flesh. (6.5, 6.6) (Played by LEON VICKERS)

Dickens, Charles John Huffam: Foremost novelist of Victorian England, he was giving a charitable seasonal reading of his novel *A Christmas Carol* in Cardiff when one of his audience, Mrs Peace, appeared to die, exhaling a translucent spirit as she did so. The tired and jaded Dickens then met the Doctor and became embroiled in the fight against the alien Gelth. It was Dickens who realised the Gelth could be drawn out of the corpses they had reanimated if overloaded with gas. He then returned to London, revitalised, ready to finish his latest novel, which he elected to name 'The Mystery of Edwin Drood and the Blue Elementals'. The Doctor sadly told Rose Tyler that this would never happen – Dickens was destined to die the next year and would leave the story of Edwin Drood unfinished. (1.3) Donna Noble unwittingly made reference to this incident at Eddison Hall. (4.7) He was interviewed on breakfast TV about his new television Christmas ghost story in the alternative timeline where time stood still after River Song changed history. (6.13) (Played by SIMON CALLOW)

Didcot: Pete Tyler won the third prize in a bowling competition. The winner and runner up got to go to the Berkshire town of Didcot. (1.8)

Die Hard: The Doctor considered the first three *Die Hard* movies to be good examples of 'escaping from difficult predicaments' movies. (DL)

D

Digger: Cleric who told Fat One the story of the Doctor sending the Atraxi off Earth in the 21st century then calling them back for a good telling off. (6.7)

Digihumans: One of the evolutionary routes taken by the humans of five billion years in Rose Tyler's future. It implied they were different from the then-extinct (bar Lady Cassandra) humans originating from Earth itself. (1.2) This was probably the same stage of human evolution as that referred to by the Doctor in the Silo base on Malcassairo, when he noted that humanity had spent time as 'digital downloads' before reverting to their basic physical shape. (3.11)

Dillane, Sylvia: One of the arrivals at 10 Downing Street after the Big Ben incident. Chair of the North Sea Boating Club, she was actually a disguised Slitheen, the real Dillane having already been killed. (1.5)

Dimensional Lesions: Tears in space created when the TARDIS was hit by a Rutan ship in space. (AG05)

Dimension Cannon: Device used by Rose Tyler to cross into different realities and dimensions, trying to find the Doctor, to warn him that the universe was collapsing. It could track timelines and Rose quickly realised all the lines led to Donna Noble so, unable to contact the Doctor, Rose concentrated on finding Donna instead. (4.1, 4.5, 4.10, 4.11, 4.12, 4.13)

Dimension Jump: The circular yellow disc device by which Mickey Smith, Pete Tyler and Jake Simmonds and his troopers travelled from 'Pete's World'

to Rose Tyler's Earth and back. (2.12, 2.13) Mickey Smith and Jackie Tyler used them to return to Earth to help Rose find the Doctor and ultimately defeat the Daleks. Their power was limited and needed thirty minutes to reboot after each use – Jackie's rebooted just in time to save her from dying in the Daleks' Reality Bomb experiment. (4.13)

Dimension Vault: Dalek technology which catapulted the user across the dimensions. The Cybermen stole this from the Daleks from within the Void where the Doctor had sealed them all and, as the Void began to collapse, they used it to vault back to Victorian London. The Doctor later used the Dimension

Vault to shunt the CyberKing into the space/time vortex where it was destroyed. The Infostamps the Cybermen used to learn about Earth, London and the Doctor were all stored within the Dimension Vault. (4.14)

Dimitri: Lady Christina de Souza's partner in crime. He was her getaway driver at the International Gallery and was arrested whilst she made her escape. (4.15) (Played by DOMENICO BALASCO)

'Ding Dong Merrily On High': Traditional Christmas Carol being sung by carollers in the London streets of 1883 when the Graske kidnapped a street urchin. (AotG) It was being played through the street speakers in Sardicktown, drawing shoals of small fish down from the clouds, because the music resonated with the fog crystals they lived on. (6.X)

Dinner Lady: A Krillitane who had taken human form and worked at Deffry Vale High School. She was killed when K-9 heated up the drums of Krillitane Oil in the school kitchen and blew the Dinner Lady, the school and himself to pieces. (2.3) (Played by CAROLINE BERRY)

Dinosaurs: Sarah Jane Smith told Rose Tyler that, during her time travelling with the Doctor, they had encountered real dinosaurs. (2.3) Donna Noble hoped they wouldn't find any at the centre of the Earth. (3.X)

Direct-to-Brain Downloads: One of the methods of accessing books at The Library. (4.8, 4.9)

Disciples of Light: The beings credited with imprisoning the Beast below the surface of Krop Tor, in a pit, before the creation of the universe. They left behind a pictorial representation of the Beast's imprisonment, in a form that resembled prehistoric cave paintings on Earth. (2.9)

'Disco Inferno': Lady Cassandra quoted the refrain 'Burn baby, burn' from this hit for the Trammps when she gloated that everyone would burn to death aboard Platform One as she teleported away. (1.2)

Discovery Drilling Project: Government-backed industrial project, operating in the village of Cwmtaff, South Wales, in 2020. The Project's head, Nasreen Chaudhry was hoping to find new energy sources below ground, but all that seemed to be happening was the local grass was turning blue. In fact the drill had started to break through into a Silurian city and was slowly waking the hibernating inhabitants. After Ambrose Northover and her dad Tony Mack put the drill into overdrive to scare the Silurians, the Doctor was forced to destroy the whole complex to stop it. (5.8, 5.9)

Disillium: The metal used by the Cybermen, which bonded their ship and the doorway to the Sanderson & Grainger department store built over them. When the ship exploded, the disillium was strong enough to protect the shop. (6.12)

Disneyland: Franchise theme parks across the galaxy, based on the creations by Walt Disney and his successors. There was even one on Clom. (6.10)

DJ [1]: Played records such as 'Love Don't Roam' and 'Merry Xmas Everybody!' at the reception to celebrate the non wedding of Donna Noble and Lance Bennett. His equipment, boosted by the Doctor's sonic screwdriver, destroyed the Roboform Santas that then attacked. (3.X) (Played by MARK HASTE)

DJ [2]: Played records such as 'Crazy Little Thing Called Love' and 'You Give Me Something' at the wedding reception of Amy Pond and Rory Williams. (5.13) (Played by SAM GOULD)

Djagradorf: Empire whose ionic flux engines aboard their Imperial Flagship were repaired by the Doctor using an old chewing gum wrapper and a mousetrap. (AG02)

D96: One of the ingredients of a medicinal compound, for helping relieve stiff bone joints, that didn't exist on 21st-century Earth. (5.7)

DNA Replication Module: The Doctor's scientific rationale for the technology behind the dolls which the Carrionites use to make puppets of menfolk. (3.2)

'Do It, Do It Again': 1978 song by Raffaella Carrà, which played relentlessly on the entertainment system of the *Crusader 50* until the Doctor disabled the system with his sonic screwdriver. (4.10)

Docherty, Professor Allison: Scientist engaged in work for the Master in Nuclear Plant Seven in southern England. Although the Resistance seemed to count her as a major player in their ranks, she was, in fact, loyal to the Master and betrayed Martha Jones, though only because the Master's people held her son captive, and she was never sure if he was truly alive or dead. When Martha gave Docherty the correct frequency to disable a Toclafane sphere, she and Tom Milligan helped Martha do this, only to discover that the Toclafane were really the last humans, from the far future. After time jumped out of sync and erased the previous year, Martha sought out Docherty at the university where she worked and gave the bemused professor flowers, explaining that she didn't blame her. None the wiser, Docherty accepted the flowers and went on to work. (3.13) (Played by ELLIE HADDINGTON)

Dock Worker: Dalek prisoner captured by the Pig Slaves and inspected by Daleks Thay and Jast in the sewers of Manhattan. They decided he was of low intellect and ordered him to be turned into a Pig Slave. (3.4) (Played by MEL TAYLOR)

Docker: East London dockworker who watched aghast as the CyberKing rose from the Thames. (4.14) (Played by MATTHEW ALICK)

Doctor, the: The last of the Time Lords and sole survivor of the planet Gallifrey, the Doctor fought on the front line of the Last Great Time War and was ultimately responsible for the destruction of the Daleks and the Time Lords, using the Moment. He had tried every other option beforehand, but was unable to save a number of worlds in the process, and had been present at the Fall of Arcadia – something he never came to terms with. With no alternative available, the Doctor's children, family and friends all perished along with his planet, and he was left to wander the universe alone in his TARDIS. He could never go back to save them.

A lonely child, when he was 8 years old the Doctor was entered into the Academy, where he became childhood friends with the Master, was taught recreational mathematics and chose his own name. He later claimed to have run from the sight of the Untempered Schism during his initiation ceremony and, years later, began roaming the universe in a TARDIS.

The Doctor's travels to Earth eventually resulted in him attracting the attention of UNIT, a top-secret intelligence organisation, for whom he worked occasionally, and who considered him to be the ultimate expert in extraterrestrial affairs. He often used the alias 'John Smith' when on Earth, and, on occasion, 'Doctor James McCrimmon' (2.2) and 'Sir Doctor of TARDIS', (3.2) while on the planet Myarr he called himself 'Doctor Vile'. (TIQ) He was also known as 'the Oncoming Storm' in the Dalek legends on Skaro. (1.13) To the Holy Roman Emperor, Winston Churchill, he was 'the Soothsayer'. (6.13)

Although he was initially reluctant to travel with company again after the Time War, the Doctor's companions over the next few years included Rose Tyler, Captain Jack Harkness, Mickey Smith, Martha Jones, Donna Noble, Amy Pond and Rory Williams.

D

Having spent 900 years travelling through time and space, the Doctor has never lived a normal life, and things have frequently happened to him in the wrong order. He has a list of rules that he is forever breaking. He is equipped with over five billion languages (including Baby), is able to identify substances through taste and has identified beings such as the Slitheen and Carrionites simply by narrowing down a series of facts relating to their species. (1.5, 3.2) Whilst on Volag-Noc, he was also discovered to have 3,005 outstanding convictions, earning him two billion years in prison. These charges included 1,400 minor traffic violations, 250 counts of evading library fines and 18 counts of planetary demolition, with 6,000 further charges to be taken into consideration at that time. (TIQ) He would never choose to kill, however, nor ask another to kill for him, and even made himself human in an attempt to spare the Family of Blood in 1913. (3.8, 3.9). A half-human version of him was created during a metacrisis when his DNA and that of Donna Noble merged – this part-human version, with all his memories, feelings and experience intact, remained on 'Pete's World', where he could grow old alongside the only person he truly ever loved, Rose Tyler. (4.13) He spent some time on Earth, both in established time and in an alternative one created by River Song, operating a robotic version of himself, the Justice Department Vehicle *Teselecta*, inside which the miniaturised Doctor and TARDIS hid. (6.1, 6.13) It was predicted that the Fall of the Eleventh would occur on the fields of Trenzalore, when no living creature may speak falsely or fail to give an answer when the Question was asked. A question that must never, ever be asked. . . (Played by CHRISTOPHER ECCLESTON, DAVID TENNANT and MATT SMITH)

Doctor of TARDIS, Sir: The title bestowed upon the Doctor by Queen Victoria after he destroyed the Haemovariform that threatened her life at Torchwood House. Victoria then exiled him from the British Empire. (2.2)

DoctorDonna: Their telepathy anticipating the future, the Ood referred to the Doctor and Donna Noble as this. At first the Doctor assumed it was just a misheard name of affection but later realised it was a precursor to the metacrisis that Donna would go through when she merged her DNA with his, creating an alternative, part-human Doctor. (4.3, 4.12, 4.13, 4.18)

Doctor Moon: A computer virus-checking program, built into the artificial satellite that powered The Library by Felman Lux to maintain the structure and stability of the operating system, CAL. CAL itself was the mental shadow of Lux's daughter Charlotte, encoded into a program and kept alive at the

DOCTOR WHO THE ENCYCLOPEDIA

heart of The Library. In her dreamscape, Charlotte saw an actual Doctor Moon, who looked after her and ensured her wellbeing along with her father. Doctor Moon also looked after Donna Noble and Lee McAvoy when they were placed into CAL's reality for what he told them was a total of seven years. (4.8, 4.9) (Played by COLIN SALMON)

Doctor Who?: Website about the Doctor that led Rose and Mickey to Clive Finch's house. (1.1) After Clive's death, Mickey Smith took it over, eventually renaming it 'Defending the Earth', until he left Earth to travel full-time in the TARDIS. (2.3)

Dolls: The Carrionites, especially Lilith, used tiny cloth or straw dolls, with the hair or skin of their victim attached to it to control his body. The Doctor described these as basic DNA Replication Modules. (3.2)

Dom: Occasional member of the King's Arms football team who was on holiday in Malta, which meant he couldn't play. The Doctor took his place. (5.11)

Dominicus: Monitoring technician on Demon's Run who was observing the Clerics and Headless Monks seeking out the Doctor when Madame Vastra and Jenny arrived on the asteroid and tied up Dominicus and his associate, Lucas. (6.7) (Played by DAMIAN KELL)

'Don't Bring Me Down': The Electric Light Orchestra's most successful single, reaching number three in 1979 (although a year later they'd have their only number one, with 'Xanadu', on which they shared the credit with Olivia Newton-John). Elton Pope and his LINDA friends used to do a cover version in the basement meeting room at Macateer Street. (2.10)

'Don't Mug Yourself': A 2002 single by The Streets which broke through onto Pete Tyler's car radio in 1987 as the time breach occurred, as a result of Rose Tyler saving her father's life earlier. This disturbed Rose, who recognised the song and knew something was wrong. (1.8)

Doomfinger, Mother: One of the Carrionites who had escaped into Elizabethan England, seeking to have William Shakespeare write the words that, when spoken at the end of his play *Love's Labour's Won*, would open a portal in time and space and release the rest of the Carrionites from the Deep Darkness into which the Eternals had cast them at the dawn of time. Mother Doomfinger could kill people with a touch but, when William Shakespeare turned their spellcasting back on them, Mother Doomfinger and the other Carrionites were trapped inside their crystal ball for eternity. (3.2) (Played by AMANDA LAWRENCE)

Doomsday Weapon: The Rutans brought two of these to Earth, planning to use them to eradicate the Sontarans once and for all. (AG05)

Doorman: Crimean War veteran, who greeted guests at the village dance in Farringham. He was disintegrated by Son of Mine's gun. (3.8) (Played by DEREK SMITH)

Doors, The: American rock band mentioned by the Doctor when he realised that the Graske's hatchery had, he reckoned, more doors than Jim Morrison, the band's lead singer. (AotG)

Dorabella: An old flame of the real Edwin Bracewell. The android version went in search of her after helping defeat the Daleks. (5.3)

Dorsal Tubercle: The Doctor had a weak one in his right wrist. (BA) When his right hand was cut off in a swordfight with the Sycorax Leader, he was able to grow a new one, presumably with a far stronger dorsal tubercle. (2.X)

Dougal: A farmer who drove the Doctor and Rose Tyler back to the TARDIS in his cart after Queen Victoria had exiled them from the British Empire. (2.2)

Downing Street, Number 10: The residence and office of the Prime Minister of the United Kingdom of Great Britain and Northern Ireland. The Doctor and Rose Tyler went there and met and befriended Harriet Jones MP. Trapped in its 18th-century Cabinet Room, they helped stop the Family Slitheen destroying Earth. When a missile strike hit the building, it was destroyed, wiping

D

out most of the Slitheen present, but the Doctor, Rose and Harriet sheltered in a small reinforced box room, built in 1991, which survived the blast. (1.4, 1.5) Downing Street had been rebuilt by the time the Master, posing as Harry Saxon, became Prime Minister. (3.12)

Draconia: Civilisation which had the concept of evil represented by a horned beast in its culture. (2.9) Draconians travelled to Stonehenge, as part of the Pandorica Alliance. (5.12)

Dragon Star: A descendant of Adelaide Brooke reached this distant celestial body. (4.16)

Drake, Sir Francis: Nobleman locked up in the Tower of London for treason. (AG05)

Drahvins: Female-dominated warrior race who travelled to Stonehenge, as part of the Pandorica Alliance. (5.12)

Dravidia: A planet in the Rexel Planetary Configuration. (3.2)

Dread, Mister: Android leader of the Men in Black, who worked for the Alliance of Shades. They were searching for a genetic weapon brought to Earth by Rivesh Mantilax, an Endymide, which would wipe out the Viperox. The weapon was disguised as an ionic fusion bar, part of her ship's power drive. Mister Dread was disabled by Night Eagle's Shoshoni tribe, but later reprogrammed by Lord Azlok to work for him and bring the weapon directly into his hands. (DL) (Voiced by PETER GUINNESS)

Dreadlock Man: The Doctor spotted him tapping out the rhythm of the Master's hypnotic signal, being beamed down from the Archangel satellites, in a street in London. (3.12) (Played by JAMES BRYNE)

Dreadnought: See *CyberKing*

Dream Lord, the: When the Doctor visited the candle meadows of Karass don Slava, a speck of psychic pollen flew into the TARDIS and got trapped

in the Time Rotor. The pollen was a mind parasite which fed on the dark sides of people's minds, taking their memories and creating dreamscapes to make them experience events that could quite easily kill them. Manifesting in the TARDIS as a being patterned roughly on the Doctor and calling itself the Dream Lord, the pollen apparently created two dreamscapes. One was of the TARDIS heading irreversibly towards destruction in a cold star. The other was five years into Amy Pond and Rory Williams's future; having left the Doctor, they were back in Leadworth, Amy was pregnant, and Rory was a successful doctor. The Dream Lord, taking his cues from the Doctor's dark thoughts, demanded that Amy choose which was actually a dream and which was real. In Leadworth, a group of Eknodines arrived and took over the older population, killing Rory. Realising that life without Rory was no life at all, Amy killed herself and the Doctor, believing the TARDIS environment was the real one. The Doctor, however, realised that both environments were unreal. Outwitted, the Dream Lord conceded defeat and reverted back to the speck of pollen, though the Doctor knew that a piece of him would always be a reflection of the Dream Lord. (5.7) (Played by TOBY JONES)

Dreaming, the: The telepathic shared consciousness of the Elder Ood, the Ood Brain and the natural Ood. They allowed the Doctor to join in and he saw visions of the Master, the Naismiths, Donna Noble, Wilfred Mott and Lucy Saxon. They also used to it sing the Doctor to his regeneration. (4.17, 4.18)

Dreamland: The colloquial name for the Groom Lake military base in Nevada, also known as Area 51, famed for allegedly storing captured aliens and their equipment. The Doctor was taken there in 1958, where he found the Senior Officer, Colonel Stark, in league with the Viperox Horde. A scientist from another race of aliens, the Endymides, had crash-landed there five years earlier and was kept in safety by the Shoshoni tribe, while the Viperox used Stark to search for the ionic fusion bar that was actually a genetic weapon. The base was badly damaged when the Viperox turned on Stark and his men and were only defeated when the Doctor used powerful sonics to deafen them. The US government only admitted to Dreamland's existence in 1994. (DL) The Doctor was 'captured' by Canton Delaware III and imprisoned there in 1969, within a cell made from dwarf star alloy. They later took President Nixon there in the TARDIS and later still, brought a wounded Silent in to be treated. (6.2)

D

Driver [1]: A coach driver took the Doctor and Charles Dickens to Gabriel Sneed's undertakers on Christmas Eve, 1869. (1.3) (Played by MEIC POVEY)

Driver [2]: Mini-owner whose car, despite being recently serviced, ceased working as it drove down Dame Kelly Holmes Close – in fact, right over the Isolus ship buried beneath the tarmac. Rose Tyler helped council worker Kel give it a push and, once it was free of that immediate area, it roared back into life. (2.11) (Played by RICHARD NICHOLS)

Driver [3]: Londoner who drove the number 200 bus during its journey from Victoria to Brixton Bus Depot on the night it went through a wormhole and ended up on San Helios. Alarmed at the damage it endured on the journey, he was anxious to get home. When the Doctor explained how the wormhole worked, he walked through it, hoping to get home. Instead, the energies within it reduced him to a charred skeleton which ended up back in London, alerting the police and UNIT that the wormhole was there, and was lethal. (4.15) (Played by KEITH PARRY)

Driver [4]: Owner of a camper van that the Doctor and Amy hijacked in the dreamscape version of Upper Leadworth. Amy later drove the van into her cottage to kill herself and the Doctor and thus break their real selves out of the Dream Lord's trap. (5.7) (Played by ALPHAEUS DANIEL)

Drone, the: Red-liveried member of the new Dalek Paradigm. (5.3) It was part of the Pandorica Alliance. (5.12) (Played by JOE WHITE and JON DAVEY)

Drumming, the: The sound in the Master's head, ever since he was 8 years old and looked into the Untempered Schism on Gallifrey. He held it responsible for making him what he was, and it only stopped when, after being shot by Lucy Saxon, he refused to regenerate and died. (3.11, 3.12, 3.13) In fact, the Time Lord President Rassilon had sent an echo of a Time Lord heartbeat back through time from the final day of the Time War to the exact moment the Master stared into the Untempered Schism – the drumming provided a link out of the Timelock via which Gallifrey would be brought back into existence. (4.18)

Drunk: A victim of the Reapers as they broke into the world after Rose Tyler saved her dad's life and created a breach in time. (1.8) (Played by COLIN GALTON)

Drunk Giraffe: Dance taught to some of the children at Amy Pond and Rory Williams's wedding reception by the Doctor. They learned it, listening to Queen's 'Crazy Little Thing Called Love'. (5.13)

Drunk Man: Believing the appearance of 26 planets in the sky signalled the end of

the world, this man got drunk and shouted out to Rose Tyler on her return to Earth. (4.12) (Played by MARCUS CUNNINGHAM)

Dry Springs: Small American town in Nevada that was besieged and badly damaged by the Viperox Horde. (DL)

DSTO: The Australian Defence Science & Technology Organisation, where Edward Gold worked prior to joining the Space Program where he met Adelaide Brooke. (4.16)

Duck and Drake, the: London tavern where the Gunpowder Plotters met to plan. (AG05)

Duck Soup: Marx Brothers film (the last to feature all four of the brothers). The film used the fictitious island of Freedonia as part of the narrative, and the Doctor borrowed the name to explain Martha Jones's origins to William Shakespeare. (3.2)

Duke of Manhattan: Charitable patron of New New York's social elite, he was taken to the Hospital and treated by the Sisters of Plenitude for the terminal illness Petrifold Regression. (2.1) Although he was cured, it seems almost certain he later died as a victim of the mutated Bliss virus that wiped out the majority of New Earth's population. (3.3) (Played by MICHAEL FITZGERALD)

Dumfries, Albert: Member of Harry Saxon's Cabinet, originally allied to another political party, but who shifted allegiance when he saw Saxon was the most likely winner. Saxon, really the Master, killed Dumfries, along with the rest of the Cabinet, using cyanide gas. (3.12) (Played by NICHOLAS GECKS)

Dundra System: Alfava Metraxis was the seventh planet here, the system being part of the Garn Belt. (5.4, 5.5)

Dunkerque: Northern French port which, whilst under German occupation in 1940, saw an astonishing 338,000 British and French soldiers successfully evacuated due to a determination not to give up, despite the odds. The Doctor

cited the 'Dunkirk spirit' to Orin Scannell while aboard the SS *Pentallian*, to convince him to keep trying to find a way out of their predicament. (3.7) A similar series of nautical evacuations took place after the world was plagued by the ATMOS devices. (4.4, 4.5)

Duplicate Doctor: After the Doctor was shot by a Dalek, he involuntarily started a regeneration cycle but rather than letting it change him, he just used the energy to heal himself and siphoned the rest of it into his severed right hand, which Captain Jack Harkness had kept in a jar since the Sycorax Leader cut it off. That hand later grew into a duplicate Doctor after Donna Noble's DNA reacted with it, creating an instant biological metacrisis between the two of them. This Doctor was part-human, having only one heart, and would age and die just like any human of his age, whilst Donna's brain power was incrementally increased until it nearly killed her. This second Doctor was more aggressive and vicious than the Gallifreyan version and thought nothing of wiping out the Daleks. Appalled at this act of genocide, the Doctor realised he needed teaching some morality and left him on 'Pete's World' with Rose Tyler where the duplicate could be all the things the real Doctor wanted to be for Rose but knew was impossible. (4.13) (Played by DAVID TENNANT)

Dury, Ian: Actor and singer who, with his band The Blockheads, had a number one hit with 'Hit Me With Your Rhythm Stick', which the Doctor was playing to Rose Tyler in the TARDIS when he suggested they could go to one of Dury's concerts, in Sheffield on 2 November 1979. (2.2)

Dwarf Star Alloy: Bricks made from this were used to construct the Doctor's cell in Area 51. This meant that no conversations held inside the completed cell could be heard or recorded, and it allowed the TARDIS to come and go unseen by the military staff. (6.2)

Dylan: One of the many crises in Melina's life requiring Sophie Benson to leave Craig Owens's flat to go and sort them out. (5.11)

Dynamite: The Master arranged to have sticks of this attached to the back of the television set in Martha Jones's flat, primed to go off on a timer. (3.12)

E

Ealing: Home district in London for Sarah Jane Smith and her adopted son Luke. (4.12, 4.13, 4.18)

Ealing Road: Road at the apex of Little Sutton Street in Chiswick. Donna Noble drove down it to get onto Chiswick High Road and thus towards HC Clements to accept a job. (4.11)

Ear pods: Communications device worn by the majority of the population of 'Pete's World', developed, like most domestic electronics, by Cybus Industries. In fact, they contained the ability to blank the wearer's mind, enabling Lumic to guide them into his Cyber-conversion factories. Mrs Moore and the Preachers had fake ear pods that could get them past Cybus staff without raising suspicion. (2.5, 2.6)

Earl Mountbatten of Burma: Louis Mountbatten was the last Viceroy of India and was assassinated by the IRA in 1979. Donna Noble's friend Alice once claimed she saw his ghost at the Boat Show. (4.11)

Earth: Also known as Sol 3, the third planet of our solar system, within the Milky Way galaxy, and the Doctor's favourite planet. It was home to the Tylers, Joneses, Smiths, Nobles, Ponds and Williamses, and any number of other friends of the Doctor. It was invaded, dominated and over time became a focus for much interest amongst alien races, as well as spearheading a number of Empires that spread across the galaxy over the centuries. The Doctor has had a lot of adventures there.

Earth Command: The military strategy centre of the Earth Empire in the 40th century. The Doctor spoke to Earth Command from Myarr, pretending to be Doctor Vile and claiming the war between Earth and the Mantasphids was his fault. Earth Command then circulated Doctor Vile's image across the Empire, demanding he be located, which he was, on Volag-Noc. (TIQ)

Earth Point 2: The name Luke Rattigan intended to give to Castor 36 once he and his students had settled there. (4.4, 4.5)

Earthdeath: The moment when the planet Earth was consumed as the sun expanded in the year 5.5/apple/26, after the gravity satellites that had held the moment in check for hundreds of years had been removed. (1.2)

East London Constabulary: Local police force in Stratford trying to ascertain the whereabouts of the children who had been disappearing from the area in 2012. (2.11)

EastEnders: BBC Television primetime soap opera, set in the fictional London borough of Walford. The Doctor made a passing reference to disasters that seemed to befall Walford each Christmas, (2.8) while the ghost of former bad guy Den Watts returned to plague Queen Vic landlady Peggy Mitchell. (2.12) Rory Williams likened the Rowbarton House estate to *EastEnders*. (6.9)

Easter Island : Polynesian island, famous for its huge statues of heads, which River Song implied might have been carved to look like the Doctor. (6.1)

Eastern Zone: Area of Messaline where pacifism broke out three generations ago, according to General Cobb. He wondered if that was where the Doctor was from. (4.6)

Ebenezer Scrooge: Main character in Dickens' novel *A Christmas Carol*, which the author read to a rapt Welsh audience on Christmas Eve 1869. (1.3)

Ectoshine: A special ghost-inspired household cleaner. (2.12)

Eczema: Skin disorder affecting humans. Posing as Victor Kennedy, the Abzorbaloff claimed that the condition he suffered from was much more extreme – 'x-zeema' – which was why no one could make physical contact with him. (2.10)

Eddison Hall: Stately home to Lady Eddison and her husband Colonel Curbishley. When the Doctor and Donna Noble visited, they found author Agatha Christie was a guest there, and a series of murders quickly followed. The Doctor helped stop the murders, committed by a shape-changing Vespiform, and eventually left the occupants of the Hall to carry on with their lives. (4.7)

Eddison, Lady Clemency: Owner of Eddison Hall, which she shared with her husband Hugh Curbishley and their son Roger. As a girl, Clemency had lived in India, where she had met and fallen in love with Christopher, a man who was in fact an alien shape-changer, a Vespiform. When she returned to England, Clemency hid herself away for six months, cared for only by her loyal housekeeper Mrs Chandrakala, because she was pregnant. The child was half-human, half-Vespiform, and she gave it away. Christopher had left Clemency the Firestone, a piece of jewellery to remember him by. In fact the Firestone boosted human thought waves and it was this gem that drew the young

Vespiform, now under the guise of the Reverend Golightly, to commit murders in the style of Agatha Christie's novels, which Lady Clemency had been reading. Both Mrs Chandrakala and Roger became victims of the Vespiform's murderous rage and, after it was destroyed, Clemency and Hugh tried to get on with their lives as best they could. (4.7) (Played by FELICITY KENDAL and HAYLEY SELWAY)

Eden: Biblical garden where life began, according to myth. Andy Stone thought they should name the bio-dome, part of Bowie Base One, on Mars after it because they had got vegetation to grow there. (4.16)

Edinburgh: Capital city of Scotland. Sir Robert MacLeish lied to Queen Victoria and said his wife, Lady Isobel, and her household were holidaying there, when they were in fact prisoners in the stables, watched over by the Host. (2.2)

Editor, the: Human in charge of Satellite Five, the broadcasting station that didn't just disseminate the news, it created it, deciding what people did or didn't need to know. Whether the Editor was a corpse reanimated by his true master, the Jagrafess, using Dalek technology, or whether he could simply cope with the sub-zero temperatures on Floor 500 is unknown. He believed he was in the employ of a consortium of bankers (in fact the future Bad Wolf Corporation) and willingly betrayed the Earth Empire to the Jagrafess. He discovered the truth about the Doctor's origins, and hoped to gain access to the TARDIS, but when one of the journalists, Cathica, increased the heat levels on Floor 500, the Jagrafess exploded. The Editor tried to resign and escape in the chaos but one of his drones, the reanimated corpse of an anarchist called Eva Saint Julienne, grabbed hold of him and they were destroyed together in the conflagration. (1.7) (Played by SIMON PEGG)

Editor-in-Chief: See *Mighty Jagrafess of the Holy Hadrojassic Maxarodenfoe*

Edwards, Daniel: One of the children drawn by Chloe Webber, who thus disappeared from Dame Kelly Holmes Close to become a friend for the Isolus.

He was given a celebratory piggyback by his overjoyed dad when he later returned to the street after the Isolus left Earth. (2.11) (Played by LEON GREGORY)

Edwards, Huw: BBC commentator, reporting on the events of the opening-night ceremonies for the Olympic Games in 2012. (2.11)

Egypt: The Doctor thought Astrid Peth might find the pyramids in Egypt more interesting than a street in Chiswick, but she was more than happy with what she saw there. (4.X) Donna Noble travelled there after she first met the Doctor but realised it wasn't the life-changing experience she had expected it to be. (4.1) Lobos Caecilius remarked that the people of Egypt loved scarab beetles. (4.2) The Doctor, Kazran Sardick and Abigail Pettigrew visited it one Christmas Eve. (6.X) In the alternative timeline created by River Song saving the Doctor's life, the pyramids of Egypt housed Area 52, and the Silence were waiting within water chambers for the Doctor's arrival. (6.13)

Ehrlich, Senior Technician Steffi: The only military-trained member of the Bowie Base One crew, who very much missed her husband and children back in Iserlohn, Germany, where she was born. When Captain Adelaide Brooke decided to evacuate the base to escape the Flood, Steffi became separated from the rest by a wall of infected water and locked herself away in the video room until the crew could rescue her. However, the water began to seep in and, knowing she was destined to be taken over, Steffi made sure the last thing she saw was a recording of her daughters saying how happy they were to be going on a trip with their father, Hans Stott, to see their grandparents. Steffi was then taken by the Flood and eventually her body died, along with the Flood, when Adelaide set off the base's nuclear core. (4.16) (Played by COSIMA SHAW)

Ehrlich, Ulrika and Lisette: Steffi Ehrlich's two young daughters on Earth who she hadn't seen in the two years since the mission began. Steffi kept video messages from them and watched one as she was killed by the Flood and her body reanimated by it. (4.16) (Played by ANOUSKA STRAHNZ and ZOFIA STRAHNZ)

Eiffel Tower: Major Parisian landmark, which the 'ghosts' (really Cybermen) materialised around, though they were later drawn back into the Void. (2.12, 2.13) The Doctor, Kazran Sardick and Abigail Pettigrew visited it one Christmas Eve. (6.X)

8.02am: The time at which the Paradox Machine attached to the Doctor's TARDIS by the Master activated. This created a rip in time and space, enabling the massed Toclafane to travel from Utopia, at the end of the universe, and destroy humanity, their own ancestors, in the 21st century. This happened seconds after the assassination of President Winters but, when the Paradox Machine was destroyed 12 months later, time jumped out of sync and returned to 8.02am, trapping the Toclafane in the future – their invasion had never happened and, to the majority of humanity, the only Toclafane incursion involved the murder of Winters, after which they vanished completely, as did Harry Saxon. (3.12, 3.13) Also the time, a year later, when the Earth was removed from its orbit and transported to the Medusa Cascade by the Daleks. (4.12)

8447: The prison cell on Volag-Noc that contained the real Governor, Locke. The Doctor was erroneously placed with Locke, and together the two escaped. (TIQ)

Eileen: A guest on Trisha Goddard's talk show, who had married a ghost. (2.12) (Played by RACHEL WEBSTER)

Einstein, Albert: 20th-century German physicist and mathematical genius who, like Elliot Northover, was dyslexic but, as the Doctor told Elliot, he never let it stop him. (5.8) The Doctor said he spent Christmas 1952 with Einstein, along with Frank Sinatra, Marilyn Monroe and Santa Claus or – as the Doctor called him – 'Jeff'. (6.X)

Eisenhower, President Dwight: 34th President of the United States – Colonel Stark had kept the existence of the Endymides and Viperox from him. (DL)

Eknodines: A proud but ancient race that inhabited other people's bodies, often gifting their new hosts with longer than average lifespans. They displayed their presence as a small eyeball on a stalk hidden in the mouths of their human hosts, and were extremely photosensitive. Angry and bitter, a group of them arrived in Upper Leadworth and took over all the pensioners who lived there, killing all the younger people in the village. However, as this was part of the dreamscape created by the Dream Lord, this never happened outside of the dream shared by Amy Pond, Rory Williams and the Doctor. (5.7)

Eldane: Elder of the Silurian City beneath Cwmtaff. He was awoken by Scientist Malohkeh, who feared that without his sound judgement, Protector Restac would start a war with the humans. Eldane indeed dismissed Restac's posturing and acted as an ambassador for the Silurians with Nasreen Chaudhry and Amy Pond representing mankind. But, just as breakthroughs seemed likely,

Rory Williams brought the body of Restac's sister Alaya back to the city. Seizing the opportunity, Restac took control and ordered the death of everyone, Eldane included. Realising that there was no way forward, Eldane put himself and his people back into hibernation, except for Restac who was killed by poison gas. (5.8, 5.9) (Played by STEPHEN MOORE)

Elder Ood: Leader of the Oodkind, who lived in an ice cave and shared his Dreaming with natural Ood and the Doctor. He warned the Doctor about the return of the Master and the lines of convergence that spread through Wilfred Mott, Donna Noble, the Naismiths and Lucy Saxon. (4.17, 4.18) (Played by RUARI MEARS, voiced by BRIAN COX)

Eldridge, USS: US naval vessel from 1943. The military tried to make the ship invisible but instead created a rent in space and time, and the *Eldridge* was sent forward to the bottom of the Atlantic Ocean in the 23rd century. The Accelerator the military used to open the Trans-Dimensional Gateway was still aboard when the *Eldridge* vanished, and allowed the Razor-Toothed Blade-Fin, the Vashta Nerada and a plague through to Earth. The Doctor deactivated the Accelerator and closed the Gateway, sending everything back home. (AG04)

Eleanor: President of the people fighting at Zarusthra Bay. Her son Arthur was injured and tended by the Sontaran nurse, Strax. (6.7) (Played by ANNABEL CLEARE)

Election Day: May 2008 – and Harry Saxon became Britain's new Prime Minister. (3.12)

Electric Light Orchestra (ELO): British rock group from the Midlands who fused traditional rock 'n' roll with classical instrumentation and structure. Elton Pope was a massive fan, often dancing along to their 1978 top ten hit 'Mr Blue Sky'. The members of LINDA sometimes got together as a tribute band, knocking out versions of other hits such as 1979's 'Don't Bring Me Down'. (2.10)

Electricity beds: The power system on New Earth which had fallen into disrepair after everyone in the New New York Overcity had been wiped out by the Bliss virus. The Face of Boe had managed to maintain some power by drawing off his own life energies, but not enough to sustain the electricity beds. The Doctor rerouted the power through the Senate computer banks and used the electricity beds to repower the covers over the Motorway, opening them and enabling those trapped down there to reclaim the Overcity. (3.3)

Electromagnetic bomb: Mrs Moore, one of the Preachers on 'Pete's World', built these as a defensive weapon. She realised they might be useful in combating Cybermen, too, and successfully stopped one, which the Doctor inspected, discovering it had once been Sally Phelan. (2.6) The Doctor was able to use the cybernetic energy transmitter from the deceased Bannakaffalatta to emit an electromagnetic pulse to destroy the Heavenly Host aboard the starliner *Titanic*. (4.X)

Elephant Inn: The place of lodgings in Southwark where William Shakespeare and latterly the Doctor and Martha Jones stayed, run by Dolly Bailey. (3.2)

Elephant Man: The Doctor joked to Queen Victoria that he'd had the choice of buying either Rose Tyler or the disfigured John Merrick for sixpence. (2.2)

Eliot, TS: Both the Doctor and Richard Lazarus quoted Eliot's poem 'The Hollow Men' to make their points about the benefits and negatives of the GMD that Lazarus had built. (3.6)

Elizabeth I, Queen: Ruler of England and Ireland when the Doctor and Martha Jones encountered William Shakespeare. The Doctor was looking

forward to meeting her but, when she arrived at the Globe theatre, she immediately sentenced him to death – clearly the result of a prior meeting between them that the Doctor had yet to experience. (3.2) (Played by ANGELA PLEASENCE) The Doctor finally experienced that moment, by eloping and marrying her, some time before heading to the Ood-Sphere when answering Ood Sigma's projected song. (4.17, 6.13) Liz Ten thought the Doctor was a 'bad boy' for what he and Elizabeth got up to. (5.2) The Dream Lord alluded to this as well. (5.7) The Gunpowder Plotters and many Londoners mourned her death. (AG05)

Elizabeth II, Queen: The British monarch being crowned on 2 June 1953 – the day that the Wire planned to unleash the full extent of its plasmic powers, feeding off the energy from people watching the Coronation on their television sets. (2.7) The Queen thanked the Doctor for stopping the starship *Titanic* crashing into Buckingham Palace at Christmas. (4.X) (Played by ANGHARAD BAXTER, voiced by JESSICA MARTIN) The Doctor claimed she didn't mind him parking the TARDIS at the Palace over Easter. (4.15) He was known to have had tea and scones with her. (5.2)

Elizabeth of Bohemia: The young princess the Gunpowder Plotters planned to marry to a Catholic and place on the throne of England after assassinating James I. (AG05)

Ellis Island: Island in New York's Hudson Bay, through which, from 1892 onwards, immigrants hoping to make a new life in New York had to pass. During that first year, Captain Jack Harkness got into an argument with a man on Ellis Island, who shot him through the heart. (3.11)

Ember: Earth colony world, whose main city was Sardicktown. The planet was surrounded by a fog created by crystals in the upper atmosphere, where a variety of fish swam about. (6.X)

Emergency Government: Administrators of Britain in the alternative world where Donna Noble never met the Doctor, who took charge after London was wiped out in a nuclear explosion caused by the crashing starliner *Titanic*. (4.11)

Emergency Programme One: When the Doctor tricked Rose Tyler into getting back into the TARDIS before he activated the Delta Wave aboard the Game Station, this emergency protocol, in the shape of a holographmatic message, automatically switched on. The protocol explained the Doctor's likely death and that the TARDIS was programmed to return to Earth, which it did. The ship would then die, ensuring that no one could ever get their hands on Time Lord technology or any of the other secrets therein. (1.13) The Doctor explained that there would be five hours between making an emergency teleport to the TARDIS, as he had done with Donna Noble, and him returning before Emergency Programme One activated. (4.9)

Emergency Protocol 417: Captain Jack Harkness instructed his onboard Chula computer to activate this protocol when he was about to die. A hyper-vodka was promptly delivered to him. (1.10)

Emergency Protocols: Top secret official documents that detailed the actions to be taken by the British government in the event of an alien invasion. Indra Ganesh gave them to the Slitheen posing as Joseph Green, the Acting Prime Minister. Under Section Five, General Asquith had the authority to remove Green from power – threatening to do so led to Asquith's death and subsequent resurrection as a Slitheen. Under the Protocols, communications were monitored for specific words and phrases, including 'blue box', 'TARDIS' and 'Doctor', which triggered a Code Nine alert. (1.4)

Emergency temporal shift: Process by which the four members of the Cult of Skaro fled the Battle of Canary Wharf when they realised it was lost. (2.13) Dalek Caan, the eventual sole survivor of the Cult, repeated this action to escape 1930s Manhattan. (3.5) Caan's shift took him back into the throes of the Last Great Time War, where he was able to rescue Davros from the jaws of the Nightmare Child. The journey drove Caan insane (4.13)

E

Emotional inhibitor: A part of the Cynaps artificial nervous system threaded through John Lumic's Cybermen on 'Pete's World'. When activated, the inhibitor prevented the human brain operating the Cyberform suit from experiencing emotions. When the emotional inhibitors were switched off en masse, the Cybermen were driven insane as they realised what had happened to them. (2.6)

Emperor Dalek: Giant immobile Dalek, the mutant suspended in a secure glass casing below the strutted body, protected by an inner cadre of black-helmeted Imperial Guard Daleks. He created the Cult of Skaro (2.13) during the Time War and took control of the Cruciform. (3.12) Absolutely despotic and insane, as a survivor of the Time War he believed himself not just the Daleks' Emperor but also their god, with all the immortality, omnipotence and arrogance such a belief could instil. He put in motion the Dalek Stratagem: he set the Jagrafess up in power on Satellite Five around the year 199,909, and manipulated mankind, first through news broadcasts, later though quiz and game shows, and gradually built up a new Dalek army harvested from the 'losing' contestants, transported there illegally by a series of Controllers, creating, in his warped mind, life from nothing — a talent only a god could possess. Over the next 191 years, he built a fleet of 200 ships, and almost half a million new Daleks, ready to dominate the galaxy. However, as the plan neared completion, the Emperor did not foresee that Rose Tyler would absorb the Time Vortex from the heart of the TARDIS and use that power to erase his Daleks, ships and finally himself from existence. (1.13) (Voiced by NICHOLAS BRIGGS)

Emperor Dalek's New Clothes, The: Allegedly a classic bedtime story from the Doctor's childhood. He tried to interest the Tenza child, 'George', in hearing it. (6.9)

Emperor Waltz, The: 19th-century dance music composed by Strauss. The TARDIS played it to Vincent Van Gogh when he entered the ship. (5.10)

Empire House: Building in Wembley outside which, in 1883, the Graske kidnapped a street urchin, replacing him with a changeling. (AotG)

Empire of the Wolf: The era the Host wished to see dawn in Scotland in1879, when he unleashed the werewolf from within himself. It had the potential to lead to a Victorian Age of starships and missiles fuelled by coal and driven by steam. (2.2)

Empire State Building: Art deco skyscraper built between 1929 and 1931 in Manhattan, New York. Motivating the speed of its construction was the Cult of Skaro, operating from a Transgenic Laboratory, secretly built beneath the building. The Cult needed the mooring mast at the top to be completed by November 1930, when they knew a solar flare would create a ball of gamma radiation. Using Dalekanium from the body of one of their number, Dalek Thay, they intended to draw lightning caused by the gamma radiation down through the mast, through the building and into their lab, where it would be used to transmit Dalek DNA from the hybrid Dalek Sec into the thousand-strong army of comatose humans they had there, as part of their Final Experiment. This would create a hybrid Dalek–Human army, enabling the Daleks to conquer first America, then the world and thus rebuild their empire. Overseeing the construction work was foreman-turned-businessman, Mr Diagoras, whose body Dalek Sec later mutated into a hybrid with his Dalek form on Diagoras's shoulders. (3.4, 3.5)

Empress of the Racnoss: The last of her ancient race, legendary foes of and destroyed by the Time Lords. One Webstar, the Secret Heart, containing her offspring escaped but was entombed at the core of the planet Earth, which formed around it. The Empress needed an organic key full of Huon particles to free her children and, as the Torchwood Institute had already drawn her attention, she recreated Huon particles artificially in its secret labs. She convinced Lance Bennett, an employee of a Torchwood subsidiary company, to force-feed a co-worker, Donna Noble, with potentially fatal doses of Huon particles, thus creating the key she required. When Donna escaped, the Empress had her Roboform mercenaries force-feed Lance, thus creating a spare key. The

Doctor realised that he had to stop these old foes once and for all and destroyed the children using small bombs to flood the chamber beneath the Thames Barrier, into which they were crawling. As her children died, the Empress escaped back to her own Webstar, swearing revenge, but a British army tank, acting on the orders of Minister of Defence Harold Saxon, blew the Webstar to pieces, presumably killing the Empress too. (3.X) In the alternative world where Donna never met the Doctor, the Empress was killed but the Doctor did not escape the resultant destruction of the Thames Barrier and died there. (4.11) Despite her memory having been wiped, after the arrival of the Master on Earth and his subsequent attempt to turn humanity into himself, Donna Noble recalled the Empress as her mind subconsciously fought the Master's influence. (4.17, 4.18) The Doctor cited his defeat of the Racnoss to the Atraxi as a reason to fear him. (5.1) (Played by SARAH PARISH)

Encounter, an: How the Clerics referred to an actual meeting between one of their number and the Doctor. A Level 1 was observation; Level 2 was an actual conversation. (6.7)

Endothermic vaporisation: Precise description of the power of the sun-possessed Korwin McDonnell, according to the Doctor after finding the remains of Abi Lerner aboard the SS *Pentallian*. (3.7)

Endtime: 100,000,000,000,000 years in the future, when the universe was nearly at its death. Few races survived, but one was humanity, which believed salvation was to be found on a planet called Utopia. (3.11) When the Doctor defeated the Master's scheme to repopulate 21st-century Earth with the Toclafane, the spheres remained trapped at the Endtime. (3.13)

Endtime Gravity Mechanics: The theory behind the system that Professor Yana had come up with to power the rocket that would take the human refugees from Malcassairo to Utopia. (3.11)

Endymides: Race of small, grey-skinned aliens with almond-shaped eyes. One of them, Saruba Velak, was shot down by space pirates in Earth's orbit and crashed in New Mexico in 1947. She was captured by the US military and taken to the Dreamland base in Nevada. A few years later her husband, Rivesh Mantilax came looking for her but was attacked by the Androids from the Alliance of Shades. The badly injured Rivesh Mantilax was saved by Night Eagle and his men from the Shoshoni tribe and kept safe in a cave, until Colonel Stark of Dreamland found him. The Endymides had created a genetic weapon with which to wipe out the Viperox Horde, who had invaded their world, but the Doctor was able to convince them not to use it. Both Rivesh Mantilax and Saruba Velak returned safely to Endymor. (DL)

Endymor: A planet invaded and devastated by the Viperox Horde. The Endymides developed a genetic weapon to use against the Viperox. (DL)

Engineer: Worker aboard the starliner *Titanic* who oversaw the repair and management of the Heavenly Host. He was killed by them after the *Titanic* was struck by meteoroids. (4.X) (Played by BRUCE LAWRENCE)

English, Dame Eve: A member of the King's Lynn Players, whose music was heard on the episode of *What's My Line?* playing on a television in Mr Magpie's shop when the Wire first appeared to him. (2.7)

Enmity of Ages, the: Description of the never-ending struggle between good and evil, from the Ancient Prophesies of Gallifrey. Rassilon believed this was personified by the endless fighting between the Doctor and the Master. (4.18)

Entity, the: A life form which the Doctor had trapped in a bottle in the TARDIS. Amy Pond accidentally broke the bottle and the Entity stalked her through the TARDIS, wanting to absorb her time energies, meaning she'd never have existed. The Doctor released it into the Vortex and it fed off the never-ending life cycles of the Chronomites. (AG03) (Voiced by SARAH DOUGLAS)

Environment Status Chip: Everyone on the Poseidon Community had one issued to them, to read their life signs at all times. The Doctor used them to trace the Vortron Radiation the Trans-Dimensional Gateway emitted. (AG04)

Eocenes: see *Silurians*

Epcot: Amusement park, run by the Disney Corporation in Florida. Famous for its recreations of different cultures and environments from places all over Earth, Donna Noble wondered if they were there rather than Ancient Rome. (4.2)

Eric: Husband of Isabella and brother-in-law to Abigail Pettigrew. The Doctor and Kazran Sardick brought Abigail home one Christmas Eve from her cryogenic suspension, and they all celebrated Christmas a day early. (6.X) (Played by NICK MALINOWSKI)

Ernie: One of the young boys Nancy looked after on the streets of Blitzed London. He had been evacuated to a family out of London but had experiences similar to another lad, Jim, and fled back home to London. (1.9, 1.10) (Played by JORDAN MURPHY)

Essex: One of the county tower blocks on *Starship UK*. (5.2) The TARDIS materialised in the original English county in 2010 – in Colchester. (5.11)

Eternal, the: Yellow-liveried member of the new Dalek Paradigm. (5.3) It was part of the Pandorica Alliance. (5.12) (Operated by SEAN SAYE and IAN HILDITCH)

Eternals, the: Legendary cosmic beings who existed outside of time and space completely, considering the inhabitants of the universe to be ephemerals, little more than playthings to amuse them. They left the universe for good after the Last Great Time War, distraught at the destruction wrought upon space and time. They referred to the Void as the Howling. (2.12) The Eternals were responsible for banishing the Carrionites to the Deep Darkness soon after the universe was created. (3.2)

Ethical Committee: Geneva-based organisation on 'Pete's World' from which John Lumic should have gained approval for the Ultimate Upgrade. Dr Kendrick threatened to report Lumic to them, and was killed. Later, Lumic told the President of Great Britain that he had prepared a paper for the Committee, but the President was not interested. (2.5)

Etruscans: Pagan tradespeople, assimilated into the Roman Empire. Lobos Caecilius wasn't keen on his son Quintus socialising with them at the Thermopolium. (4.2)

Europa: The Emperor Dalek's forces bombed this Earth continent in 200,100. (1.13)

European Safety Inspectors: A group of French experts unfortunately killed, apparently because they couldn't read the sign in Welsh warning them that they were investigating items marked 'Danger Explosives'. (1.11)

European Space Agency: Steffi Ehrlich studied with them before joining the Bowie Base One Mars mission. (4.16)

Evac Tower: Part of the St John's monastery where the Captain would fly the helicopter to retrieve the contractors working at the Morpeth-Jetsan alpha-grade industrial facility on the island. (6.6)

Evangelista, Miss: Strackman Lux's personal assistant and secretary and Everything. She wasn't an especially bright person (she had problems differentiating between toilets and escape pods on the spaceship that took her to The Library), and knew that she had got where she was in life through her looks rather than her brains. The rest of Lux's team treated her with contempt because she didn't pull her weight, but Donna Noble felt sorry for her and tried befriending

her. Miss Evangelista was the first victim of the Vashta Nerada and Donna talked to her as her brain patterns, locked into a 'data ghost' on her spacesuit, degraded and she faded away. When Donna herself was downloaded into CAL's reality, Miss Evangelista tried to help her because she appreciated Donna's kindness earlier. Although her looks had been corrupted by a transcription error by The Library's Data Core, her intelligence had been boosted significantly because, in the simulation, everyone was really just a string of numbers and a decimal point in her construction had been moved in error. Miss Evangelista was able to help Donna escape back to the real world. When the Doctor saved the Data Core, Miss Evangelista's face was restored but she kept her new intellect. (4.8, 4.9) (Played by TALULAH RILEY)

Evans, Gareth: An operative at the Torchwood Institute, based in the Lever Room in the Torchwood Tower. He and his colleague Adeola Oshodi went to the upper floors for an illicit snog, only to find that the area still under construction was in fact the new conversion site for the Cybermen. Like Adeola, Gareth was killed and reanimated via a Cybus Industries ear pod that was connected directly into his cerebral cortex. When the Doctor discovered this, he jammed the signal to all the converted ear pods, and the already dead Gareth died once again. (2.12) (Played by HADLEY FRASER)

Evening News: Local newspaper in Colchester in which the Doctor read about the disappearances in the area – and also about Nina's talent show experiences. (6.12)

Evening Standard: London newspaper that told its readers that the Big Ben-Slitheen incident had all been one big hoax. Mickey Smith was appalled, but the Doctor was unsurprised, saying that humanity wasn't ready to accept the idea of alien invaders. (1.5) The paper was also available on 'Pete's World'. (2.5)

Examiner, The: Daily newspaper. John Smith, the schoolteacher the Doctor became for a few weeks in 1913, read it regularly. (3.8) It reported on the disappearance of Agatha Christie in 1926. (4.7) Nearly 60 years later, its then editor (played by NICKY RAINSFORD) was offered a piece telling the inside story of the Torchwood Institute by a freelancer called Atif. She betrayed him to Torchwood, whose operatives removed him from the newspaper's offices and provided a replacement front-page story for the next day's edition. (2.12T) Wilfred

Mott was selling the papers from his stand when the Doctor and Astrid Peth visited London from the starliner *Titanic*. (4.X)

Exedor: See *Alignment of Exedor, the*

Exeter: Devonshire city. Craig Owens got it confused with Exedor. (6.12)

Exoglass: The glass aboard Platform One was shattered when the sunfilters were lowered. Exoglass had a self-repair system and once the filters went back up, the Exoglass was renewed. (1.2) According to Lynda Moss, the Exoglass that was used on the Game Station (and, by default, Satellite Five) would require a nuclear bomb to break, although she was proven fatally wrong when a Dalek hovering in space used its blaster to shatter it, killing her. (1.12, 1.13)

Expelliarmus: Martha Jones suggested this word from the Harry Potter books by JK Rowling would help William Shakespeare send the Carrionites back into the Deep Darkness. It did. (3.2)

Eye Drive: What appeared to be eyepatches – worn by envoys of the Silence such as Madame Kovarian, Gantok and Father Gideon Vandaleur – were in fact devices that enabled the wearer to always remember the Silence. The Silence communicated telepathically with their envoys through them and could use them to cause the wearer extreme pain or kill them. (6.2, 6.3, 6.5, 6.6, 6.7, 6.13)

Eye of Orion, the: Restful place where the Doctor suggested going after defeating House. (6.4)

Eye of Time, the: A unique, naturally occurring energy field controlled by the Time Lords, more powerful than the heart of every TARDIS ever grown. It was lost during the fall of Gallifrey during the Last Great Time War, and fell into the clutches of the Daleks who used it to manipulate the time continuum and create a new timeline where they were never defeated. The Doctor used a magnetic field generator to disrupt the Eye's power, and allow him and Amy Pond to pass through it and so put history on the right track. (AG01)

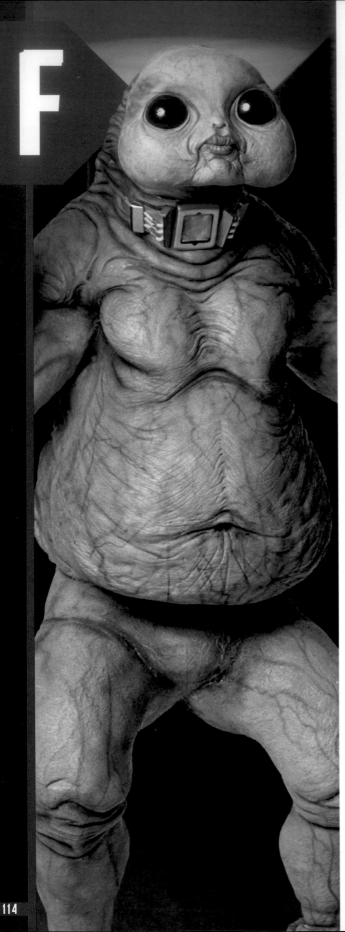

Face of Boe, the: A 1.5 metre alien head, suspended in a glass tank and wreathed in smoke, the Face of Boe was the oldest inhabitant of the Isop galaxy, and apparently the last member of Boekind. Believed to be millions of years old, legends stated that the Face of Boe had watched the universe grow old, and that before his death he would impart a great secret to a homeless wanderer like himself, a lonely god. Although he was reported to be pregnant with Boemina by the *Boewatch* programme on Bad WolfTV in 200,000, (1.7) the Face of Boe was alone again in the year five billion, by which time he had based himself on the Silver Devastation, and acted as sponsor of the Earthdeath spectacle on Platform One, when the Lady Cassandra attempted to stage her fraudulent hostage situation. (1.2) Twenty-three years later, the Face of Boe summoned the Doctor to meet him in Ward 26 of the New New York Hospital, where he was dying of old age. Here, he was under the care of Novice Hame, a Catkind nurse with whom he would communicate telepathically as he slept, singing songs in her mind whilst she kept him company and maintained his smoke. When the Doctor eventually came to hear Boe's final secret, the Face willed himself away using pure mental power, keeping his secret until their next, and final, encounter. (2.1) He then remained on New Earth, in the city of New New York, where the Bliss virus wiped out the population of the Overcity. The Face of Boe then ensured Hame's protection from the virus by shrouding her in his smoke, before wiring himself into the city's mainframe, giving his life force to maintain the Motorway and its inhabitants until the Doctor returned. He gave the last of his energy to help release the population from the Undercity, and was released from his tank by the Doctor and Hame one final time before he perished. (3.3) His dying words – 'You Are Not Alone' – were later revealed to be a warning of the Master's presence at the end of the universe. (3.11) The Doctor's occasional travelling companion, the immortal Captain Jack Harkness, fondly remembered being nicknamed the Face of Boe, leading to speculation that he would live to become the Doctor's other old friend. (3.13) Davros taunted the Doctor about how many people had died trying to help him over the years, and this made the Doctor think of Boe. (4.13) (Voiced by STRUAN RODGER)

Fairchild, Reverend Aubrey: The local priest in East London whose house Jackson Lake was investigating, believing himself to be the Doctor. Fairchild had been killed by the Cybermen, and all the local wardens and proprietors of the workhouses which the clergyman supported were in attendance at his funeral. Miss Hartigan arrived, needing four of the workhouse proprietors and brought with her the Cybermen, who massacred the other mourners. (4.14)

Fall of the Eleventh, the: A mysterious event that Dorium Maldovar warned the Doctor was yet to come. (6.13)

Family: A family held hostage by the Cybermen, but who were eventually freed when the Cyberman guarding them was recalled to fight the Daleks. The family consisted of Dad (SIMON CORNISH), Mum (LIZ EDNE), a son (FINNIAN COHEN-ENNIS) and a daughter (CIARA COHENENNIS). (2.12, 2.13)

Family of Blood, the: Short-lived family of murderous aliens who sought the Doctor, his time-travel capabilities and his Time Lord life essence so that one of the Family, Son of Mine, could live for ever. They had never seen the Doctor's face, just his TARDIS, so they had no idea what he looked like but, using a stolen Vortex Manipulator, they were able to pilot their invisible ship and chase the TARDIS from 2007 to 1913, to the village of Farringham in Herefordshire. There they would try to sniff him out with their acute olfactory senses. To escape them, the Doctor took on the physical form of a fictitious human, John Smith, a teacher at the local boys' school. One by one, the Family found bodies to inhabit — Mother of Mine taking on the body of Jenny, a maid, Son of Mine taking schoolboy Jeremy Baines's life, Daughter of Mine usurping the body of Lucy Cartwright, and Father of Mine becoming Farmer Clark. They attacked the village, killing and maiming at random, until eventually the Doctor came out of hiding. He tricked them, making them believe he was still human, and set their ship to blow up. Fleeing the ship as it did so, the Doctor then, one by one, gave the Family exactly what they wanted — eternity, but in individual prisons of his choosing. (3.8, 3.9)

Family Slitheen, the: A crime syndicate originally from the planet Raxacoricofallapatorius — although they have set up bases on other worlds too.

Hiding in Britain for some months, they infiltrated the police, military forces, even Parliament, by killing people of large stature and wearing their skins as suits, fitting themselves in by use of a slipstream compression field generator worn around their necks. They planned to instigate a third — nuclear — world war, by faking an alien incursion on British soil. With the world in panic, they persuaded the UN to allow nuclear weapons to be launched at supposed 'massive weapons of destruction'. Their plan was then to sell the resultant radioactive slag that had once been Earth to the highest bidder, to be used as fuel for interstellar spaceships. The Doctor managed, with Mickey Smith's help, to locate launch codes for sub-Harpoon missiles and so destroyed 10 Downing Street with the Family Slitheen inside. Jocrassa Fel Fotch Pasameer-Day Slitheen, and all the other Family members — except Blon Fel Fotch Pasameer-Day Slitheen, posing as MI5 operative Margaret Blaine — were killed in the explosion. (1.4, 1.5) Blon Fel Fotch ended up in Cardiff as Lord Mayor, hoping to use initially a nuclear accident, and then the energy from the Doctor's TARDIS to force open the rift in space and time that coursed through the city. She could then escape from Earth. The power in the heart of the TARDIS reverted Blon Fel Fotch Pasameer-Day Slitheen to an egg, which the Doctor took home to be given a second chance. (1.11) The Doctor identified another member of the Family Slitheen as having been captured by a Graske on the planet Griffoth. (AotG) (Played by ELIZABETH FOST, PAUL KASEY, ALAN RUSCOE) Sarah Jane Smith defeated members of the Family Slitheen too, which caused Captain Jack Harkness to admire her. A lot. (4.13)

Fancy, the: Henry Avery's ship, originally called the *Charles II*. When Avery mutinied and became a pirate, he stole the ship and renamed it. It became caught in a temporal rift, unable to move as it now shared the same space as a Skerth ship. When he and all his crew stayed aboard the Skerth ship, the deserted *Fancy* sailed on and into history. (6.3)

Farisi, Rosita: Young woman befriended by Jackson Lake, after he saved her from a Cyberman at Osterman's Wharf. She believed him to be an adventurer called the Doctor. She was Jackson's companion and later, after he regained his memories, she remained with him to help bring up his son Frederic. (4.14) (played by VELILE TSHABALALA)

Farringham: Village in Herefordshire which came under attack from the Family of Blood on Tuesday 11 November 1913. A number of its inhabitants died, before John Smith accepted he really was the Doctor and changed back into the Time Lord. (3.8, 3.9)

Farringham School for Boys: The Doctor, having turned himself human to escape the Family of Blood, taught history there as John Smith, with Martha Jones acting as his maid. Smith's colleagues included the Headmaster, Mr Rocastle, the Bursar, Mr Phillips, and the school's nurse, Joan Redfern, who he began a romance with. Amongst the pupils were the gifted Timothy Latimer and Hutchinson, the school captain. The Family eventually attacked with their Scarecrow army, but the boys survived, although neither Rocastle nor Phillips was so lucky. (3.8, 3.9)

Fast Lane: The legendary bottom lane of the Motorway, only accessible with three adults aboard a car. It was rumoured that speeds of up to 30 miles per hour were achievable down there, although Cheen's friend Kate said there were legends of monsters beneath the Fast Lane. Kate was correct – the Macra which had escaped from the New New York Zoo years before had settled there, living off the exhaust fumes, and swatting any cars that disturbed them. (3.3)

Fat One: One of the Clerics from the Vatican, stationed on Demon's Run. Married to Thin One, Fat One opted to attend a conversion tutorial to become one of the Headless Monks, unaware that it would literally cost him his head. (6.7) (Played by CHARLIE BAKER)

Father of Mine: Leader of the Family of Blood, who sought out a Time Lord body to enable Son of Mine to live for eternity. He brought the Family in their invisible spaceship to Earth, where they believed the Doctor was hiding in the village of Farringham. The Doctor had in fact turned himself wholly human to

avoid being sniffed out by the Family. Father of Mine took on the body of a local farmer, Mr Clark, and was responsible for tracking down the Doctor's TARDIS, as well as the murder of bandleader Mr Chambers. Once the Doctor had regained his Time Lord form, he tricked the Family and blew up their spaceship. The Doctor threw Father of Mine, trapped in Clark's form, into an underground chamber for eternity, binding him in unbreakable chains forged in a dwarf star. (3.8, 3.9) (Played by GERARD HORAN)

Fawkes, Guido 'Guy': One of the 13 plotters who planned to blow up the House of Lords in 1605. (AG05) (Voiced by RALF LITTLE)

FBI: Federal Bureau of Investigation. American security service who worked on American soil. Canton Delaware III was a former agent who had quit because he couldn't marry his black boyfriend. (6.1, 6.2)

Fear, Mister: One of the Alliance of Shades' Men in Black androids. He was put out of action by an arrow fired by one of Night Eagle's Shoshoni tribesmen. (DL)

Felman Lux Corporation: The company responsible for building The Library, which Strackman Lux inherited about a hundred years later. (4.8, 4.9)

Felspoon: A planet with mountains that sway in the breeze. When Donna absorbed the Doctor's knowledge after undergoing a metacrisis, she knew of Felspoon and asked to go there. (4.13)

Female Crewmember: Realising that the *Madame de Pompadour* was about to be caught up in an ion storm, she and her fellow crewman sent a mayday back to Earth. When the storm struck, she survived and was momentarily relieved when a Clockwork Robot appeared on the bridge to help her. Then she realised the Robot was looking for spare parts . . . (2.4T) (Played by LIZ ARMON-LLOYD)

F

F

Female Programmer:

One of the administrators of the Game Station, alongside her male counterpart Davitch Pavale. They answered to the Controller but, when the Doctor exposed the Game Station as a fraud and the Controller was transmatted aboard the Dalek mothership and exterminated, the two programmers joined forces against their foes. They joined Captain Jack Harkness on Floor 499 and were still flirting outrageously with one another when they were both exterminated. (1.12, 1.13) (Played by NISHA NYAR)

Female Student:
Attended the Rattigan Academy and was amongst those who challenged Luke Rattigan after the world was poisoned by the ATMOS devices. She went off to find her brother while the other students also abandoned Luke and went home. (4.5) (Played by MERYL FERNANDES)

Feng Shui:
According to Lance Bennett, Donna Noble talked excitedly about this Chinese concept of harmonically spacing furniture and other household items. (3.X)

Fenning, Sir Roderick:
Musical arranger for the episode of *What's My Line?*, playing on a television in Mr Magpie's shop when the Wire first appeared to him. (2.7)

Ferdinand, Franz:
Austrian Archduke, whose assassination by a Serb in June 1914, was the event that led directly to the First World War, according to the Doctor. (3.9)

Fermat's Last Theorem:
The Doctor showed the proof of Pierre de Fermat's work with positive integers to demonstrate to the world's scientists that he was worth listening to. (5.1)

Fetch, Mr:
Master of a Workhouse in Victorian London. He was captured by the Cybermen and put under their control via an earpiece control device. He then took all the children in his Workhouse to the Cybermen where they were used to build the engine for the CyberKing. Mr Fetch's usefulness over, Miss Hartigan killed him, via the earpiece. (4.14) (Played by ROGER BAILEY)

Fiction-Mist:
A method of accessing books at The Library. (4.8, 4.9)

Fifteen-Dash-Ten-Barric Fields:
Discovered by the mathematician San Chen not San Hazeldine. Rodrick didn't know this when asked by the Anne Droid in *The Weakest Link* aboard the Game Station. (1.12)

15.39:
The scheduled time for Earthdeath. (1.2)

Fifteenth Broken Moon of the Medusa Cascade:
The Doctor wanted to take Donna Noble there. (4.4)

58.2 North 10.2 East: The coordinates of the *Valiant* when the Doctor, Captain Jack Harkness and Martha Jones teleported aboard, using Jack's Vortex Manipulator. (3.12)

58.5 kiloamperes, transferred charge 510 megajoules: The precise electrical pulse needed to bring down a Toclafane sphere. (3.13)

56 Squadron: One of the RAF squadrons mobilised to protect London when the Daleks forced the city's lights to come on during a German air raid. (5.3)

Fighting the Future: Title of the biography of Joshua Naismith which Donna Noble bought for Wilfred Mott, although she wasn't sure why. It was an example of the convergence of reality, bringing the Doctor, Donna, Wilfred and the Naismiths together for the Master's return. (4.17)

Final Experiment, the: Audacious plan by Dalek Sec and the Cult of Skaro, trapped in 1930s New York. They intended to create a new form for themselves, realising that humanity now vastly outnumbered them. As humans had the advantage of mobility, Sec reasoned that if the human form could be imprinted with Dalek mentality, the Cult would have the ultimate army. As a precursor to this, Sec experimented on his own form, physically merging his Dalek body with that of a human – Mr Diagoras – via a special chromatin solution and thus became the genetic template for the Dalek-Human army. The Final Experiment required a thousand comatose humans, each of whom would receive a pulse of DNA-rewriting gamma radiation, imbued with Sec's new DNA. This was foiled when the Doctor placed his own DNA into the mix, diluting the hybridisation process and the Dalek-Human army questioned their orders and engaged in a battle with the Daleks. After they had destroyed Daleks Thay and Jast, Dalek Caan wiped out the entire species with a mental bolt that fried their brains. (3.4, 3.5)

Finchley: North London area where Adelaide Brooke was born. (4.16)

Financial Family Seven: Origin of the Adherents of the Repeated Meme, who travelled to Platform One to witness Earthdeath. However, as the Adherents were later exposed as robot servants to Cassandra, the true existence of 'Financial Family Seven' is in some doubt. (1.2)

Finch, Caroline: Clive's wife, who put up with his obsession about the Doctor. She and her son (played by ADAM McCOY) later witnessed Clive's death at the hands of the Autons. (1.1) (Played by ELLI GARNETT)

Finch, Clive: Enthusiastic website-runner, who was obsessed with sightings of the Doctor. Rose visited him for more information but wasn't sure if he was completely sane. He was killed in front of his family when the Autons rampaged through a London shopping arcade. (1.1) (Played by MARK BENTON)

Finch, Hector: Assumed name of Brother Lassar of the Krillitanes, who adopted human form. He posed as the headmaster of Deffry Vale High School, using Krillitane Oil in the food to enhance the minds of his pupils, so that they could solve the Skasas Paradigm. He was killed when K-9 heated up the drums of Krillitane Oil in the school kitchen and blew Finch, the school and himself to pieces. (2.3) (Played by ANTHONY HEAD)

Finch's: Butcher's shop in South East London. Jackie Tyler suggested to Rose she should get a job there. (1.1)

Finitoglass: Protective glass that surrounded the cabin of the *Crusader 50* – it would offer about two minutes of protection from the X-tonic rays if the *Crusader 50*'s shields were raised. (4.10)

Fire Island: The Brannigans driving on the New New York Motorway were heading to Fire Island, hoping to find work in the laundries. (3.3)

Firestone: Purple jewel given to Lady Clemency Eddison by the Vespiform she knew only as Christopher in Delhi in 1885. It was actually a Vespiform Telepathic Recorder, and it linked with Clemency's brain as a way of keeping Christopher alive in her memory. It also however became so attuned to her mind that it projected her strongest thoughts back out to any other Vespiforms. The only other one on Earth, forty years later, was their son, now living as Arnold Golightly, causing him to commit murders in the style of the Agatha Christie novels Clemency was such an aficionado of. The mysterious high-society thief the Unicorn briefly stole the Firestone from Clemency, breaking the link with Golightly. Agatha Christie later took the jewel, as it was beginning to bond with her, and threw it into a lake, and the Vespiform followed and drowned. (4.7)

Firing Stock 15: Bullets used by the humans on Sanctuary Base 6; not powerful enough to pierce the hull of the station, but lethally effective on organics, such as the Ood. (2.8, 2.9)

First Antigravity Olympics: The Doctor told Rose Tyler that he could take her to witness this. (2.2)

First Contact Policy: An agreement ratified by the UN in 1968, regarding protocol surrounding contact with alien species. Harry Saxon ignored it, gaining the contempt of US President Winters. (3.12)

First Officer: Bridge officer aboard the starliner *Titanic*. He was presumably killed when the meteoroids struck the ship. (4.X)

Finnegan, Florence: Elderly patient admitted to the Royal Hope Hospital apparently suffering from a salt deficiency. In fact, the real Florence Finnegan was probably dead, killed by a shape-shifting Plasmavore who had stolen her identity and entered the hospital, hoping to source a rich supply of blood, off which it lived. This Plasmavore was always accompanied by two Slabs to do its strong-arm work and was in hiding because it had murdered the Child Princess of Padrivole Regency Nine, and thus was hiding from the Judoon Platoon sent to execute it. Because the Judoon were forbidden to land on Earth, the Plasmavore believed itself safe, until the Judoon transported the hospital to the moon. The Plasmavore then absorbed as much blood as it could, including blood corrupted by fat, alcohol and rich foodstuffs, to disguise itself as a human when the Judoon scanned everyone's physiognomy. When it drank the Doctor's blood, it registered as a non-human and was swiftly executed by the Judoon. (3.1) (Played by ANNE REID)

Fiona: Young woman who was jogging through Leadworth when her MP3 player started playing the Atraxi message instead of her music. (5.1) (Played by FAYE LOUISE NORIEGA)

Firbourne House Hotel: Place where the Noble family spent Christmas Day in the alternative world where Donna never met the Doctor. A Spanish maid there claimed she saw something on Donna's back, and the family watched in horror as London was destroyed by the falling starship *Titanic*. (4.11)

Fire extinguisher: Needing to disable a Clockwork Robot aboard the SS *Madame de Pompadour*, the Doctor used what Mickey Smith thought was an ice gun, but was in fact a fire extinguisher, although it proved very effective at freezing the repair androids. (2.4)

Fish: Many different varieties of fish lived in the cloud belt of Ember, able to fly because of the electrical charges flowing through the fog crystals up there.

Occasionally small shoals would drift closer to the surface, either when their nets broke or one of the Sardick family let them in because he was in a foul mood, which excited the population, especially the youngsters, despite some of the larger fish being predatory. (6.X)

Fitch: One of the players of *The Weakest Link* aboard the Game Station. When she lost a round, the Anne Droid appeared to disintegrate her but, in truth, she was transmatted over to the Dalek mothership to be turned into part of the growing Dalek army created by the Emperor. (1.12) (Played by KATE WINCHESTER)

5.02pm: The time at which River Song murdered the Doctor on 22 April 2011 on the shores of Lake Silencio. (6.1, 6.2, 6.8, 6.13)

5.6.1.434 sigma 777: The incomplete coordinates of the Dalek fleet from the Game Station, given to the Doctor by the Controller the instant before the Daleks transmatted and exterminated her. (1.12)

5/930167.02: The coordinates of an area within the Rexel Planetary Configuration known as the Deep Darkness. (3.2)

Five-Straighten Classabindi Nursery Fleet, Intergalactic Class: Matron Cofelia was one of their members. (4.1)

Flannagan, Martin: Young farmer from one of Poseidon's outer communities. He was the sole survivor of his group, who had mostly been wiped out by a plague. He was later killed by the Vashta Nerada. (AG04) (Voiced by BARNABY EDWARDS)

Fledgling Empires: A grouping of planetary empires from the Dark Times. The Empires included Gallifrey, which fought a war against the Racnoss, and won. (3.X)

Flesh, the: The Morpeth-Jetsan company had alpha-grade industrial stations across the world farming crystal-diluric acid under military contracts. Because the acid was so instantly lethal to humans, even encased in protective suits, the Morpeth-Jetsan company developed a substance called the Flesh, from which they created Gangers, duplicates of their staff with exact memories and skills downloaded into them to farm the stuff. When Gangers were damaged, they were discarded into Fleshmounds, the humans unaware that the damaged Gangers were still alive and in pain. When gamma radiation from a solar tsunami hit the St John's monastery, the Gangers working there gained greater sentience and independence, and the well of Flesh they were formed from also started to feel alive, thinking and reacting even before a human form was duplicated. The Doctor introduced his DNA into the mixture accidentally, creating a Ganger of himself. After escaping St John's, the human foreman, Miranda Cleaves and a flesh Ganger, Dicken, went to the Morpeth-Jetsan Board to open discussions about Ganger rights. (6.5, 6.6)

Fletcher, Tom: Member of pop group McFly, who endorsed Harry Saxon's campaign to become Prime Minister. (3.12)

Flight Leader: US airman who, in 1958, pursued the retro-fitted Endymide ship stolen by the Doctor and later reported that it had crashed near the town of Solitude. (DL) (Voiced by RYAN McCLUSKEY)

Flintlock: Codename for one of the three spitfire pilots sent into outer space via Bracewell's gravity bubble to destroy the Daleks' transmitter. He was the second pilot to be killed during the attack. (5.3)

Flood, the: Microscopic Martian entity that thrived in water, which it could control and duplicate. On contact with flesh, the Flood could possess a body and begin turning it into living water. The Flood were frozen, immobile and impotent beneath the surface of Mars, possibly deliberately by the Ice Warriors before they fled the planet. When the World State sent Captain Adelaide Brooke and her team to Mars to establish a base and determine if Mars could be colonised, the Flood were released and one by one began taking over the base crew until only three were left. The Doctor got the survivors off Mars in the TARDIS and the Flood were destroyed in the nuclear explosion set off by Adelaide. (4.16)

Floor Manager: Part of the production team making *The Weakest Link* aboard the Game Station in 200,100. When the Daleks attacked the Station, she joined Captain Jack Harkness's team and led the defence of Floor 494, but the Bastic bullets in her gun had no effect on the invaders and she was exterminated. (1.12, 1.13) (Played by JENNA RUSSELL)

Flora: 15-year-old maid to Lady Isobel MacLeish, she avoided being captured in the initial attack by the Brethren upon Torchwood House. After meeting Rose Tyler, they were both captured and chained up to face the Host as he transformed into a werewolf. Flora later helped her mistress prepare mistletoe as a defence against the creature and was still present when Rose was invested by Queen Victoria and then exiled. (2.2) (Played by RUTHIE MILNE)

Florida: Southern American state, famous for good weather, and where Mr Stoker had hoped to retire to before being murdered by the Plasmavore disguised as Florence Finnegan in the Royal Hope Hospital. (3.1) Cape Kennedy was based there, from which America launched Apollo 11 to land on the moon. The Silence had manipulated NASA into making this mission happen as they needed an astronaut's suit to protect the mysterious little girl they had 'adopted' from Graystark Hall Orphanage. The Doctor realised she was in Florida because she identified Jefferson St, Adams St and Hamilton Avenue as being outside the warehouse she was hiding in. (6.1, 6.2)

Florizel Street: North London street and home to the Connolly family, the Gallaghers and the Bells amongst many others in 1953. After the Queen's Coronation, it was decked out for a massive street party. (2.7)

Flowers, Alice: Londoner who sold herbs and remedies. (AG05) (Voiced by LIZZIE HOPLEY)

Flydale North: The constituency for which Harriet Jones was MP, campaigning for Cottage Hospitals to be considered as Centres of Excellence. (1.4) As Prime Minister, she successfully implemented her New Cottage Hospital Scheme. (2.X)

Flying Deuces, The: Laurel and Hardy movie made in 1939. The Doctor made a brief cameo. Wearing a fez. (6.1)

Fob watch: Escaping from the Family of Blood, who wanted his body so they would have access to all of time and space, the Doctor used a chameleon arch in the TARDIS to turn himself human for approximately three months, knowing that, if the Family hadn't found him by then, they would die. The fob watch, decorated with Gallifreyan symbols but otherwise looking like a common-or-garden Earth fob watch, was a special vessel, containing the very essence of his Time Lord existence. When the now-human John Smith was

exposed to the interior of the watch, the cells of his body would once more be rearranged and he would become his old self, literally. The fob watch was briefly in the possession of Tim Latimer, a pupil at the school where John Smith taught, and some of the Time Lord energy leaked out, giving him a glimpse of the Doctor and Martha Jones's real lives. Realising that the Family of Blood would happily slaughter everyone in the village of Farringham, John Smith opened the watch and became the Doctor once more. (3.8, 3.9) On the planet Malcassairo, the Doctor and Martha met the human scientist Professor Yana, who had an identical watch, which Martha spotted and warned the Doctor about. The Professor's close proximity to both the Doctor and his TARDIS reawakened something in Yana, and he unconsciously found himself opening the watch – whereupon his Time Lord personality re-established itself, and the Doctor's old foe the Master was reborn. (3.11) Jackson Lake possessed a fob watch and, briefly believing Lake might be a future incarnation of himself suffering from amnesia, the Doctor opened the fob watch to see if it would restore Lake's Time Lord persona. But it was really just a fob watch. A broken one at that… (4.14)

Fog Shark: Large predators that usually lived amongst the fog cloud belt above Sardicktown. Attracted by the Doctor's sonic screwdriver, a Fog Shark entered the young Kazran Sardick's bedroom and swallowed half the screwdriver, which poisoned it. As it lay dying, Kazran realised it would be fine if it could be returned to the sky, encased in fog-ice. He took the Doctor to the Cryo-Cave and they used Abigail Pettigrew's cryogenic chamber to save the Shark. For the rest of its life, it still had the piece of the screwdriver within it, which the Doctor used to draw it down, attach to a rickshaw and take himself, Abigail and Kazran for a trip through the Ember night sky. Later the same Shark took the elder Sardick and the dying Abigail for one last sky trip. (6.X)

Fontana-Brooke, Susie: Granddaughter of Adelaide Brooke who was so inspired by her grandmother's exploits in space that even Adelaide's death couldn't stop her becoming one of Earth's space pioneers. Susie was one of the most important human beings in history – she was the pilot of the first lightspeed ship to Proxima Centauri, and her own offspring would create many other important milestones in human space development. Fearing that her survival could affect Susie's future, Adelaide committed suicide rather than allow the Doctor to change established history. (4.16) (Played by JENETTE CLOTHIER and CAITLIN SMITH & JOSH PEMBURY)

Footprint Impeller System: Part of the system that Professor Yana had come up with to power the rocket that would take the human refugees from Malcassairo to Utopia. (3.11)

'For the Fallen': Poem by Laurence Binyon, read at the Remembrance Day service Tim Latimer attended as an old man, where he saw the Doctor and Martha Jones for the first time since he had been a schoolboy at Farringham School for Boys in Herefordshire. (3.9)

Foreman: Mr Diagoras, charged with overseeing the construction of the upper floors of the Empire State Building by the Cult of Skaro, demanded of the workers' foreman that his men work harder. The foreman pointed out that this was impossible and, if need be, he'd happily tell Diagoras's masters that too. He was horrified when he met Dalek Caan and was taken down to the Transgenic Laboratory beneath the streets of Manhattan. He became part of the Final Experiment, leading the Dalek-Humans to the Laurenzi theatre, but asked why he had to obey without question, only to be exterminated by Dalek Jast. (Played by IAN PORTER)

Forest of Cheem: Collective name for the revered tree-people of Cheem. As living wood, they were understandably frightened of fire. (1.2)

Forget: Coming in varying strengths, this was one of the Mood Patches on sale in Pharmacytown in the Undercity of New New York. A patch was bought by the Pale Woman so that she could forget the disappearance of her parents on the Motorway. (3.3)

Fort Cecil: The Arctic relay station that would send supplies and help out to the Zebra Bay Geological Base in the Arctic Circle. The Doctor was able to radio them for help. (AG02)

Fortes: British café where people watched the murder of President Winters by the Toclafane and then, on leaving, were slaughtered by the invading Toclafane spheres. (3.12)

Fortune Teller: A trader on Shan Shen who was in thrall to a Time Beetle and sought out Donna Noble, to enable the Beetle to feed off her chaotic memories which were caused by her reliving an alternative history in which the Doctor died before they ever met. Because Donna was able to put time on its correct path, the Beetle was killed and the Fortune Teller became more frightened of Donna than she ever was of the Beetle. (4.11) (Played by CHIPO CHUNG)

41 Squadron: One of the RAF squadrons that headed towards the south coast of England to engage German fighters in battle during the Second World War. Lillian Breen's boyfriend Reg was part of this squadron, and was killed. (5.3)

Foss Street: Road in Pompeii where Lobos Caecilius and his family lived and conducted his business. (4.2)

Foster, Miss: See *Cofelia, Matron*

Foundries: Industrial units in the Brooklyn area of New New York, where Milo had learnt there were jobs going. (3.3)

Fountain Six: Internet search engine developed by Luke Rattigan when he was 12 years old, which made him a millionaire overnight. (4.4, 4.5)

467-989: The specific DNA-type of the failed Dalek embryos artificially created and then discarded by the Cult of Skaro in the sewers beneath Manhattan. (3.4)

426: River Song's cell number in the Stormcage 1 facility. (5.12)

F

Fourth Great and Bountiful Human Empire, the:
The era in which the Doctor, Rose Tyler and Adam Mitchell landed on Satellite Five. (1.7)

Fox, Oswald: De facto leader of Poseidon once the apparent sickness had taken hold and begun killing people. He eventually allowed the Doctor and Amy Pond to help once he realised that the true enemy were the Vashta Nerada, and the Doctor was able to cure him of the sickness, which he too had contracted but told no one about. (AG04) (Voiced by NICHOLAS BRIGGS)

Frame, Midshipman Alonso: Young and dedicated bridge crew officer aboard the starliner *Titanic*. He realised that meteoroids were going to strike the ship, but Captain Hardaker shot and wounded him to stop him raising the alarm. Hardaker was killed in the collision, and Frame was one of the few crewmen left alive. In an effort to stop the murderous Heavenly Host reaching him, he sealed himself off from the rest of the ship. He formed a friendship with the Doctor over the internal comms and did his best to help the survivors. When the Doctor eventually made it to the bridge, he and Frame stopped the damaged ship crashing into Earth. Frame appeared to be the only member of the crew to have survived to tell the authorities on Sto what had happened. (4.X) The Doctor next saw him in a bar on Zog and introduced him to Captain Jack Harkness. (4.18) (Played by RUSSELL TOVEY)

France: The European country where Rose had been working as an au pair for a year, or so Jackie Tyler had told Rose's grandmother. (1.5) The Doctor, Rose and Mickey Smith visited it – both Paris and Versailles – on a few occasions while dealing with the Clockwork Robots' hunt for Madame de Pompadour. (2.4) One of the early ATMOS victims died there. Their nuclear weapons were primed and ready to strike the Sontaran mothership in Earth's orbit. (4.4, 4.5) The Doctor and Amy Pond visited the Musée D'Orsay in Paris, and then travelled back to Auvers-Sur-

Oise to meet artist Vincent Van Gogh. (5.10) Van Gough's painting *The Pandorica Opens* was found in France. (5.12) Holy Roman Emperor Churchill had recently visited there. (6.13)

Frane, Hoshbin: Rodrick knew that this was the President of the Red Velvets when asked by the Anne Droid in *The Weakest Link* aboard the Game Station. (1.12)

Frank: 18-year-old from Tennessee who took the railroad to find enough work in New York to feed his family after his father died. He ended up living in Hooverville and joined the Doctor, Martha Jones and Hooverville's de facto leader Solomon in their exploration of the Manhattan sewers. Frank was captured by the Pig Slaves and, along with Martha Jones, selected to become part of the Final Experiment but, due to the Doctor's interference, they were able to escape back to Hooverville. The Daleks pursued them, and Frank was traumatised when Solomon, brokering peace, was murdered. Frank later helped Martha defend the Empire State Building against the Pig Slaves and was present in the Laurenzi theatre when the Dalek-Human army destroyed the two Cult of Skaro Daleks there. Frank stayed on in Hooverville, negotiating with the survivors for the semi-Pig Man Laszlo to live among them. (3.4, 3.5) (Played by ANDREW GARFIELD)

Franklin, Benjamin: American inventor (as well as acclaimed politician, abolitionist and diplomat), who conducted early experiments into electricity, aided by the Doctor, who got burned. (3.1)

Freedom Fifteen: Anarchist group dedicated to exposing Satellite Five as corrupt and working against the interests of the Earth Empire. Their last

surviving member was Eva Saint Julienne, who disguised herself as Suki Macrae Cantrell and reached Floor 500, intending to destroy what she found there. (1.7)

Freedonia: The Doctor told William Shakespeare that Martha Jones was from Freedonia, borrowing the fictitious name from a Marx Brothers' film, *Duck Soup*. (3.2)

Freud, Sigmund: Austrian psychologist who the Doctor cited when teasing Henry Avery about his reliance on big guns. (6.3)

Friends List: Inter-car networking system used by the likes of the Brannigans and the Cassinis to stay in touch with one another as they drove the Motorways of New New York. (3.3)

Friends of the Ood:
Movement throughout the Earth Empire of the 42nd century that objected on ethical and moral grounds to the enslavement, however willingly, of the Ood. (2.8) Dr Ryder of Ood Operations was secretly a member and had been trying unsuccessfully to access Warehouse 15 on the Ood-Sphere, where the Ood Brain was housed, so he could free it and thus free the Ood. (4.3)

Frost, David: BBC reporter and presenter who, some years after President

Nixon's dealings with the Silence, would come to America to interview him. The Doctor tipped Nixon off about him. (6.2)

Frost, Colonel Muriel: UNIT officer killed, alongside many other experts on alien incursion, at the 10 Downing Street briefing by the Family Slitheen. (1.4)

Fumigator gas: The Silurian Warriors used this on the Doctor and Nasreen Chaudhry when they first entered the Silurian City. Later, Eldane used a toxic version to send the warriors back into hibernation, killing Restac in the process. (5.9)

Fusion Mills: Martha Jones walked across the Earth telling her story about the Doctor, preparing people for the right moment to chant his name. Amongst the places she went to were the Fusion Mills of China. (3.13)

Futurekind: Mutated humans living on Malcassairo who had become cannibals, living a nomadic existence on the plains near the old Coral City of the Malmooth and hunting any humans foolish enough to venture there. To many, the Futurekind represented everything humanity might become if they allowed themselves to. Human guards at the rocket silo would check approaching humans for pointed teeth – if they had fangs, they were Futurekind and were refused admission. After the rocket launched, taking the humans to Utopia, the Futurekind Chieftain realised the power was off and his people could get into the base and ransack it. The Doctor, Martha Jones and Captain Jack Harkness were still in the silo base and the Futurekind hunted them, still trying to get at them even as they teleported back to 21st-century Earth. (3.11, 3.12)

G

Gable: Commander of the Hath on Messaline. He led his troops to the Source at the same time as the humans got there, and the Doctor revealed the truth of their war to them all. Gable agreed to a ceasefire after the Doctor's daughter, Jenny, was murdered by the human leader, General Cobb. Gable and one of the other humans, Cline, were present

when Jenny's Time Lord DNA, boosted by the Source, enabled her to heal her body and she stole a shuttle and escaped to the stars before their startled eyes. (4.6) (Played by RUARI MEARS)

Gachet, Doctor Paul: Vincent Van Gogh's favoured physician – Van Gogh's second painting of him was part of the Great Exhibition at the Musée D'Orsay. (5.10) Gachet was at Vincent's bedside when Madame Vernet discovered his latest painting, *The Pandorica Opens*. (5.12) (Played by HOWARD LEE)

Gadget: Service robot used by the humans on Bowie Base One to do menial tasks or those that would be awkward or lethal to human life. It was controlled remotely by Roman Groom, via Auto-Gloves. Gadget discovered the Doctor on the surface of Mars and led him to Bowie Base One. Later when fleeing the Flood-infected humans, the Doctor used the sonic screwdriver to boost Gadget's engine capacity, making him go significantly faster and carry himself and

Adelaide Brooke to safety. The Doctor used Roman's automated system to direct Gadget to the TARDIS and transport it back to the Base so he could get Adelaide, Mia Bennett and Yuri Kerenski home to Earth before the base blew up. Cut off from his controlling radio signal from Mars four minutes later, Gadget ceased to function. (4.16) (Voiced by PHILIP HURD-WOOD)

Gaffabeque: A dish which originated on the planet Lucifer, not Mars. Rose Tyler didn't know this when asked by the Anne Droid in *The Weakest Link* aboard the Game Station. (1.12)

Gainsborough, Thomas: British painter. The Doctor reckoned he would have drawn a more realistic Krafayis than Vincent Van Gogh managed. (5.10)

Galaxy M87: Location of New Earth. (2.1)

Gallagher, Edward: Television-owning resident of Florizel Street, who lost his face to the power of the Wire and was reported to the police by Eddie Connolly. Ted was taken away one night by Detective Inspector Bishop and his officers, but returned home after the Wire was defeated and his face had returned to normal. (2.7) (Played by JOHN JENNER)

Gallagher, Mrs: Anxious neighbour whose husband was taken away by the police after losing his face to the Wire. (2.7) (Played by MARIE LEWIS)

Gallifrey: Not a town in Ireland, as Joan Redfern assumed, (3.8) but the home world of the Doctor, and the Time Lords. It was known to some as the Shining World of the Seven Systems. Destroyed in the Last Great Time War, which only the Doctor and the Master survived, the Doctor recalled it as having fields of deep red grass, silver-leafed trees and a burnt orange sky. It had two suns, one of which rose in the south, causing the snow-capped mountains to shine. The Citadel of the Time Lords was enclosed in a transparent dome and was situated on the continent of Wild Endeavour, between the mountains of Solace and Solitude. Outside the Citadel could be found the Untempered Schism, which was a tear in the fabric of reality. Time Lord children would be forced to gaze through this before they could enter the Academy – the experience caused some Novice Time Lords to flee, while others were driven mad. (3.X, 3.3, 3.11, 3.12, 3.13, 4.X) As part of his Ultimate Sanction, Lord President Rassilon planned to move Gallifrey out of its Timelock and across space and time, re-establishing it in the skies above planet Earth. He almost succeeded, but the Doctor and the Master stopped the plan, and Gallifrey was returned, along with the Time Lords, to its rightful place in time and space, Timelocked for eternity. (4.18) The last surviving Sister of the Water knew of Gallifrey and that it no longer existed. (5.6)

Galvanic Radiation: Lethal radiation that flooded the surface of Midnight, due to the X-tonic sun rays (4.10)

Game Room 6: The studio on Floor 407 where *The Weakest Link* was being made on the Game Station. (1.12)

Game Station: See *Satellite Five*

Game Station Syndicate: The authority under which the Doctor was arrested aboard the Game Station. (1.12)

Gamma Forests: Arboreal planet, considered heaven-neutral to the Clerics of the 51st century. The people there had their own language; they had no word for water, other than 'river', and 'Doctor' meant 'mighty warrior', as that was what he was to them. Lorna Bucket, who came from the Gamma Forests, sewed a prayer leaf for Amy Pond with Melody Pond's name on it, but in Lorna's own language. She wanted to see the Doctor again – their 30-second encounter had happened when Lorna was a child. Lorna died trying to protect Amy and Melody – and the TARDIS finally translated the words on the prayer leaf into the name Lorna knew Melody by – River Song. (6.7)

Gamma Radiation: Electromagnetic radiation known to be able to damage or rewrite human DNA. The Daleks trapped in 1930s New York planned to attract a massive bolt of gamma radiation to Earth after a solar flare, via the mooring mast atop the Empire State Building. Dalek DNA would then be bled into the comatose humans who formed part of the Final Experiment. The DNA-corrupting gamma pulse would rewrite the humans' DNA, imprinting Dalek DNA as well, thus creating a mobile Dalek-Human hybrid army – with the physical freedom of humans but the unquestioning amorality and obedience of rank-and-file Daleks. The Doctor placed himself in the path of the lightning bolt, so, as well as Dalek Sec's already mutated DNA, a fragment of Time Lord DNA went into every Dalek-Human hybrid, leading them to turn on their masters. (3.4, 3.5)

Gandalf: Fictional aged wizard in the *Lord of the Rings* trilogy of books. The Master called the Doctor this after ageing him by 100 years. (3.13)

Ganesh, Indra: A junior secretary with the Ministry of Defence, working at 10 Downing Street during the Big Ben incident. There he met Joseph Green MP and briefed him on the situation, informing him that he was now Acting Prime Minister. He supplied Green with the Emergency Protocols and later, along with Harriet Jones and Rose Tyler, discovered the dead body of the Prime Minister. The Slitheen posing as Margaret Blaine then killed him. When the Doctor asked about him, Harriet Jones realised she had talked to him and given him a cup of coffee but never asked his name. (1.4, 1.5) (Played by NAVIN CHOWDRY)

Gangers, the: Created from the Flesh by the Morpeth-Jetsan Company, a Ganger was a copy of a human original. When the Flesh was manipulated at a molecular level, its structure could be programmed into any form – a Ganger. Everything was identical to the original human, hair, nails, eyes and memories. The Gangers were exact duplicates – with the eyes and minds forming first, giving Gangers a slight obsession with eyes. There were stories about Gangers going rogue, but no one paid them much heed. However in the St John's monastery, at a crystal-diluric acid industrial facility, gamma radiation from a solar tsunami gave the Gangers there more independent thought and they turned on the humans. One Ganger in particular, an unstable one based on Jennifer Lucas, tried to kill the humans and other Gangers but was destroyed by a Ganger of her boss, Miranda Cleaves, and a Ganger of the Doctor. The reason the Doctor had taken Amy Pond and Rory Williams to St John's in the first place was because he suspected Amy was a Ganger – and had been since before their reunion in America – her pregnancy readings varied between positive and negative, suggesting the TARDIS was scanning two different Amys simultaneously. He needed to understand how the Gangers worked and why. After leaving Morpeth-Jetsan, the Doctor revealed to Amy and Rory that Amy was fake – that the real Amy was elsewhere, experiencing everything the Ganger Amy had experienced because they were connected by something linking into the TARDIS. He deactivated the Ganger Amy, and the real one awoke on Demon's Run, in a birthing chamber overseen by Madame Kovarian. (6.5, 6.6) Rescuing Amy, the Doctor and Rory realised Kovarian had placed the Ganger Amy aboard the TARDIS to distract them while she induced Amy's labour. Amy gave birth to Melody Pond, who Kovarian wanted to turn into a weapon against the Doctor. Rory retrieved Melody from Kovarian and reunited her with Amy. But Kovarian had fooled them all – and by using a codeword beamed across space, Melody was reduced to Flesh – Kovarian having successfully stolen the real Melody. (6.7)

Gangsters: A 1970s BBC drama series about Birmingham's underworld. DVD store-owner Banto was watching Episode 6 when Sally Sparrow went to see Larry Nightingale (3.10)

Gantok: Warrior and envoy of the Silence. The Doctor allowed him to win at Live Chess on Vegas 12 provided he took him to Dorium Maldovar. Gantok tried to kill the Doctor on behalf of the Silence, but was instead devoured by the carnivorous skulls that guarded the Seventh Transept. (6.13) (Played by MARK GATISS)

Gardener: The first victim of the Reapers as they broke into the world after Rose Tyler saved her dad's life and created a breach in time. (1.8) (Played by KEN TEALE)

Gardner: Head of Security at Kennedy Space Center, who was in the process of questioning the Doctor on his apparent sabotage of the Apollo command module when President Nixon intervened. (6.2) (Played by GLENN WRAGE)

Gareth: Husband-to-be of Sally Phelan on 'Pete's World'. Sally was converted to a Cyberman and died the night before their wedding. (2.6)

Garn Belt: Area in space which contained the planet Alfava Metraxis. (5.4, 5.5)

Gas-mask zombies: Nanogenes, subatomic robots leaking from a crashed Chula medical ship in 1941, which were programmed to seek out damaged life forms and aid their recoveries. What they found first in London was a recently deceased child victim of an air raid, Jamie, who had been wearing a gas

G

mask when he died. Assuming all humans were 'empty' of life in the same way, they reanimated him, the gas mask now blended into his flesh, and proceeded to make contact with other humans at the local Albion Hospital, making gas masks and scars identical to Jamie's appear on their bodies – within a week everyone in the hospital bar one consultant, Dr Constantine, had been affected and completely transformed. When the nanogenes later saw the DNA of both dead Jamie and his living mother, they recombined to bring Jamie back to full health. The Doctor then programmed them to revert all the other affected humans back to perfect health, which included making a lot of them fitter than they had been before. (1.9, 1.10)

Gate Room, the: Area in Joshua Naismith's house which he had converted into a store for the Vinvocci's so-called Immortality Gate. Surrounded by scientific apparatus and computer banks, the team Naismith had employed to perfect the Immortality Gate worked long and hard. Beneath the Gate Room was a basement area, which the Gate was also built into, through the floor where more machinery existed, although that was operated solely by the two disguised Vinvocci, Addams and Rossiter, who were actually trying to teleport the Gate back to their ship in orbit, the *Hesperus*. The Gate Room became the site of the final battle between the Doctor, the Master and the Time Lords, who used the Whitepoint Star the Master had incorporated into the Gate's mechanisms to lock onto and bring themselves to Earth. (4.17, 4.18)

Gates III, William Henry: American entrepreneur and co-founder of Microsoft, the world's largest and most prolific computer software company. Professor Docherty rued his death at the hands of the Toclafane when her computers wouldn't work properly. (3.13)

Gates of Elysium, the: Location of a battle during the first year of the Time War. Davros was lost there when his command ship entered the jaws of the Nightmare Child. (4.13)

Gaul: See *France*

Gauntlet of Rassilon, the: Powerful glove worn by Time Lord President Rassilon during the Time War, which emitted destructive energies that could vaporise his enemies. (4.18)

Gavin: A red-headed boy Rory knew from school (AG05)

Gedes: The Torchwood Archive sent and lost an expedition there. Amongst the things that were found were a book of hieroglyphs, maps and drawings which inspired the Empire to instigate a mission to the legendary impossible planet, known as Krop Tor. (2.8T)

Gelth: An alien life form that was reduced to a non-corporeal state during the Time War. They arrived on Earth in Victorian times via the space and time rift which existed across Cardiff. As gaseous creatures, they used the gas from recently deceased humans, as well as the gas in the lighting and heating pipes that were threaded through local housing, to exist in. They convinced the Doctor to let them use a local psychically gifted maid, Gwyneth, to enable them to inhabit dead bodies until they could establish a new form. In truth, they were an invasion force, and Gwyneth had to ignite the gas and blow them, and herself, up. (1.3) (Voiced by ZOË THORNE) Rose Tyler pretended to have authority granted to her by the Gelth Confederacy to demand the Sycorax leave Earth. (2.X) Rose wondered if the ghosts breaking through on Earth could be the Gelth, but the Doctor was convinced they weren't as they were all over the planet rather than just around the Cardiff rift. (2.12)

G

Gemini: Codename for the mole in Cybus Industries on 'Pete's World' who fed the Preachers with their information. It was in fact Pete Tyler. (2.5, 2.6)

Genesis Ark: Conical device the Daleks had stored inside their Void Ship. It was stolen Time Lord technology from the Time War, although the Doctor didn't recognise it. It required the cellular imprint of a time traveller to activate it and, when Mickey Smith fell against it, his touch was enough. When it opened, the Doctor discovered that it was a Gallifreyan prison, dimensionally transcendental

like the TARDIS, and it stored millions of Daleks that the Time Lords had imprisoned. The Cult of Skaro immediately sought to get it free of Torchwood Tower, raising it into the sky as it needed a clear radius of 30 square miles, and let the captive Daleks loose to begin a pitched battle with both Cybermen and humans. When the Doctor was able to breach the Wall for one last time and rip open the Void, the Ark and all its Daleks were sent back into the Void, for ever. (2.13) (Operated by STUART CROSSMAN)

Genetic Manipulation Device (GMD): A sonic micro-field manipulator, using hypersonic sound waves to create a state of resonance that would destabilise the cell structure of someone's DNA and enable them to literally hack into their genes and, with a metagenic program, instruct them to change. This is exactly what it did to its creator, Richard Lazarus. Its main effect was shaving 40 years off Lazarus's age, but the side effect was to unleash previously dormant cells within his DNA that caused him to change into a primordial beast that lived off the life forces of others. The Doctor reversed the polarity of its flow of neutrons, which wrecked the machine with one final pulse of hypersonic waves, with which he believed he had reversed Lazarus's DNA changes. However, this was only temporary and the Lazarus Creature rose again. (3.6)

Geneva: Swiss city and home to many United Nations departments. A flight from Geneva, containing recognised experts in extraterrestrial affairs, arrived in the aftermath of the Big Ben incident. (1.4) On 'Pete's World', Dr Kendrick threatened to report back to Geneva, as the Ultimate Upgrade project contravened the Ethical Committee's Bio-Convention. (2.5) UNIT Control in Geneva was attacked by the

Toclafane; when those events were erased, UNIT Control contacted the *Valiant*, demanding to know what was going on following the assassination of President Winters. (3.12, 3.13) UNIT Control issued a worldwide Code Red alert as Dalek ships approached Earth. (4.12) The Master took control of UNIT there. (4.18)

Genghis Khan: 13th-century Mongolian warlord who created the Mongol Empire. His warriors once tried to break into the TARDIS but failed. (1.1)

Geocomtex: Henry Van Statten's software and hardware company. It had made him a billionaire, most probably through his use of illicit alien tech he had acquired. (1.6) A web page about Geocomtex was seen by the Doctor when he accessed a mobile phone with his sonic screwdriver to search for HC Clements. (3.X)

George [1]: Mikhail Kerenski's husband who, instead of saving their money, bought Mikhail a car for his birthday. (4.16)

George [2]: Seemingly terrified young son of Claire and Alex, residents of the Rowbarton housing estate. In fact George was an alien, a Tenza, who had placed himself in their family, and both affected their 'parents' feelings towards him, but also reflected those feelings too – and suffered from pantaphobia as a result. Believing that he was always being spied on by monsters, his psychic panic drew the Doctor to him. George, feeling rejected, created a nightmare world inside a toy doll's house, creating menacing Peg-Dolls that transformed the other residents, as well as Amy Pond, into dolls. Alex was able to prove to George that he loved him, that he was forever part of the family and the nightmare world was erased, with

everyone reverting to normal. George then remained happily with Alex and Claire, who promised to bring him up as their own son. (6.9) (Played by JAMIE ORAM)

George [3]: Security guard at Sanderson & Grainger, a department store in Colchester. He tried to intervene when shop worker Kelly claimed that Craig Owens was hassling her, until the Doctor interceded. George was later murdered by the Cybermen, and his body parts harvested by them. (6.12) (Played by CHRIS OBI)

George IV, King: English monarch for whom the Coronation Coach used by Elizabeth II was built. (2.7)

George, the: A pub on 'Pete's World' where Jackie Tyler had celebrated her 21st birthday. (2.5)

German Officer: Nazi in Berlin who challenged River Song shortly after she had regenerated. His soldiers tried to shoot her but she was still in her regeneration cycle and was unharmed, and knocked the soldiers down with the energy she was expelling. (6.8) (Played by MARK KILLEEN)

German Woman: An old woman who was stationed at Osterhagen Station One some distance from Nuremberg. She greeted Martha Jones when she arrived with an Osterhagen Key, and had seen the Daleks scouring the woods. When she realised Martha intended to use the Key, she held a gun on the Englishwoman, but realised she couldn't actually kill anyone, and therefore Martha was able to continue her mission. (4.13) (Played by VALDA AVIKS)

Germany: European country which, according to Lance Bennett, Donna Noble couldn't even find on a map. (3.X) Martha Jones ended up there after using the Project Indigo device, to find Osterhagen Station One in Nuremberg. (4.13) Melody Zucker caused the TARDIS to go there by shooting the Time Rotor. (6.8)

G

Ghosh, Atif: 19-year-old Colchester resident who was killed by the Cybermen and his body used for spare parts. (6.12)

Ghost Energy: Form of energy that Torchwood monitored each time a Ghost Shift occurred. (2.12)

Ghost Field: The area of distortion around one of the 'ghosts' as they broke through into the world from the Void. The Torchwood Institute believed they were responsible for creating the ghost fields, whereas all they were doing was enhancing a pre-existing gap in reality. (2.12)

Ghost Shift: Term used by the Torchwood Institute when they activated the Lever Room to bring the ghosts into the world, hoping to utilise them, little realising what they were actually doing was giving the Cybermen the opening they needed to cross the Void from 'Pete's World'. (2.12)

'Ghost Train': Title of Colin Skinner's unpublished novel, which he read in chapters to the other members of LINDA. (2.10)

Ghostbusters: The Doctor quoted the theme song, written and performed by former Raydio frontman Ray Parker Jnr, to

this 1984 movie when building the ghost triangulator that he used on the Powell Estate to try and entrap a ghost, and learn the source of its emergence. (2.12)

Ghosts: Apparently friendly spirits that began appearing all over planet Earth, much to the delight of its inhabitants. In truth, they were Cybermen, breaking through the Void as a means of travelling to Earth from 'Pete's World', with the unwitting help of Yvonne Hartman and the Torchwood Institute. (2.12)

Ghostwatch: Television show, which examined the phenomenon of the ghosts appearing all over the world, presented by Alistair Appleton. (2.12)

GI Jane: 1997 movie starring Demi Moore as an American who is the first woman to join the US Navy Special Warfare Group. Donna Noble likened Jenny to her, on Messaline (4.6)

Gibbis: Tivolian, whose school motto was 'Resistance is Exhausting'. Instinctively cowardly, his automatic response to being brought aboard the God Complex was to run and hide. However, he also had a great deal of cunning, using his cowardice to protect himself and convince others, such as Joe Buchanan, to face the Minotaur rather than him. Gibbis was a town planner on Tivoli and his biggest fear was the Weeping Angels but it was his faith in his race's innate ability to be dominated that almost killed him. However, he was the only survivor of the God Complex and was in fact its final prisoner before heading home. (6.11) (Played by DAVID WALLIAMS)

Gideons: Unit of currency on Ember. (6.X)

Ginger: Yorkshire lad living rough on the streets of London. He was mates with Tommo and together they got food from Sarah. When the Master arrived, Ginger thought he looked like Harry Saxon, but after Tommo realised the Master was a threat, he and Ginger ran for their lives. However the Master's new powers enabled him to catch up with them, and he killed both Ginger and Tommo. (4.17) (Played by DWAYNE SCANTLEBURY)

G

Girl: Young member of a family whose Christmas was almost ruined when her parents were kidnapped by the Graske and replaced with changelings. But the real parents were swiftly returned, none the wiser. (AotG) (Played by MOLLY KABIA)

Gita: London resident scooped up by the Daleks and transferred to the Crucible in the Medusa Cascade. Along with Jackie Tyler and some others, she was placed in a sealed room and although Jackie escaped, Gita and the others were dissolved when the Daleks tested their Reality Bomb on them. (4.13) (Played by SHOBU KAPOOR)

Gladwell: South London road tunnel which the number 200 bus entered but didn't come out of, because it had gone through a wormhole to San Helios.

The police and later UNIT set up their mobile bases there, waiting for it to return, which it eventually did, flying, followed by three Stingrays which UNIT dealt with. (4.15)

Glasgow: In the alternative world where Donna Noble never met the Doctor, the starliner *Titanic* crashed onto Southern England, turning it into a radioactive wasteland. Donna hoped her family could get moved to Glasgow because she believed there were job opportunities there. They ended up billeted in Leeds. (4.11)

Glasgow Water Riots: These were in their third day on Caledonia Prime, according to Channel McB, when the TARDIS first visited Satellite Five. (1.7)

Glasmir Mountains: Popular tourist destination in Apalapucia. (6.10)

Glass Pyramid of San Kaloon: The landmark that made San Kaloon famous. (1.11)

Glen Canyon Dam: Water-plant in Arizona where Canton Delaware III tracked Rory Williams down and apparently shot him. (6.2)

Glen of St Catherine: Area of Scotland where an alien Haemovariform crashed in 1540. The Monks in the local monastery worshipped the creature from then on. (2.2)

Globe, the: Theatre designed by Peter Streete, working under the influence of the Carrionites, as a tetradecagon, 14 being an important number in Carrionite science. The Lord Chamberlain's Men performed William Shakespeare's works there and, on the opening night of *Love's Labour's Won*, the Carrionites' plan came together as their Tide of Blood opened a portal to the Deep Darkness, allowing the rest of the Carrionites to descend to Earth. From the stage,

Shakespeare himself came up with the right words to seal the portal, exiling the Carrionites for ever. (3.2)

Gloria's Golden Grill: Roadside diner where the Doctor, River Song, Amy Pond and Rory Williams met up both before and after his death. On their second visit, a younger Doctor arrived, having received the same invitation as the others from his older self, although he was unaware who it was from. (6.1)

'Glory to Insert Name Here': National anthem of Tivoli. (6.11)

Gloucester: Cathedral city in the west of England. Leadworth was about thirty minutes away. (5.1)

God Complex, the: Holographic prison into which people were teleported until the Minotaur creature that guarded it could die. The prison floated through space on an endless journey, collecting people it considered to have a strong faith in something (religious or otherwise) – and converted that faith into nourishment for the Minotaur. (6.11)

'God Rest Ye Merry Gentlemen': Traditional Christmas Carol being sung by carollers in the Cardiff streets of 1869 when Charles Dickens was giving a reading. (1.3) It was heard on the streets of London in 1883 when the Graske kidnapped a street urchin, (AotG) and the Santa Roboforms were playing it when they attacked Rose Tyler and Mickey Smith (2.X) and again when one of them kidnapped Donna Noble a year later. (3.X) The Doctor listened to carollers sing this in London, 1851. (4.14) The Salvation Army band Wilfred passed on his way to church were playing it. (4.17)

'God Save The Queen': National Anthem for Great Britain. Magpie heard it after the closedown moments on his television set shortly before he was visited by the Wire. (2.7)

Goddard, Diana: Polkowski's replacement as chief aide to Henry Van Statten, the American billionaire. Goddard initially supported Van Statten's actions, until the Dalek he was keeping prisoner broke free and systematically slaughtered over 200 staff. After the Dalek was destroyed, Goddard had Van Statten mind-wiped and left to live his life as a brainless junkie on the streets of a random American city. (1.6) (Played by ANNA-LOUISE PLOWMAN)

Goddard, Trisha: The presenter of her own TV chat show, she interviewed a woman called Eileen in an episode entitled 'I Married a Dead Man'. (2.12)

G

G

Godmother: The Doctor had a dull one, with two heads (twice the bad breath) but a useful propensity for gift-giving. (5.10)

Goffle: The measurement of length defined by Emperor Jate as being from his nose to his fingertip is a paab, not a goffle. Rodrick didn't know this when asked by the Anne Droid in *The Weakest Link* aboard the Game Station. (1.12)

Gold, Deputy Edward: Australian second-in-command of Bowie Base One on Mars. He was a stickler for regulations, although this may have been more to do with knowing how Adelaide Brooke, the captain (who he had romantic feelings towards, and something darker in their past that he reckoned she could never forgive him for) would react if rules were broken or time and energy wasted. When the Flood infiltrated the Base, Ed went to check on the shuttle rocket, to ready it to take everyone back to Earth. However, the Flood-infected Maggie Cain was aboard the craft and infected Ed. Determined not to lose his humanity and to protect Earth, Ed blew the rocket up with himself locked inside (4.16) (Played by PETER O'BRIEN)

Golden Age: An era of prosperity and peace that the Doctor believed would be ushered in for Britain when Harriet Jones became Prime Minister. (1.5) In fact, he was later directly responsible for her downfall after she murdered the Sycorax by having Torchwood destroy their retreating spaceship. (2.X) On 'Pete's World', as Britain's President, she did indeed bring forth a Golden Age, but one marred by climatic disaster. (2.13)

Golden Locust: When Elton Pope stood up to the man he believed to be Victor Kennedy, bemoaning the fact that Victor had stopped LINDA being fun, he announced that he was walking out, along with Colin Skinner and Ursula Blake. Elton and Ursula would then head for a Chinese dinner at the Golden Locust. Before they could get there, both Skinner and Ursula were absorbed by the Abzorbaloff. (2.10)

Golightly, Reverend Arnold: Brought up in an orphanage by the Christian Fathers and now a friend of the Curbishleys. He was the local vicar in the village where Eddison Hall was situated. He was a guest there when a series of brutal murders took place — murders committed by Golightly as he was in fact half-Vespiform, and a telepathic Firestone jewel from his home planet and worn by his natural mother, Lady Eddison was beginning to fill his mind with murders from the books of Agatha Christie, which Lady Eddison was reading. After he was exposed, Golightly's instinct was to be reunited with the Firestone whatever the cost, and when Agatha Christie threw it into a lake, he dived in, in his Vespiform state, and drowned. (4.7) (Played by TOM GOODMAN-HILL)

Goodheart, Netty: One of Wilfred Mott's friends and part of the Silver Cloak. (4.17)

Gooding Jnr, Cuba: American actor who shared a birthday with Jackie Tyler on 'Pete's World' — 1 February. On Rose Tyler's version of Earth, although Jackie's birthday was still 1 February, Cuba Gooding Jnr's wasn't (it was 2 January). This was just one of many minor differences between the two versions of Earth. (2.5)

G

Gorilla: Simian creature from a book Lucy Hayward read as a child, which scared her. Once she had conquered that fear, by seeing the gorilla brought to life in a hotel room in the God Complex, Lucy was enraptured and died. (6.7) (Played by ROGER ENNALS)

Governor, the: Woman who became the administrator of HMS Broadfell, the prison where Lucy Saxon was secretly detained. She had arranged for the previous governor to have an accident, leaving the way open for her to take charge and, with her associates, including Miss Trefusis, restored the Master at the cost of their own lives. (4.17) (Played by TERESA BANHAM)

Graduate, The: Rom-com novel by Charles Webb, about Benjamin, a young student seduced by an older woman, Mrs Robinson. It was made into an award-winning movie by Mike Nichols. The Doctor likened River Song to Mrs Robinson, (6.1) and River referred to him as Benjamin. (6.8)

Gran [1]: Jackie Tyler hoped that after the defeat of the Family Slitheen she and Rose could go and visit Rose's grandmother. Jackie had told her that Rose had been in France, working as an au pair, for the twelve months when she was actually missing. (1.5)

Gran [2]: Senior member of a family whose Christmas was almost ruined when his daughter and son-in-law were kidnapped by the Graske and replaced with changelings. But the real couple were swiftly returned, none the wiser. (AotG) (Played by GWENYTH PETTY)

Gran [3]: Rory Williams's grandmother, who used to say 'You never miss the water till the well runs dry.' (6.9)

Grand Central Ravine: This was named after the Ancient British city of Sheffield, not York. Rose Tyler didn't know this when asked by the Anne Droid in *The Weakest Link* aboard the Game Station. (1.12)

Granddad: Senior member of a family whose Christmas was almost ruined when his daughter and son-in-law were kidnapped by the Graske and replaced with changelings. But the real couple were swiftly returned, none the wiser. (AotG) (Played by ROBIN MEREDITH)

Grandma: Rita Connolly's mother, who lived with Rita and her husband, Eddie, and their son Tommy in a home that Grandma actually owned. She was excited at the prospect of seeing the Queen's Coronation on television, and was present when the TV set was delivered from Magpie Electricals. However, it was playing up and the Wire appeared and stole her face. (2.7T) Eddie Connolly, unbeknownst to his family, then reported Grandma to the police, who took her faceless body away and stored it in a lock-up with all the other locals who had suffered a similar fate. When the Wire was defeated,

G

Grandma's face returned and she went home. (2.7) (Played by MARGARET JOHN)

Grant: Security officer at Kennedy Space Center, who was in the process of questioning the Doctor on his apparent sabotage of the Apollo command module when President Nixon intervened. Grant's wife was expecting a baby. (6.2) (Played by JEFF MARSH)

Graphite: Principal material within a standard pencil. The Scribble Creature that Chloe Webber created, which attacked Rose Tyler in London in 2012, was made of this, as the Doctor demonstrated by rubbing some of it out with an ordinary eraser. (2.11)

Graske: Diminutive aliens from the planet Griffoth, they either worked for themselves or, more often than not, were employed to do a specific job. Amongst their technology was the ability to kidnap creatures from different times and space and replace them with changelings. These were then controlled by the Graske and used to abduct further victims. (AotG) A Graske was able to access the TARDIS through a portal and then escaped into a concert at the Albert Hall on Earth, but the Doctor got him back and sent him home. (MotS) There was a Graske in the Zaggit Zagoo bar. (4.18) (Played by JIMMY VEE, voiced by PHILIP HURD-WOOD)

Gravitissimal Accelerator: Part of the system that Professor Yana had come up with to power the rocket that would take the human refugees from Malcassairo to Utopia. (3.11)

Gravity Bubble: Edwin Bracewell believed he had invented these flying devices to enable life to survive in space. In fact, the Daleks had planted the secret into his android brain. However, Bracewell used them to protect the spitfires that Churchill sent into space to attack the Dalek ship. (5.3) The Silurians had similar technology. (5.8, 5.9) More spitfires used them again when they strafed Demon's Run. (6.7)

Gravity Globe: Device used for illuminating cavernous areas by rising to the uppermost area of the cave. Ida Scott used one to illuminate Krop Tor's core. (2.8) The Clerics used them in the Maze of the Dead on Alfava Metraxis. The Doctor shot one to use the gravity force in it to help those present in the Maze fall into the Byzantium. (5.4, 5.5)

Gravity Pockets: Familiar disturbance in space, they are rarely threatening but can cause starships and space stations to judder if hit by one. (1.2)

Gravity Satellites: Devices placed around the sun to hold it back as it expanded, slowing the destruction of Earth and other planets in the solar system. (1.2)

Gravity Well: The Tritovore ship had a gravity well, at the bottom of which were the ship's engines. The crystal nucleus which powered it was at the very bottom and, as Lady Christina de Souza entered the well, she realised a number of sleeping Stingrays had snuck in. (4.15)

Gray, Private Steven: UNIT soldier who along with Private Harris discovered the Sontaran involvement with the ATMOS situation. Harris and Gray were hypnotised by General Staal into working for him, alongside a clone of Martha Jones. When his usefulness was at an end, Commander Skorr shot him dead. (4.4, 4.5) (Played by WESLEY THEOBOLD)

Graystark Hall: An orphanage in Florida where the Silence nested. They used a young girl they found there, encasing her inside a NASA astronaut's spacesuit for protection. The Silence believed she was important to their future. Graystark Hall's proprietor Doctor Renfrew was driven insane by his constant exposure and memory wipes by the Silence, scrawling hostile messages over the walls and his own skin, although never understanding the significance of them. (6.2)

Great Atlantic Smog Storm: According to Lynda Moss, this pollution cloud had been raging for 20 years by 200,100. (1.12)

Great Colbalt Pyramid: Built on the remains of the Torchwood Institute on Old Earth.

G

Broff didn't know this when asked by the Anne Droid in *The Weakest Link* aboard the Game Station. He thought it was built on the remains of Touchdown. (1.12)

Great Exhibition, the: European touring display of Vincent Van Gogh's paintings. The Doctor and Amy Pond visited it in Paris, (5.10) while Craig Owens had an advert for the London stop attached to his fridge. (5.11)

Great Expectations: A book cited by the Doctor as one of Charles Dickens's works that he'd read. (1.3)

Great Exterminator, the: The Dalek Emperor taunted the Doctor while he battled with his conscience over using the Delta Wave, which would destroy Earth as well as the Dalek fleet, by calling him the Great Exterminator. (1.13)

Great Flood: A natural disaster in the 23rd century that briefly enveloped London. (AG03)

Great Old Ones: According to the Doctor, the legendary Great Old Ones existed from the creation of the universe right up to and including the Dark Times, about 4.6 billion years ago. One of the Great Old Ones had a spaceship, the *Infinite*,

and used its great powers to grant the Heart's Desire of anyone who boarded the ship. By the 40th century, the *Infinite* was just a crumbling wreck, with only an echo of the long-dead Great Old Ones' power left in it. (TIQ)

Great One, the: Mythological goddess to the humans and Hath on Messaline. They believed a fragment of her breath, contained within the Source,

would bring life to Messaline, and whoever had access to it controlled the destiny of the planet. (4.6)

Great Vampires: One of the legendary races from the Dark Times, mentioned by the Doctor. (TIQ)

Green Anchor: One of the two time streams co-existent on Apalapucia. (6.10)

Green Crescent: The emblem of medicine by the year 5,000,000,000. It was seen on the side of the Hospital on New Earth and on posters and Mood Patches in New New York. (2.1, 3.3)

Green Mile, The: Elton Pope misquoted a passage from this Stephen King novel when summing up his new outlook on life after meeting the Doctor. (2.10)

Green, Joseph: The MP for Hartley Dale, and chairman of the Parliamentary Commission on the Monitoring of Sugar Standards in Exported Confectionery. The real Green had been murdered and replaced by a member of the Family Slitheen, Jocrassa Fel Fotch Pasameer-Day Slitheen. As Green, he was the most senior Member of Parliament in London and assumed the temporary role of Acting Prime Minister as the real one was missing, having been killed by another Slitheen. Jocrassa Fel Fotch Pasameer-Day Slitheen died when a sub-Harpoon missile struck 10 Downing Street. (1.4, 1.5) (Played by DAVID VERREY)

Greeves: Butler at Eddison Hall, as his father had been before him. He got caught up in the murders that occurred there but, because he was with Donna Noble when Roger Curbishley was killed, she was able to ascertain that in this case, the butler didn't do it. (4.7) (Played by DAVID QUILTER)

Grexnik: A married character from the holovid series *Jupiter Rising*. (1.12)

Greyhound: UNIT call sign used by non-commissioned officers. Martha Jones was Greyhound Six. Private Gray was Greyhound Sixteen. Private Jenkins was Greyhound Forty. (4.4, 4.5) Private Harris was Greyhound Fifteen. (4.11)

Griffin's Parade: Street off Ealing Road. In the alternative world where Donna Noble never met the Doctor, she took that route towards Merchant Street where she accepted a job at Jival Chowdry's photocopying shop. (4.11)

Griffoth: Home world of the Graske. (AotG)

Groom, Andrea: Essex girl spotted snogging Sanderson & Grainger worker Don Petherbridge. (6.12)

Groom, Junior Technician Roman: American on Bowie Base One, and the youngest of the crew. A child prodigy, he was responsible for overseeing the technical requirements of the Mars mission, especially Gadget, the robot he created and controlled remotely via a pair of Auto-Gloves. He was the last of the crew to be infected by the Flood, by just a single drop of infected water

landing on his cheek. His body was destroyed, along with the Flood, when Bowie Base One was destroyed in a nuclear explosion. (4.16) (Played by MICHAEL GOLDSMITH)

Groom Lake Army Air Base: See *Dreamland*

Ground Force: One of the programmes broadcast from the Game Station. Losing contestants get turned into compost. (1.12)

Gruffalo, The: 20th-century children's book by Julia Donaldson. Elliot Northover was trying to read it with his dad, Mo, but his dyslexia held him back. (5.8)

Guantanamo Bay: Donna Noble likened UNIT's treatment of the hypnotised ATMOS workers to that of the prisoners held at Guantanamo Bay in South America. (4.4)

Guard [1]: In charge of keeping the Futurekind out of the Silo base on Malcassairo, he let the Doctor, Martha Jones, Captain Jack Harkness and Padra Fet Shafe Cane in, but only after checking they didn't have fangs. He and his men later left on the rocket to Utopia. Whether he or his descendants were turned into Toclafane by the Master is unknown. (3.11) (Played by ROBERT FORKNALL)

Guard [2]: New officer in charge of watching River Song in cell 426 at the Stormcage One Prison Facility. River apologised for kissing him with her hallucinogenic lipstick on, but he believed it hadn't worked and was found keeping his gun trained on a stick-man-like drawing of her. (5.12) (Played by JOE JACOBS)

Guard [3]: Worked at the Stormcage One Prison Facility and reported to his superiors that River Song was packing her bags to leave again. (6.1) (Played by KIERON O'CONNOR)

Guard [4]: Worked at the Stormcage One Prison Facility. River Song suggested he take the night off once it was time for her to head to Demon's Run. (6.7) (Played by SAM STEEPER)

Guard [5]: Arrested Guy Fawkes in the cellars under the House of Lords. (AG05) (Voiced by CHRIS JOHNSON)

G

G

Guido: Down-on-his-luck Venetian boat builder, who helped build warships. He realised that the only chance his daughter Isabella had for a good life was to join Rosanna Calvierri's School and become one of the famed Calvierri Girls. Neither he nor Isabella had bargained on never seeing each other again, and Guido tried to get her back, but to no avail. The Doctor offered to help, and Amy Pond joined the school to find Isabella. Isabella helped Amy avoid becoming a Saturnyne but it was too late for her and she couldn't escape with Amy and be reunited with her father. Grief-stricken at this, Guido led the rest of the Calvierri Girls into a trap within his rooms and detonated barrels of explosives from the arsenale, killing all the vampiric girls along with himself. (5.6) (Played by LUCIAN MSAMATI)

Guinevere One: A British space satellite sent to Mars, financed by the government under Harriet Jones and overseen by Daniel Llewellyn. It was taken aboard the Sycorax ship en route, and they used its transmitters to make contact with Earth. (2.X) Another Guinevere satellite was used to transmit footage of the *Titanic* space cruiser crashing towards Earth in the alternative world where Donna Noble never met the Doctor. (4.11)

Gunpowder Plot: A plan by 13 Catholics to blow up King James I as he entered the House of Lords. The Plotters were infiltrated by a Rutan spy in the guise of Lady Elizabeth Winters, and the Doctor realised she planned to use their gunpowder for different reasons. (AG05)

G

Gurney, Constantine Ethelred: He claimed to be the Governor of the prison on Volag-Noc but was actually an impostor. Previously a prisoner on the planet, his old enemies still wanted him dead after he was freed, so he returned to prison and, with the help of technology he acquired from Ulysses Mergrass, rewired the robot Warders, so they saw him as Locke and Locke as Gurney and imprisoned the real Governor. When the Doctor brought an end to Gurney's new lifestyle after releasing Governor Locke, Gurney fled to the surface, taking with him the final datachip the Doctor and Martha Jones needed to locate the *Infinite*. Gurney was then attacked and killed by Baltazar after he shot and mortally wounded Baltazar's companion, Caw. (TIQ) (Voiced by STEPHEN GRIEF)

Gusev Crater: Geological area on Mars, under which solid ice was detected in the early 21st century. By 2059, Bowie Base One had been established on Mars, built right atop the crater, to use that ice. However, the ice contained the dormant microscopic life force the Flood, which the Base accidentally reawakened. (4.16)

Gwyneth: Orphaned maid in the service of Gabriel Sneed, she was gifted with the ability to contact what she believed were departed human spirits – a natural talent enhanced by her growing up close to the space and time rift that crossed Cardiff. In fact, the spirits were an alien species who called themselves the Gelth. They sought bodies to inhabit as they crossed to Earth via the rift, before beginning their intended conquest of the planet. Pretending to be angels, they tricked both Gwyneth and the Doctor into allowing her to act as a conduit for them. As they emerged, they revealed their true forms, killing Gwyneth but leaving enough of her spirit intact that she was able to strike a match and ignite the Gelth's gaseous forms so they, along with her, were destroyed in a massive explosion. (1.3) (Played by EVE MYLES)

Gypsies: Group of Earth colonists in Sardicktown who were famous for singing to the fish. (6.X)

H

H₂O Scoop: Colloquial name for the Judoon device that enabled them to take the Royal Hope Hospital from Earth (where they had no jurisdiction) to the moon. The scoop, in breaking through the atmosphere, created meteorological disturbances and then, as it activated, it drew all the moisture upwards, followed by the instant transmission of the Hospital. The scoop was reversed by the pedantic Judoon to avoid any complaints, and the Hospital was returned (with the rain) to exactly where it had come from. The Judoon used plasma coils that they had, two days previously, placed around the Hospital to power the scoop. (3.1)

Haemo-Goth: Aliens who travelled to Stonehenge, as part of the Pandorica Alliance. (5.12)

Halke, Commander: Sontaran warrior who died in the God Complex. His greatest fear was defeat. (6.11) (Played by CHRISTOPHER RYAN)

Hallucinogenic Lipstick: Used by River Song – one kiss and the compound in the lipstick seeps through the skin and affects the mind, creating illusions and leaving the victim open to suggestion. River used it on Josh, a guard aboard the *Byzantium*, (5.4) and later her guard at the Stormcage Facility, plus the Roman Autons stationed near Stonehenge who believed her to be Cleopatra and the Doctor to be Caesar. (5.12)

Halo: Ornamental headdress worn by the Heavenly Host, which became a lethal weapon after the Host had been reprogrammed by Max Capricorn. (4.X)

Halpen, Klineman: Chief Executive Officer and owner of Ood Operations. He liked neither the Ood nor the Ood-Sphere, nor many of his employees, and was only interested in making money through the company his father founded. He always kept an Ood at his side, Ood Sigma, ostensibly to be bullied and to supply him with drinkable hair tonic, but he actually had a grudging respect for Sigma and was willing to let him rejoin the other Ood before killing them all.

Ood Sigma, however, had actually been giving Halpen a drink, Ood-Graft, that was altering his biochemistry and changing him into a natural Ood. After the transformation happened, the Halpen-Ood lived the rest of his life on the Ood-Sphere. (4.3) (Played by TIM McINNERNY)

Hame, Novice: A young nun, a member of the Sisters of Plenitude, who was seen in advertisements for the Hospital on New Earth saving a human suffering from Hawtrey's Syndrome. (2.1T) She was charged with looking after the Face of Boe in Ward 26. When the Sisters' plan was exposed, Hame was arrested and taken away. (2.1) Her penance was to be returned to the Face of Boe to minister to him for the rest of their lives, and he protected her from the mutated Bliss mood that eradicated the Senate and everyone else in the Overcity of New New York. She found the Doctor on the Motorway and brought him back to the Senate Building to save New New York and restore those trapped on the Motorway to the City once the danger had passed. When Boe died, the Doctor and Martha Jones left Hame in charge of the city. (3.3) (Played by ANNA HOPE)

Hamilton, Alexander: One of the Founding Fathers of the USA. An avenue in Florida was named after him, and the Doctor realised that the little girl trapped inside a NASA spacesuit was located nearby. (6.1)

Hamilton Colt: Maker of radios in the 1930s. The Doctor cannibalised a Hamilton Colt radio Solomon found in the basement of the Laurenzi theatre to make a DNA scanner, which revealed that his old enemies the Daleks were at work. He then converted it back to a radio receiver, switching it on in the Daleks' Transgenic Lab. The noise temporarily disabled the Daleks, the Dalek Sec Hybrid and the Pig Slaves, so he, Martha Jones and the captured humans could escape. (3.4, 3.5)

Hamlet: *The Tragedy of Hamlet, Prince of Denmark*, a play by William Shakespeare. Shakespeare considered writing it after defeating the Carrionites, as a way to honour his dead son, Hamnet. He also got a line for the play from the Doctor – 'The play's the thing' – although he didn't realise it at the time. (3.2)

Hammill, Mrs: Pensioner from Upper Leadworth who suffered from depression. Like all the local old folk, Mrs Hammill appeared to have been taken over by an Eknodine. She was amongst those who attacked the Doctor in the butcher's shop and Amy and Rory in their cottage – Rory thwacked her with a plank of wood, but it had no effect. Whether a real Mrs Hammill actually existed in the real Leadworth was unconfirmed, although as the psychic spore that created the Dream Lord fed on dark thoughts and memories, it seemed likely she was someone known to Amy and Rory back home. (5.7) (Played by JOAN LINDER)

Hamnet: William Shakespeare's only son, who died from the Black Death while Shakespeare was away from home. Shakespeare's grief at the loss caused him such despair, bordering on madness, that it enabled the Carrionites to gain a foothold on Earth. The defeat of the Carrionites prompted Shakespeare to consider honouring his dead son with a new play, which would later become *Hamlet*. (3.2)

Handbots: Automated robots which maintained the Twostreams Facility on Apalapucia, who 'saw' via their organically grown hands as their faces were completely blank. They anaesthetised then sterilised the infected victims of the Chen7 virus and, not realising she was human and thus immune, they tried to sterilise Amy Pond after she was placed into a different time stream to the Doctor and Rory Williams. Thirty years passed for Amy – but only an hour for the Doctor and Rory – during which she became adept at fighting, destroying and reprogramming the Handbots, including one she lived with which she called Rorybot. (6.10) (Voiced by STEPHEN BRACKEN-KEOGH)

Hannibal: Carthaginian military commander whose legendary exploits included taking his troops to face the Romans over the Alps.

Legend has it that to get through difficult rocky terrain with his troops and elephants, he used vinegar to corrode the calcium-based boulders. Harriet Jones MP was reminded of this when the Doctor was trying to devise a means to defeat the calcium-based Raxacoricofallapatorians. (1.5)

Happy: Coming in varying strengths, this was one of the Mood Patches available in Pharmacytown in the Undercity of New New York. (3.3)

'Happy Days Are Here Again': One of the show tunes used as part of the New York Revue at the Laurenzi theatre in 1930s New York, when it was still a new song to most people. (3.4)

Happy Prime Numbers: One of the passwords Martha Jones and Riley Vashtee needed to gain access to the next area aboard the SS *Pentallian* was the next in a sequence of numbers which the Doctor realised was a series of happy primes, the number required being 379. Happy numbers are any number which reduces to 1 when you take the sum of the squares of its digits and

continue iterating until it yields 1. A happy prime is any number that's both a happy number and a prime number. (3.7)

Harcourt, Captain: Human officer at the battle of Zarusthra Bay. He got the Sontaran nurse Strax to help save a human boy, Arthur. (6.7) (Played by RICHARD TRINDER)

Harcourt, Mrs: A patient at Albion Hospital who was transformed into a gas-mask zombie by the Chula nanogenes. Her DNA was rewritten properly by the reprogrammed nanogenes, returning to normal, but also replacing the leg she had lost that probably put her in the hospital in the first place. (1.10) (Played by VILMA HOLLINGBERY)

Hardaker, Captain: Officer in charge of the luxury cruise liner *Titanic* on its voyage from Sto to Earth. Hardaker was at the end of his career, aware he was dying and so had come to an arrangement with Max Capricorn, owner of the shipping fleet, to let the *Titanic* be destroyed, providing his family were financially well rewarded. When he met Midshipman Frame, he was disappointed that someone that young was to die, as Capricorn had promised him a final crew of men nearing retirement. He was killed on his bridge when the *Titanic* was struck by meteoroids after he had deliberately lowered the shields. (4.X) (Played by GEOFFREY PALMER)

Hardinger Seals: Hermetic airtight seals used on doorways in the Bowie Base One construction. The Flood were able to get past them. (4.16)

Hardy, Oliver: American actor, real name Norvell Hardy. The Doctor appeared alongside him in the movie *The Flying Deuces*. (6.1)

Harkness, Captain Jack: Originally a Time Agent from the Boeshane Peninsula in the 51st century, Captain Jack Harkness woke one morning to find that two years of his memories had been stolen by his employers, leaving him with no knowledge of what had happened to him during this period. On account of this, Jack set himself up as a freelance conman, travelling to locations such as first-century Pompeii and Second World War London, salvaging alien space junk and selling it back to the Time Agency before pre-known and natural causes resulted in their destruction.

Basing himself in Westminster in 1941, Jack served as an American volunteer for the Royal Air Force, assuming the identity of the real Captain Jack Harkness. Having previously stolen a Chula vessel for himself, Jack conned the Doctor and Rose into believing a Chula hospital ship was actually a warship. A German bomb was scheduled to destroy it soon after. Jack prevented the bomb from falling on the crash site by suspending it in stasis on board his own ship, but was unable to jettison it. He was then rescued from his ship's destruction by the Doctor and Rose Tyler, who invited him aboard the TARDIS as their travelling companion, even giving him his own TARDIS key. (1.9, 1.10) He then helped them stop a Slitheen from destroying Cardiff, (1.11) and was then transported from the TARDIS to the *What Not To Wear* studio aboard the Game Station. Following an attempt to rescue Rose from *The Weakest Link*, he was arrested alongside the Doctor and Lynda Moss, and sentenced to imprisonment on the Earth's Lunar Penal Colony. When they eventually escaped and uncovered an army of ships hidden from the Game Station transmitters, Jack recognised them as Dalek ships, which he had seen during the Tenth Dalek Occupation. Jack served as the Doctor's last line of defence, ultimately being exterminated by the Daleks, although he was later resurrected by Rose, who used the power of the Time Vortex to bring him back to life, making him immortal in the process. The Doctor instinctively reacted against Jack's immortality, and abandoned him on board the Game Station. (1.12, 1.13)

Stranded in the year 200,100, Jack used his Vortex Manipulator to travel to Earth in 1869 but, when the Manipulator burnt out, was forced to live through the entire 20th century, waiting for a version of the Doctor that coincided with his own timeline. Jack took this opportunity to visit Rose when she was growing up on the Powell Estate in the 1990s, though without making contact with her. Knowing that the Doctor would have to return one day to refuel, Jack based himself in Cardiff, on top of the rift that ran through the city. Jack joined Torchwood Cardiff and, following the Battle of Canary Wharf, rebuilt it in the Doctor's honour to defend the Earth. He had retrieved the Doctor's severed hand after the Sycorax attack, and kept it in order to detect the Time Lord's presence. He then travelled to the end of the universe by clinging to the TARDIS exterior as it dematerialised from Cardiff in 2008, (3.11) before helping the Doctor and Martha Jones defeat the Master upon their return to Earth. Though the Doctor offered to let

him continue travelling in the TARDIS once more, Jack returned to his team at Torchwood, but not before the Doctor had disabled his Vortex Manipulator's travel capabilities for a second time. Charming and flirtatious with everyone he met, regardless of gender or species, Jack revealed that he'd been a poster boy where he grew up in the Boeshane Peninsula, and was the first of his people ever to be signed up for the Time Agency. As a result, he told them, he had been nicknamed the Face of Boe, leaving the Doctor and Martha wondering whether Jack would live to become their other old friend, billions of years in the future. (3.12, 3.13)

In the alternative world where Donna Noble never met the Doctor, Jack was captured by the Sontarans and transported to Sontar, leaving Gwen Cooper and Ianto Jones to destroy the Tenth Sontaran Battle Fleet, giving their lives in the process. (4.11) Jack, Gwen and Ianto were in the Torchwood Hub when Earth was moved to the Medusa Cascade and the Daleks invaded Earth. Leaving his friends to deal with a Dalek, Jack took the Defabricator Gun and teleported to London in time to destroy the Dalek that shot the Doctor during his reunion with Rose. He, Rose and Donna Noble watched in the TARDIS as the Doctor used regeneration energy to save himself and then they all travelled to the Medusa Cascade where the Daleks exterminated Jack. This was a ruse to allow Jack to infiltrate the Crucible, and he met up with Jackie Tyler, Mickey Smith and Sarah Jane Smith. Together they helped defeat Davros and the Daleks and he returned to Earth and left the TARDIS with Martha Jones and Mickey. (4.12, 4.13) Jack was in a bar on Zog when the Doctor came to say goodbye, but left him a note, telling him to introduce himself to the man sat next to him, Midshipman Alonso Frame, which Jack did. (4.18) The Doctor thought he might go to all of Jack's stag parties in one night. (6.13) (Played by JOHN BARROWMAN)

Harmonic Filter: Part of the TARDIS which, if the gravity patterns of the galaxies are fed through it, creates music. (MotS)

Harper, Owen: Torchwood Three's medic. He died in action, and was remembered by Gwen Cooper and Ianto Jones as they faced a Dalek entering the Hub. (4.12)

Harriet: In charge of the art department aboard the *Teselecta*, she was responsible for ensuring that, every time the ship duplicated a human, the dimensions and external clothing were spot on (unlike with Rasputin). When the Anti-Bodies began attacking the crew, Harriet was teleported safely back to the Mothership. (6.8) (Played by ELLA KENION)

Harris, Private: UNIT soldier who, along with Private Gray, discovered the Sontaran involvement with the ATMOS situation. Harris and Gray were hypnotised by General Staal into working for him, alongside a clone of Martha Jones. When his usefulness was at an end, Commander Skorr shot him dead. (4.4, 4.5) In the alternative world in which Donna Noble never met  the Doctor, Donna overheard Private Harris reporting the Doctor's death after fighting the Empress of the Racnoss. (4.11) (Played by CLIVE STANDEN)

Harrogate: North Yorkshire town where Agatha Christie turned up after vanishing for eleven days. She had amnesia when she arrived at the Harrogate Hotel – all memories of her adventure with the Doctor and the Vespiform gone. (4.7)

Harry: One of the inhabitants of Hooverville in 1930s Manhattan. Solomon told him to stay with the rest of the people there when they were attacked by the Pig Slaves. (3.5)

Harry Potter and the Deathly Hallows: Final book in the seven-novel run by British author JK Rowling. The Doctor had read this, although Martha Jones hadn't, and it made him cry. Martha used a word from the Harry Potter books – 'Expelliarmus' – to help William Shakespeare send the Carrionites back into the Deep Darkness. (3.2)

Hart, Mrs: Cook at Eddison Hall, and a bit of a gossip, much to Mrs Chandrakala's chagrin. (4.7) (Played by CHARLOTTE EATON)

Hartigan, Miss Mercy: Brilliant but bitter woman who had been Matron of the St Joseph's Workhouse in Victorian London. She formed an alliance with the Cybermen, hoping that their victory over humanity would bring an end to men's social and sexual domination over women. She was tricked by the Cybermen, and her mental capacity increased a hundredfold. She became the pilot of the CyberKing, powering it by thought, passion and fury. Still in possession of her human emotions despite her conversion, she took revenge by destroying the Cyberleader that had betrayed her. The Doctor used the Cyclo-Steinham core energy within all the Cybermen's Infostamps to free her mind from Cyber control and, horrified by what she had become, she wiped out her personal guard of Cybermen. Independent again, but still with all the power in her mind, Miss Hartigan died as the engines she controlled exploded at her command. (4.14) (Played by DERVLA KIRWAN)

Hartley Dale: Constituency for which Joseph Green was MP until he was murdered by Jocrassa Fel Fotch Pasameer-Day Slitheen, and his body used as a disguise. (1.4, 1.5)

H

Hartman, Yvonne: CEO of the Torchwood Institute, fiercely patriotic and loyal to Queen and Country. Arrogant and self-assured, Yvonne made the mistake of assuming that she understood all the alien tech that Torchwood had accumulated over the years, but had no real idea of what exactly her Ghost Shifts were doing to the fabric of reality. Nor did she understand the Void Ship that Torchwood had secreted in one of their research labs. When the 'ghosts' revealed themselves to be Cybermen, and Daleks emerged from the Void Ship, she was hopelessly out of her depth and unable to resist when taken away for the Ultimate Upgrade. However, even in her Cyberform, Yvonne's duty took precedence, and she turned on the Cybermen and began shooting them down. It is likely that, along with the rest of the Cybermen, she was drawn into the Void for ever. (2.12, 2.13) (Played by TRACY-ANN OBERMAN)

Hartnell, Norman: Designer of the dress worn by the future Queen Elizabeth II on her Coronation day. (2.7)

Haruspex: Unlike the augurs and soothsayers of Pompeii, who foretold the future through their minds, the haruspex used animal entrails to read the future. However in Pompeii, after the Pyrovillian incursion 17 years prior to the Doctor's arrival, their readings had become highly accurate. (4.2)

Harvard University: Massachusetts-based establishment. Tarak Ital studied medicine there before joining the Johnson Space Center. (4.16)

Hath: Piscine life form. Some Hath travelled with humans to the planet Messaline, but their shared colony ship crashed and, over a seven-day period that seemed like centuries to those involved, a war raged between the two races. Martha Jones teamed up with a Hath called Peck to survive Messaline's harsh surfaces whilst the Doctor and Donna Noble tried to stop the war. Eventually the Doctor learned the truth and began the terraforming process on Messaline and the two species were reconciled. (4.6) There were two Hath in the Zaggit Zagoo

he alone knew the truth about the star whale at the base of the spaceship. (5.2) (Played by TERENCE HARDIMAN)

Hawtrey's Syndrome: One of the diseases successfully cured by the Sisters of Plenitude in their Hospital on New Earth. (2.1T)

Hayler, Kate: Hockey player at school with Amy Pond in Year 10. Amy smacked Kate's shins with her hockey stick after she tried chatting up Rory Williams. (6.10)

Hayward, Lucy: One of the humans, a police officer, transported to the God Complex, which was holographically altered to resemble an Earth hotel. Lucy died when her faith – in her ability to overcome her fear of a brutal gorilla from a book she had read as a child – enabled the Minotaur that prowled the Complex to drain her life energy. (6.11) (Played by SARAH QUINTRELL and ELLA WILTON-STROUDE)

Hayward, Mr: Married to Lucy Hayward. She remembered him before she died. (6.11) (Played by ANDREW JAY)

Hazel Street Workhouse: A Victorian Workhouse for orphaned children. Its Master was Mr Cole and, under Cyber control, Cole led his charges to the place where the Cybermen were building the engine for their CyberKing. The children were forced to work there, while Mr Cole was killed. (4.14)

Hazeldine, San: In physics, San Chen, not San Hazeldine, discovered the 15-10 Barric Fields. Roderick didn't know this when asked by the Anne Droid in *The Weakest Link* aboard the Game Station. (1.12)

Hazlehead: The Royal Jewellers, Hellier & Carew, were based in this Aberdeenshire town. Queen Victoria was taking the Koh-I-Noor diamond there for its annual re-cutting when she stopped for the night at the Torchwood Estate. (2.2)

bar. (4.18) The Doctor cited his encounter with the Hath as a reason for the Atraxi to fear him. (5.1)

Haven Road: Street in Chiswick in which St Mary's Church stood. The church was where Donna Noble and Lance Bennett were getting married when Donna vanished. (3.X)

Haverstock, Mr: London butcher who was having an illicit liaison with Arthur Lloyd, and also supplying him with meat to feed his family. (1.10)

Hawk Major: UNIT call sign for the command centre of the UNIT Carrier Ship *Valiant*. (4.5)

Hawkes, Howard: Movie director, allegedly responsible for the 1951 version of *The Thing From Another World*, which the Doctor referred to when he and Amy Pond approached the deserted Arctic Geological Survey Base in Zebra Bay. (AG02)

Hawking, Professor Stephen William: British theoretical physicist and author of *A Brief History of Time*, confined to a wheelchair due to ALS and only able to speak via a voice synthesizer. Mickey Smith commented on the similarity between Hawking's speaking voice and that of a Dalek. (2.13)

Hawthorne: Chief Winder of *Starship UK*, who reported directly to the Queen, Liz Ten. He alerted her to the presence of the Doctor and later revealed that

HC Clements: Security firm where Donna Noble was temping as a secretary when she met the company's head of Human Resources, Lance Bennett. Donna believed they had fallen in love and she asked Lance to marry her. HC Clements had actually been a subsidiary of the Torchwood Institute for 23 years, supplying Torchwood with various security systems and specialised locks. An underground tunnel linked the basement of HC Clements with a Torchwood facility beneath the Thames Barrier. (3.X) Donna Noble was heading there for a job interview when she changed her mind and went to Jival Chowdry's shop instead, creating an alternative timeline for Donna in which she never met the Doctor and he died fighting the Empress of the Racnoss. (4.11)

Head Chef: Food dealer on Floor 139 of Satellite Five, selling, amongst other delicacies, Kronkburgers. (1.7) (Played by COLIN PROCKTER)

Head Servant: Major Domo to Kazran Sardick. He resigned his post after the Doctor 'arranged' for him and all the other staff to win the lottery, even though there wasn't a lottery on Ember. (6.X) (Played by TIM PLESTER)

Headless Monks: Mysterious 51st-century order of monks overseen by the Papal Mainframe, whose final resting place was in the Delerium Archive (5.4) No one knew what was under a Headless Monk's hood – it was a Level One Heresy to remove a hood to find out. The Monks were literally headless – lifeless meat puppets controlled by their hearts, because they believed the domain of faith was there, not in the head, which always contained doubt. They could take people's heads and reanimate their bodies instantly, as they did with the Cleric called Fat One and Dorium Maldovar. On the asteroid Demon's Run, they entered an uneasy truce with the Clerics from the Vatican to find the Doctor, but he tricked both groups and almost set them against one another. When the Clerics were taken away by the Judoon and Silurians, a number of Monks took up their power-swords and engaged some of the Doctor's friends in fierce close-quarters battle, but the Monks were defeated and killed. (6.7)

Headteachers: The young Melody Zucker was sent to see her Headmaster after telling her History teacher that the Doctor failed to stop the RMS *Titanic* sinking. The older Melody Zucker was sent to see the Headmistress after telling her History teacher that Hitler's rise to power wasn't halted because the Doctor wasn't around to stop it. (6.8) (Played by ANDREW MARCHANT and PINA HARRINGTON)

Heat: Celebrity gossip magazine which the Tylers had a copy of in their living room. The Doctor glanced through it, pointing out that one of the celebrities therein was gay, another an alien. (1.1)

Heath, Tim: Human who died in the God Complex. His greatest fear was having his photograph taken. (6.11)

Heathrow: The Doctor told Adam Mitchell to head there on a 3pm flight from the USA when beginning his journey home to Manchester, before agreeing to give him a trip in the TARDIS. (1.6)

'Heaven And Hell': Show-stopping number at the heart of the New York Revue at the Laurenzi theatre in Manhattan during November 1930. It was sung by Tallulah after the original singer, Heidi Chicane, broke her ankle. (3.4)

Heavenly Host: Robotic servitors and guides aboard the Max Capricorn starliner *Titanic*. Capricorn had reprogrammed them to kill everyone aboard, mainly by attacking people with their razor-sharp halos. The Hosts could be deactivated with an EMP pulse but, once Capricorn was dead, they recognised the Doctor as the most senior person aboard ship and followed his instructions to fly him to the bridge and thus save the ship from crashing onto Earth. (4.X) (Voiced by EWAN BAILEY)

Hell: A name often used to describe the Void. (2.12)

Hellier & Carew: Royal Jewellers, based in the Aberdeenshire town of Hazlehead. Queen Victoria was taking the Koh-I-Noor diamond there for its annual re-cutting when she stopped for the night at the Torchwood Estate. (2.2)

Henderson, Mr: Resident of Leadworth and friend of Amy's. Amy used his car door to trap the Doctor while discussing what was going on in Leadworth with him. (5.1) (Played by ARTHUR COX)

Henrik's: Chain of London department stores, part of the JC Howell group. One branch, in which Rose Tyler worked, was damaged when the Doctor blew up a Nestene relay device on its roof and was later demolished. (1.1) Elton Pope had been shopping at a branch when he got caught up in the Auton attack. (2.10) Another branch in West London was passed by the Doctor and Donna Noble when he tried to get her to her wedding in Chiswick. (3.X)

Henry V: Play by William Shakespeare. The Doctor used the phrase 'Once more unto the breach' to the writer, which Shakespeare recognised as one of his own. (3.2)

Henry VIII, King: 15th-century English monarch. The Doctor offered Martha Jones the chance to meet him, but she declined. (3.13)

Henry XII, King: British monarch at some, as yet unrecorded, point in Britain's future. He and the Doctor shared a tipple or two. (5.2)

Hercule Poirot: Fictional Belgian detective created by Agatha Christie. His first few cases had been published when she visited Eddison Hall and fought the Vespiform alongside the Doctor and Donna Noble. (4.7)

'Here Comes The Sun': After being asked a trivia question about The Beatles while heading towards a sun aboard the SS *Pentallian*, the Doctor quoted this George Harrison composition from the group's *Abbey Road* album. (3.7)

Herefordshire: Rural English county that borders east Wales. One of its villages was Farringham, which, in 1913, was the scene of a battle between the Family of Blood and the Doctor. (3.8, 3.9)

Hermethica: Home world of the Wire, leader of a criminal gang there who could transform themselves into pure plasmic energy. (2.7)

Hermits United: The Doctor joked to Professor Yana that he, Martha Jones and Captain Jack were all members of Hermits United to explain why they knew nothing about the Utopia project. (3.11)

Hesperus, the: Vinvocci salvage ship, in orbit around Earth. It was operated by Addams and Rossiter but the Doctor used it, and them, to take him

back to the Naismith mansion, to face the Master and ultimately the Time Lords. It was equipped with laser cannons to get rid of meteors, which the Vinvocci and Wilfred Mott used to take out nuclear missiles fired at them by the Master. The Vinvocci then left Earth in it. (4.18)

Hesperus Galaxy: Initial location of the *Infinite*, provided by the datachip possessed by Gurney. (TIQ)

Hicks, Dale: Boy who vanished while playing football on a front lawn with Tom on 29 July 2012. His was the last of the children's disappearances caused by the lonely Isolus and Chloe Webber, who drew him because they needed a friend to play with. He later returned to Tom's front garden after the Isolus left Earth. (2.11) (Played by JAXON HEMBRY)

Hicks, Mr [1]: The distraught parent who added a poster of his son Dale to the posters on a lamp post asking for information about the missing children from Dame Kelly Holmes Close. (2.11) (Played by IAN HILDITCH)

Hicks, Mr [2]: Villager at the dance in Farringham when the Family of Blood attacked, killing Mr Chambers and demanding the Doctor hand himself over to them. John Smith told Hicks to warn the villagers that they should evacuate immediately. (3.9)

High Content Metal: The specific steel John Lumic invented on 'Pete's World' to build his Cyberforms from. (2.5, 2.6)

High Priestess: Elder of the Sibylline Sisterhood, who ruled her fellow sisters and had been completely turned to living stone by breathing in Pyrovillian dust. It was her psychic link with the Pyroviles that gave them their greatest power in Pompeii. (4.2) Watching her mother and fiancé change into the Master in front of her, Donna Noble remembered the High Priestess as her memories started to return. (4.17) (Played by VICTORIA WEEKS)

Highbury, Ellen: Bought Adipose capsules from Adipose Industries (4.1)

Higher Species: Term used by the Shadow Architect to describe the more powerful entities of the universe. (4.12)

Himalayas: Mountain range in Tibet, where Harry Saxon sent Captain Jack Harkness's Torchwood teammates, including Toshiko Sato, on a worthless mission, to stop Jack from contacting them. (3.12)

History teachers: One asked the young Melody Zucker about the RMS *Titanic*, and Melody told her it sank because the Doctor wasn't there to save it. When Melody was older, another History teacher quizzed her on Hitler and, again, she said his rise to power wasn't halted because the Doctor didn't stop him. (6.8) (Played by TOR CLARK and IAN DARLINGTON ROBERTS)

'Hit Me With Your Rhythm Stick': 1979 number one single for Ian Dury and the Blockheads. The Doctor was playing it to Rose Tyler in the TARDIS when he suggested they go to one of Dury's concerts. (2.2)

Hitchingson, Tom: A news reporter trying his best to report from Westminster Bridge on the Big Ben incident. (1.4) (Played by JACK TARLTON)

Hitler, Adolf: Austrian-born leader of the Nazi Party, Chancellor and then Führer of Germany in the years leading up to and during the Second World War. Wartime posters in London proclaimed that Hitler would give no warning before German air raids during the Blitz. (1.9) Winston Churchill said he would prefer the Devil in Hell to Hitler. (5.3) After Melody Zucker shot the TARDIS's Time Rotor, it wound up in 1938 Berlin, crashing into Hitler's Grand Office. It arrived at the same time as the Justice Department Vehicle *Teselecta*, which had arrived to kill him, although a few years too early. Hitler was a lousy shot, and instead of shooting the apparent assassin, Zimmerman (really the *Teselecta* in disguise) he missed and hit Melody Zucker, causing her to regenerate into River Song. Hitler himself was punched on the nose by Rory Williams, who then locked him in a cupboard. (6.8) (Played by ALBERT WELLING)

Hobbes, Professor Winfold: Pompous, opinionated and rather dull expert on Midnight who was taking his 14th trip across the planet's surface aboard the *Crusader 50*. When an entity took over the mind of one of his fellow passengers, Sky Silvestry, Hobbes veered from dogmatic insistence that nothing could live on the planet's surface to fear and paranoia, eventually causing him to join in the attempt to throw the Doctor out onto the surface. However, after Sky's villainy was revealed and she was destroyed, Hobbes sat in silence until they were rescued and returned to the Leisure Palace. (4.10) (Played by DAVID TROUGHTON)

Hockley Terrace: In the fiction created for John Smith's background, John believed this street was adjacent to Broadmarsh Street, where he thought he remembered growing up, in Nottingham. (3.9)

Hoix: Race of aggressive exoskeletal aliens with an aversion to certain warm liquids. Elton Pope encountered the Doctor and Rose Tyler trying to contain one in Woolwich, London. (2.10) Some travelled to Stonehenge, as part of the Pandorica Alliance. When the Pandorica opened and history was stopped, the Alliance members were reduced to fossils. (5.12, 5.13) (Played by PAUL KASEY and ANDY JONES)

Holland: Home country of Vincent Van Gogh. (5.10)

'Hollow Men, The': Both the Doctor and Richard Lazarus quoted this poem by TS Eliot to make their points about the benefits and negatives of the GMD that Lazarus had built. (3.6)

Holovid: One of the methods of accessing books at The Library. (4.8, 4.9)

H

Holy Writ: The official testaments, conventions and treaties of the Shadow Proclamation. (4.12)

Home Box: Equipment aboard starships that records all the information necessary during an emergency and then leaves the ship, homing in on its home world, ensuring the information gets back. River Song used the one aboard the *Byzantium* to call for help from the Doctor by leaving it in the Delerium Archive. (5.4)

Homer Simpson: 20th-century cartoon character. Ood Operations had a Translator Ball accessory for the Ood that could make the Ood sound like Homer. (4.3)

Homeworld Security: UNIT were charged with overseeing this, a programme designed to ensure Earth was safe from alien invasions. (4.4, 4.5)

Homo Reptilia: See *Silurians*

Honesty: Coming in varying strengths, this was one of the Mood Patches available in Pharmacytown in the Undercity of New New York. Cheen was wearing a patch of this, even though she was pregnant. (3.3)

Honeymoon Planet: The Doctor suggested dropping Amy Pond and Rory Williams off on this because it was a moon actually made of honey — although he then remembered it wasn't actually a moon but a carnivorous life form. But the views were lovely. . . (6.X)

Hoob: In the Pan Traffic culture, the month of Hoob is followed by Pandoff, not Clavadoe. Fitch didn't know this when asked by the Anne Droid in *The Weakest Link* aboard the Game Station. (1.12)

Hoodie: The Doctor spotted him tapping out the rhythm of the Master's hypnotic signal, being beamed down from the Archangel satellites, in a street in London. (3.12) (Played by RYAN PROBERT)

Hooper, Minnie: Friend of Wilfred Mott's and one of his Silver Cloak. She took a shine to the Doctor and pinched his bum. She was a guest at Donna Noble's wedding to Shaun Temple, and suggested she and Wilfred might be next. She once got locked inside a police box in 1962! (4.17, 4.18) (Played by JUNE WHITFIELD)

Hoover, Herbert Clark: The 31st President of the USA, holder of that position at the time of America's Wall Street Crash. All over the States, shantytowns were erected for the homeless and penniless to live in. These were called Hoovervilles, and the one in Manhattan's Central Park, run by Solomon, was attacked by the Cult of Skaro. (3.4, 3.5)

Hooverville: All over the United States of America, shantytowns were erected for the homeless and penniless to live in during the Great Depression. These were called Hoovervilles, named after the then President, Herbert Hoover. The one in Manhattan's Central Park was run by a former soldier, Solomon. Most of the people in Hooverville respected Solomon, but sometimes he had to break up fights between some of the inhabitants, such as the time one man (played by PETER BROOKE) had stolen a loaf of bread belonging to another (played by EARL PERKINS). The bread-owner was the first person to see the Daleks' Pig Slaves when they attacked Hooverville at night, shortly before the Daleks themselves arrived. (3.4, 3.5)

Hop Pyleen: Brothers who invented Hyposlip Travel Systems. They were guests aboard Platform One to see the Earthdeath spectacle. (1.2)

Hopper, Idris: Margaret Blaine's secretary. He tried, unsuccessfully, to stop the Doctor entering her office as she fled through an open window. (1.11) (Played by ALED PEDRICK)

Hoppledom 6: Planet where the fruit flies live for only twenty minutes and never mate for life. (5.12)

'Horatius': A poem by Macaulay, quoted by Mr Jefferson in tribute to Scooti Manista after she had been murdered by the possessed Toby Zed. (2.8)

Horde of Travesties, the: Participants in the Time War. (4.18)

Horsehead Nebula: The Doctor offered to show this to Rose, pointing out that, due to a galactic storm, there were fires a million miles wide burning there, but he could safely fly the TARDIS into the heart of it. (1.5)

Hoskins, Sonny: Father of the groom, Stuart, at the wedding Pete Tyler was due to attend when he was killed. Sonny was very proud of his new mobile phone. He was 'eaten' by a Reaper, one of the creatures that broke into the world after Rose Tyler's actions in saving Pete's life created a breach in time. Sonny was returned to life after Pete died again, with no memory of the incidents. (1.8) (Played by FRANK ROZELAAR-GREEN)

Hoskins, Stuart: It was on the way to Stuart's wedding to Sarah Clark that Pete Tyler was killed in a hit-and-run accident. However, when Rose Tyler saved her father's life, time was disturbed, enabling antibody-like wraiths, the Reapers, to spill into the world of 1987, wiping people out of time and feeding off the resultant chronal energy. Stuart and Sarah had met outside the Beatbox Club. Stuart's father Sonny was a victim of the Reapers but, after Pete Tyler sacrificed his life, Sonny was returned and the wedding took place, with no one recollecting what had occurred, other than the unfortunate death of Pete outside the church. (1.8) (Played by CHRISTOPHER LLEWELLYN)

Hospital: Massive complex on an island in the bay of New New York run by the Catkind Sisters of Plenitude. In fact the Sisters were breeding a whole new sub-species of humanity with every known plague, virus and illness genetically contained within them, creating a vast store of natural antibodies which could potentially cure any disease. The Hospital was also the secret lair of Lady Cassandra O'Brien and, in Ward 26, the Face of Boe waited to see the Doctor. (2.1)

Host, the: Young sickly lad, abducted from his village and forcibly infected with the Haemovariform virus, turning him into a huge werewolf. He was released on the Torchwood Estate by the moonlight which the Brethren of St Catherine had arranged for him to be bathed in. When trapped by the Torchwood telescope, and burnt by moonlight via the Koh-I-Noor diamond, the Host briefly asserted control again, begging the Doctor to kill him and destroy the Haemovariform for ever, which the Doctor did. (2.2) (Played by TOM SMITH)

Hostess: Employee of the Leisure Palace Company, whose job was to ensure the comfort of the passengers aboard the *Crusader 50* as it crossed the surface of Midnight. When an alien entity entered the mind of passenger Sky Silvestry, it began to turn everyone else against the Doctor and they were willing

to throw him out into the lethal X-tonic sunlight until the entity made a mistake and used the Doctor's catchphrase, 'molto bene', and the Hostess realised they had been tricked. She quickly grabbed Sky and threw her and herself out of the vehicle, where they were destroyed instantly by the X-tonic radiation. Afterwards, the Doctor asked if anyone knew the Hostess's name, but no one did. (4.10) Davros taunted the Doctor about how many people had died trying to help him over the years, and this made the Doctor think of the Hostess. (4.13) (Played by RAKIE AYOLA)

Hotel Adlon: Berlin hotel where River Song stole clothes from the well-to-do diners and Nazi officials and was later trapped by the *Teselecta*. (6.8)

Hotel Rooms: In the holographic hotel created within the God Complex, each room contained someone's specific fear. Room 7 was where Amy Pond saw her younger self. The Doctor saw his fear in Room 11. Howie Spragg's fear of ridicule by girls was in Room 155, while the PE Teacher came out of Room 158. The Clown and Lucy's Gorilla were both in Room 214, Tim Heath's photographer was in Room 215, and Gibbis's Weeping Angels were in 216. The Doctor rang Room 311 to attract Rita Jalal's attention. (6.11)

Houdini, Harry: 19th-century escape artist, real name Erik Weisz. Donna Noble assumed the Doctor must have met him and taken lessons in removing handcuffs. (4.3) The Doctor certainly learned how to relax his muscles, and so escape straps, from him. (DL) The Doctor judged the Calvierri Girls' ability to be invisible in mirrors worthy of Houdini. (5.6) The Doctor also used those skills to escape Oswald Fox's ropes on Poseidon. (AG04)

'Hound Dog': Blues song first recorded in 1952 by Big Momma Thornton. Elvis Presley recorded a cover version in 1956, and he later sang it on *The Ed Sullivan Show*, watched in eager anticipation by 60 million people in the USA. The Doctor wanted to take Rose Tyler to see this event live in New York. (2.7)

Hounslow Library: Donna Noble temped there for six months and mastered the Dewey Decimal System in just two days. (4.6)

Hour of Woven Words: The time at which the portal linking Earth to the Deep Darkness would open, enabling the Carrionites to dominate Earth, creating a Millennium of Blood. The Woven Words were given to a sleeping Shakespeare by Lilith to be spoken at the end of his play, *Love's Labour's Won*. (3.2)

House: Alien sentience that possessed an asteroid tucked away in a bubble universe, accessed by crossing the Void via a rift in time and space. In ages past, House would lure Time Lords to the asteroid, and while his Patchwork People would distract the Time Lords, House would drain the TARDISes of the rift energy that powered them, which he fed off. The wrecked TARDISes would then fall apart, while the Patchwork People would be constantly renewed by the bodies and organs that House would extract from the Time Lords (and any other passing travellers). As time went by and the supply of TARDISes dried up after the Time War, House began to get desperate, wanting to find a way into the main universe. When the Doctor's TARDIS came into the asteroid's universe, House sacrificed one of the Patchwork People, Idris, and drew the TARDIS's eleven-dimensional personality matrix into her. Placing his own consciousness into the TARDIS, he took control of it and piloted it back to the Doctor's universe, tormenting the imprisoned Amy Pond and Rory Williams to amuse himself. The Doctor and Idris built a new TARDIS from the junked ones on the asteroid and caught up with the TARDIS. The Doctor's TARDIS then re-established herself within the Ship, and destroyed House's sentience completely. (6.4) (Voiced by MICHAEL SHEEN)

House of Calvierri: Stately waterside mansion which the last Sister of the Water of Saturnyne had taken over, disguising herself and her son as Rosanna and Francesco Calvierri, hiding their piscine form from the locals by means of a perception filter. The device that Rosanna needed to generate a storm to drown Venice once her plan to create breeding partners for her people was complete was kept atop the mansion's bell tower. (5.6)

Household Gods: The Romans believed every home was protected by certain gods and each building had a small shrine, where effigies of the gods were blessed each morning to keep the occupants safe. Quintus Caecilius was

H

disrespectful towards the gods until the Doctor and Donna Noble saved him and his family from the destruction of Pompeii. Each morning, once his family had moved to Rome, he blessed the gods – stone effigies of the Doctor, Donna and the TARDIS. (4.2)

Housewife: Character in a television advert for a new ghost-inspired cleaning agent, Ectoshine. (2.12) (Played by MADDI CRYER)

Housing Officer: Administrator responsible for sending the Noble family to Leeds in the alternative world where Donna never met the Doctor. (4.11) (Played by SANCHIA McCORMACK)

Houston: American city in Texas, where the Johnson Space Center was based. Mia Bennett was born there, and met Andrew Stone there. Adelaide Brooke went there after graduating from Rice University. (4.17)

Howard: Market-worker that Jackie Tyler had been seeing whilst Rose was off travelling with the Doctor. He left a pair of pyjamas and a dressing gown in Jackie's flat in which she dressed the post-regenerative Doctor. Its pockets were filled with fruit, apparently for when Howard got hungry during the night. (2.X)

Howling, the: The name the Eternals gave to the Void. (2.12)

Howling Halls: The Doctor was pursuing a Living Shadow that had escaped from there when he found himself at the Pope household. Mrs Pope had been killed by the Shadow and her 4-year-old son Elton saw the Doctor with her body. (2.10)

HP Sauce: An advert for this suggested to Rose Tyler that the TARDIS had brought them to England and not 1956 New York. (2.7)

Hub, the: Torchwood Three's base, under Roald Dahl Plass in Cardiff. When Captain Jack Harkness left them to help the Doctor fight the Daleks, Ianto Jones and Gwen Cooper remained to defend their base, protected by a time lock created by Toshiko Sato. (4.12, 4.13)

Hubble Array: Colloquial name for instrumentation aboard the Hubble Space Telescope. Strictly speaking, the arrays aboard the telescope are solar reflectors used to power the device, but Sally Jacobs of UNIT used the phrase as shorthand to report that the telescope was following the course of the Sycorax ship. (2.X)

Huddersfield: West Yorkshire town where Ginger originally came from. (4.17)

Hull: Humberside city to which Kathy Nightingale was transported by the Weeping Angel that touched her in Wester Drumlins house. She met her future husband, Ben Wainwright, in a field there. (3.10)

Hull Times: Ben Wainwright showed Kathy Nightingale a copy of this newspaper to prove she was in Hull when she first arrived. (3.10)

Human Point Two: The designation Cybermen gave themselves after receiving the Ultimate Upgrade. (2.5)

Humanish: Name for one of the evolutionary routes taken by the humans of five billion years in Rose Tyler's future. It implied they were different from the now extinct (bar Lady Cassandra) humans originating from Earth itself. (1.2)

Huon Energy: Ancient energy, used in the early technology of the Time Lords. However, the Time Lords believed they had rid the universe of it billions of years ago, having realised it was lethal. The Racnoss, an enemy from the Dark Times, thrived off the energy, and the Empress, the last of her race, needed an organic key full of it to free her children, trapped at the core of the Earth. When the Torchwood Institute drew the Empress's attention, she recreated Huon particles artificially in its labs, subsequently convincing an employee of a Torchwood subsidiary company, Lance Bennett, to force-feed a co-worker, Donna Noble, with potentially fatal doses of Huon particles over six months, thus creating the key she required. Because Donna was getting married, her body became a melting pot of adrenalin and acetylcholine, setting off her endorphins and heating the theoretically inert Huon particles. This caused Donna to be almost magnetically drawn to the only other similar particles in the area, inside the Doctor's TARDIS. (3.X)

Hutchinson: Bullying school captain, who got Timothy Latimer to do his prep for him, including Latin. Latimer was a disappointment to Hutchinson, not the sort of chap he wanted in his House. When Tim had the Doctor's fob watch, he saw a future where he would save Hutchinson's life on a battlefield, and knew therefore that Hutchinson would not die in the battle with the Family of Blood. This vision came true as, a few years later in the trenches of First World War France, Tim did indeed save an injured Hutchinson from a falling German shell. (3.8, 3.9) (Played by TOM PALMER)

Hyde Park: Central London green space, where a group of children were attacked by a pterodactyl. (6.13)

Hydra Combination: The door to the Game Station's *Weakest Link* studio was strengthened by this, as was the one to the Observation Deck on Floor 056, although the Daleks still managed to cut through. (1.12, 1.13)

Hydrokinometer: Device aboard the Family of Blood's spaceship that registered the massive energy feedback going through the retrostabilisers and feeding it back through the primary heat converters, because the Doctor had pushed so many buttons. The ship then exploded. (3.9)

Hydroxiding Ribicola: A metal-eating virus the Doctor added to Baltazar's ship, which was made from Pheros living-metal. The race which had developed the virus had long become extinct, but the Doctor possessed a teaspoon, passed through generations of chefs and cooks, made from the virus. When Baltazar broke the spoon, the virus escaped and consumed his ship. (TIQ)

Hyperplex: Specially toughened glass used on 51st-century spaceships that was, all things considered, pretty unbreakable. (2.4)

Hyper-Vodka: The result of Captain Jack Harkness instructing his Chula ship's computer to activate Emergency Protocol 417 was the arrival of this drink. Jack recalled that, the last time he had faced execution, he'd had four for breakfast and, instead of dying, ended up in bed with both his executioners. (1.10)

Hyposlip Travel Systems: A form of transportation invented by the brothers Hop Pyleen. (1.2)

Hywel, King of the Welsh: Presented the Cup of Athelstan to the English King Athelstan at his coronation in the tenth century. (4.15)

'I Can't Decide': Song by the Scissor Sisters, from their *Ta-Dah* album. The Master played and sang it one morning aboard the *Valiant* as he pushed the artificially aged Doctor around in a wheelchair. (3.13)

'I Could Have Danced All Night': The Doctor returned from a Versailles party with Madame de Pompadour, pretending to be drunk, to fool the Clockwork Robots into letting him pour anti-oil into them. To aid the deception, he sang this song from *My Fair Lady*, the musical version of *Pygmalion*. (2.4)

'I'm Confessin' That I Love You': One of the gramophone records, performed by Al Bowly, played by Greeves the butler at Lady Eddison's garden party in honour of Agatha Christie. (4.7)

'I Wish It Could Be Christmas Everyday': Perennial Christmas song by Wizzard that was played aboard the starliner *Titanic* on its journey between Sto and Earth. (4.X)

Ice Cream Man: He was confused by the Atraxi voice booming out of his van's speakers instead of the expected *Clair de Lune*. (5.1) (PLAYED BY PERRY BENSON)

Ice Warriors: Militaristic and noble indigenous population of Mars who may have discovered the Flood and been responsible for freezing them centuries ago, before leaving the planet for ever. (4.16)

Iceland: The city of Pola Ventura, not Reykjavik, hosted Murder Spree 20. Rose Tyler didn't know this when asked by the Anne Droid in *The Weakest Link* aboard the Game Station. (1.12) Lord de Souza lost all his money during the Icelandic bank crisis of the early 21st century (4.15)

Idris: One of the Patchwork People, a humanoid woman trapped on the sentient asteroid House. She was kept alive by House over many centuries to act as a lure for Time Lords and other travellers that were drawn into House's pocket universe. House fed off the rift energy that powered TARDISes and it would reuse limbs and organs from the dead pilots to keep the Patchwork People alive. Idris finally died when House, running low on energy, had to sacrifice one of his Patchwork People and her soul and mind were drained by Nephew, allegedly, into his translator ball. House drew the eleven-dimensional personality matrix out of the Doctor's TARDIS, and placed it in her dead body, while placing its own consciousness into the TARDIS. Idris's body, now possessed by the TARDIS, helped the Doctor to build a new TARDIS from all the junked TARDIS remnants on House's now deserted asteroid. Together they followed the Doctor's TARDIS, now possessed by House, as it crossed the Void from House's bubble universe towards the Doctor's universe and eventually the matrix was drawn out of Idris's body and back into the TARDIS, while House was destroyed. Idris's human body then finally died – but not before telling Rory rather cryptically that 'the only water in the forest is the river' – a reference to the people of the Gamma Forests. (6.4) (Played by SURANNE JONES)

IE24: News channel on 'Pete's World'. An IE24 newscaster (played by DUNCAN DUFF) tried to warn the population about the Cybermen. (2.5, 2.6)

Il Divo: Multinational pop-opera singing group, of which Jackie Tyler was a fan. When she was flirting with Elton Pope, she played their song 'Regresa A Mi'. (2.10)

Immortality Gate, the: Device which Joshua Naismith stole from the Torchwood Institute and installed on two storeys of his mansion. He believed that, with the Master's help, the Gate would give his daughter Abigail immortality. In actual fact, the Gate was a medical device created by the Vinvocci and used to restore people after illness or injury. But rather than one at a time, it would take the biological imprint of a species and restore whole groups of people at once. The Master reprogrammed it to read his genetic imprint and flood that over every human on Earth, turning them into him, both mentally and physically, at a cellular level. Two Vinvocci on Earth, masquerading as part of Naismith's team, were scavengers, trying to get the Gate off-planet and back home (it had originally come in another Vinvocci ship that had crash-landed in Wales). The Gate itself was powered by a Nuclear Bolt, controlled from two identical glass booths which maintained the feedback levels at all times, one booth locked and occupied, the other unlocked and empty, with booth shifts changing at regular intervals. Wilfred Mott was trapped inside one of these booths after the Time Lords were vanquished, and he was in danger of absorbing all the lethal radiation, so the Doctor went into the second booth, freeing Wilfred but absorbing all the Nuclear Bolt's radiation himself, which caused his regeneration. The Gate itself was presumably dismantled and taken by the authorities once Joshua and Abigail Naismith were arrested and imprisoned. (4.17, 4.18)

'In The Bleak Midwinter': Christmas song, based on a Christina Rossetti poem, set to music by Holst. Abigail Pettigrew sang this to the injured Fog Shark to calm it while the Doctor turned her cryogenic chamber into a container so they could take the Fog Shark home. (6.X)

'In The Mood': The Doctor and Rose danced to this swing number composed by Glenn Miller, watched by Captain Jack Harkness in the TARDIS control room. (1.10)

India: Their nuclear weapons were primed and ready to strike the Sontaran mothership in Earth's orbit. (4.4, 4.5) Lady Clemency Eddison met an alien shapeshifter called Christopher there and fell pregnant by him, returning ashamed to England with only Mrs Chandrakala as her confidante. (4.7) According to Dicken's Ganger, there were over ten million Gangers in India working for Morpeth-Jetsan. (6.6)

Inducer: Computer system at Adipose Industries which Matron Cofelia used to induce parthenogenesis in Adipose Capsule users, turning them into Adipose young. The Doctor deactivated it, saving nearly everyone's life. (4.1)

Infinite Temporal Flux: Time is not linear and, as the Doctor explained to Martha Jones, the future can be changed. Although in Martha's world, the Carrionites did not destroy Earth, that didn't mean it couldn't happen in 1599; if it did, the future Martha was from would just fade away, as would she, as time corrected itself to cope with the temporal change. (3.2)

Infinite, the: A mysterious ship from the Dark Times of the universe. Lost for millennia, the ship once contained an ancient entity that could offer someone their Heart's Desire. When the Doctor, Martha Jones and Baltazar located it, the Great Old One who inhabited it had long since died, and only an echo of its power remained, enough to show Martha her Heart's Desire (the Doctor) and

Baltazar his (gold and treasures). But these images were illusory, and the Doctor used his sonic screwdriver to deliver a final sonic pulse which weakened the ship and broke it apart for ever. (TIQ)

Infostamps: Primitive devices used by the Cybermen trapped in Victorian London to learn all they could about Earth. Each Infostamp contained a certain amount of information about the history of London from 1066 up to the mid 1800s – the information most likely originally gleaned by the Daleks, as the Infostamps also contained everything the Daleks knew about the Doctor. The Infostamps were powered by a Cyclo-Steinham core, which could disable a Cyberman when released directionally. Jackson Lake was having a nervous breakdown after the death of his wife and his susceptible mind absorbed all the information about the Doctor from an Infostamp, causing him to believe he was actually the Doctor, albeit an amnesiac version of the Time Lord. The Doctor used all of them at once to free Miss Hartigan's mind from Cyber control when she was piloting the CyberKing. (4.14)

Ingleby Workhouse: A Victorian Workhouse for orphaned children. Its master Mr Cole came under Cyber control and led his charges to the place where the Cybermen were building the engine for their CyberKing. The children were forced to work there, while Cole was killed. (4.14)

Inspector: Venetian official, who initially tried to stop the Doctor, Amy Pond and Rory Williams from entering the city, believing they might be plague carriers. When the Doctor's psychic paper told him that the Doctor was the Pope, he let them in. (5.6) (Played by MICHAEL PERCIVAL)

Intensive Care: Massive area concealed in the Hospital on New Earth where the Sisters of Plenitude had grown human clones, riddled with every disease, virus and contagion known to them. They planned to use the clones as stock for cures, but Lady Cassandra O'Brien let the patients out and they rampaged through the Hospital until the Doctor cured them with their own antibodies mixed into a massive cocktail of drugs. (2.1)

Interface: Automated system within the Twostreams Facility which acted as a guide to Amy Pond when she was trapped in the Green Waterfall time stream on Apalapucia. Amy was able to reprogram it to help her avoid the Handbots. (6.10) (Voiced by IMELDA STAUNTON)

Intergalactic Rules of Engagement: Possibly an edict from the Shadow Proclamation, the Doctor cited Jurisdiction Two of these to General Staal aboard the Sontaran mothership. (4.5)

International Electromatics: One of the Cybus Industries dummy companies on 'Pete's World' – and the name on the side of the pantechnicon which Mr Crane used to collect people and bring them for Cyber-conversion at the Battersea Power Station factories. (2.5)

International Gallery: South London art gallery and museum which was hosting an exhibition including the Cup of Athelstan. Cat burglar Lady Christina de Souza managed to break in and steal the cup from under the noses of the Security Chief and his staff. (4.15)

International Olympic Committee: News commentator Huw Edwards believed the IOC would have to hold an enquiry into how 80,000 people had disappeared then reappeared at the Olympic Stadium in Stratford, East London in 2012. (2.11)

International Rescue: Fictional organisation that helped people in distress. The Doctor told the avatar hologram from the time engine that he was Captain Troy Handsome from the organisation. (5.11)

Ionic Fusion Bar: The genetic weapon designed to wipe out the Viperox and brought to Earth by Rivesh Mantilax was disguised as this, a piece of his ship's power drive. (DL)

Ionic power: The power the Isolus used, via Chloe Webber, to transport the children (and cats) away from Dame Kelly Holmes Close and transmute them into living drawings, drawn by Chloe. (2.11)

Iowa: State in America where Andrew Stone was born. (4.16)

Ipswich: City in Suffolk, UK. Rose Tyler caustically commented that maybe she could go there instead of being trapped inside a Viewing Gallery on Platform One. (1.2)

Ironside Project: Professor Edwin Bracewell developed what he thought were a duo of war machines he called the Ironsides, to help Winston Churchill win the Second World War. The Ironsides actually created Bracewell themselves and set the whole plan in motion – and the Doctor immediately recognised them for what they were – Daleks (5.3)

Isabella [1]: 17-year-old daughter of the Venetian boat builder, Guido. She agreed to join the Calvierri School for Girls, unaware that to do so would result in her slowly having her blood replaced by Rosanna Calvierri's and becoming a 'vampire', ultimately destined to become a Saturnyne and breed with the thousands of male Saturnynes living in the canals. Shortly after her transformation began, she found Amy Pond and helped free her from Rosanna's clutches. However, she was already becoming a Saturnyne herself. As a result,

she couldn't survive in pure sunlight and so remained in the House of Calvierri. Rosanna punished her for the betrayal by throwing her into the canal, where she was eaten by the piranhic Saturnyne males. (5.6) (Played by ALISHA BAILEY)

Isabella [2]: Sister of Abigail Pettigrew. She, her nephew Benjamin and Benjamin's children visited Kazran Sardick to beg to be allowed to 'borrow' Abigail for Christmas Day but, because they still owed 4,500 Gideons, Sardick refused. When the Doctor went back through time, trying to change Sardick's past, he took Abigail to the family on Christmas Eve, when Isabella was younger and they enjoyed an early family Christmas. (6.X) (Played by MEG WYNN-OWEN and LAURA ROGERS)

Iserlohn: German town where Steffi Ehrlich was from. (4.16)

Ishem, Sergeant: US Air Force officer at Dreamland who was alarmed to see Canton Delaware III emerge from the Doctor's cell days after he went in, and was more amazed to see President Nixon follow Canton out. (6.2) (Played by TOMMY CAMPBELL)

Isle of Dogs: Where Blon Fel Fotch Pasameer-Day Slitheen ended up after teleporting away from the destruction of 10 Downing Street, finding herself in a rubbish skip. (1.5, 1.11)

Isle of Sheppy: According to Morpeth-Jetsan contractor Buzzer, a Ganger working on Sheppy had been electrocuted and gone rogue, killing his sleeping human template in his rig-harness. (6.5)

Isle of Wight: Watching the creation of Earth as it formed around a Racnoss Webstar over four billion years ago, Donna Noble joked to the Doctor that one particular piece of rock was the Isle of Wight, the small island off the British south coast. (3.X)

Isolus: Empathic beings of intense emotion, who drifted through space after leaving the Deep Realms. The Mother Isolus jettisoned roughly four billion offspring, which rode the solar tides in their ovoid podships for thousands of years, their empathic link keeping them connected no matter how far apart they were physically. They could not survive for long if they were alone. They used ionic energy to create make-believe worlds and survived on the love they felt for one another. One Isolus child fell to Earth after its podship encountered a solar flare and, separated from its craft, it sought refuge in the lonely Chloe Webber and used her drawing abilities to create images of the local children. The Isolus then used ionic energy to transport the children away from reality and into an ionic holding pen, where it played with them. This manifested itself in the real world as animated images of the children and animals that Chloe drew. When Rose Tyler located the podship, she returned it to a heat source, the Olympic Torch that was passing by Dame Kelly Holmes Close. Transported warmly in that, the Isolus was then able to return to its collective once the Doctor added the Torch to the Olympic Bowl, creating a massive influx of heat and energy. (2.11)

Isop Galaxy: The oldest inhabitant of this galaxy was the Face of Boe. Rose Tyler knew this when asked by the Anne Droid in *The Weakest Link* aboard the Game Station. (1.12)

'It Had To Be You': Song being sung in the drinking den that the Doctor entered shortly before an air raid, until when he had been unaware of when the TARDIS had landed. (1.9)

Ital, Doctor Tarak: Senior medical officer aboard Bowie Base One on Mars. When the team lost contact with the bio-dome, he went with Captain Adelaide Brooke and the Doctor to try and locate Maggie Cain and Andy Stone. In the bio-dome, Tarak was himself captured by Andrew Stone and infected by the Flood, becoming its third agent on the base. Tarak's body was destroyed along with the Flood that possessed him when Bowie Base exploded. (4.16) (Played by CHOOK SIBTAIN)

ITV: Collective name for a consortium of British independent television channels. The Doctor suggested that the galaxy would implode if their programming was viewed on Christmas Night. He may have been telling a fib. (AotG)

Jabe: Charming and flirtatious lead representative from the Forest of Cheem, who visited Platform One to witness Earthdeath. Her ancestors were from a tropical rainforest on Earth. She could project a liana from her wrists. She presented the Doctor with a sapling of her grandfather and later, after learning of the Time Lord's heritage, devoted herself to helping him save the space station. Jabe died when the sunfilters protecting Platform One collapsed and the sun's heat flooded through the Ventilation Chamber, burning her wooden body in seconds. (1.2) Davros taunted the Doctor about how many people had died trying to help him over the years, and this made the Doctor think of Jabe. (4.13) (Played by YASMIN BANNERMAN)

Jack the Ripper: Notorious serial killer in Victorian London. His reign of terror was brought to an end in 1888 by the Silurian, Madame Vastra, who ate him. (6.7)

Jackson [1]: A footman in the service of the MacLeish family in Torchwood House. He was killed by the Werewolf. (2.2)

Jackson [2]: Schoolboy at Farringham School for Boys in 1913, who hid alcohol in the cricket pavilion. (3.8)

Jackson [3]: DI McMillan's driver. (4.15) (Played by VICTOR RICHARDS)

Jackson, Alan: Neighbour of Sarah Jane Smith's in Ealing, whose daughter was Luke Smith's best friend. Alan and Maria were holidaying in Cornwall when 26 planets appeared in the skies above Earth. (4.12)

Jackson, Maria: Young girl who lived opposite Sarah Jane Smith and became friends were her and Luke, Sarah Jane's adopted son. In the alternative world where Donna Noble never met the Doctor, Maria died alongside them in the Royal Hope Hospital after the Judoon moved it to the moon. (4.11) She was holidaying in Cornwall with her father when 26 planets appeared in Earth's sky. (4.12)

Jackson, Michael: American pop star infamous for having cosmetic surgery. Rose Tyler likened Lady Cassandra to him. (1.2)

Jackson, Mr: Villager at the dance in Farringham when the Family of Blood attacked, killing Mr Chambers and demanding the Doctor hand himself over to them. (3.9)

Jacob [1]: One of the Lever Room operators responsible for bombarding the Wall with particle energy via the giant Levers during a Ghost Shift. He was killed by Cyberleader One, who arrived to take over Torchwood Tower. (2.12)

Jacob [2]: Son of Benjamin who, along with other members of his family, visited Kazran Sardick on Christmas Eve to try and secure the release of his great aunt, Abigail Pettigrew, for Christmas Day. When Sardick refused, Jacob threw a lump of coal at him. Sardick nearly hit Jacob, but stopped himself, and seeing this made the Doctor realise that the potential existed to change Sardick's character by altering his past. (6.X) (Played by BAILEY PEPPER)

and this provoked him into confronting the Minotaur and destroying it. (6.11) (Played by AMARA KARAN)

Jalandra: UNIT soldier in New York who was knocked over when Earth was moved to the Medusa Cascade. He was later exterminated by the Daleks alongside General Sanchez as Martha Jones escaped with the Osterhagen key. (4.12) (Played by MIKE FREEMAN)

James Bond: Fictional spy featured in many popular movies. Martha Jones likened the Doctor to him as they walked to the LazLabs reception because the Doctor was wearing a tuxedo. (3.6) Sean Connery's performance as Bond in the movies was one of the highlights of 1963, according to the Doctor. (AG01) Rory mentioned him to Black Rod when discussing spies. (AG05)

James I, King: Protestant King of England, also James VI of Scotland. The Gunpowder Plotters planned to murder him and marry the future Elizabeth I off to a Catholic. (AG05)

James, Group Captain Tennant: One of the arrivals at 10 Downing Street after the Big Ben incident. An RAF officer, he was actually a disguised Slitheen, the original James having been killed previously. (1.5)

Jamie: A young boy who had been wearing his gas mask during an air raid in the Blitz. He was killed (massive head trauma on the left side, partial collapse of his chest cavity on the right and a gash on the back of his right hand) but was reanimated by the Chula nanogenes that had leaked out of a crashed medical transport ship. His only thought was to be reunited with his mother, and he wandered the streets of London, a gas mask of flesh and bone grown from his face, asking everyone, 'Are you my mummy?' Because the nanogenes were unaware of what a human looked like, they began transforming all humans they came into contact with into gas-mask zombies. In the end the nanogenes were able to use DNA from both him and his mother, Nancy, and restore him to normal. (1.9, 1.10) (Played by ALBERT VALENTINE, voiced by NOAH JOHNSON)

Jacobs, Sally: An operative in UNIT's Mission Control base beneath the Tower of London. As her blood group was A+, she was hypnotised by the Sycorax. (2.X) (Played by ANITA BRIEM)

Jaggit Brocade: A conglomeration of planets, of which Crespallion was a member. (1.2)

Jagrafess: See *Mighty Jagrafess of the Holy Hadrojassic Maxarodenfoe, the*

Jahoo: One of the planets stolen by the Daleks and secreted a second out of sync within the Medusa Cascade. The Doctor eventually returned it to its rightful place in space and time. (4.12, 4.13)

Jailer: Unpleasant man who guided the Doctor's party around Bedlam as they sought out Peter Streete, the architect of the Globe theatre. (3.2) (Played by STEPHEN MARCUS)

Jalal, Doctor M: Parent to Rita, who she saw in her hotel room within the God Complex. He was castigating her for her lapses in school, claiming she brought disgrace onto the family. (6.11) (Played by RASHID KARAPIET)

Jalal, Rita: A human doctor and de facto leader of a group of prisoners who found themselves aboard the God Complex. The Doctor took a liking to Rita because she was determined and smart and refused to panic. Her Muslim faith kept her strong, although she believed she was in Jahannam, or Hell. Her biggest fear was the disappointment of her father, but also losing her faith – and when she was finally killed by the Minotaur, she had found peace within herself. The Doctor, who had offered to take her aboard the TARDIS was furious at her death,

Jamieson, George: Lord Provost of Aberdeen in 1879. Queen Victoria believed, thanks to the Doctor's psychic paper, that he had assigned the Doctor as her protector for her journey to Balmoral Castle. (2.2)

Janitor: German cleaner in the Chancellery in Berlin, 1938. He had been replaced by the *Teselecta* at some point. The original man's fate was undisclosed. (6.8) (Played by JOHN JENNER)

Japan: The Doctor, Rose Tyler and Captain Jack Harkness visited Kyoto when it was still the capital city of Japan in 1336, the year that the civil wars of the Yoshino period began. The Doctor explained that they only just escaped. (1.12) During the year that the Master and the Toclafane ruled Earth, the islands of Japan were destroyed, and Martha Jones was the only survivor. (3.13) The Daleks landed there. (4.12) The Doctor told Lady Christina de Souza that he had observed the war between China and Japan (whether this was the First or Second Sino-Japanese War wasn't clear). (4.15)

Japanese Girls: Three vox pops students who loved the ghosts and wanted to be ghosts because they were really spooky. (2.12) (Played by KYOKO MORITA, ERIKO KURASAWA, MARI YOSHIDA)

Jask, Commander: Sontaran officer on Earth, engaged in a battle with Martha Jones and Mickey Smith. The Doctor stopped him with a swift blow to the probic vent. (4.18) (Played by DAN STARKEY)

Jason: Neighbour of Jackie Tyler's who had A+ blood and was thus affected by the Sycorax's blood control. After the threat had passed, he and his partner Sandra watched as the Sycorax ash fell over the Powell Estate, mistakenly believing it to be snow. (2.X) (Played by PAUL ANDERSON)

Jast, Dalek: Former Force Leader of the Outer Rim Defensive Dalek Battalion, later one of the Cult of Skaro, who brought the Genesis Ark to Earth in a

Void ship after the Time War ended. (2.12, 2.13) After fleeing the Battle of Canary Wharf via an emergency temporal shift, along with the rest of the Cult, Jast ended up in Manhattan in 1930. Jast accompanied Dalek Caan for their attack on Hooverville. The Cult used gamma radiation to activate their new Dalek-Human army but, when the army turned on their creators, Jast was destroyed on the stage of the Laurenzi theatre. (3.4, 3.5) (Operated by ANTHONY SPARGO (2.12, 2.13) and DAVID HANKINSON (3.4, 3.5), voiced by NICHOLAS BRIGGS)

Jate: Guard working in the Radiation Room in the Silo base on Malcassairo. When the Futurekind Wiry Woman sabotaged the power systems, all the safety devices went down and Jate died, vaporised by the stet radiation. (3.11) (Played by OLIVER HOPKINS)

Jate, Emperor: The Emperor who defined the measurement of length from his nose to his fingertip as a paab, not a goffe. Rodrick didn't know this when asked by the Anne Droid in *The Weakest Link* aboard the Game Station. (1.12)

Jathaa Sun-Glider: An alien ship that flew across the Shetland Islands ten years before the Battle of Canary Wharf. Torchwood shot it down, accusing it of crossing into Britain's airspace, and then stripped it for resources, including its weaponry, which was subsequently used to destroy the Sycorax ship as it left Earth's atmosphere. (2.X, 2.12)

Jatt, Sister: One of the Sisters of Plenitude, she monitored the experiments on the humans in the secret Intensive Care Unit beneath the Hospital on New Earth. Trying to escape from the infectious patients, Jatt became their first victim when a patient's hand brushed against her face, spreading its numerous viruses into her immunity-free body, killing her instantly. (2.1) (Played by ADJOA ANDOH)

Javit: Catkind car driver in the Fast Lane on the New New York Motorway who tried to warn Milo and Cheen that the Fast Lane was dangerous. (Played by DAISY LEWIS) She had two vestal virgin girls with her (played by HOLLY DYMOCK, HALEY JONES), and all three died when the Macra clawed their way into their car. (3.3)

JC Howell: Parent company for the Henrik's chain of stores. (1.1, 2.10, 3.X)

Jed: Worker at the Mutton Street gasworks who Jackson Lake paid to help repair his 'Tardis'. (4.14) (Played by NEIL McDERMOTT)

Jeff: Name by which, so the Doctor claimed to Jacob on Ember, he knew Santa Claus. (6.X)

Jefferson, Colonel: Commander of Area 51 in 1969. (6.2)

Jefferson, John Maynard: The Torchwood Archive's Head of Security aboard Sanctuary Base 6. A tough, no-nonsense officer, he was greatly impressed by Zachary Cross Flane's leadership after their original captain, Walker, died. He was once married, but something traumatic occurred and, according to the Beast, his wife never forgave him for it. Jefferson led Danny Bartock, Toby Zed and Rose Tyler through the ventilation ducts of Sanctuary Base 6 to escape the pursuing Ood, who were possessed by the Beast. Each duct needed to be flooded with oxygen before they could enter and, as one area was delayed, he volunteered to keep the Ood away while his compatriots escaped. Realising he would not be able to reach his friends in time, Jefferson asked Cross Flane to remove all the air

from the area he was in, giving him a quicker death than he'd have had if the Ood had caught him. After his death, Cross Flane entered a commendation into his personal file. (2.8, 2.9) (Played by DANNY WEBB)

Jefferson, Thomas: Second President of the United States of America and one of the Founding Fathers. A street in Florida was named after him and the Doctor realised that the little girl trapped inside a NASA spacesuit was located nearby. (6.1)

Jeffrey: A Welsh civil servant, and father to Cathy Salt's unborn child. (1.11)

Jehovah: Judaeo-Christian deity cited by both Javit and Thomas Brannigan on the New New York Motorway. (3.3)

Jenkins: Schoolboy at Farringham School for Boys in 1913, who had been sent to see the school's Matron with a cold, although he was actually missing his mother. (3.8)

Jenkins, David: A friend of Melina's, who she was threatening to kill for reasons Sophie Benson never revealed to husband Craig Owens. (6.12)

Jenkins, Matilda: Private Jenkins's mother. He struggled to remember her name as he began his transformation into a gas-mask zombie. (1.10)

Jenkins, Private: Married soldier who was ill at the Chula ship crash site. Algy left him to guard Nancy, but Jenkins had been infected by Chula nanogenes and transformed into a gas-mask zombie. He was kept quiet by Nancy singing 'Rock-A-Bye-Baby'. (1.10) (Played by MARTIN HODGSON)

Jenkins, Private Ross: UNIT soldier who accompanied the Doctor to the Rattigan Academy and helped him overcome the SatNav that tried to kill them after they left. He died fighting Sontarans at the ATMOS factory when his gun wouldn't fire due to the Sontarans' Cordolaine Signal. (4.4, 4.5) (Played by CHRISTIAN COOKE)

Jenner, Sergeant Ian: UNIT officer and Captain Magambo's number two at the Gladwell road tunnel situation. (4.15) (Played by JAMES LAYTON)

Jenny [1]: A maid at Farringham School for Boys, she befriended Martha Jones, who was pretending to be in domestic service. Together they suffered the taunts of the boys and early 20th-century society's attitudes and mores. Jenny was a happy-go-lucky girl, always smiling, until she encountered a group of Scarecrows, who kidnapped her and took her to the Family of Blood's invisible spaceship, where she died screaming as Mother of Mine took on her form. (3.8) (Played by REBEKAH STATON)

Jenny [2]: An artificially created Generation 5000 soldier cloned from the Doctor's DNA on Messaline, effectively making her his daughter. She was militaristic and driven, but she and the Doctor gradually warmed to one another, and Jenny quickly learned to take aboard his morals and compassion. When the Doctor exposed the truth on Messaline to both the human and Hath soldiers, General Cobb of the humans tried to murder him, but Jenny took the bullet instead and apparently died. Heartbroken, the Doctor, Donna Noble and Martha Jones left Jenny interred on Messaline, but she was revived by the gaseous compound released by the recently activated third-generation terraforming

device the humans called the Source. Stealing a shuttle from the humans, Jenny took off into space, hoping to have adventures just like her father's. (4.6) Davros taunted the Doctor about how many people had died trying to help him over the years, and this made the Doctor think of Jenny. (4.13) (Played by GEORGIA MOFFETT)

Jenny [3]: Human aide to the Silurian Madame Vastra in Victorian London. Capable with most forms of hand-held weaponry, she joined her mistress in helping reunite the Doctor and Amy Pond when the TARDIS took them both to Demon's Run. She was later returned home by River Song. (6.7) (Played by CATRIN STEWART)

Jericho Street Junior School: Where Rose Tyler went to school, and joined their Under-7s gymnastics team. (1.1)

Jethro: One of the inhabitants of Hooverville in 1930s Manhattan. Solomon told him to stay with the rest of the people there when they were attacked by the Pig Slaves. (3.5)

Jim [1]: Prospective boyfriend for Jackie Tyler, that Rose presumably disapproved of – Jackie promised she'd ditch him if Rose stayed at home and stopped travelling with the Doctor. (1.5) He caused Rose and Jackie to miss their New Year's Eve parties because his car axle broke. (4.18)

Jim [2]: One of the young boys Nancy was looking after on the streets of Blitzed London. He had been evacuated to a family in the country, but fled back home to London. Although he couldn't read or write, Jim was determined to send a letter to his missing dad using an old typewriter. After he stopped typing, the 'Empty Child' began psychically using the typewriter. (1.9, 1.10) (Played by JOSEPH TREMAIN)

J

Jim [3]: One of the bridge crew aboard the *Teselecta*. He collected Amy Pond and Rory Williams when they first arrived aboard, and was later attacked by the Anti-Bodies and teleported away to safety, back to the Mothership. (6.8) (Played by DAVOOD GHADAMI)

Jim the Fish: Someone River Song and the Doctor knew and liked. He was building a dam. (6.1)

Jimbo [1]: Nickname given to one of Lady Cassandra's robotic spiders aboard Platform One by the Doctor. (1.2)

Jimbo [2]: Adipose Industries worker who kept the printers stocked with paper. (4.1)

'Jingle Bells': The popular name for a song called 'One Horse Open Sleigh', composed by James Pierpont. It was played by the lethal Christmas Tree placed in the Tylers' flat by the Roboform Santas. (2.X) They played it again while waiting to attack at Donna Noble's wedding reception. (3.X) It was played by the band aboard the *Titanic* during its journey from Sto to Earth. (4.X)

Jodrell Bank: UK-based radio telescope installation which traced the ATMOS activation signal to the Sontarans in Earth's orbit. (4.4, 4.5) The Doctor contacted them to set up his trap for Prisoner Zero. (5.1)

Joe [1]: One of the employees at Clancy's Garage, working alongside Mickey Smith. (2.X) (Played by PHILL KIRK)

Joe [2]: Jocular driver of the *Crusader 50*. He was killed when the creature from the surface of Midnight ripped his cabin away. (4.10) (Played by TONY BLUTO)

Johannesburg: Largest city in South Africa. Hutchinson, House Captain at Farringham School for Boys, heard that his father was going there. Timothy Latimer's uncle had been there on a six-month posting and loved it. (3.8)

John, Elton: British singer and pianist (real name Reginald Dwight), who Elton Pope's parents named him after. (2.10)

John Rambo: American soldier in a series of movies based on the book *First Blood*. Donna likened the human soldier Cline to him, on Messaline. (4.6)

John Steed: Fictional character from the British TV series *The Avengers* who was one of the highlights of 1963, according to the Doctor. (AG01)

John, Uncle: Eddie Connolly's brother-in-law, who was present at the Connollys' house when Rita threw Eddie out. (2.7) (Played by RICHARD RANDELL)

John-Joe: Boyfriend to Sanderson & Grainger shop worker Kelly. (6.12)

Johnny Franzetta: Character in Colin Skinner's unpublished novel, 'Ghost Train', as read by Skinner to the other members of LINDA. (2.10)

Johnson Space Center: Houston-based facility, which looked after most NASA space flights, as 'Main Mission Control'. Adelaide Brooke, Tarak Ital, Yuri Kerenski and Mia Bennett trained there. (4.16)

Jolco and Jolco: Firm of solicitors who sent the Moxx of Balhoon to represent them at the Earthdeath ceremony on Platform One. (1.2)

Jolie, Angelina: According to Lance Bennett, Donna Noble talked excitedly about this American actor and her on/off relationship with actor Brad Pitt. (3.X)

Jolly Roger, the: Flag that marked a ship which had fallen into pirate hands. Henry Avery was amongst the first to use the skull and crossbones flag, aboard the *Fancy*. (6.3)

Jonathan: Young London boy who, like his father and sister, had A+ blood and was thus affected by the Sycorax's blood control. (2.X) (Played by JOSH HUGHES)

Jones: The sentient computer that ran the systems on the Poseidon sub-aquatic base. It was a Class 14 AI, with a Nexus Prime processor. (AG04) (Voiced by SARAH DOUGLAS)

Jones, Catherine Zeta: Tish Jones compared the age difference between herself and Professor Lazarus to that between the Welsh actress and her husband Michael Douglas. (3.6)

Jones, Clive: Martha Jones's father, who had abandoned his wife Francine to set up home with a younger woman, Annalise – a source of considerable bitterness among the Jones family. After a row between his girlfriend and estranged wife at his son Leo's 21st birthday party, Clive had an argument with Annalise. Whether they remained a couple after this is unknown. Clive was later captured by Harry Saxon's minions and taken to his old house. There, along with Francine, he tried to persuade Martha to return home, so that she and the Doctor could be captured. Clive warned Martha, though he knew it would mean his own imprisonment. He was also unaffected by the subliminal hypnotic sound being beamed down from the Archangel satellite network, and realised that Saxon was not exactly what he seemed. After being taken aboard the *Valiant*, he spent a year as a cleaner on the lower decks. As such, when the Paradox Machine was activated, he was one of the few people on Earth for whom the previous 12 months wasn't erased. Martha quit travelling with the Doctor to look after Clive and Francine, who were understandably in shock, although the year's events had brought them closer again. (3.1, 3.12, 3.13) (Played by TREVOR LAIRD)

Jones, Danny: Member of pop group McFly, who endorsed Harry Saxon's campaign to become Prime Minister. (3.12)

Jones, Francine: Businesswoman and mother of Martha Jones. Separated, acrimoniously, from her husband Clive, Francine detested Clive's new girlfriend Annalise, who she saw as an ignorant gold-digger. Francine attended the demonstration of the GMD at LazLabs as a guest of her other daughter, Tish, who was head of PR there. She took her son, Leo, as her escort for the night, and he was injured when the Lazarus Creature attacked. Already suspicious of the

J

Doctor and Martha's friendship, she was distraught when both Martha and Tish remained with the Doctor and pursued Lazarus. A Mysterious Man, who had approached her during the demonstration, returned to warn her about the Doctor – although she was most likely fed a number of lies, as the Mysterious Man was a minion in the employ of future Prime Minister Harry Saxon (aka the Master). Having failed to contact Martha – who had left with the Doctor in the TARDIS – Francine agreed to help Saxon's people if it would rid her daughter of the Doctor's

influence, and she allowed a number of her phone calls from Martha to be recorded by a Sinister Woman in an effort to trace the time travellers. Eventually Saxon's people found Clive and brought him home, hoping that a fake reunion between her parents might persuade Martha to break cover. But Clive warned his daughter and, to Francine's horror, the Sinister Woman revealed her true colours and had both of them arrested, along with Tish. Taken aboard the *Valiant*, Francine spent a year as a maid serving the Master, after he had unleashed the Toclafane on Earth, and she had to watch as he slaughtered millions. When the Doctor eventually defeated the Master, the distraught Francine was prepared to shoot him dead, but the Doctor quickly talked her out of it. Because she had been aboard the ship when the Paradox Machine was activated she was one of the few people on Earth for whom the previous 12 months wasn't erased. Martha quit travelling with the Doctor to look after her parents, who were understandably in shock. (3.1, 3.6, 3.7, 3.12, 3.13) When Martha used the Project Indigo prototype to escape New York, it brought her home to Francine and the two of them were contacted by former Prime Minister Harriet Jones. Martha left her mother hiding from the Dalek onslaught when she teleported to Germany. Francine survived the invasion and joined the celebrations when the Earth was returned from the Medusa Cascade. (4.12, 4.13) (Played by ADJOA ANDOH)

Jones, Harriet: MP for Flydale North, she arrived at 10 Downing Street for a meeting about Cottage Hospitals (her mother was sick in Flydale Infirmary), but was ignored and ended up hiding in the Cabinet Room. There she discovered that the Family Slitheen had replaced the most senior people in Downing Street. She eventually helped the Doctor and Rose to defeat the Slitheen. (1.4, 1.5) In the wake of these events, she went on to become Prime Minister of Britain, although an Act of Parliament banned her from writing an autobiography. Once in office, she successfully implemented her New Cottage Hospital Scheme. She and the Doctor met again after she had made first contact with the alien Sycorax. However, her time as Prime Minister was cut short when she angered the Doctor by destroying the fleeing Sycorax spaceship. He used just six words, spoken to her aide, to bring down her government. (2.X) On 'Pete's World', she became President of Great Britain, ushering in a Golden Age that actually saw severe climate change as hothouse gases, exacerbated by the breaches that led through the Void, weakened the planet. The Doctor warned Pete Tyler to be wary of her. (2.13) Some years later, down but not out, Harriet used technology obtained from the Mr Copper Foundation to develop the Subwave Network and communicated with some of the Doctor's old friends in an attempt to contact the Doctor. Although tracing Torchwood, Sarah Jane Smith and Martha Jones, Harriet never got to see the Doctor again as the Daleks traced her and exterminated her. (4.12) (Played by PENELOPE WILTON)

Jones, Ianto: Operative working for Jack Harkness at Torchwood Three in Cardiff. In the alternative world where Donna Noble never met the Doctor, he died aboard the mothership of the Sontaran Tenth Battle Fleet. (4.11) He and Gwen Cooper worked with Jack in their base, the Hub, to try and stop the Daleks and later helped the Doctor bring Earth back to its correct place in space, using the power of Cardiff's rift. (4.12, 4.13) (Played by GARETH DAVID-LLOYD)

Jones, Leo: 21-year-old brother of Martha Jones. Because of the circumstances surrounding his parents' bitter separation, he was despairing of his proposed birthday party, suggesting to Martha that it be cancelled. It went ahead but, after an argument between his mum, Francine, and his dad's new girlfriend,

Annalise, he was forced to head off after Clive to try and smooth the waters. The next night, he accompanied Francine to the LazLabs' party because his eldest sister, Tish, was working for Professor Lazarus. He met the Doctor there, who Martha was travelling with. Having been injured during the attack by the Lazarus Creature, he stayed with his distraught mother while Martha and Tish helped the Doctor defeat Lazarus. When Harry Saxon (aka the Master) began to round up the Jones family to get at Martha, Leo and his girlfriend Shonara and their daughter Keisha were in Brighton with a mate, Boxer. Just before the Master broke through into their phone conversation, Martha warned Leo to stay there, as far away from the authorities as possible, which he did. This meant that, unlike the rest of his family, he wasn't taken aboard the Valiant and so had no memory of living through the Year of Hell. He was present at his parents' London home when Martha elected to stop travelling with the Doctor. (3.1, 3.6, 3.12, 3.13) (Played by REGGIE YATES)

Jones, Letitia ('Tish'): Martha Jones's elder sister (by a year). She witnessed the Judoon's removal and return of the Royal Hope Hospital, with Martha inside it. Tish had a job as Head of PR at LazLabs, working for Richard Lazarus. When Lazarus hit on her, she rejected him but, once he had been rejuvenated into his younger self, realised that a little flirting could be a good career move. As a result, she was with him to witness his transformation into the deadly Lazarus Creature, and ended up helping the Doctor and Martha destroy it at Southwark Cathedral. Soon afterwards, Tish took a new PR job, ostensibly overseeing public relations for the new Prime Minister's wife, Lucy Saxon. It transpired that both this job and her post at LazLabs had been set up by Harry Saxon (aka the Master) as part of his plan to bring the Jones family under his control in his pursuit of Martha and, ultimately, the Doctor. Captured by Saxon's minions and herded aboard the Valiant, when the Master unleashed the Toclafane onto Earth, Tish was a witness. She spent a year as a maid aboard the Valiant alongside her parents, serving food to the incarcerated Captain Jack Harkness. As such, when the Paradox Machine was activated she was one of the few people on Earth for whom the previous 12 months wasn't erased. Martha quit travelling with the Doctor to look after Tish and their parents, who were understandably in shock. (3.1, 3.6, 3.12, 3.13) (Played by GUGU MBATHA-RAW)

J

Jones, Martha: Daughter of Clive and Francine Jones, sister to Letitia and Leo, aunt to Keisha, and cousin of the late Adeola Oshodi, Martha Jones was a medical student at the Royal Hope Hospital when she first met the Doctor. Under the tutelage of Mr Stoker, she worked alongside Julia Swales and Oliver Morgenstern, and was able to employ CPR to resuscitate the Doctor when a Plasmavore drained his body of blood. (3.1) She was also able to recognise and treat concussion, (3.6) demonstrated the bones of the human hand to Joan Redfern, (3.9) and had worked the late shift in Accident and Emergency. (3.2)

Following her transportation to the moon and subsequent return to Earth, Martha accepted the Doctor's offer of a single thank-you trip in the TARDIS, despite concerns about her rent and exams. (3.1) Upon materialising in 1599, she was initially cautious about changing history, but quickly learned to embrace the Doctor's time-travelling lifestyle, using her knowledge of Harry Potter to help Shakespeare defeat the Carrionites. (3.2) The Doctor then took Martha to New New York in the far future, (3.3) before travelling back to old New York in the 1930s, a city she had always wanted to visit. She was identified as possessing superior intelligence by the Daleks, and was taken for their Final Experiment, before being rescued by the Doctor and Laszlo. (3.4)

Following the Daleks' defeat, (3.5) the Doctor took Martha home to 2008, just 12 hours after their departure the previous evening. They attended the reception for Professor Lazarus's rejuvenation demonstration, where Martha introduced the Doctor to her family as one of her work colleagues, and Martha's mother, Francine, became increasingly suspicious of her daughter's behaviour. (3.6) The Doctor then invited Martha to join him as a proper companion, giving her a key to the TARDIS, and providing her mobile phone with Universal Roaming. (3.7) Together, they embarked on a quest to find the legendary vessel the *Infinite*. (TIQ) When the Doctor made himself human, Martha was left responsible for the safety of his alter ego, John Smith, in 1913. Smith found Martha employment alongside him at Farringham School for Boys, where she worked as a maid for several weeks, and befriended fellow staff member Jenny. (3.8) She then protected Smith from the Family of Blood's attack in the village hall, and ultimately helped persuade both him and Joan Redfern that the Doctor should be brought back into existence. (3.9)

The Doctor and Martha also watched the moon landing no fewer than four times, (3.10) and, when they were transported to 1969 by the Weeping Angels,

Martha had to find employment as a shop assistant in order to support the Doctor. (3.10) On a trip to the planet Malcassairo at the end of the universe, she met first Captain Jack Harkness and then Professor Yana, who was revealed to be the Master in human form. (3.11) Eventually they returned to Earth only four days after her first meeting with the Doctor. Martha's flat was destroyed by the Master, who then took the Jones family into custody in an attempt to lure the Doctor's party into a trap. Having never engaged in any criminal activity, Martha became an unlikely fugitive as part of the Master's plans. She teleported aboard the *Valiant* with the Doctor and Jack, where they were taken prisoner. Escaping with Jack's Vortex Manipulator, Martha was then left on Earth to defeat the Master alone. (3.12)

Unable to return to Britain for an entire year, Martha travelled the world, carrying out the Doctor's instructions. She sailed the Atlantic single-handed and walked across America, travelling from the ruins of New York, to the Fusion Mills of China, and across the Radiation Pits of Europe. She was said to be the only person to have escaped Japan alive, and legends claimed that she had travelled the world in search of a weapon capable of killing the Master. In reality, she had been telling her tale of the Doctor to the world, and used her knowledge of Docherty's son to ensure she was on board the *Valiant* for the Doctor's victory. Following the Master's defeat, Martha Jones decided to remain on Earth to look after her family, and to seek out Thomas Milligan, who had sacrificed his life for Martha in the year that never was. She also reminded herself of the advice she had given to her friend Vicky, and took the opportunity to escape her unrequited love for the Doctor, her self-confessed Heart's Desire. (TIQ) Parting on good terms, Martha then left her phone with the Doctor, determined that she would see him again one day soon . . . (3.13)

They next met when she called him to Earth to help deal with the ATMOS deaths. The Doctor then discovered that the Sontarans were planning to turn Earth into a clone breeding planet, helped by a clone of Martha they had infiltrated into UNIT. Martha was with the clone when it died, realising they shared the same memories, thoughts and emotions. After the Sontarans were defeated, Martha went into the TARDIS to say goodbye to the Doctor and Donna Noble, but the TARDIS took off before she could leave. (4.4, 4.5) She was transported to the planet Messaline, where the Doctor's cells were used to create a young warrior girl, Jenny,

as part of the war effort between the human colonists and the Hath. Martha was separated from the Doctor and Donna while helping an injured Hath, who helped her cross the planet's hostile surface to reunite her with her friends. The Hath, Peck, sacrificed his life to save Martha. The Doctor then returned her to Earth. (4.6)

Martha was one of the things the Doctor mentioned to Sky Silvestry on Midnight which she repeated back at him. (4.10) Her work with UNIT took her to New York where she was the medical specialist working on Project Indigo, when the Manhattan HQ was attacked by Daleks. Using Indigo to take her home to her mother, Martha was one of the people contacted by Harriet Jones via her Subwave Network. Martha then travelled to Germany, to possibly use the Osterhagen Key UNIT had given her, but was teleported to the Dalek Crucible in the Medusa Cascade instead, as one of the Children of Time. Alongside the Doctor, Donna, Sarah Jane Smith, Captain Jack Harkness, and Rose Tyler, she defeated Davros and the Daleks and was returned to Earth in the TARDIS. Leaving with Jack, they were both joined by Rose's ex-boyfriend Mickey Smith. (4.12, 4.13) Some time later, Martha broke off her engagement to Tom Milligan and married Mickey. She left UNIT and worked with him, tracking down dangerous aliens on Earth, including a Sontaran Commander, Jask. Jask was close to killing them both, when the Doctor arrived and stopped him. Mickey and Martha realised this was the very last time they would see the Tenth Doctor – he had come to say goodbye. (4.18) When trying to create a voice interface with the TARDIS, while dying from the poison from the Judas Tree, the Doctor considered talking to a hologram of Martha. (6.8) (Played by FREEMA AGYEMAN)

Joofie Crystalle: Soap opera character from the Sto show *By the Light of the Asteroid*. Joofie had many husbands. (4.X)

Joplin, Janis: American singer, originally part of the blues group Big Brother and the Holding Company before finding fame as a solo artist. She had given the Doctor his overcoat. (3.3)

Jordan Road: A street near the Powell Estate in South East London. Pete Tyler was killed there in a hit-and-run accident. (1.8) The TARDIS landed there when the Doctor sent Rose Tyler back to Earth before the Daleks invaded the Game Station. (1.13)

Jørgensen, Mr: One of Craig Owens's regular customers at the BIS call centre where he worked. The Doctor dealt with him after getting rid of the rude Mr Lang. (5.11)

Josh: Security guard aboard the starship *Byzantium* who was affected by River Song's hallucinogenic lipstick and believed he was standing in a meadow. He was killed when the *Byzantium* crashed onto Alfava Metraxis. (5.4) (Played by MIKE SKINNER)

'Journal of Impossible Things, A': Believing that the Doctor and his exploits were just fantasies he was dreaming up, John Smith kept a notebook full of his stories and drawings of all the fabulous places he had seen. He loaned the book to Joan Redfern (and drew a picture of her in it), not realising it was all completely real. When trying to determine if Martha Jones was telling the truth about John's true origins, Joan read to the very end of the book, and its stories convinced her that the consequences of the Family of Blood's victory would be terrible for everyone. After the Doctor was returned, Joan asked him to leave her alone, but kept the journal as a record of John Smith, the man she loved with all her heart. (3.8, 3.9)

Journal of Impossible Things, A: Biography of Joan Redfern, written by her great granddaughter, Verity Newman. (4.18)

Jovanka, Tegan: Companion of the Fifth Doctor at the time he encountered the Tenth Doctor during a time collision. (TC)

Joy: Woman who worked at the White House who Amy Pond met in the women's restroom. When she saw a Silent, she assumed it was her colleague Ben wearing a *Star Trek* mask. The Silent killed her. (6.1) (Played by NANCY BALDWIN)

Jubilee: Code name for one of the three spitfires sent into outer space via Bracewell's gravity bubble to destroy the Daleks' transmitter. He was the first pilot to be killed during the attack. (5.3)

Judas Tree: Source of a lethal poison with which River Song almost killed the Doctor by kissing him with it. (6.8)

Judd, Harry: Member of pop group McFly, who endorsed Harry Saxon's campaign to become Prime Minister. (3.12)

Judoon: Rhinocerotini species of large-lunged galactic law enforcers, intelligent but over-methodical, frequently missing important details in their determination to do a job quickly and efficiently. The Doctor encountered a Judoon platoon on the moon, searching out a Plasmavore that had murdered the Child Princess of Padrivole Regency Nine. Because they had no jurisdiction on Earth or for hunting humans, they had used plasma-coil technology to move the Royal Hope Hospital to the moon. (3.1) A platoon was stationed on the Shadow Proclamation. (4.12) . As she saw her mother and fiancé change into the Master in front of her, Donna Noble remembered the Judoon as her memories started to come back. A Judoon officer was in the Zaggit Zagoo bar. (4.18) A platoon travelled to Stonehenge, as part of the Pandorica Alliance. When the Pandorica opened and history was stopped, the Alliance were reduced to fossils. (5.12, 5.13) The security software necessary to help the Headless Monks kidnap Amy Pond was extracted from a Judoon's frontal lobe. (6.7P) A troop was brought to Demon's Run by the Doctor to arrest the Clerics in the 51st century. (6.7) A Judoon had once been killed inside the God Complex and his photograph mounted on the wall. (6.11)

Judoon Captain: Commander of the Judoon on Earth's moon, sent to execute the Plasmavore hiding on Earth. He led his troopers through the Royal Hope Hospital, ensuring that everyone was scanned, logged as human (and given compensation forms for their trouble if necessary). Upon locating the Plasmavore,

Judoon justice was swiftly meted out, and the Judoon Captain led his troops off the moon, safely returning the Hospital to Earth, presumably to avoid litigation later. (3.1) A Judoon Captain led the security detail for the Shadow Proclamation. (4.12) There was a Judoon Captain amongst the Pandorica Alliance. (5.12) (Played by PAUL KASEY, voiced by NICHOLAS BRIGGS)

Jumna: River in Delhi that burst its banks during the 1885 monsoon, drowning a Vespiform that had adopted the identity of Christopher. (4.7)

Junction 19: The area of ventilation ducts on Platform One where the Crespallion plumber Raffalo was killed by Cassandra's robot spiders. (1.2)

Junctions: Parts of the New New York Motorway. Junction 5 had been closed for three years, according to an irate White Man. Legend had it that a woman had stood at Junction 47 breathing in the fumes for 20 minutes and her head swelled up to 50 feet. According to Sally Calypso, a multiple stackpile (i.e. crash) had occurred at Junction 509. (3.3)

June: One of the Silver Cloak whose sister lived on Dent Road, opposite HMP Broadfell, and told June she'd seen the TARDIS there. (4.17)

Juniper Avenue: East London road where Ellen Highbury lived, at number 45C. (4.1)

Jupiter Rising: A holovid series. Rose Tyler was asked a question about it by the Anne Droid in *The Weakest Link* aboard the Game Station. (1.12)

Justice Department: Time-spanning organisation that saw itself as a champion of law and order and so sent fleets of shape-changing robots throughout time to arrest, replace and execute notorious criminals. The *Teselecta* was one of their vehicles. (6.8)

Justicia: A prison planet visited by the Doctor and Rose Tyler. It was the first alien world that Rose went to. (1.11)

K 37 Gem 5: Official designation for the black hole in space, connected by a gravity funnel to the planet Krop Tor, which was impossibly in orbit around it. When the funnel finally collapsed, Krop Tor was drawn back towards the black hole. The survivors aboard Sanctuary Base 6 tried to use an escape shuttle to flee the black hole but were drawn towards it after the Beast, in its human host Toby Zed, was sucked into the event horizon. Using the TARDIS, the Doctor pulled the shuttle to safety, but Krop Tor was eventually destroyed within the black hole's event horizon. (2.8, 2.9)

Kaarsh, Field Major: Commander of the Sontaran forces on Earth in 1605. (AG05) (Voiced by DAN STARKEY)

Kaata Flo Ko: The Doctor wanted to take Donna Noble there to see the diamond coral reefs. (4.4)

Kahari, Mooky: In the alternative world where Donna Noble never met the Doctor, Mooky was one of the mates Donna was drinking with. She suggested moving on to the Boardwalk but they were interrupted because the Empress of the Racnoss attacked. (4.11) (Played by MARCIA LECKY)

Kalaann: City of the Daleks on Skaro. The Doctor once visited it when it had been destroyed, but when the Daleks changed time, it became a powerful power base once again. (AG01)

Kalahari Desert: South African plain, where Lady Christina de Souza had holidayed and as a result learned how to get vehicle tyres out of deep sand. (4.15)

Kaled God of War: The inhabitants of Skaro had the concept of evil represented by a horned beast in their culture. (2.9)

Kaliko, Captain: In command of the *Black Gold*, a futuristic pirate ship on Bouken, a desert planet overrun by the oil rigs owned by OilCorp. OilCorp were sucking the planet dry of its natural resources in an oil-starved 40th century then selling it at inflated prices. OilCorp's biggest opponents were pirates like Kaliko, who would attack the rigs and steal the oil, selling it at low prices to poorer planets. Kaliko was betrayed by her Skeleton Crew but, after an attack by the OilCorp rigs, she was able to flee her damaged ship in an escape pod. This though was shot down. She crash-landed on the desert floor, and was then murdered by the despot Baltazar. The Doctor and Martha found her body, retrieving the first datachip they required for their quest to find the *Infinite*. (TIQ) (Voiced by LIZA TARBUCK)

Karachi: City in Pakistan where Tarak Ital was born and attended Aga Khan University before heading to Harvard in America. (4.16)

Karass don Slava: The Doctor found a speck of psychic pollen trapped in the TARDIS, which he reckoned must have drifted in from the candle meadows of Karass don Slava and become the Dream Lord for a short time. (5.7)

Kardania: The Doctor needed a Kardanian Vortex Tuner to help stabilise the Dimensional Lesion in the TARDIS. (AG05)

Kasterborous: Star system which contained the Doctor's home planet, Gallifrey. (4.X)

Kate: A friend to Cheen, who had told her of the rumours that something lived below the Fast Lane of the New New York Motorway. Milo put the noises they were hearing down to faulty ventilation ducts, but Kate was proven correct when they were attacked by the Macra. (3.3)

Katherine: Friend of Jeanne-Antoinette Poisson in France. During 1744, they had a conversation about Louis XV's paramour Madame de Chateauroux, who was close to dying, and wondered whether Reinette could catch the King's eye at the Yew Tree Ball. (2.4) (Played by ANGEL COULBY)

Katusi, Winston: One of the Silver Cloak and, like Wilfred Mott, an old soldier. He witnessed people changing into the Master from his housing estate and rang Wilfred to tell him before succumbing to the transformation himself. (4.17) (Played by ALLISTER BAIN)

Keisha: The daughter of Leo Jones and his girlfriend Shonara. She was safely with Leo and Shonara in Brighton when the Master began rounding up the rest of the Jones family. (3.1, 3.12) (Played by BAKARI SMART)

Kel: Council worker who had been digging up the road around the time that kids began disappearing from Dame Kelly Holmes Close. Initially accused by some of the neighbours of abducting them in his van, he helped Rose Tyler find the Isolus ship, which had been tarmacked over in the road at a point where cars passing over it lost all their power for a few metres. (2.11) (Played by ABDUL SALIS)

Kelly: Lazy shop worker at Sanderson & Grainger. She worked in the ladieswear department and was in a hurry to get out on a date with her boyfriend John-Joe, leaving her supervisor Shona to do Kelly's after-hours clearing up. (6.12) (Played by HOLLI DEMPSEY)

Kelvin, Pilot: A human fighter pilot originally from Myarr who was dedicated to destroying the Mantasphids. However, when the Doctor averted the war, Kelvin ended up brokering the peace deal between the insects and humanity. (TIQ) (Voiced by STEVEN MEO)

Kempe, William: Actor, of the Lord Chamberlain's Men. He played Costard in both *Love's Labour's Lost* and *Love's Labour's Won*. (3.2) (Played by DAVID WESTHEAD)

Kendrick, Dr: On 'Pete's World', Kendrick was a scientist employed by Cybus Industries to oversee the

Ultimate Upgrade project. After the first Cyberman was 'born', John Lumic had Kendrick killed by his own creation to stop him reporting Lumic to the Ethical Committee in Geneva for contravening the Bio-Convention. (2.5) (Played by PAUL ANTONY-BARBER)

Kennedy, John Fitzgerald: The 35th President of the United States of America, he was assassinated on 22 November 1963, an event witnessed by the Doctor. (1.1) Rose Tyler said the word 'assassination' automatically made her think of Kennedy. (2.2) The Doctor repaired his Cadillac on 22 November 1963. (AG02) Cape Kennedy was named for Kennedy. (6.1, 6.2) Anita, a crewmember aboard the *Teselecta* cited Kennedy's death as a moment where time could be rewritten. (6.8) In the alternative timeline created by River Song not killing the Doctor, Kennedy was still President, and River used her hallucinogenic lipstick on him to help set up Area 52 in Egypt. (6.13)

Kennedy, Victor: Needing to disguise himself as a human, the Abzorbaloff created this eccentric human guise, insisting that he had a virulent skin disease so that no one would be inadvertently absorbed into him before he wanted them to be. He carried an ornate cane which was actually a limitation-field device that stopped the Abzorbaloff stretching his physical form too far. (2.10T, 2.10) (Played by PETER KAY; DEAN HARRIS)

Kenny: Schoolboy, not very popular with the other kids at Deffry Vale High School. For medical reasons, he was not allowed to eat chips and so was unaffected by the Krillitane Oil and was not forced to work on the Krillitane plan to solve the Skasas Paradigm. He helped the Doctor and

K

his friends escape the Krillitanes when he realised that, bat-like in their natural form, they wouldn't like loud noises, so he set off the school fire alarms. Later, with the school blown up, he was hailed as a hero by Melissa and the other kids for his involvement in the day's events. (2.3) (Played by JOE PICKLEY)

Kent: One of the county tower blocks on *Starship UK*. (5.2)

Kent, Doctor: In the alternative timeline created by River Song, Doctor Kent worked in Area 52, monitoring the frozen timeline and the Silence. She was killed when the Silence attacked her via the Eye Drive she wore over her eye. (6.13) (Played by EMMA CAMPBELL JONES)

Kerenski, Mikhail: Yuri Kerenski's brother, who moved from Moscow to Dagestan to live with his husband George. (4.16) (Played by MAX BOLLINGER)

Kerenski, Nurse Yuri: One of the crew of Bowie Base One on Mars, when the Flood attacked. Muscovite Yuri was in a clandestine relationship with

geologist Mia Bennett and the two of them were saved by the Doctor, slightly changing the established future timelines where they died on Mars. (4.16) (Played by ALEKSANDAR MIKIC)

Kess, Guard Commander: Head of security for Ood Operations on the Ood-Sphere. He loathed the Ood and had no problem slaughtering them at the slightest provocation. He tried to kill the Doctor with a pneumatic claw and was planning to gas the Ood, but they trapped him and he died, a victim of his own plan. (4.3) (Played by ROGER GRIFFITHS)

Kessler Chart: Mathematical table, which the Doctor thought Jones may have used to solve the Anghelides Equation. Jones hadn't, because the Kessler Chart didn't allow for four-dimensional drift. (AG04)

Kew Gardens: South London botanical gardens. Donna Noble likened the 'Lost Temple' area on Messaline to it. (4.6)

Keycoder: Device used by Ulysses Mergrass to activate the weaponry he sold to the Mantasphid Queen. After she betrayed him, he fled, taking the keycoder with him, leaving the weapons useless. (TIQ)

Keyes, Robert: One of the 13 plotters who planned to blow up the House of Lords in 1605, who had an aversion to rats. (AG05) (Voiced by CHRIS JOHNSON)

Kilburn: North London area where Donna Noble's mate Matthew Richards lived with his boyfriend. (4.4)

King Kong: Fictional giant ape. The Doctor was beating on his chest once, trying to mime 'press' but Amy Pond thought he was doing 'King Kong'. (AG03)

King Lear: One of William Shakespeare's best-known plays. Dr Black likened the quality of it to painter Vincent Van Gogh's artistic output. (5.10)

King of Despair: Legendary demon name, one of many attributed to the Beast throughout the galaxies. (2.8, 2.9)

King of Sweden: When Rory Williams pretended to pass his 'sister', Amy Pond, off to Rosanna Calvierri as a potential candidate for her School, he showed her the psychic paper, claiming it was a reference from the King of Sweden. Rosanna saw straight through this, but played along, intrigued that a human had access to psychic paper. (5.6)

King, Stephen Edwin: American novelist most popularly associated with the horror genre, although he has written outside that sphere many times. Elton Pope misquoted a passage from his novel *The Green Mile* when summing up his new outlook on life after meeting the Doctor. (2.10)

King's Arms, the: Colchester pub which boasted a Sunday soccer league team of which Craig Owens was a player. The Doctor played one match for them against the Rising Sun, and they won. (5.11)

King's Lynn Players: Assembly whose music was heard on the episode of *What's My Line?* playing on a television in Mr Magpie's shop when the Wire first appeared to him. (2.7)

Kinks, The: London Mod band, who were one of the highlights of 1963, according to the Doctor. (AG01)

Kirsty: Friend of Trish Webber's who phoned her for a chat. Trish told her Chloe was ill but that a Doctor had come to help. (2.11)

Kiss Me, Kill Me: Novel allegedly written by Harry Saxon before he became Prime Minster of Great Britain. (3.12)

Kitchenhand: Worker in Kitchen Five aboard the starliner *Titanic*. He and most of his co-workers survived the impact of the meteoroids that crippled the ship but were subsequently massacred by the Heavenly Host. (4.X) (Played by STEFAN DAVIS)

Klein, Alex: UNIT operative assigned to Prime Minister Harriet Jones during the Guinevere One expedition to Mars, he was with her when she was teleported aboard the Sycorax ship. Her premiership crumbled when the Doctor whispered to Alex, 'Don't you think she looks tired?' – six words that began a political chain reaction leading to her downfall. (2.X) (Played by ADAM GARCIA)

Klein, Ludovic: Artist whose latest installations were amongst the *Crusader 50*'s entertainment options. (4.10)

Klempari defence: According to the Doctor, this is an interrogation technique where the prisoner claims to be the last of their kind. Alaya the Silurian

Koh-I-Noor: Indian jewel, presented to the British monarchy by Prime Minister Disraeli when Queen Victoria was declared Empress of India. It was said that whoever owned it must surely die. 'Koh-I-Noor' means 'Mountain of Light'. The diamond was regularly resized by Prince Albert until it was ready to be added to the telescope he and Sir George MacLeish had built at Torchwood House to destroy the Haemovariform that had lived in the area for more than 300 years. (2.2)

K1: A Giant Robot the Doctor once defeated when working for UNIT. When he learned that his successor, Malcolm Taylor had read and enjoyed all the files about his work, the Doctor asked if the K1 incident was his favourite. (4.15)

Kontron Crystal: The Doctor needed one to build the Chronon Blocker. (AG01)

'Kookaburra': Traditional song by Australian composer Marion Sinclair, popular with societies such as the Girl Guides. The song was sung by Chloe and Trish Webber to bond over, thus keep the drawing of Chloe's abusive dead father from coming to life and hurting her. (2.11)

Warrior tried it, but the Doctor didn't believe her. (5.8)

Klingons: According to the local newspaper reports that drew Mickey Smith's attention to the UFOs above Deffry Vale High School, the invaders were not Klingons from the TV show *Star Trek*. (2.3T) In his nightmare scenario in the God Complex, a girl taunted Howie Spragg by asking him whether 'loser' was in the Klingon language. (6.11)

K-9: Specially built version of the Doctor's one-time companion, K-9 Mk III was a gift for Sarah Jane Smith, which she received at Christmas in 1981. K-9 was a mobile computer created in the image of a dog, with circuitry and intelligence far beyond Earth technology of the time. K-9 Mk I had remained on Gallifrey with the Doctor's former companion, Leela, whilst the second K-9 stayed with another companion, Romana, in a pocket universe called E-Space. Sarah Jane was very fond of her friend, with his unique and strong personality, but she had been unable to get spares for him, so, by the time they were reunited with the Doctor at Deffry Vale High School in 2007, he was in serious need of repair. K-9 then sacrificed himself to destroy the Krillitanes that had taken over the school, and Sarah Jane was left sad and alone. However, the Doctor had built her a brand new model, K-9 Mk IV, with all the latest non-degrading parts and an omniflexible hyperlink facility, and the two headed back to her London home ready for new adventures together. (2.3) He, Mr Smith and Luke Smith helped the Doctor return Earth back to its proper place in time and space. (4.13) (Voiced by JOHN LEESON)

Knitting for Girls: Magazine the Doctor was reading while waiting to meet Father Gideon Vandaleur. (6.13)

Kovarian, Madame: Mysterious envoy of the Silence who was in charge of looking after the pregnant Amy Pond on Demon's Run. The Ganger Amy kept getting flashes of Kovarian at odd moments when the real Amy awoke. Whether Madame Kovarian was part of the Anglican Clerics or merely working with them is unclear, but she had been charged with devising a weapon with which the Clerics could destroy the Doctor in the 51st century on behalf of the Silence. Kovarian realised that, since Melody Pond had been conceived within the TARDIS, she was the best weapon possible, so she kidnapped the baby. Replacing Amy

with a Flesh Ganger Amy before the Doctor's first meeting with the Silence gave her access to the real, pregnant Amy who she took to Demon's Run. Kovarian oversaw Melody's birth, planning to bring the baby up on Earth and programme her to track the Doctor down and kill him. She also replaced Melody with a Ganger. She escaped Demon's Run with the real Melody and later left the baby in

the care of the Silence in America. When the baby regenerated into River Song, Kovarian trapped her within a NASA spacesuit in 2011, leading to River killing the Doctor at Lake Silencio. In the alternative world created when River broke her conditioning and did not kill the Doctor, River had Kovarian held prisoner in Area 52 in Egypt. Kovarian's eye patch, like everyone else's, was actually an Eye Drive to enable humans to constantly perceive the Silence. The Silence turned against Kovarian and tried to kill her through her Eye Drive, but she managed to get it partially off. However, as a last act of revenge for everything she had done to Amy, Rory and Melody, Amy put Kovarian's eye patch firmly back into place, leaving her to die in agony. Amy later confessed this to River, who implied that what happened in an alternative reality did not count – suggesting that Kovarian was still alive somewhere. (6.2, 6.3, 6.5, 6.6, 6.7, 6.12, 6.13) (Played by FRANCES BARBER)

Krafayis: A race of alien hunters and scavengers. Invisible to most of their victims, they are ruthless, even to their own and will abandon an injured, blinded Krafayis rather than slow the pack down. One was stranded in France and was only visible to Vincent Van Gogh. The Krafayis killed a number of the locals before the Doctor, Van Gogh and Amy Pond cornered it in a church at Auvers, hoping to stun it with crosactic energy. In trying to defend his friends, Van Gogh accidentally stabbed the Krafayis with his easel and killed it. (5.10)

Krakatoa: Volcanic Indonesian island, which suffered a terribly destructive eruption in August 1883. The Doctor was present but survived by swimming towards the neighbouring island of Sumatra. (1.1)

Krillitanes: A race of aliens who could reconstitute themselves over generations, by taking on features, both physical and mental, of the races they conquered. After many centuries, the Krillitanes now resembled bat creatures (their characteristics absorbed from the inhabitants of a planet called Bessan) but could morph into above average strength humans at will. A side effect of this evolution was that their own Krillitane Oil was toxic to them, acting as an acid poison if it touched them. However, they needed the Oil, safely stored in sealed drums, to enhance the intelligence of the human children at Deffry Vale High School where they based themselves. With their knowledge and imaginations expanded, the children ought to have been able to solve the Skasas Paradigm, providing the Chosen Few, as these Krillitanes called themselves, with the ability to harness the basic energies that made up the universe and become gods. Aware of the Last Great Time War, the Krillitane leader, Brother Lassar, offered to share this knowledge with the Doctor, perhaps enabling him to go back and stop the destruction of the Time Lords. The Krillitanes were eventually destroyed when K-9 heated up and then exploded the drums of Krillitane Oil stored in the school kitchens (2.3)

Kronkburger: Item of food for sale on Satellite Five. It came ungarnished, or with cheese or pajato. (1.7)

Krop Tor: Ancient Veltino name for the planet beneath which the Beast was imprisoned, which translated as 'the bitter pill'. The planet generated a natural

gravity field which, boosted by a gravity funnel, connected it to the nearby black hole K 37 Gem 5. This enabled the black hole and Krop Tor to remain in synchronous orbit around one another, a hitherto impossible situation. A team was sent from the Torchwood Archive on Earth to explore Krop Tor, because an energy spike had been recorded ten miles beneath its surface, but the mission went awry as their ship encountered the funnel and, although the crew successfully landed on Krop Tor, a number of their personnel died, including their captain, Walker. When the TARDIS brought the Doctor and Rose Tyler to the humans' base, they were just completing their drilling procedure. The Doctor and Science Officer Ida Scott went down in spacesuits to discover the source of the energy readings – which was a huge trapdoor in the surface. Krop Tor's connection to the gravity funnel weakened drastically as they did this and, while the humans aboard the base had to cope with this and the mentally controlled Ood, the trapdoor opened. Leaving Ida by the entrance, the Doctor lowered himself into the depths of the planet and encountered the Beast, whose consciousness was currently split between the Ood and archaeologist Toby Zed. As Krop Tor's orbit finally decayed, the Doctor escaped with Ida aboard the TARDIS, leaving the planet and the Beast to be destroyed within the event horizon of K 37 Gem 5. (2.8, 2.9)

Kurhan: Cold planet where, the Doctor suggested, he and Martha Jones could go ice skating on its mineral lakes. (3.7)

Kyoto: The Doctor, Rose Tyler and Captain Jack Harkness visited Kyoto in 1336, the year that the civil wars of the Yoshino period began, when it was still the capital city of Japan. The Doctor explained that they had only just escaped. (1.12)

K

La Viva: Coffee house which the Doctor, Rose Tyler, Mickey Smith and Sarah Jane Smith took K-9 to. Later, they were startled by a Krillitane outside. (2.3)

Lab 003: Torchwood laboratory beneath the Thames Barrier where the Doctor explained to Donna Noble what Huon particles were. (3.X)

Labour Camps: Established across Earth by the Master, overseen by the Toclafane, to ensure the building of his war rockets went to schedule. (3.13)

Labyrinth of Skulls, the: Outer chamber leading to the Headless Monks' Seventh Transept. The skulls were the still alive heads of those the Monks had beheaded and were carnivorous, attacking and eating anything they could. (6.13)

Lad [1]: Occupant of the slave house in Bexley, South London. He listened to Martha's story and was later on the streets saying the Doctor's name, along with the rest of mankind. (3.13) (Played by TOM GOLDING)

Lad [2]: Young London boy who wondered who the Doctor was, and was told by Jackson Lake. (4.14) (Played by ASHLEY HORNE)

Lady Announcer: BBC continuity announcer who announced the credits for *What's My Line?* and then declared the end of transmission, while Magpie worked in his shop. The Wire adopted her image to communicate with Magpie and, later, Rose, the Doctor and Tommy. (2.7) (Played by MAUREEN LIPMAN)

Lake, Caroline: Wife of Jackson Lake and mother to their son Frederic. She was killed by the Cybermen, an event that shattered Jackson's mind and made him susceptible to the influence of the Infostamps. (4.14) (Played by MARIA HONNEKER)

Lake, Frederic: Son of Jackson and Caroline Lake, kidnapped by the Cybermen and put to work building the engines that would control the CyberKing. When the Cybermen finished with Frederic and the other children, they left them to die in an explosion, but the Doctor and Jackson Lake freed them, and Frederic and his father were reunited. (4.14) (Played by TOM LANGFORD)

Lake, Jackson: A Mathematics teacher from Sussex who travelled with his wife Caroline and son Frederic to London to take up a new post. However, the home they had bought was also the arrival point of the Cybermen who had used a Dimension Vault to bring them from the Void to 1851. Within the Dimension Vault was Cyber technology, including Infostamps, primitive devices for rapid dissemination of information. After the Cybermen killed Caroline and kidnapped Frederic, Jackson defended himself, using an Infostamp to destroy the Cybermen. But the resultant backlash from the Infostamp filled his head with information about the Doctor. Believing he was the Doctor, he created his own 'sonic screwdriver' and 'Tardis' over a three-week period, and even found a companion, Rosita Farisi. With the real Doctor and Rosita's help, Jackson eventually regained his own, tortured memories and helped defeat the Cybermen, rescuing Frederic in the process. He managed to convince the Doctor to share Christmas

dinner with him, his son and Rosita to honour the memory of those they had lost. (4.14) (Played by DAVID MORRISSEY)

Lake Silencio: Lake in Utah where the Doctor was shot dead by a mysterious astronaut. The area was a still point in time, which made it easier to create a fixed point, ensuring the Doctor's death had to happen. When River Song tried to change that fixed point, it created an alternative still point in which time never moved. (6.1, 6.13)

Lamb and Flag, the: Sarah Clark's local pub – a number of her fellow regulars were expected at her wedding, but they did not show up. (1.8)

Lammasteen: The Doctor used technology from this world to build a scanner in Craig Owens's spare room. (5.11)

Lancashire: British county. The Doctor guessed he and Amy Pond might be there when, aboard *Starship UK*, they found themselves in the mouth of the star whale. (5.2)

Lang, Mr: One of Craig Owens's best customers at the BIS call centre where he worked. When the Doctor stood in for Craig, he found Mr Lang very rude and told him to take his custom elsewhere. (5.11)

Langer, Carla: She and her son Clyde were together when 26 planets appeared in the skies above Earth. (4.12)

Langer, Clyde: Best mate of Luke Smith, adopted son of Sarah Jane Smith. In the alternative world where Donna Noble never met the Doctor, Clyde

died alongside his friends in the Royal Hope Hospital when it was transported to the moon. (4.11) He and his mum were together when Earth was transported to the Medusa Cascade. (4.12) Luke was on the phone to Clyde when he was nearly run over by a car on Bannerman Road, only to be pulled to safety by the Doctor. (4.18)

Las Vegas: American city in Nevada, famous for its luxurious hotels and casinos. It also played host to a famous concert by Elvis Presley, and the Doctor was taking Rose Tyler to see Elvis – she wanted his 'Vegas' period, he opted for seeing him perform on *The Ed Sullivan Show* during the late 1950s – but they actually ended up in Muswell Hill in 1953 instead. (2.7)

Laser screwdriver: The Master's lethal version of the Doctor's sonic screwdriver, with isomorphic controls, ensuring only he could operate it. It could kill with a laser beam (as it did Thomas Milligan and Captain Jack Harkness) or, when adapted with technology from Professor Lazarus's Genetic Manipulation Device, be used to temporally alter DNA. The Master used it to increase the Doctor's age, first by 100 years and then, after suspending his regenerative abilities, he physically aged his body to its full 900 years, leaving him a stunted, shrivelled humanoid. (3.12, 3.13) The Doctor had one aboard the TARDIS. (AG03)

Laser spanner: Tool that the Doctor claimed he used to have until it was nicked by suffragette Emily Pankhurst. (3.1)

Lassar, Brother: Leader of the Krillitanes based at Deffry Vale High School. He sought to use the children there, having expanded their minds with Krillitane Oil, to solve the Skasas Paradigm, providing the Krillitanes with the ability to harness the basic energies that make up the universe and become gods. Aware of the Time War, Brother Lassar offered to share this knowledge with the

Doctor, perhaps enabling him to go back and stop the destruction of the Time Lords. Brother Lassar was eventually destroyed when K-9 heated up and then exploded the drums of Krillitane Oil stored in the school kitchens. (2.3) (Played by ANTHONY HEAD)

Laszlo: Young, good-looking stagehand at the Laurenzi theatre, who had a relationship with Tallulah the singer. He was kidnapped by one of the Daleks' Pig Slaves and was being turned into one himself when he escaped halfway through the transformation, leaving him neither one thing nor the other. He met up with Tallulah again in the sewers and realised she wasn't going to abandon him. He helped the Doctor escape from the Daleks, although he knew he was dying. When the Daleks were defeated, the Doctor used their Transgenic Laboratory to find a way to halt the decay and save Laszlo's life. Laszlo opted to live in Hooverville, hoping to continue his romance with Tallulah. (3.4, 3.5) (Played by RYAN CARNES)

Latimer Street: London road. The Lake family had bought number 15 after moving to London from Sussex, only to discover a Dimension Vault, Infostamps and other alien technology in the cellar. The Cybermen had established a base there after falling out of the Void. They killed Caroline Lake, sending her husband Jackson into a fugue state, unaware of her death or the subsequent kidnapping of their son Frederic, until the Doctor cured his shock and depression. (4.14)

Latimer, Timothy: Schoolboy at Farringham School for Boys, easily bullied and pushed round by the bigger boys, forced to do their prep, useless at cadet training and deliberately flunking his lessons so as not to look too bright and become a bigger target for thugs like Baines and Hutchinson. He was mildly psychic, born with a low-level telepathic field, which drew him to the fob watch that schoolteacher John Smith kept on his mantelpiece. The watch contained the

essence of the Doctor and, when Tim tried to open it, bits of the Doctor would leak out and give Tim either glimpses of the future, or warnings, with the aim of keeping the fob watch out of the hands of the Family of Blood. One specific warning concerned Tim's own fate, a few years into the future, when he and his schoolboy nemesis, Hutchinson, would be caught in a bombing raid somewhere in the trenches of the First World War — the watch warning him to step to the right and out of a bomb's path. Realising that John Smith needed the fob watch back, he took it to the Cartwrights' cottage where Smith, Martha Jones and Joan Redfern were hiding. Later, having survived the war, Tim lived to a very old age and, at a Remembrance Day ceremony decades later, he saw the Doctor and Martha, unchanged by the ravages of time. (3.8, 3.9) (Played by THOMAS SANGSTER, HUW REES)

Launch Day: The day when the Master planned to launch his two thousand war rockets at the rest of the universe, via a rift in Braccatolian space, and so begin the New Time Lord Empire. (3.13)

Laura: Chiswick resident whose husband Alan disobeyed the Daleks and took her and their son Simon back into their house. The Daleks then blew the house to pieces with them inside as an example to the other humans. (4.12) (Played by JENNIFER FAUBEL)

Laurel, Stanley: British actor, real name Arthur Stanley Jefferson, who the Doctor appeared alongside in the movie *The Flying Deuces*. (6.1)

Laurenzi, the: New York theatre where the New York Revue was playing. Tallulah was a solo singer there; Myrna and Lois were dancers for the 'Heaven And Hell' routine. Tallulah was also having a relationship with one of the

stagehands, Laszlo. Beneath the theatre were the New York sewers, where the Daleks' Pig Slaves roamed, stealing people for use in the Daleks' Final Experiment. The Doctor used the auditorium of the theatre for a final showdown with the Cult of Skaro and their Dalek-Human army, in which three members of the Cult and all of the Dalek-Humans died. (3.4, 3.5)

Lava Snakes: Clerics Angelo and Christian remembered chasing them on a mission once. (5.4, 5.5)

Lazarus, Professor Richard: Creator of the Genetic Manipulation Device, with which he claimed he could change what it meant to be human. He entered the machine aged 76 and came out nearly 40 years younger, his DNA having been rewritten. In undoing his DNA, however, he brought to the surface a series of molecules that were otherwise dormant in humanity and these quickly became dominant in him, transforming him into a savage arthropod, needing to draw the life energy out of other humans to survive. Believing he had the changes under control, Lazarus continued to maintain that what he was doing was essential to the future of mankind but, with each change, more people had to die. Eventually he sought refuge in Southwark Cathedral, just as he had done as a boy during the Second World War. There the Doctor magnified the sonic resonance of the cathedral's organ, disorienting Lazarus, who fell from the bell tower, dying for good at his true 76 years of age. (3.6) (Played by MARK GATISS)

LazLabs: Aka Lazarus Laboratories, the company run by Professor Richard Lazarus, who unveiled his Genetic Manipulation Device at a gala reception in the

foyer of the LazLabs building to the press and potential investors. (3.6)

Leadworth: Gloucestershire village where Amy Pond and Rory Williams lived. It was split into two parts, Leadworth Village and Upper Leadworth. It had a pub, a post office, a duck pond (minus ducks) a ruined castle, a church and other traditional aspects of rural village life. Prisoner Zero escaped to Earth into Leadworth, using coma patients in the Hospital to create multiforms for itself to escape the Atraxi. (5.1) Amy dreamed of married life with Rory, five years after leaving the TARDIS, in Upper Leadworth. (5.7) Amy and Rory were married there after the Doctor rebooted the universe (5.13)

L

Leadworth Chronicle: Local newspaper whose front-page photograph of the word 'DOCTOR', drawn in a crop circle, was seen by the Time Lord and so brought him back into Amy Pond and Rory Williams's lives. (6.8)

Lear, Edward: British writer, most famous for his 'nonsense' poetry, which Agatha Christie recalled, likening much of what the Doctor said to her as sounding like Lear's work. (4.7)

Leeds: British city in Yorkshire, which had elected one of the ghosts (in reality, a Cyberman still semi-existing within the Void) as their MP. (2.12) The Noble family were billeted there after the nuclear accident that wiped out Southern England in the alternative world where Donna never met the Doctor. (4.11)

Legend of Pandora's Box, The: Storybook based upon the Grecian poems of Hesiod, from his collection *Works and Days*, the story of Pandora – the first woman on Earth – concerns her being forbidden to open a jar. She did, and all the evils of the world escaped into the mortal world leaving hope still trapped in the jar. This was a story that intrigued Amelia Pond as a little girl, and the Pandorica Alliance used that story to create the legend of the Pandorica and spread it through time, eventually trapping the Doctor within the physical Pandorica they had constructed as a prison for him. (5.12, 5.13)

Legion of the Beast: The eyes and ears of the Beast, in this case, the entire stock of Ood aboard Sanctuary Base 6, led by the possessed human archaeologist Toby Zed. (2.8, 2.9)

Leisure Palace, the: Metal structure on the planet Midnight, run by the Leisure Palace Company, dedicated to relaxing holidays, pleasure and amusement. Donna Noble took full advantage of it while the Doctor opted for a

cruise across the planet to see sights such as the sapphire waterfall and the Cliffs of Oblivion. The building itself was lowered into its location from orbit due to the planet's lethal Galvanic radiation. The Doctor hoped to convince the corporation to close that specific Leisure Place down and rebuild elsewhere. (4.10)

Lennon, John: Singer-songwriter and musician with 1960s group The Beatles. Amy Pond hoped to meet him in 1963. (AG01)

Lent: Liturgical period of abstinence. The Cleric Fat One asked the Headless Monks if they practised it, as he wasn't good at giving things up. (6.7)

Leonardo: 16th-century Italian artist and designer who, like Elliot Northover, was dyslexic but, as the Doctor told Elliot, he never let it stop him. (5.8)

Lerner, Abi: Medical officer aboard the SS *Pentallian*, she was trying to diagnose what had happened to Korwin McDonnell when he allowed some of the sun that had possessed him to leak out of his eyes, reducing her to an ashen shadow on the wall. (3.7) (Played by VINETTE ROBINSON)

Lethbridge-Stewart, Brigadier Sir Alistair Gordon: Former commander of the British branch of UNIT and one of the Doctor's oldest friends. Colonel Mace knew and respected him, and was disappointed that he was stranded in Peru when the Sontarans invaded Earth. (4.4) He later died in a nursing home, where he had often talked about the Doctor and always had a glass of brandy ready for him should he ever drop by. The Doctor was utterly devastated by the passing of his old friend, and it was this news that made him finally accept it was time to go to Lake Silencio and meet his pre-ordained death. (6.13)

Level 5: Earth was considered a Level 5 planet by the people of Sto. (4.X) The Doctor reported Matron Cofelia to the Shadow Proclamation because seeding a Level 5 planet was illegal. (4.1) The Doctor said something similar to the Atraxi. (5.1)

Level One Heresy: To remove the hood of a Headless Monk was a Level One Heresy amongst the Clerics of the 51st century. (6.7)

Level One Security Clearance: Martha Jones had this, making her the perfect person for the Sontarans to clone so she could infiltrate UNIT. (4.4, 4.5)

Lever Room: Vast area dominating the top of Torchwood Tower with two huge levers operated by Jacob and Andrew, and a massive blank Wall at one end, through which the Torchwood Institute hoped ghosts would materialise whenever particle energy was fired at it. However, unbeknownst to Torchwood, the ghosts were Cybermen, which had already infiltrated the Tower. These Cybermen used reanimated Torchwood operatives to push the Lever Room to its fullest capacity, enabling tens of thousands of Cybermen to fully materialise on Earth and take over the planet. Following an attack by the Daleks, which had also emerged from the Void via Torchwood, the Doctor reversed the power of the Lever Room, keeping the levers erect long enough for all of the Cybermen and Daleks to be sucked back into the Void from which they had come. Rose Tyler very nearly joined them after losing her grip on one of the levers and was only saved by the 'Pete's World' version of her father, who rescued her and transported her to his home, sealing Rose off from the Doctor. (2.12, 2.13)

Levitation Post: Matron Cofelia used the office block that housed Adipose Industries as a levitation post, a gravity-free invisible tether, so that the Adipose young could be raised into the Adipose First Family's spaceship. However, the first family switched off its power while she was in mid air, causing her to drop to her death. (4.1)

Liao Dynasty: The Doctor sent Amy Pond and Rory Williams to the Liao Palace for a Chinese takeaway – it wasn't a restaurant but the actual 12th-century palace. The guards were not happy. (AG05)

Liberian Man: Possessor of an Osterhagen Key at Osterhagen Station Four. He refused to tell Martha Jones his name because he didn't want history to know what he was going to do. (4.13) (Played by MICHAEL PRICE)

Library, The: A planet that was, quite literally, one vast building containing every book ever written throughout the galaxy, kept both digitally and physically. A number of the books had been printed on paper which contained the Vashta Nerada. To escape the Vashta Nerada, the staff and visitors in The Library were digitised and stored in The Library's hard drive until the Doctor was able to free them. The Library was the creation of Felman Lux in the 51st century, and at the heart of its operating system was an electronic brain pattern digitised from that of his youngest daughter, Charlotte, known colloquially as CAL. (4.8, 4.9)

Life and Adventures of Martin Chuzzlewit, The: A book cited by the Doctor as one of Charles Dickens' canon that he'd read. The Doctor told Dickens that he didn't like the section set in America. (1.3)

Lilith: Carrionite daughter to Mother Bloodtide and Mother Doomfinger, and leader of the three aliens trying to create their Millennium of Blood – a resurgence of the Carrionite Empire. Lilith was an expert in spellcasting via word-shaping, naming and the use of dolls laced with human hair. When William Shakespeare turned their spellcasting back on them, Lilith and her mothers were trapped inside their crystal ball for eternity. (3.2) (Played by CHRISTINA COLE)

Limehouse Green Station: Railway station close to Albion Hospital and the area of the crashed Chula medical ship that the military were guarding. (1.9, 1.10)

LINDA: Acronymic name created by Elton Pope for the band of Doctor-hunters who met up beneath the old library on London's Macateer Street. The London Investigation 'N' Detective Agency used to meet and spend more time having fun with their singalongs than searching out aliens – until  Victor Kennedy arrived and took charge, giving each member a job. Kennedy was in fact the Abzorbaloff and, one by one, he absorbed the group until only Elton was left to face him, aided by the Doctor and Rose Tyler. (2.10) The Fifth Doctor mistook the Tenth Doctor for a member of LINDA as he knew so much about him. (TC)

Linda [1]: Housemate alongside Strood, Crosbie and Lynda in the *Big Brother* house some time prior to the Doctor's arrival there. She was forcibly evicted for damaging a camera. Presumably, she ended up on the Dalek mothership and was turned into a Dalek. (1.12)

Linda [2]: One of the Master's minions, working in 10 Downing Street. (3.12)

L

Lion, the: Pub frequented by Wilfred Mott. (4.17)

Lion King, The: Disney movie (their first full-length animation not based on a pre-existing work) which featured a song, 'The Circle Of Life', that the Doctor quoted to the Sycorax Leader. (2.X)

'Lion Sleeps Tonight, The': Originally a South African song written by Solomon Linda in 1939 as 'Mbube' (Zulu for 'lion'). Various lyrics were added over the years by western musicians. The most popular version was recorded in 1961 by The Tokens, and it was this song which Mr Crane played loudly to cover the screams as Morris and the other homeless people were given the Ultimate Upgrade on 'Pete's World'. It was not The Tokens' recording, however, but the 1981 Tight Fit cover version – track 19 on Crane's CD. (2.5)

Lissak, Erina: One of the crew aboard the SS *Pentallian*, killed by the sun-possessed Korwin McDonnell. (3.7) (Played by REBECCA OLDFIELD)

Little Girl: Small child who, along with her parents (played by DARIUS WALKER, DURINE HOWELL), was caught up in the Racnoss attack on London, and stood in the path of an energy weapon from the Webstar. She was pulled to safety by her father. (3.X) (Played by ZAFIRAH BOATENG)

Little Lord Fauntleroy: Aspirational 19th-century novel by Frances Hodgson Burnett about an American boy who goes to live in England and becomes part of the aristocracy. Henry Van Statten referred to Adam Mitchell as 'Little Lord Fauntleroy' in a derogatory sense. (1.6)

Little Nell: Heroine from *The Old Curiosity Shop*, a novel by Charles Dickens. The Doctor asked Dickens to read the section in which she dies to him, because it made him laugh. Unsurprisingly, Dickens didn't. (1.3)

Little Sutton Street: Chiswick street where Sylvia and Donna Noble had a conversation about whether Donna was going to seek a job with Jival Chowdry or HC Clements. (4.11)

Live Chess: Potentially lethal game that the Doctor played against Gantok on Vegas 12. The Doctor, winning, agreed to throw the game if Gantok took him to Dorium Maldovar. (6.13)

Liverpool: City in England's north west. The Doctor was proud to find out that Bowie Base One stood up to the Flood because it was constructed in Liverpool. (4.16)

Livingston, Ken: Mayor of London at the time of the Big Ben incident, during which one stranded motorist blamed him for the gridlocked streets. (1.4) When the Empress of the Racnoss came to Earth in the alternative world where Donna Noble never met the Doctor, her mate Veena reckoned the Mayor was responsible for putting the Webstar in the sky as a Christmas treat. (4.11)

Liz Ten: The British Queen aboard *Starship UK*, who knew of the Doctor and his past involvements with members of the British royal family throughout history. She was not surprised to discover that he was aboard the ship, nor that he, like her, was intrigued by the lack of vibrations. She allied herself with him and, together with Amy Pond and Mandy Tanner, they tried to investigate the mystery at the heart of the place. Hawthorne, her Chief Winder, revealed, as the Doctor suspected, that Liz Ten had had her body clock slowed and was over 300 years old and had many times chosen to forget the truth of the star whale that carried the ship through space. (5.2) Many years later, she was still the ruler of the colony, when River Song came aboard to steal a painting called *The Pandorica Opens* by Van Gogh from the Royal Collection. (5.12) (Played by SOPHIE OKENADO)

Llewellyn, Daniel: Project Manager at the British Rocket Group, charged with overseeing the *Guinevere One* Space Probe on its mission to Mars. When the Sycorax transported him aboard their ship, he volunteered to make contact with them as the probe had been his responsibility. The Sycorax Leader murdered him with his whip. (2.X) (Played by DANIEL EVANS)

Lloyd, Arthur: London householder who reluctantly joined his wife and son in their air-raid shelter when the sirens started during his dinner, in late January 1941. When the raid was over, the Lloyds discovered Nancy attempting to leave their house, after she had allowed the stray children she was protecting to eat the family's evening meal. Nancy then blackmailed him into giving her other things she needed, including a torch and some wire-cutters, by threatening to expose that it was Arthur, not his wife, having an affair with Mr Haverstock, the butcher. (1.9, 1.10) (Played by DAMIAN SAMUELS)

Lloyd, Mrs: London housewife who hurried to get her husband and son into their air-raid shelter when the sirens started during their evening meal, in late January 1941. Many of the locals assumed she was having an affair with the local butcher, which explained how she always had lots of meat to feed her family. (1.9, 1.10) (Played by CHERYL FERGISON)

Lloyd, Timothy: Son of the owners of the house which Nancy broke into, bringing with her the stray former evacuees to eat the Lloyds' food. Nancy was also spooked by the child wearing a gas mask who was wandering the streets, seeking his lost mummy. When Timothy returned to his house, wearing his, Nancy was understandably alarmed. (1.9, 1.10) (Played by LUKE PERRY)

Lloyd George, David: The Doctor tells Rose that he used to go drinking with this early 20th-century Liberal Prime Minister, renowned for his campaigning against alcohol. (1.4)

Loch Ness Monster: Sarah Jane Smith told Rose Tyler that, during her time travelling with the Doctor, they had encountered the Loch Ness Monster – in reality, a creature called the Skarasen. (2.3)

Locke, Governor: The real Governor of Volag-Noc. Locke was a robot, and he was sadly lacking in compassion. When the Doctor met him, he'd been rewired under the orders of the new Governor, former inmate Gurney. When the Doctor freed Locke, the robot Governor decided to murder all the inmates of Volag-Noc. This was not part of his deal with the Doctor, who disabled him, returning later and reprogramming him to run a better prison. (TIQ) (Voiced by DAN MORGAN)

Lockley: Schoolboy at Farringham School for Boys in 1913 who was placed in charge of the gathering before the Family of Blood attacked (3.9)

Lois: Dancer at the Laurenzi theatre in 1930s New York, taking part in the New York Revue. When Martha Jones needed to get across the stage to find Laszlo, she accidentally trod on Lois's costume's tail, causing Lois to tumble. (3.4) (Played by ALEXIS CALEY)

Londinium Cotide: Newspaper on sale in the London in which time stood still after River Song created an alternative timeline due to her attempts to change history. (6.13)

London: Capital city of the United Kingdom. Rose Tyler, Mickey Smith, (1.1) Martha Jones, (3.1) Donna Noble (3.X) and their respective families all lived there. The Doctor met Captain Jack Harkness there. (1.9) Alien visitors and invaders at

various times have included: Autons, the Nestene Consciousness, (1.1) the Family Slitheen, (1.4, 1.5) Reapers, (1.8) the Chula nanogenes and the resultant gas-mask zombies, (1.9, 1.10) Roboform mercenaries disguised as Santas, (2.X, 3.X) Graske, (AotG, MotS) Krillitanes, (2.3) the Wire, (2.7) a Hoix, the Abzorbaloff, (2.10) an Isolus, (2.11) Cybermen, (2.12, 2.13, 4.14) Daleks, (2.12, 2.13, 4.12, 4.13, 5.3) the Racnoss, (3.X) Slabs, a Plasmavore, (3.1) Carrionites, (3.2) the Weeping Angels, (3.10) the Master using the remnants of the human race disguised as the Toclafane, (3.12, 3.13) passengers and crew, including a Zocci, from the starliner *Titanic*, (4.X), Adipose, (4.1) Sontarans, (4.4, 4.5) Stingrays (4.15), and an Ood (4.16, 4.18). The 'Pete's World' London was overrun by Cybus Industries' Cybermen. (2.5, 2.6) Amongst the London landmarks involved in alien activity have been the London Eye, (1.1) Big Ben, (1.4, 1.5, 2.X) 10 Downing Street, (1.4, 1.5, 3.12) 30 St Mary Axe, (2.X) Alexandra Palace, (2.7) the 2012 Olympic Stadium, (2.11) Canary Wharf, (2.12, 2.13) the Thames Flood Barrier, (3.X) the Globe theatre, (3.2) and Southwark Cathedral. (3.6) On 'Pete's World', Battersea Power Station was where Cybus Industries set up their Cyber-conversion factories. (2.5, 2.6) Ursula Blake took the Doctor's photo in Trafalgar Square on New Year's Eve. (2.10) Martha Jones claimed she had returned to London to collect from a disused UNIT base the final phial of liquid needed to arm the gun she was supposedly preparing to kill the Master with. (3.13) Adipose Industries was based there, and was building a client base throughout Greater London. (4.1) The Rattigan Institute was in North London. (4.4, 4.5) The city was totally wiped out in the alternative reality where Donna Noble never met the Doctor. (4.11) Much of it was damaged by the invading Daleks. (4.12, 4.13) The CyberKing stomped over Victorian London. (4.14) The International Gallery was in London. Three Stingrays escaped San Helios to London via a wormhole. (4.15) The TARDIS took Adelaide Brooke and the other survivors of Bowie Base One home to North London. (4.16) The Master confronted the Doctor across London. (4.17, 4.18) The damaged TARDIS flew over the city with the Doctor hanging outside. (5.1) London was one of the main cities on *Starship UK*. (5.2) The Cabinet War Rooms were

situated beneath the city. (5.3) The National Museum visited by Amelia Pond, and where the Lone Centurion guarded the Pandorica, was in the heart of the city. (5.12, 5.13) The Daleks used the Eye of Time to change history and destroy London in 1963, but the Doctor reversed this. (AG01) The Doctor took River Song to the frozen River Thames for her birthday in 1814 – and had Stevie Wonder sing for her under London Bridge. (6.7) The Doctor visited the Rowbarton House estate there. (6.9) After River Song changed established history, an alternative London was created in which time stood still and the Roman culture never fell. In Hyde Park, a group of children were attacked by a Pterodactyl. (6.13) The Doctor, Amy Pond and Rory Williams visited 17th-century London to stop a Rutan and Sontaran war breaking out. (AG05)

London Credit Bank: Financial institution whose cashpoint machine the Doctor soniced to get it to spew thousands of pounds into the street to distract the Santa Roboforms, giving him the chance to pursue the taxi which had kidnapped Donna Noble. (3.X)

London Eye: Also known as the Millennium Wheel and situated on London's South Bank, near Westminster Bridge. The Nestene Consciousness had set up a base below it, and used the shape of the wheel to transmit its activation signal to the dormant Autons throughout London. (1.1)

London Market: Area of London within *Starship UK*. The Doctor and Amy Pond observed Mandy Tanner there, and the Doctor began to realise that something was wrong with the ship as glasses of water didn't vibrate. He was followed through London Market by a Winder, Peter. (5.2)

Londoners: Townsfolk who helped the Doctor, Amy Pond and Rory Williams in 1605. (AG05) (Voiced by DAVID AMES, AMELDA BROWN and ALEXANDER VLAHOS)

Lone Centurion, the: The legendary Roman guardian of the Pandorica, sighted throughout history, though no one ever knew why he watched over the box. After the London Blitz in 1941, the Lone Centurion was never seen

L

again. It was actually the Auton duplicate of Rory Williams, who was guarding the Pandorica because it contained Amy Pond's body. He later assumed the identity of a security guard at the National Museum, to keep a closer eye on the Pandorica. (5.13) Rory liked the Lone Centurion armour, though, as he wore it on his and Amy's honeymoon (6.X) and when confronting the Cybermen and River Song. (6.7)

Lonely Assassins: See *Weeping Angels*

Lonely God, the: Legendary name for the traveller to whom, it was believed, the Face of Boe would impart a great secret. This traveller was in fact the Doctor. (2.1, 3.3)

Lord Provost: Queen Victoria believed, thanks to the psychic paper, that the Lord Provost George Jamieson had assigned the Doctor as her protector for her journey to Balmoral Castle. (2.2)

Look-In: Children's magazine from the 1970s, which featured comic strip stories based on television shows. Copies of this were kept in the hair salon in the Pasiphaë Spa inside the God Complex. (6.11)

Looters: Two thieves who were trying to steal laptops from Megabyte City and were stopped when Rose Tyler confronted them with her big gun. (4.12) (Played by OLLIE BRYAN and ALEX LUCAS)

Lorry Driver: Guilt-ridden Walcott's Haulage truck driver who killed Donna Noble when she stepped out in front of him, to cause a diversion, meaning her other self had to turn left out of Little Sutton Street and eventually meet the Doctor. (4.11)

Los Angeles Crevasse: Area on Earth where Lady Cassandra grew up. (1.2)

Lost Dimension, the: A term used by the Doctor to describe the Void, through which the TARDIS passed to arrive on 'Pete's World'. (2.5)

Lottery: Public method of legalised gambling on many worlds. Kazran Sardick's entire staff won the lottery and quit his employ, and many years earlier his babysitter Mrs Mantovani did the same, despite the fact that Sardicktown did not run a lottery – the Doctor, however, made sure they still won. (6.X)

Lou: Louis was the husband of Carmen and was with her when the number 200 bus they were travelling on was transported to San Helios. He tried to ease her discomfort when her sensitivity to voices in her head began upsetting her. He was very grateful to the Doctor for getting them both home safely. (4.15) (Played by REGINALD TSIBOE)

Louis XV, King: Ruler of France and Navarre, and lover of Reinette in her later life, he was dubious about the Doctor until he was saved by him from the Clockwork Men. When the Doctor arrived back in France in 1764, it was in time to see Reinette's hearse leaving Versailles for the last time, and the King gave the Doctor a letter from his mistress. (2.4) (Played by BEN TURNER)

'Love Don't Roam': Song played at Donna Noble and Lance Bennett's reception to celebrate their non-wedding, which made the Doctor think of Rose Tyler. It was sung by Neil Hannon. (3.X)

Love's Labour's Lost: A play by William Shakespeare. The Doctor and Martha Jones attended a performance at the Globe theatre, after which William Shakespeare announced the sequel, *Love's Labour's Won*. (3.2)

Love's Labour's Won: A play by William Shakespeare, thought lost by Martha Jones's time. In fact, Shakespeare had nearly finished it, but the Carrionites influenced the final scene, coercing him to write words that would open up a portal between the Globe theatre and the Deep Darkness, freeing the other Carrionites trapped there. When Shakespeare used the Carrionites' methods against them and defeated them, all copies of the manuscript were sucked into the Deep Darkness along with the Carrionites. The Doctor convinced Shakespeare not to start the play again. (3.2)

Lovely Bones, The: Novel by Alice Seabold, which the Doctor speed-read in Rose Tyler's flat. (1.1)

Lucas: Monitoring technician on Demon's Run who was observing the Clerics and Headless Monks seeking out the Doctor when Madame Vastra and Jenny arrived on the asteroid and tied up Lucas and his associate, Dominicus. Lucas tried to raise the alarm, but Vastra stung him into unconsciousness with her tongue. (6.7) (Played by JOSHUA HAYES)

Lucas, Jennifer: Morpeth-Jetsan contractor, working at the St John's crystal-diluric acid farm. She was in her rig-harness, asleep while her Ganger was working, when the solar tsunami hit St John's and gave her Ganger a sense of individuality and a desire to be a separate living person. As the Gangers and the human originals found themselves in conflict, Jennifer's Ganger became more and more obsessed with destroying the humans, initially winning the rest of the Gangers over, especially after the real Miranda Cleaves killed one of the Gangers. Realising they needed an ally, Jennifer pretended to be the human original and tricked Rory Williams into helping her 'escape' the Gangers. This Ganger told him her history, showing him images of her as a little girl. Unaware that this was a Ganger, Rory tried to help her as best he could. The real Jennifer, injured earlier during the tsunami, was murdered by another Jennifer Ganger, which in turn was killed by the one Rory believed to be real. This Ganger showed Rory the mound of discarded Gangers, now a mass of abused Flesh, but still sentient and in pain. Losing her control over the other Gangers, Jennifer transformed into a savage monster, determined to destroy the humans and Gangers in St John's. Letting the survivors of both teams escape in the TARDIS, the Ganger versions of the Doctor and Cleaves stayed behind to destroy Jennifer by blowing up the whole monastery, possibly dying alongside her. (6.5, 6.6) (Played by SARAH SMART and HOLLIE JONES)

Lucifer [1]: The dish Gaffabeque originated on the planet Lucifer, not Mars. Rose Tyler didn't know this when asked by the Anne Droid in *The Weakest Link* aboard the Game Station. (1.12)

Lucifer [2]: Legendary demon name, one of many attributed to the Beast throughout the galaxies. (2.8, 2.9)

Lucker, Tom: 58-year-old Colchester resident who was killed by the Cybermen and his body used for spare parts. (6.12)

Lucky: Title of a book by Jackie Collins, not Jackie Stewart. Rodrick didn't know this when asked by the Anne Droid in *The Weakest Link* aboard the Game Station. (1.12)

Lucy [1]: One of the catering staff employed by Pete Tyler on 'Pete's World' to serve at the party for his wife Jackie's birthday. Whilst preparing to serve the salmon pinwheels, she told the Doctor who the President of Great Britain was. If she wasn't killed when the Cybermen attacked the party, she was most likely taken to Battersea Power Station and her brain placed into a Cyberform. (2.5)

Lucy [2]: A diabetic stripper booked by Rory Williams's mates for his stag night. The Doctor took her place, leaving her outside the venue in only a bikini. (5.6)

Luke: Schoolboy at Deffry Vale High School, selected by Mr Wagner to help solve the Skasas Paradigm. (2.3) (Played by BENJAMIN SMITH)

Luke Gold, Royston: Human who died in the God Complex – his greatest fear was Plymouth. (6.11) (Played by MARCUS WILSON)

Lumic, John: On 'Pete's World', Lumic was the owner of Cybus Industries. Suffering from a terminal degenerative illness, Lumic had developed the Ultimate Upgrade process. This was a process by which human brains would be transplanted into a Cyberform (or Cyberman) – a body made of Lumic's High Content Metal steel. He tried to sell this concept to the President of Great Britain, not just as a commercial venture but also hoping that, with more research, it might solve his own health problems. When the President refused to support his proposals, Lumic sent the Cybermen that were already operational to kill the President at Pete Tyler's house during Jackie Tyler's birthday party. He then sent his Cybermen out onto the streets, ready to forcibly upgrade the population. After he had been fatally injured by Mr Crane, the Cybermen disregarded his orders and placed his mind inside that of a Cyberform – he became their Cyber Controller. If anything of Lumic was still there after that, it was lost when the Cyber Controller was destroyed. (2.5, 2.6) (Played by ROGER LLOYD PACK)

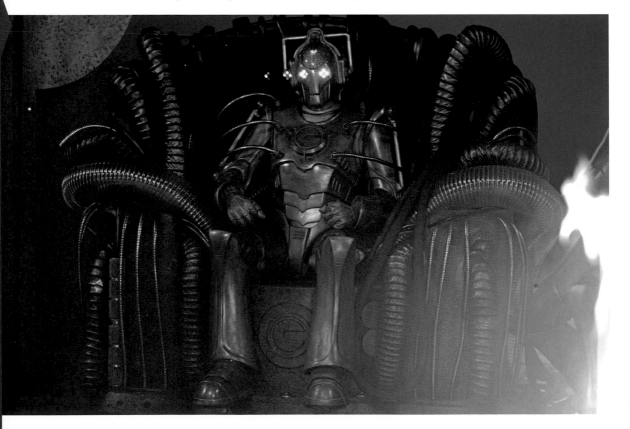

Luna University: River Song studied archaeology there for two centuries, some of that time under the tutelage of Professor Candy. (6.8)

Lunar Penal Colony: Where the Game Station Security Guard told the Doctor, Captain Jack Harkness and Lynda Moss they would be sent to, without trial. (1.12)

Lupine-Wavelength-Haemovariform: According to the Doctor, this was the correct name for the werewolf that prowled Torchwood House. (2.2)

Lute: Taller of Jabe's two associates from the Forest of Cheem aboard Platform One. He was distressed to hear of Jabe's death from the Doctor. (1.2) (Played by ALAN RUSCOE)

Lux, Charlotte Abigail: Youngest daughter of Felman Lux, creator of The Library. Booklover Charlotte was dying and so, to give her a kind of immortality, Lux used her living mind to create CAL, the central data core of the triple-grid security processor at the heart of The Library, with a doctor moon virus checker to protect her, located on the artificial satellite in orbit above. Fiercely protective of her father's work, CAL downloaded all the staff and visitors to The Library, storing them digitally on the hard drive when the Vashta Nerada attacked. However, her own programming was corrupted as a result and she began believing she was a real little girl, living in a big house with her father and Doctor Moon, who was there to help her. She claimed she lived in an imaginary library and was frustrated that people kept breaking in. She could see what was going on in The Library through her television set (her father could not see anything, though, and Doctor Moon claimed he couldn't either). In fact, she was observing The Library via the security nodes dotted throughout the building. When Donna Noble was downloaded, Charlotte created a fake reality for her where she was married to Lee McAvoy, who she met at the CAL hospital run by Doctor Moon. The Doctor was able to stop the corruption of CAL. She continued to live what she believed was a happy existence in her dreamscape alongside Doctor Moon, her father, and Professor Song and her friends, who had all been downloaded via the neural relays on their suits. (4.8, 4.9) (Played by EVE NEWTON)

Lux, Felman: Creator of The Library, he secretly used his dying daughter's living mind to give the data core of The Library a personality, CAL. In CAL's visions, her father lived with her in a big house, visited often by Doctor Moon. (4.8, 4.9) (Played by MARK DEXTER)

Lux, Strackman: Pompous, rich inheritor of The Library, designed by his grandfather. Lux financed an archaeological expedition to find out the truth behind what had happened in The Library a hundred years earlier. He was protective of his grandfather's legacy and CAL; it had taken three generations of Luxes just to have enough money to finance the expedition. After the Doctor stopped the Vashta Nerada and brought everyone back from where CAL had stored them, Lux greeted them personally, delighted to see them before they teleported away to safety. (4.8, 4.9) (Played by STEVE PEMBERTON)

Lynam, Des: Former presenter of the Channel 4 quiz show *Countdown*. After the Toclafane invasion, *Countdown* was cancelled, much to the chagrin of Professor Docherty. (3.13)

Lyndstep Crescent: Road close to the Powell Estate where the Doctor walked with Rose Tyler after the Auton arm had attacked them both in her mum's flat. (1.1)

Lynley: Master of the Revels in 1599, whose job it was to read and approve plays and decide if they were fit to go before the public. He threatened to ban *Love's Labour's Won* from being performed as he'd not had the chance to read it, so Lilith the Carrionite used her spellcasting to drown him in a dry street, then give him a heart attack. (3.2) (Played by CHRIS LARKIN)

Lynn, Auntie: Guest at the wedding of her nephew Stuart Hoskins and Sarah Clark. She hadn't arrived, and neither had her husband Steven. (1.8)

Lynne, Jeff: British producer, composer and singer for the Idle Race, The Move and the Traveling Wilburys, plus solo artists such as Tom Petty, Roy Orbison and George Harrison. However, he was most famously associated with the Electric Light Orchestra, of which Elton Pope was a huge fan. (2.10)

M

Ma: Passenger in a car on the New New York Motorway. Tired of the endless delays, her husband overrode the onboard computer that registered how many adults were in the vehicle and lied to the computer at the Transit Authority. Saying that there were three adults in his car gave them access to the Fast Lane, where they were attacked and killed by the Macra. (3.3) (Played by JUDY NORMAN)

Mabel: School classmate to Mandy Tanner and Timmy Winters. (5.2)

'Macarena': A song, originally a hit for Los del Rio in 1995, which the two Amy Ponds remembered because it was the dance they did when they first kissed Rory. Focusing on the hand movements from the dance enabled them to stay attuned to one another across time on Apalapucia. (6.10)

Macateer Street, Unit 4b: Location of the basement room beneath a deserted library where LINDA had their fun-filled meetings until Victor Kennedy arrived and forced them to work harder at hunting down the Doctor and Rose Tyler. (2.10)

Macbeth: One of William Shakespeare's best-known plays. Shakespeare had yet to write it when he met Martha Jones and the Doctor in 1599. (3.2) Doctor Black likened the quality of it to painter Vincent Van Gogh's artistic output. (5.10) It had just been performed for the first time according to Geoffrey Plum in 1605. (AG05)

Mace, Colonel Alan: UNIT officer in charge of dealing with the potential threat to Earth from ATMOS. He was working on information from journalist Jo Nakashima, who then vanished. He realised that the first wave of deaths from people using ATMOS occurred simultaneously all over the world and led the investigation into the ATMOS factory that eventually turned into a pitched battle with the Sontarans. After a shaky start, he and the Doctor grew to respect and like one another and, using the Doctor's information, he found a method of overriding the Sontarans' Cordolaine signal ability to stop the copper-coated UNIT weaponry working by using bullets coated with rad steel, and used the *Valiant* to disperse the ATMOS fumes. (4.4, 4.5) (Played by RUPERT HOLLIDAY EVANS)

Mack, Tony: Drilling engineer in Cwmtaff who had worked closely with Nasreen Chaudhry, with whom he became romantically involved, to set up the

Discovery Drilling Project. When his son-in-law and later grandson were both kidnapped by the Silurians, Tony remained composed, listening to the Doctor and trying to keep his anxious daughter Ambrose calm. Tony was attacked by a Silurian captive, Alaya, who wanted to provoke an all-out war with the humans. Poisoned by her tongue, Tony realised his flesh was starting to turn green and scaly and his heart was suffering. When Ambrose found out, she unintentionally killed Alaya. Tony, Ambrose and Rory Williams then had to take the body down to the Silurian city. Alaya's death destroyed the peace process the Doctor was establishing, and Tony and his family only just escaped with their lives. As the Silurian elder, Eldane, put his people back into hibernation, Tony revealed his venom-infested body and the Doctor realised there was no cure at this stage. Tony volunteered to join the Silurians in hibernation hoping they would cure him in the future – and Nasreen agreed to join him. (5.8, 5.9) (Played by ROBERT PUGH)

Mackeson: One of the soldiers under Captain Reynolds protecting Queen Victoria in 1879. (2.2)

MacLeish, Lady Isobel: Wife of Sir Robert and lady of Torchwood House, she bravely tried to keep spirits up among her staff when they were imprisoned by the Brethren of St Catherine and faced the Haemovariform. She led her maids and cook to the kitchens where they filled pans and buckets with mistletoe to ward off the werewolf. After her husband's sacrifice, Lady Isobel opted not to remain at Torchwood House, and it passed to the Crown. (2.2) (Played by MICHELLE DUNCAN)

MacLeish, Sir George: Father to Sir Robert, and friend of Prince Albert. A polymath, equally as au fait with science and legends and folklore as was the Queen's consort, he designed and built a huge telescope which, when linked to the Koh-I-Noor diamond, would create a beam of light powerful enough to destroy the Haemovariform. (2.2)

MacLeish, Sir Robert: Having inherited his home from his father, Sir Robert did not understand the work his father and Prince Albert, the Queen's

consort, had undertaken in the Observatory of Torchwood House. When the Brethren came, he was unable to stop them taking the house over and setting a trap for the Queen – his wife, Lady Isobel, and the entire household were held captive. After the Haemovariform escaped, Sir Robert realised the only way to salvage his family name and reputation was to sacrifice himself to protect the Queen – and so he held the werewolf off for a few vital seconds outside the Observatory before becoming its final victim. (2.2) Davros taunted the Doctor about how many people had died trying to help him over the years, and this made the Doctor think of Sir Robert. (4.13) (Played by DEREK RIDDELL)

MacNannovich, Cal 'Spark Plug': He and an unnamed companion were guests aboard Platform One to see the Earthdeath spectacle. (1.2)

Macra, the: Massive crustaceans which had most likely escaped from the New New York Zoo at some point and were living beneath the lanes of the enclosed New New York Motorway, feeding off the exhaust fumes. The Macra had once run an empire of enslavement and terror centuries before, but over the aeons had devolved into mindless brutes, acting only on instinct. As a result, cars reaching the lowest level, the Fast Lane, tended to be swatted down by the Macra, who regarded them as pests to be knocked aside. When the Doctor opened the covered Motorway and freed the cars trapped inside, the Macra were left down there, presumably to be rehoused in the Zoo at some point as the exhaust fumes they thrived on would soon dissipate. (3.3)

Macrae Cantrell, Suki: An eager young journalist, hoping that her work would get her noticed. Born in the Independent Republic of Morocco in 199'89, her hobbies included reading and archaeology and she took a job on Satellite Five to cover her

sister's university fees then applied for a promotion to Floor 500. This was successful but, when Suki got there, she discovered what was really in control of Earth – the Jagrafess. The Editor, the Jagrafess's human associate, revealed that he knew the truth about Suki; that she was not the humble journalist she pretended, but was in fact self-declared anarchist Eva Saint Julienne, the last known member of the Freedom Fifteen, a group determined to prove that Satellite Five was being manipulated by outside sources. The Jagrafess killed Suki/Eva and reanimated her corpse via her chip implant to work for him. However, when the Jagrafess was destroyed, a tiny spark of Suki/Eva still existed and she stopped the Editor from escaping the carnage, resulting in both their destructions. (1.7) (Played by ANNA MAXWELL-MARTIN)

Madame Cholet: Fictional cook, one of the Wombles, and featured in the novels by Elizabeth Beresford before transferring to television in the 1970s. The Doctor referred to her as one of the greatest chefs on Earth. (TIQ)

Madame de Pompadour, SS: Spaceship in the 51st century, run by Clockwork repair robots, which were using time-window technology to travel back to 18th-century France to find the real Madame de Pompadour and, in their skewed logic, remove her brain to enable them to complete repairs to the damaged ship – at a point when she was 37, the same age as the craft. The crew had already been sacrificed, their body parts integrated into the ship's workings. When their mission failed, the Clockwork Robots were all deactivated, and the lifeless SS *Madame de Pompadour* continued floating aimlessly through space. (2.4)

M

Maddock Way: Road running through the middle of the Powell Estate in South East London, with shops along it such as Maddock Cleaners and the Maddock Way Surgery. The TARDIS landed there a year after taking Rose away (1.4) and later crash-landed there after the Doctor's regeneration. (2.X) It returned there one last time to allow the Doctor to see Rose again before he regenerated. (4.18)

Madrid: Spanish resort that the Doctor declared to be a bit of a dump. (5.11)

Maeve: Elderly resident of Dame Kelly Homes Close who suspected that the disappearances of the neighbourhood kids weren't natural and had her suspicions about Chloe Webber. She thanked Rose when the kids were returned safely. (2.11) (Played by EDNA DORÉ)

Mafeking: South African town that was the scene of a 217-day siege in 1899–1900, during the closing months of the Second Boer War, which was decisive in the British victory in that conflict. The definitive account of the siege was written by Aitchinson Price, according to history teacher John Smith. (3.8) Colonel Hugh Curbishley claimed to have been there. (4.7)

Magambo, Captain Erisa: UNIT commander in the alternative world where Donna Noble never met the Doctor. She and Rose Tyler had come up with a method, based on the Doctor's dying TARDIS, to project Donna back in time to the exact moment she made a decision that changed the future. This used Chronon energy bounced off perfectly aligned mirrors, that enabled Donna to finally see the Time Beetle on her back that so many people she had encountered

had almost seen. (4.11) In the 'real' world, Magambo was in charge of the UNIT operation at the Gladwell road tunnel and was honoured to work alongside the Doctor, although quite prepared to sacrifice him and the other passengers on the number 200 bus, if saving them resulted in an infestation of Stingrays. (4.15) (Played by NOMA DUMEZWENI)

Magna-clamp: Alien magnetic technology that made anything heavy virtually weightless and therefore easy to move. Jackie Tyler thought that would be handy for carrying the shopping. The Doctor used them to hold himself and Rose Tyler to the wall when opening the Lever Room entrance to the Void, as the Daleks and Cybermen were sucked back in. Rose Tyler lost her grip on hers while trying to operate a Lever and was only saved by the 'Pete's World' version of her father, who rescued her and transported her to his home, sealing Rose off from the Doctor. (2.12, 2.13)

Magnatron: Dalek device used to hold 27 planets in perfect synchronous orbit within the Medusa Cascade, to power the Reality Bomb. The Doctor then used the Magnatron to free the planets and send them back to their rightful places in time and space. In an attempt to stop this, the Supreme Dalek destroyed the Magnatron, leaving Earth the only planet unable to be sent home. (4.12, 4.13)

Magpie, Mr: Small businessman, running his own shop selling electrical goods such as radios and televisions in Muswell Hill during the early 1950s. The alien criminal known as the Wire inhabited one of his television sets, spreading its

influence across many others in his store, which he then sold across the area. He worked for the Wire out of fear — the creature promised not to steal his face if he followed her orders. Under the Wire's guidance, he built a primitive portable television which he took to the Alexandra Palace television mast, through which the Wire would be able to spread itself further afield. When Magpie finally decided to fight back, the Wire vaporised him. (2.7) (Played by RON COOK)

Magpie Electricals: Retail business based on Mafeking Road, in Muswell Hill in North London, and owned by Mr Magpie in the 1950s, specialising in the then-new television sets and aerials. Thanks to the upcoming Coronation and his own very low prices, Magpie saw an upswing

in sales. (2.7) The business continued running successfully after Mr Magpie's death, reportedly taken over by his son. The loudspeakers used by the DJ at Donna Noble's wedding reception were supplied by Magpie Electricals, and the Doctor saw its website on a borrowed mobile phone as he searched for information on HC Clements. (3.X) Martha Jones had a Magpie television set in her flat (3.12) and Wilfred Mott had another in his newspaper stall. (4.X) There was a Magpie Electricals store on board Starship UK centuries later. (5.2) The regenerated TARDIS control room apparently utilised several pieces of Magpie equipment on its new console, including the monitor screen. (5.1, 5.10) River Song used an EMF meter labelled 'Magpie Technology'. (6.2) One of its delivery men set up the television set for the Connolly family. (2.7T) (Played by KEVIN HUDSON)

Main Street: Long strip leading from Dry Springs town out to Sammy's Pitstop Diner and beyond. The Doctor left the TARDIS there. (DL)

Mair, Susie: A friend of Donna Noble's and her mate Veena. Susie may have been on the plumpish side, and was known to use on-line dating sites, where she spotted a man who Veena fancied from their local off-licence. (4.13)

Majorca: Balearic island resort where, according to the Doctor, lots of Britons go to open English-themed pubs. (6.11)

Malcassairo: Planet on the very edge of the universe, where the human refugees of the year 100,000,000,000,000 had gathered. The Malmooth who originally dominated the planet were all but gone and, after the humans' rocket took off, the effectively dead world of Malcassairo was left in the hands of the bestial Futurekind. (3.11)

Maldovar, Dorium: Large, blue-skinned morally ambiguous bar owner, who supplied River Song with a Vortex Manipulator and unwittingly swallowed a micro-explosive. River gave him a Calisto Pulse to disarm it. (5.12) The Headless Monks were old customers of his — he supplied them with the security software to kidnap Amy Pond. (6.7P) He was in the process of closing down his bar and moving on when Madame Kovarian and Colonel Manton paid him a visit, to ask about the Doctor. Once they had left, Dorium was horrified to see the TARDIS out back — the Doctor had come for him, to repay a debt. Dorium was taken to Demon's Run because he had supplied the security systems there to the Clerics. When the Headless Monks made their attack, Dorium was convinced they wouldn't hurt him, but they beheaded him and reanimated his body, turning it into a meat puppet. (6.7) The Doctor later found Dorium's still-sentient head in a box (complete with wi-fi) in the Labyrinth of Skulls known as the Headless Monks' Seventh Transept. Dorium warned the Doctor that he would fall when the question that must never, ever be answered was answered. The Doctor took Dorium's head, in its box, aboard the TARDIS. Once the universe believed the Doctor dead at River Song's hand, just as the Silence intended, he returned Dorium to the Seventh Transept. (6.13) (Played by SIMON FISHER BECKER)

Maldovarium, the: The bar owned and run by Dorium Maldovar, from where River Song obtained her Vortex Manipulator. (5.12) The bar was being closed down when Dorium received visits firstly from Kovarian and Colonel Manton and then from the Doctor (6.7)

Male Crewmember: Realising that the SS *Madame de Pompadour* was about to be caught up in an ion storm, he and his fellow crewmember sent a mayday back to Earth. When the ion storm struck, he was left unconscious but safe, until a Clockwork Robot arrived on the bridge. (2.4T) (Played by DAVID MARTIN)

Male Student: Attended the Rattigan Academy and was the first to challenge Luke Rattigan after the world was poisoned by the ATMOS devices. He and the other students abandoned Luke and went home. (4.5) (Played by LEESHON ALEXANDER)

Malmooth: Blue-skinned insectoid race which once dominated Malcassairo but had almost died out. Only Chantho survived, helping Professor Yana for 17 years as he tried to launch a rocket that would take the human refugees to Utopia. (3.11)

Malohkeh: Silurian scientist. Many generations of his family had stayed awake and alone over the centuries, dedicating their lives to examining the flora and fauna of Earth and the surface world above the Silurian City beneath Cwmtaff. Malohkeh had taken dead bodies from the cemetery to examine and finally a live specimen, Mo Northover, who he carefully dissected and repaired perfectly, so Mo felt no ill effects. He was planning to do the same on a human female, Amy Pond, when she and Mo escaped. Malohkeh soon realised that the humans were not that different from his own culture and he happily released Mo's son Elliot back into his father's care. However, his liking of humans brought him into conflict with the warrior Restac, who murdered him rather than let him warn the Doctor that she was going to wipe mankind out. (5.8, 5.9) In the alternative London created by River Song's refusal to kill the Doctor and consequent disruption to established history, Malohkeh was attendant physician to Winston Churchill. (6.13) (Played by RICHARD HOPE)

Malta: Mediterranean holiday destination, where Dom, a mate of Craig Owens who sometimes filled in on the King's Arms football, team was vacationing, which meant the Doctor had to take his place in the match. (5.11)

'My Mammy': Song popular in the 1920s, written by Donaldson, Young and Lewis. When the Doctor had been poisoned by cyanide and was trying to mime what would help him, Donna Noble suggested he was miming this song, later made famous by Al Jolson. (4.7)

Man [1]: Passer-by in the street in 1883 at Christmas, when a young street urchin was kidnapped by the Graske. (AotG) (Played by ROGER NOTT)

Man [2]: One of the visitors to The Library who was restored from the hard drive by the Doctor and River Song. Strackman Lux greeted him shortly before the man was teleported off the planet to safety. (4.9) (Played by JONATHAN REUBEN)

Man in Pub: Bloke who ran into the pub where Donna Noble, Veena Brady, Mooky Kahari and Alice Coltrane were drinking to tell them about the Webstar, in the alternative world where Donna never met the Doctor. (4.11) (Played by NEIL CLENCH)

Manchester: Metropolis in North West England. Home of the Mitchell family, including Adam, who briefly travelled with the Doctor and Rose Tyler. (1.7)

Manchester Suite [1]: Where Platform One held the reception for alien dignitaries to observe Earthdeath. Its sunfilters were momentarily lowered, causing the deaths of some visitors, including the Moxx of Balhoon. (1.2)

Manchester Suite [2]: Where the reception for the non-wedding of Donna Noble and Lance Bennett was held. The reception guests were attacked by Roboform mercenaries searching for Donna. (3.X)

Manchester United: English football team, famed for wearing a red strip. The Doctor initially thought the US military personnel at Dreamland were frightened of them until he realised 'the Reds' meant the Soviet Union. (DL)

Manhattan: Island district of New York City, often separated into three areas, Lower, Midtown and Upper. The Cult of Skaro ended up there after fleeing the Battle of Canary Wharf and began plotting to create a New Skaro from a Transgenic Laboratory they had converted in the sewers beneath the Empire State Building. (3.4, 3.5) Martha Jones was seconded to the UNIT headquarters there, and was involved with the Project Indigo trials. It was attacked by Daleks and

M

most of the UNIT personnel exterminated, but Martha escaped. (4.12) The Doctor, Kazran Sardick and Abigail Pettigrew visited it one Christmas Eve. (6.X) River Song threw herself off the 50th floor of a building there rather than be captured by Canton Delaware III. The Doctor materialised the TARDIS beneath her and she fell into the TARDIS's swimming pool. (6.2)

Manista, Scootori: 20-year-old Torchwood trainee Maintenance Officer on Sanctuary Base 6. She discovered the possessed Toby Zed standing unharmed on the exposed surface of Krop Tor but, when she tried to report this, he psionically locked the doors, trapping her in one area, which he then opened to the elements, sending Scooti to her death in the vacuum of space. (2.8) (Played by MyANNA BURING)

Manservant: Sent by Madame Poisson to retrieve her daughter from her room, he was shocked to discover the Doctor there. (2.4) (Played by GARETH WYN GRIFFITHS)

Mantasphid Queen: A manipulative insect. She controlled the hive mind of the Mantasphids, an incredibly intelligent insectoid race, who colonised fertile planets full of dung. The Queen set up home on Myarr, then exiled the human colonists already there and thus found herself leading her people into a war with the Earth Empire of the 40th century. Ultimately she faced defeat and total annihilation at the hands of the humans until the Doctor stepped in and pretended to Earth Control that it was he, Doctor Vile, who had forced the Mantasphids to attack the humans on his behalf. The Doctor then fled Myarr, leaving the Mantasphids and humans to broker a peace deal. (TIQ) (Voiced by LIZZIE HOPLEY)

Mantasphids: An incredibly intelligent alien insectoid race. They colonised fertile planets full of dung, including Myarr, then exiled the human colonists already there and thus found themselves at war with the Earth Empire of the 40th century. (TIQ)

Manton, Colonel: Commander of the Clerics who, along with Madame Kovarian, plotted to kidnap Amy Pond and bring her back to the asteroid Demon's Run on behalf of the Silence. There Amy gave birth to Melody Pond, while Manton stirred his troops up into hunting for the Doctor, alongside their quasi-allies, the Headless Monks. Manton lost control when the Doctor infiltrated the Monks and one of his troopers killed a Monk. Manton managed to calm everything down, pacifying the Monks by unloading his weapon. His Clerics did likewise, but that was also part of the trick and the Doctor had the Clerics arrested by the Judoon and the Silurians. The Doctor taunted Manton into telling the Clerics waiting in space to run away, suggesting that, in history, Colonel Manton would be remembered for giving that exact order and forever known as Colonel Run-Away. (6.7) (Played by DANNY SAPINI)

Mantovani, Mrs: Babysitter for the 12-year-old Kazran Sardick. She resigned her post after the Doctor 'arranged' for her to win the lottery, even though there wasn't a lottery on Ember. (6.X)

Mara: The Tenth Doctor tried to work out where in the Fifth Doctor's timeline they were meeting by asking if he'd encountered the Mara yet. (TC)

Marbella: Popular beach resort in Spain's Costa del Sol. The Doctor told Rose Tyler that they could easily head there in 1989, and leave the Daleks to destroy humanity in 200,100. (1.13)

Marcellus: Auton Roman officer in AD 102, who greeted the Doctor and Amy Pond when they arrived, believing the Doctor to be Caesar. This may have been because he had been kissed by River Song wearing the hallucinogenic lipstick. (5.12) (Played by DAVID FYNN)

M

Marcie: Front Desk Officer at the police station where Billy Shipton was a detective inspector. (3.10)

Marco, Cleric: One of Father Octavian's troopers. He was killed in the *Byzantium*'s Forest Vault when he approached the time field. (5.4, 5.5) (Played by DARREN MORFITT)

Marconi's Disease: An illness that took years to recover from but, by using a cell-washing cascade, the Sisters of Plenitude on New Earth had developed a cure that took two days. (2.1)

Margaret: Aggressive Londoner who the Doctor woke up by throwing stones at her windows. (AG05) (Voiced by AMELDA BROWN)

Maria: Shakespearean character from *Love's Labour's Lost* and later *Love's Labour's Won*. (3.2)

Maria Leszczynska, Queen: Wife of King Louis XV of France and friend to Madame de Pompadour, despite her being the King's lover. She was present when Clockwork Robots from the 51st century attacked a party at the Palace of Versailles and the Doctor saved Madame de Pompadour's life. She died in 1768. (2.4) (Played by GAYLE ANN FELTON)

Mark: Craig Owens's previous flatmate, and owner of the flat, who had inherited a lot of money when an unknown uncle died, and so moved out. The Doctor took over his room while investigating the time engine posing as the upstairs apartment (5.11)

Mark, John: Olympic Torch-bearer at the 1948 Olympic Games in North London whom the Doctor admired. (2.11)

Market Tavern: Pub where the Jones family celebrated Leo Jones's 21st birthday, until a row erupted between Francine Jones and Clive's new girlfriend, Annalise. (3.1)

Marley, Jacob: Ghostly character in *A Christmas Carol*, which Charles Dickens read to an rapt Welsh audience on Christmas Eve 1869. (1.3)

Marr, Andrew: BBC reporter outside 10 Downing Street after the Big Ben incident, who wondered where the Prime Minister was. (1.4, 1.5)

Mars: Jackie Tyler and her friends drunkenly toasted the supposed 'Martians' that crashed a spaceship into Big Ben and then the Thames. (1.4) Adam Mitchell pretended to be a student visiting Satellite Five from the University of Mars. (1.7) The *Guinevere One* space probe was headed to Mars when the Sycorax ship intercepted it. Major Blake of UNIT knew the Sycorax weren't natives of Mars because Martians looked completely different. (2.X) When unexpectedly travelling in the TARDIS, Jackie told the Doctor that, if he took her to Mars, she'd kill him. (2.12) Donna Noble assumed the Doctor was from Mars when she first met him. (3.X) Bowie Base One was based on Mars, led by Captain Adelaide Brooke. The science survey team there were, according to history, all killed when an inexplicable nuclear explosion occurred, destroying the base. Mars was host to at least two indigenous life forms: the long-departed Ice Warriors and the Flood, which thrived in the ice beneath the planet's surface. Bowie Base One was infiltrated by the Flood, who planned to conquer Earth next, so the nuclear explosion was Adelaide Brooke destroying her base, her team and the Flood. Before the explosion, the Doctor took the survivors back to Earth, slightly changing the future. (4.16)

Marsey Street: East London street where Stacy Campbell lived at number 23. (4.1)

Martian Boondocks: Area on Mars known to be associated with the university there. (1.7)

Martian Drones: In social security, the payment given to Martian Drones was Default. Colleen knew this when asked by the Anne Droid in *The Weakest Link* aboard the Game Station. (1.12)

Marty McFly: The Doctor used the 1985 movie *Back to the Future* and its time-travelling lead character Marty McFly to explain to Martha Jones the complexities of the Infinite Temporal Flux. (3.2)

Mary I, Queen: 16th-century ruler of England, until she was replaced by her half-sister, Elizabeth. Commonly known as 'Bloody Mary'. (AG05)

Mary Poppins: Fictional babysitter and governess created by Pamela Lyndon Travers (a pseudonym for writer Helen Goff). The Doctor, pretending to be Kazran Sardick's replacement babysitter, was keen not to be likened to her. (6.X)

Master, the: Plagued by the never-ending sound of drumming in his head, the Master was one of the Doctor's childhood friends, driven insane after looking into the Untempered Schism on Gallifrey when he was just 8 years old. Just as the Doctor did, the Master chose his own name, and stole a TARDIS in order to flee Gallifreyan society and explore the universe. Unlike the Doctor, however, the Master craved domination, and sought alliances with a number of alien races during his early attempts to conquer the Earth – including the Nestene Consciousness, Axons, Daleks and Sea Devils. It was also during this time that he and the Doctor came to the attention of organisations such as UNIT and Torchwood. Despite running out of regenerations and eventually dying, the Master's consciousness was revived by the Time Lords during the course of the Time War, when he was resurrected to serve as the perfect warrior. The Master was present when the Dalek Emperor took control of the Cruciform, but fled to the end of the universe in order to escape, making himself human in the process.

After years hiding as Professor Yana on Malcassairo, it was a chance encounter with the Doctor, Martha Jones and Captain Jack Harkness that caused the Master to regain his identity, encouraged by echoes of his past incarnations contained within the Professor's fob watch. He promptly seized the opportunity to steal both the Doctor's severed hand and the TARDIS, and return to Earth – but not before suffering a fatal gunshot from the Professor's companion, Chantho, and undergoing a regeneration. (3.11) Abandoning the Doctor in the far future, the Master travelled to Earth in 2007, shortly after the downfall of Harriet Jones PM. He then met Lucy Saxon, and took her to the end of the universe to see Utopia, where the human race had devolved and were converted into the Toclafane. Returning to Earth, the Master married Lucy and assumed the role of Harry Saxon, creating an entire history for his alter ego. As Saxon, the Master claimed to have attended and graduated from Cambridge University, gone into business, succeeded in his athletics career, and even to have written a novel, *Kiss Me, Kill Me*.

During this time, the Master cannibalised the TARDIS and converted it into a Paradox Machine, as well as starting work for the Ministry of Defence, where he was responsible for launching the Archangel mobile phone network, shooting down the Racnoss Webstar on Christmas Eve, (3.X) and funding Richard Lazarus's rejuvenation experiments. (3.6) He also assisted in designing the *Valiant* aircraft carrier for UNIT. He would later incorporate Lazarus's findings into the functions of his own laser screwdriver, enabling it to age individuals beyond their natural life spans, whilst also dispensing deadly laser bolts at his attackers.

The Master was elected Prime Minister of Great Britain in 2008, assisted by the mesmeric influence of the Archangel network, which tricked the Earth into believing his deceits, whilst also concealing his presence from the Doctor. His supporters at this time included Sharon Osbourne, pop group McFly and Ann Widdecombe MP. As Saxon, the Master also ensured that Tish Jones was able to secure jobs with both LazLabs and himself, whilst simultaneously using his operatives to spread disinformation about the Doctor to Francine Jones. (3.6, 3.7) In the role of Prime Minister, his first unofficial duty was to oversee the execution of the Cabinet in his office, before publicly announcing his relationship with the Toclafane to the world. It was during first contact with the Toclafane on board the *Valiant* that the Master revealed his true identity and ordered the assassination of US President Winters by the Toclafane. Assuming authority over the entire Earth, the Master then used the Paradox Machine to allow the Toclafane to invade from the end of the universe, and ordered the decimation of the planet's populace, keeping an aged Doctor, Jack and the Jones family prisoner aboard the *Valiant* in order to watch his victory. (3.12) Over the course of a year, the Master constructed an army of 200,000 war rockets in shipyards around the world, and was planning to open a rift in Braccatolian space as part of his bid to launch a new Time Lord Empire, and adopt a new Gallifrey alongside it. Egotistical and overindulgent, the Master had his likeness carved into the face of Mount Rushmore and recreated across the globe in the form of colossal statues. He also collected wives from across the continents in addition to Lucy, and would insist upon receiving a

massage every day at three o'clock. It was through such predictability – the Doctor knew he couldn't resist a countdown – that the Doctor was able to rejuvenate himself and defeat the Master, restoring time to a point before the Toclafane ever invaded. As a fellow Time Lord, the Doctor took responsibility for the Master's actions, and intended to spend the rest of his lives caring for him within the safety of the TARDIS. When the Master was shot dead by his abused wife, he refused to regenerate in spite of the Doctor's wishes, willingly allowing himself to die in order to secure one final victory over his opponent. His body was then set upon a funeral pyre and burned by a devastated Doctor, though his ring was later removed from the embers by the mysterious Miss Trefusis... (3.13)

The Tenth Doctor tried to work out where in the Fifth Doctor's timeline they were meeting by asking if the Master still had a beard. (TC)

Although he was apparently dead, Saxon's followers, including Miss Trefusis, now a prison guard at HMP Broadfell where Lucy Saxon was imprisoned, wanted to return him to life. Using the Books of Saxon, Miss Trefusis, the Governor and others sacrificed their lives to return the Master to life, but Lucy Saxon also knew about the Books and, using her powerful family, had obtained an antidote. Lucy died as she threw the antidote at the Master, stopping his full re-emergence, creating a terrible half-life for him, where his body went from solid to energy at irregular times sending him more insane than ever before. Permanently hungry, and wasting the energies holding his corporeal form together when fighting the Doctor, the Master was eventually taken to Joshua Naismith's home, where a Vinvocci medical device they called the Immortality Gate was positioned. The Master used the device not to just repair his body but to send his own template across the Earth, turning every human being into him. Only Wilfred Mott (protected by the Nuclear Bolt room), two Vinvocci, the Doctor and Donna Noble remained unchanged. The Master then learned that his madness, everything he had ever done in his life, had been at the whim of Lord President Rassilon who, far in the future, had sent the sound of a Time Lord heartbeat (the sound of drums) back in time to the moment the Master had looked into the Untempered Schism. Rassilon sent a Whitepoint Star diamond to Earth, linked to the heartbeat sound in the Master's mind. The Master used it to open up a dimensional gateway, through

M

219

which the Time Lords returned to time and space – bringing Gallifrey with them. But when Rassilon prepared to destroy him, the Master, angry, embittered but possibly sane for the first time in his life, used the last of his life energies to blast the Time Lords back to Gallifrey, while the Doctor destroyed the Whitepoint Star's housing, and thus severed the link between Gallifrey, Earth and the Master's mind, sealing them all back within the timelocked Gallifrey. (4.17, 4.18) (Played by ROGER DELGADO, ANTHONY AINLEY, DEREK JACOBI, JOHN SIMM, WILLIAM HUGHES)

Master of the Revels: Official 'censor' of the Elizabethan era, based in Clerkenwell. The holder of the job had the power to halt any entertainment if, in his opinion, it failed to meet the criteria of good taste. Lynley, the Master of the Revels when William Shakespeare was writing *Love's Labour's Won*, was murdered by one of the Carrionites. (3.2)

Matilda: Young woman who painted a nude portrait of the Doctor, 'My Mysterious Doctor', and was discovered doing this by an annoyed Charles. Amy Pond and Rory Williams read about this incident in the book *Myths and Historical Impossibilities*. (6.1) (Played by HENRIETTA CLEMETT)

Matrix: The Type 40 TARDIS the Doctor had contained an eleven-dimensional personality Matrix – 'the soul of the TARDIS', as the Doctor described it. This was drawn out of the TARDIS by House and placed inside a dead humanoid called Idris. House then transferred its own sentience into the TARDIS, but when the Doctor's own TARDIS re-established itself, House was destroyed. (6.4)

Matron: Venetian woman who was employed by Rosanna Calvierri to look after her Calvierri Girls. (5.6) (Played by HELEN CHILCOTT)

Matt: Driver of the car that killed Pete Tyler in Jordan Road in 1987. Rather than checking on his victim, Matt panicked and drove away, never reporting the crime or being caught. When Rose Tyler's actions saved Pete's life, a breach in the fabric of time opened up and Matt and his car were projected a few miles down the road to St Christopher's Church. Matt was caught in an endless cycle of driving and panicking around the church until Pete Tyler realised what had happened. He ran out in front of the car and was killed. This time Matt did the right thing, and stayed put, while Pete died in the arms of a mysterious blonde no one ever traced. In fact, this was Rose Tyler. (1.8) (Played by CRISPIN LAYFIELD)

Matter Lines: One of the mechanisms within the Pandorica to ensure it remained sealed. (5.12)

Maurice: Manager of the café where Vincent Van Gogh hung out in Auvers. Van Gogh tried to pay for his wine with a painting, but Maurice was having none of it and threw him out. (5.10) (Played by NIK HOWDEN)

Mauve: The universally recognised colour for danger, according to the Doctor as the TARDIS pursued a Chula warship through the Time Vortex. (1.9)

Max: See *Mighty Jagrafess of the Holy Hadrojassic Maxarodenfoe*

Max-Box: Crude cybernetic transport device which contained all that remained of Max Capricorn aboard the starliner *Titanic*. (4.X)

Max Capricorn Cruiseliners: Firm in financial trouble, run by the eponymous Max Capricorn. They boasted that they were 'the fastest, the furthest, the best…' The galaxy-class luxury starship *Titanic* was part of their fleet. (4.X)

M

Maze of the Dead: The catacombs beneath the surface of Alfava Metraxis, built by the Aplans as a mortarium across six levels, one for each ascent of the soul. As the Doctor, Amy Pond, River Song and Father Octavian's Clerics passed through it on their way to the flight deck of the crashed *Byzantium*, they realised that all the statues around them were regenerating Weeping Angels. (5.4, 5.5)

McAllister, Ewan: One of the arrivals at 10 Downing Street after the Big Ben incident. The Deputy Secretary for the Scottish Parliament, he was actually a disguised Slitheen, the original McAllister having been killed previously. (1.5)

McAvoy, Ella and Joshua: Apparent daughter and son of Lee McAvoy and Donna Noble in the fictional reality created by CAL in The Library's data core. However, when Donna was shown the truth by Miss Evangelista (she demonstrated that every child in the reality looked the same as Ella and Joshua), Lee and their two children ceased to exist. (4.9) (Played by ELOISE RAKIC-PLATT and ALEX MIDWOOD)

McAvoy, Lee: In the fictional world created by CAL within the data core of The Library, Donna Noble was introduced to fishing-fan Lee. In actuality he was one of the people rescued by CAL one hundred years earlier from the Vashta Nerada but he had no memory of his former life and, like Donna, believed he had lived in suburbia for years. When Donna and he first met, he, like Donna, was a patient of Doctor Moon, who was trying to cure Lee's stammer – and once Lee

and Donna married, his stammer faded. However, when Donna was shown the truth by Miss Evangelista, Lee and their two children ceased to exist. Nevertheless, when Lee was restored back in The Library, he saw Donna and remembered her but was unable to contact her due to the re-emergence of his stutter. (4.9) (Played by JASON PITT)

McCrimmon, Dr James: Pseudonym the Doctor adopted for the benefit of Queen Victoria. Jamie McCrimmon had been a travelling companion of the Doctor during his second incarnation. (2.2)

M

McDonnell, Kath: Acerbic and quick-witted captain of the SS *Pentallian*, and ultimately responsible for the decision to use a fusion scoop to get matter from the living sun that then threatened her crew, because it was too expensive to scan for life first. As the sun-possessed version of her husband Korwin began murdering her crew, she tried to understand what had happened, but it was only when the Doctor made contact with the living sun and became sun-possessed himself that she finally realised what had to be done. She led Korwin into an airlock and opened it into space, allowing herself and her husband to be sucked into the sun, where they died together. (3.6) (Played by MICHELLE COLLINS)

McDonnell, Korwin: Husband of Kath, the captain of the SS *Pentallian*, and member of the ship's crew. They had been married for 11 years and chose the ship together. He was the first victim of the living sun, angry that the *Pentallian* had scooped out part of its body – so it consumed Korwin and used him as a walking weapon aboard the ship, wrecking engineering and so setting the ship on a course into the sun, thus regaining what it had lost. Korwin also began killing the crew one by one, although he infected Dev Ashton rather than killing him, needing a partner. However, the sun-possessed Korwin was notably weaker for doing this and Orin Scannell believed he had killed Korwin by freezing him with the ice vents. Korwin soon defrosted himself and began his relentless march through the ship, so Kath led him into an airlock, and opened it into space, allowing herself and her husband to be sucked into the sun, where they died together. (3.6) (Played by MATTHEW CHAMBERS)

McFly: British pop group, who endorsed Harry Saxon's campaign to become Prime Minister. (3.12)

McGinty, Mary: Small, dark haired woman who worked in the local newsagents near the Nobles' house in Chiswick. In the alternative world where Donna never met the Doctor, she was killed when the starship *Titanic* hit London. (4.11)

McGrath [1]: One of Avery's pirate crew aboard the *Fancy*. Whilst away in the rowboat, he scratched himself and shortly after a black spot appeared on his palm. He was then taken by the Siren from the ship's deck. He was later found alive aboard the Skerth ship, being tended to by the Siren. He joined Avery exploring the universe. (6.3) (Played by CARL McCRYSTAL)

McGrath [2]: Highwayman hung on the Tyburn Tree. (AG05)

McKenzie, Julie: Resident of Rowbarton House, one of Jim Purcell's tenants. She had twin daughters, Ruby and Daisy (played by MADDISON and SAYA KARAUNA) (6.9) (Played by SOPHIE COSSON)

McKillan, Jane: One of the children drawn by Chloe Webber, who thus disappeared from Dame Kelly Holmes Close to become a friend for the Isolus. She

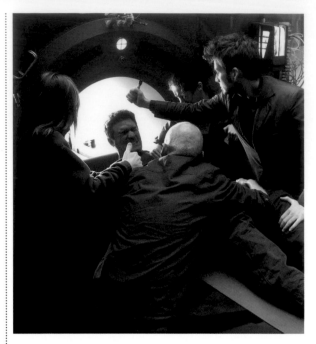

later returned to the street after the Isolus left Earth. (2.11) (Played by GABRIELLE EVANS)

McKillan, Mrs: Mother of missing child Jane, who wept with joy when her daughter was returned to her after the Isolus left Earth. (2.11) (Played by KAREN HULSE)

McLintock's Candy Burgers: Food suppliers who sponsored the Vator Verse on *Starship UK*. (5.2)

McMillan: Torchwood Archive representative who sent Captain Walker and his crew to Krop Tor to examine the energy source detected ten miles beneath its surface. (2.8T) (Played by RI RICHARDS)

M

McMillan, Detective Inspector: Hard-bitten British policeman who had been after cat burglar Lady Christina de Souza for ages and was waiting to arrest her when she came back to Earth from San Helios. He was delighted when he finally got his hands on her and placed her under arrest, but the Doctor freed her with his sonic screwdriver and Lady Christina stole the flying bus to escape McMillan once again. (4.15) (Played by ADAM JAMES)

Meadows, Daisy: Daughter of Professor Elizabeth Meadows, whose birthday was 5 May. (AG02)

Meadows, Professor Elizabeth: Senior Scientist and leader of the Geological Survey at the Arctic Circle when it was attacked by Cybermen. She claimed to be trying to find a cure for the Cybermen's nano-virus, despite being infected herself, but was in fact working for the Cybermen all along and sent the SOS that drew the Doctor to Zebra Bay in the first place. She was killed by the Cyberleader once it awoke. (AG02) (Voiced by SARAH DOUGLAS)

Measure for Measure: New play by William Shakespeare, which had just been performed for the first time, according to Geoffrey Plum in 1605. (AG05)

Medical: The area on Floor 016 of Satellite Five where Adam Mitchell went to receive an implant to give him access to the technology of the Spike Rooms. (1.7)

Med-Scanner: River Song attached one of these to Amy Pond's arm to monitor her vitals after she was infected by a Weeping Angel. (5.5)

Medusa Cascade: The Doctor once visited this astrological feature when he was a child, aged 90. The Cascade was at the centre of a space/time rift which some time later he would single-handedly seal. The Master reminded the Doctor of this when taunting him over his current defeat. (3.13) Evelina Caecilius of Pompeii foretold that the Cascade would hold some importance for the Doctor in his future. (4.2) The Doctor told Donna Noble it was one of the places he still wanted to show her. (4.4) It was one of the things he mentioned to Sky Silvestry on Midnight which she repeated back at him. (4.10) The Daleks placed their Crucible at this Rift point and drew 27 planets there, placing them in a specific orbit and then moving them a second out of sync with the universe. This was to power their Reality Bomb which ultimately failed due to Donna's actions after she underwent a metacrisis. (4.12, 4.13)

M

Megabyte City: Shop being looted by two chancers during the Dalek invasion of Earth. Rose and her big gun stopped them, and then she used one of the PCs there to watch the Dalek ships approaching. (4.12)

Melina: Friend of Sophie Benson, who was always having crises with her friends and relations. (5.11) She was having problems with David Jenkins when Sophie went to visit her, leaving Craig to look after baby Alfie alone for the first time. (6.12)

Melissa: Schoolgirl at Deffry Vale High School, she was one of the students mesmerised into helping solve the Skasas Paradigm. (2.3) (Played by LUCINDA DRYZEK)

Melissa Majoria: Home to a subset of bees that had relocated to Earth. When they sensed the build-up of the Daleks' Magnatron, they communicated with each other, using the same Tandocca Scale as the Magnatron did, and decided to head back home before Earth was shifted to the Medusa Cascade. (4.12)

Mellow: Coming in varying strengths, this was one of the Mood Patches available in Pharmacytown in the Undercity of New New York. (3.3)

Memphis: One of the cities Van Statten suggested dumping the mind-wiped Polkowski in. (1.6)

Ménière's Disease: Infection of the inner ear that causes vertigo. Martha Jones wondered if Florence Finnegan's dizzy spells were a symptom of this. (3.1)

Merchandani Family: One of the dislocated families from the South of England in the alternative world where Donna Noble never met the Doctor. Along with the Nobles, they were sent to a street in Leeds, to live at number 29. They were taken away to a labour camp alongside the Colasanto family. (4.11)

Merchant Street: Road in Chiswick where Jival Chowdry had a photocopying business. (4.11)

Mercurio, Solana: Head of Marketing and Galactic Liaison Officer for Ood Operations on the Ood-Sphere, she had arranged a group of sales reps to visit the factory and place an order for new Ood. When the Red-Eye Ood revolted, Solana tried to escape but was killed by an Ood. (4.3) (Played by AYESHA DHARKER)

Mergrass, Ulysses: A freelance military adviser and gunrunner, Mergrass had a reputation for finding anything for anyone, and was especially popular with the inmates of Volag-Noc. An amphibious lizard from Anura, he could only survive in non-water-based atmospheres by travelling everywhere with a liquid breathing tank. After selling weapons to the Mantasphids on Myarr but being betrayed by their Queen, Mergrass opted to flee, only to encounter his old enemy Baltazar, who murdered him by shattering his water tank. When the Doctor and Martha Jones found his dehydrated corpse, all they could do was retrieve the second datachip they needed to complete their quest to locate the *Infinite*. (TIQ) (Voiced by PAUL CLAYTON)

Merrick, John: The Doctor joked to Queen Victoria that he'd had the choice of buying either Rose Tyler or the disfigured Merrick, aka the Elephant Man, for sixpence. (2.2)

'Merry Xmas Everybody': Christmas 1973 number one hit for Slade. It was playing on the radio in Clancy's Garage when Mickey Smith heard the TARDIS landing in the Powell Estate. (2.X) It was also being played a year later at the disco to celebrate the non-wedding of Donna Noble and Lance Bennett. (3.X) It was being played in the pub where Donna was drinking with her mates on the night the Empress of the Racnoss attacked in the alternative world where Donna never met the Doctor. (4.11) It was playing on the radio in the Nobles' kitchen on Christmas Day. (4.17)

M

Messaline: Planet due to be colonised by humans and Hath. When their colony ship crash-landed, however, the two races separated in the confusion. Myths grew up regarding the planet's history – how the Hath betrayed the original human colonists and the humans began using the Progenation machines to create soldiers rather than colonists. They believed that the Great One had breathed life into the universe and a fragment of that breath, called the Source, was what both human and Hath alike were searching for. Once located, it would destroy their enemies and give them control of Messaline. The truth was that the war had broken out just seven days previously, and the myths and legends only grew up because each generation of human and Hath were born, fought and wiped out in a matter of minutes. Each had false memories, genetically encoded, that led them to believe they had lived for as long as they looked and felt. In truth, they could have gone through twenty generations in a day. The legendary Source was in fact a third-generation terraforming device, waiting to be activated and accelerate Messaline's ecosystem and make the planet habitable. The Doctor activated the Source, and Messaline began changing, adapting to suit both the humans and the Hath, who made peace and prepared for their lives on the surface. (4.6)

Meta Sigmafolio: The Doctor suggested taking Martha Jones there, to see a burst of starfire over its coast. (3.13)

Metacrisis: After the Doctor was shot by a Dalek, he involuntarily started a regeneration cycle but, rather than letting it change him, he just used the energy to heal himself and siphoned the rest of it into his severed right hand, which Captain Jack Harkness had kept in a jar since the Sycorax leader cut it off.

That hand later grew into a duplicate Doctor after Donna Noble's DNA reacted with it, creating an instant biological metacrisis between the two of them. This new Doctor was part human, whilst Donna's brain power was incrementally increased to Time Lord level – an event that reverberated back through time and alerted Dalek Caan to the significance of Donna to the Doctor's life. Rose Tyler's Dimension Cannon was able to follow those patterns and timelines too, and even the Ood were aware of it, referring to the metacrisis as 'the DoctorDonna'. The extra brainpower enabled Donna to shut down the Reality Bomb (she used an internalised synchronous back-feed reversal loop to close all the Z-Neutrino relays), to short-circuit Davros's metallic hand (with a bio-electric dampening field with a retrogressive arc inversion), and to power down the Dalek weaponry and send them out of control (by macrotransmitting a k-filter wavelength to create a self-replicating energy blindfold matrix). However, all that Time Lord mental power in her human brain very nearly killed her, so the original Doctor reabsorbed most of the power from the metacrisis into himself, blocking off Donna's memories, and causing her to forget everything about him, his very existence. Taking the unconscious Donna home, he warned Wilfred Mott and Sylvia Noble that if Donna ever remembered him in any way, the metacrisis would be triggered again, and kill her. (4.12, 4.13) He did, though, put a slight fail-safe into her – and when she began to recall their adventures due to the Master trying to turn her into himself, it put Donna into a short-term coma. When she awoke she once again, she had no memories of the Doctor or their time together. (4.17, 4.18)

Metaltron: The name given to the Dalek in Henry Van Statten's underground Vault, because it refused to speak and reveal its identity. (1.6)

Metastatic Energy: Energy that should, in theory, deactivate a Cybermat. 'Bitey', the one that attacked the Doctor and Craig Owens at Craig's house was shielded from it, however, so the Doctor used a different app on his sonic screwdriver to stop the Cybermat. However, it only pretended to be deactivated afterwards. (6.12)

Meteorological Department: The Doctor told Foreman Cleaves in the St John's monastery that he was from this department and that he was a weatherman. (6.5, 6.6)

Metropolitan: Sarah Jane Smith wrote features for this magazine. (4.11)

M4: London to South Wales motorway the Roboform taxi driver took Donna Noble on instead of turning off for Chiswick. (3.X)

MI5: A division of the British Security Service, focusing on counterintelligence. One of its operatives, Margaret Blaine, was murdered by Blon Fel Fotch Pasameer-Day Slitheen, and her body was used as a disguise. (1.4, 1.5) The fake Blaine later became Lord Mayor of Cardiff. (1.11)

Michael [1]: Child at the reception for Donna Noble and Lance Bennett's non-wedding. Donna checked up on him after the attack by the Roboform Santas. (3.X)

Michael [2]: Manager of the BIS team that Craig Owens worked for. He was suitably impressed with the Doctor. (5.11) (Played by JEM WALL)

Michelangelo: 15th-century Italian artist who the Doctor met when he was painting the ceiling of the Sistine Chapel. He was, apparently, scared of heights. (5.10)

Mick: Soldier based at Albion Hospital who led the search for the augmented pig that the Slitheen had launched into space, ensuring the subsequent crash back to Earth would cause a huge distraction and enable them to take over the British government. (1.4)

Mickey Mouse: Cartoon mouse created by Walt Disney. Captain Jack Harkness referred to Mickey Smith as Mickey Mouse. (4.12, 4.13)

Micropetrol: Fuel-source for vehicles, including the *Crusader* buses used by the Leisure Palace Company. Micropetrol doesn't stabilise. (4.10)

Midnight: Essentially a giant diamond in space, on which the Leisure Palace Company had set up one of their Leisure Palaces, despite the beautiful but lethal X-tonic radiation from the sun that bathed the planet's surface. While Donna Noble enjoyed all the Leisure Palace had to offer, the Doctor took a seat aboard the *Crusader 50* tour-craft for a journey across the planet. However, a creature existed in the diamond mountains that could enter people's minds and take them over, slowly working its way into the mind, initially by repeating language, then mastering it and finally anticipating thoughts and speech, to become ultimately a complete individual. The Doctor encountered the creature after it took over a businesswoman, Sky Silvestry. It played on the fears and paranoia of their fellow passengers to turn on the Doctor, who it perceived as the only threat. One by one, they became convinced that he was the threat, enabling the creature to grow in strength and confidence, until they attempted to throw him out onto the surface

M

of the planet. However, the *Crusader 50*'s Hostess realised that Sky was the true villain and she sacrificed herself by pulling Sky, and the creature within, to their deaths out on the planet's lethal atmosphere. (4.10)

Mighty Jagrafess of the Holy Hadrojassic Maxarodenfoe:
Vast gastropodic creature that lived in the freezing ceiling of Floor 500 aboard Satellite Five. Its vast metabolism required very low temperatures and it could potentially live for 3,000 years. As Editor-in-Chief, it controlled, via its human associate the Editor, the news and information gathered and disseminated around the Fourth Earth Empire. It had thus significantly weakened the Empire, making it xenophobic and closing humanity off from other species. The Jagrafess had actually been installed at the behest of the Bad Wolf Corporation, and was controlled by the Daleks as part of a grand master plan by the Dalek Emperor. It was destroyed when the temperature, normally carefully controlled, was raised considerably, and the Jagrafess exploded. (1.7) Rose Tyler pretended to have authority granted to her by the Mighty Jagrafess to demand the Sycorax leave Earth. (2.X)

Military Policeman:
Responsible for handcuffing and subsequently freeing the Doctor at the Kennedy Space Center. (6.2) (Played by ALAN GILL)

Milk Market:
Mainly automated industry on Sto where the Van Hoffs worked together. (4.X)

Milkman:
Was delivering milk one Saturday morning when he witnessed the sky change as Earth was shunted into the Medusa Cascade, one moment out of sync with the rest of the universe. (4.12) (Played by ANDREW BULLIVANT)

Millennium of Blood:
The state of chaos the Carrionites wished to create on Earth by bringing the rest of the Carrionites to Elizabethan London. (3.2)

Miller, Alton Glenn:
American jazz musician who seemingly died in 1944 while en route to France to entertain the troops. Captain Jack Harkness and

Rose Tyler danced before the face of Big Ben atop an invisible Chula ship to Miller's composition 'Moonlight Serenade'. (1.9) Jack played 'Moonlight Serenade' to the Doctor and Rose while they were trapped in the hospital storeroom, and Rose called it 'our song'. The Doctor and Rose, watched by Jack, later danced to Miller's 'In the Mood' tune in the TARDIS control room. (1.10)

Milligan, Mr: Master of a Workhouse in Victorian London. He was captured by the Cybermen and put under their power via an earpiece control device. He then took all the children from his Workhouse to the Cybermen, and they were used to build the engine for the CyberKing. Mr Milligan's usefulness over, Miss Hartigan killed him, via the earpiece. (4.14) (Played by ANTHONY BRANNAN)

Milligan, Thomas: Former paediatrician who had survived the Toclafane purges because he was considered useful as a member of the Peripatetic Medical Squad. In fact, he was part of the British resistance and helped bring Martha Jones back to Britain after a year away, believing she was assembling a special gun with which to kill the Master. Thomas was killed defending Martha on the streets of London, but after time jumped out of sync and erased the previous year, Martha was delighted to discover that Thomas was alive again and working in a children's hospital. (3.13) (Played by TOM ELLIS) Martha Jones revealed to the Doctor and Donna Noble that she and Tom were engaged to be married, although they never actually went through with it and Martha ended up marrying Mickey Smith. (4.4, 4.5, 4.13, 4.18)

Milo [1]: Studious boy at Deffry Vale High School, who knew much more information than he should have done, due to eating chips cooked in Krillitane Oil. (2.3) (Played by CLEM TIBBER)

Milo [2]: Young man in New New York who was heading to Brooklyn for a job in the Foundries there, thus creating a new home for himself, Cheen and their unborn son, away from the Undercity. He and Cheen kidnapped Martha Jones so that they could legitimately register as having three adults aboard their car and gain access to the Fast Lane. Once down there, the car was attacked by the Macra, and Milo switched off everything in the vehicle to avoid attracting their attention. Realising that they would run out of air, Milo reactivated the car and they took their chances at trying to get away from the creatures. When the Doctor reopened the cover of the Motorway, Milo and Cheen were able to drive up to the Overcity and start a new life up there. (3.3) (Played by TRAVIS OLIVER)

Ming Dynasty: Chinese restaurant favoured by the Doctor, because they did the best dim-sum. (DL)

Ministry of Art and Artiness: The Doctor pretended to be working for this fictitious government department when he arrived at the Musée D'Orsay and needed information on Vincent Van Gogh from the museum's expert, Doctor Black. (5.10)

Ministry of Asteroids: The Doctor planned to pretend to be a Doctor John Smith working for this fictitious government department when he arrived in London during the Blitz. (1.9)

Ministry of Drills, Earth and Science: The Doctor pretended to be working for this fictitious government mega-department when he explored the Discovery Project in Cwmtaff in 2020. (5.8, 5.9)

Minneapolis: One of the cities Van Statten suggested dumping the mind-wiped Polkowski in. (1.6)

Minogue, Kylie: Australian actress and singer. The Doctor quoted her song 'Never Too Late' to Tommy Connolly as they headed to Alexandra Palace to put a stop to the Wire's Time of Manifestation. (2.7)

Minotaur: The creature guarding the God Complex. As much a prisoner as those it pursued within its holographic prison, the Minotaur fed on the 'faith' its victims had in their strongest beliefs. It showed them their biggest fears, enabling their faith in something to protect them. Once triggered, the creature could feed on this faith (religion, a belief in conspiracies, luck or the Doctor), killing the victim in turn. The Minotaur actually wanted nothing more than to die itself, to be as free of the God Complex as its victims, and the Doctor, by cutting off its supply of faith, killed it. Originally the creature was one of a race of similar species, such as the Nimon, who moved from planet to planet, being treated as gods. The Doctor hypothesised that the God Complex was constructed by one of those planets who rejected their gods, and imprisoned the Minotaur within it for revenge. (6.11) (Played by SPENCER WILDING)

Minto Road: Trying to interest Rose Tyler, Mickey Smith asked Jackie Tyler if she'd been to a new pizza parlour on Minto Road, which had previously been a Christmas shop. (1.13)

Mirror, The: National UK tabloid paper. They were prepared to pay £500 to interview Rose Tyler after the explosion at Henrik's department store. (1.1)

Miss Jane Marple: Fictional detective, often inaccurately attributed to creator Agatha Christie basing the character upon herself. At the time of the incidents at Eddison Hall, Agatha had yet to create Marple. (4.7)

Miss Saigon: A theatre musical loosely adapted from Puccini's opera *Madame Butterfly*, about a doomed romance between a soldier and a Vietnamese villager. The Doctor, Donna Noble and Martha Jones arrived on Messaline in the middle of a ferocious war and, when Donna noted that the human's war chamber was an old theatre, the Doctor quipped that they may be putting on *Miss Saigon*. (4.6)

Missouri: American state where some of the citizens of Manhattan's Hooverville were from. (3.4)

Mr Smith: A Xylok computer embedded into the chimney breast of 13 Bannerman Road, Sarah Jane Smith's house. Aided by Luke Smith and K-9, Mr Smith helped the Doctor return Earth back to its proper place in time and space. (4.12, 4.13) He put out a story explaining that everyone's shared memory of becoming the Master was just a series of hallucinations caused by a wi-fi error. (4.18) (Voiced by ALEXANDER ARMSTRONG)

Mistletoe: The Brethren of St Catherine had trained the Haemovariform they unleashed to hate mistletoe, and they wore the plant for protection against it. Lady Isobel MacLeish and her staff filled buckets and pans with mistletoe and threw it over the werewolf, disorientating it for long enough to gain a brief respite from its attack. (2.2)

Mitchell, Adam: English genius, fresh out of university, and working for Henry Van Statten. He had hacked into the Pentagon's computer systems when he

M

was 8 years old. Van Statten employed Adam to go through the flotsam and jetsam of alien tech he collected and discover what it was, how it worked and to suggest ways of utilising it for Geocomtex. Adam was a bit of a dreamer and was fascinated by the universe, wondering what it was like out there. He and Rose Tyler were pursued by the Dalek once it had escaped the Vault in Henry Van Statten's underground base and, although Adam got away, Rose was captured. After the Dalek was destroyed, Rose persuaded the Doctor to take Adam in the TARDIS. (1.6) The TARDIS then took him to visit Satellite Five. Wandering off by himself, Adam had a technological implant grafted into his forehead that gave him access to a knowledge database. Using information from the future, Adam planned to make a fortune back home and, via Rose's Universal Roaming enabled mobile phone, began leaving messages on his parent's answerphone. When the Doctor discovered this, he furiously escorted Adam home, destroyed the messages and abandoned him, still with the implant grafted into his head. (1.7) (Played by BRUNO LANGLEY)

Mitchell, Geoff: Wife of Sandra, father to Adam. He was out when his wife found that Adam had returned to their home in Manchester, complete with the Type Two info-spike chip in his forehead. (1.7)

Mitchell, Sandra: Adam Mitchell's mother who, on his return home to Manchester, discovered to her horror that her son had alien tech permanently grafted into his skull. (1.7) (Played by JUDY HOLT)

Mo, Cousin: Relative of Jackie and Rose Tyler, who had left London and gone to live in the Peak District. (2.X) Before leaving for New Earth with the Doctor, Rose reminded Jackie to call Mo. (2.1)

Mobile phone: Communications device popular on 21st-century Earth. The Doctor adjusted both Rose Tyler's (1.2) and Martha Jones's (3.7) so they had

Universal Roaming, which meant that they could make and receive calls to and from anywhere in space and time.

Mobile Phone Man: A guest at the reception for Donna Noble and Lance Bennett's non-wedding. The Doctor borrowed his phone and souped it up with his sonic screwdriver to learn more about HC Clements. (3.X) (Played by BEN McLEAN)

Mogul of India, the: Indian monarch whose treasure Henry Avery had stolen shortly before his ship the *Fancy* and the Skerth ship became trapped in the same spatial coordinates due to a temporal rift. The Doctor threw the treasure overboard to stop the Siren using it as a conduit. (6.3)

Mohammad, Jason: BBC News reporter, who covered the *Guinevere One* space probe. (2.X) He reported on the *Titanic* seemingly crashing down onto Buckingham Palace. (4.X) In the alternative world where Donna Noble never met the Doctor, he reported the same news but with a different outcome, where the *Titanic* crashed, presumably putting Mohammad amongst the millions of casualties. (4.11) He reported on the Dalek spaceships approaching Earth. (4.12)

Molecular fringe animation: The science used by Son of Mine to create and activate his army of straw Scarecrows. (3.8, 3.9)

Moment, the: The Doctor used this to end the Last Great Time War, once and for all, wiping out the Time Lords and the Daleks. (4.18)

Mona Lisa, the: Painting by Leonardo. A duplicate was on display on Apalapucia. Rory Williams smashed the painting over the head of a Handbot. (6.10)

Mongrels: How Lady Cassandra O'Brien referred to humans who were, unlike her, not born on Earth. (1.2)

Monroe, Marilyn: Stage name of the 20th-century actress Norma Jeane Mortensen. She met the Doctor at Frank Sinatra's lodge at Christmastime in 1952, and shortly afterwards, during a Christmas Eve party, dragged him to a chapel to get married. He later protested that it wasn't a real chapel and the marriage was invalid. Probably. (6.X) (Played by CHARLOTTE HOWARD)

Monteagle, Baron: The title of William Parker, who received a warning of a plot to assassinate King James I and so warned the monarch. (AG05)

Monty Python's Big Red Book: One of the books found in The Library. (4.8)

Moon, Doctor: See *Doctor Moon*

Moon, the: Natural satellite which orbits the Earth. The Judoon used plasma coils to transport the Royal Hope there, so they could gain access to the fugitive Plasmavore they knew was hiding in the hospital. (3.1)

'Moonlight Serenade': Captain Jack Harkness and Rose Tyler danced before the face of Big Ben atop a Chula ship to this swing number composed by Glenn Miller. (1.10)

Moore, Mrs: Member of the Preachers on 'Pete's World', who was their driver, their techie and very good at building electromagnetic hand grenades. Her real name was Angela Price, but she adopted the 'Mrs Moore' identity from a book she'd read, hoping to protect her husband and children. She used to work for Cybus Industries but realised what they were doing was illegal as well as immoral, going on to join the Preachers when the information she knew made her a target. She accompanied the Doctor into the Battersea Power Station Cyber-conversion factory, accessing it via Deepcold Six. There they discovered that the Cyberforms had emotional inhibitors, shortly before Mrs Moore was electrocuted by the grip of a Cyberman. (2.5, 2.6) Davros taunted the Doctor about how many people had died trying to help him over the years, and this made the Doctor think of Mrs Moore. (4.13) (Played by HELEN GRIFFIN)

Moore, Sir Patrick: Television astronomer and expert on the heavens. Rose Tyler cheekily suggested to the Doctor that Moore was the biggest expert in alien knowledge. (1.4) He was one of the experts the Doctor contacted to help set up his trap for Prisoner Zero. (5.1)

Morgan: The UK official who was the face of the message that told the inhabitants of *Starship UK* the truth behind the ship. (5.2) (Played by CHRISTOPHER GOOD)

Morgenstern, Oliver: Intern at the Royal Hope Hospital who coped better at being transported to the moon than most. He was the first person to communicate with the Judoon Captain and, as a result, followed him as the Judoon troopers went through the Hospital scanning people, Morgenstern advising everyone they'd be safe. Once back on Earth, Morgenstern became the person the media went straight to for comments about the ordeal. (3.1) In the alternative world where Donna Noble never met the Doctor, he was the only survivor of the incident, commenting that Martha Jones had died giving him the last of her oxygen. He also mentioned the death of *Metropolitan* reporter Sarah Jane Smith. (4.11) (Played by BEN RIGHTON)

Morocco: North African country where Donna Noble and Lance Bennett were planning to go to for their honeymoon. (3.X)

Morpeth-Jetsan: Multinational company, with contracts from the military to farm crystal-diluric acid. Like many companies across the world, Morpeth-Jetsan used the Flesh to create a series of Gangers to save the original humans from doing dangerous work. After a solar tsunami gave the Gangers on the St John's monastery independent thought, and a journey in the TARDIS solidified their state as perfect, unchanging replicas, foreman Miranda Cleaves (human) and one of her contractors Dicken (Ganger) approached the Board in an effort to build a new understanding between the two species. (6.5, 6.6)

Morphic Residue: Honey-like genetic material left behind each time the Vespiform at Eddison Hall changed between its human and Vespiform identities. (4.7)

M

Morris [1]: A homeless man on 'Pete's World' lured into the back of Mr Crane's pantechnicon on the promise of limitless food. He was later turned into a Cyberman. (2.5) (Played by ADAM SHAW)

Morris [2]: Schoolboy at Farringham School for Boys in 1913, who was told to maintain a position over the stable yard before the Family of Blood attacked. (3.9)

Morrison, Jim: Lead singer of The Doors, mentioned by the Doctor when he realised that the Graske's hatchery had, he reckoned, more doors than Jim Morrison. (AotG)

Mortlock, Madame: A medium who worked in the Butetown district of Cardiff in the 1860s. (1.3)

Morton, Charlie: Sent Sylvia Noble a naughty Christmas card. (4.17)

Moscow: Russian capital city. One of the early ATMOS victims died there. (4.4) Yuri and Mikhail Kerenski originally came from there. (4.16)

Moss, Lynda: Contestant on *Big Brother* aboard the Game Station in 200,100, being broadcast on Channel 44,000. Like all the contestants in all the *Big Brother* houses and other games on the Station, Lynda was selected to be on the show, rather than having had to apply. When the Doctor decided to break out, Lynda followed him, eager to discover the truth behind the Game Station – and saw him as a possible way out of her drab life by travelling in the TARDIS. When the Daleks were revealed to be behind everything, Lynda enthusiastically worked with the Doctor to stop them. She was reporting back from an observation deck on Floor 056, when a Dalek appeared outside, floating in space, and blasted the Exoglass away, killing her instantly. (1.12, 1.13) Davros taunted the Doctor about how many people had died trying to help him over the years, and this made the Doctor think of Lynda. (4.13) (Played by JO JOYNER)

Most Haunted: Television show about ghost hunters. With the world populated by friendly ghosts, its presenter Derek Acorah lamented that he was out of a job. (2.12)

Mother: One of the coma patients at Leadworth hospital, who dreamt of her two daughters while unconscious. When Prisoner Zero took her form, it created images of her two girls too, although because it still hadn't mastered the art of speaking, her voice also came out of one of the children. (5.1) (Played by OLIVIA COLEMAN)

Mother of Mine: Mother of the Family of Blood, who verbally greeted schoolboy Jeremy Baines when he stumbled across their invisible spaceship in Cooper's Field, Farringham. Baines was killed, his body inhabited by Son of Mine, and one by one the Family found themselves bodies. Mother of Mine was the last to do so, taking on the form of Jenny, a maid at the school. Posing as Jenny, she encountered Martha, sensing she had something to do with the Time Lord the Family sought. She later joined her Family at the village dance, enjoying the carnage they created there and shortly afterwards at the school itself. Having regained his Time Lord form and blown up the Family's spaceship, the Doctor threw Mother of Mine into the event horizon of a collapsing galaxy where she would remain for eternity. (3.8, 3.9) (Played by REBEKAH STATON)

Mothership [1]: A sentient Cyberman ship that crashed in Earth's Arctic Circle during the Ice Age. It sent out Cybermats to convert local humans into Cyberslaves and was eventually blown up by the Doctor, who overloaded its circuitry. (AG02)

Mothership [2]: The Justice Department's main vehicle, orbiting Earth. The *Teselecta* crew were beamed aboard it in an emergency when Amy Pond activated the Anti-Bodies but deactivated the crew's defensive wrist-bracelets. (6.8)

Motorway: Vast series of tunnels and road lanes, including the legendary Fast Lane, beneath New New York's Undercity. The drivers believed they were actually getting somewhere, albeit only a couple of feet a day, but in fact they had been kept down there by the Face of Boe until such a time as the Overcity was contamination-free. It had been for quite a while, but Boe lacked the energy to reopen the covered tunnels and set the drivers free. (3.3)

Motorway Foot Patrol: When the Doctor jumped from the base of Brannigan's car and into the White Man's vehicle on the New New York Motorway, he told Whitey that he was from the Motorway Foot Patrol, doing a survey. He used this excuse a couple more times as he jumped from car to car. (3.3)

M

Mott, Wilfred: Old soldier and grandfather to Donna Noble, father of Sylvia. He first encountered the Doctor on Christmas Day when the Doctor teleported to Earth with a group of tourists from the Sto-based starliner *Titanic*. This was a fleeting meeting, with no hint of the significance Wilfred was soon to play in the Doctor's life. (4.X) He was a keen amateur astronomer, and would sit for hours on his allotment watching the stars, and he saw the TARDIS take Donna away from Earth. (4.1) He was supposed to be on a macrobiotic diet, and missed Donna's wedding to Lance Bennett due to a spot of Spanish Flu. He was trapped in an ATMOS gas-filled car but saved by Sylvia. He was overjoyed that Donna was off with the Doctor, exploring the universe and encountering aliens – and very proud of her. (4.4, 4.5) In the alternative world where Donna never met the Doctor, he was having a Christmas break with his daughter and granddaughter out of London when the south of England was devastated by a nuclear explosion. Forced to move to Leeds and billeted in a house with the Colasanto family, he formed a good friendship with Rocco Colasanto – only to despair when the Italian was taken away to a labour camp. Wilfred was prepared to sell his telescope to make ends meet. (4.11) When the Daleks invaded Earth, Wilfred was all for fighting back, but when Rose Tyler arrived looking for Donna, he could only say he had no idea where she and the Doctor were. He didn't vote for Harriet Jones, but admired her. He wasn't able to help Rose use Harriet's Subwave Network as Sylvia thought webcams were naughty and wouldn't let him have one. When the Doctor took Donna home, her mind empty of all her experiences with him, Wilfred was heartbroken but promised the Doctor he would keep an eye on the stars, remembering him on Donna's behalf. (4.12, 4.13) He set up the Silver Cloak, a network of old-age pensioners, to keep an eye out for the Doctor in case he ever needed their help. When a mysterious woman approached him in a church and told him the Doctor was returning, Wilfred put the Silver Cloak in motion and they did track the Doctor down. He tried to get the Doctor to meet up with Donna, hoping he could safely bring her memories back, but the Doctor refused, knowing it would kill her. He went aboard the TARDIS when the Doctor went after the Master, ending up a prisoner at the Naismith mansion and then finally getting to go to outer space on the Vinvocci ship, the *Hesperus*. His old soldier skills came to the fore as he fired the *Hesperus*'s laser cannons to stave off a wave of missiles and tried to help the Doctor stop the Time Lords unleashing their Ultimate Sanction. Trying to save one of Naismith's Gate Room technicians, Wilfred went into the Nuclear Bolt control room, and was locked in. The Doctor realised that Wilfred was trapped when he heard him knocking four times on the glass, and remembered what Carmen had said to him on the 200 bus. Releasing Wilfred, the Doctor absorbed 500,000 rads himself, which destroyed his body, triggering a regeneration cycle. The last time Wilfred saw the Tenth Doctor was at Donna's wedding, where he gave him and Sylvia a lottery ticket for Donna, paid for by his late son-in-law, Geoffrey. (4.17, 4.18) (Played by BERNARD CRIBBINS)

Moulin Rouge: Parisian nightclub, famed for its wild parties and shows. The Doctor suggested taking Amy Pond and Rory Williams there in 1890 as a potential wedding present. (5.6)

Mount Perdition: Mountain on Gallifrey where the Master's family had estates which he and the Doctor used to play in as children. (4.17)

Mount Rushmore National Memorial: Vast sculpture in the rock face of Mount Rushmore, in South Dakota, with four former US Presidents carved into it. The Master had his face added. (3.13)

Mount Snowden: A Vinvocci salvage ship found buried at the foot of this North Wales mountain contained a couple of Magna-clamps, which the Torchwood Institute appropriated. (2.12) The Immortality Gate was also found on that ship. (4.17, 4.18)

Mount Stuart Square: London road in which was located the police station where Sally Sparrow met DI Billy Shipton. (3.10)

Moxx of Balhoon, the: Representing the firm of solicitors Jolco and Jolco, he was sent to observe Earthdeath from Platform One. He died after Lady Cassandra O'Brien had the sunfilters around the Manchester Suite lowered. (1.2) (Played by JIMMY VEE, voiced by SILAS CARSON)

'Mr Blue Sky': Number six hit for the Electric Light Orchestra in 1978, a song often danced to by Elton Pope in the privacy of his own room, as he was a huge fan of the band. (2.10)

MRI: Magnetic Resonance Imaging, a process used at the Royal Hope Hospital for non-invasive observation of patients. The Plasmavore intended to use the MRI there as a weapon – to increase its magnetic output to 50,000 tesla, which would fry the brains of everything within 250,000 miles. The Plasmavore, protected by a screen, would be safe and, with the humans and Judoon dead, could make its escape. After the Judoon executed the Plasmavore, they left the MRI still building up its power – the results of the mono-magnetic pulse of no interest to them as they would be long gone and out of range. The Doctor was able to disconnect the scanner and save everyone. (3.1)

Mr Copper Foundation: A business set up by Sto ex-pat Mr Copper after the Doctor left him on Earth with a million pounds. Amongst the things Mr Copper invented was sentient software which he provided to Harriet Jones so she could develop her Subwave Network. (4.12, 4.13)

Mr Spock: Character from the science fiction TV series *Star Trek*, played by Leonard Nimoy. Rose commented to the Doctor that his non-technological approach was 'not very Spock', which she later contrasted with Captain Jack Harkness's high-tech methods. She introduced the Doctor to Jack, having told him the Doctor's name was Mr Spock. (1.9, 1.10)

Mrs Golightly's Happy Travelling University and Dry Cleaners: Establishment on Sto where Mr Copper obtained his diploma in Earthonomics. (4.X)

Mrs Robinson: Fictional character from Charles Webb's novel *The Graduate*. Mrs Robinson was famous for being an older seductress who corrupted the younger hero. The Doctor referred to River Song as Mrs Robinson when introducing her to President Nixon. She was not amused. (6.1)

Muffin the Mule: Children's puppet show, which ran between 1952 and 1955, presented by Annette Mills. An episode of this was among the first things watched by the Connollys on their new television set. (2.7)

Mulligan: One of Avery's pirate crew aboard the *Fancy*. He initially agreed with the Boatswain to mutiny against Avery but when the Boatswain was injured, he left his friend behind. Chased by the Doctor and Avery, Mulligan hid in the ship's stores but burned his hand on a lamp, so the Siren got him anyway. He was

later found alive aboard the Skerth ship, being tended to by the Siren. He joined Avery exploring the universe. (6.3) (Played by MICHAEL BEGLEY)

Multifaceted Coast: Area on the planet Midnight where the Waterfall Palace was based. (4.10)

Multi-grade anti-oil: The Doctor poured this into one of the Clockwork Robots, pretending it was red wine, to save Rose Tyler and Mickey Smith from being dissected by them. (2.4)

Mum [1]: London woman whose family had A+ blood and thus were affected by the Sycorax's blood control. (2.X) (Played by CATHY MURPHY)

Mum [2]: A London woman kidnapped by the Graske at Christmas, and replaced with a changeling. She was eventually returned home with no memory of her experiences. (AotG) (Played by LISA PALFREY)

Mummies: Sarah Jane Smith told Rose Tyler that, during her time travelling with the Doctor, they had fought Egyptian Mummies – in reality these were powerful Servo Robots, created by the Osirans. (2.3)

Munchkin-Lady: A bizarre alien who, the Doctor and Rose Tyler recalled, had breathed fire from her mouth. (2.5)

Muppet Movie, The: Listing things of importance that happened in 1979, the Doctor told Rose Tyler that this film was released. (2.2)

Murder of Roger Ackroyd, The: Classic Agatha Christie novel which Lady Clemency Eddison was reading when the Firestone jewel she wore began to telepathically transmit her thoughts and ideas to her Vespiform son, posing as the Reverend Golightly. (4.7)

Murder Spree 20: The city of Pola Ventura hosted Murder Spree 20, not Reykjavik. Rose Tyler didn't know this when asked by the Anne Droid in *The Weakest Link* aboard the Game Station. (1.12)

Musée D'Orsay: Parisian museum of modern art. The Doctor and Amy Pond took in *The Great Exhibition*, a touring Vincent Van Gogh retrospective there, when the Doctor noticed an alien painted into Van Gogh's *Church At Auvers*. Checking with Van Gogh expert Doctor Black to pinpoint when it was painted, the Doctor and Amy went to meet the painter. After they had sorted out the alien, they took Van Gogh to the museum, where he heard Doctor Black explaining how he thought Van Gogh was the greatest painter ever, and he saw his paintings being admired by academics and schoolchildren alike. (5.10)

'Music of the Spheres': A piece of music the Doctor composed and asked the Conductor of the Proms to play in the Albert Hall. (MotS)

Mussolini, Benito: Italian leader during the Second World War. In the alternative world where Donna Noble never met the Doctor, she referred to Rocco Colasanto rudely by calling him Mussolini because Rocco was Italian. (4.11)

Muswell Hill: North London area, in the shadow of Alexandra Palace and home to streets such as Florizel Street and Damascus Street in 1953. (2.7)

Mutt and Jeff: American comic-strip characters created by Bud Fisher in the 1920s. Mutt was the tall rich one, Jeff, his shorter insane companion. The Doctor likened Rose Tyler and Adam Mitchell to them when aboard the space station Satellite Five. (1.7). He later used the same name to describe Rose and himself working as a team in the Torchwood Institute Lever Room as they prepared to destroy the invading Cybermen and Daleks. (2.13)

Mutton Street: East London street, which was home to both a gasworks and Jackson Lake's hot-air balloon, which he called his 'Tardis'. (4.14)

My Invasion Blog: Ursula Blake's online diary about the Doctor's involvement with alien incursions on Earth, which drew her and Elton Pope

together, and thus led to the formation of LINDA. (2.10)

'My Mysterious Doctor': The saucy painting created by Matilda, the 17th-century nobleman's daughter. Her father was less than happy with both the painting's nakedness and the fact that he found the Doctor hiding under Matilda's skirts. (6.1)

Myarr: Arable planet colonised by humans generations before the Mantasphids invaded and threw them out. This was the final straw in an ongoing war between the Earth Empire and the Mantasphids, and Earth Control opted to obliterate the planet and sacrifice it, thus eliminating the Mantasphids once and for all. The Doctor intervened and saved Myarr, leaving the humans and Mantasphids to find peace. (TIQ)

Myrna: Dancer at the Laurenzi theatre in 1930s New York, taking part in the New York Revue. When Martha Jones needed to get across the stage to find Laszlo, she used Myrna to shield her from the audience. (3.4) (Played by FLIK SWAN)

Mysterious Man: An employee of Harry Saxon who approached Francine Jones at the cocktail reception at LazLabs to plant seeds of doubt in her mind about the Doctor's ability to keep her daughter Martha safe from harm. (3.6) (Played by BERTIE CARVEL)

Mystery of Edwin Drood and the Blue Elementals, The: Charles Dickens decided to finish his serialised novel as soon as he returned to London after his adventure with the Doctor in which they defeated the Gelth, who inspired the blue elementals he elected to use in the new title. The story was never finished, as Dickens died six months later. (1.3)

Myths and Historical Impossibilities: A book Amy Pond was reading aloud to Rory Williams which contained a number of stories that seemed to be about the Doctor. (6.1)

Nainby, Mr: Old man who used to run the sweetshop in the dreamscape-future created by the Dream Lord. Like all the local pensioners, Mr Nainby appeared to have been taken over by an Eknodine. He was amongst those who attacked the Doctor in the butcher's shop and Amy Pond and Rory in their cottage. Whether a real Mr Nainby actually existed in the real Leadworth was unconfirmed, although as the psychic spore that created the Dream Lord fed on dark thoughts and memories, it seemed likely he was someone known to Amy and Rory back home. (5.7) (Played by NICK HOBBS)

Naismith, Abigail: Spoilt, rich daughter of Joshua Naismith, who was familiar with the Books of Saxon. She wanted immortality, and Joshua went to extraordinary lengths to get it, by kidnapping the Master and getting him to re-power the Immortality Gate. When the Master used the Gate to imprint himself on every human on Earth, Abigail became the Master too. When she was restored, she fled the family home but was later arrested and imprisoned. (4.17, 4.18) (Played by TRACY IFEACHOR)

Naismith, Joshua: Vain, arrogant businessman, with a private army and a huge mansion. A self-made billionaire via his communications company, he was willing to do anything for his daughter Abigail, and he tracked the Master from Broadfell Prison and had him snatched and taken to him as a Christmas present for her. He ordered the Master to re-power the Immortality Gate, which he had stolen from Torchwood but when the Master used the Gate to imprint himself

on every human on Earth, Naismith became the Master too. When he was restored, he was so terrified by the arrival of Gallifrey in Earth's sky that he couldn't escape with Abigail. Wilfred Mott later told the Doctor that Naismith had been arrested and imprisoned. (4.17, 4.18) (Played by DAVID HAREWOOD)

Nakashima, Jo: Freelance journalist who realised that ATMOS was potentially lethal and tried to talk to Luke Rattigan about it. He threw her out of his Academy and the Sontarans took control of her car's SatNav and drove her into a river, drowning her. She had, however, already been in contact with Colonel Mace at UNIT with details of her investigations. (4.4) (Played by ELEANOR MATSUURA)

Naming, the: A Carrionite spell in which powerful words ended with an object or person being named, which in turn caused injury or even death to the target. The Doctor, when he worked out that Mother Doomfinger was a Carrionite, named her and transported her back where she came from. Martha tried the same trick on Lilith, but a Naming didn't work when it was repeated. Instead Lilith knocked Martha out by Naming her, and tried to stop the Doctor's heart by Naming Rose Tyler. (3.2)

Nancy: Teenage girl who took it upon herself to look after various children who had been evacuated from London during the Blitz but had returned as strays. She told the Doctor this was because her younger brother Jamie had died during

an air raid. She also explained about the strange 'empty' child walking the streets, wearing a gas mask and asking everyone 'Are you my mummy?' She suggested the Doctor should talk to a doctor at Albion Hospital, the nearest hospital to Limehouse Green Station where an unexploded bomb had fallen shortly before the child began walking the streets. Nancy later went to the site of the bombing and revealed to the Doctor that the child was Jamie – not her brother but her son. The Chula nanogenes that had brought the dead Jamie back to life then conjoined Nancy and her son's DNA, returning Jamie to normal. (1.9, 1.10) (Played by FLORENCE HOATH)

Nanodentistry: One of the areas within the Hospital on New Earth run by the Sisters of Plenitude. (2.1)

Nanogenes: Smart subatomic robots that inhabited all Chula ships and could restore living tissue to its pristine form, provided they had been programmed with what that pristine form was. The nanogenes aboard Captain Jack's ship were familiar with humans, due to his presence; the ones aboard the medical ship he had forced to crash in war-torn London were not. They reanimated a dead boy and assumed that was how all humans should be, so rewrote the DNA of all those they encountered to resemble that child. They were reprogrammed when they encountered mother and son together, recognising the mother's superior DNA, and they repaired all the damage they had done, actually improving the health of many they had infected. (1.9, 1.10)

Nano-Recorder: The Doctor implanted tiny recorders into the palms of River Song, Amy Pond, Rory Williams, Canton Delaware III and himself. They tuned themselves directly into the speech centres of their brains to pick up their voices every time they activated the recorders. This meant they could record any Silent sightings before forgetting. The Silence took Amy's out and Rory found it and could hear Amy's panic when she was in the Silent's base. (6.2)

Nano-Synthesiser: Machine used by the Doctor to reverse the nano-virus in the bodies of the Cyberslaves to make them human again. Used on Cybermen, it actually killed them. (AG02)

Nano-Termites: Installed in Adam Mitchell's throat as part of the Vomit-o-Matic when he had the Type Two chip inserted into his head. As soon as the doors in his forehead whirred open and he saw his own brain, Adam threw up, but the Nurse told him that the nano-termites had frozen the waste created by his gag reflex. (1.7)

Nano-virus: Injected into humans by Cybermats, this turned them into Cyberslaves. (AG02)

Naples: The Doctor hoped to take Rose Tyler there in 1860, for the first Christmas of the newly unified Kingdom of Italy. They ended up in the Cardiff of 1869. But still at Christmas. (1.3) Lobos Caecilius of Pompeii believed there was a restaurant there called San Francisco in AD 79. (4.2)

NASA: National Aeronautic Space Agency, based in America. The Doctor contacted them to set up his trap for Prisoner Zero. (5.1) The Doctor broke into the Saturn 5 rocket silo at NASA's Cape Kennedy to reprogramme Apollo 11's cameras to receive and re-broadcast the clip of the Silent demanding humanity kill it. He was captured by the security detail there, led by Mr Gardner, but was released by President Nixon. (6.1, 6.2)

Nathan: Recently unemployed teenager aboard the number 200 bus to Brixton when it wound up on San Helios. He was quick-thinking and calm in a crisis, so the Doctor recommended him to Captain Magambo as a potential recruit for UNIT. (4.15) (Played by DAVID AMES)

National Grid: The UK's electrical power transmission network – Torchwood hacked into it to boost Mr Smith's ability to access the world's mobile telephone network. (4.12) Morpeth-Jetsan contractor Jimmy Wicks reckoned he'd had the National Grid run through his body when the solar tsunami radiation hit the rig-harness he was asleep in. (6.5)

National Herald: Newspaper that reported on the disappearance of Agatha Christie in 1926. (4.7)

National Museum: Exhibition hall in London, where the Pandorica was on display as part of the Anomaly Exhibition. It had a video monitor, with a voice giving background information to the exhibits. (5.13) (Voiced by NICHOLAS BRIGGS)

National Trust: Preservation authority which owned Earth five billion years in Rose Tyler's future and had artificially prolonged its life with gravity satellites, as well as reversing continental drift to maintain a 'Classic Earth'. (1.2)

NATO: The North Atlantic Treaty Organisation – a military alliance which went to red alert when the Sycorax ship approached Earth. (2.X) Their Defence Systems were disrupted by the Sontaran clone of Martha Jones. (4.5) The Master controlled their nuclear arsenal and fired it at the *Hesperus*. (4.18)

Naturists: A nude couple driving on the New New York Motorway, encountered by the Doctor as he jumped from car to car. (3.3) (Played by CHRIS ILSTON, GRÁINNE JOUGHIN)

Navarre, King of: Character from Shakespeare's *Love's Labour's Lost* and *Love's Labour's Won*, played by Richard Burbage. (3.2)

Nav-Com: The Chula navigational system on Jack's stolen ship. (1.10)

Neighbour [1]: A resident of number 3 in the same street as the Finch family, he put out a wheelie bin near Mickey Smith's car while Rose Tyler was visiting Clive Finch. The bin was used by the Nestene Consciousness to kidnap Mickey and replace him with an Auton facsimile. (1.1) (Played by ALUN JENKINS)

Neighbour [2]: An anxious mother who suggested that council worker Kel was responsible for kidnapping the missing children of Dame Kelly Holmes Close. (2.11) (Played by ERICA EIRIAN)

Neo-Classic Congregational and Neo-Judaism: Two of the many religions practised in the 42nd century. (2.9)

Nephew: One of the Patchwork People, an augmented Ood trapped on the sentient asteroid House. He was kept alive by House over many centuries to act as a lure for Time Lords and other travellers who were drawn into House's bubble universe. House fed off the rift energy that powered TARDISes, and it would reuse limbs and organs from the dead pilots to keep the Patchwork People alive.

Nephew channelled House's energy and communicated with House via his translator ball, which was also used to drain, allegedly, the souls from dying patchwork people. House took Nephew aboard the Doctor's TARDIS when it possessed it, using Nephew to terrorise Amy Pond and Rory Williams to amuse itself as they crossed the Void. Nephew was killed, his atoms disseminated throughout the TARDIS, when the Junk TARDIS built by the Doctor and Idris materialised in the exact spot he was standing inside the old control room. (6.4) (Played by PAUL KASEY, voiced by MICHAEL SHEEN)

Nerys: One of the guests at Donna's wedding. Donna assumed that Nerys had arranged her transportation from the church to the TARDIS. When Donna finally got to her reception, she was not amused to find Nerys moving in on Lance Bennett, her fiancé. (3.X) According to Donna, Nerys had twins after using a turkey baster. (4.6) She was at Donna's wedding to Shaun Temple, wearing peach, unlike everyone else in the wedding party. (4.18) (Played by KRYSTAL ARCHER)

Nestene Consciousness: Disembodied energy form that could manipulate any form of plastic and use it as a weapon. It fled the Time War after the destruction of its home planet, and may have been a signatory to the Shadow Proclamation. It had attempted to invade Earth more than once but, after it took on a liquid-plastic form, the Ninth Doctor used antiplastic to destroy it. (1.1) The Consciousness was part of the Pandorica Alliance, and placed Auton replica Roman Legionaries around Stonehenge in AD 102. The Nestenes used psychic residue of Amy Pond's memories from her home in 2010 to create the Pandorica myths and legends as well as the Auton Romans, including Rory Williams, drawn directly from those memories. (5.12) (Voiced by NICHOLAS BRIGGS)

Nevada: American state, where the towns of Dry Springs and Solitude were situated. Also the home to Dreamland. (DL, 6.2)

'Never Can Say Goodbye': Cover version of the Jackson 5 hit, performed by The Communards and being played nearby when the TARDIS materialised in 1987 prior to Pete Tyler's death in a hit-and-run accident. (1.8)

'Never Gonna Give You Up': Number one hit for Rick Astley in 1987. It was playing on Pete Tyler's car radio as he took Rose to St Christopher's Church for the wedding of Stuart Hoskins and Sarah Clark. (1.8)

'Never Too Late': 1989 hit for Kylie Minogue, quoted by the Doctor to Tommy Connolly as they headed to Alexandra Palace to put a stop to the Wire's Time of Manifestation. (2.7)

New American Alliance: The Emperor Dalek's forces bombed this Earth continent in 200,100. (1.13)

New Amsterdam: Original name for New York. (3.4)

New Atlantic: Ocean off the coast of New New York where, according to Sally Calypso, the sun was blazing high in the sky, creating a perfect setting for the Daily Contemplation. (3.3)

New Byzantine Calendar: Method of date measurement used by the human colonists on Messaline. (4.6)

New Earth: A planet the same shape, size and orbit as the original Earth, but 50,000 light years away, in the Galaxy M87, and settled on by humans nostalgic for their home world, which had been destroyed by the expansion of the sun. The Doctor took Rose Tyler to visit it in 5,000,000,023, and they encountered

Lady Cassandra O'Brien trying to blackmail the Sisters of Plenitude. (2.1) The Doctor returned there with Martha Jones in 5,000,000,053, by which time the planet had been quarantined for 24 years after the Mood Patch Bliss had mutated and wiped out most of the planet's inhabitants. (3.3)

New Fifth Avenue: Street intersection on the New New York Motorway where, according to Sally Calypso, a spate of car-jackings had occurred. (3.3)

New Gallifrey: Once the Master had created his New Time Lord Empire, he hoped to found a new home planet for himself. (3.13)

New Germany: European country on 'Pete's World', which Pete Tyler suggested to John Lumic as an alternative place to establish the Ultimate Upgrade project. (2.5)

New Humans [1]: Name for one of the evolutionary routes taken by the humans of five billion years in Rose Tyler's future. It implied they were different from the then-extinct (bar Lady Cassandra) humans originating from Earth itself. (1.2)

New Humans [2]: In a massive Intensive Care Unit beneath the Hospital on New Earth, the Sisters of Plenitude had grown new humans, riddled with every known disease, virus and contagion. Their plan was to use the humans as stock for cures, but Lady Cassandra O'Brien let the patients out of their cells, and they rampaged through the Hospital until the Doctor was able to cure them with their own antibodies in a massive cocktail of drugs. Once they were cured, the Doctor described them as a new species. (2.1)

New Mexico: American state where an Endymide ship crashed near Roswell in 1947, after being shot down by space pirates. (DL)

New New Jersey Expressway: Part of the New New York Motorway where, according to Sally Calypso, 15 extra lanes had been opened to assist traffic flow. (3.3)

New New York: The 15th place to bear the name New York, this city was located on New Earth in Galaxy M87, and everyone on New Earth lived in the city and its environs, surrounded on one side by the New Atlantic and on the other by the New Pacific. New New York was ruled over by a Senate and was an ultra-sophisticated, high-rise cityscape, dominated by two main species, humans and Catkind. The areas of New New York, usually named after those of the 21st-century New York on Earth (such as Brooklyn, Battery Park and Manhattan), were linked by a series of covered motorway tunnels. Over the years, the city had become divided into two distinct areas, the Overcity and the Undercity. While the rich and powerful, such as the Senate and the Duke of Manhattan, lived above, the lower levels became home to the poor, the dispossessed and the dealers of Mood Patches in Pharmacytown. The Doctor and Rose Tyler's visit to New New York in 5,000,000,023 centred on a small headland where a vast Hospital had been built, run by the Sisters of Plenitude, an order of Catkind nuns. (2.1) Thirty years later, he took Martha Jones to the Undercity and learned that a new mood, Bliss, had mutated and wiped out the Overcity, leaving the people on the Motorway the only survivors apart from Novice Hame and the Face of Boe, who were striving to maintain the city's energy levels. The Macra, which inhabited the lowest levels of the Motorway, were rumoured to have escaped from the New New York Zoo. (3.3)

New Roman Empire: The Empire that ruled Earth in the year 12,005. (1.2)

New Skaro: The Cult of Skaro intended to use their Dalek-Human army to turn Earth into New Skaro. (3.5)

New South America: Devastated area of 'Pete's World' with a huge homelessness problem. (2.5) According to the mysterious Gemini, 265,000 people had disappeared from New South America since 2004. (2.5T)

New Time Lord Empire, the: The Master intended to set this up by going to war with everyone else in the universe, aided by the Toclafane. To this end he was using labour camps across the Earth to build 200,000 massive war rockets, each with a black hole converter inside. Time Lord technology had been based on the harnessing of black holes, and the Master reasoned that this would be the perfect foundation for his New Empire. (3.13)

New Times Square: The Businessman driving his car on the New New York Motorway compared the arrivals of first the Doctor and then Novice Hame in his car with the hustle and bustle of New Times Square. (3.3)

New Venus Archipelago 27: Place where 200 people died in sandstorms, according to Bad Wolf TV. (1.7)

New York: Colloquial name for New York City, the largest city in America, and the main city of New York State. Base of the United Nations, who were debating what to do in light of the massive weapons of destruction the faux British government (in reality, the Family Slitheen) had convinced them existed in space, requiring a nuclear strike to destroy them. (1.5) Location of the studios for *The Ed Sullivan Show*, where the Doctor planned to take Rose Tyler to see Elvis Presley perform 'Hound Dog' live in 1956. (2.7) Captain Jack Harkness tried to enter New York during the year Ellis Island became the immigration entry point – Jack was shot while there, and discovered then that he couldn't die. (3.11)

Martha Jones walked across the Earth, including New York, telling her story about the Doctor, preparing people for the right moment to chant his name. (3.13) ATMOS devices reportedly went off there. (4.4) Martha Jones was posted there by UNIT as Medical Director on Project Indigo. (4.12) Melody Pond ended up in an alleyway in New York, injured and exhausted, until she began to regenerate. (6.2)

New York Record: Daily newspaper, which alerted the Doctor and Martha to the disappearances from Hooverville in 1930s Manhattan. (3.4)

New York Revue: The musical show playing at the Laurenzi theatre in 1930, which featured Tallulah singing 'Heaven And Hell'. (3.4)

New Zealand: The Doctor thought Astrid Peth might find New Zealand more interesting than a street in Chiswick, but she was more than happy with what she saw there. (4.X)

Newman, Verity: Great granddaughter of Joan Redfern, who wrote a biography of Joan, entitled *A Journal of Impossible Things*. The Doctor went to her book signing to ask after Joan. (4.18) (Played by JESSICA HYNES)

Newport: On 'Pete's World', the name of the London Borough which, on Rose Tyler's version of Earth, was called Lambeth. (2.6)

Newsreaders: A male BBC newsreader commented on the Big Ben incident. A female newsreader reported on the arrival of UNIT officers from Geneva. (1.4) Another reported on the Sycorax's contact with Earth. (2.X) (Played by SAGAR ARYA) A French presenter told viewers that the President of France had decided that ghosts would not receive the Légion d'honneur. (2.12) (Played by ANTHONY DEBAECK) An Indian newsreader warned visitors to the Taj Mahal that the ghosts should be treated as sacred guests. (2.12) (Played by HAJAZ

N

AKRAM) In Japan, a newsreader explained that the ghosts were the latest craze to sweep Japan. (2.12) (Played by TAKAKO AKASHI) A young newsreader tried to warn her viewers and her family about the Dalek and Cyberman invasion, but was cut off mid-broadcast by one of the alien invaders. (2.13T) (Played by ADRIENNE O'SULLIVAN) A News 24 anchor warned the public about the Doctor, Martha Jones and Captain Jack Harkness after the Master arranged for them to be declared public enemies. She later commented on the Toclafane arrival. (3.12) (Played by OLIVIA HILL) A Chinese newsreader warned the People's Republic that watching British newscasts about the Toclafane was illegal. (3.12) (Played by DANIEL MING) A newsreader commentated on Holy Roman Emperor Winston Churchill's return from Gaul. (6.13) (Played by MEREDITH VIEIRA)

Night Eagle: Shoshoni Indian leader, and grandfather to Jimmy Stalkingwolf. In 1953, he and his people witnessed Rivesh Mantilax's ship crash and saved him, tending to him in a cave in the Nevada desert. Over the years the Alliance of Shades' androids had often come looking for him, but the tribe had seen them off. When Night Eagle introduced Rivesh Mantilax to the Doctor, they were all found by Colonel Stark, arrested and taken to Dreamland. (DL) (Voiced by CLARKE PETERS)

Nightclubber: Young woman who answered the time engine avatar's call for help at 79B Aickman Road and was unintentionally killed, ultimately adding to the stain on Craig Owens's ceiling below. (5.11) (Played by KAMARA BACCHUS)

Nightingale, Katherine Costello: Best friend of Sally Sparrow. When Sally came to her flat late one night, spooked about the message she had found addressed to her at Western Drumlins, Kathy agreed to accompany her back to the house the next day for another look. They were then disturbed by the arrival of a man claiming to be Kathy's grandson, just as Kathy was touched by a Weeping Angel and sent back in time, to 5 December 1920. She found herself in Hull and eventually settled there, with a young farmer called Ben Wainwright. They married (although Kathy lied about her age, claiming to be only 18) and had three children, one of whom was named Sally in Sally Sparrow's honour. After Ben died, Kathy had grandchildren, one of whom was Malcolm Wainwright, and she wrote a letter explaining what had happened and asked him to deliver it to Sally at the exact moment she had disappeared from Wester Drumlins in 2007. She died in 1987, not long after writing the letter. (3.10) (Played by LUCY GASKILL)

Nightingale, Lawrence: Brother to Kathy, who had been wandering around his sister's flat naked the first time he met Sally Sparrow. After Kathy disappeared and Sally received a letter from her from 1987, she tracked Larry down to Banto's DVD shop where he worked, and tried to explain that Kathy had had to go away. She was intrigued by the DVDs that Larry had — he was a bit of a geek about 17 particular DVDs all of which had Easter eggs on them, each with clips of a man called the Doctor apparently having one half of a conversation. When Sally next contacted Larry and told him the 17 discs matched all the DVDs she owned, he agreed to meet her at Wester Drumlins with copies of them. Together they learned about the Weeping Angels, and were promptly attacked by one. While Sally looked for a way out of the house, Larry tried not to blink, but he eventually gave in and followed Sally to the cellar where they found and entered the TARDIS. After they'd inserted one of the DVDs into the console, the TARDIS

dematerialised around them and went back to 1969 to locate the Doctor and Martha Jones. Larry was relieved to realise that it had been a lure for the Weeping Angels, which had been holding the TARDIS as it vanished – with the police box gone, they had been left staring at one another, freezing them for eternity. During the next 12 months, Larry and Sally bought Banto's store and set up their own shop selling old books and rare DVDs, naming it Sparrow and Nightingale, and the two briefly met the Doctor in the street. Sally handed the Time Lord all her files on their encounter, realising she was now starting off the chain of events. (3.10) (Played by FINLAY ROBERTSON)

Nightmare Child, the: Participant in the Time War. Davros, creator of the Daleks, was lost when he flew his command ship into the jaws of the Nightmare Child during the first year of the War. (4.13, 4.18)

Nimon, the: Race of bull-like aliens who the Doctor discovered were distantly related to the Minotaur creature that patrolled the God Complex. (6.11)

Nina [1]: Orphaned schoolgirl eaten by Hector Finch at Deffry Vale High School. (2.3) (Played by HEATHER CAMERON)

Nina [2]: Essex girl who was rejected from talent show *Britain's Got Talent*, which made the front page of the local paper in Colchester because of her emotional journey to seek fame. (6.12)

92 Squadron: One of the RAF squadrons that headed from Biggin Hill towards the south coast of England to engage German fighters in battle during the Second World War. (5.3)

Nitrofine: Strong metal from which the interior of the starliner *Titanic* was constructed. (4.X)

Nixon, Richard Milhous: 37th President of the United States of America. He was relatively new to office in 1969 when, in the months leading up to Apollo 11's mission to land a man on the moon, he became aware of the Silence and their power over humanity. Taking his cue from former FBI agent Canton Delaware III, Nixon supported the Doctor and travelled in the TARDIS a few times to get him out of sticky situations. When the Silence were defeated, he asked the Doctor if the future would remember him. Without revealing quite why, the Doctor assured Nixon that his place in history was guaranteed. (6.1, 6.2) (Played by STUART MILLIGAN)

NNYPD: The New New York Police Department arrested the Sisters of Plenitude on New Earth after their scheme had been thwarted. (2.1) By the time the Doctor and Martha Jones investigated the Motorway on New New York in 5,000,000,053, the NNYPD had ceased to exist, and drivers were fooled into thinking they were still there via a series of recorded messages going out automatically. (3.3)

Noakes, Robert: Murderer hung on the Tyburn Tree. (AG05)

Noble, Donna: The daughter of Sylvia and Geoff Noble, granddaughter to Wilfred Mott (who used to call her the Little General) and fiancée to Lance Bennett, Donna was halfway up the aisle of St Mary's Church when she found herself accidentally transported aboard the TARDIS, a side effect of the Empress of the Racnoss's plans hatched with her accomplice, Lance. Donna first recalled meeting Lance when she was temping as a secretary for HC Clements, six months before their eventual wedding day, when he offered to make her a simple cup of coffee. In reality, he was dosing her with Huon Energy in liquid form on behalf of the Empress, who was using her body to catalyse the Huon particles, enabling her to release the remaining Racnoss from the centre of the Earth. The Doctor later deduced that it was when these particles inside Donna had magnetised with those inside the TARDIS that she was initially drawn on board, and was then able to reverse the process, summoning the TARDIS to materialise around them. The Doctor confirmed that all the Huon Energy, deadly to humans, had been drained from Donna by the Empress before she returned home. Prior to HC Clements, Donna lived alone with her dog in London, where she worked as a temp, and had a tendency to show off — even her mother noted that, on her first day at school, she had been sent home for biting. She liked Pringles, lifestyle fads and celebrity gossip, and disliked Christmas to the extent that she deliberately scheduled her wedding for Christmas Eve, with a honeymoon to follow in Morocco. The Doctor also observed Donna's tendency to miss big events playing out around her, having been hung over during the Sycorax invasion at Christmas and scuba-diving in Spain when the Cybermen manifested across the globe. Although her time with the Doctor helped put everything into much greater perspective, Donna turned down the opportunity to travel with him following their encounter with the Racnoss, choosing instead to give up temping and go travelling instead. She did, however, hope that their paths might cross again, one day... (3.X) Donna's plans to travel came to nothing more than a quick holiday to Egypt before

temping again. But she never forgot the Doctor and began investigating unexplained phenomena, hoping to bump into him — which she did while posing as a health and safety inspector at Adipose Industries. (4.1) After stopping the Adipose, Donna revealed that she'd kept her mum's car permanently packed, ready to go off in the TARDIS, and the Doctor took her to Pompeii (4.2) and the Ood-Sphere (where the Ood christened the two of them the DoctorDonna), (4.3) before they returned to Earth to meet Martha Jones and stop the Sontarans' stratagem involving the ATMOS devices. (4.4, 4.5) With Martha, they travelled to Messaline, (4.6) and then Donna and the Doctor met Agatha Christie (4.7) and visited The Library, where they met River Song. River knew who Donna was but wouldn't explain how or why. (4.8, 4.9) Donna was one of the things the Doctor mentioned to Sky Silvestry on Midnight which she repeated back at him. (4.10) Shortly before leaving Earth with the Doctor, Donna had her first meeting with Rose Tyler, although she didn't know it — but Rose was tracking Donna, because she knew she was integral to reaching the Doctor, to warn him that the universes, all of them, were collapsing. She was able to talk to Donna in the alternative reality where Donna never met the Doctor, telling her the phrase 'Bad Wolf', knowing this would get the Doctor to search for her. (4.11) When Earth and 26 other planets were transported to the Medusa Cascade, the Doctor and Rose were finally reunited, but a Dalek shot and wounded the Doctor, almost jump-starting a regeneration. The Doctor deflected the regeneration energy into his spare hand and later Donna touched this, creating a metacrisis. The result of this was the creation of an extra, part-human Doctor, while Donna found her brain now filled with all the Doctor's knowledge and awareness of time and space. She used this to stop Davros and the Daleks but the metacrisis was destroying her, and the Doctor had to erase all memories of him and everything they had ever seen and done together from her mind. Heartbroken, he took Donna home to Wilfred and Sylvia, telling them that if Donna ever remembered anything about him, she would die. (4.12, 4.13) The following Christmas, when the Master tried to create

the Master race, the metacrisis prevented Donna from being turned into the Master; instead it protected her, sending out waves of mental energy as her memories started to come back, stopping the local Masters and putting Donna into a coma until, once again, the memories faded for ever. Months later, the Doctor watched her wedding day, as she married Shaun Temple and gave her a wedding gift, via Wilfred and Sylvia – a lottery ticket, bought with a pound he'd borrowed from her late father, which meant she and Shaun were set up for life. (4.17, 4.18) When trying to create a voice interface with the TARDIS, while dying from the poison from the Judas Tree, the Doctor considered talking to a hologram of Donna. (6.8) (Played by CATHERINE TATE)

Noble, Geoffrey: Somewhat henpecked (by his wife Sylvia) father-of-the-bride (Donna). He took charge of seeing to the injured in the wake of the Roboform Santas bombing the wedding reception, and was overjoyed when Donna returned home after her adventures with the Doctor, having feared his daughter was dead. (3.X) He died sometime between the failed wedding and the time that the Judoon stole the Royal Hope Hospital and placed it on the moon, and the family moved house shortly afterwards. (4.11) Some time before he died, he gave the Doctor a pound and the Doctor bought a lottery ticket which had a triple rollover, giving it anonymously to Donna as a wedding gift. (4.18) (Played by HOWARD ATTFIELD)

Noble, Sylvia: Donna's mother, quick to criticise and used to getting her own way, but ultimately overjoyed when Donna returned home after her adventures with the Doctor, having feared her daughter was dead. (3.X) After Geoff, her husband, died, she, Donna and her father Wilfred Mott moved to a new house in Chiswick and was cross that once again Donna chose to run off without saying goodbye. (4.1) She was not happy to realise that Donna's travels were with

the Doctor, nor that Wilfred and the Doctor were friends. However, she was relieved when the Doctor stopped the ATMOS pollution. (4.4, 4.5) In the alternative world where Donna never met the Doctor, Sylvia convinced Donna to take a job with Jival Chowdry rather than at HC Clements. Spending Christmas out of London, they were saved when it was destroyed in a nuclear explosion, but having lost their home and possessions, Sylvia, Wilfred and Donna were forced to move to Leeds, where Sylvia became more and more depressed. (4.11) She finally learned the truth about where exactly Donna and the Doctor were when the Daleks invaded Earth and, with Wilfred, tried to fight back. When Rose Tyler arrived at their house, looking for Donna, they watched Harriet Jones contacting all the Doctor's friends, but Rose couldn't participate in the conversation because Sylvia wouldn't allow a webcam in the house. Sylvia now gained a new respect for her daughter and, when the Doctor returned the amnesiac Donna to her, she was furious with him and said she was so proud of her daughter. (4.12, 4.13) However, when the Doctor and Wilfred met up on Christmas morning, she was livid, knowing that if Donna saw the Doctor, her mind would burn. Sylvia was turned into the Master but later returned to normal. The last time she saw the Tenth Doctor was at Donna's wedding to Shaun Temple, where he gave them a lottery ticket bought with Geoffrey Noble's money that was destined to make her daughter rich. (4.17, 4.18) (Played by JACQUELINE KING)

Noble Corporation PLC Limited, Intergalactic: Company that Donna Noble and the Doctor claimed to be sales reps for on the Ood-Sphere. (4.3)

Noddy: Fictional taxi driver created by author Enid Blyton for very young children. Donna Noble assumed it was unlikely that she and the Doctor would encounter him having tea with Enid. The Doctor assured her that wasn't going to happen as Noddy was definitely fictional. (4.7)

Node 710/aqua: A Courtesy Node in The Library, it warned the Doctor and Donna to flee and to count the shadows. (4.8) (Played by SARAH NILES)

Nodes: In both Courtesy and Security variations, these were found all over The Library, to help visitors find their way around. They had faces projected on them, often of deceased people who donated their image to The Library, such as Mark Chambers. After being digitised and 'saved' by CAL, Donna Noble's face was used on a Security Node. (4.8, 4.9)

North Korea: Their nuclear weapons were primed and ready to strike the Sontaran mothership in Earth's orbit. (4.5)

Northover, Ambrose: Meals on Wheels driver for the Cwmtaff Volunteer Service and rather highly strung mother of Elliot and wife of Mo, who lost first her husband and then her son to the Silurians. Fearing the worst, when her father, Tony Mack, was poisoned by Silurian venom, she finally snapped and attacked a Silurian warrior, Alaya, with a taser. The shock killed the Silurian and, just as the Doctor and Amy Pond were brokering peace in the Silurian city below ground, Ambrose, Tony and Rory Williams had to return Alaya's corpse to them. The Doctor was furious with Ambrose – her loss of control had jeopardised everything he had tried to achieve, and the Silurian warriors then attempted to kill them all. The Northovers all escaped in the TARDIS, although Elliot was none

too impressed with his mother. Nor was the Doctor. (5.8, 5.9) (Played by NIA ROBERTS)

Northover, Elliot: Young son to Mo and Ambrose. A good artist but dyslexic, Elliot loved listening to talking books and, after his father had been kidnapped by the Silurians, he raced home to get his earphones before the Doctor could seal them safely inside the church. As a result, Elliot was also captured and placed in suspended animation. Mo later convinced the Silurian scientist Malohkeh to release Elliot, and the Doctor hoped that the boy would be the kind of person who in later life would help steer humanity towards seeking peaceful coexistence with the Silurian race. (5.8, 5.9) (Played by SAMUEL DAVIES)

Northover, Mo: Drill technician at the Discovery drilling project in Cwmtaff. He was married to Ambrose and had a son, Elliot, who they doted on. Working the nightshift, Mo was dragged beneath the ground by Silurian Malohkeh's gravity discs. When Mo awoke, he realised the Silurian had done invasive surgery on him, but left him feeling fine. When Amy Pond was similarly drawn down to the Silurian city, she and Mo escaped, discovering Elliot, unharmed but in suspended animation. Malohkeh happily released Elliot but after

Warrior Restac tried to kill all the humans, Mo led Elliot and Ambrose into the TARDIS with the Doctor and Amy, and then fled back to Cwmtaff while the Silurians returned to hibernation. (5.8, 5.9) (Played by ALUN RAGLAN)

Norway: Having been trapped on 'Pete's World' for some months, Rose Tyler heard the Doctor calling to her in a dream. She, Mickey, Jackie and Pete followed the voice, driving from Britain all the way to Norway, where the Doctor, as a hologram, and Rose were reunited for two minutes on the beach at Dårlig Ulv Stranden, able to say a final, heartfelt goodbye. (2.13) The Doctor took Rose and his human double back to Norway to start a new life together. (4.13) Howie Spragg reckoned the hotel he was locked in was in Norway because he believed the US government had cities hidden under the mountains there. (6.11)

Nottingham: Midlands city where, in the fiction the Doctor created for John Smith's background, John believed he came from. He told Joan it lay on the River Leen and other basic details, but couldn't give her more personal recollections of it. (3.8, 3.9) The *Daily Courier* reported a major influenza outbreak there in 1926. (4.7)

Novice: Rank of young Time Lords as they entered the Academy on Gallifrey for the first time. (3.12)

Nuclear Bolt: Radioactive energy which powered the Immortality Gate, controlled from two identical glass booths which maintained the feedback levels at all times, one booth locked and occupied, the other unlocked and empty, with booth shifts changing at regular intervals. (4.17, 4.18)

Nuclear Plant Seven: Research area where Professor Docherty worked for the Master, although the Resistance counted her as a major player in their ranks. (3.13)

Nuclear Storm Drive: Engines aboard the starliner *Titanic*. The Doctor managed to stop the stricken ship crashing into Buckingham Palace after reigniting the secondary drives. (4.X) In the parallel world where Donna Noble never met the Doctor, the *Titanic* struck London and destroyed the south of England in a massive nuclear explosion. (4.11)

Nuremberg: Bavarian city in Germany. Martha Jones found herself in woods, about 60 miles away from Nuremberg, when searching for Osterhagen Station One. (4.13)

Nurse [1]: She looked after Adam Mitchell on Floor 016 of Satellite Five and oversaw the implantation of the Type 2 chip into his forehead. (1.7) (Played by TAMSIN GREIG)

Nurse [2]: A Krillitane who had taken human form and worked at Deffry Vale High School. She was killed when K-9 heated up the drums of Krillitane Oil in the school kitchen and blew the Nurse, the school and himself to pieces. (2.3) (Played by SUZANNE CASENOVE)

Nurse [3]: The Doctor left River Song in a hospital run by the Sisters of the Infinite Schism after she sacrificed her regenerations to save him. The Nurse there promised to make sure River got plenty of rest. (6.8) (Played by EVA ALEXANDER)

Nurse [4]: Working at the nursing home where Sir Alistair Lethbridge-Stewart passed away, she had to break the sad news to the Doctor. (6.13) (Played by KATHARINE BURFORD)

Nyssa: Companion of the Fifth Doctor at the time he encountered the Tenth Doctor during a time collision. (TC)

'O Little Town of Bethlehem': Victorian carol by Philips Brooks. It was played during Christmas Eve at Isabella and Eric's home when the Doctor, Kazran Sardick and Abigail Pettigrew joined them for an early Christmas. (6.X)

O'Brien Dot Delta Seventeen, Lady Cassandra: The last 'pure' human alive at the time of Earthdeath, although she was nothing more than a thin area of skin hung tautly across a wire frame, with only her eyes and mouth left functioning. Her vain, selfish and arrogant brain was kept safely in a jar beneath her skin, and she was regularly moisturised by her two surgeons. She resented all the various hybrid humans and mutations that existed across the cosmos that, ironically, kept the human race alive. She claimed she'd been married a number of times, that her father was from Texas, her mother from the Arctic Desert, and they were the last humans buried on Earth. She boasted that she had undergone more than 700 operations to preserve and refine herself, and that she was born male. Using her robot spiders and the Adherents of the Repeated Meme, Cassandra's plan was to stage a hostage situation, with herself as one of the victims, then collect all the ransom and insurance monies herself. When the Doctor exposed her plan, she teleported away, leaving Platform One to be destroyed, and intended to take over each of the deceased dignitaries' holdings. However, the Doctor brought her back to the space station without her surgeons to moisturise her, so her skin, now dry, snapped. (1.2) Cassandra didn't die, however – her servant, a force-grown clone she called Chip, rescued her brainmeat and her eyes, and she had her face rebuilt using skin from her posterior. The Doctor encountered her again on New Earth 23 years later, where she was able to use a psychograft to place her mind in Rose. Cassandra had discovered the Sisters of Plenitude's attempts to breed clone humans with every disease in their systems, thus creating perfect anti-serums, and intended to blackmail the Hospital. After leaving Rose, she took over the Doctor's body and even one of the clone patients before finally accepting her time was up. The dying Chip volunteered his own body for Cassandra's final resting place and, before she died for good, the Doctor took Cassandra to witness her real self many years earlier. 'Chip' died in the younger Cassandra's arms, after telling her how beautiful she was. (2.1) (Played by ZOË WANAMAKER, BILLIE PIPER, DAVID TENNANT, JOANNA CROZIER, SEAN GALLAGHER)

O'Connell, Pat: One of Oswald Fox's friends on Poseidon. Leader of the Community's farmers, he was killed by the Razor-Toothed Blade-Fin. (AG04)

O'Connor, Des: Presenter of Channel 4 quiz show *Countdown*. After the Toclafane invasion, *Countdown* was cancelled, much to the chagrin of Professor Docherty. (3.13)

O'Grady, Paul: Ianto Jones of Torchwood was watching Paul O'Grady's TV show when the chat show host mentioned the planets in the sky. (4.12)

Oakham Farm: Farm owned by Mr Clark, who was murdered by the Family of Blood. (3.8, 3.9)

Obama, President Barack: Was about to give a speech on Christmas Day concerning his new financial plan to rescue the global economy, when his body was turned into the Master. He reverted back to normal once Rassilon had reversed the Master's work. (4.17, 4.18) (Played by ROGER HAYNES)

Obego Family: One of the dislocated families from the South of England in the alternative world where Donna Noble never met the Doctor. Like the Nobles, they were sent to a street in Leeds, to live at number 31. (4.11)

Oblivion Continuum: The energy device used to power the android that believed itself to be Edwin Bracewell. The Daleks, which built Bracewell, later used it as a bomb but Amy Pond was able to convince Bracewell to disarm it. (5.3)

Observatory: Room atop Torchwood House containing a telescope designed and built by Sir George MacLeish and Prince Albert. (2.2)

Observer, The: National Sunday newspaper for which Penny Carter was Science Correspondent. (4.1)

Octavian, Father: Bishop, Second Class, of the team of Clerics that arrived on Alfava Metraxis at the request of River Song to find the Weeping Angel that had escaped from the crashed *Byzantium*. Many of his clerics died during the crossing of the Maze of the Dead, and Octavian warned River that he'd have her shipped back to the Stormcage if she betrayed him. In the end, Octavian was captured by the Angels and he sacrificed himself so that the Doctor could carry on and destroy the Angels — warning him about River's duplicity before he died. (5.4, 5.5) (Played by IAIN GLEN)

Oddie, Bill: British comedian and ornithologist, famous for his bird conservation television programmes. When the TARDIS arrived on Pheros, Martha Jones saw the bird eyrie and suggested they were in Bill Oddie heaven. (TIQ)

Ofsted: UK quango dedicated to overseeing educational establishments. Amy Pond pretended to represent them when she investigated Rosanna Calvierri's School. (5.6)

Oil Apocalypse: 21st-century event that almost led to the extinction of mankind. It's fallout was one of the reasons why Adelaide Brooke was content to take a mission away from Earth for some years and take command of Bowie Base One on Mars (4.16)

OilCorp: Galactic corporation that was sucking planets such as Bouken dry of their natural resources in the oil-starved 40th century, then selling the oil at inflated prices. OilCorp's biggest opponents were a number of pirates who would attack the rigs and steal the oil, selling it at low prices to poorer planets. OilCorp created sentient robotic rigs that could defend themselves against the pirates, and on Bouken they placed a spy, Swabb, aboard the *Black Gold*, the ship commanded by Captain Kaliko. (TIQ)

Oklahoma: The Trine-E android aboard the Game Station described Captain Jack Harkness's outfit as having an 'Oklahoma farm boy look' during the *What Not to Wear* programme. This was a reference to the 46th American state, famed for its farming and oil production. (1.12) Some of the residents of Manhattan's Hooverville were from this state. (3.4)

Oklahoma!: A Rodgers and Hammerstein musical, beloved of amateur dramatic societies, such as the bad one in Upper Leadworth. Amy Pond did not want to see their version of the show at any cost. (5.7)

Old Curiosity Shop, The: A novel by Charles Dickens that includes a celebrated scene in which the heroine, Little Nell, dies. The Doctor asked Dickens to read that specific section for him, but he didn't. (1.3)

Old Earth: Referred to in questions by the Anne Droid aboard the Game Station, during *The Weakest Link*. (1.12)

'Old Rugged Cross, The': Every day at the same time, the drivers of the cars on the New New York Motorway took a few moments to sing together, as one voice, a hymn to celebrate their lives. When the Doctor was with the Brannigan family, and Martha Jones with Milo and Cheen, the hymn sung was this 20th-century Christian anthem — perhaps suggesting that the New New Yorkers were primarily Christians (Thomas Brannigan and Javit both mentioned Jehovah, and the occupants of the cars later sang another Christian anthem, 'Abide With Me'). (3.3)

Olive Woman: One of the posh guests at the LazLabs reception party, who thought that choking on an olive was a greater threat than anything that the GMD experiment could have created, until she became the second victim of the Lazarus creature. (3.6) (Played by LUCY O'CONNELL)

Oliver Twist: A book cited by the Doctor as one of the Charles Dickens canon that he'd read and loved. (1.3)

Olympia: Location of the very first Olympic Games in 776 BC. The Doctor offered to take Amy Pond and Rory Williams there as a wedding gift. (5.6)

Om-Com: The communications system on Chula ships. It allowed both Captain Jack Harkness (when he was on his ship) and the 'empty' child (because he was infused with Chula nanotechnology) to communicate through anything with a speaker grille. (1.9, 1.10)

Omnistate Impact Chamber: The Doctor found one of these on Deck 31 of the starliner *Titanic*. Within it was the Max-Box, a cybernetic carriage which contained the head of Max Capricorn, who had engineered the meteoroid

strike that crippled his ship. The Chamber kept him secure, and he planned to remain safe within it even after the ship had crashed to Earth and detonated its nuclear engines. (4.X)

Oncoming Storm, the: The name the Daleks gave to the Doctor in their own legends. (1.13) Rose Tyler sarcastically reminded him of this when he turned up in the 51st century, apparently drunk after partying in the 18th. (2.4) The Dream Lord referred to him as this. (5.7)

106: Number of River Song's cell in the Stormcage Prison Facility. (6.1, 6.2, 6.7)

1,306: Amy Pond's age by the time she visited *Starship UK* in the 33rd century. (5.2)

133 Squadron: The RAF Squadron that Captain Jack Harkness was a volunteer member of. (1.9)

Ood Brain: All of Oodkind were linked telepathically to one another via three brains — one in their heads, one carried in their hands and one shared brain. This massive separate Ood Brain had originally lived beneath the Northern Glacier on the Ood-Sphere but was found and brought to the surface by Ood Operations, where they enslaved it and kept it alive to ensure the survival of their Ood slaves. Klineman Halpen tried to blow up the Ood Brain in an effort to destroy all Oodkind, but the Doctor rendered his bombs useless. (4.3) The Ood Brain was later troubled because it sensed the return of Gallifrey and placed snatches of telepathic imagery into the minds of the Ood, which they could then show the Doctor. (4.17)

Ood-Graft: Drink ingested regularly by Klineman Halpen. He believed it was hair tonic but in fact Ood Sigma was using it to turn him into an Ood. (4.3)

Ood Operations: Human company based on the Ood-Sphere, which took natural Ood, lobotomised them and turned them into slaves for selling throughout the Earth Empire. When it became too difficult to stop the Red-Eyed

and rabid Ood, the company's Chairman Klineman Halpen decided to shut the company down and destroy all his livestock, but the Ood stopped him and the company was ruined without any further loss of life. (4.3)

Ood-Sphere: Home world to the Ood and neighbour to the Sense-Sphere. (4.3)

Oodkind: Hive-minded race of aliens, who believed they were bred to serve, and thus were treated as slaves by humanity in the 42nd century in both domestic and military situations. They were considered so unimportant that human computers were not even programmed to recognise Oodkind as proper life forms. They communicated on a low-level telepathic field with one another, and with their human masters via cybernetically attached communication spheres called interface devices. Sanctuary Base 6 had a complement of 50 Ood and, although they were docile, when the Beast of Krop Tor awoke, he raised their telepathic field to Basic 100. Normally this would kill any sentient being, but it allowed the Beast to use the Ood as mobile eyes and ears in the Base, as well as enabling the Ood to deliver a lethal pulse of psychic energy via their interface devices. When the Beast was stopped, the Ood were left free of its mental control but abandoned on Sanctuary Base 6 as it was drawn into the singularity of a black hole, where they all undoubtedly perished. The human survivors of Sanctuary Base 6 awarded them all posthumous commendations. (2.8, 2.9) The Doctor and Donna Noble visited their home world, the Ood-Sphere, where humans had set up a company

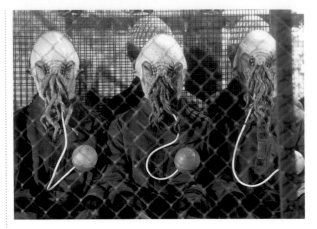

called Ood Operations, supplying enslaved Ood across the empire. There they encountered Oodkind in their natural state – timid and trusting, carrying a hindbrain in the palm of their hands. The Doctor realised that the Ood actually had three brains, the one in their heads, the one in their hands and a third gestalt one on the Ood-Sphere that they shared contact with, the Ood Brain. When Ood Operations began severing the hindbrains and replacing them with the translator balls, the Ood Brain reached out telepathically, gradually infecting more and more Ood with its anger at this butchery, slavery and mistreatment – a contact which caused the otherwise passive Ood to behave similarly, their eyes turning red. This

Operation Fallen Angel: The codename used by the US military at Dreamland to describe their mission to find any aliens which had arrived on Earth. They examined, classified and stored all artefacts in the Vault. (DL)

Operation Market Stall: Part of Detective Inspector Bishop's scheme to solve the mystery of the faceless people appearing in Muswell Hill in 1953. When he and his associate Crabtree drove a newly captured victim back to the cage where he was keeping them, two undercover policemen would cover the entrance to his base with a fake set of market stalls, creating a dead end littered with trucks and signage, including a removals firm, B Clancy and Son, and two business estate agents: W Carter & Co and Gardiner Lawson of 27 Paddock Street. (2.7)

Orb of Healing, the: Endymide device which Saruba Velak brought to Earth as part of her Ambassadorial trip. After she crashed near Roswell, the US military transferred the Orb to the Vault in Nevada. She later retrieved it and used it to cure her husband Rivesh Mantilax's injuries. (DL)

Orient Express: An Egyptian Goddess, who had escaped her imprisonment within the Seventh Obelisk, was loose on this space train, presumably named after the original one on Earth. (5.13)

Orion: Constellation in the Milky Way. In the alternative world where Donna Noble never met the Doctor, the stars started disappearing and Wilfred Mott noticed Orion had disappeared first. (4.11)

Osbourne, Sharon: Television personality who endorsed Harry Saxon's campaign to become Prime Minister. (3.12)

Red-Eye state was seen as unsellable by Ood Operations, so they slaughtered any Red-Eyed Ood. Eventually the Head of Ood Operations, Halpen, decided to kill off his 'livestock' by destroying the massive Ood Brain. Once this was stopped, the Ood, both natural and enslaved, settled down to a peaceful coexistence on Ood-Sphere. (4.3) The Doctor returned to the Ood-Sphere one hundred years later at the behest of Ood Sigma and was surprised to discover that they had evolved far faster than was natural. The imminent return of Gallifrey had created massive ripples back through the Time Vortex, and the sensitive Ood were able to read these future-echoes – and show the Doctor those involved in this incident: Wilfred Mott, Donna Noble, the Naismiths, Lucy Saxon and the reborn Master. Despite her memory having been wiped, after the arrival of the Master on Earth and his subsequent attempt to turn humanity into himself, Donna recalled the Ood as her mind subconsciously fought the Master's influence. As he neared his regeneration, the Doctor saw Sigma once more, singing him to his death.. (4.17, 4.18) (Voiced by SILAS CARSON) The Doctor cited the Ood to the Atraxi as one of the races he had encountered and therefore why the Atraxi should be afraid of him. (5.1) An enslaved Ood ended up in a bubble universe, on the asteroid inhabited by the entity known as House. House called the Ood Nephew and imbued him with some of his energy, making his translator ball and his eyes glow green. (6.4)

Oshodi, Adeola: Torchwood operative based in the Lever Room in the Torchwood Tower. She and her colleague Gareth went to the upper floors for an illicit snog, only to find that the area under construction was a new conversion site for the Cybermen. Adeola was killed, then reanimated via a Cybus Industries ear pod that was connected directly into her cerebral cortex. When the Doctor discovered this, he jammed the signal to the ear pod and the already dead Adeola died once again. (2.12) Her cousin, Martha Jones, later became the Doctor's companion, and commented that Adeola had vanished during the Battle of Canary Wharf. The Doctor opted not to confirm Adeola's death or his part in it. (3.1) (Played by FREEMA AGYEMAN)

Operation Blue Sky: The UNIT codename for their investigation of the ATMOS factory. (4.4, 4.5)

Osterhagen Key: Five devices that, used simultaneously, would detonate a chain of 25 nuclear warheads placed strategically beneath the surface of Earth by the United Nations as a final method of denying the planet to any would-be extraterrestrial conquerors should the suffering of the human race become too great. Only three keys needed to be operated in unison to activate the devices. Martha Jones was given one of these and ordered to use it when Earth was overrun by the Daleks. (4.12, 4.13)

Osterhagen Stations: A series of bases scattered across the globe from which Osterhagen Keys could activate the nuclear devices they were programmed for. Station One was in Germany, Station Four in Liberia and Station Five in China. (4.13)

Osterman's Wharf: London dock where Jackson Lake, believing himself to be the Doctor, saved Rosita Farisi from a Cyberman. (4.14)

Ostrich: Cassandra brought gifts aboard Platform One, including the last ostrich egg from Earth. She mistakenly believed the ostrich had a wingspan of 50 feet and breathed fire from its nostrils. (1.2)

Othello: One of William Shakespeare's best-known plays. Doctor Black likened the quality of it to painter Vincent Van Gogh's artistic output. (5.10)

Other Dave: One of the archaeologists (so named because there was already a member of the team, the pilot, called Dave) in the team that Strackman Lux brought to The Library. He was killed by the Vashta Nerada but his brain patterns were saved onto the data core and when River Song found herself living in the core's fantasy world, Other Dave was there too. (4.8, 4.9) (Played by O-T FAGBENLE)

Ouroboros Snake: Mythological serpent on many worlds, symbolised by the creature always being seen eating its own tail. The Corsair always had an Ouroboros tattoo on his (or sometimes her) body. (6.4)

Oval: One of the scheduled London destinations of the bus, number 200, during its journey on the night it went through a wormhole and ended up on San Helios. (4.15)

Oval Office: Main Presidential office in the White House. The Doctor parked the invisible TARDIS in it while President Richard Nixon was telling ex-FBI agent Canton Delaware III about the phone calls he had been receiving from a scared child. Nixon and his aides and security staff watched Neil Armstrong's moonwalk from there on TV. (6.1, 6.2)

Overcity: The upper echelons of New New York. Ruled by the Senate, everyone there was killed by a virus when a mutated Mood Patch called Bliss infected the very air of New New York. (3.3)

Owens, Alfred aka Alfie: Baby son to Craig Owens and Sophie Benson. The Doctor was able to communicate with him, learning that Alfie preferred to be called Stormageddon, Dark Lord of All. When the Doctor and Craig got involved in a Cyberman plot centred around a local department store in Colchester, it was Craig's love for his son that saved him from becoming the new Cyber Controller. (6.12) (Played by LUCAS and WILLIAM MORRIS, ISABELLE and JOSIE JAMES, DARCY and JAKE EVANS, and ELLIS POMEROY)

Owens, Craig: 27-year-old non-smoker living at 79A Aickman Road in Colchester. He was looking for a flatmate after his previous one mysteriously inherited a lot of money from a previously unknown relative. The Doctor then conveniently arrived with £3,000 in cash and took the room. He was investigating the apartment above Craig's from which he had detected strange energy emissions, which were also leaving a stain on Craig's ceiling. Craig and the Doctor formed quite a good team at first, although Craig's friend, Sophie Benson, began to compliment the Doctor more than Craig liked. Craig was madly in love with Sophie, and she with him, but neither of them would admit to it. When Sophie, encouraged by the Doctor, announced she was leaving to go and work with orang-utans abroad, Craig decided he had to get rid of his new flatmate. He discovered that the Doctor had built a bizarre scanner in his room, and the Doctor was forced to share everything with Craig, by implanting his recent memories and experiences in Craig's head. Realising what the Doctor was trying to do with what turned out to be a lethal time engine upstairs, he offered to help. Sophie then ventured upstairs and nearly became the new pilot of the ship as she was willing to leave, which was a power the ship psychically needed. However as she and Craig talked, they realised that they both loved one another and agreed to stay. This conflicting information destroyed the time engine, and the Doctor left the young lovers to start a new life together. (5.11) After getting married, Craig and Sophie had a baby son, called Alfie. While Sophie was away, Craig, determined to prove he could cope with the baby, met up with the Doctor, who was investigating a Cyberman incursion at a local department store. When trying to save the Doctor, Craig was taken by the Cybermen and they attempted to turn him into a new Cyber Controller. However, his love for Alfie broke their conditioning and overloaded all the Cybermen's emotional inhibitors, destroying them all. The Doctor left Craig and Alfie to wait for Sophie's return, after painting and decorating their home for them. (6.12) (Played by JAMES CORDEN)

Oxford Street: Avenue in London Market where the Doctor first noticed that *Starship UK* did not vibrate as it moved. (5.2)

Oxygen Pockets: The Silurian City had these strategically placed around the city, to keep the hibernating Silurians alive. (5.9)

Pa: Driver of a car on the New New York Motorway. Tired of the endless delays, he overrode the onboard computer that registered how many adults were in the vehicle and lied to the computer at the Transit Authority. Saying that there were three adults in his car gave him access to the Fast Lane, where he and his wife were attacked and killed by the Macra. (3.3) (Played by GRAHAM PADDEN)

Paab: The measurement of length defined by Emperor Jate as being from his nose to his fingertip was a paab, not a goffle. Rodrick didn't know this when asked by the Anne Droid in *The Weakest Link* aboard the Game Station. (1.12)

Pacifica: The Emperor Dalek's forces bombed this Earth continent in 200,100. (1.13)

Padrivole Regency Nine: The society which had employed the Judoon to trace the Plasmavore that had murdered its child princess. (3.1)

Paisley: Scottish city from where Edwin Bracewell came. (5.3)

Pakoo, Mr and Mrs: They were guests aboard Platform One to see the Earthdeath spectacle. (1.2)

Pakistan: Their nuclear weapons were primed and ready to strike the Sontaran mothership in Earth's orbit. (4.5)

Pale woman: A young, depressed woman who came to Pharmacytown to buy a Forget Mood Patch after her parents had left the Undercity to travel on the Motorway. (3.3) (Played by LUCY DAVENPORT)

Palestine Mandate, the: The legal treaty that made Palestine subject to British rule, which failed in 1948 during a civil war between the Jewish and Arab societies. Wilfred Mott took part in this campaign when he was in the Paratroopers. (4.18)

Palin, Michael: Actor and presenter, famed for his TV shows about travelling the world. Sylvia Noble sarcastically likened Donna to him. (4.4)

Pallidome Pancrosis: A lethal disease that killed its victims in ten minutes. The Sisters of Plenitude on New Earth found a cure. (2.1)

Pallushi: A mighty civilisation which spanned a billion years and was destroyed for ever when its solar system, the Scarlet System, was destroyed by the black hole, K 37 Gem 5. (2.8)

'Palm Waltz': Music to which Lady Clemency Eddison and her beau Christopher danced in Delhi in 1885. (4.7)

Pan Traffic Culture: In their calendar, the month of Hoob is followed by Pandoff, not Clavadoe. Fitch didn't know this when asked by the Anne Droid in *The Weakest Link* aboard the Game Station. (1.12)

Pandoff: In the Pan Traffic culture, the month of Hoob is followed by Pandoff, not Clavadoe. Fitch didn't know this when asked by the Anne Droid in *The Weakest Link* aboard the Game Station. (1.12)

Pandorica, the: Shortly before being taken away by the Atraxi, Prisoner Zero warned the Doctor that the Pandorica would open. (5.1) On Alfava Metraxis, River Song told the Doctor that the next time they saw one another would be when the Pandorica opened. (5.5) The Pandorica itself was a massive cube, which legend said was a prison built to contain the most feared thing in the universe. Those legends were actually created in the past by an alliance of alien races using ideas and thoughts from Amy Pond's childhood memories of her favourite stories, the Pandorica being based upon Pandora's Box. The Pandorica Alliance created the prison to entrap the Doctor because they realised that the destruction of the TARDIS exploding, as depicted in Vincent Van Gogh's painting *The Pandorica Opens*, would signify the annihilation of time itself — the explosion opened a time field that erased time completely and detonated every sun at the start of time, so no stars ever existed. The Pandorica's interior was a restorative

field that had within it a few atoms of matter from when the Doctor was imprisoned. That way, it actually restored life, and so kept the Doctor, Amy Pond and even a Stone Dalek alive. Realising that if he could spread this throughout creation he could effectively reboot the universe, the Doctor flew the Pandorica into the exploding TARDIS, so that the detonation restarted the universe, instead of erasing it. The Doctor was thrown into the Void by the explosion, and all the time field cracks were simultaneously sealed. Exactly what changes were made to the universe as a result (other than bringing Rory Williams, River Song and Amy's parents back to life) remains unknown. (5.12, 5.13)

Pandorica Alliance, the: A gathering of thousands of different alien races who decided to work together to trap the Doctor within the Pandorica believing this would stop history being destroyed by the time field that appeared as a crack across the universe. The Alliance were utterly destroyed when they shut the Doctor inside the Pandorica as that began the chain of events they sought to stop — and a wave of total event collapse wiped them out. Some remained as fossils close to the Pandorica, caught fractionally in its restorative field. The aliens in the Alliance included Daleks, Cybermen, Nestenes, Sontarans, Drahvins, Silurians, Draconians, Zygons, Terileptils, Chelonians, Slitheen, Roboforms, Sycorax, Hoix, Weevils, Judoon, Uvodni, Blowfish, Atraxi, Haemo-Goths and many others. (5.12, 5.13)

Pandorica Chamber, the: Specially constructed area within the Under Henge in Wiltshire, where the Pandorica Alliance placed the Pandorica itself. It remained at the eye of the storm as the universe was destroyed when the Doctor was locked within it, destroying the Alliance. (5.12, 5.13)

Pandorica Opens, The: One of the last paintings Vincent Van Gogh completed before his death, it showed the TARDIS exploding. It passed through a number of hands, including Winston Churchill and Liz Ten before River Song took it to show the Doctor. (5.12)

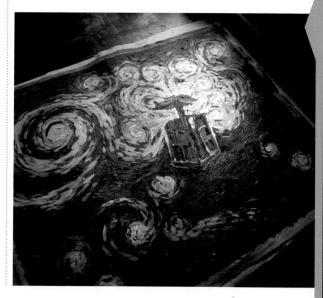

Pandovski, Private: UNIT soldier at the Gladwell road tunnel who escorted DI McMillan and Sergeant Dennison away from the area. (4.15)

Pankhurst, Emmeline: One of the founders of the British Suffragette movement in the early 20th century. She stole the Doctor's laser spanner. Allegedly. (3.1)

Pantheon of Discord: Extra-dimensional enclave of which the Trickster and the Time Beetle were a part. (4.11)

Papal Mainframe: The computer system which oversaw the Headless Monks in the 51st Century. It had a presence on Demon's Run during the preparations for the battle against the Doctor. (6.7) (Voiced by EMMA FEENEY)

Papua New Guinea: Their Olympic Team surprised everyone in the Shot-Put in the Games of 2012, according to the Doctor. (2.11)

Paradox Machine: Device built by the Master and fitted to the TARDIS whilst aboard the *Valiant*, after he travelled, with Lucy Saxon, to Utopia in the year 100,000,000,000,000. With the TARDIS's unlimited power, the Paradox Machine created a rent in time and space, enabling the Toclafane to travel to 21st-century Earth from Utopia, to wipe out their own ancestors. When Captain Jack Harkness destroyed the Paradox Machine, the rent closed, sealing the Toclafane in the future. Because time needed to heal, the *Valiant* was shunted back to the exact moment the Paradox Machine had begun to operate. This erased the previous year for everyone on Earth, though not for those aboard the *Valiant*. (3.12, 3.13)

Paris: Capital of France. Jeanne-Antoinette Poisson was living here as a child when the Doctor first met her. (2.4) Mickey Smith and Jake Simmonds set off in

P
Q

the Preachers' van towards Paris to liberate it from whatever Cybermen still existed there. (2.6) ATMOS devices reportedly went off there. (4.4) The Doctor and Amy Pond met Vincent Van Gogh in the north-western quarter of the city, at Auvers-sur-Oise. (5.10) The Doctor told Craig Owens he learned to cook there, although he was vague as to which century that was in. (5.11) The Doctor had a bad holiday experience there once. (AG03) The Doctor, Kazran Sardick and Abigail Pettigrew visited it one Christmas Eve. (6.X)

Parker: Madame Vastra's coachman in Victorian London. (6.7) (Played by DAVID WEST)

Parker-Bowles, Camilla: Rose Tyler likened Madame de Pompadour's determination to get on in the 18th-century French Royal court as similar to that of Prince Charles's second wife in the Britain of the 21st century. (2.4)

Parsons, Luke: Technician in UNIT's Mission Control base beneath the Tower of London. As his blood group was A+, he was vulnerable to the Sycorax's blood control. (2.X) (Played by JOHNIE CROSS)

Parsons, Mr: A history teacher at Deffry Vale High School who was a bit dubious about new Headmaster Finch and some of the other members of staff who had also arrived in the previous three months. He was, along with the other human teachers, eaten by the Krillitanes. (2.3) (Played by ROD ARTHUR)

Partisan, the: Member of Lord Rassilon's Time Lord Council during the latter stages of the Time War. She disapproved of the continuance of the Time War and suggested it might be advisable to let Gallifrey finally fall and release them all from the endless dying. Rassilon angrily destroyed her with the Gauntlet of Rassilon. (4.18) (Played by JULIE LEGRAND)

Pash Pash: One of the many religions practised in the 42nd century. (2.9)

Pasiphaë Spa, the: Part of the fake hotel constructed within the God Complex, which contained a beauty salon, hairdressers and aroma therapy areas. (6.11)

Passenger 57: Identity adopted by the Doctor aboard the starliner *Titanic*. (4.X)

Parthenogenesis: Biological occurrence when a human body rids itself of excess fat which then turns into a living Adipose child. (4.1)

Patchwork People: Humanoids trapped on the sentient asteroid House. They were kept alive by House over many centuries to act as a lure for Time Lords and other travellers that were drawn into House's pocket universe. House fed off the rift energy that powered TARDISes and it would reuse limbs and organs from the dead pilots to keep the Patchwork People alive. (6.4)

Patient: A human suffering from Hawtrey's Syndrome, who was cured by the Sisters of Plenitude in the Hospital on New Earth. She was subsequently threatened by an unknown force, and may have been killed. (2.1T) (Played by SOPHIE HIGGS)

Patients: The New Humans being bred by the Sisters of Plenitude on New Earth. One of them (played by SIMON JUDDERS) awoke in his incubation tank, and Sister Jatt incinerated him. Another (played by JOANNA CROZIER) killed Matron Casp and was briefly inhabited by the consciousness of Lady Cassandra O'Brien. (2.1)

Pavale, Davitch: One of the Programmers on the Game Station. Like his female counterpart, he answered to the Controller but, when the Doctor exposed the Game Station as a fraud and the Controller was transmatted aboard

the Dalek mothership and exterminated, the two Programmers joined forces against their foe. They joined Captain Jack Harkness, who took a shine to him, and Davitch was still flirting outrageously with the Female Programmer when she was exterminated defending Floor 499. Angrily, he returned fire but was likewise cut down by the Daleks. (1.12, 1.13) (Played by JO STONE-FEWINGS)

PC Plod: Fictional policeman created by Enid Blyton for her 'Noddy' books. The name has come to refer to dim-witted policemen in general and the Doctor cited this when he declared he, rather than the traditional authorities, would solve the murders at Eddison Hall. (4.7)

PE Teacher: One of the 'fears' in a hotel room within the God Complex. It interacted with the Doctor but had no effect on him. (6.11) (Played by DAFYDD EMYR)

Peace Treaty 5.4/cup/16: A treaty which forbade the use aboard Platform One of weapons, religion and teleportation devices, such as the TARDIS and the one possessed by Lady Cassandra. (1.2)

Peace, Mrs: Elderly lady who died and was laid to rest at Sneed and Company. An alien Gelth took over her corpse, reanimating it. Mrs Peace then murdered her grandson and fled to the Taliesin Lodge where Charles Dickens was giving a
reading – the last place the real Mrs Peace had been intending to visit prior to her death. When the Gelth left her body to return to its gaseous form, Mrs Peace's body collapsed in the auditorium. (1.3) (Played by JENNIFER HILL)

Peach, Professor Gerald: Friend of Lady Clemency Eddison and a guest in her house. He suspected that the Reverend Golightly might be Clemency's illegitimate child but was murdered by Golightly in his Vespiform state before he could reveal the truth. (4.7) (Played by IAN BARRATT)

Peck: One of the Hath soldiers on Messaline, injured in a battle with the human soldiers. Separated from the Doctor and Donna Noble, Martha Jones rescued Peck and restored him to health and they formed an uneasy alliance. Together, they crossed the surface of the planet to try and get to the Doctor faster than going through the damaged encampments, but got caught in a bog. Peck pushed Martha to safety but at the cost of his own life. (4.6) (Played by PAUL KASEY)

Pedro, Cleric: One of Father Octavian's troopers. He was killed in the *Byzantium*'s Forest Vault when he approached the time field. (5.4, 5.5) (Played by MARK MONERO)

Peg-Dolls: Toys within a doll's house given life by the Tenza powers of George. He was able to transport his family and neighbours, along with the Doctor, Amy Pond and Rory Williams, into the doll's house to be menaced by the Peg-Dolls. The dolls were led by a Dancer (played by LOUISE BOWEN) and a Soldier (played by BARBARA FADDEN). The Dolls could transform humans into Dolls, as they did with Mrs Rossiter (played by NATALIE CUZNER and BEAN PEEL), Jim Purcell (played by RUSSELL CUZNER) and Amy (played by RUTH WEBB). After George was convinced by his 'father' Alex that he was loved, just as he himself was about to be transformed, George shut the doll's house down and all the people were returned to normal and the Peg-Dolls reverted to just being toys. (6.9) (Voiced by GABRIELLA GILLESPIE, MAX LONGMUIR, SONNY ASHBOURNE-SERKIS)

Peggy Mitchell: Fictional owner of the Queen Vic pub in the BBC soap opera *EastEnders*, set in Walford. Jackie Tyler explained to the Doctor that, in recent episodes of the serial, Peggy had heard a noise in the cellar which had turned out to be the ghost of former publican Den Watts. (2.12) (Played by BARBARA WINDSOR)

P Q

PQ

Pemberton: Schoolboy at Farringham School for Boys in 1913 who took part in the war games there, manning the Vickers Gun. He was later charged with loading the spare magazines with real bullets before the Family of Blood attacked the school. (3.8, 3.9)

Pen-y-Fan: Punning title for Ambrose Northover's Meals-on-Wheels service around Cwmtaff. (5.8)

Penhaxico Two: World sympathetic to cyborgs, where Max Capricorn planned to retire to. (4.X)

Pentallian, SS: Cargo ship touring the Torajii system, it was separated into a series of Areas which, in an emergency, could be individually locked, requiring a two-man team to open the deadlock-sealed doors using machinery and a special password. Run-down and battered, the crew were similarly exhausted and overworked, which led the captain, Kath McDonnell, to use an illegal fusion scoop to steal vast amounts of energy from a sun without doing the standard procedure of scanning for life beforehand — scanning taking time, and time costing money. As a result, the living sun took over the bodies of two of her crew, including her husband, and they sabotaged the ship, ensuring it would crash into the sun, thus returning what had been taken. The Doctor was able to

discover the truth and convince the surviving crew to jettison the fuel back into the sun, and thus avoid a fiery death. The Doctor and Martha Jones departed, leaving the *Pentallian* and its two surviving crew awaiting rescue by the authorities. The areas on the ship included: Area 31, where the TARDIS materialised; Area 30, the main area which engineering, medcentre, etc., spread out from; Area 28, where Kath McDonnell used the airlock to eject herself and the sun-possessed Korwin McDonnell into space; Area 27, which Lissak was nearly locked into when the secure closure occurred; and Area 22, where the sun-possessed Doctor crawled to after leaving the medcentre. In Area 17, Korwin McDonnell transferred some of his sun-possession to Dev Ashton, who then threatened Martha and Riley, forcing them to hide in an escape pod, which he then jettisoned. The Doctor later left the ship via the Area 17 airlock to remagnetise the outer hull and draw the pod back in — seen by McDonnell from Area 10. Area 1 was where the auxiliary controls for the ship were stationed, allowing Vashtee and Scannell to vent the fuel, so saving their lives. (3.7)

Perception Filter: The Doctor surrounded the Gallifreyan fob watch into which he downloaded his essence from the chameleon arch with a perception filter. This meant that it could only be seen if the observer really wanted to see it, otherwise it would always seem to be just on the periphery of their vision. This meant that John Smith could never inadvertently pick the fob watch up and open it, thus restoring the Doctor and alerting the Family of Blood to his whereabouts. (3.8, 3.9) Martha Jones realised Professor Yana had never really noticed the fob watch he carried, because of its perception filter. (3.11) The Doctor created a similar field on each of their TARDIS keys, using bits from Martha Jones's mobile phone and Captain Jack Harkness's laptop. When they wore these keys around their necks, people didn't really notice them. The Master was unaffected by perception filters, however, and was aware of all three of them on the deck of the *Valiant*. (3.12) When Martha escaped from the *Valiant* using Jack's Vortex Manipulator, her key's perception filter allowed her to travel the Earth unnoticed by the Toclafane. (3.13) Prisoner Zero used one within Amy Pond's home, to stop people noticing the door to the room it was hiding in. (5.1) The Weeping Angels used a low-level filter to stop those passing through the Aplan Maze of the Dead from realising all the statues were of single-headed figures, rather than two-headed Aplans. (5.4, 5.5) Rosanna and Francesco Calvierri used portable perception filters to hide their natural Saturnyne forms from the Venetians amongst whom they lived. Amy Pond damaged Rosanna's with a kick and, as it failed, her staff saw who she really was and fled. (5.6) The time engine that landed on Aickman Road used a perception filter to give everyone the impression that the building was a two-storey house when in fact It was a single-storey building, the upper floor actually being the time engine. (5.11) The Doctor theorised that the Tenza used one whenever they placed themselves amongst a family, to change everyone's memories and perception of where they had really come from. (6.9)

Percy, Thomas: One of the 13 plotters who planned to blow up the House of Lords in 1605. (AG05) (Voiced by DAVID AMES)

Perganon: A civilisation lost during the Great Time War. (2.3)

Peripatetic Medical Squad: A mobile group of doctors, given permission by the Master and the Toclafane to go between labour camps, administering their services where necessary. Thomas Milligan worked for one, which was useful cover for his Resistance activities. (3.13)

Personal Clerics: Kovarian's personal body guards, who carried the Flesh version of Melody Pond that Rory Williams retrieved, unaware that Kovarian still had the real Melody. (6.7) (Played by MARCUS ELLIOTT and SION PRICE)

Personal Experience Contract: Strackman Lux asked Miss Evangelista to get the Doctor and Donna Noble to sign one of these each when he found them in The Library. (4.8)

Personal Guards: Matron Cofelia's two guards, who followed her everywhere and did whatever she told them. (4.1) (Played by RUARI MEARS and CLAUDIO LAURINI)

Peru: South American country. Brigadier Lethbridge-Stewart was stranded there when the Sontarans invaded Earth. (4.4) Amy Pond found some blankets aboard the TARDIS and made them into ponchos, suggesting they looked like they belonged in a Peruvian folk band. (5.7)

Peshwami: A Shan Shen trader tried to sell this to Donna Noble. (4.11)

'Pete's World': The Doctor gave this name to the parallel Earth on which he, Rose Tyler and Mickey Smith fought the Cybermen. The Cybermen and other humans from 'Pete's World', including Pete Tyler himself, then went back and forth between it and the Earth where Rose was born. The two Earths were almost identical, but there were subtle differences: Mickey Smith was Ricky Smith; his

grandmother Rita-Anne was still alive; Cuba Gooding Jnr was born in February not January; Cybus Industries dominated the business world from their Zeppelin airships; Pete Tyler was a millionaire, married to Jackie Tyler but without a daughter (instead, their terrier was called Rose). The Britain of 'Pete's World' was a Republic, run by a President, and was suffering not just from severe global warming but also from the breaches created by the Cybermen and Jake Simmonds' troopers travelling back and forth between the two Earths. The Doctor was able to repair these breaches, sealing off both worlds for ever and trapping millions of Daleks and Cybermen in the Void between the two. However, this meant that Jackie, Mickey and Rose had to stay on 'Pete's World' for the rest of their lives, officially listed among the dead after the Battle of Canary Wharf on Rose's home Earth. (2.5, 2.6, 2.12, 2.13)

Peter: One of the Winders aboard the London part of *Starship UK*. He watched the Doctor in London Market and reported back to Hawthorne, his boss. He later came to collect the Doctor, Amy Pond, Liz Ten and Mandy Tanner from Buckingham Palace and take them to the Tower of London. He revealed that he, like most Winders, was actually cybernetic – part human winder, part Smiler. (5.2) (Played by DAVID AJALA)

Peterson: Schoolboy at Farringham School for Boys in 1913, who did something his headmaster found unacceptable before the Family of Blood attacked. (3.9)

Peterson, Carl: One of President Nixon's Secret Service guards. He accompanied an agent called Phil to find Canton Delaware III in a bar and take him back to the Oval Office. Canton later pointed out that, since he had somehow got the TARDIS into the office, the Doctor was more worth listening to than Peterson, who he had somehow bypassed. Peterson later reacted to the broadcast of the Silence telling humanity to kill them on sight and when he saw a Silent outside the Oval Office, he drew his pistol to follow the order. (6.1, 6.2) (Played by CHUK IWUJI)

Peth, Astrid: Waitress aboard the starliner *Titanic*, who always dreamt about being out amongst the stars but had only so far managed three years serving in a starport restaurant until she got the job aboard ship. She quickly became friends with the Doctor and he sneakily took her down to Earth so she could see it in person, and she was overjoyed to be on an alien world. Soon after their return to the starliner, it was struck by meteoroids and Astrid was amongst the survivors, helping the Doctor stop the Heavenly Host. When the Doctor went to confront Max Capricorn, she followed him and, learning what Capricorn intended to do, she drove a fork-lift truck into the cyborg's Max-Box and sent Max and herself to their deaths in the heart of the nuclear engines. The Doctor later tried to save her by attempting to draw out her body from within the transporter device that had sent her briefly to Earth but the pattern was already too degraded and all he could do was send her dissipating body out through the ship's portholes and literally amongst the stars where she drifted for eternity. (4.X) Davros reminded the Doctor of what Astrid had sacrificed for him, while taunting him within the Dalek Crucible. (4.13) (Played by KYLIE MINOGUE)

Petherbridge, Don: Sanderson & Grainger worker spied by Mary Warnock snogging Andrea Groom on his day off. (6.12)

Petrichor: The name of the perfume created and advertised by Amy Pond and Rory Williams, using a name given to them by Idris, to attract the Doctor's attention. (6.12)

Petrifold Regression: A terminal disease of the flesh that turns people to stone. The Duke of Manhattan on New Earth was suffering from it and, although the Doctor believed there wouldn't be a cure for another thousand years, the Sisters of Plenitude cured him. (2.1)

P Q

Pettigrew, Abigail: Young woman from Sardicktown on Ember. Some years earlier, when her sister's family got into financial debt to money-lender Kazran Sardick, she had volunteered to be cryogenically frozen and kept as 'security' on his loan. Abigail was in fact dying and had only a few days left to live. When the Doctor went back in time to attempt to change Kazran Sardick's past, he introduced the 12-year-old Kazran to Abigail when releasing her for a day, Christmas Eve, as they needed her cryogenic chamber for a sick Fog Shark. Abigail's perfect singing voice had the same effect on the beast as the ice crystals in the cloud belt where it usually lived, resonating with the Shark. Kazran and the Doctor visited Abigail every Christmas Eve over the next few years, unwittingly using up her life, but she didn't mind as she and Kazran eventually fell in love. However, when Abigail revealed to Kazran that the next time they met would be the last as she would die at the end of that day, Kazran elected to leave her untouched for ever after that. A space cruiser was about to crash on Sardicktown and the elder Kazran didn't care until the Doctor introduced him to his younger self. Realising that he wanted to change and not be the man he had become, he agreed to help the Doctor, but his Sky-Mast Weather Controller would not open the cloud belts and let the ship in. They realised the only way to resonate the ice crystals effectively was to broadcast Abigail's singing into the sky. Abigail was woken and successfully helped guide the ship down to safety and spent her last day of life with the elder Kazran, riding a rickshaw through the skies on Christmas Day. (6.X) (Played by KATHERINE JENKINS)

Pharmacists: Stallholders in Pharmacytown, part of the Undercity of New New York. They sold Mood Patches and were told by an angry Doctor to be prepared to be closed down. After freeing the cars from the Motorway, the Doctor returned to Pharmacytown and found they had moved on voluntarily. (3.3) (Played by TOM EDDEN, NATASHA WILLIAMS, GAYLE TELFER STEVENS)

Pharmacytown: Part of the Undercity of New New York where stallholders sold Mood Patches and were told by an angry Doctor to be prepared to be closed down. After freeing the cars from the Motorway, the Doctor returned to Pharmacytown and found the stallholders had moved on voluntarily. (3.3)

Phelan, Sally: When the Doctor and Mrs Moore went further into Deepcold 6 on 'Pete's World', they stopped a Cyberman with an electromagnetic bomb. When the Doctor tried to examine the fallen Cyberform, he realised its emotional inhibitor was damaged. The human within tried to reassert its personality, revealing itself to be a girl, Sally Phelan, who had been Cyber-converted the night before her wedding to Gareth. Using his sonic screwdriver, the Doctor sorrowfully switched off the life support in the Cyberform, giving Sally final peace. (2.6) (Voiced by NICHOLAS BRIGGS)

Pheros: Planet of living metal, a huge eyrie for the giant metal birds that dominated the planet. Baltazar used the living metals to build himself a vast warship from which he became the scourge of the galaxies, along with his first mate, Caw, one of the Pheros bird creatures. (TIQ)

Phil: One of President Nixon's Secret Service guards. He accompanied an agent called Carl Peterson to find Canton Delaware III in a bar and take him back to the Oval Office. Phil accompanied Amy Pond to and from the women's restroom and later, alongside Peterson, drew his firearm on a Silent stood outside the Oval Office after the Silence told humanity to kill them on sight. (6.1, 6.2) (Played by MARK GRIFFIN)

P
Q

Philip, Cleric: One of Father Octavian's troopers. He was killed in the *Byzantium*'s Forest Vault when he approached the time field. (5.4, 5.5) (Played by GEORGE RUSSO)

Philippines: Margaret Cain reckoned only the Philippines would have the resources to send up an opposing Mars mission. Or the Spanish. (4.16)

Phillips, Mr: The bursar at Farringham School for Boys, who was murdered by Son of Mine, inhabiting the body of schoolboy Jeremy Baines. (3.8, 3.9) (Played by MATTHEW WHITE)

Phosphorous Carousel of the Great Magellan Gestalt: The Doctor visited this on his way to the Ood-Sphere when answering Ood Sigma's projected song. (4.17, 4.18)

Photafine Steel: The hull of the Tritovore ship was constructed from this because it ensured the temperature within the ship remained comfortably frozen regardless of the external temperatures. (4.15)

Photographer [1]: Responsible for taking the wedding pictures at Donna Noble and Shaun Temple's wedding. (4.18) (Played by GWEN JENKINS)

Photographer [2]: Victorian gentleman found in a hotel room within the God Complex. He was there to represent Tim Heath's fears. (6.11) (Played by GARY DOBBS)

Picasso, Pablo: 20th-century Spanish painter. The Doctor claimed that he tried to get him to paint normally rather than in his more famous Cubist stylings. (5.10)

Pick-up truck: Jackie Tyler borrowed one from her friend Rodrigo, and Mickey Smith used it to wrench open the TARDIS console, flooding Rose Tyler with the Time Vortex. (1.13) Mickey later recalled this when deciding to fight Cybermen in Paris with Jake Simmonds. (2.6)

Picosurgeon: Surgeon who administered the Type Two chip to Adam Mitchell to give him full access to the information spikes on Satellite Five. (1.7)

Pig Slaves: When they first arrived in Manhattan, the Daleks began a series of genetic experiments, initially attempting to create new Dalek embryos. When that failed, Dalek Sec realised the way forward was to merge himself with a human but, to ensure they would be compatible, the Cult began using kidnapped humans and merging them with pigs, porcine flesh being the closest to human,

creating a race of Pig Slaves. The resultant physical trauma meant that the Pig Slaves had a limited life span, but it was long enough to use them to kidnap more humans, the less intelligent of which were also turned into Pig Slaves. The more intelligent ones went on to join the other aspect of the Final Experiment: the creation of a hybrid Dalek-Human army. Most of the Pig Slaves were killed in the Empire State Building when Martha Jones used iron poles to conduct electricity from a lightning strike into their ranks. Once the Daleks were defeated, any survivors would have roamed the sewers until they died naturally. (3.4, 3.5)

Pilot: One of the crew of the *Thrasymachus*, whose job it was to try and land the ship safely on the planet Ember, without killing any of the 4,003 people aboard. (6.X) (Played by LEO BILL)

Pilot Fish: The Doctor likened the mercenary Roboforms, who disguised themselves as Santa Clauses during two consecutive Christmases, to pilot fish. (2.X, 3.X)

Pirates: A regular fear of the drivers on the New New York Motorway was that they might be car-jacked by pirates. (3.3)

Pit, the: The area on Krop Tor sealed by a 30-foot metal trapdoor. The trapdoor opened when the humans from Sanctuary Base 6 drilled through to the cavern it was in, revealing the Pit, within which lived the body of the Beast. (2.8, 2.9)

Pitt, Brad: According to Lance Bennett, Donna Noble talked excitedly about this American actor and his on/off relationship with actor Angelina Jolie. (3.X)

Pizza Geronimo: Establishment accidentally called by the Doctor instead of UNIT HQ. (4.15)

Place du Forum: French street with a terraced café in it. The Doctor and Amy Pond recognised it from one of Van Gogh's paintings and met Vincent there for the first time. (5.10)

Planet of the Hats: If ever she visited it, Donnas Noble was well-prepared, going by the luggage she took aboard the TARDIS. It probably didn't actually exist… (4.1)

Planet One: The oldest planet in the universe. On a cliff face there, River Song had etched the message 'Hello Sweetie' and a series of coordinates in Old High Gallifreyan. (5.12)

Plasma Coils: Artificial energy source, used throughout the galaxy. A platoon of Judoon transported a set to Earth and placed it around the Royal Hope Hospital. Over two days it began creating electrical storms that would power the H_2O Scoop that they would use to transport the hospital to the surface of Earth's moon. (3.1)

Plasmavores: Race of shape-changing aliens who lived off the richest veins of haemoglobin they could find. A Plasmavore was hiding in the Royal Hope Hospital on Earth, disguised as Florence Finnegan. (3.1)

Plasmic Energy: The energy that the Wire was composed of, which it also used to drain the life force out of its television-viewing victims. (2.7)

Platform One: Vast space station, overseen by a computerised Control (voiced by SARA STEWART), consisting of Suites, Viewing Galleries, ventilation ducts, private rooms, a massive Ventilation Chamber and other areas. On Platform One, a number of alien dignitaries arrived to observe Earthdeath, as did the Doctor and Rose Tyler. Although nearly destroyed when the protective force field was temporarily shut off by Lady Cassandra O'Brien, Platform One survived. Other Platform space stations included Platform Three, Platform Six and Platform Fifteen. (1.2)

PlayStation: Mickey Smith told Rose Tyler that he had learned to fly a Zeppelin on his PlayStation games console. (2.6)

Pleasure Gardens: An area of the Hospital on New Earth. Access to it required coloured ID cards, and taking cuttings from the Gardens was forbidden. (2.1)

Plough and Pheasant, the: London pub in the alternative world where Donna Noble never met the Doctor. Mooky Kahari, Veena Brady and Alice Coltrane were having Christmas drinks there with Donna when the Racnoss Webstar crossed the night sky. (4.11)

Plum, Geoffrey: Town crier of London in 1605, who befriended the Doctor. (AG05) (Voiced by PHIL DANIELS)

Plump Man: Customer in the pub where the Wednesday Girls were meeting, who was affected by unexpected Adipose parthenogenesis in the pub, along with a number of other customers, but was safe after the Doctor stopped Matron Cofelia's scheme. (4.1) (Played by GREG BENNETT)

Plymouth: City in Devon, on the south-west coast of the UK with the largest naval docks in Western Europe. The submarine HMS *Taurean* was just ten miles away from Plymouth when Mickey Smith helped the Doctor launch one of its sub-Harpoon missiles at 10 Downing Street. (1.5) Luke Gold was frightened of it. (6.11)

Poem Girl: A pre-recorded image that recited a poem about the Beast Below which Timmy Winters heard shortly before the floor of his vator dropped away. (5.2) (Played by CATRIN RICHARDS)

Poggit, Mrs: Resident of the Upper Leadworth nursing home Rory Williams worked at in the dreamscape-future created by the Dream Lord. Like all the local pensioners, Mrs Poggit appeared to have been taken over by an

Eknodine. She was amongst those who attacked the Doctor in the butcher's shop and Amy Pond and Rory in their cottage, killing Rory. Whether a real Mrs Poggit actually existed in the real Leadworth was unconfirmed, although as the psychic spore that created the Dream Lord fed on dark thoughts and memories, it seemed likely she was someone known to Amy and Rory back home. (5.7) (Played by AUDREY ARDINGTON)

Poisson, Jeanne-Antoinette: As an adult, Reinette, as she had been known when a child, met the Doctor in her bedroom for the first time since 1727, having previously assumed he was a dream. They next met face to face in 1745 when he, Rose Tyler and Mickey Smith went through a time window from a ship in the 51st century to stop a Clockwork Robot attacking her in the palace at Versailles, where she had recently moved. Sending Rose and Mickey back, the Doctor strove to find out why they were interested in Reinette and they linked minds – she gaining access to his as much as he to hers. Their friendship seemed to be growing deeper (he stayed for a good party). Her next encounter with the

P
Q

future was via Rose in 1753, by which time she had become Madame de Pompadour. Rose told her that the Robots would be back one last time, in 1758, when she would be the same age as the spaceship. Sure enough, at a party in Versailles, the Clockwork Robots were back, and the Doctor crashed through a mirror on the back of Arthur the Horse, breaking the Robots' link to the 51st century and cutting them off from their power source. They collapsed, inert. Reinette was told by the Doctor he could never go back – she, however, had had the Paris fireplace moved to Versailles, and the mechanism connecting it to the future still worked. The Doctor asked her to accompany him to the stars and she agreed, preparing for his return once he'd found Rose and Mickey. She never saw him again and died in 1764. (2.4) (Played by SOPHIA MYLES)

Poisson, Madame: Mother to Jeanne-Antoinette Poisson, aka Reinette, who was anxiously waiting to take her away from their Paris home for the evening, when the Doctor encountered the adult Reinette for the first time. (2.4)

Pok Baint, Stella: She was famous for her hats, not for shoes. Rose Tyler didn't know this when asked by the Anne Droid in *The Weakest Link* aboard the Game Station. (1.12)

Pola Ventura: The city of Pola Ventura, not Reykjavik, hosted Murder Spree 20. Rose Tyler didn't know this when asked by the Anne Droid in *The Weakest Link* aboard the Game Station. (1.12)

Police: A young officer took notes from Rose Tyler when she returned home after being missing for a year. (1.4) (Played by CERIS JONES) A police officer observed the A+ hypnotised victims of the Sycorax making their way to the tops of tall buildings. (2.X) (Played by SEAN CARLSEN) A policeman tried to stop Rose Tyler reaching the Olympic Torch so she could power the Isolus spaceship. (2.11) (Played by STEPHEN MARZELLA) Two police officers stopped members of the public, including Tish Jones, getting to the site where the Royal Hope Hospital had stood until the Judoon took it to the moon. (3.1) (Played by BRIAN MORGAN and SONAL MANTA)

Police Commissioner: Metropolitan officer who asked the public to remain calm as more 'ghosts' appeared. When the ghosts transformed into Cybermen, he urged people to stay in their homes. (2.12) (Played by DAVID WARWICK)

Polkowski: Henry Van Statten's chief aide, who warned his boss against having the US President replaced. As a result, Van Statten had Polkowski fired and mind-wiped, leaving him to live his life as a vagrant. (1.6) (Played by STEVEN BECKINGHAM)

Polycarbide: The alloy used to create the outer casing of a Dalek. It is usually combined with Dalekanium, although Dalek Sec's was made from Metalert. (2.13, 3.4, 3.5)

Pompeii: Captain Jack Harkness likened London during the Blitz to Pompeii as a great place to put things you want destroyed surreptitiously. Pompeii was destroyed when a volcano buried it in lava and ash in AD 79. (1.10) The Doctor and Donna Noble visited it at the time Vesuvius erupted, due to the Pyrovillian incursion. The city was completely destroyed in the resultant disaster although the Doctor and Donna were able to save the Caecilius family. (4.2) The Doctor remembered these events when discussing temporal cause and effect with Adelaide Brooke. (4.16)

Pool, Mr: Teacher at Farringham School for Boys who didn't want his afternoon tea, so Cook gave it to Martha Jones. (3.8)

Pond, Amelia Jessica (Amy): Born in Scotland, Amelia moved to England with her parents, Augustus and Tabetha, some time before her 7th birthday. They had a big house in the Gloucestershire village of Leadworth, where, on the wall of Amelia's bedroom, there was a menacing crack, which scared the little girl. This was a splinter of the time field caused by the explosion of the Doctor's TARDIS. Identical cracks appeared across the universe, through which time was absorbed and erased. Amelia's parents were erased from existence so neither she nor her Aunt Sharon, who came to look after her in Leadworth,

actually recalled them. One night, just after Easter 1996, alone in the house, Amelia was asking Santa Claus for help with the crack when the Doctor crash-landed the TARDIS in her garden. Newly regenerated and a bit erratic, the Doctor still impressed Amelia as he tried to explain the time field. He went back to the TARDIS, saying he'd return in five minutes. She waited in the garden all night, eventually falling asleep. (5.1) She awoke in her bed (put there by a slightly later version of the Doctor) (5.13) and found that no one believed her stories of the 'raggedy Doctor', including her school friends Mels Zucker and Rory Williams, (6.8) and she was taken to four different psychiatrists.

Twelve years later, the Doctor returned, but Amelia — now calling herself Amy and working as a kissogram — could not believe it was him. Pretending to be a policewoman (using one of her work outfits), she attacked the Doctor. He revealed that a room she had never noticed in the house contained a multiform, Prisoner Zero, who had escaped through the time field. Prisoner Zero's Atraxi jailers were coming for their charge, happy to destroy Earth if necessary. Teaming up with Rory, now her boyfriend, she and the Doctor stopped Prisoner Zero and sent the Atraxi away. Amy hoped the Doctor would now take her with him in the TARDIS, but he vanished for another two years. By the time he returned, Amy and Rory were engaged to be married and it was the night before the wedding, but she went with him, (5.1) and was taken to Starship UK, (5.2) and wartime London, where the Doctor discovered she had no knowledge of the Daleks, (5.3) later realising this was because the time field had erased them from her memory. A trip to Alfava Metraxis followed where she met River Song for the first time and became infected by Weeping Angel dust. Emotionally exhausted at the end of this escapade, she made a pass at the Doctor and he realised he needed Rory back in her life. (5.4, 5.5) After collecting him from his stag night, the Doctor took the

couple to 17th-century Venice. (5.6) Together the trio faced the Dream Lord (5.7) and the Silurians. As they fled the Silurian city, Rory was shot and killed by a Silurian, and his body was absorbed by a time field crack. Despite her best efforts, Amy forgot Rory ever existed. (5.8, 5.9) At the back of her mind, however, she knew something was missing from her life, a suspicion further expanded when she found her engagement ring in the Doctor's pocket. After a meeting with Vincent Van Gogh (who dedicated his famous *Sunflowers* painting to her) (5.10) and being stuck in the TARDIS while the Doctor was in Colchester, (5.11) they received a message from River Song. They met up with her in Ancient Britain, Amy's favourite period of history, and at Stonehenge found the legendary Pandorica. Amy commented this was similar to Pandora's Box, her favourite story as a child. While the Doctor and Amy explored, the TARDIS took River back to Amy's Leadworth home where she found the Pandora's Box book and also a book of Roman soldiers, which looked very like the Romans they had encountered at Stonehenge — the whole thing was a trap set up by the Pandorica Alliance as part of a plan to prevent the TARDIS's destruction and the time field's threat to the universe. Amy was reunited with Rory, but he was actually an Auton replica and, when his Nestene programming took over, he shot her. After the Pandorica opened, time was erased, along with most of the Alliance, and only the Doctor, Rory and the dying Amy survived. The Doctor placed her inside the Pandorica and Rory loyally stood guard over it for 2,000 years. (5.12)

As time was erased by the exploding TARDIS, the young Amelia was now seen by a number of psychiatrists, including Christine, because she believed in 'stars' in the sky — nobody else did because the time field had erased them all from reality so they had never existed. Amelia got a note telling her to visit the Pandorica exhibit in the National Museum. She did, slipping away from Aunt Sharon and hiding there overnight, until she saw her future self emerge from the Pandorica. The young Amelia stayed with Amy and the Doctor until winking out of existence as the time field caught up with her. The Doctor later went to her bedside and talked to her about the future until he was erased from time. He had realised that the only way to stop the TARDIS destroying the universe was to fly the Pandorica into the explosion and contain it. This rebooted the universe, restoring everything: Amy's parents came back, Rory was human again, but the Doctor was removed from history completely and no one remembered him. On her wedding day, Amy was given a strange blue diary that resembled the TARDIS by a later version of River Song, and this triggered Amy's memories. All that time subjected to the time field in her bedroom had given Amy the ability to break through timelines and alternative realities and she willed the Doctor back into existence. Rory simultaneously regained all of his memories of his past adventures and the centuries he'd spent as Auton Rory. Once married, they returned to the TARDIS and continued travelling with the Doctor, (5.13) conceiving their daughter aboard the TARDIS. After a honeymoon period, (6.X) the Doctor left Amy and Rory back in Leadworth, at which point Amy was, unknown to Rory, kidnapped by Madame Kovarian, working for the Silence and the Academy of the Question. Amy was replaced with a Ganger, a Flesh duplicate, that was psychically connected to the real Amy who was now a prisoner on Demon's Run, while Kovarian waited for her to give birth. The Doctor soon contacted the unaware Rory and Ganger Amy, inviting them and River Song to Lake Silencio in Utah. They travelled to America and witnessed what they believed was his death. A younger Doctor later arrived, unaware of what had happened and River Song told them all to keep it quiet. After stopping the Silence, (6.1, 6.2) the Siren, (6.3) House (6.4) and the Gangers, (6.5, 6.6) the Doctor exposed the Ganger Amy for what she was – he had suspected for a while as the TARDIS could not read her properly and Amy had kept seeing flashes of Kovarian's face at odd moments – reality breaking through. As he destroyed the fake Amy, the real one gave birth to a daughter, who she named Melody after her old school friend Mels Zucker. Melody was stolen from her and Rory by Kovarian (6.7) and taken to Earth to be trained as a killer – to destroy the Doctor. River Song revealed that Melody would be all right in the end – because River was Melody. River took Amy and Rory home to Leadworth, where they waited for the Doctor to take them away again. When he did, they took along their old friend Mels Zucker, who was actually Melody Pond. Part of Melody's

inheritance from being conceived aboard the TARDIS was the ability to regenerate, and Mels regenerated into River, who donated her remaining regenerations to save the Doctor and was left to continue her life in the 51st century until she became the woman Amy and Rory would know. The TARDIS used a projection of the young Amelia as a voice interface to communicate with him after the Judas Tree poison left him dying. (6.8) After an adventure with a Tenza, (6.9) Amy was separated from Rory and the Doctor at the Twostreams Facility and spent thirty years alone, training herself as a warrior to keep at bay the Handbots that wanted to kill her, mistakenly believing she was carrying a plague. Rory eventually found both her and the original Amy before she had been trapped in the other time stream and the older one was sacrificed so that the original could continue to travel with the Doctor and Rory. (6.10) Exploring the God Complex, the Doctor tried to explain to Amy why he had taken her aboard the TARDIS as they attempted to escape and he briefly caught a glimpse of the younger Amelia. Escaping the God Complex, the Doctor left Amy and Rory in a new home in Leadworth. (6.11) Hoping to catch his attention, Amy and Rory set up a brand of perfume called Petrichor, and used themselves on all the advertising. (6.12) When River Song tried to change history and not kill the Doctor at Lake Silencio, she accidentally created a new reality where time was frozen at 5.02 on 22/04/11. In this new reality, River and Amy teamed up to get the Doctor to Area 52 in Egypt, where the Silence were interred. However, it was a trap – the Silence and Madame Kovarian had planned this and the Silence broke out and attacked. Rory was Amy's Captain, unaware they were married, but Amy had a feeling they were – again, an effect of her exposure to the time field in her bedroom all those years ago, she could recognise the altered reality for what it was. As they fled Area 52 and the attacking Silence, Amy had the chance to save Kovarian – instead she left the woman who had kidnapped her baby so many years earlier to die. The Doctor put time back on its path by apparently sacrificing himself at Lake Silencio, although River told Amy and Rory that it was in fact a Teselecta Justice Vehicle that had 'died' and the real Doctor was still out in the universe. Amy asked River about the way she had killed Kovarian, and River pointed out that it was an alternative reality, so the real Kovarian was probably still alive – but that didn't stop Amy being concerned that she had been willing to kill. (6.13) (Played by CAITLIN BLACKWOOD and KAREN GILLAN)

P
Q

Pond, Augustus: Amy Pond's father whose existence had been erased by the time field but was brought back when the Pandorica's restoration field rebooted the universe. He gave a father-of-the-bride speech at his daughter's wedding to Rory Williams. (5.13) (Played by HALCRO JOHNSTON)

Pond, Melody: See *Song, River*

Pond, Tabetha: Amy Pond's mother whose existence had been erased by the time field but was brought back when the Pandorica's restoration field rebooted the universe. She was at Amy's wedding to Rory Williams. (5.13) (Played by KAREN WESTWOOD)

Poosh, Lost Moon of: Dee Dee Blasco wrote a paper about this, which Professor Hobbes read and so took her on as his personal researcher. (4.10) The moon itself was one of the planets that Davros had taken to the Medusa Cascade to use as part of his Reality Bomb. (4.12, 4.13)

Pope, Clare: Telesales worker at Adipose Industries who flirted with the Doctor when he tried to get a list of customers from her. (4.1) (Played by CHANDRA RUEGG)

Pope, Elton: As a 4-year-old, Elton found his mother dead, and the Doctor standing over her body. The Doctor had been trying to track a Living Shadow which had escaped the Howling Halls. The Shadow had killed Elton's mother, but Elton's memories of exactly what had happened remained blurred for many years. However, as Elton found himself in the same shopping centre as Jackie Tyler during the Auton invasion, watching the Slitheen ship smash through Big Ben, and had his windows blown out by the passing Sycorax ship, he gained an interest in alien incursions on Earth. He found a blog on the net, 'My Invasion Blog', set up by Ursula Blake to record such things, which led him to join a like-minded group of gentle people all searching for the Doctor. They called themselves LINDA and, before long, they were all close friends. Elton was especially close to Ursula Blake. After their group was infiltrated by the Abzorbaloff, posing as Victor Kennedy, Elton was forced to make friends with

Jackie Tyler (who he actually really liked) and ultimately betray her as he searched for information about her daughter Rose. Rebelling against Kennedy, Elton ended up as the only survivor of LINDA, although Ursula lived on as a face embedded in concrete, so she still stayed with him in his flat. Finally meeting the Doctor gave Elton the closure he needed over his mother's death and he was able to continue with his life. (2.10) (Played by MARC WARREN)

Pope, Mrs: The Doctor was pursuing an elemental shade that had escaped from the Howling Halls when he found himself at the Pope household. Mrs Pope had been killed by the Shadow, and her 4-year-old son Elton saw the Doctor with her body. (2.10) (Played by LAMORNA CHAPELL)

Poseidon: Sub-aquatic research base and community on the seabed under the Atlantic Ocean in the 23rd century. Separated into a variety of different independent communes but all linked by a series of pressurised transparent tunnels. (AG04)

Posh Mum and Posh Dad: Visitors to Ward 26 in the Hospital on New Earth. They were leaving the ward when the infected New Humans tried to burst through the door, and the mum was killed. (2.1) (Played by HELEN IRVING and DAVE BREMNER)

Posh Woman and Posh Boyfriend: Couple aboard the starliner *Titanic* who spotted the approaching meteoroids and were killed instantly when they struck the ship. (4.X) (Played by RACHEL ANTHONY and GILES CLAYDEN)

Postman: Delivered post to the people of Leadworth. He was killed by the Eknodine-possessed Mrs Poggit in Amy's dream. (5.7) He later delivered the

PQ

Doctor's invitations to Amy Pond and Rory Williams which led them to Utah, in America. (6.1) (Played by ANDY JONES)

Post-Op: One of the areas within the Hospital on New Earth run by the Sisters of Plenitude. (2.1)

Potions of Life: Recipes listed in the Secret Books of Saxon that would recreate the Master. Lucy Saxon had people who also had access to the Potions so she could prepare an antidote, which she used on him. (4.17)

Powell Estate: Part of the North Peckham Estate in South East London, postcode SE15 7GO, where the Tyler family lived, and where Mickey Smith lived (at number 90 Bucknall House) after the death of his grandmother, Rita-Anne. The Tylers lived at 48 Bucknall House. Other estate residents included Debbie, the Changs, Tina the Cleaner and Sandra and Jason. (1.1, 1.4, 1.5, 1.8, 1.13, 2.X, 2.1, 2.6, 2.10, 2.12, 3.X) The Tenth Doctor spoke to a younger Rose there just after midnight on New Year's Day 2005. (4.18)

Powyll, Alun and Gladys: Uncle and Aunt to Ambrose Northover. Gladys died in 2014 and was buried in the Cwmtaff churchyard. When Alun died in 2020, the family went to bury his body next to Gladys's but found her body had vanished. It had been taken beneath the ground, into the Silurian City by Malohkeh the scientist, to dissect. (5.8)

Poynter, Dougie: Member of pop group McFly, who endorsed Harry Saxon's campaign to become Prime Minister. (3.12)

Prayer Leaf: Lorna Bucket created this tapestry for Amy Pond. It was a ritual of her people from the Gamma Forest, and woven into it was the name Melody Pond in her language. When the TARDIS was finally able to translate it, it read 'River Song'. (6.7)

Praygat: Tritovore trader whose shop crashed on San Helios. Along with his commander, Sorvin, he befriended the Doctor and Lady Christina de Souza but was killed by a Stingray hiding in the ship's gravity well. (4.15) (Played by RUARI MEARS)

Preacher: Gloomy predictor of Earth's imminent destruction in 1599. When the portal to the Deep Darkness opened, he seemed curiously delighted that his prophecies were about to come true. (3.2) (Played by ROBERT DEMEGER)

Preachers, the: Underground resistance group on 'Pete's World', dedicated to bringing down Cybus Industries, aided by the mysterious Gemini. They took their name from the fact they planned to tell the world 'the gospel truth' about John Lumic's plans. Amongst its members were Mrs Moore (the group's driver and techie), Jake Simmonds (reconnaissance), Ricky Smith (planning) and Thin Jimmy (leader). After Thin Jimmy's capture, Ricky became leader. When Ricky

P
Q

and Mrs Moore died fighting the Cybermen, Mickey Smith took Ricky's place and headed to the continent with Jake to locate more Cybermen. (2.5, 2.6) Jake Simmonds later led an armed group from 'Pete's World' to the real Earth to fight Cybermen. Whether these were newly recruited Preachers or an entirely new group is unknown. (2.13)

Prentice, Granddad: Jackie Tyler's father, who died from a heart attack in the late 1980s, but according to Jackie came back as a friendly ghost. The 'ghost' was in fact a Cyberman, breaking through the Void as a means of travelling to Earth from 'Pete's World'. (2.12)

Presenter: TV personality who alerted the public to the disappearances of the children from Stratford in 2012. (2.11T) (Played by DANIEL ROCHFORD)

President, the: Administrative head of Ember – although Kazran Sardick was de facto ruler of the planet, due to his control of the fog clouds. (6.X)

President of the People's Republic of Great Britain: On 'Pete's World', Britain was a republic. The President refused to fund the Ultimate Upgrade project, so Lumic had him killed. (2.5) (Played by DON WARRINGTON) He was succeeded by Harriet Jones, under whom the People's Republic took over the Torchwood Institute. (2.13)

President of the United States of America: The President was due to address the American nation live from the White House on the evening of the Big Ben incident. (1.4) The President wanted to bypass Harriet Jones and make contact with the Martians that later turned out to be Sycorax. (2.X) See also *Eisenhower, President Dwight*; *Hoover, President Herbert*; *Kennedy, President John F*; *Nixon, President Richard Milhous*; *Obama, President Barack*; and *Winters, President Arthur Coleman*

Presley, Elvis Aaron: American singer, generally considered the King of Rock 'n' Roll. The Doctor suggested the Sycorax could hypnotise someone to sing like Elvis, but not convince them to die. (2.X) The Doctor and Rose were on their way to see Elvis in New York but ended up in Muswell Hill. (2.7) The crew of the SS *Pentallian* had set a trivia question on one of their door seals, regarding who had the most UK number one hits, before the download era, out of Elvis and The Beatles. (Elvis won!) (3.7) The Doctor taught him to play guitar. Badly. (AG02)

Price, Angela: On 'Pete's World', Angela Price worked for Cybus Industries until she learned their secrets and fled, joining the

Preachers to try and bring the corporation down. To protect her husband and children, she assumed the name Mrs Moore. After her death, the Doctor told Jake Simmonds and Mickey Smith to find Mr Price and tell him how brave his wife had been. (2.5, 2.6)

Price, Captain Marion: Colonel Mace's second-in command during the assault on the ATMOS factory. She kissed Mace in delight when the Sontarans were defeated. (4.4, 4.5) (Played by BRIDGET HODSON)

Price, Sergeant: Police officer who oversaw security at 10 Downing Street in the wake of the murder of the UNIT personnel, academics and military officers, unaware that the murderers were actually the people he took his orders from – Slitheen family members disguised as humans. When the Doctor managed to have a sub-Harpoon missile launched at the building, it was Price's job to get everyone out but, when he saw the Slitheen in their true forms, he happily left them to their fate. (1.5) (Played by MORGAN HOPKINS)

Prime Minister: The head of the British Government, the Prime Minister disappeared at the start of the Big Ben incident. Margaret Blaine of MI5 told General Asquith that she personally saw the PM into his car, but Margaret was really a disguised Slitheen, and the Prime Minister had actually been murdered and stuffed into a cupboard in 10 Downing Street. He was replaced by Acting Prime Minister

PQ

Joseph Green, in reality another Slitheen. (1.4, 1.5) Once the Slitheen attack had been defeated, Harriet Jones was elected Prime Minister by a landslide. She then had to deal with the Sycorax spaceship over London, until the Doctor intervened. Using Torchwood to destroy the alien craft after it began its retreat, she angered the Doctor, who whispered the phrase 'Don't you think she looks tired' to her aide. Within hours, Harriet Jones's leadership was crumbling, (2.X) an event that enabled the Master to create a fake personality, Harry Saxon, and begin his campaign to become Prime Minister and destroy Earth via the mysterious Toclafane. (3.12, 3.13) Saxon's successor was seemingly killed when his plane was shot down by Daleks. (4.12)

Prin, Novice: Catkind who died in the God Complex. Her greatest fear was sabrewolves. (6.11) (Played by ANNA HOPE)

Pringles: According to Lance Bennett, Donna Noble got excited over a new flavour of these crisp snacks. (3.X)

Prisoner Zero: Long-lived multi-form, whose natural state was a gelatinous serpent but which could take on any number of other forms once it had created a psychic link with them. It was escaping from the Atraxi and hiding on Earth after escaping through a portion of the time field that manifested itself as a crack in Amelia Pond's bedroom wall. After killing a number of staff at Leadworth Hospital, Prisoner Zero was stopped when the Doctor drew the Atraxi's attention to it and they recaptured it. (5.1)

Private Gallery 15: Area aboard Platform One where the TARDIS landed. (1.2)

Private Legislation 16: The rule under which the Doctor was arrested aboard the Game Station. (1.12)

Probic 5: Part of the chemical compound that the Sontarans used in the ATMOS devices. (4.4, 4.5)

Probic Vent: Aperture on the back of a Sontaran's collar where they plug in to take nutrients such as Probic 5. It is a Sontaran's only weak spot, so it guarantees Sontarans have to face their enemies at all times. (4.4, 4.5, 4.18)

Progenation Machines: Devices brought to Messaline by the colonists with the intention of genetically cloning human and Hath colonists to populate the planet. However, as the war between the Hath and humans progressed, the machines were used to create ready-made warriors. The Doctor's DNA was sampled and a machine generated a clone of him in the form of a teenaged girl. Donna Noble called her Jenny and it seemed she was, in essence, the Doctor's daughter. (4.6)

Progenitor Devices: Many thousands of these egg-shaped devices, which contained Dalek DNA, were scattered through time and space. They could only be opened, to create new Daleks, when other Daleks activated them.

However, the last few Daleks in the universe that found a Progenitor in the 20th century were ones that had escaped the destruction of the Crucible in the Medusa Cascade and as such were created from cells from Davros's body. The Progenitor device would not recognise these Daleks as pure Daleks and thus could not be operated. The Daleks knew that if the Doctor correctly identified them as Daleks, such a testimonial from their oldest foe would be enough – the Progenitor would recognise him and the veracity of his words. When the Doctor did this, the Progenitor activated and created a new Dalek Paradigm that exterminated the last of Davros's Daleks and escaped to the future via a Time Corridor. (5.3)

Project Indigo: A UNIT programme, for which Martha Jones was appointed Medical Director. It used Sontaran technology to try and create a teleportation device, using brainwaves as a guidance system. Martha used the prototype to escape the Daleks and because she was thinking of Francine, it took her home. (4.12, 4.13)

Project Midas: Russian space programme that Maggie Cain took part in, making her only the second British woman to land on the moon. (4.16)

P
Q

Project Rainbow: In 1943, the US Navy conducted an experiment attempting to make the aircraft carrier *Eldridge* invisible. Instead they accidentally created a rent in space and time and the *Eldridge* was sent back and forward in time, either killing the crew or sending them insane. Due to the Time Lords' interference, the experiment was stopped but this caused the *Eldridge* to disappear for good – in fact it ended up on the bottom of the Atlantic Ocean in the 23rd century. (AG04)

Proms, the: Popular run of promenade concerts held annually at the Royal Albert Hall in London. The Doctor actually played the tuba there once in 1895. His own composition, 'Music of the Spheres' was played there over a hundred years later. (MotS)

Proper Dave: Pilot aboard the ship that took Strackman Lux's archaeological team to The Library. He was killed by the Vashta Nerada but his brain patterns were saved onto the data core and, when River Song found herself living in the core's fantasy world, Proper Dave was there too. (4.8, 4.9) (Played by HARRY PEACOCK)

Prophecy: One of the tenets of the Sibylline Sisterhood was their prophecy that foretold the arrival of the TARDIS in Pompeii. The accuracy of their predictions was actually due to the timelines being corrupted after the eruption of Vesuvius, an explosion so great it caused a rift in time, which echoed back seventeen years and enhanced the Sisterhood's abilities. The Pyroviles living within Vesuvius exploited the Sisterhood, Augurs and other soothsayers in the area, to keep abreast of what was happening in the outside world while they prepared to change Earth to suit their needs. (4.2)

Protean Energy: The energy used by the medical interface that resembled a sea siren to move herself and her victims across into her own ship's dimension. (6.3)

Protein One: One of the foodstuffs eaten by the inhabitants of Sanctuary Base 6. Other Protein supplements included Protein Two and Protein Three. (2.8, 2.9)

Protohumans: One of the evolutionary routes taken by the humans of five billion years in Rose Tyler's future. The name implied they were different from the then-extinct (bar Lady Cassandra) humans from Earth itself. (1.2)

Provence: Region of south-eastern France where Vincent Van Gogh became famous, and prolific, shortly before his death in Paris in 1890. (5.10)

Proxima Centauri: Red dwarf star, the nearest to Earth's own sun. Space pioneer Susie Fontana-Brooke was the pilot of the first lightspeed ship between Earth and Proxima Centauri. (4.16)

Psychic Containers: Small cubes that could be built by Time Lords using their minds. Into these cubes they could seal psychic messages and send them anywhere in time and space to be received by other Time Lords. The Doctor was drawn to House by one, and later discovered a large number of them, all calling out for help, in the TARDIS junkyard on House's surface. (6.4)

Psychic paper: Special paper, apparently blank, housed in a wallet, and used by the Doctor, and also by Captain Jack Harkness. It projected a low-level telepathic field that caused its viewer to see on it whatever they expected to see (e.g. an invitation, a security pass or a business card). This enabled the Doctor and his companions to access many places they would otherwise not have been allowed to enter. (1.2, 1.7, 1.9, 2.2, 2.5, 2.7, 2.11, 3.5, 4.X, 4.1, 4.3, 4.7, 4.10, 4.15, 5.8, 5.10, 5.11, 6.5, 6.7) It could also on occasion receive messages. (2.1, 4.8, 5.1) The employees of the Torchwood Institute, (2.12) William Shakespeare

(3.2) and Rosanna Calvierri (5.6) were among those immune to the psychic paper. The Doctor also used it to discover other people's identities by getting them to hold it and then reading whatever they unwittingly projected onto it, as he did with Gurney, the fake Governor of the prison on Volag-Noc. (TIQ) When the Doctor visited the young Kazran Sardick and used the psychic paper to suggest he was universally recognised as mature and responsible, the paper finally gave up the ghost. (6.X)

Psychograft: A device activated by Chip to transplant the consciousness of Lady Cassandra O'Brien into Rose Tyler's body on New Earth. The psychograft's energy remained within Cassandra's mind, enabling her to jump from body to body for some while afterwards. (2.1)

Purcell, Jim: Aggressive, unpleasant landlord of a number of properties on the Rowbarton House estate, who owned a bulldog called Bernard. Disliked and feared by his tenants, he was drawn into George's nightmare world, and transformed into a Peg-Doll. He was later returned home safe and well. (6.9) (Played by ANDY TIERNAN)

Pyroviles: Huge stone and lava-based aliens from Pyrovillia. A scout craft landed on Earth thousands of years past, and once they awoke they discovered their home world had vanished so attempted to claim Earth as theirs. When Vesuvius erupted, it destroyed the Pyroviles but sent a shockwave back 17 years in time, creating a massive rift. The dust particles from the Pyroviles turned the people of Pompeii slowly but surely into living rock. The Doctor realised that, with the help of an energy converter constructed by the City's Augur, Lucius Petrus Dextrus, the Pyroviles could use the volcanic energy to heat up the planet, boil away the seas and ultimately make Earth their new home. The Pyroviles and their ships were destroyed when the Doctor set history on the right track, ensuring Vesuvius did erupt, sealing the rift and removing all trace of the Pyrovillian incursion from the minds of any soothsayers, augurs or haruspex who survived the city's destruction. (4.2) Despite her memory having been wiped, after the arrival of the Master on Earth and his subsequent attempt to turn humanity into himself, Donna Noble recalled the Pyroviles as her mind subconsciously fought the Master's influence. (4.17, 4.18)

Pyrovillia: Home world of the Pyroviles that had vanished thousands of years ago. (4.2) It was one of the planets the Daleks had stolen and placed a second out of sync with the universe, to help power the Reality Bomb. (4.12, 4.13)

Quant, Mary: Fashion model and style icon who was one of the highlights of 1963, according to the Doctor. (AGOT)

Quantum Enfolding: Method by which the Doctor accessed the recordings from the 12-year-old Kazran Sardick's computer drive and projected them onto the elder Sardick's living room walls. (6.X)

Queen's Arcade: Shopping mall in South London where Rose Tyler's mother and Clive Finch's family were attacked by Autons. (1.1) Elton Pope was also shopping there when the attack began. (2.10)

Queen Street: Location of Banto's DVD store, where Larry Nightingale worked. After defeating the Weeping Angels together, Larry and Sally Sparrow bought Banto out and turned the shop into an antique book and rare DVD store. (3.10)

Queen Victoria, the: Fictional Walford pub featured in the BBC soap opera *EastEnders*. Publican Peggy Mitchell had discovered the ghost of previous tenant Den Watts in the cellar of the pub, in episodes being watched by Jackie Tyler. (2.12)

Quizmania: ITV Play television series of which Annalise, the girlfriend of Clive Jones, presumably watched repeats. According to Clive's estranged wife, the show was too difficult for Annalise to handle. (3.1)

Quoldonity: One of the many religions practised in the 42nd century. (2.9)

P
Q

Rachett: Highwayman hung on the Tyburn Tree. (AG05)

Racnoss: Omnivorous, giant, eight-legged, semi-humanoid race from the Dark Times, who devoured entire planets because they were born starving. Believed destroyed by the Fledgling Empires, a Webstar ship carrying Racnoss young, the Secret Heart, was caught in the gravity field of a star, and a world was formed around it – the Earth. Billions of years later, the last of the Racnoss, their Empress, returned to Earth, eager to free her ever-hungry young, using an organic key charged with Huon particles. However, the Doctor blew up the walls of the Torchwood base under the Thames, flooding the tunnel through which the children were escaping, wiping out all the Racnoss young. The Empress herself was aboard her Webstar when it was destroyed moments later, bringing an end to one of the longest-surviving races in the universe. (3.X)

Radford Parade: Area of Nottingham where, in the fiction the Doctor created for John Smith's background, John believed he grew up. (3.9)

Radiation Pits of Europe: Martha Jones walked across the Earth telling her story about the Doctor, preparing people for the right moment to chant his name. Amongst the places she visited were the Radiation Pits of Europe. (3.13)

Radiation Room: Part of the Silo base on Malcassairo, where stet radiation was being used to power the rocket's drives. Stet radiation was utterly lethal to humans – and when the Futurekind's Wiry Woman turned the power off, Guard Jate was instantly vaporised by it. (3.11)

Radio Enthusiast, The: Magazine about radio and the burgeoning television industry. Tommy Connolly was reading a copy when trying to persuade his father to buy a television set. (2.7)

Raffalo: A Crespallion maintenance worker aboard Platform One who Rose talked to. She was killed when Cassandra's robot spiders dragged her into a ventilation duct. (1.2) (Played by BECCY ARMORY)

Rage: Coming in varying strengths, this was one of the Mood Patches available in Pharmacytown in the Undercity of New New York. (3.3)

Rago Rago Five Six Rago: Location of a famous university. Chosen Scholars from Class 55 were guests aboard Platform One to see the Earthdeath spectacle. (1.2)

Raleigh, Sir Walter: Nobleman during the reign of Elizabeth I who reportedly laid his cloak across a puddle to avoid his monarch's feet getting wet. This chivalrous act seeped into history and Queen Victoria likened Sir Robert MacLeish to Raleigh when he offered to climb through a window first, better to help her out afterwards. (2.2)

Ralph: One of the Lord Chamberlain's Men, an actor and stagehand in Shakespeare's company at the Globe theatre. He was charged with distributing drafts of *Love's Labour's Won* to the rest of the company. (3.2)

Ramsay: One of the soldiers under Captain Reynolds protecting Queen Victoria in 1879. (2.2) (Played by CHARLES DE PAULA)

Ramsden, Doctor: Medic at Leadworth Hospital who did not believe Rory Williams's claims that coma patients had been seen out and about in the village. She was later killed by Prisoner Zero. (5.1) (PLAYED BY NINA WADIA)

Ranjit: School classmate to Mandy Tanner and Timmy Winters. (5.2)

Rasputin, Grigori: Charismatic Russian mystic, legendarily hard to kill. The Justice Ship *Teselecta* encountered him, although initially they made the *Teselecta*-copy of him green. (6.8)

Rassilon, Lord President: Legendary Time Lord, brought back into existence to lead the Gallifreyan armies in the Last Great Time War. He considered the Doctor his enemy after the Doctor destroyed the Time Lords to stop Rassilon's plan to unleash the Ultimate Sanction. Realising that the only way out of the Timelock they were trapped within was to push ahead with the Ultimate Sanction anyway, Rassilon sent an echo of a Time Lord heartbeat back through time to the exact moment the Master stared into the Untempered Schism, ultimately driving him insane because only he could hear the drumming sound. The Time Lords then tracked this sound to Earth where the Master had been reborn and sent him a Whitepoint Star so they could link to the physical reality of Earth and so leave the Timelock, bringing Gallifrey back into the universe with them. The Doctor destroyed the mechanism powering the Whitepoint Star and, furious to discover that everything he had done in his life was down to Rassilon's interference, the Master attacked Rassilon, driving him back into the Timelock, and himself in the process. (4.17, 4.18) (Played by TIMOTHY DALTON)

Rattigan, Luke: Millionaire egocentric child prodigy, who famously invented the Fountain Six search engine when he was just 12 years old. He entered into an arrangement with the Sontarans. They perfected his ATMOS and in return, promised to take him and his Rattigan Academy students to Castor 36,

or Earth Point Two as he called it, as the Sontarans were going to destroy the existing Earth by turning it into a clone-breeding world. However, when Luke learned that the Sontarans planned to kill him and use his students as target practice, he was left lonely and friendless in his Academy until the Doctor arrived and built an Atmospheric Converter from the equipment there to save Earth. When he realised the Doctor was going to blow the Sontaran ship up with him aboard, Luke teleported onto the ship, sent the Doctor to safety and blew himself and the Sontarans to pieces. (4.4, 4.5) Davros taunted the Doctor about how many people had died trying to help him over the years, and this made the Doctor think of Luke. (4.12, 4.13) (Played by RYAN SAMPSON)

Rattigan Academy, the: Establishment in North London set up by child prodigy and multimillionaire Luke Rattigan, ostensibly to train the brightest and best of British youth, both mentally and physically. What the students were not completely aware of was that Luke had set it up to create a group who would travel to a new planet, Castor 36. With the help of the Sontarans, they had constructed revolutionary new equipment for terraforming new worlds, and Luke planned to lead them there and start human civilisation all over again. (4.4, 4.5)

Ravan-Skala: Planet the Doctor intended to take Amy Pond and Rory Williams to, before ending up in the God Complex. The people there were apparently 600 feet tall, and the Tourist Information Centre was built into one of their hats – tourists needed hot air balloons to communicate with them. (6.11)

Ravel, Maurice: French composer whose most famous work, *Boléro*, was being listened to by Toby Zed while working on the ancient Veltino inscriptions he found on the surface of Krop Tor. It switched off when the Beast contacted his mind. (2.8)

Raxacoricofallapatorius: A world whose primary inhabitants were the calcium-based Raxacoricofallapatorians, separated into different families, including the exiled ruthless criminals, the Family Slitheen. Criminals were executed by being boiled alive in acetic acid until they became soup. Female Raxacoricofallapatorians had lethal defence mechanisms: a poison dart that could be ejected from their claws, and they could exhale poison gas. (1.4, 1.5, 1.11)

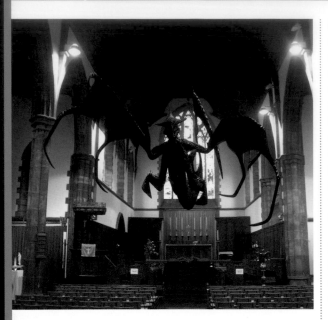

Henry Van Statten had the arm of a Raxacoricofallapatorian in his exhibit room in Utah. (1.6) Rose Tyler pretended to have authority granted to her by the Raxacoricofallapatorian Parliament to demand the Sycorax leave Earth. (2.X) The Graske held a Raxacoricofallapatorian, which the Doctor identified as a member of the Family Slitheen, prisoner in his base on Griffoth. (AotG) Raxacoricofallapatorius had a sister planet, Clom, and the Abzorbaloff came from there. (2.10) There were two Raxacoricofallapatorians in the Zaggit Zagoo bar (4.18) A Raxacoricofallapatorian ship, from the Family Slitheen, travelled to Stonehenge, as part of the Pandorica Alliance. (5.12)

Razbahan: The Weeping Angel carried by the *Byzantium* had been found in the ruins of Razbahan and been in private hands ever since. (5.4)

Razor-Toothed Blade-Fin: Alien aquatic predator that besieged the Poseidon base, and killed Pat, leader of the farming community. (AG04)

Reality Bomb: Device created by Davros at the behest of the Supreme Dalek. By placing 27 planets in perfect balance within the heart of the Medusa Cascade, at the edge of a rift in time and space, he used the alignment of the planets to create a compressed string of Z-Neutrino Energy. By focusing that beam onto a subject, the energy cancelled out the electrical field that surrounded every atom in existence. When it was fired through the Medusa Cascade rift, everything in the universe would disintegrate, each atom becoming unattached from all others and then themselves ceasing to exist. Only the Daleks, safe within the Cascade, would remain safe and untouched. The Reality Bomb was eventually shut down by Donna Noble after the metacrisis increased her brainpower. (4.12, 4.13)

Reapers: When Rose Tyler stopped her dad dying in a hit-and-run accident on the day of Sarah Clark and Stuart Hoskins' wedding in 1987, she caused a tear in the fabric of time, allowing the antibody-like wraiths the Reapers to spill into the Earth of 1987, wiping people out of time and feeding off the resultant chronal energy. The survivors hid within St Christopher's Church, a building so old the Reapers had a hard time getting in, with the Doctor's age being an added protection. However, when Rose met her younger self, as a baby, and they touched, the safety net broke as the additional surge of chronal energy from this paradox weakened the Church. The Reapers burst in, and the Doctor became their next victim, although one of them was destroyed when it touched the TARDIS. Pete Tyler, having worked out who Rose really was and why the Reapers were there, sacrificed his life, putting time back on track and expelling the Reapers, and returning to life all those they'd taken. No one there was left with any memory of the events, except the Doctor and Rose. (1.8) The Doctor cited his encounter with the Reapers to the Atraxi as a reason to fear him. (5.1)

Receptionist: Crewmember aboard the Max Capricorn cruiseliner *Titanic*, who tried to keep calm after the ship was struck by meteoroids but was killed by a girder that crashed down on top of her. (4.X) (Played by STEPHANIE CAREY)

Receptor Room: Chamber built on top of the Area 52 pyramid in Egypt, which was established in the alternative timeline created by River Song after she changed time. The room contained a huge beacon from which River had asked the universe for help in saving the Doctor's life. The Doctor, inside his *Teselecta* duplicate, and River got married there in what appeared to be a Gallifreyan ceremony. (6.13)

R

Red Carnivorous Maw: The Doctor saved a planet from this on his way to the Ood-Sphere when answering Ood Sigma's projected song. (4.17)

Red Division: A troop of security guards under the command of Bywater, working for Henry Van Statten in his Vault, deep below Utah. (1.6)

Red Falls Five: Place that the Shafe Cane family came from before arriving as refugees on Malcassairo. (3.11)

Red Hatching: According to Martha Jones, she and the Doctor were in a hurry and couldn't speak to Sally Sparrow in 2008 because a migration had begun and the red hatching would be starting within 20 minutes. Exactly what the red hatching was remained a mystery to Sally, but she discovered from the Doctor that it involved four things and a lizard. (3.10)

Red People: A number of the humans who lived on New Earth came in extreme colours, including red and white. In the Hospital on New Earth, a Red Woman was being repainted as a cure for Marconi's Disease by some of the Sisters of Plenitude. (2.1) (Played by CLAIRE SADLER) As the Doctor dropped from car to car on the New New York Motorway, he encountered a Red Man driving one vehicle. (3.3) (Played by ANDREW CAMERON) There was a Red Man in the Zaggit Zagoo bar, (4.18) and he was also a visitor to the Maldavorium. (5.12) (Played by JASON COLLINS)

Red Six Seven: Tickets that allowed a trip to Earth from the starliner *Titanic*, organised by historian Mr Copper. The Van Hoffs and Bannakaffalatta were ticket holders and, thanks to the psychic paper, the Doctor and Astrid Peth were able to join in, too. (4.X)

Red Velvets: Rodrick knew that Hoshbin Frane was the President of the Red Velvets when asked by the Anne Droid in *The Weakest Link* aboard the Game Station. (1.12)

Red Waterfall: One of the two time streams co-existent on the planet Apalapucia. (6.10)

Redfern, Nurse Joan: Matron at Farringham School for Boys and charged with overseeing their welfare. Over the few weeks that John Smith had been teaching history at the school, Joan had become attracted to him and he to her, and they began a courtship, much to the chagrin of Martha Jones. She knew their relationship was doomed because, before long, she would have to open the fob watch containing the essence of the Doctor, so John Smith would no longer exist. When the Family of Blood attacked first the village and then the school, Joan found herself tested. She deplored the fact that the boys were educated in the art of war, because her husband Oliver had died during the Boer War, and yet she accepted that the school needed to defend itself from the Family and their Scarecrow foot soldiers. She eventually led Smith and Martha to the Cartwrights' cottage, where she and John discussed the fact that he clearly was this Doctor that the Family and Martha had claimed he was. Eventually, John opened the fob watch, and the Doctor was reborn. Joan realised that, no matter how much she had loved John Smith, the Doctor was a wholly different person, and one she did not like at all. The Doctor offered Joan the chance to travel with him, because somewhere inside him whatever had drawn John Smith to her still existed. But Joan was resolute and asked him to leave, keeping his 'Journal of Impossible Things' as a reminder of the second man in her life to have died. (3.8, 3.9) Her great granddaughter Verity Newman wrote a biography of her, based on her diaries. Verity told the Doctor that Joan had lived a happy life. (4.18) (Played by JESSICA HYNES)

Redfern, Oliver: Late husband of Joan Redfern, Matron at Farringham School for Boys. He died at Spion Kop, one of the famous battles of the Boer War, in January 1900. (3.8)

Redford: Schoolboy at Farringham School for Boys in 1913, who was told to secure the courtyard before the Family of Blood attacked. (3.9)

Redmond, Robina: Young society girl, impersonated by the Unicorn at Eddison Hall. The real Robina never even left London. (4.7)

Redpath, Mr: Young grandson of Mrs Peace, whose body was lying in Gabriel Sneed's Chapel of Rest. When the Gelth inhabited Mrs Peace's body, she throttled Redpath to death and another Gelth later took over his corpse. (1.3) (Played by HUW RHYS)

Reg: Fighter pilot boyfriend of Lilian Breen, he was shot down and killed over the English Channel by German fighter planes. (5.3)

Registrar: Council official who married Jackie Prentice to Pete Tyler in a registry office. (1.8) (Played by ROBERT BARTON)

'Regresa A Mi': Spanish-language version of the song 'Un-Break My Heart', sung by Il Divo and played by Jackie Tyler to Elton Pope in her flat. (2.10)

Reinette: Nickname given to Jeanne-Antoinette Poisson, better known in later life as Madame de Pompadour. As a 7-year-old, Reinette met the Doctor for the first time when he talked to her from the 51st century via the fireplace in her Paris bedroom. He later crossed through to see her, but some months had passed for Reinette. Together they discovered a Clockwork Robot hiding under her bed. (2.4) (Played by JESSICA ATKINS)

Rels: Dalek measurement of time. (2.13, 3.5, 4.12, 4.13, 5.3)

Remembrance Day: Annual service held across Britain each November to remember and honour the dead of the wars of the 20th century. As a very old man, Timothy Latimer was at one when he saw the Doctor and Martha Jones for the first time since he was 14. (3.9)

Renfrew, Doctor: The man in charge of Graystark Hall Orphanage, where the Silence made a base for themselves to protect a girl they found there, who they believed was important to their future. Renfrew was driven insane by his constant exposure to, and subsequent memory wipes by, the Silence. He thought it was still 1967 (it was 1969) and had taken to scrawling hostile messages over the walls of the building, as well as his own skin, trying to remind himself to escape but then forgetting why. He was present when Canton Delaware III shot and wounded a Silent and brought it to the Doctor's attention. (6.2) (Played by KERRY SHALE)

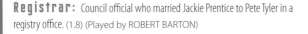

Rep: Sales Representative who travelled to the Ood-Sphere to have the latest Ood tech displayed to him and his fellow reps. He, along with all the other reps, was killed by the Red-Eyed Ood. (4.3) (Played by TARIQ JORDAN)

Reporter: News hound who told the story of the disappearance of the Royal Hope Hospital, and its subsequent return in the alternative world where Donna Noble never met the Doctor. (4.11) (Played by CATHERINE YORK)

Resistance: A network of resistance cells formed after the Master and the Toclafane took over the Earth. Amongst their members were Professor Allison Docherty, Thomas Milligan and Martha Jones. (3.13)

Restac, Protector: Military Commander of the Silurian Warriors. She had great antipathy towards humanity as a whole but this was increased when they murdered her sister Alaya. She opposed Eldane's plans to co-exist peacefully with the mammals, and killed Malohkeh, the scientist, when she reallsed he was also siding with them. When Eldane concluded that the human and Silurian cultures would always be at war, he put his people back into hibernation, driving the warriors back to their safe chambers by releasing toxic fumigator gas into the atmosphere. Restac, furious with her fleeing soldiers, refused to give up and, as the gas finally suffocated her, she tried to gun the Doctor down, killing Rory Williams instead. (5.8, 5.9) (Played by NEVE McINTOSH)

Rex Vox Jax: Planetary home of the Hop Pyleen brothers, inventors of Hyposlip Travel Systems. (1.2)

Rexel 4: A planet in the Rexel Planetary Configuration. (3.2)

Rexel Planetary Configuration: The home system of the Carrionites. Legend had it that the specific alignment of the configuration was the

prison door created by the Eternals to seal the Carrionites within the Deep Darkness. (3.2)

Reykjavik: The city of Pola Ventura hosted Murder Spree 20, not Reykjavik. Rose Tyler didn't know this when asked by the Anne Droid in *The Weakest Link* aboard the Game Station. (1.12)

Reynolds, Captain: Commander of the soldiers charged with guarding Queen Victoria against would-be assassins on her way to Balmoral in 1879. He was killed by the Haemovariform at Torchwood House. (2.2) (Played by JAMIE SIVES)

Rhodri: Official wedding-video recordist for Donna Noble and Lance Bennett. He recorded Donna's disappearance and showed it to the Doctor, who realised she had been fed Huon particles and that the biodamper she wore wouldn't therefore protect her. Rhodri was considering selling the tape to the TV show *You've Been Framed*. (3.X) (Played by RHODRI MEILIR)

Rhombus: Major Domo in the household of Lobos Caccilius of Pompeii. He was killed by the Pyrovile that entered Villa Caecilius. (4.2) (Played by GERARD BELL)

Rhondium: Energy particles the Doctor was seeking out while on the number 200 bus in London. The wormhole that took the bus to San Helios contained Rhondium particles. (4.15)

Rice, Cassie: Young woman who worked as a waitress in her mother's old diner in Dry Springs, Nevada. The Doctor realised that a piece of alien 'junk' in the diner was actually genuinely alien and when it was tracked down by the Alliance of Shades, Cassie, her friend Jimmy Stalkingwolf and the Doctor found themselves taken to Area 51 and discovered a plot by the US military to team up with the Viperox Horde. After the Doctor stopped the Viperox, Cassie and Jimmy headed back to the now-devastated Dry Springs together. (DL) (Voiced by GEORGIA MOFFETT)

Rice University: Education facility in Houston, Texas. Adelaide Brooke went there. (4.16)

R

Richard, Cliff: British singer (real name Harry Webb) who Jackie Tyler was a fan of. The Doctor was not surprised by this. (2.7)

Richards, Matthew: Potential boyfriend of Donna Noble's when she was younger. Probably a bit emo, he ended up living with a man. (4.4)

Ricky: Deliberately trying to wind him up, the Doctor often referred to Mickey Smith as Ricky. (1.4, 1.5, 1.11) On 'Pete's World', Mickey's counterpart really was called Ricky Smith. (2.5, 2.6)

Rift, the: An unexplained space and time phenomenon that crossed through the centre of Cardiff, its exact start and end points unknown. Various kinds of energy bled through it and, in 1869, it formed a gateway to Earth for would-be invaders called the Gelth. (1.3) The Doctor's TARDIS was re-energised by absorbing rift energy. When it was connected to a tribophysical waveform macro-kinetic extrapolator, energy beamed up from the TARDIS into the rift, tearing it open and causing a series of earthquakes across Cardiff. (1.11) The Doctor and Martha Jones later returned to Cardiff to refuel the TARDIS. Captain Jack Harkness had previously begun working at the Torchwood base beneath Cardiff, knowing that the Doctor would return eventually for this purpose. (3.11) When Earth was shunted to the Medusa Cascade, Jack wondered if it was rift activity. Torchwood used the rift energy to boost Harriet Jones's Subwave Network and later to help move all the stolen planets back to their own space and time, including Earth. (4.12, 4.13) Aliens that Torchwood referred to as Weevils were known to have come to Earth via the rift, some of which at one point joined the Pandorica Alliance. (5.12, 5.13)

Rigs: Robotic oil rigs patrolled the planet Bouken, harvesting its rare oil reserves. They had a low level of sentience and advanced weaponry. (TIQ)

Ring: The Master wore a ring, with the LazLabs logo on it, which he habitually tapped out the pulse-beat his Archangel Network was hypnotising humanity with. After his death and immolation, Miss Trefusis removed the Master's ring from his funeral pyre, later using it as part of the ceremony to restore the Master to life. (3.12, 3.13, 4.17)

Rio de Janeiro: City in Brazil where Great Train Robber Ronald Biggs fled to. (3.1) Martha Jones decided to visit it. (TIQ) The Doctor promised to take Amy Pond and Rory Williams there but instead they ended up in Cwmtaff. (5.8, 5.9)

Rising Sun, the: Essex pub whose football team lost to the King's Arms team when the Doctor joined them briefly. (5.11)

Rita Logistics: Haulage company that Elton Pope worked for. (2.10)

Rita-Anne: Mickey Smith's blind grandmother, who took Mickey in after his mother left and Jackson Smith, his father, moved to Spain. She was a strict disciplinarian, but loved Mickey a lot. She died about five years before Mickey met the Doctor, by tripping over loose stair-carpet. Mickey felt guilty about this – she

Rivesh Mantilax: Endymide scientist, who came to Earth in search of his wife Saruba Velak. Endymor had been overrun by the Viperox Horde and Rivesh Mantilax had developed a genetic weapon designed to wipe them out. The Viperox followed him to Earth, trying to stop him using the weapon, but Rivesh Mantilax had been safely hidden away by the Shoshoni Native American tribe. However, after five years in a cave, Rivesh Mantilax was dying, and he was only saved when Saruba Velak brought him the Orb of Healing. Together with his wife, Rivesh Mantilax returned to Endymor in her repaired spaceship. (DL) (Voiced by NICHOLAS ROWE)

Robert Lewis: Fictional character created by Colin Dexter for his range of Inspector Morse novels, later successfully translated into a major television series. Lewis later got his own TV show. The Doctor called Rose Tyler 'Lewis' when he pretended they were both police officers investigating the disappearances of the children in Dame Kelly Holmes Close. (2.11)

Robinson: London policeman who was sent to clear the roads close to the International Gallery when they were looking for Lady Christina de Souza before DI McMillan spotted that she was on the number 200 bus to Brixton. (4.15)

had asked him to repair it a few times. On 'Pete's World', Mickey was delighted to see she was still alive, although her grandson was called Ricky and, much to her consternation, hung out with the Preachers. (2.5) He decided to remain on 'Pete's World', partly because she was there. (2.6) After she died, Mickey opted to return to his original reality. (4.13) (Played by MONA HAMMOND)

Roboforms: Robotic scavenging mercenaries based on Earth, camouflaged as Christmas Santas. They carried weapons disguised as musical

'Rockin' Around The Christmas Tree': A seasonal 1958 hit song for Brenda Lee, this was playing in the house where the Graske replaced the parents with changelings. (AotG)

Rocky: Series of six American movies about a boxer, Rocky Balboa, created by Sylvester Stallone. Donna Noble referred to one of the Pyroviles as 'Rocky 4' because he was made of rock. (4.2)

Rodrick: One of the players of *The Weakest Link* aboard the Game Station. He was ruthless and tactical, getting rid of the stronger links so he would go head to head with Rose Tyler, who he thought was a bit thick. He did indeed win, by default, but never received his money. He was amongst the angry contestants and Game Station staff gathered on Floor 000 when the Daleks invaded the station, and he was exterminated. (1.12, 1.13) (Played by PATERSON JOSEPH)

Rodrigo: Male friend of Jackie Tyler's who, she claimed, owed her a favour. She borrowed his pick-up truck, with which Mickey Smith was able to wrench open the TARDIS console. (1.13)

Roedean: Exclusive British girls' school in Sussex. Lucy Saxon went there. (3.12)

instruments and attacked Rose Tyler (and Mickey Smith by default, as he was with her) and later the Doctor because they were drawn to him and the TARDIS and intended to replenish their batteries from his chronon energy. (2.X) A year later, the Doctor encountered them again, this time being used by the Empress of the Racnoss, who had sent them to kidnap Donna Noble. (3.X) Some travelled to Stonehenge, as part of the Pandorica Alliance. When the Pandorica opened and history was stopped, the Alliance were reduced to fossils. (5.12, 5.13)

Rocastle, Mr: Headmaster of Farringham School for Boys. A strict disciplinarian, he could nevertheless be quite fair when necessary. As a former soldier in the Boer War, he saw it as his duty to instil in his boys an aptitude for warfare, fearing that it would not be long before they would need those skills. When the Family of Blood attacked first the village and then the school itself, the initially sceptical Rocastle, along with Mr Phillips the school's bursar, went to investigate. Phillips was murdered by the aliens, and Rocastle realised the danger his school and pupils were in. He organised the defence against the Family's Scarecrow soldiers. However, he refused to believe that the body of 6-year-old Lucy Cartwright could be host to an alien – a mistake, as she promptly disintegrated him. (3.8, 3.9) (Played by PIP TORRENS)

'Rock-A-Bye Baby': American lullaby, generally accepted as the first written on American soil, but based on the British ballad 'Lillibullero'. Nancy sang it to Private Jenkins to keep him calm after he had become a gas-mask zombie. (1.10)

Roentgen radiation: A form of radiation transmitted by the X-ray machine installed in the Royal Hope Hospital. The Doctor used a huge amount to flood the room, destroying a Slab and filling his body as well, though Time Lords were immune to its destructive capabilities. He managed to shake the radiation

out through his foot, soaking his shoe with it in the process – he threw away the shoe. When he was a child, the Doctor used to play with Roentgen blocks. (3.1)

'Rolling In The Deep': 2010 single by Adele that was playing in Gloria's Golden Grill Diner in Utah, when the Doctor and River Song were comparing diaries. (6.1)

Rolling Stones, the: British rock band who were one of the highlights of 1963, according to the Doctor. (AG01)

Rook, Vivien: British journalist, working for the *Sunday Mirror*. Claiming to be doing a story about Lucy Saxon, she made her way through Downing Street to warn Lucy about Harry Saxon. As one of the two per cent of the population not affected by the Master's hypnotic pulse beaming down from the Archangel network (like Lucy Saxon and Clive Jones),  she had discovered he was a fake. Realising this, the Master had her killed by the Toclafane, but Vivien had already uploaded a message and all her files to Torchwood, hoping someone would stop Saxon. (3.12) (Played by NICHOLA McAULIFFE)

Room 802: Room in Albion Hospital where Dr Constantine made taped recordings of his sessions with Jamie, the gas-mask-wearing 'empty' child. When the gas-mask zombies tried to surround the Doctor, knowing they were all behaving like a 4-year-old boy, he told them to go to their rooms. Eventually Jamie made his way to Room 802, believing it to be his room. (1.10)

Rorybot: The nickname Amy Pond gave to the Handbot she reprogrammed to keep her company in Green Anchor on Apalapucia. (6.10)

Rose: In 'Pete's World', Jackie Tyler's pet Yorkshire Terrier was called Rose. This Tyler family had never had a daughter. (2.5) (Played by TINKERBELL)

Rose of the Powell Estate, Dame: The title bestowed upon Rose Tyler by Queen Victoria after the Doctor destroyed the Haemovariform that threatened her life at Torchwood House. Victoria then exiled Rose and the Doctor from the British Empire. (2.2)

Rossetti, Christina: Dee Dee Blasco quoted her poem, 'Goblin Market', whilst the Doctor tried to work out what was controlling Sky Silvestry on Midnight. (4.10)

R

Rossiter: Vinvocci salvager, whose ship the *Hesperus* was in orbit while he and his fellow Vinvocci, Addams, pretended to be humans, using a Shimmer. They seemed to be working for Joshua Naismith, attempting to repair the Immortality Gate, but in fact they knew exactly what it really was, since it was Vinvocci-built. They were trying to transport it off Earth. Instead, Rossiter helped free the Doctor from the Master and teleported him to the *Hesperus*. When the *Hesperus* flew down to Earth, Rossiter manned the laser guns along with Wilfred Mott to shoot down the warheads the Master fired at them. After the Doctor and Wilfred left the ship, Rossiter and Addams flew it home. (4.17, 4.18) (Played by LAWRY LEWIN)

Rossiter, Mrs Elsie: Elderly resident of Rowbarton House, who was drawn into the terrifying doll's house by 'George', the alien Tenza posing as a human child on the estate. Mrs Rossiter frequently chided George for apparently scaring her, and she was the first person to be absorbed into the doll's house and transformed into a Peg-Doll, although she later reverted to normal. (6.9) (Played by LEILA HOFFMAN)

Roswell: City in New Mexico, famed for its alleged alien sightings and activity. Henry Van Statten had a milometer from a Roswell spaceship in his exhibit room deep under the surface of Utah. (1.6) Saruba Velak's ship crashed near Roswell and was found by the US military and taken to Dreamland, in Nevada. (DL)

Rough Lads: Two chancers who tried to steal from the Reverend Golightly's church. This made him so angry that the genetic lock which kept his Vespiform side in check broke and he dealt harshly with them. (4.7) (Played by ROBERT PRICE and STEPHEN BARRETT)

Rowbarton House: Housing estate where the Tenza known as George placed himself, with his 'parents' Claire and Alex. Other residents included Mrs Rossiter, the McKenzie family, a traffic warden from Croatia and a man with ten cats, along with spiteful landlord Jim Purcell. (6.9)

Rowling, Joanne aka JK: Author of the Harry Potter novels. The Doctor told Martha Jones he had cried at the end of *Harry Potter and the Deathly Hallows*. Martha used a word from the books, 'Expelliarmus', to help William Shakespeare send the Carrionites back into the Deep Darkness. (3.2)

Royal Collection, the: Art gallery aboard *Starship UK*, watched over by Liz Ten. Van Gogh's painting *The Pandorica Opens* ended up there, and River Song convinced Liz Ten to part with it. (5.12)

R

Royal Hope Hospital: Thameside hospital where Martha Jones was training to become a doctor and which was unwittingly harbouring a fugitive Plasmavore. As a result it was transported wholesale to the moon, where the alien Judoon, who had no jurisdiction to land on Earth, came searching for the Plasmavore. Once the Plasmavore had been executed, the hospital was returned safely to Earth. (3.1) In the alternative world where Donna Noble never met the Doctor, it was Sarah Jane Smith who gave the Plasmavore to the Judoon, ensuring the hospital's safe return, although at the cost of her own life. (4.11)

Royal Leadworth Hospital: Facility where Rory Williams worked as a nurse. He was concerned by the fact that he had seen a number of supposed coma patients walking out and about in Leadworth, but this was not believed by Doctor Ramsden, who suggested Rory needed a holiday. In fact Rory was correct, although what he was seeing was Prisoner Zero using a psychic link with the comatose people to create mobile forms for itself. The Doctor drew the Atraxi to Leadworth Hospital, and they recaptured Prisoner Zero. (5.1)

Rubicon: North Italian river which, according to legend, Caesar crossed as a deliberate act of war. The Doctor told Rose he could take her to witness this. (2.2)

Run-Away, Colonel: See *Manton, Colonel*

Russell, Kurt: American actor, who starred in the 1982 version of *The Thing*, which the Doctor referred to when he and Amy Pond approached the deserted Arctic Geological Survey Base in Zebra Bay. (AG02)

Russia: The largest country on Earth, turned into the massive Shipyard Number One by the Master and the Toclafane. The shipyard ran from the Black Sea to the Bering Strait. (3.13) Colonel Stark, like many American military leaders from the 1950s, was concerned by the Soviet Union and allied himself with Lord Azlok of the Viperox, believing Azlok would help him if America and the USSR ever went to war. (DL)

Rutan Host: The war between the shapeshifting Rutans and the Sontarans had raged for at least 50,000 years. (4.4, 4.5) A Rutan ship collided with the TARDIS in the 11th century over Earth and crashed into the planet below. Trapped beneath ground for 500 years, only one Rutan remained awake, and infiltrated the Gunpowder Plotters under the guise of Lady Elizabeth Winters. They planned to use a doomsday weapon to wipe out the Sontarans for good. (AG05)

Ruth: Daughter of Benjamin, who, along with other members of her family, visited Kazran Sardick on Christmas Eve to try and secure the release of her great aunt, Abigail Pettigrew, for Christmas Day. (6.X) (Played by LAUREN ROWLANDS)

Rutherford, Ernest: Often associated with splitting the atom (he didn't; that was actually John Cockcroft and Ernest Walton), and generally seen as the main exponent of that branch of science. Richard Lazarus likened the importance to mankind of his own work with the Genetic Manipulation Device to Rutherford's work. (3.6)

RWTH: University in Aachen, Germany. The Rheinisch-Westfälische Technische Hochschule was where Steffi Ehrlich studied before moving to join the Space Program in America. (4.16)

Rydall Street: Road near Donna Noble's home, where the Doctor and Ross Jenkins dropped her off before they went to the Rattigan Academy. (4.4)

Ryder, Dr: Head of Ood Management on the Ood-Sphere, seemingly working for Ood Operations, but in fact a spy for Friends of the Ood. Over ten years with the company, he had sought access to the Ood Brain to find a way of freeing the Ood from enslavement. He was thrown onto the surface of the Ood-Brain by Klineman Halpen and died when the brain swallowed him. (4.3) (Played by ADRIAN RAWLINS)

Sabre-toothed gorillas: Alien creatures which the Doctor warned Martha Jones about when they arrived on the planet Myarr. (TIQ)

Sabrewolves: Catkind Novice Prin was frightened of these. (6.11)

Sacramento: One of the cities Goddard suggested dumping the mind-wiped Henry Van Statten in. (1.6)

Sahara Desert: The Doctor likened trying to find the Tandocca Scale to looking for a speck of cinnamon in this African desert. (4.12) Lou wondered if that was where the number 200 bus he and the Doctor were aboard had been transported to. (4.15)

St Christopher's Church: Location of the wedding between Stuart Hoskins and Sarah Clark. As an old building, it was the final refuge of the survivors on Earth hiding from the Reapers as they broke into the world after Rose Tyler saved her dad's life and created a breach in time. (1.8)

St John's Monastery: Situated on an island off the coast of Britain, the 13th-century monastery was converted to an alpha-grade industrial facility, supplying the military with crystal-diluric acid for the Morpeth-Jetsan company. The humans working there tended to use Gangers, duplicate humans made from the Flesh, to do the work because much of it was hazardous as the acid was extremely corrosive. When St John's was struck by solar tsunami energy, the existing Gangers became independent from their prime humans and rebelled. The Flesh supply was similarly affected. (6.5, 6.6)

St Joseph Workhouse: A Victorian Workhouse for orphaned children. Its Matron was Miss Hartigan. (4.14)

Saint Julienne, Eva: See *Macrae Cantrell, Suki*

St Mary's Church: Chiswick church situated in Haven Road, where Donna Noble and Lance Bennett were getting married when Donna vanished. (3.X)

St Paul's Cathedral: London place of worship that was damaged during the Blitz when the Daleks caused all the lights of London to illuminate. (5.3)

St Stephen's Church: Rosita Farisi sent the children she, the Doctor and Jackson Lake evacuated from the CyberKing's engine room there, to be looked after by the Warden. (4.14)

Sainted Physician: Name that Londoners in the 13th century gave to the Doctor when he rid them of a 'demon'. They put a stained glass window into their church showing the TARDIS to celebrate him. (4.17)

Salisbury: Wiltshire town, on whose plains stands Stonehenge, under which the Pandorica was hidden, in the Under Henge. (5.12, 5.13)

Salisbury, Lord: Robert Cecil, the first Earl of Salisbury, was King James I's spymaster. The Doctor discussed him with Black Rod. (AG05)

Sally: Neighbour of the Nobles in Chiswick who greeted Donna when she came back to visit. (4.4) She was one of the Silver Cloak, and had contacts at the Bridge Club. (4.17) (Played by ANGHARAD BAXTER)

Salt, Cathy: Reporter for the *Cardiff Gazette*, who read some of Mr Cleaver's postings about the Blaidd Drwg project's shortcomings. She confronted Margaret Blaine, the Lord Mayor of Cardiff, with her story, not realising Blaine was actually responsible for the design faults. Blaine was preparing to kill her when she learnt that Cathy and her boyfriend Jeffrey were expecting a child. (1.11) (Played by MALI HARRIES)

Salt Lake City: The nearest populated area to Henry Van Statten's underground base. The Doctor predicted that, if the Dalek escaped the Vault, Salt Lake City's one million inhabitants would be just the first to die. (1.6)

Salvain: Rickston Slade's secretary on Sto. (4.X)

Sammy's Pitstop: Diner in Dry Springs, run by Cassie Rice and previously owned by her mother. The diner had on display something that Cassie's mother thought was just a piece of junk, though she told everyone it was from a crashed spaceship near Roswell. In fact it was a weapon carried aboard an Endymide ship that had actually crashed there in 1953. Android Men in Black from the Alliance of Shades came to retrieve it, but the Doctor escaped with it. (DL)

Samson: A horse owned by Gabriel Sneed, used to pull his undertaker's cart. (1.3)

Samuel: Identity assumed by Mickey Smith once back in his home reality, so he could infiltrate the Torchwood Institute as one of Dr Singh's associates. (2.12)

San Andreas Fault: An 800-mile stretch of geological fault line in California caused by tectonic plates moving northwards and southwards, often resulting in earthquakes. The Doctor likened the rift threaded through Cardiff to the San Andreas Fault. (3.11)

San Claar: One of the many religions practised in the 42nd century. (2.9)

San Diego: One of the cities Goddard suggested dumping the mind-wiped Henry Van Statten in. (1.6) Martha Jones claimed to have gone there and collected one of the phials of liquid needed to arm the gun she was allegedly preparing to kill the Master with. (3.13)

San Francisco: North Californian city renowned for its earthquakes. The Doctor likened it to Pompeii. Lobos Caecilius believed it was the name of a restaurant in Naples. (4.2)

San Helios: Planet in the Scorpion Nebula with three suns, which the number 200 bus was transported to. It should have been a thriving lush planet, especially San Helios City itself, but instead had been reduced to sand and dust by the Stingrays which had devastated it, devouring everything living there. A Tritovore ship planning on doing business with San Helios City had also crashed there. (4.15)

San Juan: County in Utah, close to where the Doctor met up with Amy Pond, Rory Williams and River Song, shortly before he was shot and killed by a mysterious astronaut at Lake Silencio. (6.1)

San Kaloon: Place visited by the Doctor, Rose Tyler and Captain Jack Harkness, famous for its glass pyramids. (1.11)

Sanchez, General: UNIT Officer in charge of their New York headquarters when the Daleks attacked. He had Martha Jones take the prototype Project Indigo device and ordered her to use the Osterhagen Key. He was then killed by the Daleks. (4.12) (Played by MICHAEL BRANDON)

Sanctuary Base: Portable kit-constructed bases that could be assembled on any planet, moon or asteroid, on surfaces or beneath water. (2.8, 2.9)

Sanctuary Base 6: Constructed on the surface of Krop Tor. The crew were explorers from the Torchwood Archive. Their ship crashed after riding a gravity funnel between the black hole which Krop Tor orbited and the surface. They were carrying out their mission, drilling ten miles below the surface of the planet, to discover the unexplained power source that had registered down there. (2.8, 2.9)

Sanderson & Grainger: Colchester Department store which was built over a crashed Cyberman spaceship. When the Cybermen revived, they began taking locals and then members of the shop's staff to harvest their body parts to replenish themselves. When they were destroyed by Craig Owens, the ship's bonded disillium shielding protected the store. Amongst its employees were Val, Shona, Kelly, Mary Warnock, Don Petherbridge, and George the Security Officer. (6.12)

Sandra [1]: Neighbour of Jackie Tyler's whose partner, Jason, had A+ blood and was thus affected by the Sycorax's Blood Control. Once the threat had passed, they watched as ash from the Sycorax ship fell over the Powell Estate, mistakenly believing it to be snow. (2.X) (Played by SIAN McDOWELL)

Sandra [2]: Passer-by who answered the time engine's avatar's call for help at 79B Aickman Road and was unintentionally killed, ultimately adding to the stain on Craig Owens's ceiling below. (5.11) (Played by KAREN SEACOMBE)

Santini Khadeni, Cathica: A journalist on Satellite Five, Cathica desperately wanted to be noticed for her work, especially in the Spike Room, and was appalled when Suki Macrae Cantrell was promoted to Floor 500. Although initially resistant to the Doctor's coaxing about what was actually wrong with Satellite Five, her journalistic instincts served her well when she made her own way to Floor 500 and discovered the truth about what was really in control of Earth – the Jagrafess. Linking via her implanted chip to an abandoned Spike

Room, Cathica disconnected the other Spike Rooms' news feeds and raised the temperature on Floor 500. This broke the link between the Jagrafess and the zombie humans operating the computers and eventually caused the creature to explode, taking the contents of Floor 500 with it, including the Editor. Cathica remained on Satellite Five, determined to return the Earth Empire's news-gathering to more honest, investigative ways. (1.7) (Played by CHRISTINE ADAMS)

Santori, Goddess: Catkind deity worshipped by the Sisters of Plenitude. Other Catkind worshipped the more traditional Christian God, referred to by them as Jehovah. (2.1, 3.3)

Sarah: Woman who operated a Stephen's Point burger van for the homeless. She was killed by the Master. (4.17) (Played by LACEY BOND)

Sardick, Elliot: Human colonist who rose to prominence on the planet Ember as an industrialist – he was the creator of the Sky-Mast Weather Controller – and money-lender. He was a strict disciplinarian, especially towards his only son, Kazran, who he sought to have follow exactly in his footsteps. When Elliot died, Kazran had a painting of him placed in a corner of his living room where he didn't have to look at it. Because his house was constructed over a fog lake, he built a cryo-cave into which he installed a number of cryogenic chambers. These contained people held in suspended animation, taken as collateral against the money he lent to the people of Sardicktown. (6.X) (Played by MICHAEL GAMBON)

Sardick, Kazran: Money-lender and industrialist on Ember who inherited his father's businesses, including the Sky-Mast Weather Controller. He refused to use the Weather Controller to save the doomed starship the *Thrasymachus*, so the Doctor travelled back in time to his childhood and showed Kazran an alternative way of thinking, full of adventure and love. The older Kazran was aware as his memories altered to adapt to the new history, in which he fell in love with one of the cryogenically suspended people, Abigail Pettigrew. However, Abigail was doomed to die and each Christmas Eve they spent together was one less day Abigail was alive. When Kazran learned of this, as a teenager, he stopped wanting to see the Doctor and had nothing further to do with Abigail for fear she would finally die. Because of this, the Doctor's plan to soften the elder Kazran failed and made him even more bitter and determined not to save the *Thrasymachus*. The Doctor finally changed his mind by introducing his younger version to his older, and the older Kazran realised what he had grown into – the bullying father he always feared. He and the

Doctor, unable to use the Weather Controller, released Abigail for her last day, and she was able to sing, resonating the crystals in the fog and using the fish to help bring the ship into a safe landing, albeit a crashed one. Kazran and Abigail spent Christmas Day, her last, together, skimming through the air in a rickshaw pulled by a Fog Shark. (6.X) (Played by MICHAEL GAMBON, DANNY HORN and LAURENCE BELCHER)

Sardicktown: Capital city of Ember, an Earth colony. It was named for Elliot Sardick, who built the Sky-Mast Weather Controller which manipulated the crystalline fog that enshrouded the planet. (6.X)

Sardicktown Chronicle: Newspaper on sale in the capital city of Ember. (6.X)

Sarn: The name of the Residential Care Home in Upper Leadworth where Rory Williams sometimes worked. The residents included Mrs Poggitt. (5.7)

Saruba Velak: Female Endymide, who crashed on Earth in 1947, after her ship was shot down by space pirates. She came as an ambassador but was instead captured by the US military and transferred to the Dreamland base, as a prisoner. Years later her husband, Rivesh Mantilax, came to Earth looking for her but was severely injured. Freed by the Doctor, Saruba Velak used the Orb of Healing to save Rivesh Mantilax and the two of them went home in her repaired ship. (DL) (Voiced by LISA BOWERMAN)

Satan: Legendary demon name, one of many attributed to the Beast throughout the galaxies. (2.8, 2.9)

S

shows directly to homes on Earth — although no one was actually dying when they lost the games. Instead they were being teleported to the Dalek mothership hovering at the edge of the solar system and, once there, they were turned into Daleks. Floor 056 housed the *Big Brother* house that the Doctor was transmatted to. Floor 229 was where Captain Jack Harkness was transported to take part in *What Not to Wear*. Floor 407 housed the *Weakest Link* studio, where Rose faced the Anne Droid.

As soon as the Dalek Emperor discovered that the Doctor had arrived on the Game Station, the Dalek stratagem was advanced. The Daleks swarmed in, starting on Floor 494, moving onto 495 (where they encountered a reprogrammed Anne Droid). They continued to fight their way up the Game Station, briefly diverting to Floor 000, where the staff and game players that had not been evacuated aboard the shuttles were gathered. Jack had already tried to enlist them in the defence of the station against the Daleks; those who refused to help were massacred by the Daleks. The Daleks then made their way to Floor 499, where they killed Jack, and then entered Floor 500 to confront the Doctor. Rose Tyler, having absorbed the power of the Vortex, erased these Daleks, their fleet and their Emperor from existence. When the Doctor and Rose left in the TARDIS, the only other living being aboard the Game Station was Jack, now revived by Rose's powers, who then had to use his faulty Vortex Manipulator to try and find his companions, but ended up on 19th-century Earth instead. (1.12, 1.13, 3.11)

Sato, Toshiko: Undercover Torchwood operative who arranged to be in charge of the investigation into the supposed alien that crash-landed in the Thames. She and the Doctor determined that it was just a normal pig that had been augmented by alien technology. (1.4) (Played by NAOKO MORI) She later died in action in Torchwood, and was remembered by Gwen Cooper and Ianto Jones as they faced a Dalek entering the Hub — it was stopped by a time lock Toshiko had developed. (4.12, 4.13)

Saturn 5: The rocket that launched the Apollo 11 capsule into orbit around the moon. (6.2)

Satellite Five: A vast space station, with 501 floors, populated almost entirely by humans. Its main remit in the year 200,000 was as a broadcaster, delivering news across the Fourth Great and Bountiful Human Empire over the previous 91 years. Floor 016 was the Medical area, which staff such as Cathica Santini Khadeni first attended when they arrived. Adam Mitchell also visited this floor, where a Nurse implanted him with a chip so he could access the information he required via a Spike Room. Floor 139 was where the TARDIS landed. The top floor, which all the workers believed to be lined with gold, was Floor 500. This was actually occupied by the true master of Satellite Five, the Jagrafess, and his minion, the Editor. Unlike the rest of Satellite Five, the temperature on Floor 500 was barely above freezing, and the humans manning it were all in fact dead journalists, just corpses being manipulated by the power of the Jagrafess via their implants. (1.7)

When the Jagrafess was destroyed, Satellite Five immediately ceased broadcasting but, instead of freeing humanity from the Jagrafess's domination, the Doctor's intervention had actually started another century of social decay for humanity. The Jagrafess was actually just one part of a long-term game plan by the Emperor Dalek, who, over the next 100 years, placed his own agents, called Controllers, aboard Satellite Five — again on Floor 500. Renamed the Game Station and operating under the auspices of the Bad Wolf Corporation, the Game Station was now a huge complex, broadcasting 10,000 seemingly lethal entertainment

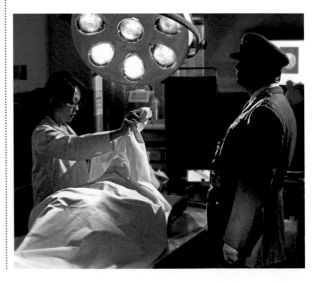

Saturnyne: Water world that was lost to the time field. Shortly before its destruction, the last of the piranhic Sisters of the Water fled to Earth with 10,000 male Saturnynes. They arrived in Venice towards the end of the 16th century, and the Sister of the Water took on the persona of Rosanna Calvierri, via a perception filter, opening a school in the House of Calvierri, where she converted local girls into Saturnynes, to breed with the males. When this plan failed, Rosanna committed suicide, leaving the male Saturnynes to fend for themselves in the canals of Venice. (5.6)

Saul: A friend of Jenny, the maid at Farringham School for Boys. When confronted by the Scarecrows about to kidnap her, Jenny briefly thought they might be a practical joke by Saul. (3.8)

Saxon, Harry: Character created by the Master to become the Prime Minister of Great Britain. See *Master, the*

Saxon, Lucy: Schooled at Roedean and St Andrews, the wife of Harry Saxon, the new Prime Minister of Great Britain, met her husband while working at the publishing house that published his book. She was well aware of his real identity as the Master, and was a willing accomplice in his plans with the Toclafane, having travelled 100,000,000,000,000 years into the future, to Utopia. She betrayed Vivien Rook to him, and danced as the Toclafane invasion began. However, as the year of Toclafane domination went on, Lucy seemed to lose favour with the Master, receiving beatings at his hands that changed her view of him, and she became more withdrawn, the spell broken. When the Toclafane were stopped and the world was sent back a year so that the majority of Earth had no idea what had transpired, Lucy remembered. As the Master surrendered, she shot him, exactly as Chantho had shot his previous incarnation. (3.12, 3.13) Imprisoned following a secret trial, Lucy was aware of the existence of the Secret Books of Saxon and the cult that had grown around them, and was always afraid that the Master could try and return. Supported by a small band of loyal followers, including a prison guard at HMS Broadfell where she was incarcerated, Lucy waited for the day the Master returned. She then prepared a liquid to counter the Potions of Life that the Secret Books of Saxon listed and threw it at the reincarnated Master. This contaminated the energies he was using, causing his body to burn up faster, but also created an explosive back-blast that destroyed the prison along with Lucy. (4.17) (Played by ALEXANDRA MOEN)

Scannell, Orin: One of the crew aboard the SS *Pentallian*, he was horrified to learn that Korwin McDonnell had destroyed the engineering equipment, setting the cargo ship on a course for a nearby sun. He and Captain McDonnell, Korwin's wife, tried to find a way to jump-start the ship using the generators. When that failed, due to the sun-possessed Ashton hacking the ship's systems, Scannell concentrated on helping the Doctor get Martha Jones and Riley Vashtee back from the jettisoned pod that was taking them closer to the sun. When Vashtee was safely back aboard, he and Scannell made it to the auxiliary controls and, on Martha Jones's orders, vented all the fuel that had been scooped from the sun. This shot straight back into the injured sun and they managed to get the ship off its predetermined collision course. When the Doctor and Martha said their goodbyes, Scannell and Vashtee stayed aboard the *Pentallian*, waiting for rescue by the authorities. (3.7) (Played by ANTHONY FLANAGAN)

S

Scarecrows: Straw-filled foot soldiers created by Son of Mine, using molecular fringe animation. Relentless, untiring, with rudimentary intelligence, even after being cut down by machine-gun fire, they could be reanimated. After the Family of Blood were imprisoned for eternity by the Doctor, the Scarecrows probably fell apart or just became traditional scarecrows, placed in fields and meadows across Britain. (3.8, 3.9)

Scarlet Junction: A conglomeration of planets and systems of which Crespallion was an affiliate, designated Convex 56. (1.2)

Scarlet System: A star system the inhabitants of Sanctuary Base 6 observed being destroyed as it was consumed by the black hole K 37 Gem 5. It was home to the Pallushi, who perished at the same time. (2.8)

Schoolchildren: Part of a school party at the Musée D'Orsay, being guided around an exhibition of Vincent Van Gogh's paintings by Doctor Black. (5.10) (Played by ANDREW BYRNE and MORGAN OVERTON)

Schwarzenegger, President: The Trine-E android aboard the Game Station described an outfit it and the Zu-Zana android had given to Captain Jack Harkness as having a 'tweak of President Schwarzenegger' during the *What Not to Wear* programme. (1.12)

Science Foundation: Human cadre of scientists who postulated the concept of Utopia and formulated the Utopia Project thousands of years before Professor Yana got the rocket launched away from Malcassairo and towards Utopia. (3.11)

Scientist, the: Orange-liveried member of the new Dalek Paradigm. (5.3) (Operated by JEREMY HARVEY)

Scooby-Doo: Famous American cartoon dog who, with a gang of human helpers, solved mysteries, usually more by accident than design. On 'Pete's World', Pete Tyler likened the Preachers to the Scooby Doo gang. (2.6) Larry Nightingale told Sally Sparrow that the Wester Drumlins house resembled something out of a Scooby-Doo episode. (3.10)

Scoones, Mr: Master of a Workhouse in Victorian London. He was captured by the Cybermen and put under their direction via an earpiece control device. He then took all the children from his Workhouse to the Cybermen, and they were used to build the engine for the CyberKing. Mr Scoones's usefulness over, Miss Hartigan killed him, via the earpiece. (4.14) (Played by EDMUND KENTE)

Scorpion Nebula: Star system on the far side of the universe from Earth. San Helios was situated there. (4.15)

Scotland Yard: Colloquial name for London's Metropolitan Police Force, derived from the location of the force's original headquarters. The Doctor told President Nixon he was from Scotland Yard when he parked the TARDIS in the White House's Oval Office. (6.1) Madame Vastra suggested calling Inspector Abberline at the Yard to let him know the Jack the Ripper menace was over. (6.7)

Scott, Ida: Science Officer on Sanctuary Base 6 who, according to the Beast, only joined the Torchwood Archive to run away from her father. She accompanied the Doctor beneath the surface of Krop Tor, but he left her safely above the trapdoor that led to the Beast's prison. However, when the planet began moving towards the nearby black hole, the atmosphere of Krop Tor was drained away and Ida collapsed unconscious, all the air in her spacesuit's tanks used up. Reunited with the TARDIS, the Doctor just had time to collect Ida, revive her and return her to the survivors of the base aboard their shuttle craft. (2.8, 2.9) (Played by CLAIRE RUSHBROOK)

Scribble Creature: A ball of literal pencil scribbles animated by the ionic energy of the Isolus channelled through Chloe Webber. Chloe inadvertently created it by scrawling on a sheet of paper in frustration when the lead in a pencil broke. The drawing became real inside a garage on Dame Kelly Holmes Close, and it attacked Rose when she opened the garage door. The Doctor later rubbed out part of it with a simple pencil eraser. (2.11)

Sea Devils: Colloquial name given to prehistoric reptile men living on Earth beneath the sea who once emerged to reclaim what they saw as their world. The Master aided and abetted them in their attempts but was defeated by the Doctor. The Master reminded the Doctor of this when taunting him over his current defeat. (3.13) The Doctor cited his defeat of the Sea Devils as a reason for the Atraxi to fear him. (5.1)

Seamus: One of the inhabitants of Hooverville in 1930s Manhattan. Solomon told him to stay with the rest of the people there when they were attacked by the Pig Slaves. (3.5)

Sean: Captain of the King's Arms football team, who was very impressed by the Doctor's soccer skills. (5.11) A Stetson that Sean had worn at his stag night was later appropriated by the Doctor and worn to Utah, to meet up with River Song, Amy Pond and Rory Williams. (6.12) (Played by BABATUNDE ALESHE)

Search-Wise: Internet search engine used by Rose Tyler to find information about the Doctor. (1.1)

Seattle: One of the cities Goddard suggested dumping the mind-wiped Henry Van Statten in. (1.6)

Sebastian: One of the Torchwood soldiers present when the Doctor first arrived at the Torchwood Tower, he showed the Doctor an alien particle gun. He later helped defend the Tower against the Cybermen on the top floor of the Tower and was presumably killed at some point during the battle. (2.12, 2.13)

Sec, Dalek: Leader of the Cult of Skaro, inhabiting a special black Dalek armoured shell, its Dalekanium enhanced with Metalert on the express orders of the Dalek Emperor during the Time War. Establishing a mobile strategy chamber within the Void Ship after fleeing the closing stages of the War, the Cult took with them the Genesis Ark, waiting to emerge on a planet and set free the millions of Daleks held prisoner within, courtesy of Time Lord technology. Needing the genetic imprint of a humanoid time traveller, the Cult waited patiently to emerge onto Earth, breaking further into Earth's reality whenever either the Cybermen or Yvonne Hartman and her Torchwood colleagues created a breach in the Void. When the Doctor found a way to send the Daleks and Cybermen back into the Void, Sec ordered an emergency temporal shift and the Cult escaped. (2.12, 2.13)

Arriving on Earth in New York, 1930, Sec realised the Cult needed to scale back their ambitions as that time zone was too primitive. He studied the millions of humans and gradually understood why the Emperor had given the Cult the capacity to think and reason. Sec masterminded the Final Experiment. Firstly, the Cult kidnapped humans – the smart ones they would use to create a Dalek-Human army, the denser ones were transformed into hybrid Pig Slaves. Another part of the experiment was to merge himself with a human, Mr Diagoras, giving him full mobility again. Unfortunately for the Cult, the Dalek Sec Hybrid began displaying human qualities such as compassion and an appreciation of morality. Sec's fellow Daleks turned on him, chaining him to Dalek Thay and dragging him to the Laurenzi theatre to confront the Doctor. Sec understood that the Doctor was possibly the only person who could help the Dalek race evolve to another level and, when Daleks Thay and Jast threatened to kill the Doctor, Sec put himself in the line of fire. Whether his death was the result of deliberate self-sacrifice or an accident remains unknown. Shortly after his death, Sec's Final Experiment failed when the Dalek-Human army turned on their creators and destroyed Thay and then Jast, before Caan killed them all and fled that time zone. (3.4, 3.5) (Operated by NICHOLAS PEGG (2.12, 2.13) and ANTHONY SPARGO (3.4, 3.5), voiced by NICHOLAS BRIGGS, (2.12, 2.13, 3.4) and ERIC LORENS (3.4, 3.5))

Second Great and Bountiful Human Empire: The Earth Empire of the 42nd century stretched across three galaxies. (4.3)

Second Officer: Bridge crew aboard the starliner *Titanic*. He was presumably killed when the meteoroids struck the ship. (4.X)

Secondary Storm Drive: Back-up nuclear engines aboard the starliner *Titanic*, which the Doctor and Alonso Frame managed to fire up in time to avert disaster. (4.X)

Secret Books of Saxon, the: Tomes that led the Cult of Saxon to find a way to rebirth the Master at Broadfell Prison. The books contained details of the Potions of Life which the prison's new Governor, with Miss Trefusis and other followers, used to bring him back, at the cost of their own lives. (4.17)

Secret Heart, the: The name of the Webstar ship that carried the Racnoss children away from the war with the Fledgling Empires. The ship later became the centre of Earth as the planet formed around it. (3.X)

Secretary: While researching sightings of the Doctor from his office, Victor Kennedy came across details of LINDA. His secretary came in with tea and was promptly absorbed. If not killed there and then, she was when the Abzorbaloff was destroyed after Elton Pope broke his cane. (2.10T) (Played by OLWEN REES)

Secretary General: Head of the Secretariat of the United Nations. He told people to 'watch the skies' in the wake of the Big Ben incident. (1.4)

Security Chief: Head of security at the International Gallery. The Cup of Athelstan, on display in the gallery, was stolen on his watch. (4.15) (Played by IAN HILDITCH)

Security Guard: He arrested the Doctor aboard the Game Station after the apparent murder of Rose Tyler by the Anne Droid. Quoting Private Legislation 16 of the Game Station Syndicate, he told the Doctor, Captain Jack Harkness and Lynda Moss that they would be transported to the Lunar Penal Colony without trial. The Doctor then knocked him out. (1.12) (Played by SAM CALLIS)

Security Guard 1: Adipose Industries officer who let Donna Noble into the front of the building. (4.1) (Played by OLIVER AGAR)

Security Guard 2: Adipose Industries officer who let the Doctor into the rear of the building. (4.1) (Played by TOBY SPERRING)

Security Protocol 712: A holographic projection of the Doctor appeared to Sally Sparrow and Larry Nightingale when they entered the TARDIS, alerting them that the DVD Larry was carrying had been recognised by the ship's systems as carrying programmed flight instructions and could be inserted into the console. Larry did so and the TARDIS began to dematerialise. (3.10)

Segway PT: Motorised one-person transport. The Doctor, Donna Noble and Lance Bennett had fun using these to get from the basement of HC Clements to the Torchwood base beneath the Thames Barrier. (3.X)

Senate: Government of New New York and, by implication, of the whole of New Earth, its members were wiped out by the mutated Bliss virus – their last act was to put the planet into a 100-year quarantine. The Face of Boe took charge of the survivors, giving his own life energies to keep the Motorway and Undercity powered so that one day, when the Motorway could be opened, the Overcity could be repopulated. (3.3)

Sense-Sphere: Neighbouring planet to the Ood-Sphere. (4.3)

Sentient Money: Wriggling currency with which the Headless Monks paid Dorium Maldovar for his services. (6.7P)

Sergeant [1]: An army sergeant at Albion Hospital who organised the search for the augmented pig that the Slitheens had launched into space. The subsequent crash back to Earth had caused a huge distraction and enabled the Family Slitheen to take over the British Government. (1.4)

S

Sergeant [2]: Colonel Stark's junior officer at Dreamland base. He monitored the Viperox attack on Dry Springs. (DL) (Voiced by RYAN McCLUSKEY)

771: The security code used by the Doctor to warn Buckingham Palace to evacuate the Queen from Buckingham Palace. She was very grateful. (4.X)

7775/34 by 10 0/acorn: The coordinates of the *Byzantium* in orbit above Alfava Metraxis, which River Song sent to the Doctor so he would know where to find her when she jumped from the ship's airlock into space. (5.4)

761390: The coordinates on Earth of the Globe theatre to which the portal from the Deep Darkness was trying to connect. (3.2)

7258: The key-code needed to open Abigail Pettigrew's cryogenic chamber in Sardicktown. (6.X)

Seventh Obelisk: An Egyptian Goddess was sealed into this, but later escaped. (5.13)

Seventh Transept: Holy chamber for the Headless Monks. It was where they stored the heads of those they had taken either in battle or when converting them to the cause. Most of the heads were left to rot into skulls, because they had still been alive when the Monks took the heads in the first place.

Richer clients tended to have ornate plush private boxes to stay within – Dorium Maldovar's even had wi-fi. Access to the Seventh Transept was through the Labyrinth of Skulls, populated by carnivorous skulls that would eat anyone they could. If not, they ate rats. (6.13) There was another Transept, much smaller, set up on Demon's Run and overseen by the Papal Mainframe. Fat One was beheaded there. (6.7)

Sexton: A churchwarden whose dead body had been reanimated by the Gelth that existed in Gabriel Sneed's Cardiff undertakers. The Sexton's corpse later walked into his own memorial service. (1.3)

Shadmoch: A planet in the Rexel Planetary Configuration, which had a hollow moon. (3.2)

Shadow Architect: Administrative Head of the Shadow Proclamation. She attempted to force the Doctor to lead the Shadow Proclamation into battle against an enemy that later turned out to be the Daleks, but he refused. (4.12) (Played by KELLY HUNTER)

Shadow Proclamation: A Federation between various interplanetary races and empires, based upon mutually accepted rules and treaties. Quoting Convention 15 enabled someone to seek peaceful contact with a potential enemy, as the Doctor did with the Nestene Consciousness. (1.1) Rose Tyler cited 'Article 15' to the Sycorax Leader in an attempt to make him leave Earth. (2.X) The Doctor cited the Shadow Proclamation when trying to communicate with the Isolus child that had possessed Chloe Webber's body in 2012. (2.11) Matron Cofelia assumed that the Doctor would report her activities to the Shadow Proclamation. (4.1) In Pompeii, the Doctor demanded to know the Pyroviles' species designation as ratified by the Shadow Proclamation. (4.2) The Doctor took Donna Noble to meet the actual people and races that made up the Shadow Proclamation on their home asteroid, where the Shadow Architect attempted to force the Doctor into leading them into battle against whoever had stolen 27 worlds. She failed. (4.12) The Doctor cited Article 57 to bring the Atraxi back to Earth so he could warn them off interfering with a Level 5 planet again. (5.1)

Shafe Cane, Beltone: Brother of Padra Fet and son to Kistane, humans on Malcassairo who, once reunited, took off in the rocket ship to Utopia. Whether they themselves or their descendants were turned into Toclafane by the Master is unknown. (3.11) (Played by MAT IRELAN)

Shafe Cane, Kistane: Mother to Padra Fet and Beltone, humans on Malcassairo who, once reunited, took off in the rocket ship to Utopia. Whether they themselves or their descendants were turned into Toclafane by the Master is unknown. (3.11) (Played by DEBORAH MACLAREN)

Shafe Cane, Padra Fet: Human spotted by the Doctor, Martha Jones and Captain Jack Harkness fleeing from the Futurekind on Malcassairo. They initially held off the Futurekind, then fled with Padra to the humans' Silo base. Padra was reunited with his mother and brother and later took off in the rocket to Utopia. Whether they themselves or their descendants were turned into Toclafane by the Master is unknown. (3.11) (Played by RENE ZAGGER)

Shakespeare, William: Elizabethan playwright, generally perceived as England's greatest ever writer but, when the Doctor and Martha Jones met him in 1599, still coming to terms with the death of his son, Hamnet. He arrived on stage after a performance of *Love's Labour's Lost* and announced he was planning a sequel, *Love's Labour's Won*. The Carrionite Lilith was in the audience and used her powers to get him to say it would be performed the next evening. He then joined forces with the Doctor and Martha Jones, who worked out that he was being manipulated by the Carrionites. Shakespeare tried to stop his play being performed, because the final words, written while under the Carrionites' spell, would open a portal to the Deep Darkness and enable a Millennium of Blood to start on Earth. With a little help from Martha, Shakespeare was able to create a new ending for the play, using the words against the Carrionites' own spellcasting and exiling them back into their prison for ever. Shakespeare was immune to the Doctor's psychic paper and quickly worked out that he and Martha were from the future. (3.2) (Played by DEAN LENNOX KELLY) Art academic Doctor Black likened the quality of Vincent Van Gogh's rapid output in his last years to Shakespeare writing *Othello*, *Macbeth* and *King Lear* over the summer holidays. (5.10) His latest plays were the talk of London town in 1605, according to Geoffrey Plum. (AG05)

Shallacatop: One of the 27 planets stolen by the Daleks and secreted a second out of sync within the Medusa Cascade. The Doctor eventually returned it to its rightful place in space and time. (4.12, 4.13)

Shallanna: Homeworld to the Shill. (6.10)

Shamboni: Aliens with prominent foreheads. One was working as a life guard at an abstract 'swimming pool' where the Cane family had once holidayed. (4.10)

S

Shan Shen: Colony world whose culture was based on Earth-Chinese. The Doctor and Donna Noble took a vacation there and Donna found herself living an alternative history after she became the victim of a Time Beetle from the Pantheon of Discord. (4.11)

Shareen: A good friend of Rose Tyler. 'Don't argue with the designated driver' was one of her pearls of wisdom. (1.2) She and Rose often used to go shopping, just to look at local boys. (1.3) Rose tried to tell her mum that she had stayed at Shareen's for the night, not realising that her first journey with the Doctor had in fact kept her away from home for 12 months. (1.4) The only time Rose and Shareen fought was over a man. (2.3)

Sharon, Aunt: Amelia Pond's aunt, who looked after her (5.1) because Amelia's parents had ceased to exist, although neither Amelia or Sharon could actually remember this. Disbelieving Amelia's stories about the 'Raggedy Doctor', she had Amelia seen by a number of psychologists – something she also did in the post-Pandorica timeline, this time because Amelia was convinced that stars existed, when they didn't. Sharon later accompanied Amelia to the National Museum and was present when the older Amy married Rory Williams. (5.12, 5.13) (Played by SUSAN VIDLER)

Shaun: Object of desire for Martha Jones's friend Vicky, who didn't reciprocate Vicky's feelings. (3.13)

Sheckley Street: Road in Colchester where Craig Owens and Sophie Benson moved to once married and brought up baby Alfie. (6.12)

Sheffield: City where the Doctor planned to take Rose Tyler to see Ian Dury and the Blockheads perform in 1979. (2.2) The Grand Central Ravine was named after the Ancient British city of Sheffield, not York. Rose Tyler didn't know this when asked by the Anne Droid in *The Weakest Link* aboard the Game Station. (1.12) Maggie Cain was born there, in Grenoside, and later attended university there. (4.16)

Sheila: Elderly resident of Leadworth, whose mobility scooter was accidentally sent haywire by the sonic screwdriver. (5.1) (Played by MARRIS HOWARD)

Shepherd, Doctor: Area 51's medical officer, who was brought in to try and heal the injured Silent that Canton Delaware III brought to the base. But every time Shepherd turned away from his patient he forgot it existed, so in the end Canton let him walk away. (6.2) (Played by PETER BANKS)

Sherlock Holmes: Fictional detective created by Sir Arthur Conan Doyle. Elliot Northover was a fan. (5.8) The Doctor claimed Conan Doyle based Holmes's powers of observation and deduction on him. (AG02)

Shetlands: A series of islands off the northern coast of Scotland. According to the Doctor, the Scots never conquered them. (6.8)

Shill Governor's Mansion, the: A building recreated on Apalapucia which Amy Pond thought was beautiful. (6.10)

Shimmer: Device worn on the wrist by the two Vinvocci working for Joshua Naismith. It made them look human. (4.17, 4.18)

Shipton, Billy: The Detective Inspector in charge of investigating the mysterious disappearances at Wester Drumlins house. Attracted immediately to Sally Sparrow, he cancelled his evening plans and instead took her to the police car pound which was filled with vehicles abandoned near the house, among them the TARDIS. The two flirted and, when Sally left, he promised to call her. Billy then noticed the Weeping Angels surrounding the TARDIS and was despatched by one of them to 1969. There he met the Doctor and Martha Jones who explained that they needed him to get a message to Sally Sparrow, but it was going to take a while. (Played by MICHAEL OBIORA) The next time Billy saw Sally, nearly 40 years had passed for him, but barely an hour for her. During the intervening years, Billy had started to work in publishing, and then moved into video and finally DVD publishing. It was he who had put all the hidden Easter egg messages onto DVDs for the Doctor, and he told Sally to look at the list she had of the 17 DVDs they appeared on; she later worked out that it was a list of her own DVD collection. He showed her a photo of his wife, also called Sally, and they gently flirted again. Sally stayed with Billy until the rain stopped and Billy passed away. (3.10) (Played by LOUIS MAHONEY)

Shipton, Sally: When flirting with Billy Shipton, Sally Sparrow accidentally referred to herself as this. In fact, Billy did end up marrying a girl called Sally, and he showed Sally Sparrow a photo of them on their wedding day. (3.10)

Shiver and Shake: Two lead characters in a British weekly comic during the 1970s. Shiver was a ghost, Shake an elephant. The Doctor likened his and Rose's partnership to theirs, implying how well they worked as a team in the Torchwood Institute Lever Room as they prepared to destroy the invading Cybermen and Daleks. (2.13)

Shona: Ladieswear supervisor at Sanderson & Grainger, a department store in Colchester. She was killed by the Cybermen, and her body parts harvested to renew them. (6.12) (Played by SEROCA DAVIS)

Shonara: Girlfriend of Leo Jones, and mother of his baby, Keisha. She was presumably at home with Keisha on the night of Leo's 21st birthday party, but she was with Leo and Keisha in Brighton when the Master began rounding up the rest of the Jones family. (3.1, 3.12) (Played by CHANNON JACOBS)

Short-range teleport: Part of the Clockwork Robots' inbuilt technology, enabling them to move short distances in space and, when the time-window technology aboard the SS *Madame de Pompadour* was activated, across the centuries as well. (2.4)

Shukina: A Shan Shen trader tried to sell this to Donna Noble. (4.11)

Shuttles: Shuttle 4 and Shuttle 6 were amongst those returning the surviving dignitaries home after the events aboard Platform One. (1.2)

Sibylline Sisterhood: Gifted with the power of accurate prophecy, due to the incursion of the Pyroviles, the Sisterhood venerated their High Priestess

and protected her from the denizens of Pompeii, where they lived. Each of them had suffered the effects of inhaling the Pyrovillian dust fragments in the city air and were in differing stages of turning into living rock. The Doctor claimed he'd met the Sibyl herself once, danced with her, and she'd had a bit of a crush on him. He also told the High Priestess that the Sibyl would be ashamed of the way she had allowed the Pyroviles to corrupt the Sisterhood's beliefs. The Sisterhood all died together when Vesuvius erupted. (4.2)

Sierpinski sequence: Trying to override Dev Ashton's attempts to eject an escape pod, Riley Vashtee opted to use a series of mathematical fractals that were self-replicating, named after Waclaw Sierpinski. In theory, these ought to have kept the computer-controlled locks busy for hours. Ashton then destroyed the controls, and the escape pod was jettisoned from the SS *Pentallian* towards the living sun with Vashtee and Martha Jones inside it. (3.7)

Sight, the: Colloquial name for Gwyneth's extrasensory skills that enabled her to communicate with the Gelth. (1.3)

Sigma, Ood: Klineman Halpen's right-hand Ood who was, in fact, feeding him regular doses of Ood-Graft, to turn him into an Ood. When the Ood were freed from Halpen's control, Ood Sigma led them. He referred to the Doctor and Donna Noble as the DoctorDonna, anticipating the forthcoming metacrisis. (4.3) Ood Sigma appeared to the Doctor after he returned to Earth from Mars, singing the Ood Song to him, and the Doctor realised his own song was ending. He later met up with Sigma on the Ood-Sphere where Sigma introduced him to the Elder Ood who revealed to the Doctor that the Master was coming back. As he neared his regeneration, the Doctor saw Sigma once more, singing him to his death. (4.17, 4.18) (Played by PAUL KASEY, voiced by SILAS CARSON)

'Signalman, The': Cited by the Doctor as one of the Charles Dickens canon that he'd read. He reckoned it was the best short story ever written. (1.3)

Silence, the: The self-appointed sentinels of history, who allegedly experience all of time at once. Prisoner Zero warned the Doctor that the Silence were coming. (5.1) Rosanna Calvierri told the Doctor that her people also fled the Silence when the planet Saturnyne was lost to the time field. (5.6) The Doctor knew the Silence still needed dealing with, even after the universe had been rebooted and the time field sealed. (5.13) The Silence was a religious order, whose

core belief was that Silence must fall when the Question was asked – the question being the oldest in the universe, but hidden in plain sight. The Silence was represented on Earth by creatures who were a part of the Silence and Academy of the Question – referring to themselves as 'the Silence' was probably as much an acknowledgement of this as it was a statement of their race's name. The Silence and the Academy of the Question was known to Dorium Maldovar and employed Madame Kovarian to create a weapon to destroy the Doctor – Melody Pond, aka River Song. The mysterious aliens had been on Earth since the dawn of mankind, making the species do its bidding. The Silence controlled people via post-hypnotic suggestion and had the ability to make anyone who saw them instantly forget about them the moment they were out of sight. That way the Silence had moved freely throughout history. They could draw electrical energy into themselves and then redistribute it through their fingers to destroy any humans they wanted to. They nested together in groups in the dark, hiding in a network of tunnels they built beneath the Earth or in caverns or on ceilings but weren't impervious to bullets. When Canton Delaware III shot and wounded one, the Doctor took it back to Area 51 in Nevada and Canton filmed it telling him that if humanity had any sense, it'd kill the Silence on sight. The Doctor used that clip of film and spliced it into the transmission of Neil Armstrong walking on the moon, ensuring that subliminal message would be seen for ever. Sure enough, whenever anyone saw a Silent, they would kill it before forgetting the instruction and deed. The Doctor did this to ensure that the Silence fled Earth for good. In Florida, the Silence operated from an identical time engine to the one the Doctor had seen at Aickman Road in Colchester. In the alternative time stream created by River, when the Doctor didn't die at Lake Silencio, the Silence waited in huge water tanks inside Area 52, in Egypt. The Doctor assumed they were captive but in fact they were just dormant, insulated, and waiting for him. When he arrived they broke out, killing Kovarian but were stopped by Amy and Rory. When time was put back on track, the events in Egypt most probably never happened, but it suggested that the Silence were still out there, waiting for the Doctor and waiting for him to fall when the Impossible Question was asked. (6.1, 6.2, 6.12, 6.13) (Played by MARNIX VAN DEN BROEKE, voiced by TOBY HAYNES)

'Silent Night': German carol by Joseph Mohr and Franz Xaver Gruber. The passengers aboard the starship *Thrasymachus* gathered together to sing it, broadcasting it into the fog clouds around Ember, hoping the sonics would resonate with the ice crystals and allow them to land safely. (6.X)

Silent Realm: A term used by the Doctor to describe the Void, through which the TARDIS passed to arrive on 'Pete's World'. (2.5)

Silfrax Galaxy: Point of origin for the Vespiform. (4.7)

Silo: The base on Malcassairo where the human refugees lived, waiting for Professor Yana to power up the rocket which would take them to Utopia. It was guarded day and night by armed guards and had electrified fences to keep the Futurekind out. (3.11)

Silurians: Millions of years ago, Earth was dominated by reptilian life – chief amongst these were reptile people, or *Homo Reptilia* (Silurians was an inaccurate name coined for them in the 20th century). With huge cities and a civilisation based on science and art, the Silurians ruled Earth. However, fearing that the arrival of an object into Earth's orbit would damage the planet, the

reptile people rebuilt their civilisation below the ground and seas and went into hibernation, waiting to awaken when the danger had passed. The danger never happened – the object in orbit became the moon and so the Silurians never woke up. Over the millennia, as Earth's continents shifted, the cities sank further and further below ground or were crushed. In 2020, when the Discovery Drilling Project was established in Cwmtaff, South Wales because of the blue grass found there (due to Silurian minerals seeping up through the ground), the drilling awoke a small group of Silurians. They were a warrior caste and decided to rid the surface world of humans by instigating a war between mammal and reptile. With their heat-ray guns and their venom-gland tongues, they planned to start with Cwmtaff. The Doctor and Nasreen Chaudhry appealed to Eldane, an elder of the civilisation to broker peace, but when the Silurian warrior Alaya was killed by the humans, war seemed inevitable. Realising this was a war neither side could win, Eldane returned his warriors to hibernation, ready to try for peace again in a thousand years. (5.8, 5.9) Some Warriors emerged close to Stonehenge, as part of the Pandorica Alliance. When the Pandorica opened and history was stopped, the Alliance were reduced to fossils. (5.12, 5.13) A troop of warriors was brought to Demon's Run by the Doctor to arrest the Clerics. (6.7) A Silurian warrior had once been killed inside the God Complex and his photograph mounted on the wall. (6.11)

Silver Cloak, the: Determined to keep an eye out for the Doctor in times of need, Wilfred Mott set up this network of OAPs across London. They would contact one another if they saw the Doctor or the TARDIS. After meeting the mysterious Woman in a church a few days before Christmas, who told him the Doctor would return, Wilfred gathered the local branch of the Silver Cloak together on Christmas Eve to try and track him down, which they successfully did. Their members included Winston Katusi, Minnie Hooper, Oliver Barnes, Netty Goodheart, Bobby, Sally, June and June's sister. (4.17)

Silver Devastation: Area in the Isop Galaxy where the Face of Boe was living when he visited Platform One to see the final destruction of Earth. (1.2)

At the start of his life as the human Professor Yana, the Master was found as a naked, orphaned child on the coast of the Silver Devastation. (3.11)

Silver Tear, Lady: Human who died in the God Complex. Her greatest fear was Daleks. (6.11) (Played by KATE WILSON)

Silvestry, Sky: Businesswoman on a break to the leisure planet Midnight to get over a breakup with her partner. An alien entity managed to enter the *Crusader* craft she and other passengers, including the Doctor, were in and entered her mind, gradually taking her over. Recognising that the Doctor was the only real threat, the creature inside Sky used the other passengers' fear and paranoia against him. They were about to throw him out of the *Crusader 50* and into the lethal X-tonic sunlight, when the bus's Hostess realised Sky was the one who had been taken over. The Hostess pushed Sky, and herself, outside, where she, the creature and Sky's body were completely destroyed. (4.10) (Played by LESLEY SHARP)

Simmonds, Jake: Member of the Preachers, a renegade group on 'Pete's World' trying to overthrow society's dependence on Cybus Industries, convinced they were up to no good. After the deaths of Ricky Smith and Mrs Moore, Jake was left as the only member of the Preachers and joined the Doctor's final assault on the Cyber-conversion factory in Battersea Power Station. He and Mickey Smith then headed to France to liberate Paris from the Cybermen. (2.5, 2.6) When the Cybermen made their way through the Void to the real world, Jake and armed troopers were sent after them by Pete Tyler, but Jake was eventually returned to 'Pete's World' for good when the Void was sealed off by the Doctor. (2.13) (Played by ANDREW HAYDEN-SMITH)

Simmons [1]: Sadistic engineer working for Henry Van Statten, charged with torturing the 'Metaltron' until it spoke. After the Doctor revealed it was in fact a Dalek, Van Statten demanded Simmons torture it further, to make it speak directly to Van Statten. Instead, the Dalek used its sucker to envelop Simmons' head, suffocating him and draining him of life. (1.6) (Played by NIGEL WHITMEY)

Simmons [2]: Captain of the English prisoners of war attempting to escape, along with the Doctor, from Stalag Luft 14. Amy Pond and Rory Williams read about this incident in the book *Myths and Historical Impossibilities*. (6.1) (Played by ADAM NAPIER)

Simon: Young Chiswick lad whose father Alan disobeyed the Daleks and took him and his mother Laura back into their house. The Daleks then blew the house to pieces, with the family inside, as an example to the other humans. (4.12) (Played by ETHAN SMITH)

Sinatra, Francis 'Frank': American crooner and actor of the 20th century. The Doctor claimed to have spent Christmas 1952 at his hunting lodge with Albert Einstein, Marilyn Monroe and Santa Claus – or as the Doctor knew him, 'Jeff'. The Doctor duetted with Sinatra at a Hollywood party there one evening and also became engaged to Marilyn. (6.X)

Sinda Callista: The Doctor and Amy Pond were on their way to this planet's fifth moon when the TARDIS actually materialised on Earth. In Colchester. (5.11)

Singer: Nightclub chanteuse singing 'It Had To Be You' in the drinking den that the Doctor went into shortly before an air raid began. Until that point, he had been unaware of exactly when the TARDIS had landed. (1.9) (Played by KATE HARVEY)

Singh, Dr Rajesh: Torchwood Institute scientist who was in charge of ascertaining the purpose of the Void Ship that Torchwood knew as 'the Sphere', but had had no luck. Once the Cybermen invaded, the Sphere activated, and four Daleks – the Cult of Skaro – emerged. Needing information, the Daleks drew it from Singh's brain, desiccating him in the process. (2.12, 2.13) (Played by RAJI JAMES)

Single Molecular Transcription: A system that replaced microprocessors on Earth in 2019. (1.7)

Sinister Woman: An employee of Harry Saxon who worked alongside Francine Jones to try and trap the Doctor. Francine wanted to keep her daughter Martha safe from the Doctor, so allowed the Sinister Woman to listen in when they talked on their mobiles. She was present when Martha spoke to Francine from aboard the SS *Pentallian*, and tried to triangulate Martha's position. (3.7) She was still working alongside Francine, aided by a number of other minions, when Martha returned to Earth after Election Day and Saxon had become the British Prime Minister. The minions had brought Clive Jones back home, but he blew the plan by warning Martha to stay away. The Sinister Woman then had the whole Jones family arrested and incarcerated and ordered her armed guards to open fire on Martha's car when she arrived at her parents' house. (3.12) (Played by ELIZE DU TOIT)

Siren, the: A holographic medical interface which, having been unable to save the crew aboard a Skerth ship, crossed to Earth through a temporal rift. She used protean energy to remove and transport injured pirates from the *Fancy* back to the Skerth ship for repair. She could only access Earth via reflective surfaces, such as water, glass, treasure or chains.

Although able to cure everyone, the cure worked only while they remained aboard the Skerth ship, so Captain Avery and his crew had to stay there and fly the ship across the stars. (6.3) (Played by LILY COLE)

Sirius: The binary star system used by many on Earth as a guide in the night sky, including Henry Avery. When Avery took control of the Skerth ship, he still used Sirius as a guide. (6.3)

Sister of the Water: See *Calvierri, Rosanna*

Sisters of Plenitude: A superfluity of Catkind nuns who ran the Hospital on New Earth. Amongst their number were Matron Casp, Sisters Jatt and Corvin and Novice Hame. (2.1) After their secret experiments on human clones were exposed, the Sisterhood was presumably disbanded, and Hame sought penance for her sins by devoting her life to looking after the ailing Face of Boe. (3.3)

Sisters of the Infinite Schism: Operated the best hospital in the universe, according to the Doctor, after leaving River Song there to recuperate in the 50th century. (6.8)

Sistine Chapel: Famous Italian house of worship, for which Michelangelo painted the ceiling frieze, watched by the Doctor. (5.10)

6,000,400,026: The number of humans left alive on Earth when the time engine imploded in Colchester. (5.11)

6879760: Using binary 9, Mickey Smith was able to hack into the Cybus Industries computers on 'Pete's World' and access the code which disabled the Cybermen's emotional inhibitors. Having found the code, he texted it to Rose

S

Tyler's mobile, which the Doctor linked into the Cyber Control mainframe, switching the inhibitors off. (2.6)

654: Security code that was used to set up the security field around the Cup of Athelstan in the International Gallery. (4.15)

6018: Designation of the Justice Department Vehicle *Teselecta*. (6.8)

Skaro: Home world to the Daleks and destroyed during the Last Great Time War. One of the Cult of Skaro's aims was to turn Earth into New Skaro. (3.5) Davros also came from there and recalled meeting Sarah Jane Smith there when he first unleashed the Daleks. (4.12, 4.13) The Doctor and Amy Pond travelled there from a devastated Earth in 1963, which the Daleks had invaded by changing time. In the Dalek city, Kalaann, the Dalek Emperor had obtained the Eye of Time and was using it to change history, including the fall of Skaro. The Doctor used a magnetic field generator to disrupt the Eye's power and put history on the right track. (AG01)

Skaro Degradations: Participants in the Time War. (4.17, 4.18)

Skasas Paradigm: A legendary mathematical problem, the solution to which would supply the ability to harness the basic energies that made up the universe and become gods – hence it's colloquial name, the God Maker. The Krillitanes on Earth at Deffry Vale High School, the Chosen Few, sought to enhance the intellect of the children there and have them solve the Paradigm for them. (2.3)

Skeleton Crew: The crew of the *Black Gold* – living skeletons who, according to Captain Kaliko, were cheaper than real people. They turned on their captain at the behest of the first mate, Swabb, in reality an OilCorp spy, but were all lost when the OilCorp rigs attacked the ship. (TIQ)

Skeletor: Villain in the *Masters of the Universe* cartoon and comic book series, with a skull for a head. The Doctor referred to the Master as this when the energy he used to bring himself back to life was disrupted by Lucy Saxon,

resulting in his body burning itself up, causing him to switch between Time Lord and skeletal form irregularly. (4.17)

Skerth: Alien race whose ship was trapped at the same spatial coordinates as the *Fancy* on Earth, neither able to move despite being in different dimensions because of a temporal rift. The Skerth captain had long since died, due to Earth germs, and the medical holographic interface that found his ship and tried to save him moved over to Earth and began bringing back injured pirates to the Skerth ship to heal them. The Skerth ship was eventually adopted by Henry Avery, who flew it back out to the stars. (6.3)

Skinner, Colin: Fiction-writing friend of Ursula Blake and founder member of LINDA. He and Bridget formed a close friendship, and he was devastated when she vanished, although Victor Kennedy told him that they could track her down together through some old phone numbers. In fact, Bridget had been absorbed by Kennedy in his true form as the Abzorbaloff, and Skinner then suffered the same fate, although he remained conscious inside the Abzorbaloff. When he combined with his fellow victims to bloat the Abzorbaloff until he exploded, Skinner died. (2.10) (Played by SIMON GREENALL)

Skintank: The Doctor suggested placing Cassandra's consciousness in one of these rather than in Chip, as her old body and brain had expired. (2.1)

Skorr, Commander (the Bloodbringer): Sontaran Commander in the Tenth Sontaran Battle Fleet and charged with the Earthbound part of the Sontaran stratagem. Cold and ruthless, like all Sontarans, he relished battle and achieved what he perceived to be a glorious death at the hands of Colonel Mace. (4.4, 4.5) (Played by DAN STARKEY)

Skorpius Flies: Ever-hungry alien insects that flew together in formation, resembling a brain and stem. The Doctor and Saruba Velak had to

hide in a box in the Vault until the Skorpius Flies grew weary of looking for them both. (DL)

Skree, Lieutenant: Sontaran officer aboard the Tenth Sontaran Battle Fleet's mothership. He died when it exploded. (4.4, 4.5) (Played by JACK STEED)

Sky-Mast Weather Controller: Device created by Elliot Sardick to give him control of the colony world Ember. It sent a pulse of electrical energy into the fog crystals that existed in Ember's cloud belt, enabling Sardick to manipulate the atmosphere of the entire planet, as well as to influence the fish that lived up there. Its controls were isomorphic, enabling Elliot and after his death his son Kazran to operate them, but no one else. After changing Kazran's past, he convinced Kazran to let the galaxy-class starship the *Thrasymachus* land safely, but because his mind had been altered, the isomorphic controls locked Kazran out, rendering the machine useless. (6.X)

Skylab: Listing things of importance that happened in 1979, the Doctor told Rose Tyler that this space station fell back to Earth, nearly taking his thumb with it. (2.2)

Slabs: Solid leather, animated by rudimentary intelligence, these drones always worked in pairs, and were therefore useful for whoever owned them. A Plasmavore hiding on Earth from Judoon justice sculpted a pair of Slabs into resembling human despatch riders so they could blend into the background at the Royal Hope Hospital, where the Plasmavore was staying. The Doctor destroyed one Slab with an overdose of Roentgen radiation from the hospital's X-ray machine, whilst the other was vaporised by the Judoon. (3.1) (Played by MAT DORMAN, MICHAEL WILLIAMS)

Slade, Rickston: Arrogant, selfish and rude businessman from Sto who had recently sold all his stock in Max Capricorn Cruiseliners. He was aboard the *Titanic* when it was struck by meteoroids, and he was one of the few survivors.

Although ultimately grateful to the Doctor for saving him, he was unaffected by the sacrifices made on his behalf by Astrid Peth, Bannakaffalatta and the Van Hoffs. Once safe, he quickly checked in on his business interests and carried on his life. (4.X) After undergoing a metacrisis, Donna Noble's mind started to overload with information absorbed from the Doctor's memories and Rickston was one of the words she muttered. (4.13) (Played by GRAY O'BRIEN)

Slater: One of Captain Rory Williams's soldiers within Area 52. He wore an Eye Drive to keep him informed at all times of the Silence. He was killed when they escaped their water chambers. (6.13) (Played by LUKE GRAHAME)

Sleep: Coming in varying strengths, this was one of the Mood Patches available in Pharmacytown in the Undercity of New New York. Martha Jones was given a patch when kidnapped by Milo and Cheen to stop her struggling. (3.3)

Slimebait: Lifeform from Sontar, whose natural predator was the speelfox. (4.5)

Slipstream Engine: The method of propulsion the Family Slitheen used in the spaceship they put into a slingshot orbit and brought back down to Earth to crash into Big Ben. (1.4, 1.5)

Slitheen, Blon Fel Fotch Pasameer-Day: One of the Family Slitheen, she murdered MI5 operative Margaret Blaine and used her identity to infiltrate the British government while everyone's attention was diverted by the Big Ben incident. She was responsible for the death of the Prime Minister. (1.4, 1.5) She was the only Slitheen to escape the bombing of 10 Downing Street by activating a short-range teleport device concealed in her earrings and brooch. She ended up on the Isle of Dogs in East London, and later made her way to Cardiff where she became the Mayor, pushing through the

S

Slitheen, Jocrassa Fel Fotch Pasameer-Day:
Leader of the Family Slitheen, he posed as Joseph Green, the Acting Prime Minister of Britain during the Big Ben incident. He then killed a roomful of UNIT experts, military officers and academics gathered to investigate the supposed alien incursion. He was killed when the Doctor arranged for a missile to obliterate 10 Downing Street with Jocrassa Fel Fotch and the rest of his family still inside. (1.4, 1.5) (Played by DAVID VERREY)

Slitheen, Sip Fel Fotch Pasameer-Day:
One of the Family Slitheen, he posed as Assistant Police Commissioner Strickland, investigating Jackie Tyler's claims to have met the Doctor. However, he was killed when, after revealing his true nature to Jackie and her daughter's ex-boyfriend Mickey Smith, they discovered the Slitheen weakness for vinegar and showered him with it, causing him to burst. (1.4, 1.5) (Played by STEVE SPEIRS)

Smilers:
Robotic devices aboard *Starship UK*. Acting as guardians, teachers, information points and sundry other jobs to make the inhabitants lives easier, the Smilers had a dark side. They had three faces: smiling, disappointed and angry – and their actions corresponded with their expressions. Most of them seemed to be just heads and shoulders encased in booths but in fact they were fully mobile and could leave their booths when necessary. Some Smilers were cybernetically attached to the Winders, the more human-looking people who patrolled the streets as policemen. (5.2) (Played by RUARI MEARS and JOE WHITE, voiced by CHRIS PORTER)

construction of the Blaidd Drwg nuclear facility. The scale model of the facility was built upon the back of a tribophysical waveform macro-kinetic extrapolator. Not having the power to use it herself, she was hoping that a nuclear meltdown would supply what she needed to open the space and time rift running through Cardiff and power up the extrapolator. As it turned out, the arrival of the TARDIS and Captain Jack's wiring up of the extrapolator to the TARDIS console supplied the very power she needed. Despite the Doctor's best attempts to get Blon to recognise the error of her ways, she still tried to kill Rose Tyler to ensure the Doctor's compliance. Instead, the extrapolator's power, mixed with that of the rift and of the TARDIS itself, opened up the heart of the TARDIS. Blon gazed into the pure energies of the Time Vortex and was reverted back to an egg. The Doctor took the egg back to Raxacoricofallapatorius in the hope that, reborn, Blon might take a different path. (1.11) (Played by ANNETTE BADLAND)

Smith, Delia:
British television cook, who first appeared regularly on TV in the 1980s, whom the Doctor referred to as one of the greatest chefs on Earth. (TIQ)

Smith, Jackson:
Mickey Smith's father who, before leaving him in the care of Rita-Anne and heading to Spain, worked at a key-cutter's on Clifton Parade. On 'Pete's World', Ricky Smith told the same story. (2.5)

Smith, John:
Regular alias used by the Doctor when on Earth, sometimes just plain 'Mr', sometimes as a 'doctor', either medical or scientific. Arriving amidst the London Blitz on 21 January 1941, he elected to be Doctor John Smith from the Ministry of Asteroids. (1.9) He used it again to pose as a physics teacher at Deffry Vale High School. (2.3) When getting himself admitted as a patient at the Royal Hope Hospital, to investigate the plasma coils that had been placed around the outside of the building, he became a patient called John Smith. (3.1) In Elizabethan England, Martha Jones jokingly continued to call him 'Mr Smith'. (3.2) After turning himself human in an attempt to escape from the Family of Blood, the Doctor actually became a man called John Smith, from Nottingham, who was a history teacher in 1913, at Farringham School for Boys. There he met and fell in love with Nurse Joan Redfern and they even had a glimpse of a future life together involving marriage, children and grandchildren, ending with John's death from old age, in 1963. However, the vision could never come true as John had to turn himself back into the Doctor to defeat the Family of Blood, and thus broke Joan's heart. (3.8, 3.9) It was the name he used as a Health and Safety inspector at

S

|

Adipose Industries. (4.1) It was the name he gave to his fellow passengers aboard the *Crusader 50*, but they dismissed it as an obvious alias. (4.10) He introduced himself as John Smith to Donna Noble after she had lost all her memories of him, (4.18) and to Jackson Lake, while unsure if Jackson was an amnesiac future version of himself. (4.14) His first incarnation's library card gave the name John Smith. (5.6) The Doctor suggested the Gangers referred to his Ganger as John Smith, although it was in fact the real Doctor posing as his own Ganger. (6.6)

Smith, Luke: Sarah Jane Smith's adopted son. In the alternative world where Donna Noble never met the Doctor, he died along with his mum, Clyde Langer and Maria Jackson when facing the Judoon on the moon. (4.11) He, Mr Smith and K-9 helped the Doctor return Earth to its proper place in time and space. (4.12, 4.13) Luke was on the phone to Clyde Langer when he was nearly run over by a car on Bannerman Road, only to be pulled to safety by the Doctor. (4.18) (Played by TOMMY KNIGHT)

Smith, Mickey: Son of Pauline and Jackson Smith, Rose Tyler's on-off boyfriend Mickey initially found himself drawn into the Doctor's world when he was just a young boy, at a point when he hadn't even knowingly met him yet. Attacked by the Reapers in a playground in 1987, this version of Mickey sought refuge in a nearby church. (1.8) He was instinctively drawn to one of the women there for protection – a woman he could always trust, and would never, ever forget: Rose Tyler. . .

As a child, he was abandoned by his mother, with his father disappearing to Spain not long after, leaving Mickey in the care of his blind grandmother, Rita-Anne. Following her death some years later, Mickey left school to become a car mechanic, and moved into a flat on the Powell Estate. When Mickey first encountered the Doctor, he was captured and replicated by the Nestene Consciousness but was later rescued although abandoned on Earth when Rose chose to explore the universe with the Doctor in his TARDIS. (1.1) Mickey didn't date anyone else in Rose's absence, and waited an entire year for her to return. During this time, he was accused by Jackie Tyler of being responsible for her daughter's disappearance, and was taken in for questioning by police five times. He started researching the Doctor, uncovering details of his past visits to Earth,

and his previous involvement with UNIT. When the Doctor and Rose did eventually return to Earth in 2006, Mickey was quickly snubbed by them both, with the Doctor nicknaming him 'Ricky' and 'Mickey the Idiot' in numerous attempts to irritate him. Although initially hesitant to support the Doctor's cause, Mickey was able to use his advanced computer skills to hack into the Royal Navy and UNIT computer systems during the Family Slitheen's fraudulent invasion of Earth, and hijacked a missile, using it to destroy the Slitheen inside Downing Street. (1.4, 1.5) Rose asked him to take her passport to Cardiff, where the TARDIS was refuelling, and he helped her, the Doctor and Captain Jack Harkness defeat the surviving Slitheen, Blon Fel Fotch. (1.11) Mickey was delighted when the Doctor sent Rose home from the Dalek invasion of 200,100, but eventually accepted that her place was with the Doctor and helped her reactivate the TARDIS and return to the Game Station. (1.13) Missing Rose terribly, Mickey took the opportunity instead to keep Jackie company, visiting her every Sunday for dinner, and helping out with odd jobs around the flat. He was with Rose when the TARDIS was transported aboard the Sycorax ship. (2.X) Now accustomed to saying goodbye to Rose, (2.1) Mickey continued to work as a garage mechanic, and considered himself to be the Doctor and Rose's 'Man in Havana', carrying out their surveillance and technical support from afar. In reality, he gradually realised, he was their 'Tin Dog'. Mickey eventually joined Rose and the Doctor aboard the TARDIS following their encounter with the Krillitanes, (2.3) travelling first to a 51st-century spaceship, the SS *Madame de Pompadour*, (2.4) before crash-landing on a parallel version of Earth in the present

day. Mickey later chose to stay behind on 'Pete's World' in order to look after 'his' grandmother following the death of her real grandson, Mickey's alter-ego, Ricky Smith. (2.5, 2.6) He then assisted Pete Tyler and Jake Simmonds in their mission to liberate the world from the remaining Cybermen scattered across the globe, but this attempt was frustrated when the Cybermen used Torchwood technology to travel across the Void and into Rose Tyler's universe. Mickey followed them, masquerading as Samuel in the Torchwood Institute, and was reunited with the Doctor and Rose in the events leading up to the Battle of Canary Wharf. He was then safely transported back to 'Pete's World' before the Doctor sealed the breach between the universes, and he lived with Pete Tyler and his adopted family, Jackie and Rose Tyler. (2. 12, 2.13) He, along with Rose and Jackie used a Dimension Jump to get back to their own universe to help the Doctor stop the Daleks. Transported to the Dalek Crucible with Jackie and Sarah Jane Smith, he narrowly avoided being killed in a testing of the Reality Bomb. His grandmother on 'Pete's World' had passed away, so he remained on his home Earth after the Daleks' defeat, leaving the TARDIS alongside Captain Jack Harkness and Martha Jones. (4.12, 4.13) Some time later, Mickey married Martha and together they worked tracking down dangerous aliens on Earth, including a Sontaran Commander, Jask, who was close to killing them both when the Doctor arrived and stopped him. Mickey and Martha realised this was the very last time they would see the Tenth Doctor – he had come to say goodbye. (4.18) (Played by NOEL CLARKE and CASEY DYER)

Smith, Pauline: Mickey Smith's mother, a victim of the Reapers as they broke into the world after Rose Tyler saved her dad's life and created a breach in time, but presumably restored to life when Pete Tyler healed the wound. (1.8) (Played by MONIQUE ENNIS) Mickey was brought up by his grandmother, Rita-Anne, because Pauline had felt unable to cope, and his father eventually left for Spain. (2.5) However, Mickey was still in semi-regular contact with his mum, so, when Rose thought Mickey had died at the hands of the Nestene Consciousness, she commented that she'd have to tell her of her son's fate. (1.1) On 'Pete's World', Ricky Smith's mother did all the same things that Pauline had done. (2.5, 2.6)

Smith, Ricky: Mickey Smith's counterpart on 'Pete's World'. Physically identical to Mickey, Ricky's life had taken much the same path. He was left in the care of his grandmother, Rita-Anne, when his mother walked out and his father, Jackson, went to Spain. Where their lives diverged was in that Rita-Anne was still alive, and Ricky was London's Most Wanted . . . for unpaid parking tickets. After Thin Jimmy's capture, Ricky became de facto leader of the Preachers and grudgingly accepted that they had to take Mickey with them. Together they tried to escape the pursuing Cybermen near Bridge Street, but Ricky was killed, leaving Mickey to overcome the hostility of Jake Simmonds, the remaining member of the Preachers, who reckoned Mickey could never replace Ricky. (2.5, 2.6) (Played by NOEL CLARKE)

Smith, Sarah Jane: A journalist who claimed to be writing a profile for the *Sunday Times* of Hector Finch and the amazing performance of Deffry Vale High School's students since his arrival as Headmaster. In truth, she was investigating for the same reasons as the Doctor, Rose Tyler and Mickey Smith – UFO sightings three months previously. Some years before, she had travelled with the Doctor, eventually leaving him abruptly when he had been summoned back to his home planet. He later left her a gift of K-9 Mark III, but that had not been enough for Sarah, who had found it difficult to go back to a normal life. After initial hostility between her and Rose, the two became friends, although Sarah tried to warn Rose of the dangers of believing that she would travel with the Doctor for ever. (2.3) In the alternative world where Donna Noble never met the Doctor, Sarah Jane, along with her adopted son Luke and his friends Clyde Langer and Maria Jackson went to the moon in the Royal Hope Hospital to face the Judoon and all four of them died. (4.11) When the Daleks invaded Earth to take people away for their Reality Bomb experiments, Sarah left Luke with Mr Smith and K-9 while she, Jackie Tyler and Mickey Smith were transported to the Dalek Crucible. There she met Captain Jack Harkness and Donna Noble and was reunited with the Doctor and Rose Tyler. Another shock for her was once again meeting the Daleks' creator, Davros, who thought it ironic they had met at both the beginning and the culmination of his campaigns. After the Daleks and Davros were defeated, Sarah went home to Luke. (4.12, 4.13) Alerted by Luke one

afternoon, Sarah Jane saw the Doctor on Bannerman Road and realised he had come to say goodbye because he was going to regenerate soon. (4.18) (Played by ELISABETH SLADEN)

Smith, Sydney: In the fiction the Doctor created for John Smith, John believed his father was a watchmaker, from Nottingham. (3.8)

Smith, Verity: In the fiction the Doctor created for John Smith, John believed his mother had been a nurse. (3.8)

Smythe: Schoolboy at Farringham School for Boys in 1913, who took part in the war games there, manning the Vickers Gun. (3.8)

Sneed, Gabriel: Undertaker that the Doctor and Rose Tyler met in Cardiff in 1869. His work had been disrupted by what appeared to be ghosts inhabiting the bodies of the recently deceased and making them walk. In fact, this was an alien species who called themselves the Gelth. They sought bodies to inhabit as they crossed to Earth via a rift, before beginning their intended conquest of the planet. One of the bodies they inhabited was Sneed's, killing him in the process. (1.3) (Played by ALAN DAVID)

Sneed and Company: Cardiff-based firm of undertakers in the 1860s, situated at 7 Temperance Court, Llandaff. It was blown up when the possessed maid Gwyneth lit a match to destroy the gaseous Gelth that occupied the premises. (1.3)

Snell, Mr: Teacher at Farringham School for Boys who Mr Rocastle told to contact the police before the Family of Blood attacked. (3.9)

'Snow White and the Seven Keys to Doomsday': Allegedly a classic bedtime story from the Doctor's childhood. He tried to interest the Tenza child, 'George', in hearing it. (6.9)

Socialist Worker: Posters advertising this newspaper, decrying Margaret Thatcher as Prime Minister of Great Britain and Northern Ireland, were on a wall close to where Rose Tyler watched her father's death, near Jordan Road outside the Brandon Estate. (1.8)

Sol 3: Name by which the Spacelane Traffic Advisers referred to Earth when warning interstellar travellers to stay away after the Toclafane had arrived – Sol 3 was considered to be entering its Terminal Extinction and was therefore closed. (3.13) The travellers from Sto aboard the *Titanic* knew Earth as Sol 3, too. (4.X)

Solace: Mountain range on the continent of Wild Endeavour, on the planet Gallifrey. The domed citadel of the Time Lords was situated between it and the mountain Solitude. It was destroyed along with the rest of Gallifrey at the end of the Last Great Time War. (3.12)

Solar Flares: The Controller of the Game Station used these to mask her conversation with the Doctor. She continued to give him the Daleks' coordinates after the solar flares had ended, and was exterminated as a result. (1.12)

Soldier [1]: On 'Pete's World', Mickey encountered this soldier at a roadblock when he went in search of his grandmother's house. (2.5) (Played by ANDREW UFONDO)

Soldier [2]: Human fighter on Messaline who was guarding the Doctor, Jenny and Donna Noble. (4.6) (Played by OLALEKAN LAWAL JR)

Soldier [3]: Young army officer in Leeds who was trying to disarm the ATMOS devices in the army vehicles in the alternative world where Donna Noble never met the Doctor. He believed he saw something on Donna's back. (4.11) (Played by PAUL RICHARD BIGGIN)

Soldier with clipboard: Army officer in Leeds who told the Noble family they had been billeted to live in a terraced house in the alternative world where Donna Noble never met the Doctor. (4.11) (Played by LAWRENCE STEVENSON)

Soldiers: Members of the US military based at Area 51 in Roswell. A couple of them took the Doctor, Cassie Rice and Jimmy Stalkingwolf to meet Colonel Stark, others tried to stop the Endymide ship from leaving the base and later fought the Viperox Horde. (DL) (Voiced by RYAN McCLUSKEY, CLARKE PETERS and ALEX MALLINSON)

Solitude [1]: Mountain range on the continent of Wild Endeavour on the planet Gallifrey. The domed citadel of the Time Lords was situated between it and the mountain Solace. It was destroyed along with the rest of Gallifrey at the end of the Last Great Time War. (3.12)

Solitude [2]: Deserted American town in Nevada. Deep below its empty streets was the Viperox Queen, constantly giving birth to new Viperox Warriors. (DL)

Solomon: The Hooverville in Manhattan's Central Park was run by former soldier Solomon. He ruled with strength but compassion and often led by example – he went with the Doctor, Martha Jones and a young Hooverville inhabitant, Frank, into the sewers, to earn a dollar from Mr Diagoras for a day's work. Solomon soon discovered that terrifying, inhuman events were occurring under the streets of Manhattan but, after Frank was lost to the Pig Slaves, he returned to Hooverville to prepare his people for battle. When the Doctor returned to Hooverville with a rescued Frank, Solomon tried to reason with the pursuing Daleks, but Dalek Caan exterminated him. (3.4, 3.5) (Played by HUGH QUARSHIE)

Son of Mine: Malicious and malevolent member of the Family of Blood, who saw the death and destruction they wrought as sport. He took on the body of schoolboy Jeremy Baines and infiltrated the school, hoping to sniff out the Doctor, whose body he wanted to inhabit and so live for ever. Not realising the Doctor had made himself wholly human, the Family followed him to the village dance, hoping to expose him. Son of Mine murdered the doorman and had both Martha Jones and Joan Redfern threatened with execution unless the Doctor changed back into a Time Lord. But the person they were dealing with believed himself to be John Smith, a teacher at the school, and couldn't understand what they wanted. Son of Mine then led an attack on the school using the Scarecrows he had created using molecular fringe animation. Not realising he wasn't dealing with Baines, Rocastle, the Headmaster, challenged Son of Mine, who then murdered the bursar, Mr Phillips, to demonstrate he meant business. After failing to get the Doctor to change, Son of Mine decided to flush him out by bombing the village from the spaceship. John Smith then arrived, offering up the fob watch which contained the Doctor's life essence, but Son of Mine discovered firstly that it was empty and was just a watch again, and secondly that the Doctor had already reasserted himself and had tricked the Family. He overloaded the ship's systems and Son of Mine led his Family out just before it blew up. The Doctor then captured him and trapped him, immobile, within one of his Scarecrows and left Son of Mine watching over one of England's fields for eternity. (3.8, 3.9) (Played by HARRY LLOYD)

Song, River: The daughter of Amy Pond and Rory Williams, whose birth name was Melody Pond. In the language of the people of the Gamma Forest, where the older River spent some time, there was no literal translation for 'Melody Pond' – 'River Song' was the closest they had. River remains one of the few people the Doctor has met who could fly the TARDIS better than him (the TARDIS taught her itself because of where she was conceived) and to know the Doctor's true name. When the Silence and the Academy of the Question learned that Amy was pregnant, the baby having been conceived whilst the TARDIS travelled through the space/time vortex, they arranged for Madame Kovarian to kidnap Amy, placing a Ganger version, made from the Flesh, aboard the TARDIS — psychically linked to the real Amy, who was now a prisoner on Demon's Run. That way, the Ganger Amy believed it was the real one, and the real one experienced all that the Ganger one did. The Silence and the Academy of the Question wanted to create a weapon to destroy the Doctor — and the human/Time Lord hybrid that was Melody Pond was the perfect opportunity as she was a human who would have certain Gallifreyan traits, including extraordinary strength and the ability to regenerate. After Melody was born, she was taken to Florida on Earth by Kovarian, and left there in the 1960s, in a ramshackle orphanage, Graystark Hall, overseen by Doctor Renfrew and the Silence that guarded her. The Silence arranged for humanity to go to the moon and thus develop protective spacesuits, which they needed to keep Melody locked inside for her own safety. When the Doctor, and her parents, along with the future version of herself arrived in 1969, the child Melody ripped her way out of the spacesuit and fled to New York. Exhausted and injured, she regenerated for the first time. Around 25 years later, in the form of a 7-year-old girl who now called herself Melody 'Mels' Zucker, she befriended both Amy Pond

and Rory Williams when she grew up alongside them in Leadworth (Amy called her baby Melody after her, not realising the irony), learning about the Doctor due to Amy's obsession with her 'raggedy Doctor'. Forever getting into trouble with authority, Mels eventually stole a car and was being chased by the police when she encountered the Doctor, Amy and Rory in a field. She took the chance to go aboard the TARDIS but shot the Time Rotor, releasing lethal gases into the ship and causing it to fly erratically through time, to 1938. There, it crashed into the chancellery of the Nazi Party in Berlin, and the time travellers encountered Adolf Hitler. Hitler, alarmed by an attempt on his life by the crew of the *Teselecta*, tried to shoot the assassin that had been sent to get him but instead mortally wounded Mels, causing her to regenerate again, this time into what the Doctor recognised as River Song. The Silence and the Academy of the Question had implanted in Mels's mind a post-hypnotic suggestion that she was to kill the Doctor as quickly as possible, which the newly regenerated River did with Judas Tree poisoned lipstick. Later, as the Doctor died in front of her, she realised her mistake and gave the rest of her regeneration cycle to him, saving his life. Injured in the process, the Doctor left her in the 51st century, giving her a TARDIS-shaped diary into which she would write her future meetings with him. She studied at the Luna University under Professor Candy, getting her doctorate in archaeology. A century later, whilst researching the Doctor's positive effect on other people's lives, she was kidnapped again by Kovarian, the Silents and the Clerics, and placed, as an adult, back inside the spacesuit at Lake Silencio, Utah, in 2011. There, she finally did what she had been conditioned to do, and shot the Doctor. However, aware that she could also influence time, River actually altered her shot, didn't kill him and instead created an alternative reality, where time was forever stuck at 5.02pm on 22/04/11. In this new world, Rome never fell and the UK was led by the Emperor Churchill, with the Doctor kept as a mad soothsayer in a cell. River teamed up with Amy and an amnesiac Rory to oversee a base in Egypt, where a number of Silence were kept in water tanks, and this alternative universe's version of Madame Kovarian was a prisoner. River had arranged for the races of the universe that were in debt to the Doctor to find a way to save him from his pre-destined

S

travelled to Amy and Rory's wedding, to help jog Amy's memory into bringing the Doctor back to the universe, and suggested afterwards to the Doctor that they were possibly married. After being freed from Stormcage, she gained the title Professor, and the Doctor later took her to the planet Darillium where he gave her an adapted version of his old sonic screwdriver, with a neural relay in it. This was because he knew that the next time they met, at The Library, she was destined to die, saving his previous incarnation, who had had no idea who she was. That earlier Doctor was able to store River's memories and personality and place them inside The Library's central processor, CAL, where she and the rest of her archaeological team that had died there were able to carry on their lives as solidified data ghosts – River now having three children (including the avatar of Charlotte Abigail Lux) to bring up. Davros taunted the Doctor about how many people had died trying to help him over the years, and this made the Doctor think of River. (4.8, 4.9, 4.13, 5.4, 5.5, 5.12, 5.13, 6.1, 6.2, 6.7, 6.8. 6.12, 6.13) (Played by LAYNA MONTICELLI, HARRISON MORTIMER, MADDISON MORTIMER, SYDNEY WADE, MAYA GLACE-GREEN, NINA TOUSSAINT-WHITE and ALEX KINGSTON)

death, and the Doctor and River appeared to get married. The Doctor apparently whispered two things to River – his true name, so that other versions of him would know to trust her, and also the secret behind the Doctor she should have murdered in Utah – it was a *Teselecta* Justice Vehicle camouflaged to look like him. Knowing this, River allowed time to go back on its rightful path, the Doctor appeared to die in Utah, and she was taken back to the 51st century and locked away in the Stormcage facility. She frequently escaped it, often returning happily after whatever escapades she had, either alone or with the Doctor. These included trips to Asgard, Planet One, *Starship UK*, and then to Earth where she pretended to be Cleopatra and helped stop the Pandorica Alliance, ice skating on the Thames in 1814, trips to the Maldovarium (where she got a Vortex Manipulator to enable her to travel through time alone), the Bone Meadows and the Delerium Archive and even an adventure with Jim the Fish and his dam-building exercise, plus an extended period when she dated an Auton. At one point she was employed by the Clerics to trace a Weeping Angel aboard the galaxy-class ship the *Byzantium*, but the ship crashed on Alfava Metraxis and, keeping her identity secret from Amy, she worked alongside her mother and the Doctor to stop the Angels. On her way back to the Stormcage from Alfava Metraxis, she stopped off on Earth in the 21st century to see Amy and Rory and let them know the truth about the Doctor's death in Utah, and therefore that he was still alive. She later received a letter from the Doctor inviting her to witness her younger self killing him, and escaped Stormcage once again. On her birthday, River went to Demon's Run, but only after baby Melody, her younger self, had been kidnapped, knowing that her time with the Doctor was coming to an end. She later

Song of the Ood, the: The mental union that connected all the Ood via their three brains was signified by a sorrowful song that only the Doctor could hear properly until he allowed Donna Noble to link into his mind. After the Ood were freed from enslavement, the song became a much happier one. (4.3)
The Doctor heard it as he approached the end of his tenth incarnation. (4.16, 4.18)

Sonic blaster: Captain Jack Harkness had one of these multi-grade guns, which the Doctor recognised as being of 51st-century construction. It was manufactured in the weapon factories of Villengard and operated on a digital basis, meaning it could reverse the damage it did. Its one weakness was that it was battery-powered. (1.10) River Song had an identical weapon, possibly taken from the TARDIS at some point in the Doctor's future. (4.8, 4.9)

Sonic cane: The Doctor carried one of these in Berlin, in 1938, after River Song poisoned him. (6.8)

Sonic pen: Device used by Matron Cofelia. Familiar with sonic technology, the fact that the Doctor had a sonic screwdriver implied to her that he too was an alien. (4.1)

Sonic screwdriver: Gallifreyan technological device carried by the Doctor, which has been used in an amazing variety of ways. It has unlocked doors (not deadlocks or wood though). It has scanned people to determine a species or identify medical flaws. It has increased or

decreased the power levels of other objects. With numerous settings or apps as the Doctor refers to them, easily controlled at the flick of a thumb, it has been used by Time Lord and humans alike. The Doctor lost one sonic screwdriver after destroying a Slab with Roentgen radiation (the sonic tried), and another when he burnt it out trying to attract the Atraxi in Leadworth, but he quickly replaced them. Just as he would be lost without his TARDIS or companions, the Doctor would be lost without his sonic screwdriver.

Sonic screwdriver (fake):
Jackson Lake, believing himself to be the Doctor, had a sonic screwdriver that was, in fact, an ordinary screwdriver. (4.14)

Sontaran Stratagem One:
The ultimate stratagem in the Sontaran war effort – a 'scorched earth' policy by which they would destroy a planet that they had failed to bring under their control, even at the cost of their own lives. General Staal adopted this after the Doctor stopped their attempt to turn Earth into a clone breeding planet. (4.4, 4.5)

Sontarans:
Cloned warrior species from the planet Sontar. The Sontarans numbered their forces in millions, with thousands of new cloned warriors hatching every few minutes. The Sontarans had been at war for millennia against the Rutan host and were bred for war and nothing else. Dying in battle was the ultimate honour, and without honour Sontarans saw no point in existing. Each Sontaran had only one weakness – the Probic Vent on the back of the neck of his armour, through which nutrients were fed. If struck, this could stun and immobilise a warrior – meaning that a Sontaran trooper would never turn his back on an enemy. Because of their love of war, the Sontarans were devastated to be ostracised by those involved in the Last Great Time War and unable to take part. The Tenth Sontaran Battle Fleet, under the leadership of General Staal, planned to transform Earth into a colony world for Sontaran clone breeding tanks, but this plan was foiled by the Doctor, Donna Noble and Martha Jones, fighting alongside UNIT. (4.4, 4.5) As she saw her mother and fiancé change into the Master in front of her, Donna remembered the Sontarans as her repressed memories started to come back. (4.17) A Sontaran Commander, Jask, threatened Martha Jones and Mickey Smith until the Doctor dealt with him. (4.18) The Doctor cited his defeat of the Sontarans as a reason for the Atraxi to be afraid of him. (5.1) A troop of Sontarans, led by Commander Strak, travelled to Stonehenge, as part of the Pandorica Alliance. When the Pandorica opened and history was stopped, the Alliance were reduced to fossils. (5.12, 5.13) Sontaran Commander Strax, forced to work as a nurse to his human enemies at the insistence of the Doctor, later teamed up with the Time Lord to defend Amy Pond on Demon's Run, but died during the battle. (6.7) A troop led by Field Major Kaarsh were on Earth in 1605. (AGO5)

Soon, Uncle:
Relative of Adelaide Brooke who popped in occasionally to check up on Emily and Susie while Adelaide was on Mars. (4.16)

Soothsayer: Member of the Sibylline Sisterhood, who saw the TARDIS materialise in the Pompeii market square and reported this to Spurrina and her other sisters. She was killed when Vesuvius erupted the following day. (4.2) (Played by KAREN GILLAN)

Sorvin: Commander of the Tritovore commerce ship that crashed on San Helios. He was killed by a Stingray, buying time for the Doctor and Lady Christina de Souza to escape back to their bus. (4.15) (Played by PAUL KASEY)

'Sound of Thunder, A': Sci-fi short story by Ray Bradbury in which a time traveller crushes a butterfly in prehistoric times and finds his world changed when he returns to the future. Martha Jones asked the Doctor if it was safe to travel through Elizabethan England in case she did something similar. (3.2)

Source, the: A third-generation terraforming device, brought to Messaline by a colony ship of humans and Hath. However, after the ship crashed and the two races separated, myths grew up about the source. It was believed that a fragment of breath from the goddess known as the Great One was contained within the Source, and would bring life to Messaline, and that whoever had access to it controlled the destiny of the planet. The Doctor activated the Source and Messaline began an accelerated terraforming procedure, as the original colonists had planned. (4.6)

South Africa: Country that Hutchinson, House Captain at Farringham School for Boys, heard that his father might be moving to. Timothy Latimer's uncle had been there, in Johannesburg, on a six-month posting and loved it. (3.8) A lightning strike in South Africa once brought down a Toclafane, and Martha Jones had gained access to the readings, so that a similar electrical pulse could be generated to stop another one. (3.13) Unlike the Britain of the alternative world where Donna Noble never met the Doctor where there was a fuel shortage, South Africa was choked by ATMOS gas. (4.11)

Southampton: Hampshire city with famous docks, from which the RMS *Titanic* sailed for New York. A local family, the Daniels, were supposed to be aboard but were apparently stopped from travelling by their friend, the Doctor. (1.1)

Southwark: Region of South London. The Powell Estate where Jackie and Rose Tyler lived was part of Southwark. (1.1) The Carrionites were based there, in Allhallows Street, close to the Globe theatre. (3.2)

Southwark Cathedral: 13th-century London cathedral, and the first Gothic church in the capital, it was a place where Londoners fled for safety during the Blitz of the Second World War. Amongst those Londoners was a young Richard Lazarus, and the positioning of his LazLabs building in full view of his beloved cathedral was not accidental. After Lazarus had been changed by his GMD, he took refuge in the cathedral, but went on an attempted killing spree once more. The Doctor used the church organ, boosted by his sonic screwdriver, to create a hypersonic wave that disorientated the Lazarus Creature, which fell to its death on the cathedral floor, the professor's transformation reversed. (3.6)

Soviet Union: See *Russia*

Space Florida: A holiday destination where the beaches cleaned themselves. It was visited by the Doctor and Amy Pond a week before finding River Song's message on Planet One. (5.13)

Space Pig: A common-or-garden Earth pig, which was augmented by Slitheen technology, dressed in a spacesuit and sent into space in a ship, the trajectory of which guaranteed it would come crashing down in Central London. The resultant panic enabled the Family Slitheen to take control of the British government. The space pig was taken to Albion Hospital, where Toshiko Sato and the Doctor tried to help it. Terrified, it ran squealing down a corridor towards a nervous Army soldier, who shot it dead. (1.4) (Played by JIMMY VEE)

Space Pirates: Mercenaries employed by the Viperox Horde to ensure Saruba Velak never survived her ambassadorial mission to Earth. They shot her ship down, but Saruba Velak survived. (DL)

S

Spacelane 77: Closed due to solar flares ranged at 5.9 according to Channel ☺+1 (1.7)

Spacelink Project: Set up by the Spanish space agency before 2059 but kept very secret. (4.16)

Spain: European country where Jackson Smith went after leaving his son, Mickey, with Rita-Anne. On 'Pete's World', the same circumstances had led to Ricky Smith living with his version of Rita-Anne. (2.5) Donna Noble was on a scuba-diving holiday in Spain when the Cybermen and Daleks came through the Void, so remained unaware of both the invasion and the Battle of Canary Wharf. (3.X) In 2059, Spain had a space agency, who Andrew Stone's sister worked for. (4.16)

Spanish Maid: Worker at the Firbourne House Hotel where the Noble family spent Christmas in the alternative world where Donna never met the Doctor. She believed she saw something on Donna's back. (4.11) (Played by LORAINE VELEZ)

Sparrow, Sally: Amateur photographer with an eye for things old and decrepit, she snuck into Wester Drumlins, an old deserted house in London, to take some photos. She was astonished to find that behind some wallpaper was a message for her, apparently written in 1969 by someone called the Doctor, warning her about the Weeping Angels. Sally came back the next day with her mate, Kathy Nightingale, but their exploration was interrupted by the arrival of a man with a letter for Sally. Just as the man identified himself to Sally as Kathy's grandson, Kathy herself vanished. Looking for Kathy, Sally found a key in the hand of one of the Weeping Angel statues. The letter purported to be from Kathy, who said she had been transported to 1920. Kathy's brother had some DVDs with a bizarre one-way conversation from a man calling himself the Doctor. He told her that this half-message had been hidden on 17 DVDs, and gave her a list of their titles. Deciding to report Kathy's disappearance to the police, Sally met DI Billy Shipton, the officer in charge of investigating a series of disappearances from Wester Drumlins. Billy showed her a number of cars, all of which had been abandoned at the old house, their owners vanished, alongside an old-fashioned police box. As she left, she wondered whether the key she had found might fit the police box but, when she returned to the car pound, she discovered that Billy had now vanished too, only to call her moments later from hospital, 40 years older and dying. Sally realised that the discs containing the one-way conversation were in fact the 17 DVDs that she owned. With Kathy's Doctor-obsessed brother, Larry, she returned to Wester Drumlins and discovered that the messages were actually a two-way conversation between the Doctor and herself about the Weeping Angels – lethal assassins that could send people into the past if they weren't being watched. The Angels attacked, but she and Larry made their way to the TARDIS, which dematerialised around them – leaving the Weeping Angels trapped. A year later, Larry and Sally had set up a shop together, but still the mystery remained – why had she been the one the Doctor had contacted? Then she saw the Doctor and Martha, who had no idea who she was. Sally gave him all her notes, realising that she was setting off the chain of events leading to what had already

happened. Sally was then able to resume her normal life, hopefully with Larry Nightingale tagging along. (3.10) (Played by CAREY MULLIGAN) The Doctor mentioned her, hoping that might jog Jackson Lake's memories when he was claiming to be the Doctor. (4.14)

Sparrow and Nightingale: When Kathy Nightingale and Sally Sparrow first went to Wester Drumlins, Kathy suggested they should form a detective agency called Sparrow and Nightingale, which Sally thought was 'a bit ITV'. A year later, Sally had opened an antiquarian book and rare DVD store with Kathy's brother, Larry, and that was the name they chose for it. (3.10)

Sparrow Lane: Organisation that put on coach tours for the over 50s. Oliver Barnes drove one of their minibuses to collect the Silver Cloak on Christmas Eve. (4.17)

Spartacus: Roman slave and subject of a movie in 1960. The Doctor and Donna Noble used the name in Pompeii, where people assumed they were brother and sister. (4.2)

S

Speelfox: Life form from Sontar, whose natural prey was slimebait. (4.5)

Spencer, Lady Diana: When Pete Tyler got Jackie's name wrong in their wedding vows, Jackie suggested they carry on, citing a similar incident at Lady Di's wedding where she had got Prince Charles's name wrong. (1.8)

Sphere Chamber: Area in the Torchwood Tower where the Sphere, or Void Ship, was stored, overseen by Dr Singh. It later became the location for the initial battle between the Cybermen, Daleks and Jake Simmonds' forces. (2.12, 2.13)

Spiders: Robotic creatures employed by Cassandra aboard Platform One to monitor the other guests and then sabotage the space station, thus contriving a hostage situation, apparently masterminded by Cassandra's other robotic slaves, the Adherents of the Repeated Meme. (1.2) Cassandra used robot spiders again, when hidden away on New Earth, to observe the Doctor and Rose's arrival there. (2.1)

Spike Rooms: Satellite Five had a number of these on its many Floors. They were areas where journalists could link, via technological implants in their foreheads, into the network of news channels and, at the speed of thought, process news to be broadcast throughout the Earth Empire. (1.7) A century later, by when the space station had become the Game Station, many of the Spike Rooms had become either storage rooms or been converted into studios. (1.12, 1.13)

Spinning Wheel, the: South East London pub where Jackie Tyler arranged to meet Tina the Cleaner to take part in a pub quiz. (2.10)

Spion Kop: A battleground in Africa, during the Boer War. Joan Redfern's husband Oliver died there. (3.8)

Spragg, Howie: Young, grungy human, trapped in the God Complex. He was obsessed with conspiracy theories and generally distrusted everyone. He was

posting a blog when he was transported to the prison along with Rita, Joe and Gibbis. His biggest fear was being ridiculed by girls for his nerdishness, but it was his conviction and faith in his conspiracy theories that eventually made him a victim of the Minotaur which guarded the holographic prison, and he died there. (6.11) (Played by DIMITRI LEONIDAS)

Spray Painter: A young lad on the Powell Estate who painted the words 'BAD WOLF' on the side of the TARDIS. The Doctor later made him clean them off again. (1.4, 1.5) (Played by COREY DOABE)

Springfield, Dusty: Iconic English singer, born Mary O'Brien, popular from the 1960s and beyond her death in 1999. Both Jimmy Wicks and Rory Williams's mum were huge fans. According to the Doctor, 'Who isn't?' (6.5)

Spurrina: Leader of the Sibylline Sisterhood, who answered only to the High Priestess. As with all the Sisters, she was slowly becoming living rock due to her inhaling Pyrovillian dust, and her gifts of accurate prophesy were actually gained due to her psychic bond with the aliens. She, along with all the other Sisters, died when Vesuvius erupted. (4.2) (Played by SASHA BEHAR)

'Squareness Gun': Rose Tyler's description of Jack Harkness's sonic blaster. (1.10)

Squawk: Caw's son – the metal bird was given to Martha disguised as a brooch, with which Caw and Baltazar could track the TARDIS's journeys as it searched out the datachips required to locate the *Infinite*. Squawk grew up to be a living metal bird just like his cunning father and, over three years trapped on Volag-Noc, was trained by the Doctor to work for him instead. When the *Infinite* was destroyed and Baltazar trapped on the decaying asteroid, Squawk, as the Doctor had instructed, collected Baltazar and returned him to Volag-Noc to be incarcerated there. (TIQ) (Voiced by TOBY LONGWORTH)

Staal, General (the Undefeated): Commander of the Tenth Sontaran Battle Fleet and leader of the project to turn Earth into a Sontaran clone-breeding world. He enlisted the help of arrogant human genius Luke

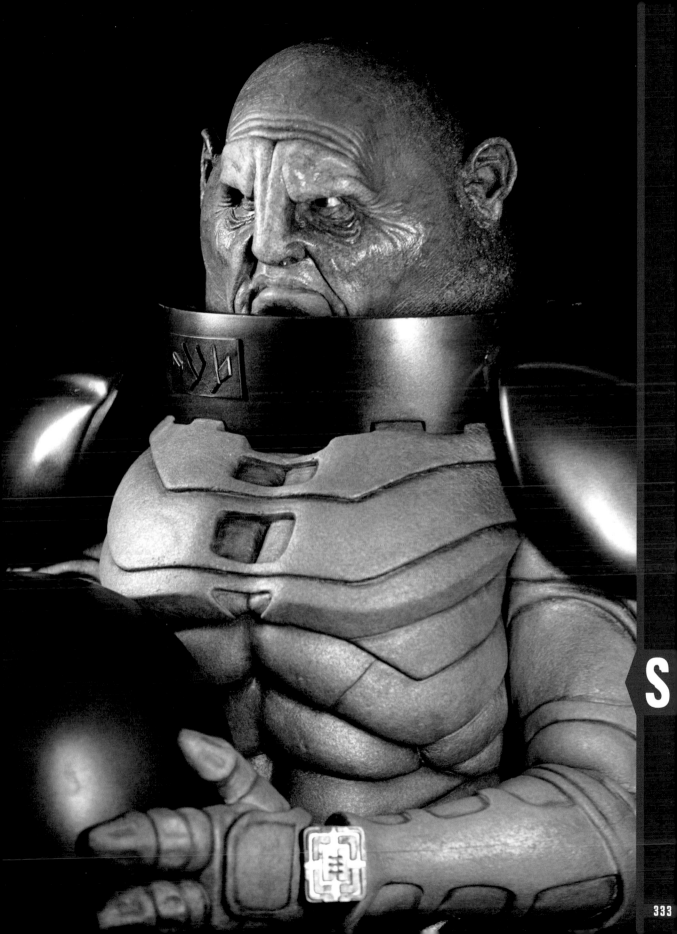

Rattigan, playing on his ego and ambition, and adapted Rattigan's ATMOS to put Caesofine gas into Earth's atmosphere. When the Doctor stopped this plan, Staal was proud to let the Doctor kill him, but was furious when it was Luke Rattigan and not the Doctor who finally defeated him and blew him, his Sontarans and their spaceship to pieces. (4.4, 4.5) (Played by CHRISTOPHER RYAN)

Stage Manager: A worker at the Taliesin Lodge where Charles Dickens was reading *A Christmas Carol*, it was his job to get Dickens on stage to begin his reading. (1.3) (Played by WAYNE CATER)

Stage 1 Disinfection: Anyone entering the Wards in the Hospital on New Earth had to go through disinfection in the elevators before they could approach the patients. (2.1)

Stalag Luft 14: Second World War prisoner of war camp in Germany, which the Doctor led a group of prisoners in an escape from. The Doctor's tunnelling expertise was a bit off, as the tunnel led directly into the Commandant's office. Amy Pond and Rory Williams read about this incident in the book *Myths and Historical Impossibilities*. (6.1)

Stalin, Josef: Leader of the Communist Party of the Soviet Union, who had seen his country through to victory against Nazi Germany during the Second World War. He was reviled by the West, however, which saw Communism as a major threat to world peace. The Doctor cited Stalin's Russia as being where he would have expected to see the police abducting people in the night, as opposed to London's Muswell Hill in 1953. Stalin was actually no longer in charge of Russia when the Doctor made the comment, having died three months earlier, power having ceded to Nikita Khrushchev. (2.7)

Stalkingwolf, Jimmy: Shoshoni Native American, who was friends with Cassie Rice and hung out at Sammy's Pitstop, the diner where Cassie worked, in Dry Springs. When android Men in Black attacked the diner, Jimmy, along with

Cassie, became embroiled with the Doctor and the alien Viperox at Area 51 in Roswell. Jimmy's grandfather, Night Eagle, introduced the Doctor to an injured Endymide called Rivesh Mantilax, and Jimmy was later captured by the Viperox leader, Azlok. After the Viperox had been defeated by the Doctor, Jimmy and Cassie returned to Dry Springs and the diner. (DL) (Voiced by TIM HOWAR)

Stallholder: Market trader in Pompeii who sold the TARDIS to Lobos Caecilius in AD 79 for 15 sestertii. He was killed when Vesuvius erupted the next day. (4.2) (Played by PHIL CORNWALL)

Stan: A mate of Mickey Smith, who might have put him and Rose up after the first attack by the Roboform Santas. (2.X)

Stanford University: Californian university attended by Mia Bennett. (4.16)

Staniland, Craig: Telesales worker at Adipose Industries who Donna pestered to get a list of customers from. (4.1) (Played by RACHID SABITRI)

Star Trek: American TV sci-fi series that ran from 1966 to 1969. Rose Tyler wanted the Doctor's methods to be a bit more like those of Mr Spock, the Vulcan, from it. (1.9) The Doctor taught Chloe Webber the Vulcan salute. (2.11) When White House worker Joy saw a Silent, she assumed it was her colleague Ben wearing a *Star Trek* mask. (6.1) Craig Owens likened the Cybermen's teleporter to the Starship *Enterprise*'s transporter. (6.12)

Star Wars: 1977 movie. The Doctor did not consider it to be a good example of an 'escaping from difficult predicaments' movie. (DL)

Star whale: Mammoth mammal that could survive in the vacuum of space. Possibly the very last of its kind, it came to Earth to offer its help evacuating the population, because it heard the cries of the children. The humans mistook its reasons and imprisoned it, hooking its brain up to *Starship UK*'s propulsion units and forcing it to fly through space, in constant great pain. Amy Pond realised that it would do the same thing happily, without being forced, so long as there were children aboard, and the star whale was released from the mechanisms. It chose to stay and carried *Starship UK* onward through space. (5.2)

Stark, Colonel: Commander of the Dreamland US military base in 1958. Believing the Viperox would help him protect America from the Soviet menace, he allowed them free rein around the local area. The Doctor was able to show Stark that Azlok, the Viperox commander, had lied to him and had no intention of upholding his end of the bargain. Stark then led his men in an attack on the Viperox Horde and, with the Doctor's help, was able to drive them off the planet. (DL) (Voiced by STUART MILLIGAN)

'Starman': Top ten hit for David Bowie in 1972. When the Doctor was trying to sneak quietly away from the Tylers' flat on the Powell Estate, the song was being played by one of their neighbours. (1.4)

Starr, Ringo: Drummer with the Beatles (real name Richard Starkey). The Doctor was disappointed that Amy Pond preferred to meet John Lennon rather than Starr. (AG01)

Stars in their Eyes: One of the programmes broadcast from the Game Station. Losing contestants would be blinded. (1.12)

Starship UK: Massive spacecraft made up from a variety of smaller ships, linked together and moved through space on the back of a massive star whale. Scotland wasn't part of *Starship UK*, as its people had wanted their own spaceship. (5.2)

Statue of Liberty: The TARDIS landed at the base of this New York landmark on 1 November 1930. (3.4, 3.5)

Steino-Magnetic tool: A tool the Doctor used to construct a portable scanner to help him find the Isolus Podship. (2.11)

Stephen's Point: Organisation that looked after London's homeless who were living on the streets. One of their volunteers, Sarah, had a burger van from which she gave food out to people like Tommo and Ginger. (4.17)

Stet Radiation: Below the Silo base on Malcassairo, stet radiation was being used to power the rocket's drives. Utterly lethal to humans (though it left

S

clothing intact), when the Futurekind's Wiry Woman turned the power off, Guard Jate was instantly vaporised by it. (3.11)

Steve: A journalist friend of Suki Macrae Cantrell's aboard Satellite Five. (1.7)

Steven: Student who answered the time engine avatar's call for help at 79B Aickman Road and was unintentionally killed, ultimately adding to the stain on Craig Owens's ceiling below. (5.11) (Played by OWEN DONOVAN)

Steven, Uncle: Guest at the wedding of his nephew Stuart Hoskins and Sarah Clark. He hadn't arrived, and neither had his wife Lynn. (1.8)

Steve-o: One of Mickey Smith's co-workers at Clancy's Garage. (2.X) (Played by PAUL ZEPH GOULD)

Stevie: Party guest at the Tyler household on 'Pete's World', when they were celebrating Jackie Tyler's birthday. Pete Tyler asked him about his work at Torchwood. (2.5)

Steward [1]: Blue-skinned Crespallion official aboard Platform One charged with overseeing the Earthdeath event. He was killed when Cassandra's robot spiders sabotaged the Control computer, resulting in the sunfliters outside his office lowering and vaporising him. (1.2) (Played by SIMON DAY)

Steward [2]: Head of the staff at Torchwood House, working to Sir Robert and Lady Isobel MacLeish. He was taken by surprise when the Brethren of St Catherine arrived and held them all prisoner, but was freed by Rose Tyler and the Doctor. He believed the Werewolf had been killed but in fact became its victim. (2.2) (Played by RON DONACHIE)

Stewart, Jackie: British 20th-century racing-car driver. Rodrick believed Stewart had written Jackie Collins's novel *Lucky* when asked by the Anne Droid in *The Weakest Link* aboard the Game Station. (1.12)

Stingrays: Metallic swarming alien life forms that used wormholes to jump from world to world, feeding by stripping everything to dust. They travelled in billions, and the sheer volume of them going around and around a planet would rupture time and space creating the wormholes so they could move on to the next, arbitrarily chosen, planet. The wormholes got larger the closer the swarm was so it could accommodate all of them. They were about to make the leap to Earth from San Helios when the Doctor and Malcolm Taylor were able to shut the wormhole down, trapping all but three of them on San Helios. Because they had already destroyed San Helios, the Stingrays were unable to feed and create the wormhole again and remained trapped there for ever. The three Stingrays that made it to Earth were gunned down by UNIT soldiers. (4.15)

Sto: Planet of origin of the starship *Titanic*. Astrid Peth, Mr Copper, Rickston Slade and most of the other passengers and crew aboard ship came from there. (4.X)

Stoker, Mr: Consultant at the Royal Hope Hospital who was in charge of medical students including Martha Jones on the day that the hospital was transported to the moon by the Judoon platoon. Observing Earth in the sky, he wondered if he'd ever see his daughter again, currently at university, or see his planned retirement in Florida. He didn't, since the Plasmavore disguised as Florence Finnegan drained his blood from his body as a screen against the Judoon's scanners. (3.1) (Played by ROY MARSDEN)

Stone, Officer Andrew: Botanist, originally from Iowa, who met geologist Mia Bennett and her father in Houston where they convinced him to become interested in the Space Program. He was responsible for overseeing the Bowie Base One bio-dome and growing fresh food. He noted in his log that the water supplies had broken down, which was in fact the precursor to the attempted takeover of the base by the Flood. Andy had a sister who worked for the Spanish space agency, and he became the first human to be infected by the Flood, subsequently responsible for converting Tarak Ital and Margaret Cain.

Andy's body was destroyed, along with the Flood, when Captain Adelaide Brooke destroyed the base in a nuclear explosion. (4.16) (Played by ALAN RUSCOE)

Stone, Jimmy: Friend of Rose Tyler's. It was because she moved in with him for a few months that she left school before sitting her A Levels. Having deprived her of £800 and broken her heart, he later ended up in prison and then started work as a door-to-door salesman. (1.1)

Stone Daleks: Three of the new Paradigm Daleks had been present in the Under Henge when the Pandorica opened. Although everything in the Under Henge was destroyed as the time field expanded and wiped the universe out, two of the Daleks were physically saved by their proximity to the Pandorica but were turned to stone. These wound up in the Anomaly Exhibition at the National Museum in 1996, alongside the Pandorica and, when it opened, a small fragment of the restorative energies within reactivated one of the Daleks and brought it back to life. It almost killed the Doctor but was destroyed by an alpha-mezon blast from River Song, despite begging for its life. (5.13) (Played by BARNABY EDWARDS, voiced by NICHOLAS BRIGGS)

Stonehenge: Ancient burial site in Wiltshire, marked by a circle of standing sarsen stones. The Doctor realised that beneath it, in the Under Henge,

was the Pandorica. He used Stonehenge itself as a transmitter to contact the thousands of alien ships that made up the Pandorica Alliance that were orbiting Earth in AD 102. (5.12, 5.13)

Stormageddon, Dark Lord of All: Alfie Owens's preferred name, according to the Doctor, who could communicate with him. Craig, his father, wasn't convinced. (6.12)

Stormcage Containment Facility 1: Prison, permanently shrouded in bad weather, where River Song had been interred before being put aboard the *Byzantium* to find the Weeping Angel there. She escaped her guards and was taken by the Doctor to Alfava Metraxis after the *Byzantium* crashed. She contacted Father Octavian, Bishop of the Clerics who had been charged with keeping an eye on her during the mission until she had earned a pardon. However, she was returned to Stormcage after Octavian's death. (5.4, 5.5) Contacted by Winston Churchill, she escaped directly from the facility, using hallucinogenic lipstick, to find Van Gogh's painting *The Pandorica Opens* and take it to Earth, via Planet One. (5.12) She also escaped it to meet the Doctor in Utah (6.1, 6.2) and was taken away from it by the Doctor for a birthday jaunt. After returning, she made another escape to go to Demon's Run. (6.7)

Stormgate: Part of the propulsion systems aboard the galaxy-class starship *Thrasymachus*. It had gone critical and, along with the failed engines, was responsible for the ship spiralling out of control, sending it crashing down towards the planet Ember. (6.X)

Story of Roman Britain, The: A book Amelia Pond had as a child, one of her favourites, which the Pandorica Alliance used as inspiration for when to place the Pandorica on Earth to trap the Doctor. The Nestenes in particular made use of the book's information, creating a whole legion of Auton Romans. (5.12)

Stott, Hans: Husband of Steffi Ehrlich and father of Ulrike and Lisette. (4.16)

Strak, Commander: Leader of the Sontaran section of the Pandorica Alliance. He was reduced to dust when the Pandorica opened and history was erased. (5.12, 5.13) (Played by CHRISTOPHER RYAN)

Strand: Street in London that links the West End to the City of London, along which the Olympic Torch-bearer headed east, towards Stratford. (2.11)

Strategist, the: Blue-liveried member of the new Dalek Paradigm. (5.3) (Operated by MATT DOLMAN)

Strategy 9: Code used by the humans on Sanctuary Base 6 to enable a lockdown, during which the humans could gather in a sealed area, and then

open all the airlocks, sucking everything else (e.g. the possessed Ood) out into space. (2.9)

Stratford: Area of East London, from which children had been disappearing in 2012. (2.11)

Stratford Olympic Park: Specially built stadium readied for the 2012 Olympic Games in East London. Eighty thousand people filled the stadium waiting for the Olympic Torch to arrive and start the games. When Chloe Webber needed to keep the Isolus which inhabited her body happy, she drew the stadium and everyone within it promptly vanished. The Doctor was able to send the Isolus home from the stadium, and the missing people all reappeared safe and sound. (2.11)

Strathclyde: Scottish city which Donna Noble intended to run away to when she was 6 years old. (4.1)

Strax, Commander: An 11-year-old Sontaran warrior forced by the Doctor to serve penance to restore the honour of his clone batch. To do this, he had gene-spliced himself to act as a nurse to humans, capable of successfully tending any wound or medical situation, including midwifery. The Doctor retrieved him from Zarusthra Bay, and took him to Demon's Run. There Strax regained his honour in battle against the Headless Monks, dying in the process, proud and satisfied. (6.7) (Played by DAN STARKEY)

Street Wize Guize 4: Music by Barrie Gledden which Donna heard when arriving in Sutton Court, played on a ghetto blaster. (4.11)

Streete, Peter: Architect of the Globe theatre who, under Carrionite influence, designed it as a tetradecagon, 14 being an important number in the

S

spellcasting of the Carrionites. After his work was completed, the Carrionites broke his mind and he was abandoned in Bedlam. The Doctor used his Time Lord abilities to clear Streete's neural pathways so he had a moment of clarity and could explain what had happened to him. This drew the attention of the Carrionites, and Mother Doomfinger arrived and killed Streete with a massive coronary to stop him speaking further. (3.2) (Played by MATT KING)

Stretton, Colin: Bought Adipose capsules from Adipose Industries. (4.1)

Strickland, Assistant Commissioner: The senior police officer who visited Jackie Tyler after she informed the authorities of the Doctor's presence. In fact, Strickland was Sip Fel Fotch Pasameer-Day Slitheen, a disguised member of the Family Slitheen, the real Strickland having been murdered previously. Revealing himself as a Slitheen, Strickland attacked Jackie in Mickey Smith's flat. The Doctor, Rose Tyler and Harriet Jones assembled enough clues about the Slitheen's physical make-up for the Doctor to deduce their weakness – Jackie threw various kinds of vinegar over Sip Fel Fotch, causing him to burst, covering them with the remains of his body. (1.4, 1.5) (Played by STEVE SPEIRS)

'Stripper, The': Traditional piece of music, performed by Joe Loss and his Orchestra, that accompanied the Doctor bursting out of Rory's wedding cake on his stag night. The actual stripper, Lucy, was outside the bar where the stag night was held, getting cold. (5.6)

Strood: Housemate alongside Crosbie and Lynda in the *Big Brother* house that the Doctor was transported to. He refused to go with the Doctor and Lynda when they escaped and may have been exterminated when the Daleks invaded the Game Station. (1.12) (Played by JAMIE BRADLEY)

Sub-Harpoon: Type of missile used by the Doctor and Mickey Smith to destroy 10 Downing Street after the Family Slitheen had occupied it and tried to start World War Three. (1.5)

Subwave Network: Using technology created by the Mr Copper Foundation, this was a sentient audio/visual communications system developed by Harriet Jones to seek out and link her up with any of the Doctor's friends on Earth. Using it, she found Torchwood, Sarah Jane Smith and Martha Jones. Eventually the Daleks traced it back to her and she passed it over to Captain Jack Harkness to utilise as the Daleks exterminated her. Afterwards, Jack and the others were able to boost the signal enough to locate the Doctor and help him jump a time track back into sync with the other planets in the Medusa Cascade and communicate with them. However, Davros was also able to tune in and the Daleks then shut the Network down. (4.12)

Sudoko #509: Puzzle book attempted by Dr Singh while waiting for something to happen to the Sphere. He rather gave the impression he'd already solved the puzzles in the previous 508 books. (2.12)

Suki: Friend of Rose Tyler and Mickey Smith's. She worked in a hospital and had told Rose there were jobs going in the canteen there. (1.1)

Sullivan, Ed: American TV star, whose entertainment series was famous for showcasing early rock 'n' roll stars, such as Elvis Presley, who performed his single 'Hound Dog' on 28 October 1956, watched by 60 million people. The Doctor was taking Rose Tyler to see this live when they ended up in London in 1953. (2.7)

Sumatra: Indonesian island where the Doctor was washed up after surviving the eruption of Krakatoa. (1.1)

Sun: Colloquial name for the star which illuminates Rose Tyler's home solar system. (1.2) A living sun was found to exist in the Torajii system, which the crew of the SS *Pentallian* had fusion-scooped living matter out of. It fought back by possessing members of the crew and letting them burn people. The crew were finally able to return the stolen material and the survivors went on their way, now aware of the possibility of living suns. (3.7)

Sunday Mirror: British tabloid newspaper, which Vivien Rook was working for when she was murdered by the Toclafane. (3.12)

Sunday Times: Sarah Jane Smith claimed to be writing a piece for this newspaper about Hector Finch and his amazing teaching methods at Deffry Vale High School. In fact, this was a ruse to get inside the school and investigate. (2.3)

S

Sunfilters: The protective screens around Platform One, which stopped the interior frying due to its closeness to the expanding sun. The sunfilters could be lowered either separately or in unison. (1.2)

Sunflowers: Painting by Vincent Van Gogh that, after leaving Vincent at home, the Doctor and Amy Pond found in the Musée D'Orsay had been inscribed 'For Amy' by Vincent in tribute, as Amy had inspired him to paint it. (5.10)

Sunita [1]: One of Sarah Clark's expected guests at her wedding, who hadn't shown up. (1.8)

Sunita [2]: Older child at the wedding reception for Donna Noble and Lance Bennett's non-wedding. Donna asked her to make herself useful after the attack by the Roboform Santas. (3.X)

'Supermassive Black Hole': Song by Muse which the Doctor was playing in the TARDIS while Amy Pond and Rory Williams played darts. Once the Doctor found the source of the Flesh, he switched the music off, and tried to convince Amy and Rory to go off on their own for a bit while he investigated. They refused. (6.5)

Supernanny: TV series about a nanny going into families with disruptive children and showing them how to cope. Donna Noble likened Matron Cofelia to her. (4.1)

Supreme, the: White-liveried leader of the new Dalek Paradigm. (5.3) It led the Pandorica Alliance. (5.12) (Operated by NICHOLAS PEGG, BEN ASHLEY and JON DAVEY, voiced by NICHOLAS BRIGGS) An alternative one was the Dalek leader on Skaro responsible for using the Eye of Time to restore the city of Kalaann along with the Emperor Dalek, so the plan to change history could commence. (AG01) Battle-scarred and severely damaged, the Supreme was

unable to defend itself when attacked by the Doctor, who opened it up to remove its data core, which contained information he required on the Silence. The Doctor then removed its eyestalk to use later when impressing upon the staff of the drinking den on Calisto B how powerful he was. (6.13) (Voiced by NICHOLAS BRIGGS)

Supreme Dalek: Red and gold Dalek who commanded the Crucible at the heart of the Medusa Cascade and enslaved Dalek Caan and Davros and made them create the Reality Bomb. The Supreme Dalek was ultimately destroyed by Captain Jack Harkness with the Defabricator Gun. (4.12, 4.13) As she saw her mother and fiancé change into the Master in front of her, Donna Noble remembered the Supreme Dalek as her memories started to come back. (4.17) (Operated by BARNABY EDWARDS, voiced by NICHOLAS BRIGGS)

Surgeons: Two white-coated figures who kept Lady Cassandra moisturised whilst aboard Platform One. (1.2) (Played by VON PEARCE, JOHN COLLINS)

Surgery: One of the areas within the Hospital on New Earth run by the Sisters of Plenitude. (2.1)

Surrey: One of the county tower blocks on *Starship UK*. (5.2)

Susan: Villager at the dance in Farringham when the Family of Blood attacked, killing Mr Chambers and demanding the Doctor hand himself over to them. (3.9)

S

Sussex: English county from where the Lake family moved to London. (4.14)

Sutton Court: Chiswick shopping street where Donna Noble arrived when returned to the correct Earth and had to try and stop herself turning right and thus never meeting the Doctor. She was then half a mile away from where she was meant to be, in Little Sutton Street. (4.11)

Suzanne: UNIT worker in New York who was knocked over when Earth was moved to the Medusa Cascade. She was later exterminated by the Daleks. (4.12) (Played by ANDREA HARRIS)

Suzie: One of Sarah Clark's friends, she greeted the car as Sarah arrived along with Bev. They informed Sarah that many of the guests had not arrived. (1.8) (Played by RHIAN JAMES)

Swabb: First mate aboard Captain Kaliko's ship, the *Black Gold*. Although just an animated skeleton, he was secretly working for OilCorp, which had promised him a new body if he betrayed Kaliko. He decided to take Martha Jones's body but, as a result of Kaliko and the Doctor's actions, Swabb was knocked overboard and last heard of swearing his revenge from the planet Bouken's sandy surface. (TIQ) (Voiced by TOM FARRELLY)

Swales, Julia: Intern at the Royal Hope Hospital and good friend to Martha Jones. Julia dealt less well with being transported to the moon than her colleague, although she was the last person to succumb to the oxygen deprivation. She was fine, however, once the hospital was returned to Earth. (3.1) (Played by VINEETA VISHI)

Sycorax: The name both of a race of long-lived scavengers and the asteroid they called home. Feared throughout the galaxy, the Sycorax were proficient in both martial artistry as well as chemical and biological manipulation. They were

eventually forced to flee Earth after the death of their Leader. The departing ship was destroyed when Harriet Jones gave the order to enable the Torchwood Institute to use stolen alien tech to blow the ship up, killing all aboard. It was reduced to a fine ash that floated back to Earth, and most people assumed this was snow. (2.X) When in Elizabethan England, the Doctor found a skull in the Globe theatre's prop store which reminded him of a Sycorax helmet. William Shakespeare liked the word, and later used it for an off-stage character in his play *The Tempest*. (3.2) Wilfred Mott referred to the Sycorax invasion when discussing aliens at Christmas with the Doctor. (4.X) The Doctor reminded Rose that when fighting the Sycorax Leader, he'd had his right hand severed and grown a new one. (4.13) There was a Sycorax warrior in the Zaggit Zagoo bar. (4.18) The Doctor cited his defeat of the Sycorax as a reason for the Atraxi to be afraid of him. (5.1) They travelled to Stonehenge, as part of the Pandorica Alliance. (5.12)

Sycorax Leader: Bullish commander of the Sycorax force that attempted to invade Earth. Onboard the Sycorax spaceship, the Doctor challenged him to a sword duel, and won, although it briefly cost him his sword-hand until he regenerated a new one. Instead of accepting his defeat, the Sycorax Leader attacked the Doctor again, who operated a control on the ship which left the Sycorax Leader plunging to his doom thousands of feet below. (2.X) (Played by SEAN GILDER)

Sydney: Australian city. ATMOS devices reportedly went off there. (4.4) The Doctor, Kazran Sardick and Abigail Pettigrew visited it one Christmas Eve. (6.X)

Sylvia: The last surviving human on Earth in 1963, after the Daleks invaded the planet. Determined to survive at all costs, she had been waging a one-woman war against the Daleks. She died saving the Doctor and Amy Pond. However, when the Doctor set time on its correct course, 1963 happened just as normal and Sylvia was still alive, talking on the phone to her mother the last time the Doctor and Amy saw her. (AG01) (Voiced by SARA CARVER)

Tabitha: School classmate to Mandy Tanner and Timmy Winters. (5.2)

'Tainted Love': Song covered by the 1980s pop duo Soft Cell, played on Cassandra's iPod (in truth, a huge jukebox) at the reception aboard Platform One in the Manchester Suite. (1.2)

Taj Mahal: Major landmark in Agra, which the 'ghosts' (really Cybermen) materialised around and later were drawn back into the Void from. (2.12, 2.13)

Take That: British boy band due to perform at the opening ceremony for the 2012 Olympic Games at Stratford. (2.11)

Taliesin Lodge: Cardiff auditorium holding a charity event in aid of a children's hospital where Charles Dickens read from *A Christmas Carol* on Christmas Eve 1869. (1.3)

Tallulah: Singer of 'Heaven And Hell', centrepiece of the New York Revue, on stage at the Laurenzi theatre in 1930s New York. Tallulah needed the job because, without it, she reckoned she'd end up living in Hooverville. She joined the Doctor in his investigation of the sewers beneath the theatre because her lover, Laszlo, had gone missing. When she discovered he had been turned  into a Pig Slave, she stood by him. After facing the Daleks in Hooverville, she and Martha Jones went to investigate the Empire State Building and met up with the Doctor and Laszlo there. After the Daleks were defeated, Laszlo opted to live in Hooverville, hoping to continue his romance with Tallulah. (3.4, 3.5) (Played by MIRANDA RAISON)

Tanaka, Dana: Poseidon's medical officer. She and Oswald Fox were the last to leave Poseidon for help after the Doctor defeated the Vashta Nerada. (AG04) (Voiced by ELEANOR MATSUURA)

Tandocca Scale: The wavelength used by migrant bees on Earth to communicate to one another the need to go home to Melissa Majoria. The same wavelength, building up over a long time, was used by the Daleks' Magnatron to shift 27 planets into the Medusa Cascade before moving them one second out of sync with the rest of the universe. The Doctor followed the Magnatron's Tandocca Scale to locate the Dalek Crucible at the heart of the Medusa Cascade. (4.12)

Tandonia: A descendant of Adelaide Brooke one day fell in love with a Tandonian Prince and together they created a whole new species. (4.16)

Tank Commander: Responsible, on orders from Defence Minister Harry Saxon, for blowing up the Webstar. (3.X, 4.11)

Tanner, Mandy: Schoolgirl in the London section of *Starship UK*. Upset by the failure of her friend Timmy Winters and aware that he was probably dead, she was seen by the Doctor and Amy Pond, alone and crying. Amy tried to befriend her. After Amy and the Doctor were 'taken' by *Starship UK*, Mandy met Liz

Ten. The Queen looked after Mandy and reunited her with the Doctor, and together they were taken by the Winders to the Tower of London, where Mandy found Timmy safe and well. (5.2) (Played by HANNAH SHARP)

Tanya: Young former UNIT officer, in the service of the Master aboard the *Valiant*. He used her as a masseuse. (3.13) (Played by EMILY MOORE)

Tarantella: Italian folk dance for a duo. The Doctor claimed he and the Sibyl danced it together once. (4.2)

TARDIS, the: TARDIS is an acronym for Time And Relative Dimension In Space. The TARDIS is to all intents and purposes the one place the Doctor calls 'home'. Capable of travelling anywhere in time and space by harnessing the power of the Time Vortex, a fully functional TARDIS can use its chameleon circuit to change its outer appearance to blend in with any environment and uses low-level perception filters to shift attention away from itself. The Doctor's TARDIS, a Type Forty, however, became stuck in the form of a 20th-century police public call box on a visit to London, and remained that way from then on. Dimensionally transcendental, the TARDIS is bigger on the inside than the outside, containing an entire world of time energy within its walls, all processed through the ship's central control console. The extent of its interior dimensions is unknown, though it does have at least an attic and a wardrobe, and probably a myriad of other rooms.

Grown by the Time Lords on Gallifrey, the TARDIS is an organic craft, linked to the Doctor and his companions by a telepathic field. It translates languages automatically inside their heads, but failed during the Doctor's regeneration into his tenth form, perhaps indicating that the Doctor himself was a key component of the TARDIS's circuitry. When the TARDIS died after falling through the Void into a parallel universe, the Doctor was able to use his own internal energies to resuscitate the TARDIS by sacrificing ten years of his own life.

Following the Time War and the loss of Gallifrey, the TARDIS had to find a new source of power, and started drawing energy from the universe around it. Having

discovered the rift running through Cardiff, the Doctor returned there on a number of occasions, allowing the TARDIS to soak up the temporal radiation and refuel itself. This power was then stored in the heart of the TARDIS, and trapped beneath the central console, emerging only in instances of severe peril. On such occasions, the TARDIS console split itself apart, enabling its soul to communicate directly with its occupants. It looked inside the minds of both Blon Fel Fotch Pasameer-Day Slitheen and Rose Tyler, interpreting their thoughts, and affording them limited control over the Time Vortex as a result.

It can be secured from the outside using a conventional Yale key, or deadlocked from with the control room itself. The Doctor has used his sonic screwdriver from outside to initiate emergency programs on the console, and also, once, to fuse the ship's coordinates, locking them permanently between locations. It also features a scanner and trim phone, and the Doctor incorporated the Slitheen extrapolator to serve as a fully functional force field, which he has used to nudge the TARDIS minor distances upon materialisation.

It has been suggested it is alive in some way, and it certainly seemed aware of the danger the Doctor was in within the Pandorica Chamber as it took River Song to 2010, to Amy Pond's house, so she could find the clues that led her to realise the Doctor had fallen into a trap. The TARDIS could be made invisible, although whenever cloaked this way, certain internal parts would not work, such as the scanner – or so the Doctor believed. He was wrong. (6.1, 6.2) The rift energy the TARDIS used for power was a source of nourishment for the alien sentience House. The TARDIS itself contained an eleven-dimensional personality Matrix which considered the Doctor to be someone it stole from Gallifrey, always taking the Doctor to where he needed to be, because it wanted to see the universe as much as he did. The TARDIS always saved back-ups of the various control rooms' desktop patterns the Doctor had created during their travels together. (6.4)

The Doctor aside, several other beings have been inside the TARDIS: Rose Tyler, Mickey Smith, Jackie Tyler, Adam Mitchell, Captain Jack Harkness, Blon Fel Fotch Pasameer-Day Slitheen, Lady Cassandra O'Brien, Sarah Jane Smith, Ida Scott, Donna Noble, Martha Jones, Sally Sparrow, Larry Nightingale, the Master, Lucy Saxon, the Caecilius family, the duplicate Doctor, Jackson Lake, Adelaide Brooke,

Mia Bennett, Yuri Kerenski, Gadget, Wilfred Mott, Amy Pond (and her Flesh duplicate), River Song, Rory Williams, the Dream Lord, Nasreen Chaudhry, Mo, Ambrose and Elliot Northover, Vincent Van Gogh, Kazran Sardick, Abigail Pettigrew, Canton Delaware III, President Richard Nixon, Henry Avery, Miranda Cleaves, the Gangers of Dicken and Jimmy Wicks, Ood Sigma, Dorium Maldovar, Madame Vastra, Jenny, Commander Strax and even a Dalek.

TARDIS (fake): Believing himself to be the Doctor, schoolteacher Jackson Lake built himself a TARDIS that was in fact a hot-air balloon, powered by the gas from the nearby Mutton Street gasworks. In this case, TARDIS was an acronym for Tethered Aerial Release Developed In Style. (4.14)

Tarzan: Fictional jungle character created by Edgar Rice Burroughs. The Doctor was beating on his chest once, trying to mime 'press' but Amy Pond thought he was doing 'Tarzan'. (AG03)

Taunton: Devonshire town. The Doctor mused that the psychic energy he had observed in Elizabethan England would require a generator the size of Taunton. (3.2)

Taurean, HMS: Royal Navy Trafalgar Class submarine, which, after hacking into the UNIT computer systems, Mickey Smith discovered was situated ten miles off the coast of Plymouth. It carried a Sub-Harpoon UGM 84A missile, which the Doctor then used to destroy 10 Downing Street and the Family Slitheen members still inside. (1.5)

Taxi Driver: A 1976 movie, starring Robert De Niro. Mickey Smith impersonated De Niro's character Travis Bickle aboard the SS *Madame de Pompadour*. (2.4)

Taxi driver [1]: Picked up Donna Noble and the Doctor, preparing to drive them to Chiswick, until he realised they didn't have any money, at which point he turfed them out. (3.X) (Played by GLEN WILSON)

Taxi Driver [2]: Arrived to collect Stacy Campbell from her house, not realising she was dead. (4.1) (Played by JONATHAN STRATT)

Taylor, Doctor Malcolm: UNIT's scientific adviser during the Gladwell road tunnel situation. A huge fan of the Doctor, he impressed the Time Lord with his out of the box thinking, especially when he found a way to reverse the wormhole. His determination to save the Doctor at any cost, however, brought Taylor into conflict with Captain Magambo. He was honoured to finally meet the Doctor at the resolution of the crisis. (4.15) (Played by LEE EVANS)

Teacher: Chaperone to a group of schoolchildren in the play area beside the ruined Leadworth Castle. She and the children were destroyed by the Eknodine-infected Mrs Poggit in the dreamscape created by the Dream Lord. (5.7) (Played by CHANNON JACOBS)

Tebb Street: Road in Hull where Kathy Wainwright lived when she wrote the letter to Sally Sparrow, detailing her life from 1920 through to 1987. She lived at number 43. (3.10)

Teenaged Mum: A victim of the Reapers as they broke into the world after Rose Tyler saved her dad's life and created a breach in time. (1.8) (Played by ZOË MARIE MORRIS)

Teenager: Emo youth who lived on the same estate as Winston Katusi and was transformed into the Master along with every other human on Earth except Wilfred Mott and Donna Noble. (4.17) (Played by MAX BENJAMIN)

Telepathic Recorder: See *Firestone*

Telepathic Translator: Device used by the Tritovores to communicate with alien species. Its limitations meant they could understand what was being spoken to them but couldn't reply likewise. (4.15)

Teleport bracelets: Mr Copper issued these to travellers on his Red Six Seven tickets to visit Earth. The Doctor later tried to retrieve Astrid Peth's form from the program stored within her bracelet, but it had degraded too much after so long. (4.X)

Telescope: Designed by Sir George MacLeish and Prince Albert in the Observatory atop Torchwood House which, when linked to the Koh-I-Noor diamond, created a beam of moonlight powerful enough to destroy the Haemovariform. (2.2)

Teletubbies: BBC children's programme, created by Ragdoll Productions. The Master watched this on a TV set and pointed out to a Toclafane sphere that the Teletubbies were wonderful because they had televisions in their stomachs. (3.12)

Television channels: Satellite Five broadcast over 600 channels, including Channel McB, Channel ☺+1 and Bad WolfTV. (1.7)

Tempest, The: A play by William Shakespeare. The Doctor used the phrase 'Brave new world' to Martha Jones when they first arrived in Elizabethan

England. He later mentioned that a skull from the Globe theatre's prop stores reminded him of a Sycorax – Shakespeare liked the word and considered using it, which he later did, naming the mother of Caliban in *The Tempest* as Sycorax. (3.2)

Temple, Mr and Mrs: Shaun Temple's parents, who were at his wedding to Donna Noble. (4.18) (Played by DENZIE PHIPPS and MICHELLE MEREDITH)

Temple, Shaun: Donna Noble's fiancé, who lived with her in a tiny flat. He and Donna spent Christmas Day at the Nobles, where Shaun was transformed into the Master for a while. The following spring, Shaun and Donna were married. (4.17, 4.18) (Played by KARL COLLINS)

Temporal Collision: The situation that arises when two TARDISes attempt to occupy the same coordinates in space and time simultaneously. (TC)

Temporal Implosion: The Doctor used a controlled temporal implosion to free the TARDIS exterior from where it had materialised inside the interior, creating a time loop. (T)

Temporal Prison: A chronon loop the Daleks placed around the TARDIS aboard the Crucible. (4.12, 4.13)

10-1: The code set up by Professor Meadows at Zebra Bay for accessing the door locks on the base. It was her daughter's birth date. (AG02)

Tennessee: Home state in America of 18-year-old Frank, one of the inhabitants of Manhattan's Hooverville. (3.4, 3.5)

Tenth Sontaran Battle Fleet: The Sontaran troopers led by General Staal made up this fleet. (4.4, 4.5)

Tenza: Alien race who hatch in their millions in the emptiness of space and drift away, searching for a 'nest' to grow in. They psychically search out foster parents and adapt themselves to whatever is required, giving off a perception filter to dull the memories of those they encounter so no one can really remember how or when they became part of the family. They assimilate their chosen race's social mores and grow up as part of whatever family they have become part of. A Tenza found a human couple called Alex and Claire, who were unable to have children, and became their 'son', called George. Alex and Claire's insecurities about their abilities as parents began to reflect back onto George, who believed he was being rejected and created a psychic prison in his cupboard where he sent anyone who threatened him, bringing his toys to life to act as guards. Assured by Alex that he was loved and wanted, George shut down the doll's house prison, and fully adapted to life as a human boy. (6.9)

Tenzing, Norgay: Tibetan explorer, often referred to as Sherpa Tenzing, 'sherpa' being a description of his job. Rowbarton House tenant Mrs Rossiter said she felt like Tenzing after climbing the stairs of the housing estate. (6.9)

Terileptils: Reptilian race whose ships travelled to Stonehenge, as part of the Pandorica Alliance. (5.12)

Terror, Mister: One of the Alliance of Shades' Men in Black androids. He was put out of action by an arrow fired by one of Night Eagle's Shoshoni tribesmen. (DL)

Terry: Soldier based at Albion Hospital and part of the search for the augmented pig that the Slitheen had launched into space, ensuring the

subsequent crash back to Earth would cause a huge distraction and enable them to take over the British government. (1.4)

Teselecta: A vehicle that could be shapeshifted into any form. Operated by a miniaturised crew of 421, and maintained in that state by a compression field, they travelled through history on behalf of the Justice Department, and replaced major criminals seconds before their death, taking the originals away for whatever punishment they felt history had made them deserve. The ships contained incredibly in-depth records of everyone throughout history, recognising River Song as a particularly major felon. The crew of the *Teselecta* was captained by a man called Carter, who tried to save the Doctor from River Song, and later felt he owed the Doctor a debt of thanks. The *Teselecta* also contained Anti-Bodies, robotic assassins that would erase the real criminals from within the ship once they were brought aboard. The crewmembers were safe from the Anti-Bodies provided they wore special wristbands that identified them as non-hostile. The *Teselecta* impersonated a Janitor at the Berlin Chancellery, a Nazi Party member called Eric Zimmerman (the real one was killed by the Anti-Bodies), Amy Pond, River Song and Gideon Vandaleur. Under the Doctor's control, the *Teselecta* impersonated him at Lake Silencio and was apparently slain by River Song there and torched by Rory Williams. Miniaturised inside, the Doctor and the TARDIS escaped the *Teselecta*, hoping the universe would now believe him dead, as his death was a fixed point in time. (6.8, 6.13)

Texas: American state where some of the citizens of Manhattan's Hooverville were from. (3.4) Lady Cassandra said that her father had been born there. (1.2)

Thalina: One of the Sibylline Sisterhood, who knew that the Thirteenth Book of the Sibylline Oracles foretold the arrival of the TARDIS in Pompeii, and that it would herald a time of storms and betrayal. She died when Vesuvius erupted (4.2) (Played by LORRAINE BURROUGHS)

Thames: London river. The Doctor took River Song ice skating there in 1814 for her birthday, and Stevie Wonder serenaded her. (6.7)

T

Thames Flood Barrier: Consisting of four huge steel gates, the Thames Barrier was built during the 1970s and 1980s because London is prone to flooding. The Doctor, Donna Noble and Lance Bennett discovered that a secret Torchwood Institute base had been built next to the flood chamber. Torchwood had drilled a hole through to the Earth's core, revealing the *Secret Heart*, a Racnoss Webstar, around which Earth had formed over four billion years earlier. When the Empress of the Racnoss enabled her trapped children to break free, the Doctor used small bombs to blow up the walls of the flood chamber, drawing water from the Thames down into the chamber and then down the tunnel. This drowned the surviving Racnoss children. Escaping the destruction, the Doctor and Donna climbed on top of one of the four barrier gates, only to find that the entire Thames had been drained of water. (3.X) In the world where Donna never met the Doctor, although the Empress of the Racnoss was defeated, the Doctor died as the Barrier collapsed on him. (4.11)

Thatcher, Margaret: Listing things of importance that happened in 1979, the Doctor told Rose Tyler that Thatcher became Britain's first female Prime Minister. (2.2) She was still Prime Minister at the time of Pete Tyler's death in a hit-and-run accident in November 1987. (1.8)

Thaw, Lady Sylvia: Benefactor of Richard Lazarus's GMD, and representative of Harry Saxon, who had put a lot of money into the project's research and development. She believed that she and Lazarus were more than just business partners and was shocked at how rapidly, once he had rejuvenated himself, he dismissed her love. When he became the Lazarus Creature, she became its first victim when it drew the life force from her. (3.6) (Played by THELMA BARLOW)

Thay, Dalek: Former Commandant of Station Alpha, later one of the Cult of Skaro, who took the Genesis Ark to Earth in the Void ship, after the Time War ended. He was the first Dalek to confront and exterminate the Cybermen in Torchwood Tower. (2.12, 2.13). After fleeing the Battle of Canary Wharf via an emergency temporal shift, along with the rest of the Cult, Thay ended up in Manhattan in 1930. Thay donated three segments of his Dalekanium-laced polycarbide armour to act as a conductor for the gamma radiation needed to activate their new Dalek-Human army. Thay stayed with the Dalek Sec Hybrid during the attack on Hooverville, observing his leader's un-Dalek-like reactions to the slaughter, and later exterminated him once Sec was chained to Thay's casing. When the Dalek-Human army turned on their creators, Thay was the first to be destroyed on the stage of the Laurenzi theatre. (3.4, 3.5) (Operated by DAN BARRATT, BARNABY EDWARDS (2.12, 2.13), NICHOLAS PEGG (3.4, 3.5), voiced by NICHOLAS BRIGGS)

Thermo-Buffer: Part of the TARDIS controls which the Doctor operated to avoid a time collision. (TC)

Thermopolium: Popular nightspot in Pompeii, frequented by Quintus Caecilius. It was destroyed along with the city after Vesuvius erupted. (4.2)

Thin Jimmy: Former leader of the Preachers, he was arrested shortly before Mickey Smith met Jake Simmonds and Mrs Moore. His arrest left Ricky Smith as London's Most Wanted... and thus leader of the Preachers on 'Pete's World'. (2.5)

Thin One: One of the Clerics from the Vatican, stationed on Demon's Run. Married to Fat One, he got talking to Lorna Bucket before Colonel Manton called the Clerics in for a briefing. When the Headless Monks were revealed to be literally headless, Thin One realised his husband was effectively dead and, when the Doctor was revealed to be posing as one of them before escaping in the darkness, the Monks got agitated and Thin One panicked and gunned one down. He later emptied his gun of bullets along with the other clerics and was taken away and off Demon's Run by a group of Judoon and Silurians working alongside the Doctor. (6.7) (Played by DAN JOHNSTON)

Thing, The: 1982 sci-fi movie directed by John Carpenter, starring Kurt Russell, which the Doctor referred to when he and Amy Pond approached the deserted Arctic Geological Survey Base in Zebra Bay. (AG02)

Thing from Another World, The: 1951 sci-fi movie, directed by Howard Hawkes, which the Doctor referred to when he and Amy Pond approached the deserted Arctic Geological Survey Base in Zebra Bay. (AG02)

37° 0'38" N 110° 14'34" W: The coordinates given to Amy Pond, Rory Williams and River Song by the Doctor, telling them where to meet him – which turned out to be just outside San Juan in Utah, near Lake Silencio. (6.1)

36 Squadron: One of the RAF squadrons that headed towards the south coast of England to engage German fighters during the Second World War. (5.3)

This Is Spinal Tap: The Doctor quoted this movie when he opted to 'turn this up to 11', meaning the volume of the organ in Southwark Cathedral he used to destroy the Lazarus Creature. (3.6)

This Is Your Life: Iconic television series that started in America in 1952, in which celebrities were joined by old friends and family to celebrate their lives and achievements. Australia, Britain and New Zealand all had their own versions. The Doctor suggested that when he found Mickey Smith and Harriet Jones aboard the Sycorax ship, it was like an episode of the programme. (2.X)

Thomas, Dylan: The Doctor quoted a line by this poet – 'Rage, rage against the dying of the light' – which Shakespeare thought he might nick, but the Doctor told him that he couldn't. (3.2)

Thompson, Ciaran: Bought Adipose capsules from Adipose Industries. (4.1)

Thought Mails: Method of communication which the suits worn by Strackman Lux's expedition were capable of transmitting. (4.8, 4.9)

Thraad: The Doctor once repaired their Great Kalxian Generators. (AG02)

Thrace: Lady Cassandra O'Brien once attended a drinks party in honour of the Ambassador of Thrace, when a dying man approached her and told her she was beautiful. She remembered this as being the last time anyone told her that. In truth, the dying man was herself, transferred into the failing body of Chip. (2.1)

Thrasymachus, the: Galaxy-class starship with 4,003 people aboard, whose engines and storm gate failed in orbit around the planet Ember, sending it crashing down through the atmosphere. (6.X)

'Three Little Sontarans': Allegedly a classic bedtime story from the Doctor's childhood. He tried to interest the Tenza child, George, in hearing it. (6.9)

£3,000: The amount, in cash, that the Doctor gave Craig Owens in advance rent. (5.11)

330C: Number of the Voting Cubicle in which Amy Pond was told the truth about *Starship UK* and then chose to forget it. (5.2)

3245: The code for Chisholm's locker in the Geological Survey Base at Zebra Bay in the Arctic Circle. (AG02)

Thwaites: Schoolboy at Farringham School for Boys in 1913 who knew the drill before the Family of Blood attacked. (3.9)

Tianzo, Emperor: Ruler of the Liao Dynasty. (AG05)

Tide of Blood: The moment when the portal between the Deep Darkness and the Globe theatre was to be opened by William Shakespeare's words, influenced by the Carrionites' spellcasting. (3.2)

T

Time Agency: Mysterious pan-galactic group who recruited from worlds across the universe those who showed a particular aptitude for undercover espionage work involving time travel. Captain Jack Harkness was an agent, the first chosen from his home on the Boeshane Peninsula, but left years later after the Agency stole two years of his memories. (1.9, 1.10, 3.13) Dorium Maldovar supplied River Song with a Vortex Manipulator that had been removed from a Time Agent — along with the Agent's wrist. (5.12)

Time Beetle: A creature from the Pantheon of Discord, one of the Trickster's Brigade. It was on Shan Shen and was drawn to Donna Noble, sensing that she was connected to time and coincidence. When Donna visited the Beetle's familiar, a Fortune Teller, it jumped on her back, feeding off the chaos created by the alternative history Donna was forced to relive. Donna, helped by Rose Tyler, was too strong and managed to restore time to its correct path, destroying the Beetle in the process. (4.11)

Time Corridor: The new Dalek Paradigm used this to escape the Doctor while they waited for the oblivion continuum within the Bracewell android to explode. (5.3)

Time Differential: Ability that TARDISes have to ensure that items/people from different times are not affected by the passage of time within the TARDIS's own internal time field. When it shorted out, the Fifth Doctor appeared to be somewhat older than the Tenth Doctor remembered him looking. (TC)

Time engine: A spacecraft that landed in Colchester which was one big TARDIS-like time engine, using a perception filter to disguise itself at 79B Aickman Road. With no crew to get it home, the ship created a series of avatars to draw passing humans in, in an attempt to find the perfect person  to merge with the controls and pilot it. Instead, each of the 17 humans it tried was killed, and burned to a stain on the floor. It recognised that the Doctor's superior Time Lord brain was the best one to relaunch the ship. However, even he wasn't perfect because the ship needed someone who wanted to leave the area to have the correct psychic energy to activate the time engine itself. Unable to convince anyone, the ship imploded, apparently destroying itself and leaving Craig's building intact, as a one-storey building again. (5.11) The Doctor subsequently saw an identical ship in Florida in 1969 and realised that the time engines belonged to the Silence. (6.1, 6.2)

Time field (aka the Crack): When the TARDIS exploded at an indeterminate point in the future, trapped within Earth's sun, it created a massive time field that manifested itself as a crack in the skin of reality at every point in time and space, slowly erasing history and reversing time so that those it touched never existed. (5.12, 5.13) Amongst the things lost to the time field were Amy Pond's parents, (5.1) the Weeping Angels on Alfava Metraxis (which tried to feed on it) and many of Father Octavian's Clerics, (5.5) the planet Saturnyne, (5.6) Rory Williams, (5.9) and ultimately the entire universe. (5.13) Vincent Van Gogh imagined an image of the destruction of the TARDIS that caused this, painting a picture of it, which he called *The Pandorica Opens*. (5.12) The Doctor used the Pandorica to go back to the point of explosion and stop it happening, effectively rebooting the universe and restoring many of the things that the time field had erased. It is unknown exactly how much was replaced precisely as it was and how much was subtly altered: Rory, for example, was returned to his human form although, like Amy and River Song, with his memories of his time with the Doctor intact. (5.13) One thing that the time field did seem to cause was the presence throughout Earth history of the Silence. (6.1, 6.2)

Time Glass: Device on Apalapucia which enabled those unaffected by the Chen7 virus to communicate with and observe those who were infected in the alternative time stream. (6.10)

T

Timelock: Temporal field that surrounded the Last Great Time War, ensuring no one could get in or out – although Dalek Caan of the Cult of Skaro managed to. A smaller, more localised version of this had been developed by Torchwood operative Toshiko Sato before her death, and it activated to protect Ianto Jones and Gwen Cooper from a Dalek that tried to enter the Torchwood Hub. (4.12, 4.13) The timelock bubble around the Last Great Time War ensured the rest of the universe was not caught up in the devastation. (4.17, 4.18)

Time Lords: Ancient and powerful race of beings from the planet Gallifrey. They tended to observe events in the universe rather than becoming involved, teaching in their Academy the importance of calm detachment. They were, however, known to have acted in wars during the Dark Times, and unwittingly instigated the Last Great Time War against the Daleks by trying to go back in time to avert, or at least significantly alter, their creation. Aeons later, Gallifrey and the entire race of Time Lords were lost from time and space, Timelocked inside the final day of the War for ever. There were two exceptions: the Doctor, whose actions eventually brought about the end of the War, and the Master, who fled and turned himself temporarily human to escape the Daleks. The Time Lords attempted to return to reality and then ascend to a new state of existence, but to do so would have brought about the end of time and the Doctor stopped them, sending them back into the Timelocked War. (1.2, 1.6, 1.12, 1.13, 2.3, 2.13, 3.X, 3.3, 3.11, 3.12, 3.13, TC, 4.2, 4.12, 4.13, 4.17, 4.18)

Time of Manifestation: The moment when the Wire would have access to the millions of people watching the Queen's Coronation in 1953 and be able to absorb their faces. (2.7)

Time Stops: One of the mechanisms within the Pandorica to ensure it remained sealed. (5.12)

Time War, the Last Great: Eventually Timelocked to prevent further universal devastation, the War was witnessed by the Eternals who fled the universe, never to return. The Forest of Cheem were terrified and saddened by it. The Sontarans were kept out of it, much to their disgust. The Time War raged across the whole of time and space, which, it has been said, saw the universe convulse. It has been speculated that the Time War was initially provoked by the Time Lords during the genesis of the Daleks, when the Doctor was sent on a mission to alter or prevent the Daleks' conception. Davros, the Daleks' creator, was destroyed at the Gates of Elysium during the first year of the War. Amongst the temporal powers each side utilised were the Nightmare Child, the Skaro Degradations, the Horde of Travesties, and the Couldhavebeen King with his army of Meanwhiles and Never-Weres. Many great civilisations were lost during the War – the Nestenes' home planet was obliterated, the Gelth Confederacy lost their physical forms, Arcadia fell, as did Perganon and Ascinta, and one turning point came when the Dalek Emperor took control of the Cruciform. The legendary final battle between the Daleks and the Time Lords led to what was possibly the final devastation of both civilisations in a single second, something caused and watched by the Doctor, after he had tried everything else he could to stop the War. Realising that to end it the Time Lord President, Rassilon, was prepared to initiate the Ultimate Sanction, the Doctor used the Moment to destroy the Time Lords and the Daleks – the Final Day, when the war ended in utter annihilation. However, small factions of Daleks escaped. The Emperor and his crippled ship fell back through time and ended up hiding invisibly on the edge of Earth's solar system for centuries before revealing itself, with a new army, during the time of the Fourth Earth Empire. One solitary Dalek fell through time to Earth in the 1960s, landing on Ascension Island, whilst the Emperor's personally selected Cult of Skaro fled into the Void, taking with them a Time Lord prison ship named the Genesis Ark, containing millions of imprisoned Daleks. The Doctor and the Master were the only surviving Time Lords away from Gallifrey and, after the destruction of the

Emperor, his ship and three of the Cult of Skaro, Dalek Caan was the only known Dalek survivor. Using an emergency temporal shift, Caan sent himself back into the Time War at the point where Davros's command ship was last seen approaching the Nightmare Child. Caan was driven insane by this crossing of his own timeline but it enabled him to see myriad splintered futures. He rescued Davros and together they created a new Dalek army, which Caan subsequently set up to be destroyed for ever, fearing what the Daleks had always been and would later become. Rassilon eventually broke free of the Timelock as well, using a Whitepoint Star delivered to the Master on Earth (this was the point at which Dalek Caan was able to cross through into the War) to create a link with Gallifrey that physically moved it across the universe to Earth. The Master and the Doctor managed to sever the link and send the Time Lords and their planet back into the Timelock for eternity. (1.1, 1.2, 1.3, 1.6, 1.12, 1.13, 2.3, 2.9, 2.12, 2.13, 3.X, 3.3, 3.4, 3.5, 3.11, 3.12, 3.13, 4.2, 4.4, 4.5, 4.12, 4.13, 4.17, 4.18)

Time Windows:

Technology aboard a 51st-century ship, the SS *Madame de Pompadour*. These enabled the Clockwork Robots to observe the lifetime of the real Madame de Pompadour. Whether they were

originally part of the ship or were added by the Clockwork Robots to aid their task is unknown. (2.4)

Tina: Potential girlfriend of Barclay. She was expecting him when he got transported to San Helios on the number 220 bus. (4.15)

Tina the Cleaner: Friend of Jackie Tyler. She lived on the Powell Estate, and she had taken in a lodger: a medical student who owned a stethoscope, which Jackie 'borrowed' to check on the Doctor's health. (2.X) Elton Pope watched her and Jackie chatting outside a laundrette. (2.10) (Played by CATHERINE CORNFORTH)

Titanic, RMS: Royal Merchant Ship *Titanic* set sail from Southampton Docks bound for New York on 10 April 1912. Four days later, it struck an iceberg and sank, claiming the lives of over 1,480 passengers and crew. (1.1) The Doctor implied to Jabe that he was aboard the ship when it went down, and he was left clinging to an iceberg for three days. (1.2) Melody Zucker told her History teacher it sank because the Doctor didn't save it. (6.8)

Titanic: After saying goodbye to Martha Jones in 2008, the Doctor parked the TARDIS in space for repairs, whereupon it was crashed into by the *Titanic*. (3.13, TC) It was a Max Capricorn galaxy-class cruiseliner, ferrying passengers

from Sto on a visit to observe the traditional Christmas holiday on Earth. However, Capricorn had deliberately sabotaged the spaceship because his company was in trouble, and he tried to crash it into Earth. He had reprogrammed the starship's robotic aides, the Heavenly Host, into killing all those aboard, and paid Captain Hardaker to allow the ship to be struck by three meteoroids. The Doctor stopped the ship crashing and it returned to Sto with a few survivors aboard. (4.X)
In the alternative world where the Doctor was killed by the Racnoss, Capricorn succeeded in his aims and the *Titanic* crashed onto London, destroying the southern half of the country in a nuclear storm drive explosion, wiping out millions of people. (4.11)

Tivoli: Planetary home to Gibbis. The Tivoli national anthem was 'Glory To Insert Name Here' – because of the race's pathological compulsion to surrender – which over the centuries had become an unconscious desire to be dominated and enslaved and therefore not to have to do any thinking for themselves. (6.11)

'To Be A Pilgrim': 17th-century hymn by John Bunyan, sung by the choir at Farringham School for Boys. (3.8, 3.9)

Toclafane: On Gallifrey, 'Toclafane' was the name given to imaginary evils to frighten children. The Master used the name for the last humans at the end of the universe in the year 100,000,000,000,000 who he discovered had, upon reaching Utopia, degenerated into cannibals, similar to the Futurekind on Malcassairo and experimented on themselves, reducing themselves to nothing more than shrunken heads, with the instincts and emotional responses of children

and armed with knives and lasers. The Master planned to use them to subjugate Earth and be the army in his New Time Lord Empire. The Doctor realised that Toclafane was not their real name because of the Gallifrey connection, and was horrified to work out who they really were. The Master was using the Doctor's TARDIS to power a Paradox Machine which enabled six billion Toclafane to reach 21st-century Earth and slaughter their progenitors but, when Captain Jack Harkness destroyed the Paradox Machine, the Toclafane were instantly propelled back to their own future, trapped on Utopia for what little time remained in the existence of the universe. (3.12, 3.13) (Voiced by ZOË THORNE, GERARD LOGAN, JOHNNIE LYNE-PIRKIS)

Todd, Group Captain: One of the RAF personnel working for Winston Churchill in the Map Room in the Cabinet War Rooms beneath London. (5.3) (Played by JAMES ALBRECHT)

Tokyo: Japanese city. ATMOS devices reportedly went off there. (4.4) The city had a Space Centre, which the Doctor contacted to set up his trap for Prisoner Zero. (5.1)

Tom: Boy playing football on his front lawn with Dale Hicks when Dale vanished in front of him. (Played by JACK PALMER) His Dad (played by TIM FARADAY) was anxious to know what the authorities were doing to find him. (2.11)

Tommo: Man living rough in London who made friends with a young lad called Ginger. He was showing Ginger the ropes, and introduced him to Sarah, who ran a burger van. While eating their burgers, they met the Master and, despite Tommo leading Ginger away from him, the Master caught up with them both and killed them. (4.17) (Played by PETER-LEE WILSON)

Tommy Zoom: CBeebies cartoon show about a boy and his dog, Daniel. Bored of listening to General Staal, the Doctor used his sonic screwdriver to change UNIT's monitor channel over to CBeebies to an episode of the show. (4.5)

Top Rank: Venue in Sheffield where the Doctor planned to take Rose Tyler to see Ian Dury and the Blockheads perform in November 1979. (2.2)

Topshop: Cardiff clothes store where Captain Jack Harkness told the Zu-Zana android that he'd bought his jeans during the *What Not to Wear* programme, broadcast from the Game Station. (1.12)

Torajii System: Quadrant of space half a universe away from Earth, patrolled by the cargo ship SS *Pentallian*, and home to a sentient sun. (3.7)

Torchwood Estate: Grounds upon which Torchwood House was built. Prince Albert was very fond of his visits there, according to his widow, Queen Victoria. (2.2)

Torchwood Institute: Founded by Queen Victoria in 1879 following her encounter with a Lupine-Wavelength-Haemovariform, the Torchwood Institute was set up with the express intention of keeping Britain great and fighting the alien hordes, including the Doctor. (2.2) Captain Jack Harkness joined Torchwood Cardiff in the late 19th century, following his return to Earth from the year 200,100. (3.11) Although a top-secret organisation, Torchwood was known to the authorities, and Detective Inspector Bishop expected the Institute to

intervene in the mystery of the faceless people at the time of Elizabeth II's Coronation in 1953. (2.7)

Independent from the government and the United Nations, by 2007 the Institute was based in Torchwood Tower, known to the public as Canary Wharf. Torchwood scavenged alien technology in order to protect and advance the British Empire. Led by Yvonne Hartman, Torchwood's operatives included Dr Rajesh Singh and Adeola Oshodi, and all of them received a basic level of psychic training. Among the technology they had acquired was the Immortality Gate, later obtained by Joshua Naismith. (4.17, 4.18) The Torchwood Institute was responsible for destroying the Sycorax ship on Christmas Day, using technology from a Jathaa Sun-Glider, on the orders of Prime Minister Harriet Jones. (2.X) They also investigated strange lights over Deffry Vale, shortly after the Krillitanes infiltrated Deffry Vale High School. (2.3T, 2.3) Victor Kennedy somehow obtained their files on the Doctor and Rose Tyler. Torchwood was the sole proprietor of HC Clements, where Donna Noble was working as a secretary when she met Lance Bennett. (3.X) Torchwood abducted a journalist who was investigating their link

with the 'ghosts'. (2.12T) Their tests on the Void Ship and Ghost Shift experiments enabled Cybermen from 'Pete's World' and the Cult of Skaro to emerge from the Void and invade Earth. In the Battle of Canary Wharf that followed, the Torchwood Institute was destroyed. (2.12, 2.13)

After the destruction of the old regime, Captain Jack Harkness continued to restructure Torchwood Cardiff in the Doctor's honour, alongside four other operatives, including Toshiko Sato. (1.4) Journalist Vivien Rook was able to contact them directly with her concerns about Mr Saxon and the Archangel network. But the Master had sent the Cardiff team to the Himalayas shortly after his election as Prime Minister, and Jack was unable to contact them. (3.12) Jack later refused the Doctor's invitation to travel aboard the TARDIS again, and returned to his work at Torchwood Cardiff instead. (3.13) He and his remaining Cardiff team helped defeat the Daleks and return the stolen Earth from the Medusa Cascade, also managing to prevent a Dalek attack on their underground base. (4.12, 4.13)

By 2012, Torchwood were well enough known for Huw Edwards to refer to them on-air following the Olympic spectators' disappearance in 2012. (2.11) The Great Cobalt Pyramid would later be built on the remains of the Torchwood Institute (1.12) and, in the far future, the crew of Sanctuary Base 6 were all representatives of the Torchwood Archive. (2.8, 2.9)

On 'Pete's World', an alternative version of Torchwood operated more publicly, and published studies into male fertility and global life spans via the Cybus mobile phone network. (2.5) One of Pete Tyler's friends, Stevie, worked for this version of the Institute before the People's Republic discovered their past misdeeds and claimed control. (2.12) Using Torchwood technology to travel across the Void, Pete Tyler, Mickey Smith and Jake Simmonds then followed the Cybermen into our universe, before returning with Rose and Jackie Tyler. Stranded on 'Pete's World', Rose joined her father at the newly reformed Torchwood, defending the Earth against alien threats. (2.13)

In the alternative world where Donna Noble never met the Doctor, Torchwood gave their lives stopping the Tenth Sontaran Battle Fleet. (4.11)

Torchwood Operative: When the editor of *The Examiner* contacted the Torchwood Institute to say she was being sold a story about them, this man came and collected the reporter from her office and took him back to Torchwood Tower. (2.12T) (Played by DAFYDD EMYR)

Torchwood Tower: The Torchwood Institute referred to One Canada Square, at the heart of the Canary Wharf business district in East London, as Torchwood Tower. Torchwood was actually responsible for having One Canada Square constructed because of the radar black spot that the breach into the Void created, 600 feet above sea level. After the destruction of Torchwood, the building was presumably returned to local businesses to use. On 'Pete's World', the Torchwood Institute used the same building but had already been brought down by Pete Tyler's people. (2.12, 2.13)

Torchwood Worker: The woman who passed a Jiffy bag full of information about the Torchwood Institute to reporter Atif in a park. (2.12T) (Played by CATHERINE HARRIS)

Touchdown Institute: Broff thought that the Great Colbalt Pyramid was built over the remains of this when asked by the Anne Droid in *The Weakest Link* aboard the Game Station. He was wrong – it was the Torchwood Institute. (1.12)

Tov: Subject of exclamation on Sto. (4.X)

Tower of London: Landmark on the north bank of the Thames. UNIT had a Mission Control base beneath it. (2.X) After discovering that ATMOS was dangerous, Jo Nakashima programmed her SatNav to take her to UNIT there, but instead it drove her into a river, killing her. (4.4) The Tower of London, like similar landmarks, was moved onboard *Starship UK*, and retained the Tower's internal appearance. This was where Chief Winder Hawthorne worked and where the star whale was directly linked into the ship's propulsion units. (5.2) In the alternative timeline created by River Song, Holy Roman Emperor Churchill locked the Doctor away in the Tower. (6.13)

T

Towering Inferno, The: Popular movie from 1974 — when the Doctor had been poisoned by cyanide and was trying to mime what would help him, Donna Noble suggested he was miming the title of this film. (4.7)

'Toxic': Song made popular by Britney Spears. When Earthdeath occurred, the observers aboard Platform One listened to this song, which Lady Cassandra O'Brien told them was a traditional Earth ballad. (1.2)

Traffic Warden: Attempted to give Donna Noble a ticket on Christmas Eve without much joy. (4.17) (Played by JUNE CAMPBELL)

Tramp: He was scavenging in a New York alleyway when the astronaut girl started to regenerate in front of him. (6.2) (Played by RICKY FEARON)

Trans-Dimensional Gateway: A flash of light on the seabed heralded this portal opening on the floor of the Atlantic Ocean, unwittingly created by the US military in 1943. Through it came a plague, the Razor-Toothed Blade-Fin, the Vashta Nerada and the USS *Eldridge*. The Gateway also emitted Vortron Radiation. The Accelerator the military used to open the Trans-Dimensional Gateway was still aboard the *Eldridge* and the Doctor deactivated it, so closing the Gateway and sending everything back home. (AG04)

Transgenic Laboratory: Huge complex the Daleks built with the last of their technology beneath the sewers at the foot of the Empire State Building in 1930s New York. In it, they planned the Final Experiment, which would see the combining of Dalek and human DNA to create a massive Dalek-Human army. After the Daleks were defeated, the Doctor used their technology to find a way of halting Pig Slave Laszlo's degeneration. (3.4, 3.5)

Translator Balls: Spherical glowing globes surgically attached to the Ood by their human masters, which acted as interface devices and enabled the two races to communicate. Once boosted to a telepathy level of Basic 100 by the Beast, the Ood were able to use the interface devices to release a lethal bolt of pure psychic energy against the humans on Sanctuary Base 6 (2.8, 2.9) and on the Ood-Sphere. (4.3)

Trap One: UNIT call sign assigned to Operational Headquarters. (4.4, 4.5)

Traveller's Halt, the: London hostelry where the Doctor shared Christmas dinner with Jackson Lake, his son Frederic and Rosita Farisi. (4.14)

Tree Borgs: Augmented vegetation kept in the Forest Vault aboard the *Byzantium*, which maintained a constant flow of fresh air on the ship between planetary stops. (5.5)

Trefusis, Miss: Tall woman with red nail varnish, who retrieved the Master's ring from his funeral pyre. She worked at HMS Broadfell, the prison where Lucy Saxon was secretly detained. She worked alongside some guards and the new Governor to restore the Master to life. Miss Trefusis willingly sacrificed her life to bring the Master back. (3.13, 4.17) (Played by SYLVIA SEYMOUR)

Trenzalore: According to Dorium Maldovar, it was predicted that the fall of the Eleventh would occur on the fields here. (6.13)

Treppa: Hypnotised ATMOS worker from Poland who Martha Jones tried to give a medical examination to. (4.4) (Played by RAD KAIM)

Tribophysical waveform macro-kinetic extrapolator: Technology obtained by Blon Fel Fotch Pasameer-Day Slitheen in an airlock sale. Rather like a pan-dimensional surfboard, it created a force field around its user, enabling them to ride the energy from a vast explosion. The Slitheen's plan was initially to combine the energy from a nuclear explosion with that of the rift running through Cardiff, though she eventually attempted to use rift energy combined with leaking TARDIS power. She hid the extrapolator beneath a scale model of the Blaidd Drwg power plant. (1.11) Captain Jack Harkness kept it and later used it to create a force field around the TARDIS to keep the Daleks at bay. (1.13) The Doctor later integrated it into the TARDIS systems completely and used it to shunt his craft away from the Empress of the Racnoss. (3.X) Captain Jack Harkness assumed its energy would act as a defence shield for the TARDIS. (4.13)

Trickster, the: One of the Pantheon of Discord, a group of beings which thrived off chaos and destruction caused by interfering in established time lines. The Time Beetle that was on Donna Noble's back was one of the Trickster's Brigade. (4.11) He was one of the beings potentially imprisoned within the Pandorica, depending which version of the legend was being told. (5.12)

Tri-Galactic: Information service broadcasting across the Earth Empire. (4.3)

Trine-E: One of the two robots, the other being Zu-Zana, which would take a human and decide how to make them look more fashionable for their TV show *What Not to Wear*. They would end the show, broadcast across Earth from the Game Station, by physically reconstructing their 'victims' with buzz saws and lasers if they weren't satisfied. Captain Jack Harkness found himself in their show and destroyed the two robots with his Compact Laser Deluxe. (1.12) (Voiced by TRINNY WOODALL, played by ALAN RUSCOE)

Triton: Home world to the 40th-century scourge of the galaxy, Baltazar, who was the planet's Corsair King. (TIQ)

Tritovores: Insectoid aliens who thrived in extreme cold and whose technology was mostly crystalline-based. Two of them travelled to San Helios to trade with the inhabitants, planning to buy their waste products. However, everyone on San Helios was dead, reduced to dust by the Stingrays, some of which got into the Tritovore ship's vents, causing it to crash. After sending out a probe to investigate a storm cloud, the two crew, Praygat and Sorvin, initially assumed the number 200 bus which had taken the Doctor to San Helios was to blame but, once they met the Doctor and Lady Christina de Souza, they agreed to join forces. Both Sorvin and Praygat were killed by Stingrays, however, and their ship was ultimately abandoned on the planet's surface. (4.15) A Tritovore had once been killed inside the God Complex and his photograph mounted on the wall. (6.11)

Troy: Legendary city in Turkey. The Doctor told Rose Tyler he had witnessed the fall of Troy, around 1183 BC. (1.3) History teacher Mr Parsons was bemused because one of his students had been able to give him the exact height of the Trojan walls. (2.3) The Doctor took Amy Pond to the Trojan Gardens. (5.10)

Turkey: ATMOS devices reportedly went off there. (4.4)

Turnbull, Bill: Breakfast TV presenter who interviewed author Charles Dickens about his new Christmas television play. (6.13)

Twelfth Cyber Legion: A Cyberfleet that monitored all the traffic in the quadrant. Rory Williams went there to find out what they knew about the whereabouts of Amy Pond. The Doctor blew the fleet up ship by ship until the Cyberleader told Rory what he wanted to know. (6.7)

Twelfth Night: A play by William Shakespeare. The lodgings house Shakespeare was in when he met the Doctor and Martha Jones was the Elephant Inn, which he later used in *Twelfth Night*. (3.2)

'20th Century Blues': Noel Coward composed song performed by Al Bowly and played on a gramophone by Greeves the butler at Lady Eddison's garden party for Agatha Christie. (4.7)

'24 Hours From Tulsa': Song made famous by Gene Pitney. Wilfred Mott was listening to Dusty Springfield's version when he missed seeing the Adipose First Family's ship pass over his head. (4.1)

22nd Century: Where the Doctor took Rose Tyler during her first trip in the TARDIS, although they didn't leave the ship to visit it. (1.2)

26 June 2010: The date of Amy Pond and Rory Williams's wedding, and therefore the date that the time field would expand and destroy the universe. River Song visited Amy's house on that date, taken there by the TARDIS to find the clues that led her to realise that the Pandorica legends, as well as the Auton replicas, including Rory Williams, were drawn from her memories. (5.13)

26 Squadron: One of the RAF squadrons that headed towards the south coast of England to engage German fighters in battle during the Second World War. (5.3)

244 Squadron: One of the RAF squadrons mobilised to protect London when the Daleks forced the city's lights to come on during a German air raid. (5.3)

200: London bus which accidently went through a wormhole from London to San Helios, where it was badly damaged in transit. The Doctor and the bus's passengers worked together to get back safely to Earth through the wormhole, pursued by Stingrays. The only way to get the bus back was by getting it to fly, and as a result the passengers all got a great aerial view of London when they returned. Later, the flying bus was stolen by one of those passengers, Lady Christina de Souza, to escape Detective Inspector McMillan and the Metropolitan Police. (4.15)

Twostreams Facility: Corporation on the pleasure planet Apalapucia, which ran the two co-existent time streams running in parallel, Red Waterfall and Green Anchor, via their robotic Handbots. (6.10)

Tyburn Tree, the: Legendary 17th-century London gallows. (AG05)

Tyler, Jacqueline Andrea Suzette [1]: Mother of Rose Tyler, fiercely protective of her daughter, she was left a widow after her husband Pete was killed on the day of their friends Stuart and Sarah Hoskins' wedding, when Rose was six months old. (1.8) Jackie and Rose lived in Bucknall House on the Powell Estate in South East London, from where Jackie ran her mobile hairdressing business. Born on 1 February 1967, she was a big fan of Cliff Richard,

(2.7) Il Divo, (2.10) and *EastEnders*. (2.12) When she married Pete Tyler, he got her name wrong during the ceremony. She was widowed in 1987, and would often talk to Rose about Pete when she'd had a few drinks. (1.8) The day before Rose first met the Doctor, Jackie got a phone call from her daughter from 5 billion years in the future, though she didn't realise it and continued to do the laundry, watch TV and hope to win the lottery. (1.2) After she was caught up in the Auton invasion, (1.1) Jackie feared Rose was missing or dead at the hands of her boyfriend Mickey Smith, as she didn't return for a year. (1.4) When she did, and explained where she had been and who the Doctor was, Jackie begged her not to carry on travelling with him. This was after Jackie and Mickey had been attacked by a member of the Family Slitheen, and she realised the Doctor was prepared to sacrifice both himself and Rose to save the world. (1.5) She felt the Doctor was a dangerous influence. But she realised she was fighting a losing battle and, when the Doctor tricked Rose into going back home, she helped Rose get the TARDIS to take her back to him. (1.13) She and Mickey became close friends, and she regularly cooked Sunday lunch for him. When Rose next came home, she was with the newly regenerated Doctor, who helped them foil the Sycorax invasion. Impressed by this new Doctor, Jackie had them all over to Christmas dinner (2.X) and was far more relaxed when Rose next went off travelling with the Time Lord. (2.1) She saw her daughter again when Rose and the Doctor returned from their first visit to the parallel Earth, 'Pete's World', to explain that Mickey was living there now, (2.6) and she got a phone call from Rose while she was flirting with Elton Pope. Jackie told Elton she would give her life for Rose and the Doctor. Soon

afterwards, she explained to her daughter how Elton had been trying to use her to get to them. (2.10) When the TARDIS next materialised at the Powell Estate, Jackie was convinced she was being visited by the ghost of her father, Granddad Prentice, which turned out to be a Cyberman. As a result of this ghostly vision, Jackie found herself being taken in the TARDIS to the Torchwood Institute where, due to a mix-up, the Doctor let everyone there believe she was Rose. (2.12) After escaping the Cybermen, Jackie met the rich and successful 'Pete's World' version of her husband, and they began to bond, although Jackie's assurance that there hadn't been anyone since him was a tad disrespectful to the legion of men she had, if not dated, certainly had the odd coffee with: Billy Croot, Jim, Howard, Rodrigo, Elton, and even a sailor. After the Doctor sent the Daleks and Cybermen back into the Void, he needed to seal off the breach between the two worlds, which left Jackie, Rose and Mickey in 'Pete's World' for ever. Jackie and Pete rekindled their romance and, after a few months, she fell pregnant with a new child. (2.13) Some time after giving birth to a son, Tony, she, along with Rose and Mickey used a Dimension Jump to get back to their own universe to help the Doctor stop the Daleks. Transporting to the Dalek Crucible with Mickey and Sarah Jane Smith, she was very nearly killed in a testing of the Reality Bomb. Then, alongside the Doctor, she was instrumental in stopping the Daleks' plans and eventually returned to 'Pete's World', along with Rose and an alternative version of the Doctor, grown from Time Lord and human DNA — a Doctor with one heart who would happily age and die alongside her daughter. (4.13) On New Year's Day 2005, Jackie and Rose were heading out to different parties, although they'd missed the turn of midnight because Jim had failed to pick them up. The Tenth Doctor watched them. (4.18) (Played by CAMILLE CODURI)

Tyler, Jacqueline Andrea Suzette [2]:
Wife of businessman Pete Tyler on a parallel Earth, 'Pete's World', where she didn't have a daughter called Rose. Instead, Rose was the name of her Yorkshire Terrier. Their

marriage was rocky, and Pete moved out. On her 40th birthday, the Cybermen invaded Jackie's party, killing many of the guests, or taking them to the Cyber-conversion factory in Battersea Power Station to receive the Ultimate Upgrade and become Cyberforms. Jackie Tyler was converted, but recognised Pete when he tried to rescue her and revealed his presence to the other Cybermen. (2.5, 2.6) (Played by CAMILLE CODURI, Cyberform version voiced by NICHOLAS BRIGGS)

Tyler, Peter Alan [1]:
Rose Tyler's father was born on 15 September 1954, and died on 7 November 1987, on his way to the wedding of Stuart Hoskins and Sarah Clark. He was hit by a car after picking up from their flat in Bucknall House a vase he and wife Jackie (the Maid of Honour) were presenting to the couple. Rose Tyler grew up hearing great stories about how Pete was a successful self-made man and a great husband. The truth, as Rose found out when the Doctor took her back to the day he died, was less romantic. Pete was a womaniser, his marriage to Jackie was rocky and all his money-making schemes, including his Vitex health drinks, were failures. But Rose wanted to see her dad, and saved his life, so he could go to the wedding as if everything was normal. This caused a tear in the fabric of time, allowing antibody-like wraiths, the Reapers, to spill into the world of 1987, wiping people out of time and feeding off the resultant chronal energy. Trapped with Jackie and Rose in a church, with the Doctor seemingly killed by the Reapers, Pete worked out the truth when he kept seeing a car driving in the area then vanishing. He left the church, and walked in front of the car. He died with Rose, who he now understood to be his baby daughter grown up, cradling him. Although the location of Pete's death, as well as the exact time, had been altered, his death was enough to heal the breach in time, the Reapers vanished and the missing people were all returned. (1.8) (Played by SHAUN DINGWALL)

Tyler, Peter Alan [2]: On 'Pete's World' (named by the Doctor in his honour), Pete Tyler was still alive in 2007, was still married to Jackie and was a hugely successful businessman thanks to his Vitex drinks. His company having been bought out by Cybus Industries in 2005, Pete was a very rich man, but his marriage was crumbling and he didn't trust Cybus's owner, John Lumic. In fact, Pete was secretly feeding sensitive information to an underground resistance movement, the Preachers, under the codename Gemini, although he believed he was in contact with the security services. When Cybus unleashed the results of its Ultimate Upgrade project, the Cybermen, Pete was forced into fighting back after Jackie was converted. He met Rose and together they worked alongside the Doctor to destroy the Cybermen. (2.5, 2.6) The few surviving Cybermen gained sympathy across the world when it became known they had once been living people, and the Cybermen were able to regroup and then cross the Void into Rose's home world. Pete was able to send Jake Simmonds from the Preachers and other armed fighters through the Void after the Cybermen, only to get caught up in a war between the Cybermen and the Daleks. Reunited with Rose and her mother, Pete helped stop the invasion. He returned to 'Pete's World' when the Doctor sealed the Void for ever, taking Jackie, Mickey Smith and Rose with him. He and Jackie decided to make a go of life together, even though neither one was the other's 'real' partner. After three months, Jackie fell pregnant. (2.13) They had a son called Tony, and Pete shared the parental duties like the nursery run. (4.13) (Played by SHAUN DINGWALL)

Tyler, Rose: The daughter of Peter and Jackie Tyler, Rose grew up with her mother on the Powell Estate in South East London, her father having been killed in a car accident when she was six months old. She left school to live with Jimmy Stone, who subsequently broke her heart and left her £800 in debt, and

then moved back in with Jackie, resumed an old relationship with a local boy, Mickey Smith, and found a job at Henrik's department store, where she was working as a shop assistant when the Doctor first met her in 2005. After the two of them had defeated the Nestene Consciousness, she was invited aboard the TARDIS. During her travels in the TARDIS, Rose met Charles Dickens in Cardiff and was made a Dame by Queen Victoria in Scotland. She saw the war-torn London of 1941 and the post war capital of 1953. She and the Doctor took a trip to the 2012 Olympics in Britain's near future and visited a spaceship some 3,000 years after her own time, chatted to a famous French aristocrat more than 250 years before Rose was born and had a narrow escape from Japan's 14th-century capital, Kyoto. She also saw what would become of television in the 200,001st century and a future for the human race of that era badly at odds with the Doctor's enthusiastic description of a Great and Bountiful Empire.

At the very start of their travels together, the Doctor had hoped to impress her with the prospect of watching the world end from the safety of an orbiting space station some five billion years in the future. They later made a return trip to that era, and visited the New Earth that the human race had gone on to establish. On each of these trips, she encountered a selection of alien races of all shapes, sizes and colours, her early wariness quickly evolving into appreciation for the different wonders the Doctor could show her — on one visit to an unnamed alien world, as they watched a new unfamiliar species wheeling in the sky, the Doctor asked her how long she would stay with him. Her answer was: for ever. However, many of the aliens that Rose and the Doctor encountered were less than friendly, among them the Gelth, Raxacoricofallapatorians, the Jagrafess, Roboform Santas, Sycorax, a Werewolf, Krillitanes, Clockwork Robots, the Wire, the Beast and the Abzorbaloff. They also endured bodily possession by the self-proclaimed last human, Lady Cassandra O'Brien.

Early in their adventures, the Doctor and Rose returned to the Powell Estate to find they had been absent for a whole year, and a distraught Jackie had thought her daughter missing or dead. Jackie pleaded with Rose not to resume her travels, but this had no effect. Rose did, though, stay in touch with her mother, either by phone — the Doctor had upgraded her mobile so she could call from any time and

T

anywhere – or on frequent return visits. Rose also persuaded the Doctor to take her back to 1987, as she wanted to be with her father as he died. She couldn't resist saving Pete's life, creating a wound in time and letting in the Reapers, which rampaged across the planet until her dad sacrificed himself for the sake of the world. Travelling later to a parallel universe, Rose discovered an Earth where Pete Tyler was still alive, and had become a successful businessman, and she had never been born – instead, the parallel Jackie doted upon a terrier named Rose. It was only after Jackie had been converted into a Cyberform that Rose revealed her true identity to Pete, but was shunned. Much later, the Doctor and Rose met this Pete again, when the 'Pete's World' Cybermen attacked Rose's Earth. The breach that they used also let through the Daleks. Rose had encountered a Dalek for the first time in 2012, in an underground museum in Utah. Unaware of its true nature, Rose felt sympathy for the imprisoned creature, and inadvertently allowed it to absorb her DNA, enabling it to regenerate. As the Dalek killed the inhabitants of the base, Rose used her connection with the Dalek to end the slaughter, ordering it to commit suicide in the process. Some time later, the TARDIS crew were transported onto the Game Station in the year 200,100, shortly before it came under attack from a huge Dalek fleet. The Doctor sent Rose home in the TARDIS, condemning himself to death alone. Desperate to return to his side, Rose forced open the ship's console hoping to communicate with the heart of the TARDIS. Instead, she absorbed the Time Vortex itself, granting her mastery over the whole of time and space, and allowing her to return to the Game Station. She confronted the Dalek Emperor and divided its fleet into atoms. The power, though, was killing her, and the Doctor absorbed it from her, sacrificing his own life.

This was the first time that Rose 'lost' the Doctor – the Vortex energy triggered his regeneration, and Rose found herself with an apparent stranger. The second time also involved the Daleks. As the Cult of Skaro and the Cybermen from the parallel Earth battled at Canary Wharf, the Doctor devised a plan that would seal both species in the Void. As Rose helped activate the levers that opened the breach and sucked the Daleks and the Cybermen into the Void, she fell towards the opening, but was saved by Pete Tyler. She was transported to 'Pete's World', where

she joined her mother and Mickey. Rose now had her whole family around her, with Pete and Jackie reunited and expecting a baby. But the breach was now closed and she could never see the Doctor again. (1.1–2.13)

Using a Dimension Cannon, she made her return to Donna Noble's Earth for the first time, arriving in Brook Street just as Donna was preparing to leave Earth with the Doctor. (4.1) She attempted to make contact with the Doctor, first via the TARDIS scanners (1.5) and then on Midnight, via the *Crusader 50*'s video screen, but he didn't notice her and the signal wasn't strong enough to allow audible contact. Ironically, she was one of the things he mentioned to Sky Silvestry on Midnight which she repeated back at him. (4.10) Rose finally made contact with the Donna of an alternative timeline and gave her a message to pass to the Doctor when that Donna died and time was put back on course: 'Bad Wolf'. (4.11) After her Dimension Cannon took her to the Nobles' home in Chiswick, Rose watched as Harriet Jones contacted all the Doctor's other friends, but was unable to join in with their online conversations. After Harriet was killed, Rose made one final jump – and was finally about to be reunited with the Doctor when a Dalek shot him. After he used regeneration energy to heal himself, the Doctor took Rose, Jack and Donna to the Dalek Crucible in the Medusa Cascade, where they discovered that the Daleks' creator Davros was building a Reality Bomb. After helping defeat the Daleks, the Doctor returned Rose and Jackie to Pete and her new brother Tony on 'Pete's World' – but left behind a part-human Doctor, created by his regeneration energy mixed with Donna's human DNA. This Doctor could confess that he loved Rose, and the two began a new life together – the Doctor and Rose, together at last. (4.12, 4.13)

On New Year's Day 2005, just after midnight, the Tenth Doctor spoke to Rose before she ever met the Ninth Doctor – his way of saying a last goodbye before he regenerated. (4.18) When trying to create a voice interface with the TARDIS, while dying from the poison from the Judas Tree, the Doctor considered talking to a hologram of Rose. (6.8) He contemplated popping back in time and helping her with her homework. (6.13) (Played by BILLIE PIPER and JULIA JOYCE)

Tyler, Tony: The son of Jackie Tyler from Earth and Pete Tyler from 'Pete's World'. (4.13)

U

Ultimate Sanction, the: President Rassilon's final manoeuvre in the Last Great Time War, which would destroy time itself, bringing about the end of all life everywhere, not just within the Timelocked War itself but throughout the universe. As the Time Vortex ripped apart, Rassilon and his Time Lords would ascend to become creatures of pure consciousness. Rassilon planned to unleash this, having used the Master to escape the War. The Doctor destroyed the housing containing the Whitepoint Star diamond, which linked the Time Lords and Gallifrey to Earth and sent them back into the Time War, to remain Timelocked into its final day for ever. (4.18)

Ultimate Upgrade: The official name for the Cyber-conversion process on 'Pete's World', whereby a human brain was soaked in chemicals, placed in a metallic head shell, connected to the steel body via Cynaps and had its natural emotional responses suppressed by an artificial inhibitor. On crossing the Void into the real Earth, the Cybermen carried out the same process on human captives there. (2.5, 2.6, 2.12, 2.13)

Uluru: Ancient site in Australia's Northern Territory, revered by the Aboriginal inhabitants, and a popular tourist destination under its English name, Ayers Rock. The Doctor, Kazran Sardick and Abigail Pettigrew visited it one Christmas Eve. (6.X)

Uncle: One of the Patchwork People, a humanoid man trapped on the sentient asteroid House. He was kept alive by House over many centuries to act as a lure for Time Lords and other travellers that were drawn into House's pocket universe. House fed off the rift energy that powered TARDISes, and it would reuse limbs and organs from the dead pilots to keep the Patchwork People alive. Uncle finally died when the Doctor's TARDIS, its personality matrix downloaded into another dead humanoid, Idris, was inhabited by House and taken across the Void towards the Doctor's universe. (6.4) (Played by ADRIAN SCHILLER)

Undercity: Lower region of New New York, untouched and unaware of the devastation in the Overcity, powered by the Face of Boe to stop it falling into the ocean. The Undercity had become a series of small towns, like Pharmacytown, where the remaining inhabitants of New New York could go for supplies. (3.3)

Under Henge, the: A hollowed-out chamber beneath Stonehenge, where the Pandorica Alliance built the Pandorica Chamber containing the Pandorica itself, as a trap for the Doctor in AD 102. It was guarded by a Cyberman, and a group of Autons who believed themselves to be human Roman soldiers. (5.12, 5.13)

Unicorn, the: Renowned East End thief who inveigled herself into high society, and had recently stolen Lady Babbington's pearls. She came to Eddison Hall in the guise of Robina Redmond, ostensibly to steal the famous Firestone gem that Lady Clemency Eddison always wore. She succeeded but was caught and had to return it. Presumably, she was arrested shortly afterwards. (4.7) (Played by FELICITY JONES)

UNIT: A special military/scientific elite force, made up of forces from across the world, specialising in threats to security of an extraterrestrial nature. A collection of UNIT specialists arrived from Geneva to attend a briefing at 10 Downing Street over the Big Ben incident, including Colonel Muriel Frost. They, along with various academics and soldiers, were killed by the Slitheen, who had electrified their ID cards. (1.4, 1.5) When the Sycorax spaceship intercepted the *Guinevere One* space probe and began to broadcast to Earth, Prime Minister Harriet Jones joined UNIT's Major Blake in the organisation's secret Mission Control base beneath the Tower of London to supervise the situation. Blake was murdered by the Sycorax when the UNIT officer, the PM and Professor Daniel Llewellyn were taken aboard the alien's vessel. (2.X) UNIT were also given authority over the British military by US President Winters after the first appearance of the Toclafane, and were initially responsible for security aboard the *Valiant*, though they were dismissed by the President as he prepared to greet the Toclafane. (3.12) In an abandoned UNIT base in North London, Martha Jones claimed, was the last of the phials of liquid needed to arm the gun she was allegedly preparing to kill the Master with. (3.13) Under the Doctor's guidance, Mickey Smith was able to access UNIT computer systems, (1.5, 2.X) and a web page about UNIT was seen by the Doctor when he accessed a mobile phone to search for HC Clements. (3.X) Realising that ATMOS was dangerous, journalist Jo Nakashima tried to reach UNIT, but the Sontarans

killed her. UNIT, however, were already aware that there was something wrong with ATMOS and investigated the warehouse where it was manufactured but got into a pitched battle with Sontaran troopers there. It was only after the Doctor told them of the method the Sontarans were using to make UNIT armaments useless, that UNIT were able to fight back and defeat the Sontarans. By this stage, Martha Jones was working for them as a Medical Adviser. (4.4, 4.5) In the parallel universe where Donna Noble never met the Doctor, UNIT investigated the death of the Doctor at the Thames Barrier and another secret team, led by Captain Erisa Magambo, alongside Rose Tyler, attempted to reverse engineer the TARDIS and send Donna back to her correct reality. (4.11) Martha Jones was UNIT's medical specialist on Project Indigo in their New York Headquarters when the Daleks moved the Earth to the Medusa Cascade. When the Daleks invaded, they targeted Earth's military installations, including UNIT's New York HQ, exterminating most of the personnel there, although Martha herself used Indigo to escape. (4.12) Under Magambo, UNIT responded to the disappearance of the number 200 bus that went through a wormhole to San Helios and later returned pursued by three Stingrays, which UNIT destroyed. UNIT HQ had an automated public phone operation system which the Doctor bypassed with Angela Whittaker's help. (4.15) The Master took UNIT over, from Geneva. (4.18) The Doctor told the survivors of the Zebra Bay Geological Survey Unit in the Arctic Circle that UNIT would debrief them later. (AG02)

United Nations Commander General: Torchwood listened to him on the radio as he surrendered to the Daleks on behalf of planet Earth. (4.12)

Units Ten/Six/Five and Ten/Six/Six: Two Cybermen sent to investigate the Sphere Room in Torchwood Tower. They encountered Dalek Thay in the corridor, who shot them down. (2.13) (Voiced by NICHOLAS BRIGGS)

Universal Roaming: The method by which the Doctor ensured Martha Jones's mobile phone could work anywhere in time and space. (3.7) He had previously given Rose Tyler's phone a similar upgrade, (1.2) although that had proved insufficient when the TARDIS took them to Krop Tor. (2.8)

Universally Speaking: TV science show upon which Richard Dawkins was a guest, talking about Earth being moved across the galaxy. (4.12)

University of California, Berkeley: Child prodigy Roman Groom was schooled there, where he invented Gadget prior to joining the Bowie Base One Mars mission. (4.16)

University of Edinburgh: Posing as Dr James McCrimmon, the Doctor told Queen Victoria he had studied in Edinburgh under Dr Joseph Bell. (2.2)

University of Mars: Adam Mitchell pretended he was a student visiting from the University of Mars, to explain away his lack of an Info Chip to the Nurse aboard Satellite Five. (1.7)

Untempered Schism: A rip in the fabric of space and time which over the centuries gave the Time Lords their physical powers such as regeneration and enhanced strength, through which eternity and the Time Vortex could be observed and absorbed. Looking into it as Novices about to enter the Academy on Gallifrey, young Time Lords would have different responses. Some would be inspired; others, like the Doctor, would flee. When the Master looked into it, he received a telepathic sound – a heartbeat, sent from the future by Lord Rassilon. The heartbeat, a rhythmic drumming, sent the Master insane as only he could hear it forever pounding in his head. (3.12, 4.17, 4.18, 6.7)

Urchin [1]: A London boy kidnapped by the Graske at Christmas 1883, and replaced with a Changeling. He was eventually returned home with no memory of his experiences. (AotG) (Played by BEN HOLLAND)

Urchin [2]: London lad who tells the Doctor that he's in 1851. (4.14) (Played by JORDAN SOUTHWELL)

Utah: America's 45th State, on the western side of the continent. Surrounded by desert plains, it was an ideal location for Henry Van Statten to build his underground base. (1.6) The Doctor asked River Song, Amy Pond, Rory Williams and Canton Delaware III to meet him there. They met near Lake Silencio, where they saw the Doctor shot dead by a mysterious astronaut. Three months later, Amy was apparently gunned down there by Delaware and her body taken to Nevada. (6.1, 6.2, 6.13)

Utopia: Legendary location where the last members of the human race planned to assemble, 100,000,000,000,000 years in the future. It was out towards the Wildlands of space, beyond the Condensate Wilderness but close to the Dark Matter Reefs. Those trapped on Malcassairo were dependent on a rocket which Professor Yana was trying to launch. With help from the Doctor and Captain Jack Harkness, the rocket took off, taking the humans to Utopia where, ultimately, they or their descendants would become the Toclafane. Later, the Master and Lucy Saxon were able to travel to Utopia to discover it was everything the humans had hoped it wouldn't be. There were no diamonds in the skies – indeed, as the universe around them began to decay, the humans on Utopia had destroyed the world, leaving it dark and cold, with only the furnaces with which they defiled their own bodies to light the darkness. (3.11, 3.13)

Utopia Project: A human cadre, the Science Foundation, postulated the concept of Utopia and formulated the Utopia Project thousands of years before Professor Yana got the rocket launched away from Malcassairo and towards Utopia. (3.11)

Uvodni: Militaristic aliens which travelled to Stonehenge, as part of the Pandorica Alliance. When the Pandorica opened and history was stopped, the Alliance were reduced to fossils. (5.12, 5.13) (Played by LEVI JAMES)

Val: Gossipy perfumery worker at Sanderson & Grainger, a Colchester department store. She liked the Doctor, who had taken a job there while investigating a Cyberman invasion. She assumed the Doctor and Craig Owens were a couple, and encouraged them to get as much 'them' time as possible as they had baby Alfie to look after. (6.12) (Played by LYNDA BARON)

Valiant, UNIT Carrier Ship: Aircraft carrier, which Harry Saxon helped design. It did not sail on the seas but flew in the skies above Earth. It was decided that Earth would greet the Toclafane there, thus not in any one country's territory. After the Toclafane invaded, the Master made the *Valiant* his base of operations for the next year, keeping Francine, Clive and Tish Jones prisoners there, working for him. Captain Jack Harkness was chained up below decks, Lucy Saxon became one of a harem of girls the Master kept onboard, and the Doctor, physically reduced to a shrunken, 900-year-old Time Lord, was held in a birdcage. The TARDIS was also stored there, cannibalised by the Master to create the Paradox Machine. After the Master had been defeated, Lucy Saxon shot him dead on the bridge. (3.12, 3.13) Colonel Mace called it in to help clear the air over London of ATMOS gas. (4.5) It was completely destroyed with all hands aboard by the Daleks. (4.12)

Valley of the Gods: Area of Utah where Canton Delaware III finally tracked Amy Pond down and apparently shot her. (6.2)

Van Cassadyne energy: The main component of a Delta Wave. Trapped on the Game Station, facing half a million Daleks, the Doctor opted to use the Station's resources as a huge transmitter, creating a Delta Wave which would fry anything in its path. The Emperor foresaw this eventuality and reminded the Doctor that, should he use the Delta Wave, he would indeed wipe out the Daleks, but before that, it would kill everything between them, including the population of Earth. In the end, faced with the choice, the Doctor resigned himself to failing, and the Wave was never activated. (1.13)

Van Gogh, Theo: Brother to Vincent Van Gogh, and a successful art dealer. Van Gogh assumed the Doctor was just the latest physician Theo had sent to check up on him. (5.10)

Van Gogh, Vincent: One of the most famous and beloved Dutch painters in history. During the latter half of the 19th century, however, Van Gogh remained fairly unknown and unsuccessful. Many of his peers and other people he interacted with in his adopted France, including his own family, believed him to be insane and incurable. Van Gogh actually suffered from bi-polar disorder, which was undiagnosed by the time he settled in Auvers. While there he painted a local church and included in it a Krafayis, which the Doctor and Amy Pond noticed over a century later at the Musée D'Orsay in Paris. Travelling back to Van Gogh's home, they realised that the invisible Krafayis was visible to the painter because of the chemical imbalance in his mind. Taking a shine to Amy, Van Gogh agreed to help them stop the Krafayis, hoping it would alleviate his 'madness'. Afterwards, the Doctor and Amy took him to 2010 to meet Doctor Black, an expert and fan of his work who lectured at *The Great Exhibition*. Overwhelmed by the realisation that his name and work would live on, he returned to Auvers an apparently contented man. But the Doctor told Amy that it wouldn't last and within a few months he would commit suicide. (5.10) A few weeks afterwards, apparently stricken again with depression and delusions, he painted a picture he called *The Pandorica Opens*, which centuries later became part of the Royal Collection aboard *Starship UK*. (5.12) (Played by TONY CURRAN)

Van Hoff, Foon: Cheerful and overweight woman from Sto who was aboard the starliner *Titanic* when it was struck by meteoroids. She confessed to her husband Morvin that she'd spent more money on entering the competition to win the cruise than it would have cost to buy the tickets directly, but he didn't mind. She was devastated when Morvin died and, upon realising that the only way to save the Doctor, Rickston Slade, Mr Copper, Astrid Peth and Bannakaffalatta was to jump into the nuclear engines, taking a lassoed Host with her, she did so, and saved their lives. (4.X) (Played by DEBBIE CHAZEN)

Van Hoff, Morvin: Avuncular and large man from Sto who, with his wife, Foon, had won a competition to take a trip on the Max Capricorn starliner *Titanic*. He and Foon were the butt of a number of jokes amongst their fellow passengers, but they didn't really mind, because they were enjoying their trip

together. With the Doctor, Astrid and Mr Copper, they took a brief trip to Earth but came back aboard just as the ship was struck by meteoroids. Morvin and Foon survived but, when trying to escape the Heavenly Host, part of the ship gave way under Morvin's weight and he plunged to his death in the nuclear engines below. (4.X) (Played by CLIVE ROWE)

Van Statten, Henry: The internet-owning American billionaire, whose intelligence was matched only by his arrogance and self-obsession. Although his main business was his Geocomtex Corporation, he was also an avid collector of any and all extraterrestrial artefacts. If he found a way to exploit them commercially through Geocomtex, he would. He kept his artefacts in an exhibit room, inside a bunker 53 storeys below Utah. He owned something he called a 'Metaltron', which he knew was alive but, no matter how much he had it tortured, he could not get it to respond. When the Doctor and Rose Tyler arrived in 2012, it did finally, and the Doctor revealed that the prize of Van Statten's collection was a Dalek. The Dalek freed itself and went on a murderous rampage, wiping out virtually all the Geocomtex security and staff, but Van Statten refused to run the risk of damaging it. Eventually, face to face with it, Van Statten revealed how terrified he was, but the Dalek spared him after a plea from Rose. After the Dalek was destroyed, Van Statten suffered a fate which had previously befallen so many of his staff – his subordinate Goddard had him mind-wiped and dumped on the streets somewhere, to live the remainder of his life as a brainless junkie. (1.6) (Played by COREY JOHNSON)

Vandaleur, Father Gideon: Envoy of the Silence, who died and was replaced by a copy, the *Teselecta*, on the orders of its captain, Carter. The Doctor wanted to find Carter and see what information he had gleaned from Vandaleur. (6.13) (Played by NIALL GREIG FULTON)

Varga Plant: Lethal vegetation native to Skaro which grew wild in the ruined city of Kalaann. (AG01)

Vashta Nerada: Carnivorous microspores, whose name literally means 'the shadows that melt the flesh'. They could only live in the darkness, so their natural habitats were forests and woods where they lived off road kill. However when Felman Lux constructed his Library planet, the trees these 'piranhas of the air' lived in were pulped for paper to make his millions of books. Over 1,000,000,000,000 Vashta Nerada escaped into the darkness of The Library's corridors, causing the central data core to save the humans by downloading them onto its hard drive. A century later, the Doctor and Donna Noble received a request to visit The Library. The message was from Professor River Song, who also arrived with an archaeological party, financed by Felman Lux's grandson, Strackman. The Vashta Nerada picked off the archaeologists one by one until the Doctor came to an arrangement – if he was allowed to get the humans off the planet, the Vashta Nerada could stay in the books in The Library. (4.8, 4.9) As she saw her mother and fiancé change into the Master in front of her, Donna Noble remembered the Vashta Nerada as her memories started to come back. (4.17, 4.18) The Doctor cited his encounter with the Vashta Nerada as a reason for the Atraxi to be afraid of him. (5.1) A swarm infested the Poseidon sub-aquatic base on Earth in the 23rd century. The Doctor sent them back through the Trans-Dimensional Gateway they had arrived through, though not until they had killed a large number of Poseidon's population. (AG04)

Vashtee, Riley: One of the crew aboard the SS *Pentallian*, he was horrified to learn that Korwin McDonnell had destroyed the engineering equipment, setting the cargo ship on a collision course with a nearby sun. He and Martha Jones headed for the auxiliary controls at the front of the ship, trying to get through the locked doors in time, answering trivia questions that the crew had set as passwords. Along the way, however, they were intercepted by a sun-possessed crewmate, Dev Ashton and, to escape him, they hid in an escape pod. Ashton jettisoned the pod, sending it towards the sun. Inside, Vashtee and Martha discussed their impending deaths, and he revealed that his father was dead and he'd run away from his mother six years before because she hadn't wanted him to sign up for work on a cargo ship. Vashtee and Martha were saved

when the Doctor remagnetised the ship and the pod. Once back aboard, Vashtee made it to Auxiliary with Orin Scannell, and they vented the scooped-up fuel from the sun, managing to get the ship back on course. Sad to say goodbye to Martha, Vashtee remained with Scannell aboard the *Pentallian*, awaiting rescue by the authorities. (3.7) (Played by WILLIAM ASH)

Vastra, Madame: Silurian warrior the Doctor met in Victorian London, when she was trying to kill tunnellers building the London Underground, who had accidentally destroyed her peoples' shelter. The Doctor calmed her and they became great friends. Vastra set herself up in a house in London, with her like-minded human aide, Jenny, and together they solved crimes and fought evil across London. In 1888, Vastra had just finished eating Jack the Ripper when the TARDIS materialised in her house, and she knew it was time she and Jenny repaid their debt to the Doctor. Going to Demon's Run to protect Amy Pond and her baby daughter Melody, Vastra and Jenny were responsible for putting the security systems offline and creating a blackout so the Doctor could escape the Headless Monks and the Clerics. They later fought beside Commander Strax, Lorna Bucket and Rory Williams to defeat the Headless Monks in hand-to-hand combat, and won. River Song later took Jenny and Vastra back to Victorian London. (6.7) (Played by NEVE McINTOSH)

Vatican, the: The coordinating organisation that the Clerics of the 51st century worked for. When Colonel Manton had finished kitting out the asteroid Demon's Run for war, he reckoned it was even more powerful than the whole Vatican itself. (6.7)

Vator: Travel between levels on *Starship UK* was by these lifts. Some vators had advertising posters in them, others had interactive screens with

poetry read out. Timmy Winters took a vator where a Vator Verse was read out as he plummeted into the ship's bowels. (5.2)

Vault, the [1]: Geocomtex's secret underground base, beneath the Utah desert, which would double as a bunker in the event of a nuclear strike above ground, had over fifty storeys of research, development and security and, below that, was the Vault, containing Henry Van Statten's exhibit room, where he kept his alien artefacts. Also in this Vault was the 'Cage' – the containment area where the 'Metaltron' was tortured. Van Statten attempted to seal the Vault off at Level 46 (his office) when the Dalek tried to fight its way out. (1.6)

Vault, the [2]: Huge storehouse of alien equipment and material, built inside a mountain in Nevada, close to Area 51, aka Dreamland. Saruba Velak's Orb of Healing was kept there, as were the dangerous Skorpius Flies, which attacked her and the Doctor when they were exploring the place. (DL)

Vaults, the: Area in the depths of the Dalek Crucible where Dalek Caan was kept in chains and Davros was confined, working for the Supreme Dalek to create the Reality Bomb. (4.12, 4.13)

Vauxhall: One of the London destinations of the bus, number 200, during its journey on the night it went through a wormhole and ended up on San Helios. (4.15)

Vegas 12: Planet which contained the Live Chess Pits, where the Doctor played against Gantok. (6.13)

Vel Consadine: Civilisation which had the concept of evil represented by a horned beast in its culture. (2.9)

Veltino: The extinct race that had once inhabited the planet Krop Tor, giving it its name, which translated from their language as 'the bitter pill'. (2.8)

Venezuela: South American country. On 'Pete's World', the diamond-studded ear pods given to Jackie Tyler as a gift from John Lumic were able to pick up signals from as far afield as Venezuela. (2.5)

Venice: Italian city, built on a system of canals. Popular with the likes of Byron and Napoleon Bonaparte, it was – according to the Doctor – founded by people fleeing Attila the Hun. The survivors of the planet Saturnyne arrived there in the 16th century and, while the males settled within the waters, the only female set herself up as Rosanna Calvierri and established a 'finishing school' for girls. The school was a front – she used her own blood to turn the girls into Saturnyne females to mate with the men and repopulate the Saturnyne species, planning on evacuating the city of humans and subsequently taking it over completely. (5.6) The Doctor, Kazran Sardick and Abigail Pettigrew visited it one Christmas Eve. (6.X)

Venom Grubs: Inhabitants of a number of planets in the Isop Galaxy. Mindless, lethal giant arthropods, Blon Fel Fotch Pasameer-Day Slitheen's father used to threaten to feed her to them when she was young. (1.11)

Venus: The second planet from the sun in Earth's solar system, named for the Roman Goddess of love. The Doctor carried a toothbrush filled with Venusian toothpaste, and he gave it to Martha Jones when they stayed in Elizabethan England. (3.2) Keen amateur astronomer Wilfred Mott told Donna Noble it was the only planet in Earth's solar system named after a woman. (4.1) Donna posed as Venus, in front of Evelina Caecilius, who thought this was sacrilegious. And amusing. (4.2)

Venus de Milo, aka Aphrodite of Milos: Ancient Grecian sculpture believed to be by Alexandros of Antioch. A copy of it was on Apalapucia. (6.10)

Vera Duckworth: Fictional character from *Coronation Street*. Although Vera was a Lancashire lady, Donna Noble accused a grumpy Yorkshire woman of being just like Vera in the alternative world where Donna never met the Doctor. (4.11)

Verger: One of Father Octavian's Cleric officers on Alfava Metraxis, who was in charge of the explosives used to access the Maze of the Dead. (5.4)

Vernet, Giselle: Young woman killed on the streets of Paris by the Krafayis. (5.10) (Played by JELENA JAKSIC)

Vernet, Madame: Mother of Giselle, who accused Vincent Van Gogh of being the reason her daughter had been murdered. (5.10) She was with Doctor Gachet when Van Gogh was ill, and together they discovered his most recent painting, *The Pandorica Opens*. (5.12) (Played by CHRISSIE COTTRILL)

Veronica of Reykjavik: Prestigious florist on 'Pete's World'. Jackie Tyler had flowers for her birthday party delivered from her. (2.5)

Verron Soothsayer: Alien who supplied Sarah Jane Smith with a Warp Star. (4.13)

Versailles: Suburb of Paris, France — and home to the legendary Palace, or Hall of Mirrors as it was known. In 1745, Jeanne-Antoinette Poisson, aka Madame de Pompadour, aka Reinette, was moved in as the King's consort. In 1758, a party at Versailles was interrupted when Clockwork Robots from the 51st century attacked, intending to remove Reinette's brain for use in the repair of their spaceship, which was named after her. The Doctor cut off their link to the future, the Robots deactivated and everyone at the Palace was saved. (2.4)

Vespa: Italian-design motorised scooter, first on the market in 1946. The Doctor had a blue Vespa parked in the TARDIS, which he and Rose used to get around North London in 1953. After defeating the alien criminal calling itself the Wire, the Doctor gave the scooter to young Tommy Connolly, telling him he was too young to ride it yet. (2.7)

Vespiform: Huge wasp-like creature from the Silfrax galaxy. Amorphous by nature, one came to Earth in the late 1880s, calling himself Christopher, and began a relationship with a human, Lady Clemency Eddison. The Vespiform

drowned in an accident and Lady Clemency returned to England, pregnant with his child. She gave the resultant changeling baby up for adoption and it began a new, unwitting, life as Arnold Golightly, who eventually became a priest. However, Christopher had given Clemency a telepathy-boosted jewel, the Firestone, and, when Golightly befriended Clemency 40 years later, he became susceptible to the Firestone's power. Unknowingly at first, Golightly changed back and forth into the Vespiform, firstly to attack two rough lads who had tried to steal from his church. At Eddison Hall, the works of Agatha Christie, being read by Clemency while she wore the Firestone, turned Golightly, in his Vespiform state, into a mass murderer. Eventually Agatha Christie lured him away from Eddison Hall, her own mind beginning to sync with the Firestone – and when Donna threw it into a lake, the Vespiform followed – and drowned, just as his father had nearly half a century earlier. (4.7) Despite her memory having been wiped, after the arrival of the Master on Earth and his subsequent attempt to turn humanity into himself, Donna Noble recalled the Vespiform as her mind subconsciously fought the Master's influence. (4.17, 4.18)

Vesuvius: A volcanic mountain by the city of Pompeii. The inhabitants had no idea it was a volcano, indeed they had no actual word for a volcano, having never witnessed such a thing. Deep within it was a crashed Pyrovillian spaceship which had arrived in AD 62. The Pyrovillian dust entered the city via the vents and flumes from the volcano that ran beneath the city and began transforming the population to stone, if they had minds capable of being psychically bonded to the Pyroviles. To destroy the Pyroviles, the Doctor had to make Vesuvius erupt, an event that otherwise the Pyroviles had stopped happening when they first landed, creating an alternative 17-year timeline. With Vesuvius erupting as history intended, the Pyroviles, their influence and Pompeii were utterly destroyed. (4.2)

Vicar [1]: Officiated at St Christopher's Church for the wedding of Stuart Hoskins and Sarah Clark. He became a victim of the Reapers as they broke into the world after Rose Tyler saved her dad's life and created a breach in time. (1.8) (Played by LEE GRIFFITHS)

Vicar [2]: Was about to perform the marriage service at St Mary's Church in Chiswick between Donna Noble and Lance Bennett when Donna vanished. During the resultant pandemonium, another wedding got delayed, and the vicar ended up calling the police to try and sort out the bedlam around him. (3.X) (Played by TREVOR GEORGES)

Vicar [3]: Gave the Remembrance Day service attended by an old Tim Latimer, the Doctor and Martha Jones. She read from Binyon's 'For the Fallen'. (3.9) (Played by SOPHIE TURNER)

Vicar [4]: Presided over the funeral of the Reverend Aubrey Fairchild. He was appalled at the arrival of Mercy Hartigan at the service, particularly because she wore red not black. He was killed by Miss Hartigan's allies, the Cybermen. (4.14) (Played by JASON MORELL)

Vicar [5]: Married Donna Noble to Shaun Temple. (4.18) (Played by JOHN CECIL)

Vicar [6]: Married Amy Pond to Rory Williams. (5.13) (Played by PAUL WHISTON)

Vicky: A friend of Martha Jones. She obsessed about a guy, Shaun, she was in love with. He never looked twice at her, but she put her own life on hold while she focused on him. Martha told her to move on and get out – and likened herself to Vicky over her feelings toward the Doctor. She and the Doctor parted company as best of friends. (3.13)

Victoria: London terminus where the bus, number 200, started its journey on the night it went through a wormhole and ended up on San Helios. (4.15)

Victoria, Queen Alexandrina: Queen of Great Britain and Ireland, Empress of India. The Doctor and Rose Tyler encountered her in 1879, at a period of her life when she spent several months each year at Balmoral Castle in

Scotland, to which she was heading when they met. She had been travelling by train until the Brethren of St Catherine blocked the line with a tree, so was now travelling by coach. Together, they all travelled to Torchwood House to stay the night as guests of her late husband's friend's son, Sir Robert MacLeish. MacLeish senior and Prince Albert had built a vast telescope in the Observatory atop the House which, it transpired, had been designed as a trap for the Haemovariform that had existed in the area for over 300 years. Victoria faced this werewolf bravely, but may or may not have been cut by its claws. The Host virus was passed by blood, and Victoria was later diagnosed with haemophilia, a hereditary illness which her forebears were not known to suffer from. She was grateful to the Doctor and Rose for destroying the Haemovariform but, after honouring them both, she exiled them from the British Empire's shores. When Lady Isobel MacLeish confessed she no longer wished to live at Torchwood House, Victoria decided to keep the place herself and set up the Torchwood Institute to defend the British Empire against further alien threats. (2.2) A web page about Queen Victoria was seen by the Doctor when he accessed a mobile phone with his sonic screwdriver to search for HC Clements. (3.X) Liz Ten knew that the Doctor had been knighted and exiled by her. (5.2) (Played by PAULINE COLLINS)

Vietnam: Listing things of importance that happened in 1979, the Doctor told Rose Tyler that China invaded Vietnam. (2.2) River Song suggested that President Nixon's stance on the Vietnam War wasn't his proudest achievement. (6.1)

Vikram: Guest at the wedding between Donna Noble and Lance Bennett. He had a mobile phone. (3.X)

Vile, Doctor: False personality adopted by the Doctor, pretending to be a galactic pirate and responsible for stirring up the war between Earth and the Mantasphids. The Empire then sent out a message across the galaxy, demanding his apprehension. (TIQ)

Villengard: Captain Jack Harkness had a digital sonic blaster, manufactured in the weapons factories of Villengard. The Doctor suggested that he had caused an accident in Villengard's main reactor, destroying the weapons factories completely and planting a banana grove in its place. (1.10)

Vinegar: See *Acetic acid*

Vinvocci: Alien race of industrial salvagers, with green, spiky skin. A Vinvocci salvage ship had crash-landed in North Wales once, with the Immortality Gate aboard. Two Vinvocci, Addams and Rossiter, later came to Earth, trying to reclaim it. They were very insistent that they were nothing like the Zocci. (4.17, 4.18)

Viperon: Homeworld of the Viperox Horde. (DL)

Viperox Horde: Insectoid warriors from Viperon. After waging war against the Endymides, they had come to Earth in search of a genetic weapon that had been designed to exterminate them. Susceptible to high-frequency noise, the Viperox were led by their Queen, whilst the army was commanded by Lord Azlok. After the Doctor used his sonic screwdriver, its frequency boosted by the TARDIS to stop them, Azlok led his Viperox Horde away from Earth. (DL)

Viperox Queen: Imperial Majesty of the Viperox Horde, 30 feet tall, with a birthing tube constantly delivering new warriors for the Horde. Lord Azlok had placed her in caves beneath the town of Solitude and she presumably fled Earth along with the rest of the Horde after the Doctor used high-frequency sonics against them. (DL)

Viro-Stabiliser: River Song used one on Amy Pond to protect her from radiation poisoning on Alfava Metraxis. (5.4)

Viscum Album: A species of mistletoe, also known as European mistletoe, used by the Brethren of St Catherine to protect themselves from the Haemovariform they had taken to Torchwood House in 1879. Sir George MacLeish had varnished the walls and doors of his library with the oil from *viscum album* to keep the werewolf out. (2.2)

Visionary, the: Time Lord seer who predicted the end of Gallifrey, declaring it would fall burning in fire. (4.18) (Played by BRID BRENNAN)

Visual Recognition System: A portable device that, when shown an image, would offer up a more accurate visual record. The Doctor used one to identify the Krafayis on a VRS given to him by his two-headed, and rather dull, godmother. (5.10)

Vitex: One of Pete Tyler's get-rich-quick schemes had involved selling a health drink called Vitex. It failed. (1.8) The 'Pete's World' version of Pete Tyler made millions out of Vitex (especially the Cherry-Lite flavour) and became a minor celebrity because of his adverts, culminating in the phrase 'Trust me on this' entering popular culture. Cybus Industries bought up Pete's Vitex company, making him even richer. (2.5, 2.6)

Void, the: The space between the dimensions separating billions of divergent realities and parallel worlds (including 'Pete's World'). (2.5) It contained absolutely nothing: no light, dark, direction, time or sense of reality. The Cybermen moved from 'Pete's World' and across the Void over a long period of time to break into Rose Tyler's reality. A Void ship containing Daleks had escaped into the Void with the Genesis Ark, then pushed itself back into the world, though with part of

it still locked into the Void. The Cybermen used the resulting breaches to ease themselves through, and Torchwood unwittingly increased these breaches with their 'ghost shifts'. When both the Cybermen and the Daleks emerged fully from the Void, the two races began an immediate war, centred on Torchwood Tower. Everything that had ever crossed the Void was contaminated with an almost undetectable substance the Doctor called Void Stuff, so he fully reopened the Void, and everything contaminated was instantly sucked back in through the Wall. Once all the Daleks and Cybermen were back inside the Void, the Doctor sealed it for ever, trapping them into an eternity of nothing. Rose Tyler had also been almost drawn in, since she had passed through the Void, but was saved by the 'Pete's World' version of her father, who transported her to his home. Rose was sealed off from the Doctor. (2.12, 2.13) Rose later reported that the Void and everything in it was dead. This turned out to be due to Davros and the Daleks constructing their Reality Bomb. (4.12, 4.13) As the integrity of the Void collapsed, a group of Cybermen stole a Dalek Dimension Vault and used it to flee the Void, arriving in Victorian London, where they built a CyberKing (4.14) The Doctor reminded the Daleks he encountered in wartime London that he had defeated them by sending them into the Void. (5.3) When the Doctor flew the Pandorica into the heart of the exploding TARDIS to reboot the universe, sealing the cracks made by the time field, he was thrown into the Void but was brought back again by the intensity of Amy's memories of him after River Song left her a wedding present – her TARDIS inspired diary. (5.13) A rift in time and space created access to a bubble universe at the bottom of what the Doctor called the plughole of the universe. Trapped there was a sentient asteroid known as House which over millennia would trap Time Lords and TARDISes there, to feed on. After the Time War, no more

TARDISes existed, and House was starving until the Doctor traversed the rift and crossed the Void into House's universe. (6.4)

Void Ship: A spheroid, 20 feet in diameter, which could be seen but not properly touched. No matter how hard anyone looked at it, it was as if it wasn't quite there. It gave off no sensory information that either humans or computers could read, and yet it was actually there. A Torchwood team led by Dr Rajesh Singh had studied it, but even a new spectrometer brought in by Torchwood's R&D team couldn't get a reading off it. Once the Cybermen had broken through into the Lever Room, the Sphere, which the Doctor identified as a Void ship, began to operate and become 'real'. But the Cyberleader in the Lever Room informed the Doctor it wasn't their technology – indeed, it had nothing to do with Cybermen at all. All parties were astonished to see four Daleks – the Cult of Skaro – emerge from within, bringing with them the Genesis Ark. (2.12, 2.13)

Void Stuff: Particles of matter which clung to anything that had passed through the Void. It was only visible through 3D glasses. The Daleks and Cybermen had had relatively lengthy excursions through the Void and were therefore coated in it. As a result, they were easily sucked back into the Void when it was fully opened by the Doctor. So would Rose Tyler have been, but she was saved by the 'Pete's World' version of her father, who transported her to his home. Rose was sealed off in 'Pete's World', where she had to remain. (2.12, 2.13)

Volag-Noc: Ice-covered planet that housed under its surface a galactic prison, run by the robotic Governor Locke and his Warders during the 40th century. Amongst the inmates were Baltazar, Gurney, Kaliko and, later, the Doctor. A regular visitor to Volag-Noc was Mergrass, who would do deals between the prisoners and other inmates or outside sources. Gurney used a device he bought from Mergrass to usurp Locke from his role as Governor. Gurney imprisoned Locke

DOCTOR WHO THE ENCYCLOPEDIA

in Cell 8447, but the Doctor freed him. Disturbed by Gurney's inhibitors, Locke tried to kill all the inmates but the Doctor stopped him and later reprogrammed him to run a fairer prison, before having Baltazar returned to the planet for incarceration. (TIQ)

Volatile Circus: English translation of the name of a planet that the Doctor told Amy Pond about. (6.11)

Vomit-O-Matic: Installed at no extra cost to Adam Mitchell when he had the Type Two chip inserted into his head. As soon as the doors in his forehead whirred open and he saw his own brain, Adam threw up, but the Nurse told him the nano-termites now implanted into his throat had frozen the waste created by his gag reflex. (1.7)

Vone: Mobile portable communication device used by the people of Sto. Although temperamental, its range reached the orbit of planet Earth. (4.X)

'Voodoo Child': Single by Rogue Traders, which was played by the Master aboard the *Valiant* as the Toclafane began their descent. Lucy Saxon danced along to it, too. (3.12)

Vortex Loop: Essential component of the TARDIS console. (AotG)

Vortex Manipulator: Wrist device supplied to Time Agents. Captain Jack Harkness owned one – he used it to teleport himself from Albion Hospital back to his ship. It had a holographic projector in it, could scan for alien tech and was capable of providing medical readouts. After the battle against the Emperor Daleks' forces on the Game Station, Jack was exterminated but brought back to life by Rose Tyler. He tried to use the Vortex Manipulator to get back to 21st-century Earth, hoping he could track the Doctor down there but, due to the damage caused by the Daleks, it fried and he was transported to 1869, the device now burnt out. When trapped on Malcassairo, the Master having stolen the TARDIS, the

Doctor used his sonic screwdriver to temporarily reboot the Vortex Manipulator's time-travelling abilities, initially to get them to 21st-century London and later as a spatial teleporter. This took Martha Jones off the *Valiant* and down to the surface of Earth. Later still, it transported the Master and the Doctor back and forth from the *Valiant*. When Captain Jack parted ways with the Doctor once again, the Doctor undid his earlier repair work, leaving the Vortex Manipulator incapable of temporal travel. With Martha Jones's help, Jack was able to make it do short teleports, but the Doctor disabled it again. (1.9, 1.10, 1.13, 3.11, 3.12, 3.13, 4.12, 4.13) Dorium Maldovar supplied one to River Song, which she used to get around the galaxy. (5.12, 5.13)

Vortron Radiation: Given out by the Trans-Dimensional Gateway that opened on the floor of the Atlantic Ocean in the 23rd century, near the Poseidon Community. (AG04)

Vossaheen, Princess: Rose Tyler did not know the surname of this royal figure during *The Weakest Link* aboard the Game Station. (1.12)

Vot: Subject of exclamation on Sto. (4.X)

Vulcan: Roman God of Fire who Lobos Caecilius assumed was angry, hence the eruption of Vesuvius. (4.2)

Vulcan Salute: From the television series *Star Trek*. The Doctor showed Chloe Webber that he could do a Vulcan salute to charm her – but it failed and Chloe was more frightened than ever because she didn't understand the Isolus that inhabited  her body. She later returned the salute as a way of telling the Doctor that she was willing to talk to him. (2.11)

Wagner, Mr: A Krillitane who had taken human form and was working at Deffry Vale High School as a Mathematics teacher. He was killed when K-9 heated up the drums of Krillitane Oil in the school kitchen and blew Wagner, the school and himself to pieces. (2.3) (Played by EUGENE WASHINGTON)

Wailing Woman: Friend of the Vernet family, who found the dead body of Giselle. (5.10) (Played by JASNA MALEC)

Wainwright, Ben: Young  farmer who was the first person Kathy Nightingale met when she was transported from the London of 2007 to the Hull of 1920. Clearly attracted to Kathy, he pursued her and eventually they got married (although she lied about her age). They had three children together, two boys and a girl called Sally, but Ben died of influenza in 1962. (3.10) (Played by THOMAS NELSTROP)

Wainwright, Katherine: See *Nightingale, Katherine Costello*

Wainwright, Malcolm: Kathy Wainwright's grandson. She asked him to find Sally Sparrow at Wester Drumlins at exactly the moment she knew she was going to be sent back in time by the Weeping Angels. Although Kathy was now dead, Malcolm did as bidden and gave Sally a letter from Kathy explaining what had happened to her and asking her to contact her brother Larry. (3.10) (Played by RICHARD CANT)

Wainwright, Sally: Daughter of Ben and Kathy Wainwright, named in honour of Kathy's old friend Sally Sparrow. She had two older brothers. (3.10)

Waitresses: Servers working in Maurice's café in Paris who were singularly unimpressed by Vincent Van Gogh, his paintings and his inability to pay his bar tab. (5.10) (Played by SARAH COUNSELL and JOLANDA TUDOR)

Walcott's Haulage: Donna Noble stepped out in front of one of their lorries in Chiswick in the alternative world where she never met the Doctor. This caused her other self to turn left and head towards HC Clements, to avoid the resultant traffic congestion, and thus put reality back on track. (4.11)

Walford: Fictional setting for the BBC TV soap opera *EastEnders*. The Doctor refers to Walford while crossing the cavern beneath Krop Tor. (2.8) Peggy Mitchell runs the show's Queen Vic pub, as seen on Jackie Tyler's television. (2.12)

Walker, Captain: Torchwood operative put in command of the mission to Krop Tor by Torchwood Archivist McMillan. It was believed that the power source detected beneath Krop Tor would be enough to power the entire Earth Empire. The only clue she could offer Walker was a book of maps, hieroglyphs, writings and drawings found by the destroyed Gedes Expedition. Walker took a ship to the K 37 Gem 5 black hole and used the gravity funnel linking it to Krop Tor as a route down. Things went wrong, however, and Walker was killed in the descent, leaving Zachary Cross Flane as acting captain. (2.8T) (Played by JASON MAY)

Wall Street Crash: The 1929 event which wiped out much of America's financial prosperity, after years of a business boom, driving the country into its Depression Era, which lasted until 1933. (3.4, 3.5)

Walterley Street, SE15: South London street running to St Christopher's Church. The Doctor landed the TARDIS there. Mickey Smith ran along it from the playground after his mother Pauline had been destroyed by the Reapers. (1.8)

War of the Roses: Battle between Yorkshire and Lancashire that was in its second year in the alternative timeline created when River Song rewrote established history. (6.13)

Ward, Shayne: British pop singer who, by 2012, had released a greatest hits CD, according to posters next to the TARDIS when it arrived in Stratford. (2.11)

Ward 26: Area in the Hospital on New Earth shared between the Face of Boe, the Duke of Manhattan and others in the upper echelons of the New New York social elite. (2.1)

Warden: Churchwarden of St Stephen's Church in Victorian London. Rosita Farisi sent the children she, the Doctor and Jackson Lake evacuated from the CyberKing's engine room to him, to be looked after. (4.14)

Warders: Robotic prison guards under the ice planet of Volag-Noc. Wired into a central network, they automatically obeyed the Governor. (TIQ) (Voiced by DAN MORGAN)

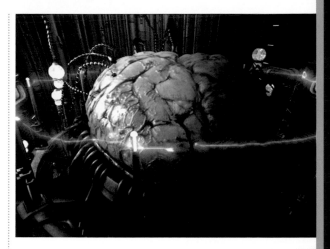

Warehouse 15: Building on the Ood-Sphere where for two centuries Ood Operations had stored the Ood Brain. Dr Ryder had tried to access it to free it, but it was restricted and he had to wait for Klineman Halpen to open it up for him. (4.3)

Wark, Kirsty: BBC newsreader who reported on the state of emergency declared after the ATMOS devices activated, filling the UK with poison gas. (4.5)

Warnock, Mary: Worker at Sanderson & Grainger. Val reported that she claimed to have seen Don Petherbridge snogging Andrea Groom on his day off. (6.12)

Warp Star: A small diamond, containing a compressed explosion, a warpfold conjunction — caught at the exact moment of detonation and given to Sarah Jane Smith as a gift by a Verron Soothsayer. (4.13)

Warp-Shunt Technology: The means of transport used by the Nestene Consciousness to flee the devastation of the Time War and reach planet Earth. (1.1)

Warpspeed Death Ride: An amusement park attraction on Apalapucia, modelled after the original one at Disneyland on Clom. (6.10)

Wash Inn: South East London launderette where Jackie Tyler met Elton Pope. (2.10)

Washington DC: American capital where, in the White House Press Room, President Obama prepared to address the world on Christmas Day. (4.17, 4.18) The Doctor befriended President Richard Nixon in the White House's Oval Office, which was plagued by the Silence. (6.1P, 6.1, 6.2)

Washington Public Archive: A photo on this website of the John F Kennedy assassination on 22 November 1963 clearly shows the Ninth Doctor watching from the crowds. (1.1)

Watchdog: BBC Television consumer programme. Roger Davey complained to them about his burglar alarm going off at 1.10am every morning. (4.1) Angela Whittaker once saw a feature on automated phone systems and learned that by keeping 0 pressed, you got transferred to a human being. (4.15)

Water pistol: The Doctor used it to threaten the High Priestess of the Sibylline Sisterhood who was by then made of living stone and lava. (4.2) It was stolen by a Graske, who ran around London's Albert Hall with it. After the Doctor reversed the polarity of the Graske's portal, he retrieved the alien and the water pistol. (MotS)

Water Snake Wormholes: A descendant of Adelaide Brooke mapped this distant celestial body. (4.16)

Waterfall Palace: Destination of the *Crusader 50*, from where the Doctor and the other passengers would be able to see the Cliffs of Oblivion. (4.10)

Watergate: American scandal in 1973 that brought down American President Richard Milhous Nixon. River Song reminded the Doctor that it wasn't Nixon's finest moment. (6.1)

Waterton Street: South-East London street on which Mickey Smith had been brought up by his late grandmother, Rita-Anne, until she tripped on a loose piece of stair-carpet and died. On 'Pete's World', Ricky Smith had continued to live there, as Rita-Anne was still alive. (2.5)

Watson, Thomas: Young electrical designer, assistant to Alexander Graham Bell and recipient of the very first telephone call. (1.8)

Watt, Joseph: Like Joseph Watt, Malcolm Taylor named a unit of measurement after himself. (4.15)

Watts, Alan: One of the geologists at the Zebra Bay Survey Unit in the Arctic Circle. He was infected by the nano-virus after being bitten by a Cybermat and was turned into a Cyberslave. He was returned to normal after the Doctor reversed the nano-virus. (AG02)

'We Plough The Fields And Scatter': Traditional Harvest Festival hymn, hummed by the Reverend Golightly at Eddison Hall. (4.7)

'We Wish You A Merry Christmas': Traditional Christmas carol being sung by carollers in the pub where Donna Noble had drinks with her mates on the night that the Empress of the Racnoss attacked Earth, in the alternative world where Donna never met the Doctor. (4.11)

Weakest Link, The: One of the many 'games' being played on the Game Station and broadcast to the whole Earth — a general knowledge quiz show, chaired by the Anne Droid — and played by Rose Tyler against Agorax, Fitch, Rodrick, Colleen and Broff. Like all the games, losing appeared to be instantly fatal, although in fact being shot by the Anne Droid involved being transported to the Dalek mothership and turned into part of the growing Dalek army created by the Emperor. (1.12)

Weatherman: As part of his television weather forecast, this presenter gave predictions of ghostly materialisations. (2.12) (Played by PAUL FIELDS)

Webber, Chloe: A 12-year-old girl who lived with her mother Trish on Dame Kelly Holmes Close. Chloe had encountered a lonely alien, an Isolus, which had merged with her, creating two intelligences in the one body. Using Chloe's natural artistic bent, the Isolus gave her the power to draw things that would then take on a life of their own, while the object or person she had drawn disappeared from reality. Chloe was the cause of the disappearances of other kids — she had drawn them to be friends for the Isolus. She also created the Scribble Creature that attacked Rose outside a car garage, and a full-sized drawing of her late, violent father, which later threatened her and her mum. Eventually the Isolus was coaxed out of Chloe when Rose found a way to release its space capsule and, using the heat from the Olympic Torch being carried past the road, was able to get the Isolus back to the rest of its family. With the Isolus gone, Chloe and her mother Trish carried on with their lives after bonding more strongly than before and defeating the last vestiges of the ionic-powered image of Chloe's dad. (2.11) (Played by ABISOLA AGBAJE)

Webber, Mr: Trish's abusive husband who had died a year before in a car crash but who Chloe kept on having nightmares about. After Chloe absorbed the Isolus into herself and gained the ability to manipulate the drawings she created, she accidentally brought a drawing of Mr Webber to life and, even though the Isolus was gone, the residual ionic energy Chloe had used continued to animate it until she and her mum bonded again by singing 'Kookaburra'. The image of Mr Webber then vanished for ever. (2.11) (Voiced by PAUL McFADDEN)

Webber, Trish: Resident of 53 Dame Kelly Holmes Close and mother of Chloe, a little girl who was having social problems, locking herself in her room to draw. Chloe had in fact been in communion with a lonely alien called the Isolus who just wanted companionship. Trish helped the Doctor and Rose Tyler find a way to free the Isolus, but not before they'd been threatened by a huge drawing

Chloe had done of her violent father, who had died a year earlier. (2.11) (Played by NINA SOSANYA)

Webstar: The distinctive ships of the Racnoss. One of these, the *Secret Heart*, was trapped at the centre of Earth. Another, filled with screens monitoring events and broadcasts across the planet, was piloted by the Empress of the Racnoss. She fired energy beams from it, trying to destroy Earth. It was eventually blown up by shells from a British army tank, just as the Empress returned to it. (3.X) Wilfred Mott referred to the Webstar when discussing aliens at Christmas with the Doctor. (4.X) In the alternative world where Donna Noble never met the Doctor, she and her friends saw it in the sky over Chiswick. (4.11)

Wednesday Girls: Group of friends who met in De Rossi's wine bar every Wednesday evening. Sylvia Noble and Suzette Chambers were amongst their group. (4.1)

Weeping Angels: Time-sensitive alien killers, as old as the universe, who thrived on chronon energy. They would send their victims back in time just by touching them, to live their lives in a different time zone, and the Angels would feed on the potential time energy created by the vanished people's preordained lives being disturbed. Once known as the Lonely Assassins, because they could

slowly convincing her she was turning into an Angel, because an image of an Angel becomes itself an Angel. The group realised that the statues in the mortarium were not Aplan statues but Angels, regenerating from the radiation and killing the Clerics one by one. Getting into the ship, the Doctor led the Angels into the onboard forest. There, a crack in reality appeared, part of the time field following Amy Pond through space. Before the Angels could escape, they fell into the time field when the Doctor shifted the ship's gravity and they were all destroyed, erased from history completely. (5.4, 5.5) Gibbis from Tivoli was frightened of them, and the God Complex projected a couple into a hotel room to frighten him. (6.11)

Weevils: Scavenging aliens that travelled to Earth via the rift in Cardiff. Some of them went to Stonehenge, as part of the Pandorica Alliance. When the Pandorica opened and history was stopped, the Alliance were reduced to fossils. (5.12, 5.13)

Wellgrove Hospice: The hospital where Sally Sparrow encountered the dying Billy Shipton. He knew he was destined to die the night he met her again, and she stayed there with him until the end. (3.10)

Wells, Trinity: American AMNN news anchor who reported on the Big Ben incident, (1.4) on the Sycorax's message being relayed to Earth, (2.X) on President Winters' address to the Toclafane, (3.12) and on the ATMOS devices giving off poison gas. (4.4, 4.5) In the alternative world where Donna Noble never met the Doctor, she reported that in America the Adipose ships were everywhere after 60 million Americans died as their body fat turned into Adipose children. (4.11) She reported on the appearance of 26 new planets in the skies above Earth, (4.12, 4.13) and was reporting on President Obama's grand financial initiative when she, Obama and everyone else were transformed into the Master. She later safely reverted to her normal form. (4.17, 4.18) (Played by LACHELE CARL)

never touch anything without sending it back in time, they could only move and attack if they weren't being observed: if they were seen, they immediately became quantum-locked and froze into solid rock. They could cross vast distances in the time it took their victims to blink. The Doctor used an unwitting Sally Sparrow to trap them – when Sally and her friend Larry accessed the TARDIS, the Weeping Angels gathered around it, hoping to feed off its energy, but the Doctor had pre-set a dematerialisation sequence, meaning it vanished from around Sally and Larry. Caught off-guard, the Weeping Angels were all looking at each other when the TARDIS dematerialised, so all four were frozen for eternity, unable to close their eyes, and unable not to see one another. (3.10) The Doctor mentioned them, hoping it might jog Jackson Lake's memories when he was claiming to be the Doctor. (4.14) The Time Lords knew of them, as President Rassilon made two of his council who did not agree with the Ultimate Sanction follow him to Earth, their faces covered with their hands, like the Angels. (4.18) A single Weeping Angel was found on the planet Razbahan and taken into private hands. Some time later, temporarily freed from the Stormcage Prison Facility, River Song was given the task of locating the Angel, and she found it in the storage hold of a galaxy-class starship, the *Byzantium*. She called for help from the Doctor and they tracked it to the planet Alfava Metraxis. The *Byzantium* had crashed on top of an ancient Aplan mortarium. With a troop of Clerics, the Doctor, Amy Pond and River led them into the catacombs, to reach the Angel before it fed off the leaking radiation from the ship. Amy watched video footage of the Angel and it scared her just enough to give it time to get into her mind,

Wembley Stadium: Venue in North London. Rose Tyler saw ABBA perform there in November 1979. (AotG) The Stadium hosted the Olympic Games in 1948, which the Doctor enjoyed so much he watched it twice. (2.11)

Werewolf: The form chosen by the Lupine-Wavelength-Haemovariform that crashed to Earth in Scotland in 1540. Its current Host was placed on the Torchwood Estate and allowed to transform, rampaging through Torchwood House, killing a number of people including the Steward, the footmen and male

staff of the House, Captain Reynolds and Sir Robert MacLeish, before being destroyed in a trap made of focused moonlight set in motion some years before by Sir Robert's father and Prince Albert. (2.2)

Wessex Lane: Alleyway in Chiswick where Donna Noble was confronted by a number of residents who had become the Master. She stopped them with a blast of metacrisis energy before going comatose herself. (4.18)

West Ham United: Football team supported by the Noble family. Donna learned to whistle on the terraces. (4.3)

West Vaughan Street: London street where Melanie Darforth lived at number 12. (4.1)

Wester Drumlins: Ramshackle old house where four Weeping Angels gathered. Having zapped the Doctor and Martha Jones back to 1969, they were seeking the TARDIS and needed Sally Sparrow to lead them to it after she took the key from them. The TARDIS was in a police car pound, surrounded by vehicles belonging to people who had gone to Wester Drumlins and never been heard from again – all sent back in time by the Weeping Angels. Larry Nightingale described Wester Drumlins as looking like Scooby-Doo's house. (3.10)

Western Mail: Cardiff newspaper on the front page of which the Doctor saw a photograph of Margaret Blaine and realised he had to investigate the Slitheen's activities. (1.11)

Westminster Abbey: Queen Elizabeth II was crowned there in 1953, watched by millions of people live on television, during which the Wire planned to steal all their faces. (2.7)

WHSmith: British chain of stationers and booksellers. Donna Noble knew she was still on Earth when she saw one in the London street the TARDIS had taken her and the Doctor to. (3.X)

What Not to Wear: One of the competitive programmes being transmitted from the Game Station to Earth. Two robots, Trine-E and Zu-Zana, would take humans and decide how to make them look more fashionable. If they weren't satisfied with the results, they would end the show by physically reconstructing their 'victims' with buzz saws and lasers. Captain Jack Harkness found himself in their show. (1.12)

What's My Line?: BBC Television quiz show in which people would mime their job before a celebrity panel who would then guess their occupation. It ran from 1951 to 1963 and was playing on a television in Mr Magpie's shop when the Wire first appeared to him. (2.7)

White House: The Executive Office of the President of the United States of America. The President was due to address the American nation live from the White House on the evening of the Big Ben incident. (1.4)

White People: A number of the humans who lived on New Earth came in extreme colours, including red and white. In the Hospital on New Earth, a White Man was cured by the Sisters of Plenitude of Pallidome Pancrosis. (2.1) (Played by PAUL ZEPH GOULD) The Doctor encountered another White Man in the New New York Motorway, when he jumped into his car from Brannigan's, claiming to be part of the Motorway Foot Patrol. Whitey was very annoyed that Junction 5 had been closed for three years. (3.3) (Played by SIMON PEARSALL) A White Man was a customer in the Zaggit Zagoo bar, (4.18) and he was also a visitor to the Maldavorium. (5.12) (Played by JASON CAPLIN)

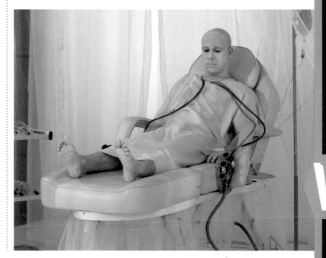

Whitepoint Star: A Gallifreyan diamond jewel. President Rassilon sent one through time and space from within the Black Void, to Earth, knowing that the Master would find and use it, thus creating a physical link between Gallifrey and Earth. The Master placed it within the Immortality Gate and this enabled the Time Lords to materialise themselves inside the Gate and restore Gallifrey itself. The Doctor later destroyed the housing that contained the Whitepoint Star, which flung the Time Lords and Gallifrey back into the Timelocked Time War, taking the Master along as well. (4.18)

Whittaker, Angela: One of the passengers aboard the number 200 bus when it travelled through a wormhole from South London to San Helios. Initially terrified, she got braver as time went on (usefully knowing that if you keep your finger on zero, you automatically get to bypass automated phone messages), and was overjoyed to get home safely, at which point she immediately called her husband Mike and 18-year-old daughter Suzanne. (4.15) (Played by VICTORIA ALCOCK)

Wickowski: UNIT soldier who led the assault on the ATMOS factory. (4.5)

Wicks: Schoolboy at Farringham School for Boys in 1913, who took part in the war games there, manning the Vickers Gun. (3.8)

Wicks, Adam: Son of Jimmy Wicks. He was anxious for his father to return from the St John's monastery in time for his 5th birthday. The Doctor made

sure that happened, although Adam was not aware it was in fact Jimmy's Ganger, the real Jimmy having been killed on the island. (6.5, 6.6) (Played by EDMOND MOULTON)

Wicks, Jimmy: Scottish Morpeth-Jetsan contractor, working at the St John's crystal-diluric acid farm. He was in his rig-harness, asleep while his Ganger was working, when St John's was hit by the solar tsunami that gave his Ganger a sense of individuality and a desire to be a separate living person. As the Gangers and the human originals found themselves in conflict, all Jimmy really wanted to

DOCTOR WHO THE ENCYCLOPEDIA

do was get home to his 5-year-old son Adam, whose birthday was the next day. In conversation with his Ganger, Jimmy realised that the two were absolutely identical, the Ganger having every memory, every feeling and every experience the real Jimmy had had. Jimmy was killed when a vat of acid expelled its contents onto him, eating straight through his heart. He passed both his wedding ring and the care of Adam over to his Ganger, realising that Adam would never know the difference. The Ganger Jimmy, his form set permanently as Jimmy after travelling in the TARDIS, returned home for Adam's birthday. (6.5, 6.6) (Played by MARK BONNAR)

Widdecombe, Ann: Conservative MP and former minister, who endorsed Harry Saxon's campaign to become Prime Minister. (3.12)

Wiggins: Young lad in Elizabethan England who tried to seduce Lilith, believing her to be a young, beautiful human. When Lilith introduced Wiggins to her parents, Mother Doomfinger and Mother Bloodtide, they literally tore him to shreds. (3.1) (Played by SAM MARKS)

Wild Endeavour: A continent on Gallifrey, the Doctor's home world, where the Time Lord citadel had sat, in the mountains of Solace and Solitude, beneath a glass dome. It was destroyed, along with the rest of Gallifrey, at the end of the Last Great Time War. (3.12)

'Wild Rover': Traditional Scottish folk song. Rocco Colasanto led everyone in a rousing chorus of it in their house in Leeds in the alternative world where Donna Noble never met the Doctor. (4.11)

Wildlands: An area of space, most likely unexplored, towards the edge of the known universe. Utopia wasn't quite as far as the Wildlands, nor the Dark Matter Reefs. (3.11)

Williams: Schoolboy at Farringham School for Boys in 1913, who was put in charge of arranging sandbags before the Family of Blood attacked. (3.9)

Williams, Mr and Mrs: Rory Williams's parents, who were at his wedding to Amy Pond. (5.13) Rory told the Doctor and Amy that his mum was a big fan of singer Dusty Springfield. (6.5) (Played by ANDY ELVIN and HELEN IRVING)

Williams, Rhys: Gwen Cooper's husband, who she was talking to on the phone about the planets that had appeared in Earth's sky. Gwen asked him to call her mother and tell her to take her pills to relax. (4.12)

Williams, Robbie: British singer who was due to perform at the opening ceremony of the 2012 Olympic Games at Stratford. (2.11)

Williams, Rory: A nurse at Leadworth hospital, and Amy Pond's boyfriend, when he first met the Doctor. Rory grew up in Leadworth, living with his parents, and going to school alongside Amy and Amy's best mate Mels Zucker.

He was in love with Amy throughout his teenage years, although Amy never twigged, assuming he was gay because he never showed the slightest interest in girls other than her. (6.8) He used to allow himself to be dressed up by Amy as her imaginary 'raggedy Doctor' and only really went into the medical profession to try and compete with what he thought was her made-up friend. Rory met the Doctor because he was taking photographs of people in and around Leadworth who shouldn't be there – they were coma patients in the ward he where he worked, who were being used by Prisoner Zero – and the Doctor noticed this and was intrigued. Shortly after this, the Doctor disappeared again from Amy's life and she agreed to marry Rory. Two years later, on the eve of their wedding, the Doctor returned and took Amy away with him, unknown to Rory. (5.1) Shortly afterwards, the Doctor turned up at Rory's stag do, inside the cake, and took Rory and Amy to Venice. The Doctor confessed Amy had kissed him but he knew it was Rory she was pining after. Rory adapted quite quickly to life aboard the TARDIS – he'd done his research on the Doctor over the preceding two years. He helped defeat Saturnynes in Venice, (5.6) the Dream Lord, (5.7) and the Silurians. As they fled the Silurian city, Rory was shot and killed by the Silurian Restac near a splinter of the time field that had been in Amy's room in Leadworth for many years. The crack absorbed Rory's body, removing him from time, erasing all memory of him from everyone, including Amy. Only the Doctor could remember him. (5.8, 5.9)

Rory's consciousness was, however, placed inside an Auton replica of a Roman Centurion, based upon one of Amy's childhood books, by the Pandorica Alliance. Believing he was the original Rory, he met up with the Doctor and Amy at Stonehenge, saving Amy from a Cybersentry. When the Alliance triggered the Auton command networks, Rory shot and killed Amy but the Doctor placed her inside the Pandorica's restorative field and locked her away for 2,000 years. (5.12) Rory, as a being made of plastic, stood watch over her, becoming known throughout time as the Lone Centurion or the Last Centurion. The Auton Rory eventually became a security guard at the National Museum, protecting the Pandorica from the Stone Daleks that came to life when the young Amelia Pond released her future self. Teamed up once more with the Doctor, Amy and River Song, Rory was present when the Doctor flew the Pandorica into the heart of the exploding sun caused by the destructing TARDIS within it. This sealed the time field for good, restoring the universe to normal, and erasing everyone's memories of the Doctor. Amy got her parents back and Rory was returned to life as a proper human being. At their wedding, Amy's memories of the Doctor brought him back into existence and, with it, all Rory's memories of their adventures, including his death and internment inside a plastic body. (5.13) He and Amy, now Mr and Mrs Williams (or Mr and Mrs Pond, as Amy and the Doctor preferred) continued travelling with him, during which their daughter Melody was conceived inside the TARDIS. After a brief honeymoon period, that ended when they were reunited with the Doctor on Ember, (6.X) Amy and Rory settled down in Leadworth for a while, waiting for the Doctor to track them down and take them away again. They received an invitation to what turned out to be the Doctor's death in Utah, but that was an older version of him. Rory was unaware that by this time Amy had been replaced by a Ganger duplicate, while the real Amy was on Demon's Run. After defeating the Silence, (6.1, 6.2) the Siren, (6.3), House, (6.4) and the Flesh, (6.5, 6.6) Rory was sent by the Doctor to find out where Amy was. He confronted the Twelfth Cyber Legion, who pointed them in the direction of Demon's Run. They rescued Amy but Madame Kovarian kidnapped the baby – and River revealed that she was their grown-up daughter, Melody. (6.7) Taken back to Leadworth by River/Melody, they waited for the Doctor again and he returned and took them to Berlin, (6.8) to an estate in London where a Tenza was living, (6.9) to the

Twostreams facility, (6.10) and finally to the God Complex. The Doctor realised he was endangering Amy and Rory too much and returned them to Leadworth, giving them a new cottage to live in. (6.11) Anxious not to be forgotten, Amy and Rory established the Petrichor perfume brand hoping to catch his attention. (6.12) When River Song tried to change established time and stop herself killing the Doctor in Utah, a new alternative timeline was created. In this version of 2011, Rory was a military captain, unaware he was married to Amy or who River was, and in charge of looking after the Silence, which were contained in watertanks at Area 52 in Egypt. However, when Amy told him the truth, he accepted it and after the timeline was erased and the universe back to normal, Amy, Rory and River met up one evening at the cottage to discuss the fact that the Doctor was still alive out in the universe somewhere and perhaps they would see him once again. (6.13) (Played by EZEKIEL WIGGLESWORTH and ARTHUR DARVILL)

Williams, Sian: Breakfast TV presenter who interviewed author Charles Dickens about his new Christmas television play. (6.13)

Willis, Bruce: American actor, famous for the *Die Hard* movies. The Doctor mentioned him to Amy as they searched for the Cybermat nest in the Arctic Circle. (AG02)

Wilson, HP: Chief electrical officer at the Henrik's store where Rose Tyler worked. He was found dead by the Doctor, presumably at the hands of the Autons. (1.1)

Winders: Cloaked humans who patrolled the streets of *Starship UK*, acting as a police force but also responsible for the upkeep of the lights, streets and Smilers. Many, if not all, Winders were actually cyborgs, part human and part Smiler. Their chief, Hawthorne, was a pure human and the only person who knew the truth about *Starship UK* and the star whale. One Winder operated the vator near Timmy Winters' school and forbade him riding with the other children as he had scored badly in class. (5.2) (Played by JONATHAN BATTERSBY)

Winter Witch Canyon: A diamond fall there, on the surface of Midnight, meant that Driver Joe had to divert the *Crusader 50*. (4.10)

W

'Winter Wonderland': Traditional Christmas song from Earth played aboard the starliner *Titanic* during its journey between Sto and Earth. (4.X)

Winters, Arthur Coleman: President-Elect of the United States of America and Representative of the United Nations to the Toclafane. He welcomed them to Earth aboard the aircraft carrier *Valiant*, but the Toclafane were interested only in the Master and, on live television, disintegrated Winters. (3.12) (Played by COLIN STINTON)

Winters, Lady Elizabeth: Human form adopted by a Rutan trapped on Earth in 1605. She brought two doomsday weapons in her ship, planning to wipe out the Sontarans once and for all. (AG05) (Voiced by EMILIA FOX)

Winters, Timmy: Schoolboy in the London sector of *Starship UK*, and friend of Mandy Tanner. He did badly at school, was forbidden to ride the vator with the other children and had to take a separate vator alone. The floor opened and he was dropped into the bowels of the ship, forced to work with others society considered a failure. Mandy found him there and he was later freed. (5.2) (Played by ALFIE FIELD)

Wipeout: One of the programmes broadcast from the Game Station. Losing contestants were, oddly enough, wiped out. (1.12)

Wire, the: Criminal mastermind from the planet Hermethica, who led a gang that could transform themselves into plasmic energy. Sentenced to death, the Wire escaped and beamed itself through space, when it was drawn into a television set in Magpie Electricals, a shop run by Mr Magpie. It used its plasmic powers to drain the life energy from its victims as they watched television, leaving them faceless, mindless husks, their basic consciousness (and faces) left trapped inside the television sets. The Wire planned to unleash its full potential via the Alexandra Palace transmitter mast as the nation sat down to watch Queen Elizabeth II's Coronation and physically renew itself, but the Doctor re-routed the Wire's broadcast frequency and used the mast to transmit the Wire onto a Betamax videotape, which he intended to record over later. (2.7T, 2.7) (Played by MAUREEN LIPMAN)

Wiry Woman: One of the Futurekind, who had evaded the normally rigorous guards and gained access to the Silo base on Malcassairo. She sabotaged the base's power systems, which killed a guard called Jate. The Doctor and Captain Jack were able to override her sabotage and the rocket eventually took off, after the Wiry Woman had been gunned down by other guards. (3.11) (Played by ABIGAIL CANTON)

Witchell, Nicholas: BBC Royal Correspondent who reported that the Queen was to remain at Buckingham Palace over Christmas, despite the now annual alien incursions that many predicted would occur again. (4.X)

Woman [1]: Occupant of the slave house in Bexley, South London. She listened to Martha's story and was later on the streets saying the Doctor's name, along with the rest of mankind. (3.13) (Played by NATASHA ALEXANDER)

Woman [2]: Bitter inhabitant of Leeds who objected to the Nobles moving into a neighbouring house in the alternative world where Donna Noble never met the Doctor. Donna likened her to *Coronation Street* character Vera Duckworth. (4.11) (Played by TERRI-ANN BRUMBY)

Woman [3]: A mysterious stranger who spoke to Wilfred Mott in a London church, talking about the Doctor, and subsequently appeared on his TV screen on Christmas Day, talking about war. She later appeared aboard the *Hesperus*. She was a Time Lord projecting an image of herself back across time from the point at which she, along with other members of the High Council, arrived on Earth, in Joshua Naismith's Gate Room. Lord President Rassilon was unaware of what she was doing – as she didn't support the Ultimate Sanction, she was forced to cover her face, like a Weeping Angel, and that was when she took the opportunity to contact Wilfred. When the Doctor, confronting both the Master and Rassilon, was unsure which to shoot, she lowered her hands, revealing her face to the Doctor and indicating that he had a third option. Shocked to recognise her, the Doctor realised his third option was to destroy the housing that contained the Whitepoint Star linking the Time Lords and Gallifrey to Earth, sending her and the rest of them back to the Time War for eternity. (4.17, 4.18) (Played by CLAIRE BLOOM)

Woman Wept: A planet visited by the Doctor and Rose Tyler. It was named this because one of its continents, if viewed from space, resembled a woman bent

over in distress. They visited a deserted beach that seemed to be a thousand miles long. (1.11) It was one of the planets stolen by the Daleks and secreted a second out of sync within the Medusa Cascade. The Doctor eventually returned it to its rightful place in space and time. (4.12, 4.13)

Woman's Realm: Women's magazine from the 1950s. Copies of this were kept in the hair salon within the fake hotel created inside the God Complex. (6.11)

Wombles, The: Fictional creatures who, in the books of Elizabeth Beresford, lived on Wimbledon Common, picking up the litter humans left behind and turning it to good use. One of the Wombles was the French cook, Madame Cholet. The Doctor referred to her as one of the greatest chefs on Earth. (TIQ)

Wonder, Stevie: Stage name of blind American singer Stevland Hardaway Morris. The Doctor took him to London in 1814, to sing for River Song on her birthday, although he never realised he had travelled in time. (6.7)

Woolf, Adeline Virginia: 20th-century English writer and society figure. The Doctor was on her bowling team. (5.4)

Woolwich: South East London location of the warehouse where Elton Pope witnessed the Doctor and Rose Tyler engaging the Hoix. (2.10)

Workers: Two hypnotised ATMOS workers were encountered by UNIT soldiers Harris and Gray beneath the ATMOS factory. (4.4, 4.5) (Played by ANDREW SLADE and JON DAVEY)

Workmen: After handing the Foreman over to the Daleks, Mr Diagoras, charged with overseeing the construction of the upper floors of the Empire State Building by the Cult of Skaro, ordered his workers to keep working until everything was completed that night. One worker (played by JOE MONTANA) protested that at that height, and late at night, they would most likely freeze and fall to their deaths instead of successfully fixing the Dalekanium slats to the mooring mast. Diagoras pointed out that he could always find other men to do the job, so the reluctant worker and a mate (played by STEWART ALEXANDER) found themselves doing it after all. (3.4)

World State, the: Governing body on Earth by 2057, who sent Adelaide Brooke and her team to Mars to establish Bowie Base One and see if the planet could be colonised. (4.16)

World War Five: The Doctor tells Rose Tyler he witnessed this war some time in Earth's future. (1.3)

Wormhole: Spatial portal created by the Stingrays speeding around and around a planet until their mass created the wormhole and they went through it to their next target. Malcolm Taylor of UNIT found a way to collapse it, trapping them on San Helios, to starve. (4.15)

Wristwatch: The Master had rigged his watch up so he could remotely activate the black hole converters within the warheads of his rockets. He threatened to set them off on Earth but the Doctor reminded him that he would die along with the planet. The Master surrendered the watch. (3.13)

X-Factor, The: According to Lance Bennett, Donna Noble talked excitedly about this reality TV show. (3.X)

X-Tonic sunlight: The sunlight filtered down onto Midnight gave off harmful Galvanic radiation, so the Leisure Company ensured that any glass in their domes on Midnight was 15 feet thick. (4.10)

Xylok: Sentient crystalline life form. One powered the computer known as Mr Smith in the attic of 13 Bannerman Road, where Sarah Jane Smith lived. Mr Smith helped in the defeat of the Daleks. (4.12, 4.13, 4.18)

Yana, Professor: Fleeing the Time War, the Master used a chameleon arch to become an orphaned human child, found naked on the coast of the Silver Devastation following a storm, and given the name Yana. The child had no possessions other than a broken fob watch – actually the receptacle that stored the Master's true consciousness. Entirely unaware that he was anything more than a real human, Yana had experienced headaches and heard the constant sound of pounding drums. He'd spent his time travelling between refugee ships, before eventually settling on the planet Malcassairo to work as a scientist, having assumed the archaic title of Professor for himself in the process. A genius across a variety of fields, he oversaw the development of the Utopia project for 17 years, with the help of his friend Chantho, and was willing to sacrifice his own life to ensure the survival of the human race when his Footprint Impeller System finally became active. It was during a conversation with Martha Jones that Yana discovered the truth about time travel, and was encouraged by her curiosity to open his fob watch, at which point the Master reasserted himself, effectively destroying both Professor Yana and his work. (3.11) The Face of Boe had tried to warn the Doctor about the Professor on New New Earth when he spoke the acronymous phrase 'You Are Not Alone'. (3.3) (Played by DEREK JACOBI)

Yappy: A brand of electronic toy dog. It yapped. A lot. (6.12)

Yew Tree Ball: Major Paris social event held on 25 February 1745, at which the young Jeanne-Antoinette Poisson hoped to catch the eye of King Louis with the intention of becoming his new mistress. (2.4)

York: The Grand Central Ravine was named after the Ancient British city of Sheffield, not York. Rose Tyler didn't know this when asked by the Anne Droid in *The Weakest Link* aboard the Game Station. (1.12)

Yorkshire: One of the county tower blocks on *Starship UK*. (5.2)

'You Don't Have To Say You Love Me': 1966 hit for Dusty Springfield which the Doctor, Amy Pond and Rory Williams could hear being played in the St John's monastery as they explored. It was put on by the Ganger of Jimmy Wicks, who shared his human original's love of Dusty. (6.5)

'You Give Me Something': Top five 2006 song by James Morrison, which was played at Amy Pond and Rory Williams's wedding. They did a slow dance to it, watched by the Doctor. (5.13)

You've Been Framed: Long-running ITV series to which members of the public sent their home videos and got a financial reward if these were shown. Rhodri, the videographer at Donna Noble's wedding, had thought of sending his footage of the bride disappearing to the show. (3.X)

Young woman [1]: Passer-by in the street in 1883 at Christmas, when a young street urchin was kidnapped by the Graske. (AotG) (Played by CATHERINE OLDING)

Young Woman [2]: Woman in the pub where the Wednesday Girls were meeting, who was affected by unexpected Adipose parthenogenesis in the pub, along with a number of other customers, but was saved when the Doctor stopped Matron Cofelia's scheme. (4.1) (Played by ABIGAIL CREEL)

Z-Neutrino Energy: The power at the heart of the Dalek Crucible, powerful enough to destroy even the TARDIS. It was the central power element of Davros's Reality Bomb (4 12, 4.13)

'Zadok The Priest': Anthem especially written by Handel for the Coronation of George II and used during the anointing ceremony at all subsequent British Coronations, including that of Queen Elizabeth II, watched by millions in 1953, when the Wire was scheming to steal their life energies in order to renew itself. (2.7)

Zaffic: An icy beef-flavoured drink Rose Tyler purchased aboard Satellite Five. (1.7)

Zaggit Zagoo: Capital city of the planet Zog. Captain Jack Harkness met Midshipman Alonso Frame in a bar there, thanks to the Doctor. (4.18)

Zardak: The Doctor needed one of their Holo-Field Traps to help stabilise the Dimensional Lesion in the TARDIS. (AG05)

Zarusthra Bay: Battlefield of a war between humanity and another race. The Doctor had placed a Sontaran, Strax, amidst the humans, forcing him to restore his honour by working to aid his enemies. (6.7)

Zebra Bay: Location of the Geological Survey Base in the Arctic Circle that was attacked by Cybermen. (AG02)

Zed, Tobias: Virginal (according to the Beast) scientist aboard Sanctuary Base 6, his specialised field was archaeology, but he was having difficulty understanding the strange hieroglyphs and inscriptions found on the objects scattered across the surface of Krop Tor after the drilling began. However, the more he studied, the more his mind drew the attention of the Beast, imprisoned deep below the planet. Transferring some of its consciousness into Toby, it used him as a tool to disrupt the Base's mission and ultimately led to the Doctor heading down to confront it. The Beast split its consciousness between Toby and the Ood – whether Toby was always aware of what he did is unknown. Eventually, not realising that the Doctor would sacrifice Rose Tyler and the other human survivors (including Toby) aboard an escape shuttle, the Beast placed all of its consciousness into Toby. Realising that Toby was dangerous, Rose Tyler ejected him into space, and both he and the Beast were destroyed in the event horizon of the black hole. (2.8, 2.9) (Played by WILL THORP)

Zeiton Crystals: The Doctor needed to heat the TARDIS power crystals up to avoid a time collision. (TC)

08081-570980: The freephone number used by the authorities after the Slitheen-augmented pig crashed its spaceship into Big Ben, in case anyone needed information about missing relatives. It was later open to any member of the public to report alien sightings. Jackie Tyler called it to report the Doctor, which set off a Code Nine alert in the government. (1.4, 1.5)

011-109-4455: The pre-booked holocall number that the Doctor used to enable birthday-boy Adam Wicks to talk to the man he thought was his father, Jimmy, whereas it was in fact his Ganger. (6.6)

0301-566-9155-76544891: Telephone number the presenter of *Crime Crackers* asked viewers to call if they had any information about the disappearances of children from Stratford in 2012. (2.11T)

0207 946000: The phone number for people to call if they had information regarding the whereabouts of Rose Tyler after her disappearance in March 2005. (1.4)

0207 946003: The phone number of the company Rodrigo worked for as a tow-truck driver. (1.13)

Zeus plugs: The Doctor needed these to close down the Time Windows aboard the SS *Madame de Pompadour*, but couldn't find them – then remembered he'd last had them in the 18th century, when he was using them as castanets at a party. (2.4)

Zhou, Anna: Possessor of an Osterhagen Key at Osterhagen Station Four in China. (4.13) (Played by ELIZABETH TAN)

Zimmerman, Eric: Member of the Nazi Party in 1938, and guilty, according to the crew of the *Teselecta*, of Category Three hate crimes. They replaced him with a *Teselecta* double, beaming the real Zimmerman aboard the ship and leaving him to die at the tendrils of the Anti-Bodies. (6.8) (Played by PHILIP RHAM)

Zocci: Small aliens with red spiky skin. Bannakaffalatta was a cybernetically enhanced Zocci. The Zocci and Vinvocci are not the same. (4.X, 4.17)

Zog: Planet that the Doctor offered to take Donna Noble to, for a party. Instead they went to Earth in the 1920s and partied with Agatha Christie. (4.7) Its capital city was Zaggit Zagoo. (4.18)

Zone One: The Master's new name for Britain after the Toclafane had helped him take over Earth. (3.13)

Zovirax: Medicinal product on Earth, used to cover cold sores. An advertising campaign used the image of a leather-clad despatch biker with a black helmet, which caused Martha Jones to suggest the similar-looking Slabs came from the planet Zovirax. (3.1)

Zucker, Mels: See *Song, River*

Zu-Zana: One of the two robots, the other being Trine-E, who would take humans and decide how to make them look more fashionable for their TV show *What Not to Wear*. They would then end the show, being broadcast across Earth from the Game Station, by physically reconstructing their 'victims' with buzz saws and lasers if they weren't satisfied with the results. Captain Jack Harkness found himself in their show and destroyed both robots with his Compact Laser Deluxe. (1.12) (Voiced by SUSANNAH CONSTANTINE, played by PAUL KASEY)

Zygons: Amphibian shape-changers, who travelled to Stonehenge, as part of the Pandorica Alliance. (5.12)

KEY TO REFERENCES

As well as the regular and special episodes themselves, this book also incorporates references from any free-to-air (in the UK) broadcast material such as the *Tardisodes*, the animated adventures *The Infinite Quest* and *Dreamland*, the interactive elements of *Attack of the Graske* and *Music of the Spheres*, the online Adventure Games, and the charity mini-episodes *Born Again*, *Time Crash*, *Space* and *Time*. This is why bonus commercial material on DVD releases such as deleted scenes or specially shot additional scenes are not included.

Throughout this book, information pertaining to a specific episode is followed by a bracketed numerical: '(3.2)' after the entry for Lilith indicates that Lilith was in 'The Shakespeare Code'. A 'T' after the number refers to the relevant *Tardisode*: '(2.8T)' in the entry for 'Chenna' indicates that the entry relates to the *Tardisode* for 'The Impossible Planet'. A 'P' after the number refers to the relevant online Prequel: '(6.7P)' in the entry for 'Sentient Money' indicates that the entry relates to the Prequel for 'A Good Man Goes to War'.

1.1	ROSE	2.10	LOVE & MONSTERS	4.5	THE POISON SKY	5.10	VINCENT AND THE DOCTOR
1.2	THE END OF THE WORLD	2.11	FEAR HER	4.6	THE DOCTOR'S DAUGHTER	AG01	CITY OF THE DALEKS
1.3	THE UNQUIET DEAD	2.12	ARMY OF GHOSTS	4.7	THE UNICORN AND THE WASP	AG02	BLOOD OF THE CYBERMEN
1.4	ALIENS OF LONDON	2.13	DOOMSDAY	4.8	SILENCE IN THE LIBRARY	AG03	TARDIS
1.5	WORLD WAR THREE	3.X	THE RUNAWAY BRIDE	4.9	FOREST OF THE DEAD	AG04	SHADOWS OF THE VASHTA NERADA
1.6	DALEK	3.1	SMITH AND JONES	4.10	MIDNIGHT	5.11	THE LODGER
1.7	THE LONG GAME	3.2	THE SHAKESPEARE CODE	4.11	TURN LEFT	5.12	THE PANDORICA OPENS
1.8	FATHER'S DAY	3.3	GRIDLOCK	4.12	THE STOLEN EARTH	5.13	THE BIG BANG
1.9	THE EMPTY CHILD	3.4	DALEKS IN MANHATTAN	4.13	JOURNEY'S END	6.X	A CHRISTMAS CAROL
1.10	THE DOCTOR DANCES	3.5	EVOLUTION OF THE DALEKS	4.14	THE NEXT DOCTOR	S	SPACE
1.11	BOOM TOWN	3.6	THE LAZARUS EXPERIMENT	MotS	MUSIC OF THE SPHERES	T	TIME
1.12	BAD WOLF	3.7	42	4.15	PLANET OF THE DEAD	6.1	THE IMPOSSIBLE ASTRONAUT
1.13	THE PARTING OF THE WAYS	TIQ	THE INFINITE QUEST	4.16	THE WATERS OF MARS	6.2	DAY OF THE MOON
BA	BORN AGAIN	3.8	HUMAN NATURE	DL	DREAMLAND	6.3	THE CURSE OF THE BLACK SPOT
2.X	THE CHRISTMAS INVASION	3.9	THE FAMILY OF BLOOD	4.17	THE END OF TIME, PART ONE	6.4	THE DOCTOR'S WIFE
2.1	NEW EARTH	3.10	BLINK	4.18	THE END OF TIME, PART TWO	6.5	THE REBEL FLESH
2.2	TOOTH AND CLAW	3.11	UTOPIA	5.1	THE ELEVENTH HOUR	6.6	THE ALMOST PEOPLE
AotG	ATTACK OF THE GRASKE	3.12	THE SOUND OF DRUMS	5.2	THE BEAST BELOW	6.7	A GOOD MAN GOES TO WAR
2.3	SCHOOL REUNION	3.13	LAST OF THE TIME LORDS	5.3	VICTORY OF THE DALEKS	6.8	LET'S KILL HITLER
2.4	THE GIRL IN THE FIREPLACE	TC	TIME CRASH	5.4	THE TIME OF ANGELS	6.9	NIGHT TERRORS
2.5	RISE OF THE CYBERMEN	4.X	VOYAGE OF THE DAMNED	5.5	FLESH AND STONE	6.10	THE GIRL WHO WAITED
2.6	THE AGE OF STEEL	4.1	PARTNERS IN CRIME	5.6	THE VAMPIRES OF VENICE	AG05	THE GUNPOWDER PLOT
2.7	THE IDIOT'S LANTERN	4.2	THE FIRES OF POMPEII	5.7	AMY'S CHOICE	6.11	THE GOD COMPLEX
2.8	THE IMPOSSIBLE PLANET	4.3	PLANET OF THE OOD	5.8	THE HUNGRY EARTH	6.12	CLOSING TIME
2.9	THE SATAN PIT	4.4	THE SONTARAN STRATAGEM	5.9	COLD BLOOD	6.13	THE WEDDING OF RIVER SONG